M000280254

Travellers' Nature Guide

Spain

Travellers' Nature Guides

Series editor: Martin Walters

This series is designed for anyone with an interest in the natural history of the places they visit. Essentially practical, each book first introduces the ecology, geology, and wildlife of the country or countries it covers, then goes on to describe where to see the natural history at its best. The entries are the personal choice of the individual authors and are based on intensive travel and research in their areas. Sites range in size from a few to thousands of hectares, be they National Parks, nature reserves, or simply common land, but all are open to the public and accessible to the ordinary visitor. The books are designed to complement each other and to build into a nature library, together giving an introduction to the natural history of Europe.

Britain: *Travellers' Nature Guide*
France: *Travellers' Nature Guide*
Greece: *Travellers' Nature Guide*
Spain: *Travellers' Nature Guide*

Travellers' Nature Guide
Spain

Teresa Farino and Mike Lockwood

Photographs
Natural Image, Teresa Farino and Mike Lockwood

Maps, animal drawings, and panoramas
Michael Wood

Plant drawings
Stella Tranah

OXFORD
UNIVERSITY PRESS

OXFORD
UNIVERSITY PRESS

Great Clarendon Street, Oxford OX2 6DP

Oxford University Press is a department of the University of Oxford.
It furthers the University's objective of excellence in research, scholarship,
and education by publishing worldwide in

Oxford New York

Auckland Bangkok Buenos Aires Cape Town Chennai
Dar es Salaam Delhi Hong Kong Istanbul Karachi Kolkata
Kuala Lumpur Madrid Melbourne Mexico City Mumbai Nairobi
São Paulo Shanghai Singapore Taipei Tokyo Toronto

Oxford is a registered trade mark of Oxford University Press
in the UK and in certain other countries

Published in the United States
by Oxford University Press Inc., New York

A catalogue record for this book is available from the British Library

Library of Congress Cataloging in Publication Data

Data available

ISBN 0-19-850435-7
10 9 8 7 6 5 4 3 2 1

Typeset by Pantek Arts Ltd, Maidstone, Kent
Printed in Italy by
Giunti Industrie Grafiche

Foreword

The primary aim of this series is to act as a guide and a stimulus to holidaymakers, be they specialist naturalist or interested amateur, and to teach them something of the wealth of wildlife that is to be found in the countryside around them, whether at home or abroad.

Despite the continued encroachment of housing and intensive farmland, and the disappearance of so much natural and semi-natural habitat over many decades, the wildlife of Europe is still remarkably varied and rewarding.

One of the major developments of recent years has been the rise of so-called 'ecotourism', which has combined the interests of the naturalist and the holidaymaker. Such tourism ranges from specialist guided tours for small groups of keen birdwatchers or botanists (often both) to more leisurely holidays that involve perhaps a sprinkling of nature study along with the more traditional goals of the tourist, such as visits to famous buildings or architectural sites. At the same time, the general traveller on a private holiday to a hotel, villa, gîte, or campsite is frequently keen to learn more about the landscape and countryside of the region he or she is visiting, and such knowledge can considerably enrich and increase the enjoyment of a holiday.

Throughout the books there is a strong emphasis on conservation and the need to ensure that a representative range of habitats remains long into the future for coming generations of naturalists and nature-sensitive tourists to enjoy.

Each book begins with an overview. This is in essence a background sketch of the country – mainly in terms of its ecology and wildlife – with a look at the major habitat types and their importance. The overview also contains some details about the state of nature conservation, and considers the various types of reserve, conservation laws, and related matters.

The overview is followed by a systematic gazetteer of selected sites, grouped by regions, of particular natural history importance. Of course, with so many fascinating areas – not all of them protected – in addition to the large numbers of reserves, our coverage cannot be comprehensive. Nevertheless, we have chosen sites that are generally not too difficult to access and which together give a full picture of the richness of each country. The choice aims to give a representative range of visitable sites, encompassing all the important habitats. The sites vary widely in status and size, but all have something special to offer the visitor, and repay a visit.

The books in this series are highly visual, and are enlivened by the use of colour photographs of landscapes, habitats, species, and locations, many showing the actual sites described. The photographs were provided by Natural Image photograph agency or by the authors where their initials (T.F. or M.L.) appear in the captions. The Natural Image photographer was Bob Gibbons except where otherwise indicated in the caption. In addition, selected animals and plants are also illustrated by black and white line drawings, accompanying the relevant text. Maps of the country, regions, and selected sites enable each site to be quickly located and placed in the context of the country as a whole.

A special feature of these *Travellers' Nature Guides* is the composite paintings, by wildlife artist Michael Wood, depicting a range of classic habitats for each country, and illustrating a number of characteristic species. These help to give a flavour of the richness of the wildlife awaiting the informed naturalist traveller.

Martin Walters
Series Editor
Cambridge, 2002

Acknowledgements

Teresa and Mike would like to offer their heartfelt thanks to the following people for their disinterested help with the research for this book:

Juan José Aja Aja, Carlos Alonso-Álvarez, Teresa Andrés, José Luis Arroyo, Xisco Avellá, Quim Bach, Vicent Boronat, Gerard Bota, Paul Buckley, María Dolores Carrasco Gotarredona, Patxi Celaya, Paco Cerdà, Sue and Neil Clarke, Jordi Dantart, Bosco Dies, Nacho Dies, Jordi Domingo Calabuig, Colin Dunster, Peter Eden, Gonçalo Elias, Tomás Escriche, Pau Esteban, Mikel Etxaniz, Carles Fabregat, Maria Farino, Ponç Feliu, Domingos Alfredo Fernandes Amaro, Fidel José Fernández y Fernández-Arroyo, Jordi Figuerola, Joan Font, Carlos García, Chus García, María Pilar García, Manuel García Tornero, Miguel Ángel Gómez-Serrano, Dani González, Felipe González Sánchez, Juan Diego González, Valentí González, Daniel Grustán, David Guixé, Ricard Gutiérrez, Sergi Herando, Víctor José Hernández, Carles Ibáñez, Loreta Jaumandreu, Joan Juan, Fernando Jubete Tazo, Xavi Larruy, Tomás Latasa, Mike Leakey, Luis Lopo, Alberto Luengo Telletxea, Luis Maillo, Javier Mañas, José María Martínez Egea, Jordi Martí, Jesús Mateos, Olga Mayoral García-Berlanga, José Manuel Meneses Canalejo, António Monteiro, Hugo Mortera Piorno, Jamie McMillan, John Muddeman, Miguel López Munguira, Rafa Múñoz, Jordi Nebot, Miguel Ángel Núñez, Rocío Ocharán, Ibón de Olana, Carlos Oltra, Alejandro Onrubia, Maribel Órgaz, Carlos Pacheco, Manuel Paez, Antonio Paredes, Jordi Parpell, Andy Paterson, Gabriel Perelló, Patricia Pérez, Miquel Rafa, Mike Read, Víctor Redondo, Enric de Roa, Isabel Roura, Andreu Salvat, Miguel Ángel Sánchez, Toni Sánchez-Zapata, Javier Santaeufèmia, Josele Sanz, Gabriel Servera, Guillém Siré, Constantí Stefanescu, Luis Suárez Arangüena, José Pedro Tavares, José Luis Tella, Ricardo Tomé, Joserra Undagoitia, Vicente Urios, Pepe Vallejo, Xabier Vázquez Pumariño, Alejandro de la Vega, Carlota Viada, Ottobrina Voccoli, Robin Walker, Sue Watt, Tobias Willett, Marcial Yuste, and Pablo Zuazua.

For Gabriel and Aneira

Abbreviations used in the text

ADENEX	Asociación para la Defensa de la Naturaleza y los Recursos de Extremadura
ANEI	*Àrea Natural d'Especial Interès*
CEAM	Colectivo de Educación Ambiental
CSIC	Consejo Superior de Investigaciones Científicas
EGRELL	Institució per a l'Estudi, Gestió i Recuperació dels Ecosistemes Lleidatans
GECEN	Grupo para el Estudio y Conservación de los Espacios Naturales
GEOTA	Grupo de Estudos de Ordenamento do Território e Ambiente
GOB	Grupo Balear d'Ornitologia i Defensa de la Naturalesa
IUCN	The World Conservation Union
NGO	Non-governmental organization
SEO	Sociedad Española de Ornitología
WWF	World Wide Fund for Nature
ZEPA	*Zona de Especial Protección para las Aves*
ZPE	*Zona de Protecção Especial*

Contents

Overview

Introduction

Spain is linked inextricably in many people's minds with sun-drenched beaches, mani-cured golf courses, *paella* and sherry, and the ideal package holiday. Dig a little deeper and you might find images of black fighting bulls, *flamenco* dancers, Don Quixote, Velázquez or Salvador Dalí, and yet there is so much more to this southwest European enclave than the glossy tourist brochures would have us believe. Spain harbours snow-capped mountains in excess of 3000 m, ancient deciduous forests that are home to bear and capercaillie, the unique wood–pasture known as *dehesa* that is the destination of thousands of cranes each winter, arid pseu-dosteppes populated by stately great bus-tards and whirring sandgrouse, and mighty rivers terminating in coastal estuaries and deltas teeming with waterbirds, not forget-ting the Balearic archipelago, adrift in the azure Mediterranean, harbouring a unique flora and prolific seabird colonies. And when you consider that this diversity of habitats contains more than 7000 species of vascular plant, 85 native terrestrial mammals, 500-odd birds cited in the past century, 70 native reptiles and amphibians and 227 butterflies – with a high level of endemism in most groups – it is clear that Spain is home to a wealth of flora and fauna unrivalled in west-ern Europe today.

Geography

The Iberian peninsula, comprising mainland Spain and Portugal, is separated from the rest of Europe by the formidable barrier of the Pyrenees and virtually closes the western end of the Mediterranean basin, its south-ernmost shores lying only a stone's throw from Africa. To the east, the Balearic archipelago (Balears), geographically and politically pertaining to Spain, falls within

1 GALICIA & ASTURIAS
2 CANTABRIA, EUSKADI & LA RIOJA
FRANCE
6 CASTILLA Y LEÓN & MADRID
3 ARAGÓN & NAVARRA
4 CATALUNYA
PORTUGAL
7 EXTREMADURA & CASTILLA – LA MANCHA
5 BALEARS
N
8 PAÍS VALENCIÀ & MURCIA
9 ANDALUCÍA
0   200 km

Opposite page: **Spring flowers in an olive grove near Ronda, Andalucía** the jurisdiction of this book, but the Islas Canarias, marooned in the Atlantic some 1150 km to the south, are not included.

Spain is divided into 17 *comunidades autónomas* (semi-federal regional administrations with a high degree of legislative autonomy), with 15 on the mainland and one each covering the Balears and Islas Canarias. Each section of this book encompasses one or more of these autonomous communities.

The Iberian peninsula covers around 581 000 square kilometres, of which some five-sixths pertain to Spain, with the Balears adding a further 5000. Population density is low, averaging only 80 inhabitants per square kilometre, with many people crowded into the principal cities – the capital Madrid, plus the coastal nuclei of Bilbao, Barcelona, València and Málaga – leaving large tracts of the interior virtually uninhabited.

As with most peninsulas, the coastline of mainland Spain is considerable, extending over some 5000 km. More than half this length pertains to the Atlantic coast, with the deeply indented shores of Galicia alone accounting for about one-third, while to the Mediterranean sector can be added the 1186 km of the Balears. On the Atlantic coast, secluded sandy coves and large estuaries alternate with rocky headlands and offshore stacks, while the virtually tideless Mediterranean shore, although plagued by the tourist industry since the 1960s, still supports a remarkable diversity of coastal wetlands, rugged cliffs and sweeping sandy beaches.

Much of the interior of mainland Spain comprises a vast upland plateau, the Meseta, gently tilted in a southwesterly direction towards the Atlantic, such that four of the five principal Iberian rivers – the Duero, Tajo, Guadalquivir and Guadiana – also flow in this direction, while the fifth – the Ebro – carries its sediments east to form a vast, arrow-shaped delta in the indolent waters of the Mediterranean. River gorges and inland wetlands are dotted across the Meseta, the latter including natural freshwater and endorheic lagoons and a multitude of artificial reser-voirs, all of which act as oases for wildlife in an otherwise largely agricultural landscape.

Spain possesses some of the highest mountains in Europe outside the Alps. In the northeast, the 400-km chain of the Pyrenees rises to 3408 m (Aneto), effectively dividing Spain from France, while further west, the Cordillera Cantábrica (highest peak: Torre Cerredo (2648 m) in the Picos de Europa), runs parallel to Spain's northern coast before curling south along the Galicia–León border and into northern Portugal. The Sistema Central, reaching 2592 m on Almanzor, splits the Meseta into north and south and is commonly referred to as the 'backbone of Spain', while the Sierras Béticas and Subbéticas occur principally in Andalucía, encompassing the roof of the Iberian peninsula: Mulhacén, in the Sierra Nevada, is 3482 m.

The Sierras Béticas continue northeastwards under the Mediterranean, terminating in a scatter of unsubmerged peaks which today comprises the Balearic archipelago, rising to just 1445 m (Puig Major) on Mallorca. Lesser mountain ranges on the mainland include the Sistema Ibérico, which runs along the southern margin of the Ebro and whose high point is El Moncayo (2313 m), the Sierra Morena, which divides Andalucía from the south Meseta but rarely exceeds 900 m in height, and the Catalan and Valencian coastal ranges. One-sixth of Spain lies over 1000 m, and it is second only to Switzerland in Europe for average land height (650 m).

Geologically, the north and west of the Iberian peninsula lies on Palaeozoic siliceous rocks – principally granite, schist and gneiss – which are immensely durable and have thus resisted erosion despite the heavy rainfall associated with these regions. As a result, a large part of Galicia and Asturias, as well as the Sistema Central and Sierra Morena, is typified by dark, rounded hills which nevertheless have been much dissected by fast-flowing rivers characterised by deep gorges and a plethora of waterfalls. Where these rivers descend to the Galician coast, rising sea levels since the last ice age have produced a series of impressive, steep-sided rias.

The Pyrenees, the eastern Cordillera Cantábrica and the Sierras Béticas are younger ranges, composed mainly of sedimentary rocks uplifted during the Alpine Orogeny, although often with a core of older, crystalline bedrock. Because of their greater height, they have been heavily glaciated and present a more rugged profile, aided and abetted by karstification where the bedrock is limestone. A third rock type is of volcanic origin, with notable outcrops at La Garrotxa and Cabo de Gata.

The Meseta, by contrast, is composed of Tertiary sedimentary rocks overlying this Palaeozoic core, predominantly limestones and sandstones. In Extremadura, the ancient rocks lie close to the surface and often break through, studding the region with quartzite crags and bluffs, while most of Castilla y León and eastern Castilla–La Mancha comprise seemingly endless plains, traversed by river gorges which harbour a wealth of wildlife, but otherwise dedicated largely to extensive cereal cultivation, vineyards and livestock rearing. Lowlands along the main river valleys harbour fertile alluvial deposits which have been much exploited for agriculture, although the vast Ebro depression once housed an enormous inland lake, which has left in its wake the largest expanse of saline steppes in Iberia, if not in Europe.

Climate

Climatically Spain can be divided into three distinct regions. Weather systems driving in from the Atlantic bring cool, moist weather to the northwestern and northern shores, creating a green, tree-clad landscape which is not dissimilar to that of Ireland or Wales, although rather warmer for much of the year, with the coastal regions generally frost-free. The abundant rains (typically in excess of 2000 mm annually) can occur at any time of year, much falling as snow in the Pyrenees and the Cordillera Cantábrica during the winter and persisting well into the summer in the higher reaches. Humidity is high and mists are frequent, often shrouding the coastal hills for days on end.

Arid badlands in the Desierto de Tabernas, Almería

The Mediterranean climate experienced by much of the eastern and southern sectors of mainland Spain and the Balearic archipelago is characterised by mild winters (in southeastern Spain, for example, the thermometer rarely drops below 13°C, even in January) and hot summers, although the worst of the heat is usually tempered by sea breezes. Rainfall is less abundant than in the Atlantic zone, and most falls during the autumn, when the normally dry watercourses (*ramblas*) can become raging torrents. A marked summer drought is responsible for the xerophytic character of the natural vegetation: pines or evergreen oaks with tough, waxy leaves to reduce water loss. Taking the Mediterranean climate to its extreme, Almería and Murcia have an emphatically hot, dry climate, with precipitation rarely exceeding 250 mm per year, maximum temperatures of almost 50°C and more than 3000 hours of sunshine annually, giving rise to the only true desert habitats in Europe.

The heart of the peninsula, however, relatively distant from the ameliorating influence of the Atlantic or Mediterranean, suffers an essentially continental climate, the long, bitterly cold winters alternating with brief, scorching summers; a situation described by Castilian Spaniards as 'nine months of winter and three of hell'. Rainfall is low, the drought period is prolonged, and temperatures range from –20°C to more than 45°C during the course of the year; even on a daily basis the variation can be extreme.

This broad scheme is of course disrupted to some extent by the various mountain ranges which traverse the Iberian peninsula. In Spain, it is estimated that the temperature drops by 0.6°C for every 100 m ascended, such that even where the temperature is in the 40s on the Almerían coast in midsummer, it could be as little as 15°C on the summit of Mulhacén, whose snows are visible from the nearby semi-desert habitats for at least 6 months of the year. In central Spain, the north flanks of the Sistema Central support extensive Scots pine forests which would look more at home in the Pyrenees, while the Sierra de Grazalema, in western Andalucía, intercepts incoming Atlantic weather systems to such an extent that it is one of the rainiest places in Spain, despite lying in the southern Mediterranean zone. Conversely, valleys which lie in the immediate rain-shadow of the Cordillera Cantábrica – such as that of Liébana, to the southeast of the Picos de Europa – are often sunny enclaves with relatively low rainfall and typically Mediterranean vegetation, in sharp contrast to the mist-swathed coast just 40 km to the north.

Climate has understandably affected land-use across the Iberian peninsula. In the north and west, for example, the mountainous terrain and high productivity resulting from abundant rainfall have led to a network of small farms (*minifundias*), often revolving around a traditional livestock-rearing system. Unfortunately this area is badly affected by emigration to the cities, such that the remaining population is sparse and elderly, resulting in a gradual abandonment of this way of life and the natural succession of species-rich haymeadows to low-diversity scrub or, worse still, their conversion into sterile tracts of non-native pines and eucalypts.

By contrast, much of the more arid southern sector of the peninsula is suitable only for low-intensity dry cereal, olive and vine cultivation, livestock-rearing (especially fighting bulls), or silviculture, with the extensive formations of *dehesa* a characteristic feature. Estates are often huge (*latifundias*), owned by absentee landlords and worked by tenant farmers, and again rural depopulation is acute. Industry and commerce are primarily confined to the larger cities and a few isolated mining areas, while the Mediterranean coast derives its income mainly from tourism. All around the shores of mainland Spain and the Balears, however, polycultural smallholdings and fishing communities persist, the latter particularly on the Atlantic coast.

History

Before humans became a permanent feature in southwest Europe, the Iberian peninsula

Dehesa of cork oaks *Quercus suber* in the Sierra de Aracena, Andalucía

was predominantly forested. The hunter-gatherers of the Palaeolithic left little evidence of their occupation, save for the paintings of remarkable eloquence which adorn the walls of caves such as Altamira in Cantabria, Tito Bustillo in Asturias and La Pileta in Andalucía. In Neolithic times, as humans became more sedentary creatures, developing the skills necessary to grow crops and domesticate wild animals, the first trees began to fall to crude axes, paving the way for the widespread deforestation that has left Spain with less than 10% of its original forest cover today.

Some anthropologists speculate that the Basques, whose language – *euskera* – is unlike any other living tongue, are the direct descendants of these Palaeolithic peoples. For the most part, however, the present-day Spaniards spring from more diverse sources. Even before the birth of Christ, Spain had been invaded by Iberos (probably from North Africa), Phoenicians (twelfth century BC), Celts (from central Europe; 800–600 BC), Greeks (seventh century BC) and Carthaginians (fifth century BC). The second century BC saw the arrival of the Romans, who proceeded to rule the

whole of the Iberian peninsula more or less unchallenged until the early fifth century.

In 409, a new wave of invasions across the Pyrenees, headed by the Vandals, Suevi and Alans, shattered Roman hegemony in the peninsula, although this was somewhat restored by a deal with the Visigoths in 415, resulting in a peaceful melding of Suevi, Visigoths and Hispano-Romans that lasted until the eighth century. But it was the arrival of the Moors from Muslim North Africa in 711 – mostly Berbers from Morocco, but also Syrians and Egyptians – that decisively changed the course of history, as they swept across the length and breadth of the Iberian peninsula in just 5 years. Asturias and parts of Cantabria never succumbed to Moorish rule, providing a foothold for the Christian reconquest of Spain that lasted almost eight centuries, ending with the fall of Granada in 1492. Not surprisingly, however, the influence of the Islamic invaders' way of life remains to this day, especially in Andalucía.

With each successive invasion, the ancient Iberian forests gradually succumbed to the need for timber, firewood and the fuelling of the war machine. Land was progressively cleared to cultivate crops to feed the burgeoning population, while the arrival of the *merino* sheep with the Moors created a need for extensive rangelands. The problem of water supply in an essentially arid environment was addressed by both Romans and Moors, who built reservoirs, aqueducts and irrigation channels throughout the peninsula, some of which are still in use today.

Since the expulsion of the Moors, Spain's history has been by no means peaceful, with a series of savage and bloody wars being fought here; for example, the War of the Spanish Succession in the early eighteenth century, the Peninsula War (War of Independence) at the beginning of the nineteenth century, and the Carlist Wars of the mid-1800s. The most recent, and perhaps the most bitter, was the Spanish Civil War of 1936–39, which resulted in a 40-year dictatorship under General Francisco Franco Bahamonde that ended only with his death in 1975, followed by the return of the monarchy and the passing of the new constitution in 1978.

During this period, which Spain spent in virtual isolation from the outside world, the country fell far behind the rest of Europe in terms of technological progress, which is undoubtedly one of the reasons why great tracts of wilderness, intact traditional agricultural systems and a rich flora and fauna have survived here until the present day. In the second half of the twentieth century, while Euro-farmers were treating their fields to a lethal cocktail of pesticides and artificial fertilisers, the Spanish peasants were still working the land in time-honoured fashion, and where tractors and combine-harvesters trundled across much of western Europe, donkeys and yoked oxen plodded through wheat fields and haymeadows teeming with wildflowers. It must be noted, however, that many of the extensive eucalypt plantations of northwestern Spain are a legacy from this period, with large tracts of semi-natural habitat having been all but destroyed by this non-native species.

In the years following its 'liberation', Spain has been rushing to make up for lost time, most significantly by gaining entry to the

Hay-making in northern Spain, 1990 (T.F.)

European Union in 1986. Access to European funding has unfortunately led to some of the most environmentally damaging projects ever to take place in Spain, not least the agricultural intensification that has occurred in response to the Common Agricultural Policy. Wetlands have been drained, arid lands have been irrigated and thousands of hectares of ancient olive groves and *dehesa* have been ripped out to make way for vast cereal monocultures. It was indeed a cruel reversal of fate that allowed such an essentially 'wild' country as Spain to embark on the destruction of its natural heritage just as the rest of Europe was starting to treat the environment seriously.

In the past few years, however, the situation has improved enormously, with the application of the Birds and Habitats Directives forcing Spain to recognise that within its borders lie some of the best-preserved landscapes and plant and animal populations in the whole of Europe, and to act accordingly to conserve them.

Habitats and Vegetation

Above the tree-line

If the seas rose a couple of kilometres above their existing level, the crests of Spain's highest mountains would still emerge from the waters by a considerable margin. At these altitudes, high levels of ultraviolet radiation, subzero winter temperatures with prolonged snow cover, high-velocity winds and a paucity of oxygen combine to make this an inhospitable world for any form of life. And yet a vast array of plants and animals are able to thrive here.

Low-growing shrubs clothe the slopes immediately above the tree-line, often taking the form of cushions or creeping carpets in an effort to outwit the elements. Some plants have densely hairy foliage which traps an insulating layer of air, like a thick winter overcoat, while others contain dark pigments to ward off damaging ultraviolet radiation emanating from the sun. Above all, these so-called 'alpine' plants are able to flower and set seed within the confines of the all-too-brief summer of the high mountain environment. Often their flowers are fantastically large and brightly coloured in comparison with their sparse foliage, such that an early summer visit to an alpine habitat dazzles the eye with sheets of sky-blue gentians, white and yellow buttercups, pink and purple primroses and narcissi ranging from pale lemon to a deep, burnished gold.

Similarly, the Iberian mountains are home to many animals which are specifically adapted to these inhospitable conditions. Sure-footed Spanish ibex and chamois scrape a meagre living from the plants which shelter among the rock crevices, moving into the middle-altitude forests and grasslands during the harshest months of winter. Alpine marmots and snow voles retreat underground with the first heavy snows, while stoats undergo a complete change of pelt to become ermine, their pristine white winter coats affording them excellent camouflage in the pursuit of their prey.

Many specialist birds also haunt the high mountains, ranging from passerines such as wallcreeper, alpine accentor, alpine chough and snow finch to veritable lords of the skies such as golden eagle and lammergeier. The ptarmigan – in Spain confined to the high Pyrenees – is the avian equivalent of the stoat, exchanging its chestnut brown summer plumage for a thick coat of purest white in the winter, which serves to conceal it from potential predators. Adaptations among the high-altitude butterflies include dark coloration in the genus *Erebia*, extreme hairiness, as displayed by the Apollo, and an extremely short flight period in most species to coincide with the height of summer.

Spain's mountain ranges are very significant from a wildlife point of view, harbouring relict enclaves of arctic-alpine plants and animals which advanced southwards during the last glacial period and were later isolated by the retreat of the ice-sheets. Even as far south as the Sierra Nevada you can find plants whose nearest known populations are in the Pyrenees today, such as glacier crowfoot and Pyrenean poppy. Plants and animals which have evolved specifically to survive in montane conditions generally

Trumpet gentian *Gentiana acaulis* (T.F.)

Parnassus-leaved buttercup *Ranunculus parnassifolius* (T.F.)

find themselves unfit for life in a lowland environment, either because of their peculiar physical, behavioural and physiological characteristics, or because they are unable to compete with species which are better adapted to this realm: humans, in the most extreme instance.

As a result, montane plants and animals find themselves as isolated as if they were truly island dwellers, often confined to a single peak in a sea of lowlands. It is not surprising, therefore, to find that creatures which have been cooped up in these mountain fastnesses for long periods have evolved independently, such that many of the Spanish endemics are closely linked with montane regions. Again taking the example of the Sierra Nevada, some 80 species of invertebrate and a similar number of vascular plants are found nowhere else in the world, while the Pyrenees is home to around 150 endemic plants and unique herptiles such as the Pyrenean brook salamander, Pyrenean frog and three species of *Lacerta*.

The land which lies above the tree-line – be it alpine grasslands, cushion scrub communities, rockgardens, screes, crags or peatbogs – is a highly sensitive environment. Faced with habitat destruction (ski installations are rife in the Pyrenees and Sierra Nevada), disturbance (four-wheel drive vehicles are becoming a real problem in the Cordillera Cantábrica), or active removal by the twenty-first-century equivalent of the hunter-gatherer (hunting and the collection of rare medicinal plants or butterflies), its inhabitants can only retreat further into the mountains until eventually they teeter on the brink of the precipice and extinction. In recognition of this fact, four of the seven national parks on the Spanish mainland protect the high mountains – the Picos de Europa, Ordesa y Monte Perdido, Aigüestortes and the Sierra Nevada – with natural parks or nature reserves covering many other montane regions.

Atlantic habitats

In contrast to the essentially Mediterranean lands of much of mainland Spain and the Balears, huge areas of the north are still clothed with native forests. The north-facing slopes of the Cordillera Cantábrica support thick stands of sessile oak, beech and downy birch (subspecies *celtiberica*), while further east, where humidity is lower, the Pyrenees are endowed with a cloak of mountain and Scots pines and European silver-fir. Little remains of the once extensive pedunculate and holm oak and bay forests which

Pyrenean oak *Quercus pyrenaica* wood–pasture (T.F.)

once clothed Spain's humid northern shores but enclaves persist, home to a rich fern flora: Killarney and royal ferns, Tunbridge filmy-fern, hay-scented buckler-fern and more typically Macaronesian species such as *Woodwardia radicans*, *Culcita macrocarpa* and *Davallia canariensis*.

A fourth species of oak – Pyrenean by name, although not by nature – is also essentially Atlantic in distribution, but extends much further into central Spain, where it forms large, almost monospecific tracts of forest on acid soils on the southern flanks of the Cordillera Cantábrica and in the Sistema Central, the Sistema Ibérico and the Sierra Morena.

Such ancient forests are defined by the characteristics of the trees themselves. Conifers do not lose all their leaves in the autumn, instead shedding them a few at a time throughout the year. Little light penetrates the dense canopy, and the soft, continuous rain of needle-like leaves forms a thick carpet on the forest floor. In the gloom, saprophytic plants such as yellow bird's-nest, ghost and bird's-nest orchids and a wealth of fungi thrive in the absence of competition from green-leaved, photosynthesising species, with summer-flowering wintergreens also characteristic.

The deciduous forests, on the other hand, present bare branches to the sky throughout the winter, such that ample sunlight filters through to the lowest levels, providing for a springtime flush of forest herbs: hepatica, wood and yellow anemones, primrose, ramsons and Pyrenean squill in the beechwoods, for example. In midsummer, when the canopy is full, more shade-tolerant plants such as narrow-leaved lungwort, herb-Paris, whorled Solomon's-seal, martagon lily and helleborines come into flower. Again there is a rich fern flora, especially on acid soils, where you might find hard, lady, lemon-scented and scaly male-ferns. Particularly associated with the Pyrenean oak woods is the western peony.

The extensive Atlantic forests of northern Spain are home to some of Europe's most endangered animals. The most remote regions provide refuge for brown bears – of which some eighty individuals remain in the Cordillera Cantábrica, plus a handful in the Pyrenees – and capercaillie, with a fast-declining population of the subspecies *cantabricus* inhabiting beechwoods in the central Cordillera Cantábrica, although the Pyrenean subspecies *aquitanicus* – characteristic of coniferous forests – is faring rather better. Forest-breeding raptors and small carnivores – pine and beech martens and wildcat – abound in both woodland types, as do Eurasian badger, wild boar and red squirrel, although edible dormice are particularly associated with lowland deciduous forests.

Woodpeckers also find one of their main strongholds here, with the humid forests of Navarra harbouring all seven Spanish species, notably white-backed, a central and northern European bird which in Spain is confined to the western Pyrenees. Tengmalm's owl is a similarly Euro-Siberian species, which in Iberia is found only in the coniferous forests of the central and eastern Pyrenees. Many other birds more typical of northern and central Europe reach their southernmost limit in Spain's Atlantic

Scything hay in the Picos de Europa (T.F.)

forests, notably woodcock, wood warbler, goldcrest, marsh tit, treecreeper and bullfinch. A rich invertebrate fauna is also associated with the Atlantic forests, particularly the broad-leaved element, including such eye-catching species as the Tau emperor moth, stag beetle and many species of longhorn beetle with wood-boring larvae, notably the steel-blue *Rosalia alpina*.

Tongue orchids *Serapias lingua* (T.F.)

Over the centuries, humans have gradually cleared land for pasture and meadow from these Atlantic forests, resulting in a mosaic of natural and semi-natural habitats that has enhanced their wildlife value by allowing species typical of more open country to flourish. At lower levels, the removal of the forest has given rise to extensive tracts of grassland which form part of a traditional livestock-rearing system – based on local breeds – across much of northern Spain. In the Cordillera Cantábrica, large tracts of haymeadow lack boundary features, individual ownership indicated only by marker stones or even sticks. Where the traditional agricultural system has been maintained, these Atlantic grasslands are among the richest in the world in terms of floristic diversity, particularly in the Picos de Europa, teeming with orchids and containing many plants which are becoming increasingly rare elsewhere in western Europe – rock cinquefoil, greater yellow-rattle, rampion and spreading bellflowers, round-headed leek and wild tulip, for example – although practices such as cutting for silage and the use of artificial fertilisers in recent years are taking their toll.

This forest–grassland mosaic is incredibly rich in butterflies, with species typical of woodland rides such as pearl-bordered, silver-washed, high brown and marbled fritillaries, purple emperor and woodland brown coexisting with those of flower-rich meadows: a virtually endless list of blues, coppers, hairstreaks and fritillaries. Red-backed shrikes also find this complex habitat to their liking, as do rock and cirl buntings and a myriad small mammals, including the Iberian blind mole, unique to the peninsula.

Higher up, close to the natural tree-line, secondary heathlands have replaced the natural forest, maintained by grazing and fire. These are particularly characteristic of northwestern Spain, where the acid soils and moist climate necessary for their development coincide. As their name suggests, heathlands are dominated by a closed canopy of ericaceous species – ling, Spanish, tree and Dorset heaths, *Erica umbellata* and green heather – accompanied by *Halimium lasianthum* subspecies *alyssoides* and leguminous shrubs, notably *Chamaespartium tridentatum* and various gorses and greenweeds. In the Pyrenees, these secondary scrub communities are characterised by echinospartum, box, alpenrose and bilberry. Where the water table is close to the surface, small peatbogs form, where cross-leaved heath abounds and insectivorous species such as sundews and butterworts find a suitable niche.

Scrublands above the tree-line in northern Spain are also home to a unique breeding bird assemblage, including hen harrier, partridge, bluethroat, ring ouzel, whinchat and yellowhammer, with the forest–scrub border the favoured haunt of citril finches. Castroviejo's hare, unique to the Asturias–León border in the western Cordillera Cantábrica, and the quasi-endemic Cantabrican viper also occupy these habitats.

Atlantic habitats are well represented within Spain's network of protected areas. The Fragas do Eume is one of the last remaining examples of coastal broadleaved forest, while beech and sessile oak wood-lands are protected in the Sierra de los Ancares, Muniellos, Somiedo, Redes and Saja–Besaya in the Cordillera Cantábrica, Señorío de Bértiz and Irati in the Pyrenees, and La Garrotxa and the Montseny in Catalunya; extensive Pyrenean oak forests occur in the enclaves of Fuentes Carrionas (Palencia) and Izki (Euskadi). The Pyrenean silver-fir and pine forests are well repre-sented in the Ordesa and Aigüestortes national parks, as well as at Benasque and Cadí-Moixeró.

Mediterranean lands

Away from the influence of the Atlantic, the potential natural forest of about two-thirds of mainland Spain, plus the whole of the Balears, is essentially Mediterranean in character, dominated by drought- and fire-resistant trees and shrubs, many of which are evergreen. The most typical species are western holm and cork oaks, lentisc, turpentine tree, Mediterranean buckthorn, myrtle, straw-berry-tree, *Phillyrea* species and laurusti-nus, as well as Spanish and prickly junipers, although some authorities con-sider the natural climax vegetation of the eastern peninsula to be Aleppo pine, accompanied by *Pinus nigra* subspecies *salzmannii* in higher areas and stone pine along the coast. It is worth pointing out here that *Quercus ilex* is nowadays consid-ered to belong to two subspecies with dis-tinct distributions in Spain: the western holm oak (*Q. ilex* subspecies *ballota*), which produces sweet acorns and occu-pies much of the western and interior reaches of the Iberian peninsula, and holm oak *(Q. ilex* subspecies *ilex*), which is principally confined to northern Spain, between Asturias and Catalunya, and the Balears.

Over the centuries of human occupation, however, these ancient Mediterranean forests have largely disappeared, confined today to the steepest slopes in the most remote corners of Spain. But the soils of the Mediterranean region are dry and unstable, such that following the removal of the pro-tective forest cover, much of this land was able to produce crops for only a few years before becoming impoverished. Once abandoned, these areas were gradually recolonised by secondary shrub communi-ties known variously as maquis and gar-rigue, depending on their vertical structure, but on the whole dominated by junipers, cistuses, leguminous shrubs, rosemary and thymes, with particularly dry regions being converted to barren pseudosteppes, their often saline soils characterised by a predominance of tough grasses. In south-western Spain, however, much of the primeval forest was converted to enormous tracts of the sparse wood–pasture known as *dehesa* (also present in northwest Africa), maintaining a viable agricultural system.

Dehesa is characterised by evergreen cork and western holm oaks – although the decid-uous Lusitanian oak is also sometimes employed in more humid regions – scattered across extensive pastureland which is tradi-tionally cultivated with cereals on a 10-year rotation to prevent the establishment of invasive shrubs, especially gum cistus. The

Gum cistus *Cistus ladanifer* (T.F.)

Extremadura e.g. Monfragüe: ❶ Black-winged kite *Elanus caeruleus*; ❷ Western holm oak *Quercus ilex* subspecies *ballota* ❸ Azure-winged magpie *Cyanopica cyanus* ❹ Common asphodel *Asphodelus aestivus* ❺ Tassel hyacinth *Muscari comosum* ❻ Gum cistus *Cistus ladanifer* ❼ Ocellated lizard *Lacerta lepida*

Picos de Europa: ❶ Rock thrush *Monticola saxatilis* (male) ❷ Amplexicaule buttercup *Ranunculus amplexicaulis* ❸ Trumpet gentian *Gentiana acaulis* ❹ Spring pasque flower *Pulsatilla vernalis* ❺ Iberian rock lizard *Lacerta monticola* ❻ Moss campion *Silene acaulis* ❼ Gavarnie blue *Agriades pyrenaicus asturiensis*

Ebro Delta: ❶ Little bittern *Ixobrychus minutus* ❷ Giant reed *Arundo donax*, ❸ Common reed *Phragmites australis* ❹ Black-winged stilt *Himantopus himantopus* ❺ Red-crested pochard *Netta rufina* (males) ❻ Little egret *Egretta garzetta* ❼ White water-lily *Nymphaea alba* ❽ European pond terrapin *Emys orbicularis*

Bardenas Reales: ❶ Griffon vulture *Gyps fulvus* ❷ Black-bellied sandgrouse *Pterocles orientalis* ❸ Stone curlew *Burhinus oedicnemus* ❹ Field eryngo *Eryngium campestre* ❺ Red horned-poppy *Glaucium corniculatum* ❻ Ladder snake *Elaphe scalaris* (juvenile) ❼ *Aizoon hispanicum*

Crown daises *Chrysanthemum coronarium* and purple viper's bugloss *Echium lycopsis* in cork oak *dehesa*

umbrella-shaped tree canopy – the result of assiduous pruning, plus browsing from below by livestock – protects the ground beneath from excessive water loss and expo- sure to frosts and wind, thus preventing the erosion of the usually poor soils. The oaks provide a copious supply of acorns – a prin- cipal food source for the black swine of the region (and for many thousands of wintering cranes) – as well as furnishing fuelwood, charcoal and a considerable proportion of the world's annual harvest of cork.

These *dehesas* are of enormous wildlife significance, the broad canopy of the oaks providing ideal nesting habitat for many raptors, notably black vulture, Spanish imperial eagle and black-winged kite, as well as for a wealth of smaller Mediterranean birds – hoopoe, roller, great spotted cuckoo, wood-chat shrike, spotless starling and azure-winged magpie, for example – while the highly diverse semi-natural grasslands beneath are a riot of colour in spring and harbour a wealth of invertebrates.

In addition, Mediterranean forests, scrub and *dehesa* habitats are home to such endangered mammals as the pardel lynx and many species of bat, particularly horseshoes and pipistrelles, as well as beech marten, wildcat, common genet, Egyptian mongoose, garden dormouse and wild boar, while *Sylvia* warblers – especially subalpine and Sardinian – are characteristic of the denser vegetation. Reptiles abound, notably Turkish and Moorish geckos, large and Spanish psammodromus, Iberian wall lizard, three-toed skink, amphisbaenian, horseshoe whip, southern smooth, ladder, false smooth and Montpellier snakes and Lataste's viper, while wetland habitats hold sharp-ribbed salamander, Iberian midwife toad, Iberian painted frog, western spadefoot and stripeless tree frog. Butterflies are at their most prolific in spring, when such eye-catching species as Spanish festoon, swallowtail, Cleopatra, Moroccan orange tip, Aetherie fritillary, cardinal, Spanish gatekeeper, nettle-tree butterfly, Provence hairstreak and black-eyed blue are on the wing, with the Spanish moon moth characteristic of the pinewoods.

Examples of the original Mediterranean evergreen broadleaved forest are protected by the Cabañeros national park and the Monfragüe natural park, with Los Alcornocales harbouring one of the largest cork oak forests in the world. Extensive *dehesas* exist in Extremadura, western Castilla–La Mancha and Andalucía, notably in the Sierra de San Pedro, Oropesa, the Valle de Alcudia, the Sierra Morena and Grazalema. The quasi-natural pine forests are well represented along the east coast and in the Balears, particularly Ibiza, and in the Serranía de Cuenca, the Sierra de Alcaraz and the Sierras de Cazorla, Segura y Las Villas.

Plains and steppes

The apparently endless plains of the Meseta, more reminiscent of the American Midwest than of Europe, occupy the heart of the Spanish mainland. Here, in Don Quixote country, the once extensive forests are but a dim and distant memory, the sky dropping abruptly to meet the bare bones of the earth in all directions. Now an essentially arable landscape, dotted with olive groves and vineyards, the far horizon is interrupted only by a small whitewashed farm or two, or a line of yellowed poplars digging deep into the parched earth in search of water.

In some cases the land is too arid or saline to support even dry cereal cultivation, and is clothed instead with tough grasses such as albardine and *Stipa* species, often accompanied by halophytic shrubs, notably *Salsola vermiculata* and shrubby orache, although on gypsum soils the flora is somewhat more diverse, swathed in pink *Ononis tridentata* and yellow *Helianthemum squamatum* in May and *Gypsophila* species in July. It is these areas that are often referred to as 'steppes', although they are almost certainly anthropogenic in origin and a far cry from

Hoopoe *Upupa epops*

the true, climactic *stepj* of Central Asia. For this reason, it is perhaps more accurate to call them 'pseudosteppes'. The most extreme examples of pseudosteppe habitats in Spain occur in the arid Ebro Depression and the badlands of Almería and Murcia. Dupont's larks are characteristic of both regions, but only the Andalucían sub-desert habitats can claim populations of desert orange tip and trumpeter finch.

Although at first sight a barren landscape, the extensive cereal fields of the Meseta are rarely treated with pesticides and artificial fertilisers, such that in many cases the crops of barley and wheat are virtually swamped beneath swathes of scarlet poppies, sky-blue cornflowers and delicate pale-pink corn-cockles. Similarly, invertebrates, reptiles and small mammals thrive here in abundance, in complete contrast to the sterile cereal monocultures so common elsewhere in Europe today.

This wealth of plant and insect life is a crucial factor in the survival of western Europe's healthiest populations of 'steppe' birds: great and little bustards, stone curlew,

pin-tailed and black-bellied sandgrouse and a wealth of larks, notably calandra and short-toed. The invertebrates and smaller vertebrates provide food for legions of Montagu's harriers, hobbies and lesser kestrels, while scavengers from further afield such as black and red kites and Egyptian and griffon vultures also feed here in some numbers. Notable concentrations of steppe birds can be found in Extremadura (La Serena, Los Llanos de Cáceres, Estepas de Brozas), Castilla y León (Villafáfila, Tierra de Campos), Madrid (Estepas de Talamanca), Navarra (Bardenas Reales), the Ebro Depression (Los Monegros, Belchite, Plana de Lleida) and southeastern Andalucía (Desierto de Tabernas, Hoyas de Baza y Guadix).

In some areas of the Meseta, the bare rock – usually limestone – is too close to the surface to permit cultivation, instead being clothed in a sparse garrigue of fragrant thymes and other low-growing shrubs, and typically dotted with Spanish junipers. Often referred to as *páramos*, these bare tablelands support a rich monocot flora –

Bardenas Reales (T.F.)

that of the Páramo de la Lora, on the Burgos–Cantabria border is quite exceptional – and are again a favoured haunt of Dupont's lark, with the Altos de Barahona a classic locality.

The Meseta is also riddled with dramatic river gorges known as *hoces*, home to exceptional assemblages of cliff-breeding birds, notably griffon and Egyptian vultures, golden eagle, peregrine, eagle owl, chough and smaller fry such as alpine swift, crag martin, blue rock thrush and rock sparrow, as well as providing shelter for a wealth of flowering plants – especially fissure-loving species known as chasmophytes – that would be unable to survive the harsh climate of the plateau above. Castilla y León is particularly well endowed with *hoces*, with notable examples including those of the Alto Ebro y Rudrón, Río Lobos, Río Riaza and Río Duratón, as well as the nearby Barranco del Dulce in Castilla–La Mancha. The most magnificent gorges in central Iberia, however, are undoubtedly those carved out by the mighty Duero and Tajo rivers along the Spanish–Portuguese border, which contain phenomenal populations of black stork, griffon and Egyptian vultures, golden and Bonelli's eagles and eagle owl.

Inland wetlands

Riverine habitats in Spain are rich and varied, ranging from the gelid, fast-flowing and well-oxygenated streams of the high mountains to the powerful, broad rivers of the five major watercourses, which often meander across wide floodplains in their middle reaches. Gallery forests are found at all levels, with shrubby willows typical of the montane sector and stately white and black poplars, small-leaved elms and narrow-leaved ashes – often referred to as *sotos*, particularly along the Ebro – characteristic of the more mature rivers. It has to be said, however, that only fragments of the latter remain today, as agriculture and dam projects have taken their toll.

Natural freshwater wetlands of any size are relatively rare in the interior of Spain today, with the drainage programmes of the mid-twentieth century having all but destroyed the former 'inland seas' of La Janda in Andalucía, Antela in Galicia and the Mar de Campos in Palencia, although the latter has been partially restored in recent years as the Laguna de La Nava. Large-scale dam projects on the principal Spanish rivers commenced at about the same time, such that nowadays the peninsula is littered with huge artificial bodies of water, several of which are of considerable wildlife significance, especially in ornithological terms: Ullivarri in Euskadi, Rosarito and Navalcán in Castilla–La Mancha and Orellana in Extremadura, to mention but a few.

Small freshwater wetlands are much more abundant, however, providing veritable oases for wildlife. Some are eminently natural, such as the glacial lakes of Aigüestortes (Catalan Pyrenees) and Sanabria (northern Castilla y León), the *galachos* (ox-bow lakes) of the middle reaches of the Ebro, or the shallow *tablas* of Daimiel and deep karstic lagoons of Ruidera in Castilla–La Mancha, while the wildlife significance of others – the Laguna de Pitillas in Navarra or the Embalse de las Cañas in La Rioja, for example – has been augmented by the construction of small dams to maintain water levels all year round.

Around the margins of these lakes and ponds, successional plant communities can be fantastically rich, home to marsh mallow, yellow flag, water-plantains and arrowhead, although they are often dominated by extensive stands of common reed and a host of sedges, galingales, club-rushes, rushes, bulrushes and bur-reeds. Open waters harbour rich assemblages of submerged and floating plants, including a wealth of pondweeds, hornworts, water-milfoils, insectivorous bladderworts, water-crowfoots and white and yellow water-lilies.

The freshwater mammal par excellence is undoubtedly the otter, relatively abundant throughout central and western Spain. The European mink, by contrast, is confined to Euskadi, Navarra, La Rioja and Burgos, notably along the margins of the upper Ebro, and is a relatively recent addition to the Iberian fauna, having been cited in Spain for

Lago de Isoba (T.F.)

the first time only in 1951, while the quasi-endemic Pyrenean desman is confined to ultra-clean, fast-flowing rivers in the northern Iberian mountains. Still and slow-moving waters throughout the peninsula are home to stripe-necked and European pond terrapins, as well as providing suitable habitat for a wide range of amphibians, with the Iberian pool frog perhaps the most ubiquitous. Spain's freshwater fish community excels in terms of diversity and level of endemism, while wetland habitats also support important assemblages of dragonflies and damselflies, including such rare and endangered species as orange-spotted and splendid emeralds.

More characteristic, however, are the so-called endorheic lagoons which are scattered across the interior of the Iberian peninsula. These are generally flat-bottomed basins lined with impermeable soils, into which flow small, rainwater-fed streams rising in the surrounding hills, creating shallow lagoons in the absence of an outlet to the sea. An important feature of many of these lakes is their seasonality, given that they usually occur in regions with very low summer precipitation and high levels of evaporation. Substrata rich in mineral salts often confer a marked salinity on the water, such that marginal and aquatic vegetation is generally of a halophytic nature and most fish and amphibians are unable to survive here. The most outstanding examples are the Lagunas de Villafáfila in Castilla y León, Gallocanta in southern Aragón and Fuente de Piedra in Andalucía.

The birdlife of the Spanish wetlands – both freshwater and endorheic – is truly phenomenal, both in terms of diversity and abundance. Reedbeds are home to healthy breeding populations of marsh harrier, purple heron, little bittern, water rail, purple gallinule and bearded tit, while riverine forests and stands of tamarisk support colonies of night herons and egrets, as well as olivaceous warbler, penduline tit and golden oriole. Spain also harbours breeding populations of several species of waterbird which are either unknown or extremely scarce in the rest of Europe, notably white-headed duck, marbled teal, red-crested pochard and crested coot, while Fuente de Piedra houses the second largest colony of greater flamingo in western Europe, after the Camargue. Huge numbers of wildfowl and waders flock to the interior wetlands in winter, with Villafáfila's tens of thousands of greylag geese a classic example.

Wetlands are extremely fragile habitats, however, and although many of Spain's classic sites are protected, both nationally and internationally, such status does not always confer survival. The Tablas de Daimiel national park, for example, has been reduced to a shadow of its former glory by interference with the rivers and aquifers that feed the lagoons and marshes, in particular dam construction and water extraction for irrigation. On the other hand, the rehabilitation of many former wetlands is currently being undertaken, notably at La Nava and La Janda, while several of those of an artificial nature, such as the gravel pits along the Río Jarama in Madrid, or the Cañada de Las Norias in Almería, are being restored with wildlife in mind.

Where the land meets the sea

With an extensive coastline bordering both the Atlantic and the Mediterranean, the Spanish shore is virtually unrivalled in western Europe for its sheer diversity of ecosystems and wildlife. Unfortunately, the Mediterranean coast was 'discovered' by the beach-oriented tourist industry in the middle of the last century, with ill-planned resorts responsible for the disappearance of large areas under wall-to-wall concrete. In the main, the Mediterranean coast is low-lying and sandy, ideal for the sun-tan brigade, while the swampy, more fertile soils around the mouths of the main rivers have long since been drained and dedicated to agriculture.

Notable exceptions are Catalunya's Delta de l'Ebre and the Marismas del Guadalquivir (Doñana): two of western Europe's foremost ornithological refuges, which harbour internationally significant breeding populations of herons, wildfowl, waders, gulls and terns, as well as attracting enormous numbers of wintering and passage birds. Other important coastal wetlands on the Mediterranean

Cliffs and offshore stacks on the Cantabrian coast (T.F.)

and southern Atlantic shores are the Marismas del Odiel and Bahía de Cádiz in Andalucía, Mar Menor in Murcia, a suite of Valencian sites – Salines de Santa Pola, L'Albufera, Marjal del Moro and Prat de Cabanes – and Catalunya's Aiguamolls de l'Empordà and Delta del Llobregat. A whole host of Iberian endemic sea-lavenders has been described from the low-lying reaches of the Mediterranean coast, with more rocky areas in Murcia and Almería harbouring relict enclaves of Afro-Iberian semi-desert vegetation: *Zizyphus lotus*, maytenus, *Periploca laevigata* subspecies *angustifolia* and *Launaea arborescens*.

Cliff-lined sectors of the Mediterranean coast – in particular the Costa Brava, northern Alacant, southern Murcia and Cabo de Gata in eastern Andalucía – have fared rather better, however, supporting small seabird colonies and important floral communities, often rich in endemic species, especially around Dénia (for example, *Silene hifacensis* and *Hippocrepis valentina*), with *Antirrhinum charidemi* and *Teucrium charidemi* notable at Cabo de Gata. The juniper- and white broom-clad dune systems of the southern Spanish coast comprise an important refuge for the Mediterranean chameleon, with spiny-footed lizards abundant in the open sands.

The northern and western Atlantic coast, by contrast, has a cooler, wetter climate and is thus less attractive to sun-seekers, such that swathes of pristine sand dunes sheltering brackish coastal lagoons persist, particularly in Galicia, at Corrubedo, Traba and Baldaio. Typical sand-dune vegetation displays physiological adaptations to a general paucity of water, such as succulence, in-rolled leaves or thick cuticles, with characteristic species including Jersey pink, *Corema album*, cottonweed and sea daffodil, as well as Iberian endemics such as the shrubby candytuft *Iberis procumbens* subspecies *procumbens*, lax viper's-bugloss and the knapweed *Centaurea corcubionensis*. Stone curlew and Kentish plover are characteristic sand-dune breeding birds, with snow buntings typical winter visitors. The reptiles of these northern dunes are

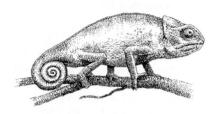

Mediterranean chameleon
Chamaeleo chamaeleon

also of interest, combining elements of both the Atlantic and Mediterranean faunas: slow-worm, Schreiber's green and ocellated lizards, Iberian and Bocage's wall lizards, large psammodromus, Bedriaga's and three-toed skinks, smooth and southern smooth snakes, ladder snake and even Cantabrican viper.

In Galicia, Asturias and Cantabria, seacliffs and offshore islets are a common feature, their relative isolation providing refuge for important seabird colonies, notably of storm petrel, shag, kittiwake, lesser black-backed gull and a last few guillemots. Far more abundant, however, is the yellow-legged gull, whose populations have snowballed in recent decades, often to the detriment of less competitive species. Salttolerant sea-cliff vegetation includes the robust Portuguese angelica and several very localised species of thrift: *Armeria pubigera* and *A. euscadiensis*, for example.

Apart from the steep-sided Galician rias, rivers discharging into the Atlantic generally terminate in estuaries of considerable significance for waterbirds, particularly in the winter and on passage, with notable examples being Umia–Grove, Ortigueira and the Ría do Eo in Galicia, Villaviciosa in Asturias, Santoña in Cantabria and Urdaibai in Euskadi. Saltmarsh vegetation is well developed in these shallower estuaries, composed primarily of halophytes which must also be able to withstand a twice-daily immersion in sea water; eelgrass meadows carpet the lower reaches, with the drier midsections of saltmarsh dominated by succulent chenopods and coloured by sea-lavenders, sea aster and golden-samphire.

Island outposts

Within the scope of this book, the only islands of any significance are the Balears of the western Mediterranean, with Eivissa lying just 85 km from the Spanish mainland. As continental islands, the Balears house a flora and fauna which has many affinities with the parent peninsula, although some 4 million years' isolation – and a prolonged human presence – has meant that some of the original animals and plants have disappeared, while others have evolved independently of those on the mainland, giving rise to high levels of endemism. Although the total flora numbers only some 1500 taxa, around 8% is found nowhere else in the world, while the Mallorcan midwife toad and Ibiza and Lilford's wall lizards are also unique to the archipelago, as are numerous races of birds, with the Balearic Marmora's warbler about to be declared a species in its own right.

Because of their warm, sunny climate, the Balears have also featured prominently in sun-and-sea travel brochures since the mid-twentieth century, although the industry has largely been confined to those parts of the islands where beaches are present. Since a goodly portion of the archipelago is flanked by sheer cliffs, the impact on wildlife has perhaps not been as great as along the Mediterranean coast of mainland Spain, such that the islands still harbour a rich flora and fauna.

The Balears are, in effect, a microcosm of the Mediterranean habitats described above. The whole archipelago lies within the Mediterranean forest biogeographic zone, here represented by holm oak and Aleppo pine. Little of this natural forest remains today, however, having been replaced with a mosaic of farmland dotted with groves of olive and carob and islands of dense Mediterranean maquis. Where the soils are too thin to support agriculture, sparse garrigue clothes the bare limestone, creating similar conditions to the pseudosteppes of the peninsula and supporting stone curlew and Thekla lark.

The highest mountains occur on Mallorca, but at a maximum of 1445 m the Serra de Tramuntana does not possess any of the typical 'alpine' elements of mainland Spain's great ranges. Nevertheless, the area above the tree-line is home to a number of endemic plants: the buttercup *Ranunculus weyleri*, the crucifer *Brassica balearica* and the umbellifer *Bupleurum barceloi*, for example. Seasonal torrents have carved spectacular chasms through this range, which are also home to an interesting flora – *Paeonia cambessedesii* and Mallorcan violet, to mention just two of the Balearic endemics found here – as well as providing refuge for the Mallorcan midwife toad. Similar defiles can be found in southern Menorca, which are utilised by breeding Egyptian vultures, peregrines and alpine swifts.

Coastal habitats are represented mainly by sand dunes and sea-cliffs, with salt-marshes all but non-existent in the absence of any major permanent rivers. The sea-cliffs – particularly those of the smaller islands such as Sa Dragonera and Cabrera – harbour a rich endemic flora and healthy colonies of storm petrel, Cory's shearwater, shag, Eleonora's falcon and Audouin's gull, while Aleppo pines clinging to the sheer marine precipices of the Serra de Tramuntana are utilised by nesting black

Paeonia cambessedesii

vultures. In addition, the Balearic shear-water breeds nowhere else in the world, but sadly its populations have declined dramatically in recent years, apparently due to predation from introduced rats and cats.

The best-preserved wetland in the Balears today is undoubtedly S'Albufera de Mallorca, its extensive reedbeds and marshes home to the western Mediterranean's largest populations of moustached warbler, as well as important heron colonies and a plethora of purple gallinules (reintroduced in 1991). Other significant wetlands are S'Albufera des Grau in Menorca and the saltpans of the Ses Salines complex, which links Formentera and Eivissa, plus those of Salobrar de Campos on Mallorca.

Wildlife

Flora

The most recent 'census' of vascular plants (ferns and flowering plants) of mainland Spain and the Balears derives from the *Flora Iberica* project (21 volumes, of which 9 have been published to date), which claims around 7000 species and subspecies (not including the Islas Canarias), of which some 1300 are endemic (over 18%). This compares very favourably with other Mediterranean countries, with only Turkey boasting a richer flora (around 8650 species), while the British Isles, by comparison, harbours about 1900.

The richness of the Spanish flora is considered to derive mainly from its climatic and altitudinal variation, with the underlying geology a third, but lesser, criterion. The fact that Spain lies at the cross-roads of Europe and Africa, and of the Atlantic and the Mediterranean, means that floristic elements of each occur here. On the one hand, many Tertiary – that is, semitropical – relics occur in warm, humid regions, notably Portugal laurel, *Rhododendron ponticum* subspecies *baeticum* and a wealth of ferns, for example, *Psilotum nudum, Davallia canariensis* and *Culcita macrocarpa*, while on the other, the highest mountains, especially the Pyrenees, are home to a number of species that also occur in the Arctic: dwarf willow, moss campion, glacier crowfoot, alpine meadow-rue, yellow mountain and purple saxifrages, mountain avens, sibbaldia, trailing azalea, blue heath, bog bilberry and snow gentian.

During the Upper Miocene, the Mediterranean existed as a series of small interior seas, with land-bridges connecting Spain with the Balears, the other western Mediterranean islands and Africa itself, such that today a good proportion of the Spanish flora is common to the Mediterranean region, while Afro-Iberian elements abound, especially in Andalucía. Nevertheless, the relative geographical isolation of the Iberian peninsula has resulted in the evolution of a myriad endemic species, particularly in montane and island habitats, notably in the genera *Dianthus, Petrocoptis, Saxifraga, Limonium, Armeria, Thymus, Linaria* and *Centaurea*. Of the 40–50 naturally occurring species of *Narcissus* in the world (numbers vary according to the taxonomy applied), no fewer than 35 occur in the Iberian peninsula, many of which are found nowhere else.

A good proportion (around one-third, excluding the Macaronesian entries) of the vascular plants which are listed on Annex II of the Habitats Directive occur in mainland Spain and the Balears, some of which are included by virtue of their endemic status, while others have a significant part of their European populations here.

Mammals

Spain is home to some 85 species of native or anciently introduced terrestrial mammal, 25 of which are bats. Among the old-established species are Algerian hedgehog, common genet and Egyptian mongoose, all of which seem to have followed the Moors into Iberia, while fallow deer were introduced even before this time. In the Balears, almost all the native mammals, with the exception of a few bats, were introduced from around 4000 BC onwards, several of

Pardel lynx *Lynx pardina* (Mike Lane)

which have evolved into unique subspecies since this time.

The twentieth century has seen a number of additions to Spain's mammalian fauna, including mouflon (although this was probably present in ancient times) and Barbary sheep, both deliberately introduced as game species, American mink, escapees from fur farms, now well established in certain areas, Alpine marmot, introduced to the French Pyrenees for food in 1948, which has since colonised the Spanish side of the range under its own steam, and coypu, with small numbers present in the wetlands of Euskadi and Navarra today. By contrast, the only extinctions in historic times have been two subspecies of Spanish ibex: *lusitanica*, which disappeared from northwestern Iberia at the end of the nineteenth century, and *pyrenaica* from the Pyrenees, the last known individual of which expired in 2000.

Unusually for a European region, Spain and Portugal boast a number of mammals found nowhere else in the world, notably the Iberian blind mole, Spanish shrew, Cabrera's vole, Castroviejo's hare, Spanish ibex and pardel lynx, with the Pyrenean desman's range extending into the French Pyrenees. Bats, cetaceans and carnivores are the most threatened mammal groups today, with the pardel lynx – whose population in 2002 was estimated at around 250 individuals – considered to be the most endangered feline in the world. On the other hand, the wolf, Egyptian mongoose, European mink and wildcat are all recover-

ing nicely after reaching an all-time low in the 1970s, while wild boar, Spanish ibex and roe and red deer are all considerably more abundant now than then. The same can be said of the chamois, the Spanish populations of which have recently been separated from those of the Alps, as *Rupicapra pyrenaica*, and which should perhaps more accurately be referred to as the isard.

Considered to be endangered at a European level and thus included in Annex II of the Habitats Directive, are Pyrenean desman, Cabrera's vole, wolf, brown bear, otter and pardel lynx, as well as all four Iberian horseshoe bats (greater, lesser, Mediterranean and Mehely's) and barbastelle, Schreiber's, Bechstein's, greater and lesser mouse-eared, long-fingered and Geoffroy's bats.

Birds

Around 240 species of bird breed regularly in mainland Spain and the Balears, with a further 100 or so habitually dropping in on passage or spending the winter here, although the complete list of species recorded exceeds 500.

Pride of place must go to the quasi-endemic Spanish imperial eagle (152 pairs in 2001; an encouraging, remarkable recovery from just 104 pairs in 1986), which is confined to the Iberian peninsula today, although it formerly bred in North Africa. In addition, the Balearic shearwater is only known to breed in the Balears (1750–2125 pairs in 2001), while various endemic avian subspecies occur on the mainland, notably *hispaniensis* of partridge, *aquitanicus* and *cantabricus* of capercaillie (in the Pyrenees and Cordillera Cantábrica, respectively) and *pyrenaicus* of ptarmigan.

Many Species of European Conservation Concern (SPECs) occur in the area covered by this book, several of which have their only European breeding populations here: Spanish imperial eagle (although a few pairs reputedly nest in Portugal), crested coot, cream-coloured courser (also Macaronesia, but bred in mainland Spain, in Almería, for

Griffon vultures *Gyps fulvus* in the Foz de Arbayún

the first time in recent history in 2001), Andalusian hemipode (probably extinct today), Dupont's lark and trumpeter finch (also Macaronesia). In addition, of the 24 globally threatened bird species which occur in Europe, 6 maintain important populations in Spain: almost all the Spanish imperial eagles, 30–40% of lesser kestrels (around 12 000 pairs in Spain), 25–50% of the European population of marbled teal, around half of all white-headed ducks, about half the great bustards and almost all the Audouin's gulls, with the largest colony in the world in the Delta de l'Ebre. Spain also harbours 66–90% of all the European black vultures, an enormous griffon vulture population – around 17 000 pairs in 1999, again the bulk of the European population – and over half of the European Bonelli's eagles.

In addition, Spain is of international importance for passage birds, especially storks and raptors, notably through the lowest passes of the Pyrenees and – of course – across the Strait of Gibraltar, and is also of significance for its wintering cranes. The north coast sees an important westward autumn passage of seabirds and waders, while the east coast is the main route of the so-called western Mediterranean flyway. In terms of waterbirds, it is considered that 77 wetlands in Spain comply with the Ramsar criteria, although only 38 have been designated to date.

Reptiles

Mainland Spain and the Balears are home to some 45 species of terrestrial and freshwater reptiles, including the Mediterranean chameleon, whose presence in Andalucía dates from at least 3000 years ago, and the long-established populations of Moroccan and Italian wall lizards in the Balears (and a few mainland localities). In addition, five marine turtles are seen sporadically off the Spanish coast, with a clutch of green turtle eggs successfully hatching for the first time here in Almería in 2001.

If we include the French Pyrenees, seven species are unique to the study area: Spanish algyroides, *Lacerta aurelioi*, *L. aranica*, Pyrenean and Iberian rock lizards, *Podarcis atrata* (on the Columbretes only) and Lilford's and Ibiza wall lizards, the latter two endemic to the Balears. Recent molecular studies have suggested that the Iberian populations of three-toed skink and green lizard are distinct from those found elsewhere in Europe, and that they be referred to as *Chalcides striatus* and *Lacerta bilineata*, respectively.

Other notable denizens are the spur-thighed tortoises in Doñana and the southeastern peninsula, which are probably of Algerian origin but introduced in ancient times (and more recently to the Balears), as well as Hermann's tortoise, which is native to L'Albera in northeastern Catalunya but introduced elsewhere. False smooth snakes, taken to the Balears by the Romans, are almost certainly responsible for the subsequent disappearance of Lilford's wall lizard on the main islands, with the introduction of the viperine snake similarly to blame for the regression of the Mallorcan midwife toad. A more recent, accidental introduction is that of the American red-eared slider to many wetland habitats in the peninsula and Balears alike, where it is said to be out-competing the native European pond terrapin.

Several Iberian reptiles are considered threatened at a European level and are thus listed on Annex II of the Habitats Directive: spur-thighed and Hermann's tortoises and European pond and stripe-necked terrapins, as well as several Iberian endemics: Schreiber's green lizard, Pyrenean and Iberian rock lizards and Lilford's and Ibiza wall lizards.

Amphibians

The amphibian populations of mainland Spain and the Balears are similarly diverse, comprising 25 native species. The green toad is a notable addition, introduced – probably as a religious totem – to the Balears in the Bronze Age, with the only other non-native species of note being the painted frog, which has colonised northeastern Catalunya since 1906 from populations introduced to southern France at the end of the nineteenth century.

As with the reptiles, several endemic species occur here, including the Mallorcan midwife toad in the Balears, *Alytes dickhilleni* in the southeastern corner and *Discoglossus jeanneae* in the southern and eastern peninsula. Golden-striped salamander, Bosca's newt and the Iberian frog are endemic to the northwestern corner of the Iberian peninsu-

la, while the Pyrenean brook salamander and Pyrenean frog are confined to the Pyrenees. Only four Spanish amphibians are listed on Annex II of the Habitats Directive: golden-striped salamander, Iberian painted frog, *Discoglossus jeanneae* and the Mallorcan midwife toad.

Freshwater fish

Spain also harbours one of Europe's most important assemblages of endemic freshwater fish. Most of these are mentioned in the various site descriptions and there is simply not room to list them all here. Many endemics are increasingly threatened by habitat destruction, pollution and predation by introduced species, and as such have been included in Annex II of the Habitats Directive, for example, the cyprinodontid Valencia toothcarp and many cyprinids: jarabugo, Iberian barbel, Iberian nase, *Iberocypris palaciosi*, bermejuela, pardilla and calandino, as well as the Spanish toothcarp, also found in Portugal and Algeria, and soiffe, whose distribution extends into France.

The northern rivers are home to significant populations of migratory fish, notably sea lamprey, Atlantic salmon and Twaite and Allis shad, all increasingly rare in Europe today, but the magnificent Atlantic sturgeon is nowadays observed only sporadically in the lower reaches of the Guadiana and Guadalquivir; all of these are also listed on Annex II of the Habitats Directive.

Butterflies and moths

Although butterflies have been well studied in mainland Spain and the Balears – with 227 species (more than half the European total) cited – the moths are only just starting to

Death's-head hawk-moth *Acherontia atropos*

attract attention, such that the only figure available is a highly conservative estimate of around 4000 species.

Once again the level of endemism is high. Among the blues unique to Spain are Carswell's little, Nevada and mother-of-pearl, as well as several members of the genus *Agrodiaetus*, of which we can cite Forster's furry blue, Catalan furry blue (sometimes referred to as Agenjo's anomalous blue) and Oberthür's and Andalusian anomalous blues. Other Spanish endemics include the Spanish argus (with a single, dubious record in the French Pyrenees), Chapman's ringlet, unique to the Cordillera Cantábrica, Zapater's ringlet, known only from the mountains of central-eastern Spain, Lefèbvre's ringlet, confined to the Cordillera Cantábrica and Pyrenees, false dewy and Gavarnie ringlets, unique to the Pyrenees, and the Spanish brassy ringlet, with widely separated populations in the Pyrenees and the Sierra Nevada. In addition, many endemic races of more widespread species occur, especially in mountainous areas.

Only a few of Spain's butterflies and moths are listed on Annex II of the Habitats Directive, notably marsh fritillary (excellent populations on the mainland), dusky large and Nevada blues and Spanish moon moth. The IUCN 2000 Red List, however, also considers the following to be endangered: Glandon blue (subspecies *zullichi*), Alcon, mountain Alcon and large blues, Zephyr blue (subspecies *hespericus*), Apollo, spring ringlet and carline skipper (subspecies *cirsii*).

Large blue *Maculinea arion* (T.F.)

Other invertebrates

The Spanish quota of dragonflies and damselflies – as a group often referred to as odonates – is 75 species, and although none of these is endemic, *Ischnura graellsii*, *Onycogomphus costae* and *Zygonyx torrida* are found only here in Europe. In addition, several endangered species listed on Annex II of the Habitats Directive occur, notably southern damselfly, *Gomphus graslini* (in Andalucía), *Lindenia tetraphylla* (albeit only five records in València) and orange-spotted and splendid emeralds.

Other invertebrate groups are not easily accessible to the amateur naturalist, as field guides covering Spain are practically non-existent. On the other hand, much work has been carried out by the Consejo Superior de Investigaciones Científicas (CSIC), and species lists for many invertebrate groups can be found on the website www.fauna-iberica.mncn.csic.es

Nature conservation

National

Although the national parks of La Montaña de Covadonga – expanded in 1995 to form the Picos de Europa – and Ordesa y Monte Perdido were among the first to be declared in Europe, in 1918, it was not until 1975 that the protection of natural habitats really took off in Spain, with the passing of the *Ley de Espacios Naturales Protegidos*; many areas were subsequently declared as *parques naturales* (natural parks) as a result. This was replaced in 1989 by the *Ley de Conservación de Espacios Naturales y de la Flora y Fauna Silvestres* (revised in 1997) under which four main categories of protected area were established: parks (including both national and natural), natural reserves, natural monuments and protected landscapes.

National parks – eight in mainland Spain and the Balears at the time of writing – continue to be declared and managed by the central government, nowadays under the auspices of the Ministerio de Medio Ambiente (Ministry of the Environment), but responsibility for the declaration and management of the remaining categories falls squarely on the shoulders of Spain's 17 *comunidades autónomas*. As might be expected, each autonomous region has chosen to exercise its freedom in environmental legislation to the full, resulting in a confusing rash of designations relating to protected areas: for example, *biotopo babestua* in Euskadi, *paraje natural* in Andalucía, *parque regional* in Castilla y León and *àrea natural d'especial interès* in the Balears. In Catalunya, 144 areas (covering 644 724 ha, 21% of the region), were identified as being of natural interest under the *Pla d'Espais d'Interès Natural* in 1993; these are usually referred to as PEINs.

International

One of the earliest international conventions dealing with wildlife was that relating to Wetlands of International Importance Especially as Waterfowl Habitat, agreed at Ramsar, Iran in 1971, which was ratified by Spain in 1982. At the time of writing, mainland Spain and the Balears have declared 38 so-called Ramsar sites covering 158 216 ha, in accordance with the criteria laid down therein.

Spain is also well endowed with Biosphere Reserves, declared under UNESCO's Man and the Biosphere programme, with 19 such sites having been declared to date (excluding the Islas Canarias), most recently that of Las Dehesas de Sierra Morena (2002).

In terms of the European Union legislation, Special Protection Areas under the Birds Directive (79/409/EEC) are known as *Zonas de Especial Protección para las Aves* (ZEPAs) in Spain, of which 231 had been declared in the peninsula and Balears in 2001. Progress with respect to the Habitats Directive (92/43/EEC) is rather slow however; although Spain has identified a massive 685 Natura 2000 sites in the peninsula and Balears alone, encompassing almost 83 000 square kilometres, their designation as such is way behind schedule.

Maps

This book has been written using the Michelin 1:400 000 series published in 2000 as base maps. Six maps cover mainland Spain and the Balears: Northwest Spain (441), Northern Spain (442), Northeast Spain and Balears (443), Central Spain (444), Central and Eastern Spain (445) and Southern Spain (446). All the localities and road numbers referred to in the site descriptions are marked on these maps; where road numbers are different on the ground (due to a major renumbering exercise in some regions), this has been indicated in the text.

More detailed maps are published by the Instituto Geográfico Nacional at 1:25 000, or by the Servicio Geográfico del Ejército at 1:50 000. The addresses of these organisations are given in the Useful contacts section, but you can also order them online at www.verdinet.com/mapas (an extremely easy-to-use website with maps to show the exact area covered by each sheet). In addition, the País Valencià and Catalunya have independently produced large-scale maps of their territories; contact the Instituto Cartográfico Valenciano and the Institut Cartogràfic de Catalunya, respectively.

Access and route-finding

In common with the rest of Europe, two types of formal waymarked footpath exist in Spain: long-distance routes (GRs) designed to be followed over several days, marked with horizontal red and white stripes, and shorter routes (PRs) with a total length of less than 50 km, which are indicated by yellow and white horizontal stripes (in Spain these are known respectively as *Gran Recorrido* and *Pequeño Recorrido*). At present, however, such waymarked trails are pretty much confined to the most-visited mountain regions of the peninsula – with the notable addition of the Camino de Santiago – with the network best developed in Catalunya, Navarra, Euskadi and Aragón. In general they are linear, not circular, and so are of limited use to the casual visitor who wishes to return to his car at the end of the day.

Farmers' track, northern Spain (T.F.)

Hunting

Hunting is a way of life in rural Spain, and when practised as a means of providing variety to a generally very spartan diet, offers no palpable threat to natural systems. Even today, this is the situation in many parts of Spain, where the majority of the more than a million licensed hunters only do so sporadically and have very little effect on wild animal populations. The exceptions are the spring hunting of north-bound migrating pigeons and doves in Euskadi, and the vast hunting estates of Extremadura, Andalucía and Castilla–La Mancha, where the behaviour and popula-tion dynamics of the local mammalian fauna are disrupted by high fences and the introduction of non-native species.

Legislation in Spain essentially restricts hunting to the months of October through to February, although the actual dates vary with autonomous community and from year to year, and also depend on the target species; hunting is usually limited to week-ends, public holidays and, in some areas, Thursdays. It has to be said, however, that some legal game species, such as the turtle dove, are in serious decline, while the illegal taking of protected species and the practice of gamekeeping by shooting, poisoning and trapping of predators in the hunting estates are both causing considerable conservation problems, especially in southern Spain.

Although hunting takes place virtually throughout Spain, who hunts where is strict-ly controlled. *Cotos privados de caza*, usual-ly indicated by rectangular signs divided diagonally into black and white triangles, are areas where hunting rights belong to one association and its members only; bags are also limited and virtually no areas are open to all-comers.

Many protected areas, such as the Delta de l'Ebre and L'Albufera de València, are still hunted over, although this activity is totally prohibited in other sites – the Laguna de Pitillas or the Lagoa de Valdoviño for exam-ple – which have been declared *refugios de caza*. These should not be confused with the *reservas regionales de caza*, which are large natural areas managed for big-game

On a less formal basis, northern Spain – where farmland is generally divided into small plots – is riddled with farmers' tracks which can be followed at will. Above the tree-line, common lands prevail, such that you can wander pretty well anywhere you choose, although it is advisable not to stray off the beaten track in the high mountains. Southern Spain is a different matter, how-ever, with large, fenced, landed estates the norm, often inhabited by fighting bulls to boot. Access is obviously much more difficult in such terrain, although the comprehensive network of drover's roads – nowadays increasingly waymarked – does get you some way into the wider countryside.

Generally speaking, you can walk any-where that is unfenced, provided that you do not trample crops – and remember, in north-ern Spain, hay is also a crop – or enter obvi-ously private property. The Sunflower series of walking guides covers much of Spain, describing routes – usually unmarked on the ground – which are specially selected for their scenic beauty and wildlife potential, as well as being circular or connecting with public transport to return you to your start-ing point.

Boar-hunting in northern Burgos (T.F.)

hunting, originally declared in accordance with 1966 legislation and nowadays often overlapping with national parks and other protected areas.

Target species vary little from one part of Spain to another: *caza menor* encompasses the usual litany of game birds – including the much prized red-legged partridge, quail and woodcock – as well as lagomorphs, while *caza mayor* – or big-game hunting – concen-trates on wild boar and red deer, with roe deer, Spanish ibex, chamois and mouflon also on the agenda where abundant. Local inconsistencies include the spring pigeon shoots in Euskadi and the anachronistic practice of bird-liming – coating the branch-es of trees with a sticky substance made from mistletoe berries to trap thrushes – which is inexplicably permitted in the autumn in parts of Catalunya and the País Valencià.

Galicia and Asturias

Introduction

The northwestern corner of Iberia is characterised by its fundamentally oceanic climate, having little in common with the Continental and Mediterranean regions of the rest of Spain. Much of the abundant precipitation here falls as snow in the upper reaches of the Cordillera Cantábrica, but the temperate, humid climate of the coast and heartland has unfortunately led to the planting of huge areas with eucalypts, all but destroying any intrinsic wildlife interest.

Most of Galicia and Asturias lies on ancient Palaeozoic bedrock, primarily acid in nature, with limestone deposits appearing only in the south and east of the region. The low-lying heartland of Galicia rises gradually southwards to the massif of Peneda–Gerês in northern Portugal, while the eastern reaches border outliers of the Cordillera Cantábrica: O Courel, Enciña da Lastra and the Ancares de Lugo (1826 m). In Asturias, the increase in altitude from the coast to the highest reaches of the Cordillera Cantábrica (here exceeding 2400 m) is more abrupt, given that the province is only some 80 km across at its widest point.

The most important river basin of the region is that of the Miño (310 km long), which discharges into the Atlantic on the Portuguese–Galician border (see p. 429). Further east, rivers descending from the Cordillera Cantábrica to the Bay of Biscay – renowned for their Atlantic salmon populations – are short and fast-flowing, their considerable erosive power often being responsible for the formation of spectacular defiles, especially where they cross the limestone outcrops of Somiedo and Redes.

The northern flanks of the Cordillera Cantábrica support some of the best-preserved deciduous forests – mainly beech and sessile oak – in Iberia, with outstanding examples at Muniellos and Somiedo.

1	Illas Cíes
2	Umia-Grove
3	Corrubedo
4	Costa da Morte
5	Fragas do Eume
6	Valdoviño
7	Ría de Ortigueira e Ladrido
8	Lagoa de Cospeito
9	Ría do Eo
10	Serra do Courel
11	Bosque de Muniellos
12	Somiedo
13	Macizo de Ubiña/Sierra del Aramo
14	Cabo de Peñas
15	Ría de Villaviciosa
16	Redes

Opposite page: **Subalpine meadows near Lago del Valle, Somiedo**

Relatively huge expanses of primeval woodland, they are home to the most important enclave of brown bear in western Europe today, as well as housing good populations of other carnivorous mammals, raptors (notably honey buzzard), woodpeckers (especially black and middle spotted) and capercaillie (here the subspecies *cantabricus*, which largely inhabits beechwoods). An interesting example of lowland deciduous forest is preserved in the Fragas do Eume, a refuge for a number of thermophilic ferns more usually associated with the semitropical forests of Macaronesia.

Above the tree-line thrives a classic high-level avifauna of alpine accentor, rock thrush, wallcreeper, alpine chough and snow finch, as well as chamois, snow vole and large numbers of plants unique to the Cordillera Cantábrica, particularly on the limestone peaks of O Courel, Somiedo, Ubiña and Redes. More acid uplands often support peatbogs and glacial lakes, again with an interesting flora and the Iberian stronghold of the alpine newt.

The Galician coast is profoundly dissected by flooded river valleys known as rias, between which finger-like promontories extend out into the Atlantic. The Rías Baixas (Bajas) to the south are separated from the Rías Altas by Cabo Fisterra – the westernmost point of Continental Spain – while to the east, the Atlantic coast is divided from the Cornisa Cantábrica by the headland of Estaca de Bares, itself the northern extremity of the peninsula. The Asturian coast, by contrast, lacks these deep inlets, with the exception of the Eo and Villaviciosa estuaries.

The west coast of Galicia harbours some of the most extensive and best-preserved sand-dune ecosystems in Iberia, notably those of Corrubedo and Baldaio, home to a number of psammophilic plants found nowhere else in the world and populated by breeding Kentish plover and stone curlew. The deep, fjord-like rías only support salt-marsh vegetation in their most sheltered reaches, as at Umia–Grove, but the Asturian estuaries are noteworthy for their diverse, halophytic plant communities. Sandwiched between these low-lying coastal areas are stretches of spectacular maritime cliffs which, together with the nearby archipelagos of Cíes, Ons and Sisargas, provide refuge for some of the most important seabird colonies in the peninsula, notably of storm petrel, shag and yellow-legged and lesser black-backed gulls, as well as the only Spanish populations of kittiwake and the all-but-extinct guillemot.

Not surprisingly, these coastal habitats attract large numbers of wintering and migratory waterbirds, with the northwest coast of Galicia often turning up Nearctic accidentals after strong westerly winds, while Estaca de Bares and Cabo de Peñas are renowned for their autumn passage of seabirds; Galicia is considered to be the most important wintering area in western Europe for oystercatcher. Wetland breeding birds are less abundant than on the Mediterranean and southern Atlantic shores, being restricted mainly to reedbed species such as little bittern, water rail and warblers, with black-winged stilt notable at Corme e Laxe and curlew at Villaviciosa.

This northwestern corner of Spain harbours internationally significant herptile populations, with the world distribution of golden-striped salamander, Iberian frog, Iberian rock lizard, Schreiber's lizard, Bocage's wall lizard and Cantabrican viper centred here. The scrubby transition zone between forest and subalpine habitats along the Asturias–León border is the stronghold of the Spanish endemic Castroviejo's hare, often accompanied by stable populations of wolf and partridge.

Galego is the first language of Galicia, with the regional dialect *bable* much used in Asturias, but most people also speak Castilian Spanish. The website www.xunta.es/conselle/cma/CMA05e/p05e01.htm gives more information about protected areas in Galicia.

SITE
1 Illas Cíes

A small archipelago harbouring large seabird colonies, an interesting sea-cliff and sand-dune vegetation and important reptile populations.

Spanish festoon
Zerynthia rumina

The diminutive archipelago of the Illas Cíes in the Ría de Vigo is all that remains today of an ancient granitic cordillera which once traversed the southern shores of Galicia, thought to have subsided during one of the frequent tectonic upheavals in the area, leaving just the tips of the highest peaks protruding from the ocean. The archipelago comprises three main islands: Illa de Monte Agudo in the north (maximum 188 m) is linked to the central Illa do Faro by the sandbar of Rodas and an artificial dyke topped by a road (these enclosing the Lagoa dos Nenos lagoon), while a channel of just 50 m separates the central island from that of San Martiño to the south. Numerous subsidiary islets speckle the surrounding seas, notably the cluster known as A Agoeiro, home to a small colony of storm petrel, despite being completely swamped by waves during winter storms.

In the 1950s, much of the natural climax vegetation of the Illas Cíes was largely replaced with non-native eucalypts and maritime and Monterey pines. Small, wind-pruned enclaves of Pyrenean oak persist, however, associated with a dense scrub of osyris, gorse, blackthorn, Mediterranean mezereon, sage-leaved cistus, white asphodel and *Asparagus aphyllus*, providing suitable breeding habitat for nightjar, tree pipit and Sardinian and Dartford warblers, while goshawks nest in the mature pines. Look out, too, for herptiles of humid, well-vegetated environments such as Bocage's wall lizard and the sleek, bronze-coloured Bedriaga's skink, both unique to Iberia, as well as fire salamander and the virtually legless three-toed skink, with rocky outcrops hosting southern smooth snake.

The sand-dune systems at Rodas and further north at Figueiras-Muxieiro harbour extensive stands of the Afro-Iberian endemic shrub *Corema album* and the pink-flowered candytuft *Iberis procumbens* subspecies *procumbens* (confined to northwestern Iberia), interspersed with sea-holly, spiny thrift, sea bindweed, cottonweed, *Helichrysum italicum* subspecies *serotinum* and sea daffodil. The rugged cliffs which characterise the seaward coastline – lashed by savage Atlantic waves for much of the year – harbour Portuguese angelica and the thrift *Armeria pubigera*, both unique to the northwestern seaboard of Iberia. Amongst the cushion-vegetation of this western shore, look out for Spanish festoons in abundance in mid-April, the larvae here feeding on *Aristolochia longa*.

These inaccessible sea-cliffs provide refuge for the largest breeding colony of shag in the Iberian peninsula, numbering more than 1000 pairs, as well as a few pairs of lesser black-backed gulls (since 1974), somewhat hampered in their nesting efforts by the enormous yellow-legged gull population: around 22 000 pairs, the largest breeding colony in Europe. Of the 400-odd pairs of guillemots which nested here at the beginning of the 1960s, however, there remains just a single pair, reflecting the spectacular decline of this species on the Atlantic coast of Iberia, although non-breeding immature birds can be seen in the area all year round, particularly during the crossing from Vigo. Other cliff-breeders include peregrine, rock dove, alpine swift and black redstart.

In winter, large concentrations of cormorants roost on the islands between fishing trips to the surrounding estuaries, while Balearic shearwaters congregate in the surounding waters from late summer

Sheltered, east-facing shore of the Illas Cíes (T.F.)

onwards. Winter is also a good time of year to encounter all three divers, gannet, great skua, Sandwich tern, razorbill and kittiwake, with a much-extended list on offer during passage periods, including the possibility of great, Manx, Yelkouan and sooty shearwaters, velvet scoter and great and pomarine skuas.

The Cíes archipelago is currently a *parque natural* and ZEPA of 433 ha (including a 100 m band of sea around the islands), but also forms the bulk of a proposed national park – Illas Atlánticas – of some 2772 ha (1637 ha of which are marine), also to include the Illas de Ons e Onza (see p. 37) and the privately owned Illa de Sálvora. Among the notable undersea habitats to be protected are the brown alga forests below 15 m on the rocky west side of the Cíes, dominated by thong-weed, furbelows, cuvie and *Laminaria ochroleuca*, which provide shel-

ter for a wealth of marine fish such as European seabass, corkwing wrasse and comber, with topknot attached to the surrounding rocks and crevice-dwelling creatures including Ballan wrasse, European conger and common octopus.

The sandy substrata of the more sheltered eastern shore of the archipelago house a wide range of burrowing molluscs plus more cryptic fish such as common sole, European plaice, brill and flounder, as well as undulate ray, common cuttlefish and long-finned squid. Of particular interest are the beds of shell debris which occur here and there, often topped by a fast-moving carpet of the brittle-star *Ophiocomina nigra* and dotted here and there with the spectacular seven-rayed starfish: an aggressive, bright-red species which can measure up to half a metre in diameter.

Access and information: Boats depart from the Estación Marítima de Ría in Vigo (tel: 986 439069), but only during Easter week and between 1 June and 15 September; there is a quota of 2200 visitors per day. The boat lands at the northern end of the Praia de Rodas (the interpretation centre is in the former monastery of San Francisco de Afora at the southern end), from which tracks lead to each of the three lighthouses on the two interconnected islands, all of which are superb observation points; access to the western cliffs is restricted.

Also in the area

The extensive sand-dune system at **Barra** is stabilised by one of the largest stone pine forests in Galicia. The cliffs of nearby **Cabo de Home** are carpeted with the Iberian endemic thrift *Armeria pubigera* and much frequented by the shags which breed in the Illas Cíes.

Enseadas de Vilaloba e San Simón The most inland section of the Ría de Vigo, to the east and north of the A9 motorway. Extensive reaches of saltmarsh in the upper levels which also house abandoned *salinas* (rare in Galicia), now sporting marsh vegetation and alder carr, good for kingfisher. Reedbeds – harbouring water rail and fan-tailed warblers – around the mouths of the rivers Verdugo and Pontenova. Wintering wildfowl include fairly regular scaup.

2 Umia–Grove

A mosaic of intertidal marshes, coastal lagoons and offshore islets of great significance for wintering and migratory waterbirds; rich sand-dune flora.

The peninsula of O Grove (in reality a former island attached to the mainland by the tombolo of A Lanzada) extends northwards into the Ría de Arousa, enclosing the large, shallow Enseada de O Grove, whose intertidal mudflats support the largest concentration of wintering waders on Spain's Atlantic coast, often numbering more than 10 000 individuals.

A Ramsar Site and ZEPA (2561 ha), Umia–Grove comprises four main habitat types: intertidal marshes, the extensive sand-dune system of A Lanzada, the small freshwater lagoon of Bodeira, behind the Playa de Mechillueira on the north side of the O Grove peninsula, and Punta Carreirón, the rocky southern headland of the Illa de Arousa: an island to the north of O Grove which is connected to the mainland at Vilanova by an artificial causeway.

The western seaboard of the isthmus of A Lanzada – 600 m wide and 3 km long – supports a fabulous dune flora comprising more than 100 species of vascular plant. The younger dunes harbour prickly saltwort, sea stock, sea rocket, sea medick, purple and sea spurges, sea-holly, sea bindweed and sea daffodil, while the stabilised, grey dunes are dotted with sand stock, coastal crucianella, *Helichrysum italicum* subspecies *serotinum* and clumps of sea wormwood, here parasitised by the lilac-flowered broomrape *Orobanche arenaria*. Look out, too, for the shrubby candytuft *Iberis procumbens* subspecies *procumbens*, *Armeria pubigera* and the toadflax *Linaria caesia* subspecies *decumbens*, all of which are endemic to the coast of northwestern Iberia, as well as for breeding Kentish plover, crested lark and fan-tailed warbler.

The seaward shore of A Lanzada can often turn up black-throated and great northern divers, black-necked grebe, long-tailed duck, scaup, common scoter and red-breasted merganser during the winter, as well as storm petrel and Manx shearwater outside the breeding season. The Punta Lanzada headland, at the southern extremity of the beach, is a good place to watch for guillemots and razorbills in winter, while the northern sector of the beach – Playa de los Pinos – often attracts sanderling, bar-tailed godwit and whimbrel on spring migration.

Immediately to the east of the tombolo lies the most sheltered sector of the Enseada de O Grove, which hosts large numbers of duck at high tide in winter – mostly mallard, teal and shoveler, but also including wigeon, gadwall, pintail, pochard and tufted duck – which are replaced by large bands of waders feeding on the mudflats at low tide. These intertidal saltmarshes are populated by purple and perennial glassworts, shrubby sea-blite, sea-purslane – parasitised by the spectacular yellow broomrape *Cistanche phelypaea*, for which this is the only site on the Galician coast – and common sea-lavender, with beds of small cord-grass, eelgrass and dwarf eelgrass in the lower reaches.

The Enseada de O Grove as a whole is of great significance for wintering waterbirds, particularly for spoonbills, with 87 birds spending the winter here in 2000. Almost half the shorebirds which winter here are dunlin, accompanied by a thousand or so grey plovers, several hundred oystercatchers and curlew, and good numbers of cormorants, little egrets and grey herons. From the southernmost point of A Toxa (La Toja) – a small island joined to O Grove by a bridge – you should add turnstone, Sandwich tern and common and great black-backed gulls to your list, with Mediterranean and little gulls a distinct possibility. Various hides exist on the southern and western shores of Arousa.

The tiny, shingle beach of Mechillueira, in the centre of the concave north coast of the O Grove peninsula (accessible from the village of Reboredo) hosts an abundance of sea sandwort, yellow horned-poppy, Portland spurge, rock samphire and cottonweed, plus the yellow-flowered shrubby crucifer *Alyssum arenarium*, found only along the coasts of southwest France and northern Spain, lax viper's-bugloss, confined to northwest Iberia, and the succulent-leaved Afro-Iberian endemic figwort *Scrophularia frutescens*. At the western end of this beach lies the small freshwater lagoon of Bodeira, fringed with a belt of common and giant reeds and harbouring small breeding populations of little grebe, mallard, coot, moorhen and water rail.

Umia–Grove saltmarshes and estuary

Also in the area

Arquipélago de Ons In the mouth of the Ría de Pontevedra. The Illa de Ons is the most extensive island off the Iberian Atlantic coast (440 ha), while to the south lies the diminutive, almost conical Illa Onza; the remainder of this granite archipelago comprises the islets of O Centolo and As Freitasas. Cliff-top flora includes sea campion, rock samphire, Portuguese angelica and thrift. Healthy shag colony (600 pairs), plus 4000 pairs of yellow-legged gull. Other cliff-breed-ers include rock dove, alpine swift, raven, jackdaw and chough. Balearic and Cory's shearwaters, great skua, Sandwich tern and razorbill around the islands in winter. Ladder snake particu-larly abundant, plus viperine, grass and southern smooth snakes, slow-worm, three-toed and Bedriaga's skinks, ocel-lated lizard, Bosca's newt and fire sala-mander. Boats run to Ons from Bueu, Marín and Portonovo from 1 June until 15 September.

The waters of the Enseada de O Grove and tidal reaches of the Río Umia are frequented by sea lamprey, Iberian nase, bermejuela, Allis and Twaite shad and Atlantic salmon, with harbour porpoise and bottle-nosed dolphins being sighted in the bay from time to time. Other mammals recorded here include Iberian blind mole, otter and greater and lesser horseshoe and greater mouse-eared bats, while among the herptiles the most notable are fire salamander, Bosca's newt, Iberian painted frog, western spade-foot, common tree and Iberian frogs, Schreiber's green lizard, Bedriaga's and three-toed skinks and ladder snake.

The marshes are also the haunt of an interesting community of odonates, includ-ing the common winter damselfly (the only European species to hibernate as an adult), and Mediterranean hawker (scarce in Iberia), as well as small, scarce and southern emerald damselflies, common blue dam-selfly, migrant hawker and red-veined, southern and common darters.

Corrubedo

One of the most important and best-preserved Atlantic dune systems in the Iberian peninsula, incorporating coastal lagoons of interest for their wintering and passage waterbirds.

The extensive sand dunes of Corrubedo (a *parque natural* of 996 ha, which encompass-es a 550-ha Ramsar Site) stretch for almost 4 km along the crescent-shaped bay between Cabo de Corrubedo and Punta de Couzo (Punta Falcoeiro) at the seaward end of the Serra de Barbanza. Unlike many Spanish dune systems, where the ancient, stabilised sands have disappeared under a rash of beach-side resorts, Corrubedo still harbours

Sea-holly *Eryngium maritimum*

a fine swathe of tertiary dunes, boasting more than 200 species of vascular plant, many of them unique to Iberia.

These so-called 'grey' dunes are carpeted with *Silene littorea*, sea medick, the dwarf,

Galicia and Asturias

0   1 km

annual umbellifer pseudorlaya, *Scrophularia frutescens*, coastal crucianella, *Helichrysum italicum* subspecies *serotinum*, sea wormwood (often heavily parasitised by the North American yellow dodder here) and sea daffodil, interspersed with swathes of the natu-

ralised American grass *Stenotaphrum secundatum*. Look out, too, for *Iberis procumbens* subspecies *procumbens*, confined to the Atlantic coast of Iberia, lax viper's-bugloss, found only in northwest Spain and Portugal, the bluish-white flowered annual *Omphalodes littoralis* subspecies *gallaecica*, endemic to Galicia, and a rather leggy dwarf sheep's-bit (subspecies *maritima*) which grows only along the coasts of southwest France and northwest Spain.

Large numbers of Kentish plover breed here, together with stone curlew, crested lark and stonechat, the tertiary dunes also providing rich hunting grounds for kestrel and barn owl all year round, hobby in summer and merlin in winter, while the pine forests along the inland margin are home to goshawk, sparrowhawk, scops and tawny owls, cuckoo and nightjar.

Towards the sea, the younger secondary dunes typically host marram, sand couchgrass, sea knotgrass, sea spurge, sea-holly, sea bindweed and some marvellous grey-felted cushions of cottonweed. Perhaps the

Corrubedo

most-visited feature of the park, however, is an enormous mobile dune at the northern end of the bay: almost a kilometre long, around 300 m wide and 15 m high. Moving in a northeasterly direction and gradually burying the older dune systems behind, this huge mass of shifting sand is virtually devoid of vegetation.

To the south of the mobile dune lies the Lagoa de Carregal, fed by three braided rivers – Longo, Sirves and Artes (Arles) – but also subject to a twice-daily influx of saltwater from the sea. The intertidal zone is populated by purple glasswort, annual sea-blite, sea-purslane, common sea-lavender, sea rush and saltmarsh-grasses, while the Carregal lagoon itself supports submerged beds of beaked tasselweed and holly-leaved naiad. Further south lies the freshwater lagoon of Vixán, isolated from the sea by dune movements in the past and today fed primarily by rainwater. The surrounding damp grasslands harbour a diverse community of wetland plants, including adder's-tongue spearwort, yellow flag and summer lady's tresses, and attract golden plover and snipe in winter.

The birdlife of the Corrubedo wetlands is best appreciated in winter and during passage periods. Censuses of wintering waterbirds over the past few years have turned up more than 35 species, the lagoons typically harbouring grey heron, mallard, wigeon, teal, pochard, shoveler, gadwall, pintail and tufted duck, while the intertidal marshes offer feeding grounds for little egret, grey and

golden plover, dunlin, bar-tailed godwit, curlew, whimbrel and greenshank, as well as an occasional spoonbill. Breeding birds of the freshwater marsh include little grebe, water rail and common sandpiper, with the surrounding reedbeds and scrub providing nesting grounds for a myriad warblers, among them Cetti's, fan-tailed, great reed, reed and melodious.

An examination of the birds occupying the beach during the winter and on migration could easily turn up oystercatcher, ringed plover, sanderling and turnstone, while gannet, shag, common scoter, Sandwich tern and razorbill are often seen just offshore. Among the less common passage migrants recorded in the lagoons and marshes are black-necked grebe, little bittern, purple heron, marsh harrier and spotted crake, with great northern and red-throated divers and Cory's shearwater off the coast.

Corrubedo also holds interesting herptile populations; amphibians include fire salamander, Bosca's newt, western spadefoot, Iberian painted frog and natterjack toad, with Bedriaga's skink, Schreiber's green lizard, Bocage's wall lizard and Cantabrican viper among the Iberian endemic reptiles. Otters are known to frequent the marshes and a few red squirrels inhabit the small belt of forest inland, while red fox, Eurasian badger, common genet and wild boar from the surrounding farmland–forest mosaic occasionally forage in the park.

Access and information: The park interpretation centre (Casa da Costa; tel: 981 878532; fax: 981 878527) lies to the west of the road which links the villages of Carreira and Artes. Just south of here, the car-park at Praia do Vilar gives access to the tertiary dunes and the Vixán lagoon, while the mobile dune and Carregal saltmarshes are best reached from the car-park near Olveira; almost opposite the turnoff (AC-550) to Oleiros.

Also in the area

Cumio da Curotiña (*sitio de interese nacional*; 50 ha) Also known as the Mirador de la Curota. A 498 m peak at the southern end of the Serra de Barbanza with fabulous views over the Ría de Arousa. Barbanza was considered sacred by the Celts and is peppered with dolmens and megalithic monuments.

Lagoa de Louro (*refuxio de caza*; 218 ha) To the north of the Ría de Muros, a brackish coastal lagoon separated from the sea by 16 m-high dunes with nesting Kentish plover. Emergent vegetation and scrub hosts breeding fan-tailed, reed and great reed war-blers. Interesting reptiles, combining elements of both Atlantic and Mediterranean faunas: slow-worm, Schreiber's green and ocellated lizards, Iberian and Bocage's wall lizards, large psammodromus, Bedriaga's and three-toed skinks, smooth and southern smooth snakes, ladder snake and Cantabrican viper. Punta Louro (227 m) is an excellent sea-watching point for birds and cetaceans alike.

SITE 4 Costa da Morte

A magnificent stretch of coast of significance for its seabird colonies and passage and wintering waterbirds, as well as harbouring many plants unique to northwestern Iberia.

Between Cabo Fisterra (Finisterre) – peninsular Spain's most westerly outpost – and Cabo de San Adrián, the convoluted coastline of the Costa da Morte encompasses precipitous granite cliffs, deep fjord-like estuaries (here pertaining to the Rías Altas) and sandy coves backed by dune systems and small coastal lagoons.

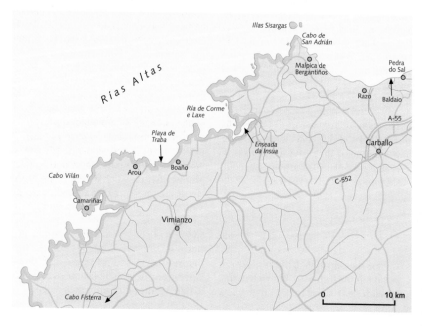

Coast near Cabo Vilán

Cabo Vilán (a *sitio de interese nacional*) is one of the more interesting headlands along this wild stretch of coast, its 80 m-high cliffs and nearby islets – Vilán de Terra (only about 60 m from the shore) and Vilán de Fora – harbouring exceptional seabird colonies. This is the most important breeding site for guillemot in Spain today, although just 7–12 pairs remain, reduced from at least 150 pairs in 1960. Vilán also hosts one of Galicia's largest colonies of storm petrel (100+ pairs), as well as one of only two Spanish colonies of kittiwake, here numbering about 40 pairs, plus some 30 pairs of shag and far too many yellow-legged gulls. Although good views (with a telescope) of the islets and their breeding birds can be had from the vicinity of the lighthouse, you could also hire a boat in Camariñas to observe them from the sea.

Other typical cliff-breeding birds here include peregrine, black redstart and chough, while in winter, waders typical of rocky coasts – oystercatcher, purple sandpiper and turnstone – can be seen foraging along the base of the cliffs. Cabo Vilán is also an excellent outpost from which to observe cetaceans and the migration of seabirds along the coast in spring and autumn. Apart from post-breeding concentrations of guillemots in the area, watch out for shearwaters (particularly Manx and Balearic), gannet, scoters, skuas, gulls, terns (chiefly Sandwich) and auks (mainly razorbills, but puffins also turn up occasionally).

The track linking Cabo Vilán with the village of Arou takes in some of the most spectacular coastal scenery in Galicia. The heathland and low gorse scrub – studded with clumps of Portuguese angelica, *Corema album* and *Armeria pubigera* – which carpets the cliff-top plateau is home to Iberian blind mole and Spanish shrew, both of which are endemic to the peninsula, as well as three-toed skink and slow-worm; seasonal pools should be examined for the presence of Bosca's newt, Iberian frog, Iberian painted frog and natterjack toad. Woodlark and Dartford warbler are typical avian residents of these coastal heaths, which also attract hunting Montagu's harriers and hobbies in summer.

Black-winged stilt *Himantopus himantopus*

Just a stone's throw from Arou lies the **Playa de Traba** (accessed from Boaño), behind the dune system of which lies the most important coastal lagoon along the Costa da Morte. The **Lagoa de Traba** (a *refuxio de caza*) is about 800 m long and encircled by a belt of common reed, bulrush and sea rush. Among the breeding birds are little grebe, water rail, fan-tailed, reed and great reed warblers, reed bunting and, more significantly, little bittern. Snipe, curlew and great black-backed gulls camp out here in the winter, but passage periods are of greater interest: apart from the regular appearance of aquatic warbler in early autumn, Traba is renowned for its Nearctic vagrants – for example, American bittern, bufflehead, Barrow's goldeneye and sora – especially after strong westerly winds.

The Traba dunes are characterised by an abundance of cottonweed in the more mobile part of the system, with the tertiary communities comprising the Iberian endemic candytuft *Iberis procumbens* subspecies *procumbens*, coastal crucianella, *Helichrysum italicum* subspecies *serotinum* and the knapweed *Centaurea corcubionensis*, unique to Galicia. Kentish plovers breed here in some numbers, with stone curlews occasional in winter.

A few kilometres to the east lies the **Ría de Corme e Laxe**, the interior of which is almost completely separated from the remainder of the wide bay by an impressive sandspit, boasting a similar flora to the Traba dunes. This sheltered section, the Enseada da Insua, empties almost completely at low tide, providing a wide swathe of sand and mudflats which attracts a myriad waders in winter – oystercatcher, grey plover, dunlin, knot, curlew and whimbrel, for example – but is best visited during passage periods; past surprises include lesser scaup, falcated duck, king eider, semipalmated plover, least, western and semipalmated sandpipers and greater yellowlegs. The Ría de Corme e Laxe is also the only place in Galicia where black-winged stilts breed, albeit in small numbers (5–10 pairs in 1996), and also harbours nesting Savi's warbler.

The easternmost point of the Costa da Morte is Cabo de San Adrián, just north of the port of Malpica de Bergantiños; look out to sea and the **Illas Sisargas** (a ZEPA of 99 ha) dominate the horizon. This small archipelago (95 ha) comprises three granite islets: Sisarga Grande (maximum 107 m) and the much less impressive Sisarga Chica and Malante (sometimes called Atalayero). The Iberian peninsula's largest colonies of both kittiwake (around 100 pairs) and lesser

Also in the area

Baldaio Dune cordon more than 5 km long backed by a coastal lagoon with saltmarsh vegetation, lying about 10 km east of Cabo de San Adrián, between the villages of Razo and Pedra do Sal. All the typical psammophiles of Spain's northern shores, plus *Seseli tortuosum*, perennial and yellow centauries, *Linaria caesia* subspecies *decumbens* and *Scrophularia frutescens*. Breeding Kentish plover and wintering snow bunting. High diversity of wintering waterbirds and of particular significance during spring passage for knot and bar-tailed godwit; occasional black-throated and great northern divers, spoonbill, and puffin. Common tree frog and Cantabrian viper.

black-backed gull are located here, as well as 65 pairs of shag, while a couple of pairs of guillemot are thought still to nest on the sheer, needle-like islet of Magnánimo, on the north side of the archipelago. There is no organised transport to the islands, but it is relatively simple to hire a fisherman's boat privately in Malpica (Sundays are best).

SITE
5

Fragas do Eume

One of the best thermophilic Atlantic forests in Europe, rich in ferns and Iberian endemic vertebrates.

The Fragas do Eume (a *parque natural* of 9126 ha) represents one of the most extensive natural forests remaining in Galicia today. The steep-sided tectonic valley which today houses the Río Eume supports a deliciously verdant jungle of pedunculate oak, cork oak (here at its northernmost Spanish outpost), sweet chestnut, hazel, bay, strawberry-tree and narrow-leaved ash, grading into a belt of alder and wych elm along the margins of the river, although even here you can't escape Galicia's omnipresent eucalypt plantations. Epiphytic ferns, mosses and lichens literally drip from the native trees, favoured by a humid microclimate where frosts are unheard of and precipitation regularly exceeds 1900 mm per year.

The forest floor is carpeted with woodsorrel, Irish spurge, bilberry, scrambling gromwell and butcher's broom, with spray-drenched rocky gullies supporting a luxuriant growth of navelwort, St Patrick's cabbage and opposite-leaved golden-saxifrage, while clumps of the pendulous-flowered *Narcissus cyclamineus*, endemic to north-western Iberia, colour the margins of the river in spring.

Some 25 fern species have been recorded here, including a number of Tertiary relics such as the enormous *Woodwardia radicans*, *Culcita macrocarpa*, a denizen of humid rock faces, and the often-epiphytic *Davallia canariensis*. Look out, too, for typically Atlantic species such as Killarney fern, hay-scented buckler-fern and Tunbridge filmy-fern. Bryophyte enthusiasts will also

be in their element here, as around 85 species of liverwort and 136 mosses have been cited in the park, as well as over 200 species of lichen.

Notable among the vertebrates of the Fragas do Eume are Iberian endemics such as golden-striped salamander (particularly abundant here), Iberian frog, Iberian rock lizard (subspecies *cantabrica*), Cantabrian viper (which just extends into southern France), Pyrenean desman and Spanish shrew, with the river itself harbouring Iberian nase, Atlantic salmon, sea trout and brown trout.

Typical forest mammals include red squirrel, wild boar, wildcat, Eurasian badger, common genet and pine marten. Particularly noteworthy is the presence of the edible dormouse, in Spain confined to mature deciduous woodland in the extreme north, while otters frequent the Eume and its larger tributaries and wolves have been recorded in the mountains around the

Golden-striped salamander *Chioglossa lusitanica*

headwaters of the river, in the aptly named Serra da Loba. Among the birds, eagle owls (extremely scarce in Galicia) breed sporadically in the gorges which characterise the higher reaches of the river, together with peregrine, while the forest harbours honey buzzard, both chiffchaff and Iberian chiffchaff and firecrest; dippers and kingfishers are a common sight along more open stretches of river.

Access: In Pontedeume (on the N-651), turn west just south of the bridge over the Eume, towards Taboada and Monfero. About 400 m after passing under the motorway, turn left (signposted Monasterio de Caaveiro and Ombre); after 8 km you come to the park's information centre. From here the road follows the left bank of the Eume for another 5 km before terminating in a small car-park, where you can cross the river and continue up to the ruins of the Romanesque monastery of Caaveiro (a *monumento histórico-artístico*) on foot. Further upstream, access is best from the north side of the river; follow the AC-141 from Cabanas to Nieves then turn right to the hydroelectric station. The area immediately below the reservoir accommodates the most precipitous river canyon, with walls up to 300 m high; carry on along the AC-141 almost as far as Goente and turn left to the village of Eume itself, close to the dam.

Also in the area

Encoro (Embalse) de Cecebre Small, two-pronged reservoir lying at the confluence of the rivers Mero and Barcés, the 'tail-ends' populated by some of Galicia's finest gallery forest. Duck abound in winter, while passage periods sometime turn up purple and night herons, little bittern, osprey and aquatic warbler. In autumn exposed mudflats attract ruff and wood and green sandpipers. Many bats hawk over the open water – greater and lesser horseshoe, greater mouse-eared, brown long-eared, pipistrelle and serotine – with other vertebrates including golden-striped salamander, Bosca's newt, Iberian painted and common tree frogs, Schreiber's green lizard, otter and western polecat. Head for Crendes (on the promontory between the arms) and explore the network of small roads and tracks which lead down to the surrounding water.

Ría de A Coruña Rocky promontories at the entrance to the estuary are good vantage points for the autumn migration of seabirds, occupied at sea-level by purple sandpiper and turnstone in winter. Sheltered estuarine waters provide refuge for divers, grebes and sea duck in poor weather, with Mediterranean and ring-billed gulls regular.

6 Valdoviño

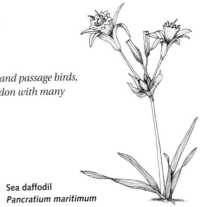

A small coastal lagoon, of interest for wintering and passage birds, separated from the sea by an extensive dune cordon with many endemic plants.

Also known as Lagoa Frouxeira, the Valdoviño lagoon (a Ramsar Site of 255 ha) measures approximately 1.6 km by 0.5 km and has a maximum depth of 1.5 m, harbouring submerged beds of beaked tassel-weed. Much of the southern third of the lagoon is swathed in thick stands of common reed – home to breeding reed warblers and reed buntings – which grade into seasonally flooded *Salix atrocinerea* and alder carr around the mouths of the small feeder streams. At the seaward end, the lagoon is closed off – all bar a narrow artificial channel – by a magnificent stretch of low dunes over 3 km long.

Sea daffodil
Pancratium maritimum

Starting at the resort of Robaleira, in the northeastern corner of the lagoon, a nature trail – complete with informative panels and two hides – allows you to make a complete circuit of the lagoon. The margins are sandy rather than muddy, attracting major gull roosts in winter as well as small numbers of waders, particularly oystercatcher, ringed,

Lagoa de Valdoviño

Kentish and grey plovers, dunlin, sanderling and redshank, occasionally joined by black-winged stilt, knot, little stint and ruff on passage. The open water is the winter haunt of little grebe, gadwall (which also breed here), mallard, pochard, tufted duck and coot, while small bands of teal skulk around the marginal growth of sea and sharp rushes. Look out, too, for small odonates such as common blue and blue-tailed damselflies and red-veined darter.

The sand-dune system is best investigated from the northwestern corner, via the village of Praia de Lago. Among the plants to look out for here are *Iberis procumbens*, *Omphalodes littoralis* subspecies *gallaecica* and the reddish-striped yellow flowers of the toadflax *Linaria caesia*, all three of which are unique to western Iberia, amid a rich mosaic of sand-stock, pseudorlaya, *Scrophularia frutescens*, coastal crucianella, *Helichrysum italicum* subspecies *serotinum* and sea daffodil. The most ancient of the dunes harbour small enclaves of the Afro-Iberian endemic *Corema album*, interspersed with twining stems of *Antirrhinum majus* subspecies *linkianum*, while summer lady's tresses occurs in the seasonally flooded dune slacks. Although the dunes are much disturbed by sun-seekers and sand extraction, they still attract wintering stone curlew, snow bunting on passage and in winter and a few pairs of breeding Kentish plover. Notable herptiles include Bosca's newt and Iberian painted and Iberian frogs, Schreiber's green lizard and three-toed skink.

Among the more interesting wintering waterbirds of Valdoviño are marsh harriers over the lagoon and all three divers in the coastal waters, while purple heron, bittern, little bittern and spotted crake use the reedbeds on passage. Between September 2000 and May 2001, notable visitors included great white egret, squacco heron, white-fronted and Brent geese, garganey, scaup, osprey, greater yellowlegs, grey phalarope, little, glaucous and ring-billed gulls and kittiwake. Punta Frouxeira and Punta Chirlateira – the rocky headlands on either side of the lagoon – are noted for their autumn passage of gannet, scoters and shearwaters, plus the occasional little auk.

Corema album (T.F.)

Also in the area

Cabo Prior A pronounced rocky promontory about 10 km to the southwest of Valdoviño, renowned for its shag colony and also hosting nesting peregrine, blue rock thrush and chough.

Laguna de Doñinos Coastal lagoon to the south of Cabo Prior, again located behind a sandbar and dunes. Winter visitors include pochard, tufted duck, golden plover, curlew and snow bunting, with black-necked grebe and scaup in coastal waters; in summer you might turn up marsh harrier, hobby and sand martin.

Illas Gabeiras Small group of islets immediately north of Doñinos, harbouring the most important breeding colony of storm petrel in Galicia (100+ pairs), as well as an important winter cormorant roost (400–500 birds). The mainland cliffs opposite harbour breeding shag, alpine swift and chough.

SITE 7 Ría de Ortigueira e Ladrido

A convoluted estuary of interest for its wintering and passage waterbirds, with the neighbouring headlands providing excellent observation points for the autumn seabird migration.

Located at the eastern end of the Rías Altas, the Ortigueira estuary (a Ramsar Site of 2920 ha and ZEPA) is one of the most sheltered on the whole Galician coast. To the west lies Cabo Ortegal, along the spine of which runs the Serra de la Capelada (maximum 620 m), while to the east the estuary is enclosed by the Punta de la Estaca de Bares: the northernmost point of mainland Spain, which is traditionally considered to separate the Atlantic Ocean from the Mar Cantábrico. In the interior of the estuary lies the extremely shallow Enseada de Ladrido, virtually closed off from the sea by the ancient sandspit of Morouzos.

The C-642 runs along the southern edge of the Ría de Ortigueira, but far better views of the intertidal mud- and sandflats in the higher reaches of the estuary are to be had from the small peninsula which extends in a northwesterly direction from the town of Ortigueira itself; follow signs to Praia de Morouzos, which lead to a recreation area amid dune slacks planted with maritime pines, from which you can also explore the **Morouzos sandspit**.

The undulating Morouzos tertiary dunes are carpeted with a humid sward of sand stock, *Iberis procumbens* subspecies *procumbens*, sea medick, *Linaria caesia* subspecies *decumbens*, coastal crucianella, *Helichrysum italicum* subspecies *serotinum* and sea daffodil. As in most of the larger Galician dune systems, a few pairs of Kentish

Ría de Ortigueira

plover breed, while snow buntings abound in winter and on passage. The extensive dune slacks are home to common tree and Iberian painted frogs and Schreiber's green lizard.

The spit also provides superb views over the Enseada de Ladrido to the south, fringed with sea-purslane, sea heath and sea-lavenders, and the haunt of large concentrations of dunlin and small flocks of grey plover and knot in winter, plus greenshank and spotted redshank on passage. The sandy beach on the north side of Morouzos attracts sanderling and great black-backed gulls in winter, with great northern diver and razorbill often seen offshore.

From Morouzos you can drive further north and west to complete a circuit back to Ortigueira, enjoying views over the middle section of the estuary, usually teeming with birds at low tide during winter and passage periods. Curlew, for which this is considered to be the best wintering location in Spain, bar-tailed godwit, avocet, oystercatcher (a couple of pairs of which hang around to breed on the rocky coast nearby) and little egret are particularly characteristic, while the river channels meandering through the mud are thronged with duck, notably shoveler, of which the *ría* hosts the largest wintering concentration on the northwest coast of Spain. Among the more interesting records for the Ría de Ortigueira between October 2000 and April 2001 were black-necked and red-necked grebes, whooper swan (maximum eight individuals), Brent goose, scaup, black duck, red-breasted merganser, osprey, greater yellowlegs and little and ring-billed gulls.

The headlands which enclose the *ría* and their associated offshore islets are of interest for their seabird colonies – 80-odd pairs of shag, a dozen or so pairs of storm petrel and a couple of pairs of oystercatcher, plus sporadic lesser black-backed gull – also harbour breeding peregrine, blue rock thrush and chough. Of far greater renown, however, is the highly visible passage of marine birds close to the tip of **Estaca de Bares** (a *sitio de interese nacional*, endowed with a small observatory), which regularly exceeds

100 000 individuals between November and March. Although almost anything could turn up, the bulk of the birds comprise gannet, Manx, Cory's and sooty shearwaters, common scoter and Sandwich tern, plus less abundant fulmar, great and little shearwaters, all four western Palearctic skuas and Sabine's gull. Notable among the influx of passerines in September 2001 were large numbers of wryneck, whinchat, bluethroat and grasshopper warbler.

To the west of the estuary, the plateau of ultrabasic rocks at the seaward end of the **Serra de la Capelada** boasts an interesting plant community. From Mera (on the C-642), follow the road along the eastern side of the headland as far as Cariño, then turn left following signs towards the wind farms (*parques eólicos*) of Capelada. This narrow road will eventually lead you to the plateau of Garita de Herbeira (620 m): a bleak landscape, filled with the eerie whine of the turbines. The carpet of Cornish, Irish and cross-leaved heaths is studded with clumps of the low-growing broom *Cytisus commutatus*, confined to the Cornisa Cantábrica, and small peatbogs coloured by heath-spotted orchids in early summer. Here you might also come across the rather scarce knapweed *Centaurea borjae*, unique to northwestern Spain, while the most notable vertebrate denizens of the Serra are Bocage's wall lizard, endemic to the northwestern corner of Iberia, the only known coastal population of Iberian rock lizard (subspecies *cantabrica*) and an isolated breeding nucleus of water pipit.

Returning to Cariño, head northwards to **Cabo Ortegal**, from where the sweep of precipitous cliffs – with a fall of around 100 m – westwards to Punta do Limo is nothing short of spectacular. Look out for black redstart and blue rock thrush here at any time of year, plus alpine swift in summer. The small fishing harbour in Cariño itself often turns up interesting birds in winter, notably great northern diver, red-breasted merganser, grey phalarope (often a score or more birds), glaucous gull, little auk, razorbill and guillemot.

SITE
8 # Lagoa de Cospeito

One of Galicia's few remaining inland wetlands, whose surrounding grasslands are one of the handful of breeding areas for lapwing and curlew in the region.

Montagu's harrier
Circus pygargus

The extensive floodplain of the Río Támoga is one of the few places in Galicia which has thus far escaped the invasion of wall-to-wall eucalypt plantations; the lush green fields are separated by deciduous hedgerows which here and there blossom into copses of pedunculate oak, often accompanied by alder, osier and *Salix atrocinerea* along the margins of the watercourses. Such is the spirit-level flatness of the terrain – known locally as Terra Cha – that the Támoga and its main tributary the Guisande meander and braid continuously, forming a labyrinth of channels that seasonally overflow to inundate large areas.

In the heart of Terra Cha, the Lagoa de Cospeito originally covered around 70 ha but was drained for agriculture in the 1960s. Rehabilitation of the lagoon in the 1990s means that today about 18 ha are more or less permanently flooded, this area increasing dramatically with the onset of the autumn rains.

Access to the main lagoon is simple: from the *Campsa* petrol station on the northern edge of the town of Feria do Monte (formerly known as Cospeito), take the LU-112 signposted 'Villalba' and 'Muimenta', turning left after 700 m to 'Lagoa de Cospeito'. This narrow road takes you through rush- and sedge-filled pastures around the margins of the lake, which attract golden plover, lapwing (up to 7000 individuals), snipe and jack snipe in winter, as well as little bustard (a small breeding population hangs on here) on autumn passage. Terra Cha still hosts a handful of nesting lapwing, curlew and hen harrier, plus a few pairs of white stork in one of their northernmost breeding localities in the peninsula. The area is a favoured hunting ground for goshawk and sparrowhawk all year round, plus black kite, Montagu's harrier and hobby in summer and hen harrier and merlin in winter. Kingfishers are frequently seen zooming along the larger rivers, while red-backed shrikes abound in summer, replaced by northern grey shrikes in winter.

The grasslands teem with *Narcissus pseudonarcissus* in spring, seasonally flooded areas host the eryngo *Eryngium viviparum*, and the delightful floating water-plantain flowers in the channels and ditches in late summer. This latter habitat is also home to marbled, palmate and Bosca's newts and Iberian, common tree and Iberian painted frogs, while golden-striped salamander occur in streams and oakwoods. Among the reptiles, look out for Schreiber's green lizard along stream margins and Cantabrican viper in scrubby areas. Apart from roe deer and wild boar, larger mammals are rare in this essentially anthropogenic landscape, but Iberian hares abound and you might also catch a glimpse

Lapwing *Vanellus vanellus* (Mike Lane)

of an elusive common genet, western polecat or otter.

Back at the petrol station, if you take the road immediately to your right and drive up through the town for about 600 m, a right turn opposite the Café/Bar Cotelo leads to a hide (always open) situated on a strategic hummock at the southwestern corner of the lagoon. From here you get the best views of wintering duck, while during passage periods you might turn up garganey and black tern, as well as waders such as ruff and green sandpiper; rarer visitors include purple and squacco herons, ring-necked duck, ruddy shelduck and wood sandpiper. Cospeito is also a noted site for aquatic warbler on migration, while a small group of cranes turned up in Terra Cha in the winter of 2000–01.

Also in the area

Serra do Xistral Small ridge running southwest–northeast and peaking at just over 1000 m. Lower levels reforested with eucalypts, but some deciduous woodland around the headwaters of the numerous small rivers which rise here (including the Guisande). High-level heaths dominated by western gorse and Mackay's heath, sprinkled with peatbogs housing oblong-leaved sundew and the only Galician population of viviparous lizard outside the Ancares. Pine plantations over the peatbogs support breeding citril finch and siskin.

SITE 9 Ría do Eo

Sheltered estuary which is one of the most important ornithological localities on the north coast of Spain, with a rich wetland flora.

The Río Eo meets the sea on the border between Galicia and Asturias, forming a long narrow estuary (a Ramsar Site and ZEPA of 1740 ha) which boasts an enormous diversity of habitats and a flora and fauna to match. At subtidal levels, the submerged eelgrass meadows are the most extensive along the Cornisa Cantábrica – possibly even in the whole of Spain – giving way to dwarf eelgrass just above the low-water mark. Moving inland, plant diversity increases as tidal influence declines, with characteristic saltmarsh species including perennial and purple glassworts, sea-purslane, sea heath, lax-flowered sea-lavender, sea aster, golden-samphire and common saltmarsh-grass. Less saline habitats support stands of sea club-rush and common reed, often associated with *Cochlearia pyrenaica* subspecies *aestuaria*, sea-milkwort, sea plantain, sea and saltmarsh rushes, long-bracted sedge and

hard-grass, as well as marsh-mallow, parsley water-dropwort, wild celery and buttonweed, a distinctive South African composite.

The diversity of bird species using the estuary during the course of the year is phenomenal. The stands of club-rushes and reeds harbour breeding water rail and reed and great reed warblers, as well as providing a refuge for wintering reed buntings and passage grasshopper warblers. The sandbanks towards the mouth of the *ría* are habitually occupied by enormous winter gull roosts, predominantly yellow-legged, black-headed and lesser black-backed, but also including a good number of common and great black-backed (80 individuals in 1995), the latter being relatively uncommon in Iberia in winter, despite breeding in France. Look out, too, for glaucous and Iceland gulls mingling with the horde, as well as Sandwich and common terns on passage. Snow buntings regularly winter on the coastal sands and surrounding scrub.

On average some 5000 duck spend the winter here; wigeon are particularly abundant, with a maximum census of around 4000 individuals, accompanied by pintail (the maximum of approximately 1500 birds represents one of the largest concentrations ever recorded in Spain) and lesser numbers of mallard, teal, shoveler, gadwall, pochard and tufted duck. Unusual records in and around the Eo estuary during the winter include greylag, Brent and barnacle geese, mute swan, red-crested pochard, ferruginous duck and scaup, while little bittern, night heron and black-winged stilt often drop in on migration.

At low tide the estuary virtually empties, exposing large swathes of glutinous mud in the higher reaches, with good views from the N-642 which runs along the western margin of the estuary, between Vegadeo and Ribadeo. Just after the road crosses the railway line, park at the entrance of the turn-off to Lourido and Vilaosende, where the exposed mudflats literally teem with waders in winter: for the most part avocet, grey plover, dunlin, curlew (present all year) and

redshank. During passage periods, water-bird numbers are burgeoned by temporary inmates such as spoonbill, ringed plover, ruff, both godwits, spotted redshank, green-shank and wood and green sandpipers.

The eastern margin of the estuary is more convoluted, boasting several pronounced inlets which can be accessed via Figueras, Castropol and Vilavedelle while a roadside picnic area at the top of a rise on the N-640 at km 10.6 gives a superb view over the interior of the *ría*. Seabirds are best located from the Punta de la Cruz, which closes the mouth of the estuary to the east (follow signs off the N-634 to Figueras and the Playa de Arnao). During exceptionally cold weather, great northern and black-throated divers are often seen in the mouth of the estuary, as well as black-necked grebe (up to 40 individuals), common scoter, eider and red-breasted merganser, with the offshore autumn migration turning up Cory's shearwater, gannet, guillemot, razorbill and even puffin.

From the Punta de la Cruz, you can follow the long-distance coastal footpath (GR-E9) as far east as Tapia de Casariego, which takes in the Playa de Penarronda. The cliff-top vegetation includes rock sea-spurrey, rock

Mouth of the Ría do Eo

samphire and thrift, while small offshore stacks are frequently occupied by shags; the coastal cliffs and islets between the Ría de Foz and the Playa de Barayo house no less than seven colonies, as well as 4 pairs of peregrine and around 1500 pairs of yellow-legged gulls.

The climax pedunculate oak and alder forest which once clothed the low hills surrounding the estuary has, for the most part, long-since disappeared under verdant farmland and plantations of eucalypts and pines, but even so this grassland–forest mosaic still provides suitable habitat for breeding birds such as hobby, turtle dove, whitethroat and red-backed shrike. In winter, look out for fieldfare, redwing and brambling in more wooded habitats and short-eared owl hunting over open areas, while the temporarily flooded fields attract golden plover, lapwing and snipe.

Notable fish in the estuary and river including migratory species such as European eel, sea lamprey, Atlantic salmon, sea trout and Twaite and Allis shad, as well as the sedentary Iberian nase, endemic to the peninsula. Amphibians recorded from the area include fire and golden-striped salamanders, Bosca's, marbled and palmate newts, midwife toad and Iberian painted, Iberian pool and Iberian frogs, while among the notable reptiles are Schreiber's green lizard and Cantabrican viper. Upstream of Vegadeo, the river and its margins are home to otter, western polecat and southern water vole.

Also in the area

Ría de Foz About 20 km west of the Ría do Eo; a small estuary at the mouth of the river Masma which attracts oyster-catcher, avocet, grey plover, lapwing, bar-tailed godwit, whimbrel and curlew, plus the odd spoonbill, Canada goose, whooper swan and crane. Red-breasted mergansers around the small fishing port.

Ría de Navia Some 25 km east of the Eo, a narrow, canalised estuary whose fringing reedbeds support breeding water rail. Fish-feeding birds abound, particularly great northern and red-throated divers, common scoter and red-breasted merganser. Look out for rarities such as great white egret and red-necked grebe, plus common, little, Mediterranean and ring-billed gulls.

Playa de Barayo (*reserva natural parcial*; 331 ha) About 9 km east of Navia between the headlands of Punta de las Romanelas and La Vaquina (Sabugo). Beach backed by embryo dunes, with the river meanders behind supporting well-developed stands of common reed and sea, sharp and grey club-rushes plus well-conserved alder carr. Adjacent headlands are good vantage points for passage Cory's and sooty shearwaters, gannet, common scoter, pomarine skua and Arctic tern, with the rocky shore below attracting purple sandpiper in winter and oystercatcher all year round (some seven pairs breed on rocky islets between here and the Eo). Coastal heaths harbour breeding tree pipit, fan-tailed warbler and cirl bunting plus wintering Richard's pipits (about 50 individuals). Resident otter.

SITE 10 Serra do Courel

Medium-altitude mountains harbouring one of the richest floral assemblages in Galicia plus spectacular fluvial valleys with a diverse herptile fauna.

Essentially a southerly extension of the Ancares (see p. 228), the Serra do Courel is a northeast–southwest-oriented ridge rising to just 1607 m (Piapaxaro) lying between the Río Lor, a tributary of the Sil, and the Galicia–León border. Despite having been brutally ravaged by slate-quarrying, planted with non-native trees and repeatedly burned, O Courel still harbours one of the richest botanical assemblages in Galicia. Lying at the cross-roads of the Euro-Siberian and Mediterranean climatic zones, with more than 1000 m separating Piapaxaro from the bottom of the Lor valley, and the acid bedrock complemented by important outcrops of limestone, the Serra do Courel harbours around 40% of all the vascular plants present in Galicia, although it covers only 1% of the total surface area.

Outstanding among the forest formations of O Courel are the so-called *devesas*, found only in the shadiest, most humid valleys, where Europe's westernmost beechwoods are accompanied by yew, pedunculate oak, downy birch (subspecies *celtiberica*), rowan and holly; the most renowned forest of this nature is the Devesa de Rogueira, to the east of the village of Seoane. By contrast, south-facing slopes support a climax vegetation of Pyrenean oak, although this has largely been replaced by pines and sweet chestnuts today. Some of these chestnut groves – known as *soutos* – are ancient indeed and support a rich fauna and flora: one notable example lies close to the hamlet of Esperante, near Folgoso do Courel.

The forests of the Serra do Courel harbour a woodland avifauna that has much in common with that of the Ancares. Resident species include goshawk and sparrowhawk, great spotted woodpecker, goldcrest and firecrest, crested tit, nuthatch and bullfinch, which are joined by short-toed and booted eagles, black kite, honey buzzard, hobby and spotted flycatcher in summer. Other creatures associated primarily with these forested habitats are Bocage's wall lizard, unique to northwestern Iberia, roe deer, wild boar, wildcat, pine marten (very abundant), common genet and wolf. Among the woodland glade butterflies, look out for dark green, high brown and small pearl-bordered fritillaries, tree grayling, purple hairstreak and turquoise and Adonis blues.

Above the tree-line a low scrub of *Chamaespartium tridentatum*, ling and Spanish heath prevails, with the highest floristic interest associated with scattered outcrops of limestone, which harbour fringed pink, *Saxifraga trifurcata*, the delightful stork's-bill *Erodium glandulosum*, the buckthorn *Rhamnus legionensis*, confined to a few limestone outcrops on the Galicia–León border, and the lemon-flowered snapdragon *Antirrhinum meonanthum*. Here *Erodium glandulosum* is the food-plant of the Spanish argus butterfly, cited only from the Iberian peninsula and one dubious record in the French Pyrenees, while other notable species include Oberthür's grizzled skipper, Queen of Spain and lesser marbled fritillaries, large wall

Queen of Spain fritillary *Issoria lathonia* (Peter Wilson)

Galicia and Asturias

brown, rock grayling, Chapman's ringlet, scarce, purple-shot and purple-edged coppers, mountain argus and chalk-hill blue.

The typical high-level birds of O Courel include those which favour scrub, such as partridge, Dartford warbler, red-backed shrike and rock bunting, as well as species more typical of rocky outcrops, namely rock thrush and blue rock thrush. Both hen and Montagu's harriers also breed, while the most notable reptiles are Iberian rock lizard and a plethora of Cantabrican vipers.

The river Lor and its tributaries sport a thick belt of alder, downy birch and sycamore. Try the road to the north of Seoane, which takes you past verdant cliffs dotted with St Patrick's cabbage and spectacular waterfalls flanked by clumps of hart's-tongue and opposite-leaved golden-saxifrage. A wide range of herptiles can be found here, including golden-striped salamander, Bosca's newt, Iberian frog and Schreiber's green lizard, all of which are endemic to northwestern Iberia, as well as

Access: The tortuous LU-651 traverses the range from the Puerto de Pedrafita do Cebreiro (on the N-VI) to the town of Quiroga (on the N-120). From the village of Moreda (just south of Seoane), a 12 km waymarked trail (PR-50) leads to the Devesa de Rogueira and up to the small glacial lake of Lucenza (1420 m).

Also in the area

Serra da Enciña da Lastra Dolomitic limestone ridge (maximum 1610 m) on the Galicia–León border to the southeast of O Courel. Some of the best-preserved Mediterranean vegetation in Galicia: extensive stands of western holm oak associated with cork oak, turpentine tree, cistuses, strawberry-tree, *Phillyrea angustifolia* and Etruscan honeysuckle, plus true service-tree and wayfaring-tree, both very scarce in the region. Notable calcicoles include the fern *Cheilanthes acrostica*, tufted catchfly, burnt candytuft, *Ononis pusilla* and *Thymus zygis*, while *Petrocoptis grandiflora* and *Armeria rothmaleri* are found only here and in the nearby Montes Aquilanos. Around 25 species of orchid, including champagne, military, man and pyramidal plus woodcock and early spider ophrys. Breeding golden, Bonelli's, booted and short-toed eagles, Montagu's and hen harriers, hobby and peregrine, plus Galicia's last pair of Egyptian vultures; also eagle owl, stock dove, red-rumped swallow, redstart, blue rock thrush, chough, rock sparrow and hawfinch. Good populations of western polecat, pine and beech martens, wildcat and common genet. Access from the N-120, on the OR-622 to Robledo and then San Tirso.

Serra de Queixa Dominated by Cabeza de Manzaneda (one of Galicia's highest peaks; 1778 m), which houses a ski-station on its northern flank and is thus accessible by road (from Puebla de Trives, on the C-536, via Coba). Scrub-clothed granite plateau (with the Iberian endemic greenweeds *Genista obtusiramea* and *G. sanabrensis*) with many peatbogs. Golden eagle, partridge, water pipit, wheatear and the only Galician locality for bluethroat.

Cañón do Sil Spectacular granitic river gorge with almost-vertical walls up to 500 m high. Thermophilic vegetation, with booted and short-toed eagles, goshawk, black kite, honey buzzard, peregrine, alpine swift, red-rumped swallow and blue rock thrush. Access off the N-120, following signs to the Monasterio de Ribas de Sil, or via the LU-601 south from Monforte de Lemos.

more commonplace species such as marbled and palmate newts and grass and viperine snakes. Pyrenean desman and otter abound in these unpolluted riverine habitats, with characteristic birds including grey wagtail, dipper, nightingale, Cetti's and melodious warblers, long-tailed tit and cirl bunting.

11 Bosque de Muniellos

One of Europe's largest and best-preserved expanses of deciduous oak forest; a Biosphere Reserve with a flora and fauna little changed since Neolithic times.

Often referred to as the 'jungle of Asturias', the ancient, lichen-festooned forest of Muniellos has been stringently protected since the 1960s and today is a *reserva natural integral* covering 5970 ha (encompassing a ZEPA of 2975 ha). Occupying a vast natural amphitheatre of Palaeozoic quartzites and slates which backs onto the Sierra de Rañadoiro and opens only to the northeast, Muniellos is a magnificent example of the climax vegetation of the western Cordillera Cantábrica.

The rugged horseshoe of the Sierra de Rañadoiro is almost entirely carpeted with forest save for the sheer walls of the glacial cirques around La Candanosa (1685 m), several of which hold small lakes. This is the haunt of a small, isolated population of chamois, which browse among a rich calcifuge flora that includes fabulous orange-flowered great yellow gentians (subspecies *aurantica*), alpine St John's-wort (subspecies *burseri*) and several montane species which are unique to northwestern Iberia: the delightful crucifer *Teesdaliopsis conferta*, the robust greenweed *Genista obtusiramea*, the spiny eryngo *Eryngium duriaei*, the daisy-like *Phalacrocarpum oppositifolium* and the diminutive *Narcissus asturiensis*. Here, too, grows a subspecies of parnassus-leaved buttercup (*muniellensis*) found nowhere else in the world.

Also above the tree-line, look out for breeding hen harrier, partridge (scarce), water pipit and Dartford warbler, as well as ring ouzel on passage and wintering wall-

Capercaillie *Tetrao urogallus*

creeper. Notable reptiles here include the Cantabrican viper (usually a melanic form) and Iberian rock lizard, both unique to the peninsula, with the most characteristic mammals being wolf, snow vole and Castroviejo's hare, the latter endemic to the mountains of northern Spain.

At the tree-line, which can reach 1600 m on occasion, downy birch (subspecies *celtiberica*) is dominant, accompanied by herbs typical of damp, shady habitats such as St Patrick's cabbage, Irish spurge and *Valeriana montana*. Where winter snows accumulate in the heads of the valleys the soils are richer and wetter, harbouring megaforb communities of lemon-scented fern, aconite-leaved buttercup, the yellow-flowered monk's-hood *Aconitum vulparia* subspecies *neapolitanum*, *Angelica major*, Pyrenean valerian, hairless blue-sowthistle, adenostyles, alpine leek and white false helleborine.

Below the birch, sessile oak predominates, with pedunculate oak found only along the lower reaches of the rivers and Pyrenean oak on the driest, south-facing slopes, while beech is confined to the most humid habitats. Other trees scattered through the forest include yew, wych elm, holly, large-leaved lime and ash, as well as planted Scots and maritime pines and sweet chestnut. Among the more colourful woodland herbs are Welsh poppy, *Linaria triornithophora*, angel's-tears, bluebell, dog's-tooth-violet, martagon and Kerry lilies and whorled Solomon's-seal. Along the river margins look out for royal fern, columbine, greater cuckooflower (the Galician endemic subspecies *gallaecia*), tutsan, *Omphalodes nitida* and rampion bellflower, with water-

Bosque de Muniellos

Dog's-tooth-violet
Erythronium dens-canis

eagles and scops and long-eared owls. Black and middle and lesser spotted woodpeckers occur in reasonable numbers, together with woodcock and nightjar, while breeding passerines such as pied flycatcher, treecreeper, nuthatch and bullfinch are joined by redwing and brambling in winter.

Muniellos is also of key significance for the endangered brown bear, particularly in the autumn, coinciding with the abundant acorn crop, as well as harbouring healthy populations of roe deer and wild boar, plus red squirrel, edible dormouse, wildcat and almost all the Iberian mustelids, notably Eurasian badger, pine and beech martens and otter. Among the 15 species of bat cited from Muniellos are Savi's pipistrelle, Leisler's bat, greater noctule (which has recently been discovered to prey on small birds) and brown long-eared, barbastelle and whiskered bats.

Golden-striped salamanders and Schreiber's green lizards are particularly associated with the watercourses of the reserve, while fire salamanders and Bocage's wall lizards are more usually found in damp forest habitats. The glacial lakes and numerous small peatbogs at altitude

falls hosting opposite-leaved golden-saxifrage, kidney saxifrage and *Saxifraga lepismigena*, the latter confined to north-western Iberia.

This vast expanse of virtually primeval forest provides refuge for all manner of woodland creatures. The capercaillie takes pride of place among the birds, with some 20 leks recorded in 1996, while forest-breeding raptors include goshawk, honey buzzard, short-toed and booted

Narcissus asturiensis

support alpine, Bosca's and palmate newts, with the high-mountain streams a stronghold of the curious Pyrenean desman.

Among the more notable woodland butterflies are purple and lesser purple emperors and purple hairstreak.

Access and information: Muniellos is accessed via a track off the AS-211 just west of Moal, which leads to Tablizas (at the entrance to the reserve) after about 4 km. Only 20 people per day are allowed beyond this point; a waymarked circular route leads up to the glacial lakes at the foot of La Candanosa (about 18 km in total). Permits should be obtained well in advance from: Reserva Natural Integral de Muniellos, Coronel Aranda s/n, 33005 Oviedo; tel: 98 5963060; fax: 98 5963715. Otherwise good views over the forest can be had from the nearby Puerto del Connio (1315 m), which might also turn up species typical of more open habitats.

Also in the area

Degaña–Hermo (ZEPA; 11 659 ha) Southeast of Muniellos, traversed by the AS-15 between the passes of Rañadoiro and Cerredo. Extensive beech and sessile oak forests, including the largest beechwood in Asturias: Monasterio de Hermo (1500 ha). Similar flora and fauna to Muniellos, although more Mediterranean species such as ladder and Montpellier snakes and common genet also occur. One of few Iberian breeding localities for wood warbler.

Cueto de Arbás (*reserva natural parcial*; 2900 ha) A 2007 m peak to the west of the Puerto de Leitariegos (AS-213/LE-631), at the foot of which lie many peatbogs with a unique flora: stag's-horn clubmoss, *Isoetes velatum* (locally endemic subspecies *asturicense*), yellow water-lily (here the only Iberian locality for the subspecies *pumilum*), round-leaved and great sundews, large-flowered butterwort and floating bur-reed. Rock fissures have Dickie's bladder-fern. Stable wolf population and a few chamois.

SITE
12 Somiedo

Dramatic montane landscape with a classic subalpine flora and fauna and the highest density of brown bears in western Europe.

One of the most emblematic protected areas in Asturias, the mountain wilderness of Somiedo lies on the northern flanks of the Cordillera Cantábrica and straddles four tributaries of the Río Narcea. A *parque natu-* *ral* of 29 120 ha (also a ZEPA), Somiedo has recently been declared a Biosphere Reserve.

Generally speaking, the park gains altitude from north to south, ranging from 395 m to 2194 m (El Cornón). Ice-sculpted features abound above 1500 m, including a number of spectacular glacial lakes, notably those of Saliencia and the Lago del Valle. Although dominated by slates, sandstones and quartzites, a broad band of limestone crosses the park from southeast to northwest, gouged into sheer defiles where traversed by rivers and adding considerably to the floral diversity of Somiedo, where more than 1100 species of vascular plant have been recorded.

Above the tree-line, swathes of subalpine pasture alternate with rugged limestone outcrops carpeted with dwarf juniper, savin, spurge-laurel and bearberry. This is the domain of species whose world distribution is restricted to the Cordillera Cantábrica: blue-leaved petrocoptis, *Anemone pavoniana*, Sequier's buttercup, *Draba cantabriae*, *Sempervivum vicentei* subspecies *cantabricum*, *Saxifraga babiana*, *Centaurea janeri* subspecies *babiana* and *Artemisia cantabrica*. More widespread taxa include tufted catchfly, pink sandwort, livelong saxifrage, the sticky-leaved stork's-

bill *Erodium glandulosum*, the rock-jasmine *Androsace villosa*, leafless-stemmed globularia, the mat-forming *Globularia repens* and *Narcissus asturiensis*, while spring-lines on the limestone are the preferred habitat of the centaury *Centaurium somedanum*, endemic to Asturias and León. On acid bedrock, look out for *Teesdaliopsis conferta* and the thrift *Armeria duriaei*, again both confined to the mountains of northern Iberia, as well as aconite-leaved buttercup, violet mountain pansy, pyramidal bugle and large-flowered butterwort.

One of Somiedo's key landscape elements is the beech forest (some 4554 ha), best developed between 800 and 1400 m and grading into a fringe of yew, downy birch (subspecies *celtiberica*), rowan and holly at its upper limit. On acid soils the beech-wood ground flora includes hard-fern, St Patrick's cabbage, bilberry, *Linaria triornithophora* and great wood-rush (subspecies *henriquesii*), with the characteristic calcareous elements including green helle-

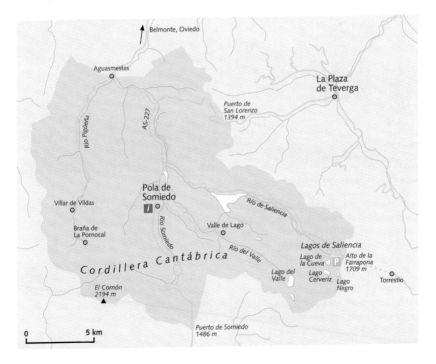

Ancient, lichen-bedecked beech trees at Somiedo

bore (subspecies *occidentalis*), Pyrenean squill and wood-sedge. Welsh poppy, wood cranesbill, *Digitalis parviflora*, Pyrenean valerian and rampion bellflower can be found along woodland margins throughout.

Pyrenean and sessile oaks flourish on nutrient-poor, acid soils, while the lowest levels of the park are the domain of pedunculate oak, often accompanied by wych elm, hazel, sycamore, large- and small-leaved limes and ash, although much of this origi-

nal forest has been cleared to create meadows or replanted with groves of sweet chestnut. The limestone river gorges in the northern reaches of the park have a markedly warmer, drier microclimate and are populated by western holm and Lusitanian oaks (subspecies *faginea*), Mediterranean buckthorn and strawberry-tree.

The Somiedo gallery forests display an interesting zonation from alder, black poplar and wych elm at the lowest levels to *Salix atrocinerea*, white and crack willows in the middle reaches, with *Salix elaeagnos* subspecies *angustifolia*, purple willow and *Salix cantabrica*, the latter restricted to northern Spain, along montane watercourses. The glacial lakes support communities of water horsetail, spiked water-milfoil (found nowhere else in Asturias), bogbean, broad-leaved pondweed and common spike-rush.

Somiedo is perhaps best known for its brown bears, with a score of individuals representing around a quarter of the Spanish total. Other notable mammals include a stable breeding population of wolf, around 500 chamois and an abundance of snow voles and the northern Spanish endemic Castroviejo's hare. Forest and scrub inhabitants include wildcat, common genet, Eurasian badger, pine marten, roe and red deer (the latter reintroduced in the 1970s and scarce today), wild boar, edible dormouse and bank vole. Rivers below 800 m are a noted haunt of otter, Pyrenean desmans have been cited from the montane streams, and riverine habitats in general are home to southern water vole, water shrew and Miller's water shrew.

Bird-wise, a noted inhabitant of the Somiedo forests is the capercaillie, although here – as in many other parts of the Cordillera Cantábrica – this endangered subspecies (*cantabricus*) is declining fast: a victim of poaching, habitat destruction, disturbance and even climatic change (heavy rains in May are responsible for high levels of chick mortality). Forest birds of prey – goshawk, booted and short-toed eagles, honey buzzard and black kite – are well represented here, with cliff-breeding species including Egyptian vulture, golden eagle, peregrine and eagle owl. The Somiedo forests also provide refuge for woodcock, nightjar, black, middle spotted and lesser spotted woodpeckers, pied flycatcher and both treecreepers.

Scrubby habitats above and around the tree-line are the haunt of breeding hen and Montagu's harriers, a stable population of partridge and isolated colonies of whinchat

and bluethroat, as well as hosting red-backed shrike, citril finch and rock bunting. At the highest levels look out for alpine swift, water pipit, alpine accentor, rock thrush, wallcreeper and snow finch, as well as both choughs.

Of the 20+ herptiles recorded here, the most noteworthy are Schreiber's green lizard, Iberian rock lizard and Cantabrican viper, all of which are endemic to the peninsula, while alpine and palmate newts and midwife toads flourish in the numerous glacial lakes, in particular the shallow Lago Cerveriz. Around the Puerto de Somiedo (1486 m), small pools harbour common tree frog, while golden-striped salamander and Iberian frog (again both unique to Spain and Portugal) are known to occur in the upper reaches of the Río Pigüeña.

Somiedo is probably the best butterfly site in Asturias after the Picos de Europa (see p. 75), home to such notable upland species as Apollo, mountain clouded yellow, shepherd's fritillary, Lefèbvre's, large, mountain and Chapman's ringlets and Gavarnie blue, with geranium argus, large and Mazarine blues and chequered skipper occurring in the mid-level forest–meadow mosaic. The Saliencia valley is of particular interest, boasting the only Asturian records for great banded grayling and dusky meadow brown, as well as harbouring a colony of Spanish argus and the only stable population of Esper's marbled white in the province.

Large-flowered butterwort *Pinguicula grandiflora*

Like the Picos de Europa, Somiedo supports a traditional livestock-rearing system that has remained unchanged for hundreds, if not thousands, of years. Outstanding among the vernacular architecture are the numerous *cabanas de teito*:

barns and dwellings with a circular or oval floor-plan and thatched broom roofs; no less than 34 of these edifices can be seen in the Braña de La Pornacal, to the south of Villar de Vildas in the Pigüeña river valley.

Access and information: The park interpretation centre is in Pola de Somiedo (tel: 98 5763758/ 5763649; fax: 98 5763704) on the AS-227 which crosses the middle of the park between Aguasmestas and the Puerto de Somiedo. The Saliencia lakes – Lago de la Cueva, Lago Cerveriz and Lago Negro – can be reached by following the minor road to Alto de la Farrapona (also called Collada de Balbarán; 1709 m) on the Asturias–León border. Lago del Valle (accessed from the village of Valle del Lago), lies in a magnificent cirque at 1570 m and is the largest natural lake in Asturias (24 ha). Access to much of the park is restricted to protect the brown bear; the higher levels are snowbound in winter.

SITE 13 Macizo de Ubiña/ Sierra del Áramo

Rugged limestone mountains harbouring a classic subalpine avifauna and many endemic plants.

One of the westernmost outcrops of Carboniferous limestone in the Cordillera Cantábrica, the precipitous Ubiña massif (*paisaje protegido*; 13 318 ha) sports more than 30 peaks in excess of 2000 m, the high point being Peña Ubiña itself, at 2427 m. Snow lies on the vertices for more than half of the year and, not surprisingly, both glacial and karstic features abound.

Beech is the most representative woodland type of Ubiña, typically confined to north-facing slopes and often associated with sessile oak, downy birch (subspecies *celtiberica*) and hazel. Important stands of holly also occur – for example in the Puertos de Agüeria and La Cubilla –

Great yellow gentian *Gentiana lutea*

interspersed with yew and bird cherry. Thef orest fauna includes goshawk, capercaillie, black woodpecker and an abundance of wild boar and roe deer, plus wildcat, Eurasian badger and pine marten, while scrubby habitats around the tree-line are a renowned haunt of partridge and wolf.

The extensive high-level calcareous pastures and rockgardens are a refuge for many plants known only from the Cordillera Cantábrica: the yellow-flowered *Draba cantabriae*, cone saxifrage, *Saxifraga canaliculata*, *S. trifurcata*, rock speedwell (subspecies *cantabrica*), *Campanula cantabrica* and *Artemisia cantabrica*. Look out, too, for the attractive *Callianthemum coriandrifolium*, a white-flowered member of the buttercup family which blooms in June and July near snow-fields. Other eye-catching species include great yellow gentian, alpine aster, English iris and the autumn-flowering *Crocus nudiflorus*.

Outstanding among the birds of these high-level habitats are alpine accentor, rock thrush, wallcreeper, snowfinch, chough,

alpine chough and peregrine, as well as griffon and Egyptian vultures and golden eagle. Chamois abound, scattered glacial lakes are the haunt of alpine newts, and Iberian rock and viviparous lizards and the Cantabrican viper are among the most notable reptiles. Butterfly-wise, look out for Apollo, silky and Lefèbvre's ringlets, Gavarnie blue and purple-edged copper at altitude, with the meadows around Tuiza de Arriba home to Escher's blue, a rare species in Asturias. Just over the border into León, tree grayling and black satyr are relatively common between 1200 and 1400 m.

Ubiña extends northwards into the 15 km-long ridge of the Sierra del Áramo (also a *paisaje protegido*; 5300 ha), dominated by a broad karstified plateau at around 1500 m from which rise a number of peaks, notably Gamoniteiro (1786 m). The low-level forests are typically dominated by pedunculate oak, groves of sweet chestnut, wild cherry,

Ubiña

sycamore, both small-leaved and large-leaved limes and ash, grading into yew, whitebeam, holly and alpine buckthorn with altitude; beech again represents the highest woodland type. The forest and scrub fauna here is similar to that of Ubiña, albeit encompassing lowland elements such as short-toed treecreeper, southern grey shrike and short-toed eagle. Lakes are less common on the karst, but being at lower altitude they support a more diverse amphibian fauna, notably palmate and marbled newts and common tree frog. The *sierra* also harbours a relict population of brown hare.

Access: The Ricabo–Lindes beechwood is accessed from Santa Marina (on the AS-230 west of Pola de Lena): the two villages are linked by a cobbled trail through the forest. The higher areas of Ubiña are best accessed from the Puerto de la Cubilla (1683 m), or Puerto Ventana (1587 m), the latter also overlooking the aforementioned beech forest.

Also in the area

Puerto de Pajares Quartzite and slate terrain rising to 1904 m (El Negrón) whose northern slopes once again have extensive beech and oak forests (Monte Valgrande; about 1000 ha), while to the south lies a mosaic of scrubby heathlands and pastures populated by aconite-leaved buttercup, *Teesdaliopsis conferta*, violet mountain pansy, pyramidal bugle, whorled lousewort, dog's-tooth-violet, angel's-tears and *Narcissus asturiensis*. Hen harrier, snowfinch, citril finch and rock bunting occur all year round, plus whinchat, rock thrush and red-backed shrike in summer. Access via the N-630, taking the turn-off for El Brañillín ski-station; the peak of Cueto Negro (1853 m) can be ascended by chair-lift.

Desfiladero de las Xanas Spectacular 3-km limestone canyon commencing near Villanueva on the AS-228. Rich flora includes maidenhair fern, fringed pink, *Saxifraga canaliculata*, Pyrenean germander, Malling toadflax, fairy foxglove and woodcock and pyramidal orchids, with more wooded areas hosting astrantia, Pyrenean valerian, rampion bellflower, martagon lily and ramsons. Crag martin, black redstart and alpine chough, plus Iberian and common wall lizards. Meadows around the village of Pedroveya at the eastern end have greater yellow-rattle (subspecies *asturicus*), large-flowered butterwort, heart-flowered serapias and early marsh orchid.

Martagon lily *Lilium martagon* (T.F.)

SITE 14 Cabo de Peñas

Cliff-top peaty heathland with an interesting flora and amphibian community; a renowned sea-watching locality with breeding seabirds on the offshore islets.

The most northerly point in Asturias, the 100 m-high cliffs of the Cabo de Peñas (a *paisaje protegido* of 1920 ha) are carpeted with a myriad wind-pruned heathers – St Dabeoc's, Cornish, Dorset and Mackay's heaths – among which flourish hoop-petticoat daffodils in spring and carpets of autumn squill from September onwards. Peaty pockets support spongy mats of sphagnum mosses, three-lobed crowfoot and alternate-leaved water-milfoil, with the margins fringed with creeping willow, many-stalked spike-rush, slender club-rush and, rarely, lesser water-plantain. The lip of

Hoop-petticoat daffodil
Narcissus bulbocodium

Cabo de Peñas

the cliffs harbours low-lying clumps of rock sea-spurrey and Danish scurvy-grass, Portuguese angelica, endemic to northwestern Iberia and here at the easternmost limit of its range, golden-samphire and wild asparagus (subspecies *prostratus*).

The cliff-top plateau is studded with seasonal pools, well worth investigating for the presence of fire salamander, marbled newt, common tree and common frogs, as well as grass snake, while drier rocky outcrops are home to common wall lizard. On the mammal front, red fox, stoat, weasel and brown hare are fairly abundant here, as is the southern water vole.

The resident bird populations of the cliff-top plateau comprise kestrel, skylark, dunnock, stonechat and black redstart, which are joined by merlin, rock and Richard's pipits, blue rock thrush, northern grey shrike and snow bunting in winter, and by tree pipit and red-backed shrike in summer. During passage periods diversity increases tremendously, with species such as hen harrier, hobby, wryneck, tawny pipit, yellow wagtail, whinchat, subalpine warbler, whitethroat and even corncrake having been recorded here. Waders such as golden plover, dunlin, ruff and snipe are also attracted by the seasonal pools, although these soon move on to less inhospitable areas. The cliffs themselves are home to a couple of pairs of peregrine.

Almost any of the headlands along the Cornisa Cantábrica – from Galicia to Euskadi – will furnish good views of the renowned autumn passage of seabirds westwards along the coast, but some localities have acquired almost legendary status among the birdwatchers of the region. Estaca de Bares (see p. 48) is one and Cabo de Peñas is another, although some claim that the Punta de la Vaca, a handful of kilometres to the east, beats Peñas hands down, despite its lower cliffs (around 60 m) and close proximity to the bustling resort of Luanco. In either case, from the end of July to the beginning of November is definitely prime time, when the passage of shearwaters, gannets, scoters, waders, skuas, terns and auks is a veritable extravaganza, although seabirds can be seen from these capes at almost any time of year. Among the more unusual species seen from Cabo de Peñas are Leach's storm-petrel, white-winged black and sooty terns and even a black guillemot off Punta la de Vaca in December 2000.

The offshore islets visible from the tip of Cabo de Peñas – El Sabín, closest at hand and connected to the mainland by a tombolo, and La Herbosa (Erbosa), a little further away to the northwest – are both home to boisterous colonies of yellow-legged gulls. La Herbosa also supports nesting shag and around 50 pairs of storm petrel, as well as an isolated population of common wall lizard; denominated subspecies *rasquinetti*, these individuals are larger and more intensely pigmented than their mainland relatives, occupying a handful of islets off the coast of Asturias, Cantabria and Euskadi.

Access: A waymarked coastal footpath (PR-AS-25) runs in a southwesterly direction from the Cabo de Peñas lighthouse to Nieva, at the mouth of the Ría de Avilés, taking in some 16.5 km of superb precipitous cliffs and sandy coves.

Also in the area

Bahía de Xixón/Gijón Busy industrial port, nevertheless harbouring large wintering concentrations of gulls, including great black-backed, common, little, Mediterranean and ring-billed (regular since 1986), as well as sporadic glaucous and Iceland. Important wintering population of purple sandpiper along the rocky shore at the eastern end of the bay (Paseo de El Rinconín).

SITE 15 Ría de Villaviciosa

An estuary of considerable ornithological significance, with an interesting halophytic flora.

One of the largest coastal wetlands in Asturias, the Ría de Villaviciosa (a *reserva natural parcial* of 995 ha) is narrowly triangular in shape, almost closed at the mouth by the headlands of El Puntal (to the west) and the enormous sandspit of Punta Rodiles, topped by a low cordon of dunes. Pioneer species here include sea knotgrass, sea rocket and the South African composite *Arctotheca calendula*, while the older dunes are stabilised by marram, aided and abetted by sea-holly, sea bindweed and sand sedge.

At high water virtually the whole valley is submerged, but the ebbing tide exposes large tracts of mud and sand around the main river channel. In the lowest intertidal areas, meadows of eelgrass and dwarf eelgrass carpet the mudflats, giving way to

perennial glasswort and small cord-grass in the middle reaches. Highest plant diversity occurs in marginal areas affected only by the spring tides, where you might encounter shrubby sea-blite, particularly on sandy soils, *Suaeda albescens*, sea-purslane, lesser sea-spurrey, sea heath, thrift, common sea-lavender, *Limonium binervosum*, endemic to the north coast of Spain, golden-samphire, sea aster and sea arrowgrass.

The upper reaches of the estuary, nowadays largely isolated from the influence of the tides by a series of dykes, have been converted to brackish grazing lands called *porreos*, harbouring a wide variety of grasses, sedges and rushes, coloured by purple loosestrife, sea-milkwort and the non-

Ría de Villaviciosa

native buttonweed. Around the mouths of the rivers Valdediós and Valbárcena, the influx of fresh water has given rise to stands of grey and sea club-rushes and common reed, interspersed with marsh mallow and wild celery.

The invertebrate diversity and biomass of Villaviciosa's intertidal area is enormous; 167 species of mollusc have been cited, a few of which – small and golden carpet-clams and sword razor – are harvested commercially. These and other subterranean invertebrates provide a wealth of food for aquatic birds, particularly waders, of which 43 species have been recorded here. The most commonplace wintering species are oystercatcher, grey and golden plovers, lapwing, little stint, dunlin, snipe, jack snipe, both godwits, curlew and redshank, while passage periods generally turn up black-winged stilt, avocet, Temminck's stint, curlew sandpiper, ruff, whimbrel, spotted redshank and green and wood sandpipers. Purple sandpiper and turnstone frequent the breakwaters at the entrance to the estuary in winter, while accidental visitors in recent years have included collared pratincole, dotterel, buff-breasted and pectoral sandpipers, great snipe and red-necked and grey phalaropes.

Among the birds which can be seen all year round are grey heron, little egret, ringed plover, dunlin, redshank and common sandpiper, although all are most abundant during passage periods or in winter. Also resident is the curlew, which bred regularly in the *porreos* until the late 1970s but does so only sporadically today, despite maintaining a sedentary population of around a hundred birds. More habitual breeding birds at Villaviciosa are water rail, fan-tailed, Savi's, reed and great reed warblers and a few reed buntings in the rush and reedbeds, with sedge, aquatic and moustached warblers, little, Baillon's and spotted crakes and even corncrake utilising this habitat on migration. Little bitterns once bred here on a regular basis, but are rare today except on passage, when you might also turn up marsh harrier, purple,

squacco and night herons, black and white storks, spoonbill (mainly in the autumn) and an occasional glossy ibis. Grasshopper warblers and whitethroats breed in the scrub between the meadows surrounding the estuary.

Grebes and duck occur here only in small numbers, although 33 species have been cited. Among the most habitual wintering wildfowl are greylag goose, teal, gadwall, pintail and wigeon, but you could also turn up scarce visitors such as white-fronted and Brent geese, shelduck, garganey, marbled teal, red-crested pochard, pochard, tufted and ferruginous duck and goldeneye, or accidentals such as the North American black duck. Only little and great crested grebes and mallard breed regularly, although shoveler does so from time to time and black-necked grebes have nested in the past. During winter storms, look out for more northern species taking refuge in the *ría*, notably great northern diver, common scoter, scaup, eider, long-tailed duck and red-breasted merganser; even smew and goosander have been recorded on occasion.

Amphibians are well-represented in the *porreos* and freshwater habitats, including golden-striped salamander, palmate and marbled newts and Iberian painted, Iberian pool and common tree frogs. Although otters disappeared from the estuary several decades ago, stoat and western polecat are still found here, while Villaviciosa is one of the few places in Spain where the presence of harvest mouse has been confirmed.

Access and information: At various points from the roads which run northwards from the town of Villaviciosa on either side of the estuary; wellington boots are a must if you want to explore the *porreos*. The reserve interpretation centre lies on the western shore (on the road to El Puntal; VV-5); closed Mondays.

Also in the area

Sierra del Sueve (*paisaje protegido*; 8100 ha) Limestone ridge (maximum 1159 m) close to the coast with a maritime climate and well-developed karst scenery. Northern slopes have stands of beech with interesting fern flora: *Woodwardia radicans*, Tunbridge filmy-fern, Killarney fern and *Culcita macrocarpa*. Large population of introduced fallow deer plus semi-wild *asturcón* horses (endangered native race), with red squirrel, edible dormouse, wildcat and common genet in beechwoods. Higher levels harbour snow vole, water pipit and both choughs, open heaths have garden dormouse, brown hare, grasshopper warbler and Cantabrian viper, and rockgardens host Iberian rock and Iberian wall lizards. Traversed by the AS-260 (Colungas– Arriondas road); Mirador del Fito boasts superb views of the Picos de Europa.

^{SITE}
16 Redes

A highly scenic mountain area topped by jagged peaks, traversed by precipitous river gorges and harbouring remote beech forest enclaves; rich bird and mammal fauna.

The Parque Natural de Redes (37 622 ha), declared a Biosphere Reserve in 2001, is centred on the broad valley of the Río Nalón in southeastern Asturias, extending from its source close to the Puerto de Tarna (1490 m) to the Ríoseco dam at around 360 m. Located on the north-facing flanks of the Cordillera Cantábrica, the park encompasses a wilderness of limestone and quartzite peaks (maximum Pico Torres, at 2104 m), ice-sculpted into more than 60 glacial cirques. A multitude of small streams rises here, carving out sheer gorges – El Alba, Los Arrudos and Monasterio – as they plunge precipitously towards the Nalón.

Broad-leaved woodlands are the focus of Redes, covering almost 50% of the park. At low levels groves of sweet chestnut have replaced much of the native pedunculate oak forest and today extend over some 2000 ha, but higher up Pyrenean and sessile oaks are still well represented, often associated with hazel, wych elm, wild cherry and Plymouth pear. Perhaps the most significant habitat, however, is the beech forest, notably that of Monte Redes around the headwaters

of the Río Monasterio. Although beech is the dominant canopy tree, it is accompanied by yew, downy birch (subspecies *celtiberica*), sessile oak, whitebeam, rowan, holly, large-leaved lime and ash, according to variations in bedrock, aspect and altitude, and hosts a characteristic ground flora of green hellebore, wood anemone, hepatica, kidney saxifrage, wood sorrel, bilberry, yellow pimpernel, broad-leaved helleborine and the saprophytic bird's-nest orchid.

Above 1700 m, a subalpine climax community of dwarf juniper prevails, accompanied by bilberry and ling on acid soils and by *Genista legionensis*, confined to the eastern Cordillera Cantábrica, spurge-laurel, bear-

Pyrenean desman *Galemys pyrenaicus*

Riaño reservoir in winter (T.F.)

berry and bog bilberry on the limestone. Calcareous fissure communities, which extend from the peaks down into the river gorges, include species such as blue-leaved petrocoptis, confined to the mountains of northern Spain, fringed pink, livelong and yellow mountain saxifrages, dragonmouth, the northern Iberian endemic snapdragon *Antirrhinum braun-blanquetii* and leafless-stemmed globularia.

The vegetation of the more acid upland grasslands, peatbogs and glacial lakes – notably that of Ubales, in a quartzite cirque at 1680 m – is also of interest, including species such as alpine clubmoss, *Isoetes velatum* (subspecies *asturicense*), fringed and great yellow gentians, large-flowered butterwort, *Narcissus asturiensis*, *N. pseudonarcissus* and the arctic-alpine hare's-tail cottongrass.

Of the 52 species of mammals which have been cited in Redes, outstanding are the 3000-odd chamois, a phenomenal figure considering that the post-Civil War population numbered only 30–50 individuals. The park also harbours the highest density of red deer in Asturias (about 2000), although these were reintroduced in the 1930s. All the carnivores present in the Cordillera Cantábrica today occur here, although brown bears are

at best accidental visitors from the small nucleus in Riaño and Fuentes Carrionas.

Many of the Redes mammals are closely associated with the forest habitats, particularly pine marten, Eurasian badger, wildcat, common genet, garden and edible dormice and red squirrel. The few wolves which occupy the park tend to occupy scrubby areas around the tree-line, where they prey mainly on roe deer and wild boar, while the upland screes are populated with snow voles, unpolluted mountain streams are the haunt of Pyrenean desman and the larger rivers host otter and western polecat. Brown hares are still sometimes spotted in the middle-altitude haymeadows, but the once impressive population of Castroviejo's hare is little more than a memory today. Among the 13 species of bat recorded here are Daubenton's and lesser horseshoe, plus Savi's pipistrelle.

The rich forest avifauna includes a fairly stable population of capercaillie, black, great spotted and middle spotted woodpeckers, pied flycatcher, goldcrest, crested tit, nuthatch, treecreeper, bullfinch and citril finch. Listen out, too, for willow and wood warblers, whose Iberian breeding populations are confined to a handful of localities in the northern peninsula. Forest-breeding birds of prey include goshawk, honey buzzard, short-toed eagle and long-eared owl, while among the notable cliff-nesters here are golden eagle and Egyptian vulture.

Above the tree-line, you can find most of the high-altitude specialities of northern Spain, notably water pipit, alpine accentor, rock thrush, wallcreeper, both choughs and snow finch, with scrublands at altitude providing a refuge for quail, whinchat, wheatear, rock bunting and yellowhammer. Riverine habitats are the haunt of kingfisher, grey wagtail and dipper, while the reservoirs at the western end of the park attract little grebe and water rail; there is a sand martin colony on the walls of the Embalse de Ríoseco.

Most of the interesting herptiles recorded from Redes are also high-level species, including Iberian endemics such as Iberian rock lizard and Cantabrican viper, while the glacial lakes harbour fire salamander (also abundant in the forests) and alpine, Bosca's and palmate newts. The same can be said for the butterfly fauna, with notable species recorded at or above the tree-line including Apollo, mountain clouded yellow, shepherd's fritillary, Chapman's, common brassy, mountain and large ringlets, purple-edged, purple-shot and scarce coppers and Gavarnie blue; the Puerto de Tarna is a particularly good locality. Among the more interesting woodland species are chequered skipper, lesser purple emperor and Duke of Burgundy fritillary.

Access and information: The AS-17 from Pola de Lavaniana to the Puerto de Tarna traverses the park alongside the Río Nalón. The Alba gorge is accessible from Soto de Agües and that of Los Arrudos from Caleao, while the Monte Redes beech forest lies to the south of Bezanes (via 11 km of track leading to Brañagallones). The park interpretation centre is in Campo de Caso (tel: 98 5608110; fax: 98 5608145).

Also in the area

Mampodre Vast mountainous area to the south of Redes, topped by the peak of the same name (2190 m). Includes two fabulous glacial lakes – Isoba, adjacent to the LE-332, and Ausente, accessible from the San Isidro ski-station – and the best-preserved native Scots pine forest in the Cordillera Cantábrica: the Pinar de Lillo (to the south of the Puerto de las Señales (1625 m) on the LE-331). This pine forest, harbouring trees more than 400 years old, covers around 200 ha and is a relic of drier, colder times. Pyrenean desman, otter, chamois, wolf, golden eagle, capercaillie, partridge, black and middle spotted woodpeckers and both choughs.

Riaño Enormous reservoir ringed by high mountains, with well-preserved beech forest in steep valleys boasting a particularly high incidence of capercaillie leks, plus black, middle spotted and lesser spotted woodpeckers and citril finch. About 40 pairs of white stork still breed here, despite the inundation of many former nest sites in nine villages in 1987. Partridge, eagle owl and sand martin also breed, with high-altitude birds including wallcreeper, alpine chough and snow finch. Castroviejo's hare, wolf and brown bear are the most notable mammals. Several colonies of bog fritillary, dusky large blue and Spanish argus are known from the area.

Cantabria, Euskadi and La Rioja

Introduction

Most of Cantabria and Euskadi (País Vasco) is a simple easterly continuation of Asturias, with the foothills of the Cordillera Cantábrica and the Montañas de Transición – the ill-defined mountain area that links the Cordillera to the Pyrenees – crowding down in many places almost to the sea, largely confining human settlements to the coastal strip or valley bottoms.

There is no doubt that the rugged limestone pinnacles of the Picos de Europa are the most outstanding feature, both physically and in terms of wildlife, since they harbour more than 1400 species of vascular plant, 280+ vertebrates and 145 butterflies. Limestone massifs in general harbour many Cantabrican–Pyrenean endemic plants, with that of Aralar home to the region's only stable pair of lammergeiers.

The watershed of the Cordillera Cantábrica pretty much coincides with the boundary between the Euro-Siberian and Mediterranean bioclimatic regions, acting as a barrier for both essentially northern species and more thermophilic ones. Taking butterflies as an example, communities on the northern flanks include large chequered skipper, Camberwell beauty, pearl-bordered fritillary, marbled white, dryad and Alcon blue. Conversely, those of a distinctly Mediterranean ilk – southern marbled and sage skippers, Spanish festoon, Iberian and Spanish marbled whites, striped grayling and southern and Spanish gatekeepers – are unable to penetrate far into these mountains from the south. The highest peaks harbour an interesting community of Apollo, mountain clouded yellow, shepherd's fritillary, Lefèbvre's, silky, mountain, large, Chapman's and almond-eyed ringlets and Gavarnie blue.

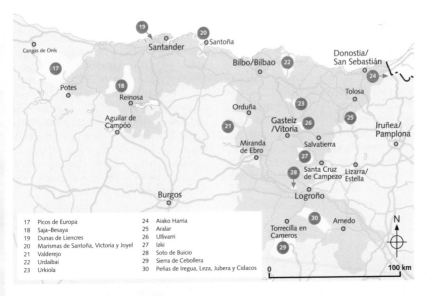

17	Picos de Europa	
18	Saja–Besaya	
19	Dunas de Liencres	
20	Marismas de Santoña, Victoria y Joyel	
21	Valderejo	
22	Urdaibai	
23	Urkiola	
24	Aiako Harria	
25	Aralar	
26	Ullivarri	
27	Izki	
28	Soto de Buicio	
29	Sierra de Cebollera	
30	Peñas de Iregua, Leza, Jubera y Cidacos	

Opposite page: **Haymeadows and limestone cliffs above Fuente Dé, Picos de Europa**

Although not as wild as the Galician shore to the west, the coastal strip contains interesting sand-dune communities, particularly at Liencres, and encompasses several important estuaries – Santoña in Cantabria and Urdaibai in Euskadi – which provide essential feeding grounds for migrating waterbirds such as spoonbill. Maritime cliffs and offshore stacks are also home to a range of seabirds, including storm petrel and shag, with Monte Candina harbouring Iberia's only coastal colony of griffon vultures.

Inland of the coastal strip, little is left of the once extensive lowland deciduous oak woodland, the most significant natural forests in the area being the scattered patches of holm oak and bay on limestone outcrops and rather more extensive beech forests in upland areas, the latter particularly well represented at Saja–Besaya. An exception to this rule is the deeply incised granite valleys of Aiako Harria, where a fine mosaic of forest formations, including Pyrenean oak and strawberry-tree, harbour an abundance of ferns. The Cordillera Cantábrica is also home to Iberia's only native alpine newts, as well as the Iberian version – *Lacerta bilineata* – of the pan-European green lizard.

The Basque province of Araba (Alava) lies to the south of the Atlantic– Mediterranean divide and is covered by large expanses of western holm and Pyrenean oaks, the latter harbouring formidable populations of middle spotted woodpecker, particularly at Izki. The southern reaches of Araba are also home to orchid-rich limestone plateaux – for example, Valderejo – and the only sizeable inland wetlands in Euskadi – notably Ullivarri – containing important populations of European mink and strategically placed on the western Pyrenean migration flyway to receive waders and black storks. The clean rivers draining south from the Gorbeia massif have remarkably diverse odonate communities, including orange-spotted and splendid emeralds, and are also one of the last refuges for the indigenous white-clawed crayfish.

In La Rioja, habitats unknown to the north of the Atlantic–Mediterranean watershed provide a stimulating contrast. The river Ebro was formerly flanked by thick gallery forests, of which the Soto de Buicio is one of the best-preserved remnants, while true Mediterranean species such as bee-eater, rosemary and holly oak abound. Affluents of the Ebro have carved out a series of impressive limestone gorges which provide a niche for important populations of griffon and Egyptian vultures, plus smaller birds such as black wheatear and alpine swift which are rare or non-existent further north.

Although La Rioja falls largely within the Mediterranean biogeographic zone, the north-facing slopes of the Sierras de Cebollera and La Demanda support typically Atlantic habitats owing to the frequency with which they are swept by humid weather systems originating in the Bay of Biscay. Beech and Scots pine dominate the forests, grading into vast scrublands of brooms, heathers and dwarf juniper above the treeline. These mountains harbour isolated breeding nuclei of a number of upland birds including partridge, alpine accentor and water pipit, and wolves still enter the area occasionally; the combination of Euro-Siberian and Mediterranean habitats again makes for a rich butterfly fauna.

Euskadi is a bilingual area and *euskera* is increasingly spoken as a first language, although Castilian Spanish is still the *lingua franca* of the whole area. Road signs usually – but not always – give place names in both languages; be prepared for signs such as 'Biasteri/Laguardia', which in fact refer to a single locality. The website www.nekanet. net/naturaleza/renp/frameprincipal.htm gives further information about protected areas in Euskadi, while www.medioambientecantabria.org/a6_2_espacios_protegidos. html deals with the Cantabrian parks.

SITE 17 Picos de Europa

Small but spectacular range of jagged limestone mountains with an incredibly diverse flora and fauna.

The Picos de Europa is one of those rare places in Europe today that combines magnificent scenery, a thriving rural economy and an enormous range of flora and fauna, the traditional methods of livestock farming practised here allowing wildlife to flourish alongside humans. A veritable pincushion of knife-edged ridges and pinnacles – the heritage of localised glacial activity and ongoing karstification – peaks at 2648 m (Torre Cerredo) and is split into three distinct massifs by precipitous gorges.

In part a *parque nacional* of 64 660 ha, the Picos de Europa houses more than 1400 species of vascular plant, 70-odd mammals and 145 butterflies, such that even a brief visit in early summer will make a lasting impression. From May to early July, the haymeadows of the Picos de Europa are simply glorious: some of the richest temperate grasslands in the world, literally teeming with orchids and butterflies. Add to this the floristic delights of the alpine rockgardens and the diversity of woodland types in the surrounding valleys – ranging from Mediterranean evergreen forests to cool, humid swathes of beech and sessile oak, from mixed deciduous canopies of ash, wych elm and small-leaved lime to extensive tracts of Pyrenean oak – and you have the recipe for the perfect natural history holiday.

One of the best things about the Picos de Europa is that you can still discover it for yourself. Roads are limited to a peripheral circuit with numerous dead-ends branching off to the villages scattered around the flanks of the main massifs, but a comprehensive network of farmers' tracks means that you

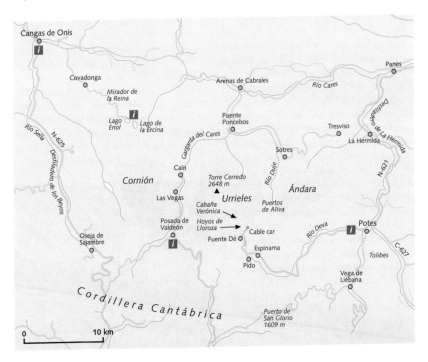

Chamois *Rupicapra pyrenaica*

can walk anywhere that you can find a path, while above the tree-line you can pretty well wander at will.

Take a trip up in the Fuente Dé cable car and you'll find yourself in a maze of limestone rockgardens and springy turf at around 1800 m. The first plants to appear with the melting snows include drifts of spring and trumpet gentians, *Narcissus asturiensis* and spring squill. As spring arrives in earnest, these are joined by the delicate bluish-white blooms of *Anemone pavoniana*, unique to the Cordillera Cantábrica, and a wealth of saxifrages – purple, neglected, cone, livelong and *Saxifraga felineri* (confined to the Picos de Europa), to mention but a few – growing amid creeping carpets of the northern Iberian greenweed *Genista legionensis*. Look out, too, for pink sandwort, moss campion, the crucifers *Draba dedeana* and *D. cantabriae*, both of which are found only in northern Spain, Pyrenean vetch, Teesdale violet, the rock-jasmine *Androsace villosa*, hyssop-leaved sideritis, fairy foxglove, prostrate, alpine and Malling toadflaxes and fluffy mats of *Globularia repens*. More elusive, however, are parnassus-leaved buttercup, spring pasque flower, *Potentilla nivalis* subspecies *asturica*, the delicate, nodding alpine snowbell and dragonmouth.

In late June the characteristic high-altitude composites start to appear, notably pygmy hawk's-beard, alpine aster, *Jurinea humilis*, large-flowered leopard's-bane and the delightful woolly leaved hawkweed *Hieracium mixtum*, but you'll have to wait until July for some of the real specialities of the Picos: the diminutive columbine *Aquilegia pyrenaica* subspecies *discolor*, unique to these mountains, the houseleek *Sempervivum vicentei* subspecies *cantabricum*, confined to northern Spain, the rock storksbill *Erodium glandulosum*, alpine skullcap and the northern Spanish endemic bellflowers *Campanula arvatica*, *C. cantabrica* and *C. legionensis*.

Early in the year chamois are relatively easy to see in the vicinity of the upper cable-car station but take refuge higher in the mountains with the onset of the summer tourist season. The same applies to wall-creepers, which can often be encountered on the main track up towards Cabaña Verónica in May, while hard winters find them in the depths of the main river gorges. The other high-altitude bird specialities of the Picos seem to be less wary of people, however, such that within a few hundred metres of the top of the cable car you should come across snowfinch, alpine accentor, chough and alpine chough, as well as good numbers of water pipit, wheatear and black redstart and the occasional rock thrush. The nearby pools of the Hoyos de Lloroza harbour an abundance of alpine newts and midwife toads, plus large red damselfly and broad-bodied chaser in June, and if you sit quietly in the surrounding rockgardens you

Spring pasque flower *Pulsatilla vernalis* (T.F.)

Upper cable car station, Fuente Dé (T.F.)

will almost certainly be inspected by a curious snow vole.

Butterfly-wise, it is late June before the first Gavarnie blues appear (here the Picos endemic subspecies *asturiensis*), along with Lefèbvre's ringlet (again a race unique to the Picos: *astur*) around the screes. Look out, too, for large grizzled skipper, Queen of Spain fritillary, large wall brown and Piedmont and common brassy ringlets, all of which are common here at this time of year, with mountain clouded yellow, shepherd's fritillary and silky ringlet appearing from July onwards.

Between the foot of the cable car and the village of Espinama lies a wonderful tract of haymeadows interspersed with beech forest which harbours a quite different assemblage of plants and animals. This is one of the best places in the Picos to look for orchids, with early June bringing out a plethora of man, pyramidal, early marsh, fragrant, lizard, bird's-nest, early purple, burnt, tongue and fly orchids, as well as dull, woodcock, early spider and sawfly ophrys.

The meadows themselves are colourful assemblages of kidney vetch (here with pink flowers), bloody crane's-bill, pale flax, musk-mallow, greater yellow-rattle (subspecies *asturicus*) and white asphodel, with other species of note including maiden pink, rock cinquefoil, round-headed rampion, the stemless, lilac-flowered 'thistle' *Carduncellus mitissimus* and round-headed leek, as well as sheets of English irises from July onwards. Wetter areas teem with globeflower, marsh marigold, whorled lousewort, marsh ragwort and marsh hawk's-beard, while the woodland margins harbour astrantia, *Pimpinella siifolia*, bastard balm, spreading and rampion bellflowers, Pyrenean rampion, spiked star-of-Bethlehem, martagon and Kerry lilies, Solomon's-seal, herb-Paris and Pyrenean squill.

The butterfly fauna of this forest–grassland mosaic is stupendous in early summer, including grizzled and mallow skippers, both Iberian swallowtails, black-veined white, Camberwell beauty, Glanville and knapweed fritillaries, Adonis, chalk-hill, turquoise, long-tailed, short-tailed, silver-studded and black-eyed blues, sooty and purple-edged coppers, blue-spot hairstreak and Duke of Burgundy fritillary. Roe deer and red-backed shrikes inhabit the edges of the meadows, wryneck, spotted flycatcher,

Digitalis parviflora

black redstart, serin and cirl bunting abound in the villages of Pido and Espinama, and middle spotted woodpecker, tree pipit, Bonelli's warbler, marsh tit and short-toed treecreeper occupy the forest, although the beechwoods along the track leading north

from Espinama towards the Puertos de Áliva are a better bet for black woodpecker, crested tit, red squirrel and pine marten.

In addition, the Picos de Europa supports healthy raptor populations, harbouring around 130 pairs of griffon vulture (plus numerous immature birds: a total of around 400 individuals), as well as several pairs of Egyptian; both species can be easily observed at the vulture feeding station visible from the Mirador de la Reina, on the road up to the glacial lakes above Covadonga. The eagles are represented by golden, short-toed and booted, the latter two in fair numbers throughout, while honey buzzard, goshawk and sparrowhawk are all common in forested areas; check out the heavily wooded Valdeón valley. Breeding black kites are particularly abundant in Cabrales, hobbies occur in the drier habitats around Potes and peregrines are regularly seen preying on choughs around Fuente Dé.

Another high-level focal point is the Covadonga glacial lakes: Enol and La Ercina. The surrounding sward is kept short by herds of the autochthonous *casina* cattle

Spring gentians near the top of the cable car

which spend the summer here, but nevertheless produces a breathtaking display of hoop-petticoat daffodils and dog's-tooth-violets in spring and merendera in late summer. Limestone outcrops around the lake are worth examining for blue-leaved petrocoptis, confined to the Cordillera Cantábrica, Pyrenean lousewort and deep purple-flowered clumps of the Picos endemic toadflax *Linaria faucicola*.

Another attraction of the lakes is the tens of thousands of common blue and azure damselflies which swarm around the margins in mid-June. The peripheral beds of bogbean and sedges should also reward you with four-spotted chaser, emperor dragonfly, keeled skimmer, golden-ringed dragonfly and red-veined and ruddy darters. Look out, too, for Iberian rock lizard in rocky habitats, rock thrush around the cliffs at the southern end of La Ercina, and citril finch in the beech forests slightly further afield.

The Garganta del Cares is probably the pick of the river gorges which dissect the Picos de Europa. An 11 km trail follows the whole length of this steep-sided chasm, often several hundred metres above the river, giving you a good chance of spotting wallcreeper in winter and black woodpecker (in small enclaves of broad-leaved forest) at any time of year. Crag martin and dipper are present all year round, plus alpine swift in summer, with blue rock thrush a distinct possibility at the northern end. Shady overhangs shelter maidenhair fern, round-leaved St John's-wort and large-flowered butterwort, while sunny limestone rockgardens host sticky flax, woodcock ophrys, fragrant orchid and dark-red helleborine. Among the butterflies which frequent the warm, sheltered reaches of the gorge in June are marbled skipper, Berger's clouded yellow, Moroccan orange tip, violet fritillary, pearly and dusky heaths, marbled white and Spanish purple hairstreak. To the south of Caín, mixed deciduous woodland around Las Vegas is a noted haunt of woodland brown, one of Europe's rarest butterflies, at a distance easy to confuse with the rather similar ringlet.

Information: Visitor centres for the Picos de Europa national park (e-mail: picos@mma.es) are located in Cangas de Onís (tel: 985 848614; fax: 985 848699), at Buferrera, up by the Covadonga lakes, and in Posada de Valdeón (tel: 987 740549; fax: 987 740587). A centre is under construction in the Cantabrian sector (near Tama), with a temporary office just west of Potes on the road to Fuente Dé (tel: 942 730555). Free guided walks (interpretation in Spanish) are offered from all four bases throughout the summer.

Also in the area

Puerto de San Glorio A 1609 m pass on the N-621 where the Picos de Europa abuts the Cordillera Cantábrica. High-level haymeadows house an acidophilic flora of common bistort, horned pansy, great yellow gentian, large self-heal, *Pedicularis mixta*, *Narcissus pseudonarcissus* subspecies *nobilis* and Pyrenean snakeshead, plus vanilla, pale-flowered, elder-flowered and frog orchids. Slaty screes host *Teesdaliopsis conferta* and *Phalacrocarpum oppositifolium*, both unique to northern Iberia, while boggy areas harbour aconite-leaved buttercup, hairy stonecrop, starry and yellow mountain saxifrages, water avens, grass-of-Parnassus, snow gentian, large-flowered butterwort and white false helleborine. Pyrenean desmans in the streams, high densities of wildcat and Eurasian badger in the surrounding forests, wolf and brown bear in the mountains to the south of the pass and red deer frequent in winter. Whitethroats, red-backed shrikes and rock buntings occupy the scrub, as do Cantabrian vipers, often sporting melanic coloration. San Glorio is a classic locality for Chapman's ringlet (endemic to the central Cordillera Cantábrica) in late June, along with marsh, mountain, pearl-bordered and Queen of Spain fritillaries, with July bringing Apollo, Esper's marbled white, rock grayling and purple-edged, purple-shot and scarce coppers.

Cork oak forest of Tolibes Between the N-621 and C-627, just to the southeast of Potes. Mediterranean forest on acid shales dominated by cork and western holm oak forest, plus prickly juniper, osyris, turpentine tree, Mediterranean buckthorn, *Cistus psilosepalus*, strawberry-tree, *Phillyrea latifolia*, wild jasmine and Etruscan honeysuckle. Dry grasslands have pink butterfly, green-winged and Sicilian orchids plus Deptford pink, spotted rock-rose, field eryngo, wild clary and cone knapweed, while rocky outcrops host rock soapwort, *Ruta angustifolia*, French lavender, daisy-leaved toadflax, *Helichrysum stoechas* and angel's-tears. Excellent for butterflies, including scarce swallowtail, Cleopatra, Moroccan orange tip, spotted fritillary and brown, purple, Spanish purple, blue-spot, ilex, false ilex and sloe hairstreaks, as well as sooty copper, black-eyed, Lang's short-tailed and Baton blues.

^{SITE}
18 Saja–Besaya

Fabulous beech and deciduous oak forest with a rich fauna; limestone outcrops add considerably to the floristic and invertebrate diversity.

From the Puerto de Palombera (1260 m), the views over the Saja–Besaya *parque natural* (24 500 ha) are simply out of this world, the tilted buttresses of bone-white limestone which punctuate the upper reaches of the Saja valley rising from the sea of beech forest like a partially buried skeleton.

Most of the park lies on the northern flanks of the Cordillera Cantábrica, directly exposed to rain-laden winds sweeping in from the Atlantic. As a result, the beechwoods – which lie predominantly between 800 and 1400 m – are sometimes referred to as 'cloud forest', the trunks and branches festooned with epiphytic mosses, lichens and ferns. Hazel is common throughout, stands of sessile oak occur where the climate is most severe, and the more lime-rich soils find whitebeam and yew mixed in with the

beech. Although the beechwood ground flora is rather poor – mainly wood spurge, spurge-laurel, bilberry, St Dabeoc's heath and butcher's broom – wetter enclaves around the many waterfalls and small streams host hart's-tongue, kidney saxifrage, opposite-leaved golden-saxifrage and ivy-leaved bellflower. Further down the valley, the beech gives way to pedunculate oak, typically associated with sweet chestnut and ash and often joined by wych elm and small-leaved lime along the watercourses.

The Saja–Besaya forests are as good a place as any in Spain to search for middle spotted and black woodpeckers, with raptors such as goshawk, sparrowhawk, honey buzzard and tawny owl also fairly commonplace. Among the smaller birds, keep an eye out for those which reach their southern limit in Iberia's

Saja, near the Puerto de Palombera (David Element)

northern forests, notably goldcrest, marsh tit, treecreeper and bullfinch, along with more widespread species such as wryneck, tree pipit, pied flycatcher and Bonelli's warbler. Although encounters with forest mammals are rare, red squirrel, roe deer, wild boar, Eurasian badger, beech and pine martens, western polecat, common genet and wildcat are all a possibility here.

Woodland butterflies (among 86 species recorded in the park) are best observed along sunny rides in late summer, notably Camberwell beauty, large tortoiseshell, silver-washed, high brown, marbled and pearl-bordered fritillaries, tree grayling and the hermit, with the spectacular Tau emperor moth flying from the end of March to early June. From July onwards, check out the Puerto de Palombera for silver-spotted skipper, Apollo, Esper's marbled white, chestnut heath, mountain ringlet and scarce and sooty coppers.

Scarce copper *Lycaena virgaureae* (T.F.)

Access: The C-625, which links Cabezón de la Sal (on the N-634) with Espinilla (on the C-628 between Reinosa and the ski resort of Brañavieja in Alto Campóo), passes through the western part of the park via the Puerto de Palombera. Many waymarked trails, indicated by signboards with maps.

Plant-wise, it is the limestone buttresses which protrude from the forest that harbour the highest diversity. A springtime exploration of the Alto de la Pedraja rockgardens, just to the north of Palombera, will reward you with hepatica, sweet spurge, thick-leaved stonecrop, livelong saxifrage, mountain currant, hoary rockrose, Pyrenean eryngo, the rock-jasmine *Androsace villosa*, trumpet gentian, Pyrenean germander, scrambling gromwell and leafless-stemmed globularia. Crag martin, wheatear, rock thrush, black redstart and both choughs are the most characteristic birds around La Pedraja, but keep an eye on the skies as golden and short-toed eagles and griffon and Egyptian vultures are often seen from here.

Close to the Alto de la Pedraja, a well-marked track leads westwards along the Sierra del Cordel (a ZEPA of 16 244 ha) to the Puerto de Sejos (10 km), renowned for its circle of sandstone menhirs, dating from around 2500 BC and carved with anthropoid figures. Most of this trail lies above the treeline, taking you across springy pastures – frequented by skylark, water pipit and wheatear – and through genista, heather and gorse scrub, home to the Iberian endemic Castroviejo's hare plus partridge, whinchat and red-backed shrike. The area around the tree-line is also the principal habitat utilised by red deer – reintroduced and numbering about a thousand individuals today – and for the wolves which have recently made a comeback; hen harriers also breed here, while bluethroat is a distinct possibility.

Also in the area

Alto Campóo At the head of the Híjar valley, west of Reinosa, peaking at Tres Mares (2175 m). Collado de la Fuente del Chivo (2008 m) affords superb views of the Picos de Europa and harbours water pipit, alpine accentor, dunnock, wheatear, rock thrush and alpine chough, with ring ouzel on passage. Spring flora includes marsh-marigold, spring gentian, oxlip, *Narcissus asturiensis*, hoop-petticoat daffodil, angel's-tears, *Romulea bulbocodium*, spring squill and dog's-tooth-violet. The extremely scarce almond-eyed ringlet has been recorded here.

Embalse del Ebro (combined ZEPAs cover 12 675 ha) Huge reservoir with breeding little bittern (2–4 pairs), white stork (some 40 pairs), great crested grebe (maximum 187 pairs), gadwall, little ringed and Kentish plovers, common sandpiper and yellow wagtail, with wintering birds including black-necked grebe and ferruginous duck. Major post-breeding congregation point for several thousand red-crested pochard in July. Spoonbill, greylag goose, garganey, avocet, little stint, ruff and both godwits on passage. Many raptors in the surrounds: honey buzzard, black kite, Egyptian vulture, short-toed and booted eagles, marsh and hen harriers and hobby in summer, plus red kite and griffon vulture all year round. Minor roads run along the margins to both north and south, giving excellent views over the open water.

^{SITE}19 Dunas de Liencres

The largest and best-preserved dune system on the Cornisa Cantábrica, with the adjacent estuary providing refuge for wintering and migratory waterbirds.

The Dunas de Liencres *parque natural* (194.5 ha) lies on a substantial sandspit which juts westwards into the mouth of the Río Pas and, despite heavy visitor pressure, supports a rich community of typical psammophiles. Immediately behind the beach, where the northwesterly winds are responsible for the continual movement of the dunes inland, vegetation is sparse, consisting primarily of sand couch-grass but, as stability increases, the tough, in-rolled leaves of marram start to appear, interspersed with sea sandwort, sea rocket, purple spurge, sea bindweed and sand sedge – all familiar members of the Atlantic dune flora – together with more Mediterranean elements such as coastal crucianella and the exquisite white trumpets of sea daffodil. Purple-tinged sea-holly abounds – often parasitised by carrot broomrape – accompanied by clumps of sea spurge whose slender stems provide food for spurge hawk-moth caterpillars, resembling fat red-and-black sausages by late June.

Beneath the scarp face of the oldest primary dunes a more humid habitat appears, supporting a luxuriant tangle of sage-leaved cistus, sharp rush and massive clumps of the South American pampas-grass, widely naturalised in northern Spain. An inspection of these dune slacks in spring should turn up bee orchid, small-flowered and heart-flowered serapias and dull ophrys, with lesser butterfly orchids appearing in early summer. Other eye-catching species here are Jersey pink, the lemon-flowered toadflax *Linaria supina* subspecies *maritima* and the everlasting flower *Helichrysum stoechas*.

The dune system harbours a small breeding population of tawny pipit, with low limestone rock outcrops along the beach providing a niche for black redstart. Much of the secondary and tertiary dunes was planted with maritime pines in 1949, nowadays attracting sparrowhawk, melodious and Sardinian warblers, crested tit and cirl bunting. These pinewoods are also the only

Dunas de Liencres (T.F.)

known site for pendulous-flowered helleborine in the Iberian peninsula, as well as hosting dark-red helleborine, violet limodore and twayblade.

The herptile interest at Liencres is focused on midwife toad and green and Schreiber's green lizards, while among the mammals the most you can hope for are wood mouse, greater white-toothed shrew, western hedgehog, weasel and the occasional red fox. The flower-rich pastures and meadows around the village of Liencres itself provide hunting grounds for short-toed eagle, hobby and red-backed shrike, while the distinctive calls of fan-tailed warbler, corn bunting, stonechat and, rarely, whinchat fill the air.

To the southwest, the intertidal mudflats of the Pas estuary provide winter feeding grounds for cormorant, grey heron, water rail, knot and whimbrel, with the protected waters attracting great northern diver, eider, common and velvet scoters and red-breasted merganser during inclement weather at this time of year; snow buntings are also regularly recorded in winter. Common sandpiper and kingfisher can be seen all year round, while black kite and little ringed and Kentish plovers are habitual summer visitors; interesting passage migrants include little bittern, spoonbill, osprey, grey phalarope, Sandwich tern, short-eared owl and grasshopper, moustached and wood warblers.

Access: The dunes lie to the west of the village of Liencres (along the S-463); take the road north signposted Playa de Valdearenas.

Also in the area

Cliffs of the Cantabrian Coast A spectacular cliff-top path (10 km) between the Playa de Valdearenas and the Isla de la Virgen del Mar features sheer limestone headlands interspersed with sandy and rocky coves, cliff-top blowholes and a sprinkling of offshore stacks. Breeding shag (7–8 pairs), peregrine and blue rock thrush, all increasingly compromised by the thousand or so pairs of yellow-legged gulls. Cliff-top scrub of Spanish gorse, burnet rose and Cornish heath, with exposed limestone outcrops hosting sea carrot, rock-samphire, sea-lavenders, thrift, sea plantain and golden-samphire. Less maritime habitats harbour round-headed leek, Pyrenean lily, spring squill, white asphodel and tongue orchid, as well as large self-heal and *Carduncellus mitissimus*, with wetter areas supporting brookweed, viper's-grass and early marsh orchid. Early summer butterflies include Lulworth skipper, swallowtail, clouded yellow, western dappled white, Cleopatra, painted lady, Provençal fritillary, Spanish brown argus and Adonis and long-tailed blues, while an examination of the small streams which breach the cliffs at intervals should turn up golden-ringed dragonfly, Mediterranean demoiselle, *Ischnura graellsii* and small red and southern damselflies.

SITE 20 Marismas de Santoña, Victoria y Joyel

Extensive estuary on the Río Asón plus two small areas of freshwater marsh, together comprising the most important coastal wetland in northern Spain for wintering and migratory waterbirds.

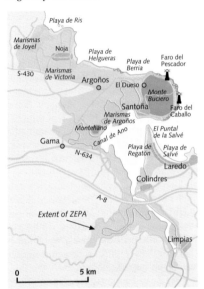

Sometimes referred to as the 'Doñana of the north', the Reserva Natural de las Marismas de Santoña, Victoria y Joyel (3866 ha; also a ZEPA of 7087 ha and Ramsar Site) is divided into three distinct units: the Santoña marshes, covering some 3005 ha in the bay of the same name; the impressive limestone outcrop of Monte Buciero (peaking at 376 m and encompassing 460 ha); and the much smaller, predominantly freshwater Marismas de Victoria (150 ha) and Joyel (251 ha), which lie either side of the resort of Noja to the northwest.

The Bahía de Santoña is almost closed off to the sea by a great sandspit – El Puntal de la Salvé – which extends northwards from the resort of Laredo and is separated from the limestone monolith of Monte Buciero by only 375 m of open water. Within the con-fines of the bay, the saltmarsh vegetation displays a marked zonation according to the degree of tidal influence. At the seaward margin, permanently submerged areas are dominated by almost mono-specific beds of eelgrass, which give way to small cord-grass and dwarf eelgrass in areas exposed occasionally by spring tides.

The upper reaches, normally inundated only at high water, possess a much more diverse halophyte community, consisting primarily of sea-purslane, annual sea-blite, common, purple and perennial glassworts, greater and lesser sea-spurreys, sea plantain, sea arrowgrass and common salt-marsh-grass. In July and August, when the common and lax-flowered sea-lavenders, sea aster and golden-samphire are in bloom, a haze of violet and yellow suffuses these upper marshes.

Where the tidal influence is diluted by an influx of freshwater, stands of sea rush and sea club-rush appear, growing together with wild celery, parsley water-dropwort, salt-marsh rush and long-bracted sedge. Here, too, you might find the scurvygrass *Cochlearia pyrenaica* subspecies *aestuaria*, unique to the coasts of northern Spain and western France, the diminutive pink-flowered sea-milkwort and slender centaury. The predominance of common reed and bul-rushes in the Victoria and Joyel marshes indicates that these wetlands are sustained primarily by freshwater sources.

Santoña's intertidal marshes are home to more than 200 species of benthic invertebrate, providing rich pickings for birds and humans alike. In addition, the shallow estuarine waters are used as a nursery by the juveniles of many fish species, while

Spoonbill *Platalea leucorodia*

European eels and Atlantic salmon, exploited by the fishing fleets of Santoña and Colindres, make annual migrations through the estuary on their way up the Asón to spawn.

Around 144 species of aquatic bird have been recorded in the reserve, with the marshes regularly housing concentrations of 20 000 individuals in winter, mainly wigeon, dunlin, curlew and hoards of black-headed gulls, as well as significant numbers of black-necked grebe, little egret, greylag goose, oystercatcher, grey plover, whimbrel and both godwits. Look out, too, for unusual species such as great white egret, Brent and pink-footed geese, shelduck, guillemot and razorbill at this time of year. During periods of severe weather, the Santoña estuary is one of the best places in Iberia to encounter some of the rarer visitors from northern Europe, including great northern, black-throated and red-throated divers, red-necked and Slavonian grebes, scaup, eider, long-tailed duck, velvet scoter, goldeneye and even glaucous gull; check out the Canal de Ano (an inlet to the south of Montehano), the main Treto channel and the Santoña harbour.

Santoña is far better known, however, for its migratory and wintering spoonbills. It is estimated that over 50% of the Dutch population of spoonbill uses the marshes as a refuelling point during the autumn migration, with no fewer than 687 individuals recorded in September 2000 (accompanied by a solitary African spoonbill!); in addition, a couple of dozen individuals usually stay put throughout the winter. At high tide these magnificent birds often congregate in the Marismas de Argoños, visible from the S-401.

At least 15 species of waterbird have bred in the reserve since 1987, with the Victoria marshes the most notable locality, harbouring nesting little bittern, purple heron (five pairs reared at least eight chicks in 2000), gadwall, shoveler, pochard, water rail, black-winged stilt, yellow wagtail and reed and great reed warblers.

Additional natural history interest is provided by the low sand-dune systems which back the beaches of Ris, Helgueras and Berria, on the coast to the west of the estuary, and that of Regatón, which runs along the inshore section of the Salvé spit. Along the Playa de Berria – in reality a tombolo linking Monte Buciero to the mainland – the strand-line hosts prickly saltwort, sea sandwort and sea rocket, with the primary dunes colonised by sea spurge, sea-holly, sea bindweed, tuberous hawk's-beard, sea daffodil and sand-sedge. The stabilised dunes inland are dominated by cushions of the sticky-leaved, yellow-flowered restharrow *Ononis ramosissima* plus *Helichrysum stoechas* and Jersey pink, with giant orchids turning up sporadically, but the native flora is threatened by the rapid invasion of tree groundsel, a North American species of which a single female bush can produce up to 900 000 seeds per season.

The more secluded Santoña dune systems provide nesting habitat for little ringed plover, tawny pipit and stonechat, also attracting large numbers of migrating passerines. Three-toed skinks and common wall and green lizards are the most characteristic reptiles, although an introduced population of Italian wall lizard at Ris has virtually ousted the common wall lizard; in Spain this species is found only in Menorca, the city of Almería and a few localities along the Basque and Cantabrian coasts.

The evergreen forest which clothes Monte Buciero's rugged flanks consists mainly of holm oak, bay, Mediterranean buckthorn and strawberry-tree, together with osyris,

Rosa sempervirens, butcher's broom and common smilax, while the more stunted vegetation atop the cliffs here is characterised by Spanish gorse, Cornish heath, bell heather, ling and St Dabeoc's heath. Where the maritime influence is greater, look out for rock sea-spurrey, bladder campion, rock samphire and sea plantain, with the splash-zone hosting sea spleenwort and thrift.

Sardinian warblers have recently (1986) colonised the Monte Buciero forests, with other typical birds including honey buzzard, black and red kites, sparrowhawk, hobby, firecrest and cirl bunting. A cliff-top path circumnavigates the whole massif; drive past the prison (Penal del Dueso) to the west and park at the lighthouse (Faro del Pescador) on the north side, or take the track from Santoña to the Faro del Caballo. Both lighthouses are good vantage points for watching gannets, shearwaters and skuas during the autumn migration, as well as for encounters with the breeding birds – shag, yellow-legged gull, chough and peregrine – of the Buciero cliffs and offshore islets.

More than 30 species of mammal have been recorded in the Santoña reserve, with the drier saltmarshes the haunt of southern water voles, here preyed on by stoats. The faunal catalogue also includes 10 species of amphibian and 12 reptiles, including viviparous lizard in the Victoria marshes.

Access: Santoña is reached via the N-634, turning north onto the C-629 at Gama, or by taking exit 177 off the A8 (E70), signposted Cicero, Treto & Santoña. The S-401 also links Cicero with Santoña across the marshes; just before the town is a hide (locked at night). The Marismas de Victoria and Joyel lie either side of the coastal resort of Noja (turn west off the S-629 at Argoños).

Also in the area

Bahía de Santander Large, deep-water estuary adjacent to the Cantabrian capital, enclosed by Cabo Mayor and the sandspit of El Puntal, the latter populated by a dune-plant community similar to that of Liencres (see p. 83) and sheltering mudflats which attract wintering and migratory waders (plus passage spoonbills and rarities such as mute swan and Brent goose). The Isla de Mouro, at the entrance to the bay, hosts the only remaining colony of storm petrel on the Cantabrian coast (20 pairs in 2000). Contains a small reserve – Las Marismas Blancas – whose freshwater lagoons and reedbeds harbour breeding gadwall, pochard, water rail, yellow wagtail, reed, great reed, fan-tailed and Cetti's warblers and reed bunting (take exit 6 off the N-635). Stone curlews winter around Maliaño airport (20–30 individuals), while the Puerto Deportivo nearby often turns up great northern diver, black-necked grebe, common scoter, red-breasted merganser, razorbill and guillemot during winter storms. The bay is the only place on the Cantabrican coast where common terns breed (since 1989), and is a noted stopover point for aquatic warbler on autumn passage.

Monte Candina Limestone headland (472 m) about 10 km east of Santoña, which extends seawards to form the Punta de Sonabia and hosts the only coastal colony of griffon vultures in Spain (87 pairs in 2000). Other cliff-breeders including shag, Egyptian vulture, peregrine, yellow-legged gull, blue rock thrush and chough; alpine accentor, alpine chough and wallcreeper in hard winters. Stunted holm oak and beech forests harbour honey buzzard, black kite and short-toed eagle in summer. Access off the N-634 or A8/E70 to Oriñón, then take the minor road signposted Sonabia.

SITE 21 Valderejo

A small valley ringed by long limestone escarpments harbouring the largest griffon vulture colony in Euskadi and a richly varied limestone flora.

The Valderejo valley (a *parke naturala* of 3496 ha) in western Araba is a delightful backwater of forests and pastures embraced by a horseshoe of jagged limestone ridges, whose main attraction is the superb gorge of the Río Purón: a short, sharp gash in the ridge which encircles Valderejo and a natural link between the Atlantic forests in the heart of the park and the Mediterranean habitats further south.

Just opposite the interpretation centre in the hamlet of Lalastra, look for signs indicating the 'Senda Purón'. The first part of this 6-km trail takes you through an attractive mixed landscape of hawthorn hedgerows, extensive grasslands and areas of encroaching *Genista scorpius* and Cornish heath, all good habitat for woodlark, Dartford warbler, red-backed shrike and rock bunting. Soon, however, you enter a mature Scots pine forest – inhabited by Bonelli's warbler, firecrest, short-toed treecreeper, crested tit, citril finch and crossbill – and start to descend through a narrow valley to the centrepiece of the walk: the river Purón itself.

Within the park, the Purón drops 700 m, its rocky course frequented by the occasional otter straying upstream from the river Ebro, kingfisher, grey wagtail, dipper, viperine and grass snakes, palmate and marbled newts, Iberian painted frog and a few white-clawed crayfish that have survived the fungal plague caused by *Aphanomyces astaci*. Less directly associated with the river are the scops and long-eared owls, wrynecks, nightingales and golden orioles that breed in the black poplars (laden with balls of mistletoe), alders and willows that line the river downstream of the abandoned village of Ribera. Look out, too, for purple toothwort parasitising the roots of the alders, abundant large tortoiseshells – some years emerging from hibernation as early as mid-February – and the holes of greater white-toothed and water shrews in the banks.

Soon the track begins to hug the side of the gorge and the river narrows to barely a metre across. Long black fingers of common ivy creep up the cliff walls, while wall-rue, rustyback, maidenhair spleenwort, thick-leaved stonecrop and an abundance of *Jasonia glutinosa* occupy cracks in the limestone. With each step, more Mediterranean elements such as turpentine tree, strawberry-tree, *Phillyrea angustifolia* and laurustinus appear.

As suddenly as it began, the defile ends and you enter a young western holm oak wood, with bearberry carpeting the ground between stands of box and many dense, bright green domes of Spanish gorse (subspecies *occidentalis*). A number of more thermophilic species find this habitat to their liking, including subalpine warbler, large psammodromus – Valderejo is one of the few places where this lizard has been recorded in Euskadi – ocellated lizard, Montpellier snake and asp.

The other classic walk in Valderejo takes you up to the Ermita de San Lorenzo – visible

Cornish heath *Erica vagans*

from Lalastra on the cliff-top to the west – and then either north along the ridge to Recuenco (the highest peak, at 1240 m), or south to Vallegrull (1226 m). Cliff-nesting raptors here include griffon vulture (around 90 pairs), Egyptian vulture, peregrine and eagle owl, accompanied by alpine swift, crag martin and both choughs. A single pair of short-toed eagles breeds here, although two more regularly hunt over the area, while the cliff-tops harbour nesting water pipit, alpine accentor, rock thrush and black redstart.

Sheer cliff faces have the early-flowering *Draba dedeana*, *Saxifraga cuneata* and cone saxifrage, here at the eastern limit of its range, in north-facing crevices, while the rare *Asplenium seelosii* and sarcocapnos choose south-facing niches. Attractive pink clumps of narrow-leaved valerian dot the screes here, along with *Ligusticum lucidum*, *Scrophularia crithmifolia* and small-flowered helleborine, while rocky ledges with just a little soil hold *Anemone pavoniana* and leafless-stemmed globularia. On Vallegrull, the bare rock at the very lip of the cliff houses sprawling mats of *Genista pulchella*, as well as an abundance of *Arenaria erinacea*, *Coronilla minima*, white flax (subspecies *apressum*) and hoary rock-rose. On the plateau, the thin limestone soils support a few holm oaks and beech trees, interspersed with stunted mats of dwarf juniper, *Spiraea*

hypericifolia subspecies *obovata*, snowy mespilus and bearberry.

Predictably, the thin limestone soils are excellent orchid habitat, as is shown by the recent discovery in the park of the Aveyron orchid, better known from southern France, and *Orchis cazorlensis*, one of the complicated Spitzel's group, never before found in the north of the peninsula. Look out, too, for bird's-nest, man, lizard, lady, bug, military and Barton's orchids, dull, yellow and sawfly ophrys and heart-flowered serapias.

Butterfly records from Valderejo indicate considerable species diversity; in the more Atlantic habitats be prepared for olive skipper, Apollo (above 1000 m), Camberwell beauty, black satyr, ilex hairstreak and large and Damon blues. On the other hand, once through the Purón gorge, more southerly species such as Portuguese dappled white and Spanish gatekeeper appear. Among the 16 species of fritillary cited here are twin-spot, lesser marbled, pearl-bordered and Spanish.

Information: The park information centre is in Lalastra (closed on Mondays; tel. and fax: 947 353146; e-mail: parquevalderejo@parques. alava. net).

Also in the area

Monte Santiago (*monumento natural*; 2411 ha, also a ZEPA) Sheer cliffs and a 300 m-high waterfall (the largest in the peninsula) where the river Nervión literally pours over the northern edge of the Meseta; breeding griffon and Egyptian vultures, golden and short-toed eagles, black kite, peregrine and chough. The turn-off to the car park (Fuente de Santiago) for the walk to the waterfall (Cañón del Nervión) is 4 km north of Berberana on the A-625. The stretch of river near the car park contains alpine

newt, while humid rock faces are studded with maidenhair spleenwort, alpine rock-cress, kidney saxifrage and opposite-leaved golden-saxifrage.

In early April, the verges of the minor roads north of **Villalba de Losa** are packed with meadow saxifrage, cowslip, Pyrenean snakeshead and sawfly ophrys, with scrubby areas home to grass-leaved buttercup, crested lousewort, spring squill and man, lady and champagne orchids. Alpine cabbage (subspecies *cantabrica*) and fairy foxglove on rocky outcrops here.

Cantabria, Euskadi and La Rioja

SITE
22 Urdaibai

A vitally important wetland for wintering and passage waterbirds, surrounded by a mosaic of campiña, *sea-cliffs and holm oak forest.*

Urdaibai – the Basque name for the estuary of the river Oka, also known as the Ría de Gernika – is by the far the best preserved of Euskadi's coastal habitat, resulting in its declaration as a Biosphere Reserve (22 041 ha) in 1984, almost a decade before the estuary was protected by Ramsar status (945 ha, also a ZEPA).

St Dabeoc's heath
Daboecia cantabrica

Urdaibai exhibits similar halophytic vegetation to the Santoña marshes (see p. 85), with dwarf eelgrass merging into meadows of small cord-grass at the lowest levels. Sea-purslane, common and purple glassworts and clumps of common sea-lavender appear in areas which spend less time under water, while above the high-tide mark sea rush and golden-samphire are common, with an abundance of tamarisk along dyke walls.

Unlike the major Mediterranean wetlands, Urdaibai has no vast colonies of breeding birds; instead its importance lies in its strategic position on the important bird migration flyway south along the French coast and then west along the Cornisa Cantábrica.

September and the first half of October are the best time for oystercatcher, avocet, ringed and a few Kentish plovers, dunlin, knot, little stint, bar-tailed godwit, curlew and *Tringa* species, while late summer and autumn also bring purple and grey herons, little egret, osprey and marsh harrier. Spring tends to see far smaller concentrations of the same species on northward migration, although there is also a good passage of red kite in March, plus a few black kites and a steady flow of common, little and Sandwich terns.

Spoonbills regularly congregate in Urdaibai in the second half of September and first half of October; up to 400 birds – between 10 and 30% of the Dutch breeding population – are recorded each year, making Urdaibai second only to Santoña as a stopping-off point for this species on the

Urdaibai estuary

Cantabrican coast. Cold snaps in northern Europe send wildfowl and waders south to the ice-free waters of the Iberian peninsula, with November seeing the arrival of the bulk of the wintering greylag geese (often with a barnacle goose or two in tow), mallard, wigeon, gadwall, teal and pintail, plus grey and golden plovers, lapwing and snipe, along with a few cranes off-course from their main cross-Pyrenean migration routes.

The less saline habitats at the head of the estuary harbour extensive beds of common reed and bulrush, good for bluethroat in autumn and nesting water rail, Cetti's, reed and great reed warblers and reed bunting. The surrounding polders, dotted with stands of sea rush, are a good place to encounter fan-tailed and grasshopper warblers, the former resident but prone to suffer population crashes in harsh winters. These marshy habitats are also home to good numbers of marbled newt, common tree and Iberian frogs and midwife toad, as well as harbouring grass snake, western polecat and, most notably, European mink.

Much of the land immediately surrounding the estuary has long since been tamed, although the few surviving enclaves of pedunculate oak are important for forest birds such as lesser spotted woodpecker, marsh and crested tits and short-toed treecreeper. The typical *campiña* (scattered farmsteads and smallholdings, with haymeadows divided by hedgerows) provides suitable breeding habitat for quail, little owl, wryneck, yellow wagtail and red-backed shrike, plus feeding short-toed

eagles, while winter brings in flocks of skylark, redwing, starling and mixed finches from northern Europe.

The limestone crags which flank the estuary are clothed in a thick tangle of holm oak, bay, lentisc, turpentine tree, Mediterranean buckthorn and strawberry-tree, tied together with traveller's-joy and common smilax; try the trail leading up to the Ermita de San Pedro, perched on a crag overlooking the eastern margin of the estuary (signposted from Kanala). Wren, robin, blackcap, chiffchaff, firecrest and chaffinch are the commonest breeding passerines in this habitat, while spring and early summer butterfly-watchers should look out for orange tip, Cleopatra, wood white, pearl-bordered and marsh fritillaries, large wall brown, sooty copper and short-tailed and Lang's short-tailed blues.

Wild boar, common genet and wildcat still frequent these relict forests and you should also be on the look out for Aesculapian snakes, avid tree-climbers which are restricted to the Cordillera Cantabrica and Pyrenees in Iberia. Open areas of bare limestone provide suitable habitat for green lizard, while Schreiber's green and viviparous lizards prefer more humid habitats nearer streams.

The entrance to the Urdaibai estuary is guarded by the craggy headlands of Cabo Ogoño to the east and Cabo Matxitxako (Machichaco) to the west, between which lies the rocky islet of Isla de Izaro; their rugged, inaccessible cliffs are the haunt of breeding storm petrel, shag, little egret, peregrine, lesser black-backed and yellow-legged gulls and blue rock thrush.

Access and information: A narrow-gauge railway runs from Bilbao to Gernika along the western margin of the estuary and on to the attractive fishing port of Bermeo (look for sea duck and auks in the harbour and purple sandpipers in winter on the breakwater). A trail and a hide with good views of the mudflats on the west bank of the estuary starts at the St Kristobal-Busturia railway station (signposted 'Urdaibaiko padurak' in the village of Busturia, 6 km south of

Bermeo) and crosses a sandy polder, home to breeding tawny pipits. Access to the polders on the east shore is by following the BI-638 north from Gernika and turning off west in Arteaga (towards the beach at Laga); tracks run down left to the polders from the road. The Urdaibai Biosphere Reserve Trust in Gernika acts as an information centre (mornings only; tel: 946 257125; fax: 946 257253; e-mail: urdaibai@ej-gv.es).

Also in the area

Cabo Matxitxako Good for sea-watching in autumn and spring, particularly after northerly weather systems: Manx and Balearic shearwaters, gannet, common scoter, great skua, kittiwake and razorbill, plus rare gulls: Franklin's, Sabine's, ring-billed and glaucous in 2001. Cetaceans commonly seen here include common and Risso's dolphins, plus an occasional fin or minke whale.

Gaztelugatxe (*biotopo babestua*; 158 ha) Headland further west with two offshore islands: San Juan de Gaztelugatxe (Gaztelugatche), connected to the mainland by a bridge, and Aketze, 2 km offshore. Flora includes rock sea-spurrey, Danish scurvygrass, Basque endemic thrift *Armeria euscadiensis* and *Limonium binervosum*, plus coastal heath of Spanish gorse, ling, bell heather, Cornish and St Dabeoc's heaths and scrambling gromwell, studded with copses of holm oak, strawberry-tree and wild olive.

SITE 23 Urkiola

Limestone upland with breeding griffon vultures and easy access to the rich high-level flora.

Pyrenean germander *Teucrium pyrenaicum*

The massif of Urkiola (*parke naturala* of 5958 ha) is one of the most popular weekend walking destinations for Basque city-dwellers and provides a great variety of contrasting habitats in a reasonably small area. Known as 'Little Switzerland', access is straightforward from the large sanctuary – the object of multitudinous processions on 13 June – at the Urkiola pass (Puerto de Urquiola) on the BI-623 between Durango and Gasteiz/Vitoria.

On the ascent from Durango you pass a huge, dark stain of holm oak on the east-facing slope up to your right. Today these relict holm oak formations – accompanied by bay, Spanish gorse (subspecies *occidentalis*), turpentine tree, Mediterranean buckthorn, strawberry-tree, tree heath, *Phillyrea latifolia*, butcher's broom and common smilax – survive only on steep limestone outcrops where they have no direct competition from deciduous species.

These evergreen forests provide good feeding for vertebrates all year round. Winter berries attract wren, robin, blackcap and thrushes from northern Europe, acorns are an important food source for jay and wild boar, and abundant invertebrates provide prey for fire salamander, common toad and garden and Bonelli's warblers and firecrest. These in turn sustain predators in the shape of Aesculapian, smooth and southern smooth snakes, sparrowhawk, wildcat and common genet.

From the Urkiola pass, a trail due east takes you up to the rounded peak of Urkiolagirre, through pasture, an exotic conifer plantation and scrubby areas of gorse, western gorse, ling, St Dabeoc's and Cornish heaths and bell heather. In early spring look out for numerous dog's-tooth-violets taking refuge within the gorse bushes from the grazing *latxa*: the Basque sheep *par excellence*.

Urkiola (M.L.)

Between Urkiolagirre and the rocky outcrops of the main limestone ridge, a saddle known as Pol-Pol lies on the spring-line between the limestone and underlying acid rocks, with streams draining south towards the Mediterranean and north into the Atlantic. A small fenced-off sphagnum bog here harbours ragged-robin, marsh-marigold, lesser spearwort, marsh gentian (common here and throughout the acid pastures), round-leaved sundew, large-flowered butterwort and bog pondweed.

Citril finch, mistle thrush and rock bunting feed around Pol-Pol, the first two nesting in the beech forest that clothes the higher, north-facing slopes, the latter at the base of rocky outcrops or bushes. Alpine newts spawn in the streams, often in the company of palmate newt, midwife toad and common frog (check out, too, the drinking trough on the broad track that leads back from Pol-Pol to the Urkiola pass), while Iberian frogs inhabit the wet meadows around the pass itself. Schreiber's green and viviparous lizards are often found near watercourses, unlike the Iberian and common wall lizards which frequent the drier, sunnier rock outcrops, or the green lizards which prefer the bracken-covered hillsides.

The upland pastures are home to skylark, water pipit, black redstart and wheatear, with rock thrush confined to the highest crags. Pyrenean pine voles burrow extensively under the pastures at the edge of the beech-woods, but are hard to track down as – unlike most sub-terranean micromammals – their tunnels are not marked by piles of earth.

The limestone outcrops house an interesting mixture of Pyrenean and Atlantic plants which will delight any botanist. An examination of the south-facing rockgardens should turn up brittle bladder-fern, alpine gypsophila, *Iberis carnosa*, chamois cress, livelong saxifrage, *Saxifraga trifurcata*, Pyrenean germander, fairy foxglove, Spanish bellflower, leafless-stemmed globularia and *Valeriana montana*. Shadier areas on the north face support *Anemone pavoniana*, Pyrenean columbine and Pyrenean lily, with megaforb communities of the pale yellow *Aconitum vulgaris* sub-species *neapolitanum*, lesser meadow-rue,

Information: The information centre is called Toki Alai ('Happy Place') and is located at the Urkiola pass, on the BI-623 between Durango and Gasteiz (tel: 946 814155). Midweek school parties mean that the centre may be temporarily closed.

adenostyles and white false helleborine at the base of cliffs. Higher up, the more inaccessible north-facing ledges are home to Thore's buttercup, alpine pasque flower (subspecies *cantabrica*), *Androsace villosa*, tozzia and vanilla orchid.

Bird-wise, keep an eye out for griffon vultures (up to 60 birds and 18 pairs, mainly on Mugarra, the first large crag to the west of the road into the park from the north), Egyptian vulture (three pairs), peregrine (three pairs) and kestrel, as well as an occasional honey buzzard, black kite or booted or short-toed eagle wandering from their nest sites lower down in the park. Both choughs and ravens also breed on the crags.

Also in the area

Neighbouring **Gorbeia** (*parke naturala*; 20 016 ha) is very similar to Urkiola. Butterflies here include Apollo, Piedmont ringlet, pearly heath, Mazarine blue and a good variety of fritillaries: high brown, marbled, pearl-bordered, marsh and Spanish. Riverine habitats and pools harbour odonates such as southern damselfly and orange-spotted and splendid emeralds. Notable bats in the park include greater and lesser horseshoe, serotine, Leisler's, Schreiber's, Natterer's, Geoffroy's, greater mouse-eared, European freetailed, grey and brown long-eared and barbastelle. Two information centres: one in Areatza (open every day), just off N-240 Bilbo–Gasteiz road (tel: 946 739279), and the second in Sarria, on the road between Murgia (Murguía) and Markina (Marquina); closed Mondays (tel. and fax: 945 430709; e-mail: parquegorbeia@parques.alava.net).

24 Aiako Harria

An abrupt granite mountain range with diverse breeding raptors and exuberant Atlantic vegetation.

Visible from the coast of Gipuzkoa, the striking granite outcrop of Aiako Harria (a *parke naturala* of 6145 ha, in Spanish known as the Peñas de Haya) shelters some of the most varied forest formations in Euskadi. Although littered with plantations of Monterey pine, European larch and red oak, enough of the original beech and pedunculate, sessile and Pyrenean oak woodlands remain to make this visually a highly attractive area, as well as harbouring a wide range of flora and fauna.

The southern flanks of the granite peaks plunge down to the thickly forested Regata de Endara, a tributary of the Bidasoa (the only river in Euskadi with a regular salmon run). In this valley, stands of Pyrenean oak (probably with middle spotted woodpecker) mingle with patches of box and strawberry-tree, while the river is lined with belts of alder, accompanied by hazel, alder buckthorn, ash and guelder-rose, all draped in traveller's-joy, common ivy, honeysuckle and black bryony.

The moist gullies flowing down to the Bidasoa provide the perfect habitat for many species of fern, notably royal, Tunbridge filmy-fern, Killarney and lemon-scented ferns, *Thelypteris pozoi*, scaly male-fern, hay-scented and narrow buckler-ferns, maidenhair fern, forked spleenwort, *Asplenium billotii*, *Cystopteris viridula* and *Woodwardia radicans*. Other humidity-seeking plants found here include French meadow-rue, coral-necklace, wood ragwort, *Senecio adonidifolius* and leopard's-bane. Around the headwaters of the river Oiartzun

Western whip snake *Coluber viridiflavus*

toed eagles, buzzard, honey buzzard, goshawk and black kite, while Egyptian and griffon vultures and peregrine are frequently seen moving to and from their nest sites on the cliffs above. Forest passerines include chiffchaff, Bonelli's warbler, firecrest and hawfinch, while among the mammals known to occur here are wild boar, red squirrel, edible dormouse, wildcat and beech marten. Fire salamanders are common in the most humid areas, and the park is also renowned for its isolated nucleus of western whip snake. The river Endara holds Pyrenean desman, otter, European mink and a few Atlantic salmon.

By contrast, the stark peaks of Aiako Harria are sparsely vegetated, although one plant to look out for is petrocoptis, unique to the westernmost foothills of the Pyrenees, often accompanied by English stonecrop and the related *Sedum hirsutum*. Few birds apart from crag martin, black redstart and rock thrush breed at the highest levels, although alpine accentor and wallcreeper often appear in winter and early spring; in September–October there is always a chance of migrating raptors and black stork.

on the northern side of the main ridge thrive healthy populations of French saxifrage and Pyrenean snowbell.

A good selection of raptors nests in the valley forests, in particular booted and short-

Access: Head west on the N-I through Irún and the *parke naturala* is indicated south along the GI-3631 at the first large roundabout. Just after the 11 km sign and a picnic spot, take a track south towards an obvious conical peak for views down into the Regata de Endara; at the base of the peak, the track leading down to the right will take you to the valley bottom. For the high peaks, 3 km further on at a saddle crossed by pylons, take paths leading southwards. Alternatively, from the nearby town of Oiartzun, take the GI-3420 towards Lesaka through the road tunnel and explore the *regata* from anywhere along the road or the track downstream from just before the dam.

Also in the area

Txingudi The estuary of the river Bidasoa, strategically situated to receive large numbers of passage migrants in September–October: all the typical coastal waders plus spoonbill, bittern, purple heron, greylag goose, osprey, aquatic warbler and bluethroat. Winter storms regularly drive grey phalarope and little and Sabine's gulls into the harbour of nearby Hondarribia, and winter also sees an influx of little egret, avocet and penduline tit, plus black-necked grebe and great northern diver to the waters of the estuary itself. Breeding birds include little ringed plover, great reed, fan-tailed and Cetti's warblers and tree sparrow. Palmate newt and natterjack toad occur here, while 20 or so coypus (unwelcome visitors from the introduced French population) take bread from visitors' hands in the Plaiaundi *parke ekologikoa* (signposted off the N-I in Irún).

SITE
25 Aralar

A large limestone massif shared by Gipuzkoa and Navarra, with extensive upland pastures, splendid beechwoods and Euskadi's only lammergeiers.

Aralar (a *parke naturala* of 10971 ha) is characterised by its high pastures, slowly won from the native beech woodlands by burning, cutting and intensive grazing. The lower slopes are more wooded, with extensive beech forests around Lizarrusti on the southern side of the massif and an important stand of holm oak to the east above the rivers Araxes and Larraun. Two other habitats to explore are the attractive *campiña* in the southeastern corner of the massif in Navarra, and the high-level limestone outcrops.

Outstanding among the rich and varied flora of the high pastures and karstified limestone are Pyrenean–Cantabrican endemics such as Pyrenean columbine, *Saxifraga trifurcata*, alchemilla-leaved cinquefoil, Pyrenean avens, *Armeria pubinervis*, violet mountain and horned pansies, dethawia, Pyrenean trumpet gentian, spiked Pyrenean speedwell, Pyrenean snakeshead, *Narcissus asturiensis* and *N. varduliensis*, growing amid a diverse array of more widespread 'alpine' species: moonwort, rigid bucklerfern, alpine pearlwort, alpine pasque flower, Thore's and Carinthian buttercups, kernera, wild cotoneaster and frog and vanilla orchids. Luxuriant megaforb communities in grikes harbouring deeper soils contain variegated monk's-hood, leafy lousewort, alpine leek and white false helleborine.

Vanilla orchid
Nigritella nigra

The Aralar beech forests cling uneasily to the bare rock, hosting a diverse ground flora of green hellebore, wood anemone, rue-leaved isopyrum, hollowroot, narrow-leaved bittercress, kidney saxifrage (subspecies *paucicrenata*), spurge-laurel, ramsons, martagon lily, lily-of-the-valley, herb-Paris and whorled Solomon's-seal. These beechwoods are considerably more extensive than those of the rest of Euskadi: a fact which surely explains the presence here of black woodpecker, an extremely scarce species in the region. Other vertebrates include fire salamander, agile and Iberian frogs, Iberian wall lizard, western whip snake at the western edge of its range, Pyrenean desman, pine marten and wildcat.

The few butterfly records that exist for Aralar talk of large chequered skipper, marbled fritillary, cardinal, water ringlet, chestnut heath and purple-shot copper, which are tempting enough to suggest that many other interesting species also occur here. It would be a surprise if the Apollo were absent from the area, given its altitude (maximum 1431 m, Irumugarrieta).

An Aralar speciality is the pair of lammergeiers that has frequented the impressive limestone cliffs southeast of Amezketa on the northern flanks of Aralar for a number of years, although breeding has yet to be confirmed. Egyptian and griffon vultures, golden eagle and peregrine do nest on these same cliffs, however, along with crag martin and both choughs. Up in the pastures, water pipits are common, whinchats perch on bushes, alpine accentors and rock thrushes nest in rock outcrops and citril finches typically feed at the edge of the beech forest. At lower levels, honey buzzards breed in the beechwoods while booted eagles and red and black kites hunt over the *campiña*.

Access and information: The Aralar information centre (Parketxea; tel: 943 582069; fax: 948 513233) is located at Alto de Lizarrusti (620 m) on the GI-120/NA-120 on the Gipuzkoa–Navarra border. Five GRs pass through Lizarrusti; GR-121 is an excellent route into the high central parts of the massif, eventually dropping down along the Arritzaga valley towards Amezketa; GR-35 takes you through an area frequented by black woodpeckers and down to the Laredoko reservoir; alternatively, the easier GR-20 circumnavigates the massif at low level, rarely surpassing 600 m. Most Gipuzkoan walkers start from the Ermita de Larraitz (on the GI-2133, to the east of Beasain; large car park signposted 'zamaoko atsedenlekua') from where a good track leads up towards the high pastures and Txindoki (Chindoqui, 1341 m), an obvious pyramidal mountain dominating the northern flank of the massif.

SITE 26 Ullivarri

Two small reserves on the shores of the extensive Ullivarri reservoir, with an interesting avifauna and rich assemblage of amphibians.

The best of the flora and fauna of the 70 km of shoreline of the Ullivarri reservoir is concentrated in the four shallow bays at its southeastern end, two of which are protected by well-planned reserves: Mendixur, whose 100 ha have been visited by no less than 225 species of bird, and Garaio (116 ha).

The shortest of the three nature trails at Mendixur leads to the Carboneros hide, overlooking an area of shallow water which is ideal for dabbling duck and greylag geese in winter and herons all year round; one pair of purple herons nested for the first time in 2000 and both cattle and little egrets are seen regularly but do not breed. The trail to the Trogloditas hide passes through an area of gallery forest which rings with the songs of wryneck, nightingale, Cetti's warbler and golden oriole in spring, and also harbours nesting scops and long-eared owls. The longer walk to the Buceadores hide gives views out over a deeper section of water

Red crested pochard *Netta rufina*

frequented by black-necked grebe, pochard, tufted duck and other diving duck in winter. Booted and short-toed eagles, hen and Montagu's harriers and hobby all breed nearby and are often seen hunting over the area, with red and black kites and marsh harrier occurring on autumn passage.

Autumn is perhaps the best time of year to visit. In September red-crested pochard numbers begin to build up and black stork and osprey drop in on passage, followed by a few cranes in November. Rather less welcome, however, are the small bands (10+) of ruddy duck which arrive each autumn; Ullivarri seems to be the principal point of entry for this highly competitive, non-native species to the peninsula, with the first Iberian breeding record hailing from here (1999).

Ullivarri as a whole (a proposed Ramsar Site) harbours an interesting aquatic vegetation, notably of holly-leaved naiad and *Najas minor*, although carpets of common water-crowfoot are more visible. The clean waters attract many amphibians, including palmate and marbled newts, common tree and parsley frogs and midwife and natterjack toads, with agile frogs especially common in this part of Araba, spawning in February–March but spending the rest of the year amid the moist leaf litter of the surrounding oak forests. The wetlands of Araba are also one of the main strongholds of the European mink in Iberia.

Around the reservoir lie copses of Lusitanian oak and dry pastures, the latter supporting dull and woodcock ophrys, fly, green-winged, lady and bug orchids and autumn lady's tresses. Wildcat, common genet, stoat and wild boar are not uncommon, while the easiest reptiles to track down are Iberian and common wall and ocellated and green lizards.

Access and information: Mendixur and Garaio are signposted off the A-3012 to Ozaeta (Barrundia); exit 367 off the N-I to the east of Gasteiz/Vitoria. The information centre for both reserves is in Garaio (best avoided at weekends); do not be put off by the fact that it is primarily a leisure park.

Also in the area

Salburua A recently restored wetland with Euskadi's primary black-winged stilt colony (59 pairs in 1999) and only breeding little bittern and tufted duck (5 pairs). Little grebe, shoveler, little ringed plover and possibly garganey also nest, while white storks regularly feed in the lagoons. Surprises on passage in 2000 included spoonbill, great white egret, purple and squacco herons, ferruginous duck, grey phalarope and aquatic warbler. Relict stands of pedunculate oak plus damp pastures with some of Iberia's best greater pond-sedge formations; aquatic plants include blunt-fruited water-starwort and the charophytes *Tolypella glomerata* and common stonewort. Important population of European mink (15–30 individuals), plus 10 amphibians, including agile frog. Salburua is signposted off the N-104 about 2 km east of Gasteiz/Vitoria.

SITE 27 Izki

A vast expanse of Pyrenean oak forest harbouring the highest density of middle spotted woodpeckers in the Iberian peninsula.

Simplifying greatly, Izki (a *parke naturala* of 9413 ha) consists of two main habitats: Pyrenean oak woodland growing on the sandy soils of the Izki river basin, which is hemmed in by limestone crags to the north and south. The monospecific stands of Pyrenean oak tend to be rather disappointing botanically, but the many peatbogs of the flat, sandy river basin harbour three species of sundew (great, rounded leaved and oblong-leaved), and two of butterwort (large-flowered and long-leaved), occasionally accompanied by marsh violet, marsh pennywort, bird's-eye primrose and marsh arrowgrass.

In what is considered to be the largest continuous expanse of Pyrenean oak in the peninsula, Izki is home to some 300 pairs of middle spotted woodpecker. The park is crossed by a series of waymarked trails, of which Senda 7 leading from the village of Urturi (north of the BU-741) is the best for these birds, but in truth any reasonably

mature stand of Pyrenean oak woodland is worth investigating, especially in spring before the trees come into leaf, when the woodpeckers noisily begin to take up territories after the winter.

Great spotted woodpeckers are also common in these woods, as are pied flycatcher, redstart, Bonelli's warbler and short-toed treecreeper, while in winter the tree canopy is enlivened by groups of mixed passerines, mainly firecrest, marsh, blue and long-tailed tits and nuthatch. Forest mammals include beech marten, common genet, wildcat, garden dormouse and roe deer, while the many bogs, streams and lakes here are home to alpine, marbled and palmate newts, common and agile frogs and Pyrenean desman, as well as increasing numbers of European mink; green lizard, ladder snake and asp occur in drier habitats.

Above the oak forest, Izki boasts a fine series of limestone crags, clothed variously

Oblong-leaved sundew *Drosera intermedia*

with beech and Lusitanian and western holm oaks. Senda 14, beyond Korres (Corres), takes you up to a limestone ridge which gives stunning views over the beech growing on the north face of the scarp. Poke around here for *Asplenium seelosii*, sarco-capnos, *Saxifraga cuneata* and Pyrenean honeysuckle before continuing down through the beech forest – past a truly enormous large-leaved lime and an equally impressive yew – and into an attractive mixed woodland of Lusitanian oak, beech, whitebeam and Italian maple.

A circular walk will take you back to Korres along the Izki river valley: one of the park's best butterfly habitats. Although no recent study has been carried out, records from the 1980s include pearl-bordered fritillary, Esper's marbled white, woodland grayling, chestnut heath and Ripart's anomalous, Forster's furry, Chapman's and Escher's

blues, with Apollo on the high limestone areas in the northwestern corner of the park.

At least 20 pairs of griffon vulture, a couple of pairs each of Egyptian vulture and golden eagle, and rather more of peregrine nest on the limestone cliffs of the park. Eagle owl, crag martin and both choughs are commoner cliff-breeders, while other raptors you might encounter include short-toed eagle, hen harrier, red and black kites, honey buzzard and long-eared owl.

A final destination in Izki should be the limestone plateaux in the northwestern part of the park, reminiscent of the high *páramos* of Castilla–León. February sees first *Narcissus minor* and then angel's-tears in flower: aperitifs for the later-flowering sawfly, woodcock, Aveyron, dull and yellow ophrys and fly, lady, man, lesser butterfly and giant orchids. In more humid habitats look out for summer lady's tresses and loose-flowered orchid.

Access and information: The park information centre is in the village of Korres (Corres), south of the A-132 which heads southeast out of Gasteiz/Vitoria (closed Mondays; tel. and fax: 945 410502; e-mail: parqueizki@parques.alava.net). The limestone plateaux can be reached via a metalled road just before the cemetery at Markiniz (Marquínez), which is accessed off the BU-741, on the west side of the park.

Also in the area

Sierra de Cantabria (ZEPA; 5160 ha) East–west limestone ridge southwest of Izki, with beech forests on the north face and western holm and Lusitanian oaks to the south. Accordingly varied butterfly populations: Spanish festoon, Moroccan orange tip, southern white admiral, marbled, lesser marbled and twin-spot fritillaries, western marbled white, scarce copper and Spanish chalk-hill, Ripart's anomalous, Escher's, Chapman's and Osiris blues.

SITE 28 Soto de Buicio

A fine example of the gallery forest that once lined the whole middle course of the river Ebro.

The term *soto* is used to describe the ribbons of forest which grow along the margins of large Iberian rivers, nowadays increasingly scarce due to the encroachment of agri-

Penduline tit *Remiz pendulinus*

nightingales compete noisily with Cetti's warblers, while great reed warblers caterwaul from the contact zone with the river. Keep an eye out for the scarce olivaceous warbler here, but beware of confusion with the very similar melodious warbler, also typical of Iberian riverine vegetation.

Different bird communities occupy the tall poplars and alders. Scops owls call on spring evenings, short-toed treecreepers and serins abound and penduline tits make their delicately domed nests from the seeds of the poplars themselves, while golden orioles are more easily heard than seen. There is a good complement of woodpeckers – wryneck, green, great spotted and lesser spotted – and you may also be lucky enough to catch a glimpse of a black kite or hobby overhead.

The Soto de Buicio is too small to hold important colonies of breeding herons, although both night and purple herons and cattle and little egrets regularly pass along the Ebro in spring and summer. Sandy banks hold bee-eater colonies and breeding kingfisher, with pebbly islands hosting little ringed plover and common sandpiper; look out, too, for white stork and migrating osprey and whiskered tern. Otters once frequented this stretch of the Ebro, although today any large mustelid encountered is more likely to be a European mink.

To the north lies an area of western holm oak, *Genista scorpius*, *Rhamnus lycioides* and rosemary scrub, worth checking in spring for *Aristolochia pistolochia*, beautiful flax, clumps of *Euphorbia serrata*, common grape hyacinth and mirror and dull ophrys. Dartford and Sardinian warblers, tree sparrow, linnet and cirl bunting frequent this habitat, while the line of cliffs up to your right as you approach the *soto* supports breeding crag martin, black wheatear and blue rock thrush. Just before the cliffs lies an area of well-preserved gypsum scrub, attractively coloured in April by pink *Ononis tridentata* and yellow *Coronilla minima*.

culture. The Soto de Buicio (a *reserva integral* of 30 ha), on a meander to the southwest of the village of Lapuebla de Labarca, is one of the best-preserved examples of this habitat remaining on the middle reaches of the Río Ebro.

The gentle flow-rate of the river permits the growth of a very lush and verdant belt of alder, particularly in the more humid areas, grading into black and white poplars as soil water content decreases with distance from the river. Small-leaved elm and narrow-leaved ash opt for the least humid soils and are here festooned with climbers, in particular traveller's-joy, hop and grape-vine. Yellow flag, reeds, rushes and sedges prosper at the water's edge, while the halfway house between water and land is occupied by willows and sallows.

These *sotos* control the river's exuberance, the roots consolidating the banks against water erosion. The jungle-like understorey of bramble, hawthorn, roses, blackthorn and elder, with its humid microclimate, also provides an important breeding and feeding refuge for many creatures, particularly birds:

Access: From Lapuebla de Labarca (west of Logroño); on the approach from Fuenmayor (LR-251), turn left at the roundabout on the edge of town. After 800 m, turn left onto a good track and left again after passing under the cliffs, through vineyards to a picnic site on the river bank (1.4 km).

Embalse de las Cañas

Also in the area

Embalse de las Cañas (Ramsar Site and ZEPA; 101 ha) Reedy reservoir boasting a long-established colony of 200+ pairs of night heron plus 20+ pairs of purple and grey herons. Also breeding bittern, little bittern, little and cattle egrets, marsh harrier and great reed and Savi's warblers, plus trans-Pyrenean migrants such as black stork, spoonbill, little, spotted and Baillon's crakes, osprey and whiskered and black terns. Winter brings duck and concentrations of marsh and hen harriers. Signposted south off the N-111 just north of Logroño. Splendid stands of lizard orchids next to the hide in June.

SITE
29 Sierra de Cebollera

One of the best-preserved sections of the Sistema Ibérico; a glaciated acid massif with a rich forest and upland fauna; around 120 species of butterfly.

Although the upper Iregua valley is well forested today, it was once maintained as pasture to provide grazing for the sheep which annually moved back and forth from Extremadura along the Real Soriana drover's-road. It was not until the system of transhumance declined in the eighteenth and nineteenth centuries that the forests

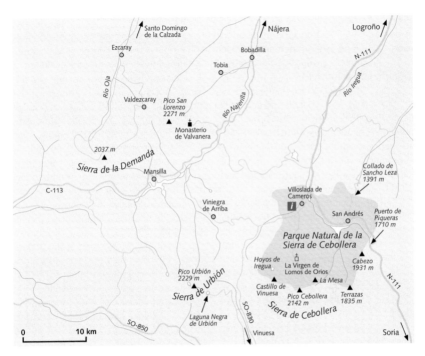

began to regenerate, initially recolonised by Scots pine and later by beech and sessile oak.

One of the best ways to get to know the Sierra de Cebollera (*parque natural*, 23 640 ha, also part of the massive Demanda, Urbión, Cebollera y Cameros ZEPA; 138 708 ha) is to follow the road from Villoslada de Cameros up the Iregua valley as far as the chapel – La Virgen de Lomos de Orios – from where another track leads up to the main ridge, which peaks at La Mesa (2164 m). Around Villoslada itself are small patches of maritime pine, accompanied by laurel-leaved cistus, plus a fine, isolated stand of western holm oak. Mature gallery forest accompanies the river, composed largely of sessile oak, large-leaved lime and ash, above a layer of olive willow, *Salix salvifolia* and *S. atrocinerea*, the river itself home to viperine snake, common sandpiper, grey wagtail, dipper, otter and an isolated population of Pyrenean desman.

Pure beech forest, slowly gaining ground as it regenerates in the shade of the Scots pine, clothes the higher slopes of the valley. Marsh tits reach their southern limit in the peninsula here, while red and roe deer, wild boar and red squirrel are common. This humid forest habitat is ideal for amphibians such as palmate newt – again at the southern edge of its range in Europe – midwife and common toads and common tree frog, while reptiles include green lizard, smooth snake and asp. Here, too, are good breeding densities of woodcock, firecrest, crested tit and both treecreepers.

With altitude, the beech woodland grades into Scots pine forest, whose more open formations sport an understorey of broom,

Apollo *Parnassius apollo*

Cantabria, Euskadi and La Rioja

Genista florida, holly, tree and Spanish heaths and ling. Wild mushrooms abound here, including the much-appreciated penny bun boletus, wood blewit, clouded clitocybe and saffron milk cap, as well as the fly agaric. Citril finches feed on the edges of the pines, goldcrests, coal tits and crossbills do so within the canopy, and honey buzzard, booted eagle and goshawk hunt overhead. The park also harbours a healthy population of genetically very pure wildcats, which prey largely on bank voles, red squirrels and occasionally small mustelids.

The Hoyos de Iregua – one of a series of glacial cirques just below the crest of the ridge – is occupied by small lagoons and peat bogs harbouring cross-leaved heath and round-leaved sundew. Look out, too, for *Saxifraga fragosoi* and common butterwort, both typically growing in areas of water seepage, as well as two attractive yellow-flowered rock roses: *Halimium lasianthum* subspecies *alyssoides* and *H. ocymoides*. Just above the Hoyos del Iregua, a small stand of La Rioja's only mountain pines clings uncertainly to the rocks below Castillo de Vinuesa.

This is also a fine place for Apollo, chestnut heath, de Prunner's and Piedmont ringlets and purple-edged and purple-shot coppers.

As the forests fade out above 2000 m, a thick mat of Pyrenean broom, ling and bilberry appears, with dwarf juniper on the highest points and an abundance of Spanish bellflower. The pasture provides poor pickings for both livestock and the botanist alike: just wavy hair-grass, common bent and the aptly named *Festuca indigesta*, plus matgrass in areas of deeper soil. Although few birds breed here, they are nevertheless of great interest, notably the isolated outposts of water pipit, alpine accentor and whinchat, along with partridge, wheatear, rock thrush and raven; bluethroats bred in the park at around 1750 m in 1996: the first record for La Rioja. Overhead, griffon vultures and golden and short-toed eagles are a possibility.

An easier, albeit less rewarding, way to access the higher areas of Cebollera is from the Puerto de Piqueras (1710 m) on the main Logroño–Soria road (N-111). Approaching from the north, splendid Pyrenean oak and then beech forests accompany you on the

Laguna Negra de Urbión

Penny bun boletus *Boletus edulis*

way up to Piqueras, home to *Digitalis parviflora*, hoop-petticoat daffodil, *Narcissus pseudonarcissus*, Pyrenean gagea, wild tulip and broad-leaved marsh, heath-spotted and frog orchids. A short walk southwest from the pass to Cabezo (1931 m) will give you a chance to see water pipit, rock bunting and, possibly, hen harrier. Retracing your steps, try the minor road (LR-250) heading north from San Andrés to the Collado de Sancho Leza (1391 m) for a wealth of summer butterflies, including marbled, twin-spot and violet fritillaries. This lower pass is also well

known for the migration of wood pigeons and thrushes; shooting pressure is intense in October and November, but is prohibited during the return migration in spring.

Information: The park information office is in Villoslada de Cameros, 2 km west of the N-111 on the LR-333 (tel: 941 468216; fax: 941 468224; e-mail: sierracebollera@larioja.org; closed Mondays).

Also in the area

Sierra de la Demanda (ZEPA) Similar to Cebollera, but more accessible. Try the road above the small ski-station of Valdezcaray for breeding partridge and rock thrush and migrating raptors and crane in autumn. The delightful Oja valley, upstream of Ezcaray, has wonderful summer butterflies and La Rioja's only haymeadows.

Follow the LR-113 south from Nájera up the **Río Najerilla valley** – first detour-

ing to **Tobia** for its conglomerate cliffs with breeding vultures – towards the headwaters of the Mansilla reservoir. On the limestone here Lusitanian oak forests are interspersed with dry pastures, where a sudden abundance of vetches, clovers and other legumes provides food for many lycaenid larvae: look out for Mazarine, Chapman's, Escher's, Ripart's anomalous, Adonis and chalkhill blues.

To the south of Cebollera and Demanda lies the **Laguna Negra de Urbión**, the most renowned of a small group of glacial lakes set in the shadow of Pico Urbión (2229 m), close to the source of the Río Duero. Around the lake grow amplexicaule buttercup, *Ranunculus gregarius*, streptopus, lily-of-the-valley, Pyrenean squill and wild tulip. Access is from the village of Vinuesa, 15 km north of Abejar on the N-234.

SITE 30 Peñas del Iregua, Leza, Jubera y Cidacos

Four right-bank tributaries of the Ebro, each with impressive cliffs holding excellent colonies of breeding raptors.

After the thickly forested siliceous rocks of the Sierra de Cebollera (see p. 102), the deforested slopes and limestone and conglomerate outcrops (or *peñas*) that characterise the lower reaches of the rivers Iregua, Leza, Jubera and Cidacos come as a sharp contrast (ZEPAs totalling 11 847 ha). Most of the high land separating the valleys was cleared many centuries ago, when warmer average temperatures permitted cereal cultivation at greater altitude, with subsequent overgrazing preventing forest regeneration; today vast expanses of monotonous scrub cover these hillsides.

On the limestone uplands, as in the Leza valley, holly oak and box form a dense scrub, with Phoenician juniper, *Genista scorpius* and rosemary appearing in the most degraded areas. Spanish gorse thrives in more humid soils, while the crests are studded with violet-flowered cushions of hedgehog broom. More acid soils to east and west are clothed with a virtually monospecific scrub of laurel-leaved cistus, interspersed with stunted copses of Pyrenean oak.

The valleys themselves, however, are veritable oases of flora and fauna. In total, around 150 pairs of griffon vulture and at least one of Egyptian vulture breed in the Iregua, Leza and Jubera gorges, along with 6 pairs of golden eagle, 12 of peregrine and 10 of eagle owl. A single pair of Bonelli's eagles breeds sporadically in the area, while short-toed eagles are frequent visitors. A further 140 pairs of griffon vulture breed in the Cidacos valley above Prejano, along with 4 pairs of Egyptian vulture. As you scan the skies for raptors, keep your eyes peeled for other cliff-nesting birds such as alpine swift, crag martin and chough.

Close to the rivers, poplars harbour scops owl, wryneck and golden oriole, with vocif-

Rock sparrow *Petronia petronia*

Griffon vulture _Gyps fulvus_

erous nightingales and Cetti's warblers staking their claim to almost any piece of cover. Lower crags, such as those in the Cidacos valley around the villages of Arnedillo and Herce, are ideal for black wheatear, blue rock thrush and rock sparrow, while beeeaters commonly breed in softer cliffs, where they can excavate tunnels for their nests. Away from the rivers, the commonest birds in the dense scrub are red-legged partridge, Thekla lark and Dartford warbler, although as the scrub changes, so do the birds. Subalpine warblers usually require some taller bushes or small trees, while tawny pipits opt for sparsely vegetated terrain with minimal cover. Rock thrushes frequent the highest crags.

There are two excellent viewpoints over the Leza gorge: 2 km and 4 km north of Soto en Cameros on the LR-250. This impressive limestone defile is often dry in summer, when the river disappears into a sinkhole just below the village and only re-emerges 4 km downstream. The dominant tree species are Lusitanian oak and Montpellier maple, with turpentine tree and box dominating the scrub. Plentiful pitch trefoil, white flax, yellow-wort, _Phlomis lychnitis_, cone knapweed, _Pallenis spinosa_, _Helichrysum stoechas_, dipcadi and bee and pyramidal orchids leave you in no doubt that this is a

Mediterranean flora, while sticky clumps of _Saxifraga cuneata_ dot the sheer cliffs.

Between the Jubera and Cidacos rivers, the siliceous rocks of the Sierra de La Hez hold the area's richest forests. Pyrenean oak and beech clothe the north-facing slopes, accompanied by tree and Cornish heaths and green heather, with common cowwheat and narrow-leaved lungwort as the basic ground cover. This is a good area for booted eagle, honey buzzard and Bonelli's warbler, with mammals including wildcat, common genet, beech marten, wild boar and roe and red deer.

Pallenis spinosa (T.F.)

> _Access_: The Iregua valley is reached via the N-111 south of Logroño, while the LR-250 follows the Leza for much of its length. For the Jubera take the LR-261 south from Murillo de Río Leza, and for Cidacos, the LR-115 west from Arnedo.

Also in the area

Dinosaur footprints of the Cidacos valley Centred on the village of Enciso, on the LR-115 southwest of Arnedo. A number of information boards are located just over the medieval bridge in Enciso, with well-marked trails leading to other sites nearby. A recently opened palaeontological centre provides more information (tel: 941 396093).

Aragón and Navarra

Introduction

For faunal and floral variety, few parts of Spain can compare with Aragón and Navarra, the latter referred to by its *euskera*-speaking inhabitants as Nafarroa. The sheer north–south extent of Aragón, stretching for over 330 km from the 3000 m-plus peaks of the main Pyrenean axis to within 50 km of the Mediterranean, makes it a likely candidate for such an accolade, while in Navarra, a journey westwards from Larra at its easternmost tip will take you from alpine habitats with ptarmigan and snow finch to the misty, fern-rich Atlantic forests of the Bidasoa valley. Euro-Siberian species such as black hairstreak and agile frog penetrate the peninsula over the low passes of western Navarra, yet a mere 100 km drive south to the Ebro valley will find you in the arid Bardenas Reales, with the chance of spotting Dupont's lark and sooty orange tip.

Aragón and Navarra together occupy the entire western half of the main Pyrenean axis. South-facing lower slopes are clad in a mixture of Scots pine and deciduous oaks, with European silver-fir and beech on shadier, north-facing slopes, grading into mountain pine up to the tree-line at around 2300 m. These forests, especially at Bértiz and Irati in Navarra, are justifiably renowned for their seven species of woodpecker, including white-backed – a scarce species in Spain – and are also home to a last few brown bears. Subalpine forests are renowned for their populations of capercaillie, Tengmalm's owl, black woodpecker and ring ouzel.

Mountain torrents host Pyrenean brook salamander and the recently described *Rana*

Pyrenean saxifrages *Saxifraga longifolia*, Ordesa national park

Opposite page: **English iris *Iris latifolia*, Benasque**

Aragón and Navarra

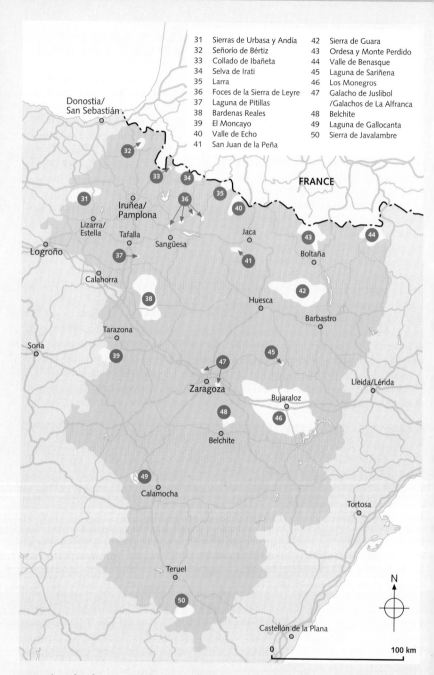

31 Sierras de Urbasa y Andía
32 Señorío de Bértiz
33 Collado de Ibañeta
34 Selva de Irati
35 Larra
36 Foces de la Sierra de Leyre
37 Laguna de Pitillas
38 Bardenas Reales
39 El Moncayo
40 Valle de Echo
41 San Juan de la Peña
42 Sierra de Guara
43 Ordesa y Monte Perdido
44 Valle de Benasque
45 Laguna de Sariñena
46 Los Monegros
47 Galacho de Juslibol /Galachos de La Alfranca
48 Belchite
49 Laguna de Gallocanta
50 Sierra de Javalambre

pyrenaica, the former widely distributed throughout the Pyrenees, but the latter virtually confined to Aragón. At altitude, vast expanses of subalpine and alpine pasture, rock outcrops and scree succeed one another – most famously in the Ordesa y Monte Perdido national park, but also well represented at Echo and Benasque – harbouring large numbers of Pyrenean endemic plants, for example Pyrenean catchfly, yellow saxifrage, cylindric rock-jasmine and Pyrenean yam, as well as characteristic high-level birds such as ptarmigan, wallcreeper, alpine chough and snowfinch.

Land-use becomes more intensive as you leave the high Pyrenees behind; few good stands of western holm oak remain and extensive livestock farming gradually gives way to the typical dry Mediterranean triumvirate of wheat, olives and vines. Rural–urban drift, above all in the Aragonese pre-Pyrenees, is widespread, with young people increasingly heading for the main cities of Zaragoza and Iruñea/Pamplona; many villages are now abandoned or dying and vast areas of mid-altitude grasslands are gradually being smothered by invasive scrub and pines.

The pre-Pyrenees are characterised by a long series of limestone ridges running east–west, rarely surpassing 2000 m, which have been sliced open by powerful Ebro-bound rivers. Both lammergeiers and griffon vultures breed in good densities in the many river gorges – as, for example, in the *foces* of the Sierra de Leyre – where rock walls are home to the attractive floral twosome of ramonda and Pyrenean saxifrage. Isolated pockets of more northerly species occur here in close proximity to Mediterranean ones; both edelweiss and black wheatear occur in the Sierra de Guara, for example.

The river Ebro – notably the ox-bow lakes of Juslibol and La Alfranca – paints a vivid green streak through the greyish pseudosteppes of the Ebro Depression, whose gypsum soils are immediately identifiable by an abundance of *Gypsophila hispanica*, *Ononis tridentata* and *Helianthemum squamatum*. Typical steppe bird communities – little bustard and both black-bellied and pin-tailed sandgrouse – can be found in both the Bardenas Reales in Navarra, north of the Ebro, and in Belchite and Los Monegros to the south; studies of the latter have revealed an incredible diversity of invertebrates, with over 100 new species described from the area in the past century. Here, too, low-lying depressions harbour a series of endorheic lagoons, notably Sariñena, Alcañiz and Chiprana, while the less saline wetlands of the Ebro basin – Pitillas and Las Cañas – are home to internationally important heron colonies.

Aragón stretches away south of the river Ebro into the Sistema Ibérico. To the west lies El Moncayo (2315 m), a veritable island of Atlantic flora in a Mediterranean sea, harbouring some of Europe's most southerly beech forests, while to the south – in the province of Teruel – immense limestone *páramos* merge into the heights of the Sierra de Javalambre (2020 m), renowned for its endemic flora. Nestling in between is Europe's largest natural salt-lake – the Laguna de Gallocanta – legendary among European birdwatchers for its huge biannual influx of migratory cranes.

Navarra boasts a network of six well-thought-out information centres in some of the region's key sites. For more information, contact Gestíon Ambiental Viveros y Repoblaciones de Navarra (see Useful contacts). Many of the Aragonese visitor centres are partly run by the local branch of SEO/BirdLife in Zaragoza (tel: 976 277638; fax: 976 373308; e-mail: aragon@seo.org), while the website www.aragob.es/ambiente/index.htm gives more information about protected areas in the region.

SITE 31 Sierras de Urbasa y Andía

Two limestone plateaux surrounded by sheer cliffs and covered by a mosaic of beech forest and pasture; one of the best areas in Navarra for herptiles, plus 107 species of butterfly.

Much of the twin *sierras* of Urbasa and Andía (a *parque natural* of 21 408 ha) is given over to intensive pasturelands, disappointing for botanists but, happily, a jewel for herpetologists. The road north from the Puerto de Urbasa (927 m) crosses an immense area of heavily cattle-grazed sward where the many drinking pools – natural or artificial – annually receive the spawn of Iberian pool, common tree, common and parsley frogs and natterjack and midwife toads. To add to the amphibian diversity, marbled, palmate and alpine newts also mate in these pools, but usually give up their aquatic life for a terrestrial existence by late June. Fire salamanders are common in the more humid beechwoods.

An excellent place for tracking down reptiles is El Espinar, an area of common juniper, Spanish gorse and hawthorn scrub which provides shelter for viviparous lizard and Cantabrian viper, typical of humid environments, as well as the more thermophilic three-toed skink and southern smooth and Montpellier snakes. Elsewhere in the park, look out for green and common wall lizards, grass and viperine snakes and slow-worm, all of which are relatively common here.

Plenty of birds take advantage of the pasturelands; both choughs feed in numbers, water pipit, wheatear and black redstart are common, whinchats perch on bushes and short-toed eagles hover in search of a reptil-

Sierra de San Donato (M.L.)

ian meal. Griffon and Egyptian vultures and Andía's recently established pair of lammergeiers cruise the plateaux on the lookout for carrion.

One of the few permanent streams in Urbasa rises at the Fuente del Arenal and flows south over sandy soils before being swallowed up by a large sinkhole. Cornish and St Dabeoc's heath, petty whin and hairy greenweed appear along the margins, together with fragrant orchid and Solomon's-seal. This is also one of the better localities for butterflies in the park, attracting small pearl-bordered fritillary, Piedmont ringlet, pearly heath, purple-shot copper and silver-studded blue in June, while other records for the park include Apollo, cardinal, pearl-bordered fritillary, Spanish argus and Mazarine and Forster's furry blues.

The most rewarding area of Urbasa's humid beechwoods is the heavily karstified northern edge of the plateau, where dolines accumulate deeper, more fertile soils and support additional woody species such as large-leaved lime and alpine buckthorn. From the chapel of Santa Marina, perched on the edge of the cliff, there are wonderful views north towards the dramatic Sierra de San Donato, plus the chance of raptors such as booted eagle, red kite, honey buzzard and goshawk. Black woodpecker, pied flycatcher, redstart and firecrest breed in the forest, while citril finches feed on the ground along the woodland edge.

In the heavy shade of the beechwoods, saprophytes such as yellow bird's-nest and bird's-nest orchid tap rotting matter in the soil, while rue-leaved isopyrum, yellow anemone, hollowroot, purple toothwort, ramsons and Pyrenean squill all flower before the canopy comes into leaf. Where a fallen tree allows a sudden influx of light to the forest floor, species such as Irish and sweet spurges and martagon and Pyrenean lilies bloom prolifically.

The neighbouring Sierra de Andía is likewise heavily grazed and the best strategy is to take the NA-120 south up to the Puerto de Lizarraga (1090 m), pausing for the view from the *mirador* (smothered with *Saxifraga trifurcata*) just before the tunnel. Once through the tunnel, take the broad track up to the right which allows you to approach the edge of the cliffs. 'Safe-to-botanise' north-facing outcrops here support a rich mosaic of chamois cress, livelong saxifrage, Pyrenean germander, fairy foxglove, the Iberian endemic toadflax *Linaria badalii*, round-headed rampion and alpine aster. Alpine accentor and wallcreeper are regularly seen here in winter.

Access and information: The NA-7182 runs north from Lizarra/ Estella over the Puerto de Urbasa to the N-I. After the pass, El Espinar lies to the north of the main grazing area (east of the road) and Fuente del Arenal to the west, 2 km north of the first right-hand bend (a sharp right angle). An information centre is being built at the camp site at Bidoiza, 4 km further north. The chapel of Santa Marina and the northern cliffs and beechwoods can be reached along the broad track which heads east 1 km before the beginning of the hairpin bends down off the plateau to the north.

Also in the area

Almost all the rain (1400 mm) falling on Urbasa and Andía is channelled through subterranean galleries into a series of powerful waterfalls – the **Nacedero del Uredarra** (*reserva natural*, 199 ha) – that burst from the sheer cliffs on the southern edge of plateau. For views from above, walk east along the edge of cliffs from the Puerto de Urbasa; look out for Egyptian and griffon vultures, alpine swift, crag martin, both choughs and rock sparrow here. Alternatively, approach the base of the waterfalls along a track leading north from the village of Baquedano (Améscoa Baja). Western holm oak woodland en route has St Lucie's cherry, snowy mespilus, wayfaring-tree and fly and Etruscan honeysuckles, followed by more uniform stands of downy oak and beech. Look out for otter and dipper along the river, Bonelli's warbler, firecrest, marsh and crested tits and bullfinch in the forests, and turtle dove and cirl bunting around the village.

^{SITE}
32 Señorío de Bértiz

A prime example of a mature Atlantic beech forest, home to seven species of woodpecker, including white-backed.

Although not actually in contact with the coast, the mountainous northern reaches of Navarra drain north into the Bay of Biscay and receive weather systems from the Atlantic. The mild, humid climate favours the development of thick deciduous forests, of which a prime example is the Señorío de Bértiz *parque natural* (2040 ha), in the heart of the Bidasoa (or Baztán) valley: a large, wooded estate with a superb botanical garden that was donated to the Navarra Government in 1949 on condition that it was left unaltered in perpetuity.

Bértiz is dominated by a magnificent beech forest which extends almost continuously from around 500 m up to the highest point of the park – Aizkolegui (842 m) – often accompanied by yew, silver birch, sweet chestnut, whitebeam, field maple and holly. Below the beech lie stands of pedunculate oak, with Pyrenean oak on drier, south-facing slopes. Greater floral diversity is offered by the *regatas* – gullies – which traverse the park, of which the most interesting is the Regata de Suspiro, lined with alder, wych elm and ash, and sheltering a luxuriant growth of royal fern, soft shield-fern, berry catchfly, bird-in-a-bush, tutsan, wild angelica, common figwort, the excessively large leaves of Pyrenean valerian and ramsons.

White-backed woodpecker
Dendrocopos leucotos

The vertebrate fauna varies little between the beech and oak forests, but pride of place undoubtedly goes to the woodpeckers: wryneck, green, black, great spotted, lesser spotted, middle spotted and white-backed (subspecies *lilfordi*), the latter two only having been detected in recent years and both requiring well-preserved mature forest. Woodcock are common, if hard to see, while passerines include crested and marsh tits, nuthatch, both treecreeper and short-toed treecreeper and bullfinch.

These forests are also home to healthy populations of red squirrel, edible dormouse, beech marten, wild boar and roe deer, with the *regatas* and main Bidasoa/Baztán river home to Pyrenean desman, otter and European mink. Fire salamanders and common and agile frogs are among the most typical amphibians. The thick forests leave little light for butterflies but are ideal for many other invertebrates, including three of Europe's most charismatic beetles: the stag beetle and two wood-boring long-horn beetles: the enormous, oak-feeding *Cerambyx cerdo*, with reddish tips to its elytra, and the rare *Rosalia alpina*, a beautiful shade of steel-blue with black spots, whose larvae eat beech.

Information: The park interpretation centre (tel: 948 592421; fax: 948 592422) is in Oieregi, close to the junction of the N-121A Hendaye–Iruñea/Pamplona road with the N-121B.

Also in the area

Peñas de Itxusi (*reserva natural*; 115 ha) Sandstone and conglomerate outcrop on the French border with Navarra, holding an important colony of griffon vultures (50+ pairs), as well as breeding Egyptian vulture, golden eagle, peregrine, chough and alpine chough. Other breeding raptors in the reserve include booted and short-toed eagles, red kite and hen harrier, as well as, possibly, lammergeier. Access information from the tourist information office next to the Bértiz interpretation centre (tel: 948 592386).

33 Collado de Ibañeta

One of a series of low passes situated on the Atlantic–Mediterranean watershed, used by thousands of raptors, storks, cranes, geese and other birds during the autumn migration.

Most birds migrating south into Iberia in the autumn avoid the high Pyrenees and either use the Mediterranean flyway (birds from central Europe) or the low passes at the western end of the Pyrenees (birds from Scandinavia, France, Britain and the Low Countries). Small birds generally migrate by night, but large soaring birds – dependent on thermals – travel by day and often 'bottleneck' at favourable places such as Gibraltar or Ibañeta as they attempt to cross large expanses of water or mountain chains.

At the Collado de Ibañeta (1057 m), late summer and early autumn are dominated by the long-distance, trans-Saharan migrants. The first black kites pass through in early July, but then little happens until white storks start arriving at the beginning of August, followed mid-month by large groups of honey buzzards. At the end of August come a few Egyptian vultures and rather more Montagu's harriers, followed by black storks and bee-eaters at the beginning of September. However, things do not really start to hot up until mid-September, probably the best time for overall variety, with osprey, booted and short-toed eagles, red kite, marsh and hen harriers, buzzard, goshawk, sparrowhawk, peregrine, hobby and merlin trickling through one-by-one or in small groups until mid-October.

Greylag geese and rooks turn up in mid-October, much at the same time as the first cranes pass through, en route to Gallocanta and thence to winter in the Extremaduran *dehesas* and elsewhere in southern Iberia. Mid- to late October is the peak time for doves and pigeons, which have to run the gauntlet of hundreds of guns from 1 October to 15 November; pigeons pass during the

Black kites *Milvus migrans*

first hour of daylight and Ibañeta is generally much quieter in the afternoon, after the hunters have gone home for lunch.

Raptors and other soaring birds generally appear once the thermals have built up, although really bad weather can stop migration altogether; the first fine day after a series of washouts can be quite spectacular. The whole of the surrounding area is good for visible migration, although Ibañeta is often the best when strong winds funnel many birds low through the pass. On the other hand, low cloud at Ibañeta can sometimes be circumvented by heading east to Astobixkar or west to Lindux, two higher points each about 2 km from Ibañeta and accessible along steep metalled tracks originating at the pass itself.

But Ibañeta and the surrounding countryside is not only about the autumn bird migration. Fine beechwoods clothe the hillsides on the southern side of the pass and a shortish walk will take you down to Roncesvalles on the Camino de Santiago, with the possibility of black woodpecker and crested tit en route. Where the beechwoods have been cleared, western gorse and Cornish heath are dominant, interspersed with groups of autumn crocus, all of which are in flower in September. Lammergeiers breed nearby, water pipits are still around in September and flocks of citril finches feed along the edges of the beechwoods. Falls of passerines also occur and the area can be alive with pied flycatchers, redstarts and whinchats, taking a break before heading further south. Much under-recorded migrants are the butterflies and moths; no records are available, but September sees both clouded yellows and hummingbird hawk-moths passing through in a southerly direction, while spring will inevitably produce far more records in the other direction, especially of painted lady.

Access and information: The Collado de Ibañeta lies on the N-135 just north of Orreaga (Roncesvalles). An information centre run by the conservation group Gurelur provides excellent advice to visitors and is open from 1 July to mid-November until dusk (see Useful contacts). As this is a border area it is wise to carry your passport at all times.

Also in the area

West of Ibañeta, the **Urkiaga (Urquiaga) pass** (890 m) on the N-138 north of Zubiri is another excellent migration watchpoint, with the added incentive of black and white-backed woodpeckers in the surrounding beechwoods of **Quinto Real**.

SITE 34 Selva de Irati

The largest continuous mass of deciduous woodland in the Iberian peninsula, including a small area of virgin forest harbouring 60% of Spain's white-backed woodpeckers.

Perhaps the description of Irati (a ZEPA of 18 684 ha) as a *selva* (jungle) is slightly over-optimistic since only a small corner of this immense mixed European silver-fir and beech forest has remained untouched by axe or chainsaw. Although timber has always been extracted from Irati, it is nevertheless still one of the best-preserved forests in Europe and has a fauna to match, especially in the upper reaches of the Río Irati valley – to the northeast of the Embalse de Irabiako – in the 20 ha of primeval forest of the Reserva Integral de Lizardoia (also known as La Cuestión).

European silver-firs begin to appear in the pure beech forests of eastern Navarra as the foggy Atlantic weather loses ground to the brighter, more continental climes of the central Pyrenees. The dark pinnacles of the light-seeking firs protrude above the paler green foliage of the beeches, sometimes in almost equal proportions, sometimes much outnumbered by the beech. Floristically, the more mixed forests differ little from the pure beech forests, although vertebrate communities are richer wherever the silver-fir takes root.

Apart from the odd yew, wych elm, white-beam or rowan, few other trees are made welcome in the Irati forests proper, although the beech forms mixed stands with Scots pine and pedunculate, sessile and downy oaks at the edges of the forest. Where some light penetrates the thick canopy, a poor understorey of hawthorn, holly, box, spurge-laurel, bilberry and elder forms, sheltering a ground flora of wood anemone, hepatica, rue-leaved isopyrum, wood-sorrel, Pyrenean squill and bird's-nest orchid. Numerous ferns – hard, hard shield- and male-, plus hart's-tongue – thrive in the dampest corners.

You need a good dose of either luck or patience to observe black or white-backed

Pyrenean squill *Scilla lilio-hyacinthus*

woodpeckers in Irati. The black woodpecker is easier to find, being a noisy creature whose loud calls tends to give it away, but 'white-backs' are quieter and scarcer, although fairly confiding, and are generally restricted to the most mature and least disturbed parts of Irati such as Lizardoia.

Stands of European silver-fir amongst the beech encourage the presence of birds such as goldcrest, crested and coal tits and crossbill, although woodcock, tawny owl, robin, firecrest, nuthatch, treecreeper, jay and chaffinch are all indifferent to the main canopy species. Likewise, pine marten and their sometime prey, red squirrels, greatly increase in number in the mixed forest. The commonest diurnal non-avian vertebrates are viviparous lizard and asp, whereas night brings out pygmy shrew, edible dormouse, bank vole, wildcat, wild boar and roe and red deer.

Another important habitat in Irati is the complex of crystal-clear streams which traverses the forest en route to the Río Irati. Brown trout, soiffe and stone loach inhabit the main rivers and are preyed upon by the highest density of otters in Navarra, as well as by western polecat and kingfisher. Pyrenean desman, water shrew, common sandpiper, dipper, grey wagtail, Pyrenean brook sala-mander and common frog, on the other hand, hunt smaller fry, while high summer sees the airspace above and around the river occupied by golden-ringed dragonfly, purple emperor, large tortoiseshell, Camberwell beauty and silver-washed fritillary.

To the east of Lizardoia, the high pastures around the peaks of Abodi (1537 m) and Orhí (2017 m) complement the claustrophobic forests of Irati. Once forested, the Sierra de Abodi is now heavily grazed and an excellent place to watch for griffon and Egyptian vultures, lammergeier and the very abundant red kite. Water pipit and wheatear are common, and woodlark, tree pipit and citril finch occur on the forest edge. Orhí (climbable from the tunnel just before Puerto de Larrau (1573 m) on the NA-140) gives a hint of the high-level botanical treasures in store in the central Pyrenees (see Larra, below) and for rock thrush, chough, alpine chough and snow finch.

> *Access and information*: There is an excellent information centre in Ochagavía (Otsagi), closed Mondays (tel: 948 890680), from which you can access the *reserva integral* de Lizardoia via the Sierra de Abodi.

35 Larra

One of the most impressive areas of karst scenery in Europe, hosting a superb alpine flora and all the classic high-level Pyrenean birds.

Larra (a *reserva natural* of 2353 ha, also a ZEPA) represents the final, westernmost fling of the high Pyrenees. The peaks of Mesa de los Tres Reyes (2438 m) and the pyramidal Anie (2504 m) – the latter just over the border in France but geologically part of Larra – are a splendid northern backdrop to the gently shelving but profoundly karstified Larra plateau.

Despite abundant precipitation and the obvious part played by water in moulding the limestone, there is practically no surface water in Larra and, unsurprisingly, a complete absence of amphibians. At altitude, plants seek out moisture in cracks, with south-facing rock faces supporting fabulous spikes of Pyrenean saxifrage and the Iberian endemics petrocoptis and *Androsace hirtella*, whereas shadier, north-facing crevices are colonised by Thore's buttercup, *Saxifraga hariotii*, *Potentilla nivalis* and fairy's thimble. Other plants such as Pyrenean

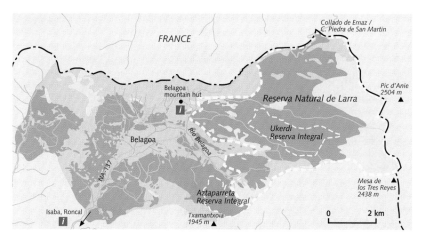

columbine, Pyrenean spurge, alpine toadflax and pygmy hawk's-beard put down long roots in unstable screes to tap underground water supplies. A third tactic is to hide away in gullies or sinkholes where snow accumulates and will remain until late summer; look out for purple saxifrage, the pink-flowered entire-leaved primrose, snow gentian and lopsided violet-blue spikes of dragonmouth.

The high-level fauna is equally specialised. Ptarmigan (about six pairs in the area) and snow finch can survive all year round at altitude, feeding on seeds and invertebrates around snow patches, while wallcreepers (look for them foraging on scree slopes) and alpine accentors make altitudinal migrations and are found at much lower levels outside the breeding season. The only other birds found above the tree-line are water pipit, rock thrush, wheatear, both choughs and, among the larger raptors, lammergeier, griffon vulture and golden eagle. Butterflies at these heights include mountain dappled white, mountain clouded yellow, Eros blue and Lefèbvre's, large and yellow-spotted ringlets. Chamois and Alpine marmots are common, although the only high-level reptiles are the common wall lizard and its natural predator, the smooth snake.

Lower down you enter a blasted forest, littered with twisted and splintered lightning-struck mountain pines, clinging improbably to the rocky terrain. Sunnier areas support an understorey dominated by bearberry,

with more sheltered localities harbouring false medlar, crowberry (subspecies *hermaphroditum*), alpenrose, Arctic bearberry and bog bilberry. Keep an eye out, too, for alpine pasque flower, narcissus-flowered anemone, white musky saxifrage, round-leaved St John's-wort, hoary rock-rose, the rock-jasmine *Androsace ciliata* and mountain thrift, here with white flowers.

Although the faunal biomass is still very low, more vertebrates can make a living here: black woodpeckers on the abundant dead-wood, and dunnock, ring ouzel, crested and coal tits, chiffchaff, citril finch and crossbill in and around the pines. A lonely male brown bear is still thought to frequent the forests of this section of the Pyrenees: one of only a dozen or so left in the western part of the range, most of which are in France.

Wallcreeper *Tichodroma muraria*

Aragón and Navarra

Larra's high limestone plateau, with Pic d'Anie in the distance

Larra is seen at its best in Ukerdi, a *reserva integral* (322 ha) that encompasses a transitional area between alpine and subalpine communities, where many species from the mountain pine forests live side-by-side with strays from the beech and European silver-fir formations. The first beeches and firs appear at around 1700 m in the bottom of gullies and depressions where more organic material has accumulated, leaving the ridges and crests to the mountain pine. The capercaillie – here at its western limit in the Pyrenees – maintains a stable population of around 20 males, while a greater variety of butterflies is on the wing than on the bare higher slopes: look out for Adonis, turquoise and Mazarine blues, shepherd's fritillary, black satyr and Spanish brassy and common brassy ringlets.

Aztaparreta – the other *reserva integral* in the area – comprises 100 ha of mixed beech and European silver-fir forest lying slightly to the south of Larra on the northern slopes of Txmantxoia (Maz; 1945 m). This is the most perfectly preserved part of the vast forest of the Selva Grande and has probably never been commercially exploited for timber. The most striking feature – aside from the gloom – is the sheer number of rotting, moss-covered fallen trees strewn across the forest floor. A few yews, rowans, *Sorbus mougeotii* and large-leaved limes take root alongside the many regenerating firs, while spring brings a carpet of pinnate coralroot into flower, with other shade-loving plants such as Irish spurge, wood speedwell, purple lettuce and bird's-nest orchid flowering later in the year. Clearings opened by falling trees are colonised by Welsh poppy, yellow pea, (subspecies *occidentalis*), *Scrophularia alpestris*, Pyrenean valerian and spreading bellflower.

Beech marten, wildcat and red deer are particularly common here, with abundant fire salamanders in the leaf litter and Pyrenean desmans known to occur in the neighbouring river Belagoa. Notable birds include woodcock, Tengmalm's owl, black and white-backed woodpeckers, goldcrest, nuthatch and treecreeper.

Access and information: Larra lies northeast of Isaba on the NA-137 and is best explored along the marked paths that head east towards Ukerdi from the very large Belagoa mountain hut (excellent information and food) or from the Collado de Ernaz on the French border. Aztaparreta can be reached along a track heading east from the hairpin bend in the NA-137, 10 km north of Isaba. The reserve information centre is in Roncal (tel: 948 475050; closed Mondays).

SITE
36 Foces de la Sierra de Leyre

Four spectacular river gorges harbouring some of the best raptor populations in western Europe plus fine limestone fissure vegetation.

The rivers Irati, Salazar and Esca chose the direct route through the limestone barriers of the Sierras de Leyre and Illón on their way down from the high Pyrenees to the Ebro, in the process carving out a number of stunning river gorges known as *foces* (all four are *reservas naturales*, totalling 1900 ha, with Arbayún (Sierra de Leyre) and Burgui (Sierra de Illón) also part of larger much ZEPAs).

A mid-June visit to the pocket-sized Foz de Lumbier is a delightful experience for the all-round naturalist. A trail through the defile follows the old route of the Iruñea/Pamplona–Sangüesa electric railway along the river Irati, with two tunnels separated by an easy 1 km walk. However, even before entering the *foz*, be sure to check out the roadside clumps of bramble and dwarf elder, which are veritable magnets for nectaring false ilex, ilex, sloe and blue-spot hairstreaks and southern white admirals. Many male *Platycnemis acutipennis* – an orange-red relative of the white-legged damselfly – also flutter around the vegetation here and all along the *foz*.

Once in the gorge, one of the first things you notice is the noise of the river, above which you should pick up the shrill calls of

Lizard orchid
Himantoglossum hircinum

speeding groups of alpine swifts, as well as those of nightingales, rock sparrows, jackdaws and, above all, choughs. Less vociferous are the rock doves, crag martins and blue rock thrushes, as well as the large raptors which sail into their nest sites on the highest ledges; about 250 pairs of griffon vulture breed in Lumbier – the largest colony in the Pyrenees – along with Egyptian vulture and eagle owl.

Within the defile, the track is lined by a splendid Mediterranean scrub of Phoenician juniper, the joint pine *Ephedra nebrodensis*, St Lucie's cherry, scorpion senna, turpentine tree and wild jasmine, all intertwined with fragrant clematis and *Lonicera implexa*. Here, too, are *Petrocoptis hispanica*, burnt candytuft, *Saxifraga cuneata* and fairy foxglove in rock fissures, as well as the splendid mauve flowers of *Phlomis herba-venti*, plus dipcadi and lizard orchid.

The Foz de Arbayún makes Lumbier look rather small, with 6 km of gorge, cliffs 385 m high and more exuberant vegetation. More

Aragón and Navarra

Foz de Arbayún (M.L.)

than 160 pairs of griffon vulture nest here, along with several pairs of other cliff-breeding species: Egyptian vulture, golden eagle, peregrine and eagle owl. Tree-nesting raptors also hunt in and around the *foz*: look out for booted and short-toed eagles, black and red kites, honey buzzard and goshawk.

The vegetation along the Arbayún defile is a strange mix of Mediterranean and montane elements, varying according to aspect: abundant western holm oak, turpentine tree, strawberry-tree (but no two-tailed pashas), *Phillyrea latifolia* and *P. angustifolia* clothe the sunny side; opposite a more luxuriant mosaic of Scots pine, wych elm, wild service-tree, *Sorbus mougeotii*, field, Italian and Montpellier maples, large-leaved lime and even the odd beech. Notable fissure plants include *Saponaria*

glutinosa, sarcocapnos, Pyrenean saxifrage and *Valeriana longiflora*.

For views down into Arbayún, visit the *mirador* just northeast of the Puerto de Iso (670 m) on the NA-178 between Lumbier and Burgui. Carry on east to the junction with the NA-2200 for access to the river Salazar where, in early June, marbled fritillaries bask on bramble banks, Spanish purple hairstreaks flutter around the ash trees, and turquoise, Escher's and silver-studded blues take moisture from the pebbly margins of the river. Look out, too, for gomphid dragonflies – yellow club-tailed and both blue-eyed and green-eyed hook-tailed – as well as the Spanish version of the banded demoiselle – *Calopteryx xanthostoma*, with dark wing tips – goblet-marked damselfly and crepuscular hawker.

The southern end of Arbayún can be reached from the village of Usún; just past the cemetery a track descends to the Río Salazar, where you can cross the bridge and follow the river as it meanders downstream to link up with Lumbier. Visitors are discouraged from entering the *foz* in a northerly direction to avoid disturbing the Pyrenean desmans, otters, beech martens, common genets, wildcats and wild boar that enjoy the solitude here.

The Foz de Benasa, tucked away behind the village of Navascués (from where paths lead into the bottom of the defile) is of note for its unique mixture of European silver-fir and western holm oak. The Foz de Burgui, south of the village of the same name and occupied by both the river Esca and the NA-137, is the only one of the four to boast an established pair of lammergeiers, with 230-odd pairs of griffon vulture, 4 of Egyptian vulture and 3 of golden eagle completing the picture. The ascent to the nearby chapel of La Virgen de la Peña (1294 m) provides stunning views over the chasm.

Access and information: All the *foces* lie to the south of the NA-178 between Lumbier and Burgui. The Foz de Lumbier is signposted in the village of Lumbier, while Usún and Navascués, for the other *foces*, are on or just off the same road. Lumbier has an interpretation and documentation centre (tel: 948 880874; fax: 948 880875; closed Mondays).

37 Laguna de Pitillas

SITE

Navarra's most important wetland, harbouring nesting bittern, purple heron, marsh harrier and bearded tit; interesting calcareous scrub and arable weeds.

The Laguna de Pitillas (*reserva natural*, Ramsar Site and ZEPA of 216 ha) lies in a large endorheic basin which once contained just a small brackish lagoon. The construction of a dyke in the eighteenth century, however, greatly increased the surface area and permanence of the lagoon and today – crucially for wildlife – reasonable water levels are maintained even in high summer.

The lagoon is fringed with extensive stands of common reed, and few other sites in the Iberian peninsula have such a complete set of reedbed breeders as Pitillas: purple and grey herons (19 and 269 pairs, respectively), little bittern (2 pairs) and bittern (two males booming), marsh harrier (30 pairs), great reed, Savi's and Cetti's warblers, bearded tit and – just possibly – spotted and little crakes. Out on the open water, great-crested and black-necked grebes display their fine plumes, and nesting duck include red-crested pochard (five pairs) and a few pairs of gad-wall, shoveler and mallard. One of the few birds not tied to the reeds is the black-winged stilt, which nests when water levels are low and sufficient mud is exposed. Purple gallinules have made an appearance recently and will probably breed in the coming years.

The lagoon lies directly on the western Pyrenean migration route and is either the first or last large freshwater body for birds using this crossing; when poor spring weather in the Pyrenees blocks the northward migratory flow, spectacular numbers of birds can build up. Groups of garganey (20+) and a mixed bag of yellow wagtail races in late March herald the beginning of the spring migration, while wader passage, best in May, sees a good variety of shanks and sandpipers plus black-tailed godwit and grey plover; both whiskered and black terns are also regular at this time. Autumn passage brings groups of up to 500 cranes, the odd spoonbill and white and black storks, while winter sees

Laguna de Pitillas (T.F.)

an influx of duck (3060 individuals in 2000), hen harrier (maximum 50), snipe, lapwing, golden plover and passerines such as water pipit and penduline tit.

If you can drag your binoculars away from the lagoon, the surrounding fields should turn up hoopoe, crested lark, spotless starling and the still fairly common tree sparrow. Little bustard, stone curlew, black-bellied sandgrouse and calandra lark all nest in the dry fields of the Pitillas basin, along with good numbers of Montagu's harriers.

Not surprisingly, Pitillas harbours important colonies of western spadefoot, as well as smaller numbers of parsley and Iberian pool frogs and natterjack toad. European pond terrapins sit out in the middle of the lagoon on beds of reeds, while both grass and viperine snakes hunt in the shallow margins. In drier areas, ladder and Montpellier snakes – the latter up to 2 m long – are quite common.

Although reedbeds make up the bulk of the marginal vegetation, seasonally flooded areas support sea, grey and triangular club-rushes, which give way to halophytes such as shrubby sea-blite and *Salicornia patula* in more saline areas, overtopped by a ring of *Tamarix canariensis*. Further afield, Pitillas is surrounded by dry cereal cultivations, interspersed with scrubby oases of prickly and Phoenician junipers, holly oak, osyris, the hare's-ear *Bupleurum rigidum*, wild jasmine, rosemary, felty germander and the everlasting flower *Helichrysum stoechas*. Sheltering amid the woody vegetation you should encounter a number of insect-imitating ophrys, namely mirror, yellow, woodcock and early spider, as well as eye-catching species such as grass-leaved buttercup, the stock *Matthiola fruticulosa*, beautiful flax, cone knapweed, blue aphyllanthes, rosy garlic and the distinctive grass albardine.

Access and information: Access to the lagoon is restricted but there is an interpretation centre topped by an observation terrace next to the NA-5330, southeast of the village of Pitillas (tel: 619 463450). The surrounding scrub can be explored by taking the first track to the left after the centre (coming from the village), from which a circuit of the whole lagoon is possible.

---

38 Bardenas Reales

A huge area of gypsum steppe and Aleppo pine forest with excellent populations of breeding raptors and steppe birds.

Although these days only mountain-bikers and 4WD vehicles are likely to approach in a swirl of dust, the seriously eroded badlands and table mountains of the Bardenas Reales really do resemble the set of a cheap Western. The most spectacular scenery is concentrated around the distinctively pale steppes of the Bardenas Blancas in the north, while the more southerly Bardenas Negras are slightly less arid and largely pine-clad.

Dupont's lark *Chersophilus duponti*

Bardenas Reales

It is wise to make an early start when visiting the Bardenas Reales (Biosphere Reserve and *parque natural*, 39 273 ha, also part ZEPA) as even in spring temperatures can soar quickly towards midday. Just south of Arguedas on the NA-134, take a narrow, metalled public road by the petrol station which heads east to the gates of a bombing range. Here, broad gravel tracks lead off to right and left, describing a complete circuit of the military estate and passing through the heart of the Bardenas Blancas.

The sparse vegetation is dominated by the grey-green tones of the halophytic shrubby sea-blite and *Salsola vermiculata*, accompanied by a range of sea-lavenders, notably the local endemic *Limonium ruizii*, the attractive grass known as albardine and several *Stipa* species. A little colour is provided here and there by *Hippocrepis multisiliquosa*, *Dorycnium pentaphyllum*, white flax (subspecies *salsoloides*), upright yellow flax, felty germander and silvery-leaved pink convolvulus. Among the typical shrubs of these arid, calcareous and often saline soils are shrubby orache, the pink-flowered

restharrow *Ononis tridentata*, white horehound, *Helichrysum stoechas* and *Artemisia herba-alba*.

Larks and pipits are much in evidence. Try using a process of elimination: the pale tawny pipit has a longer and thinner bill than the larks, no crest and an unmarked breast. A marked crest means crested or Thekla lark, while small and fairly nondescript indicates short-toed or lesser short-toed lark, the former having a distinctive rufous crown and the hint of a dark patch on its breast-side. Calandra larks, more tied to cereal fields, are much larger and have a distinctive white trailing edge to their wings. The real prize, however, is Dupont's lark; around 400 pairs breed in Bardenas, one of the best areas being around the foot of Castildetierra, an unmistakable rock pinnacle resembling an inverted funnel which is set next to the main track just to the north of the bombing range.

The larger steppe birds – stone curlew, little bustard (10+ pairs) and pin-tailed and black-bellied sandgrouse (both 30+ pairs) – are more likely to be observed in flight, particularly to and from drinking pools every morning. Just a few great bustards breed in the Bardenas; within Navarra as a whole numbers bottomed out at a mere dozen birds in 1985, although a tentative recovery is underway and some 30 birds were recorded in 1999.

Halfway along the circuit you approach an area of much-eroded cliffs which are often used by roosting griffon vultures. Spectacled warblers nest in the low halophyte vegetation here, while alpine swift, black wheatear, chough and rock sparrow all breed on the cliffs themselves. Cliff-nesting raptors include Egyptian vulture (50+ pairs) – at times remarkably common with summer roosts of up to 200 birds recorded – golden eagle (6+ pairs), peregrine and eagle owl (15+ pairs). The wealth of small vertebrate prey in general in the Bardenas also attracts short-toed eagle, both kites and Montagu's and marsh harriers.

For those working anti-clockwise, not long after passing Castildetierra a small, tamarisk-fringed lagoon appears on your right. Great reed and melodious warblers sing in a spring frenzy and, surprisingly, some of the many similar lagoons in the Bardenas are large enough to hold breeding bittern. Iberian pool frogs are very much in evidence, with other amphibians including marbled and palmate newts, midwife and natterjack toads, western spadefoot and parsley and common tree frogs.

Aside from the circuit of the bombing range, the three *reservas naturales* within the Bardenas are also well worth visiting. The Vedado de Egüaras (500 ha) is a horseshoe-shaped ridge in a transitional area between the Bardenas Blancas and the dry cultivation to the north, which is good for red-necked nightjar (access on the track leading north from the chapel of Nuestra Señora del Yugo). The Rincón del Bu (460 ha; also a ZEPA of 3651 ha), to the south of the bombing range, has similar flora and fauna to the main circuit and can be reached down a marked cycle track signposted off to the right just after the sign reading 'Bardenas Reales de Navarra' on the road in from Arguedas. The Caídas de la Negra (1926 ha) are the southerly pine-clad slopes of the Bardenas Negras, which are good for booted eagle, Bonelli's warbler, firecrest and crested tit, with *Paeonia officinalis* subspecies *microcarpa* growing in the shade of the few remaining patches of western holm oak (access is via tracks leading north from the Santuario de Sancho Abarca, some 20 km east of Tudela).

Also in the area

Arrozales de Arguedas The rice-paddies on both sides of the NA-134 south of Arguedas are excellent for white stork, black kite and passage waders in April–May and September–October: typically black-winged stilt, spotted redshank, greenshank, black-winged godwit and curlew.

Sotos along the Ebro North of **Tudela**, the Ebro is easily accessible at the end of the tracks running west off the NA-134 through the rice-paddies; look out for bee-eater, nightingale, melodious warbler, penduline tit, short-toed treecreeper, golden oriole and cirl bunting, with night, purple and grey herons and kingfisher fishing the banks of the Ebro itself. Common sandpiper and little ringed plover also breed, and overhead keep an eye out for booted eagle, black kite, sparrowhawk and hobby. Northwest of **Alfaro** lies a rather wild *soto* (*reserva natural*; 473.6 ha), that harbours most of the above-mentioned species plus olivaceous warbler and an important grey heron and cormorant roost in winter. European mink and possibly otter occur. In the town of Alfaro, 110 pairs of white stork (1999) breed on the church of San Miguel Arcángel.

SITE
39 El Moncayo

The highest peak in the Sistema Ibérico, displaying remarkable vegetation zonation on the north-facing slopes and harbouring diverse bird and butterfly faunas.

From an ecological viewpoint El Moncayo (a *parque natural* of 1389 ha) lies at a crossroads of biogeographic zones: by latitude it lies clearly within the Mediterranean region, but owing to its considerable altitude (maximum 2313 m) and location, the peak intercepts a good number of the cloudy fronts emanating from the Atlantic which are subsequently channelled down the Ebro valley.

As you climb the northern side of the massif, Mediterranean species are found up to about 1000 m: the limit for the small pockets of western holm and holly oaks where Dartford and subalpine warblers are common. Within this zone, tawny pipits and black-eared wheatears prefer open habitats, while Thekla rather than crested larks frequent rough, rocky areas, ortolan buntings the hedgerows and golden orioles scattered

El Moncayo beechwoods (T.F.)

trees near rivers. Both short-toed and Bonelli's eagles hunt over the piedmont of El Moncayo, the three or four pairs of the latter making this the best area for the species in the whole of Aragón.

From 900 to 1300 m, higher rainfall and deeper soils offer appropriate conditions for mature Scots pine and Pyrenean oak forest – the former often planted – which shelter an understorey of the delightful *Arenaria grandiflora*, bitter vetch and common cowwheat. Where more light penetrates, Montpellier and field maples appear, together with snowy mespilus and secondary communities of laurel-leaved cistus, *Halimium umbellatum*, Cornish heath and bell heather. Booted eagles hunt over these forests and great spotted woodpeckers abound, but the most obvious of the disappointingly few songbirds in the Pyrenean oaks is Bonelli's warbler.

Between 1300 and 1800 m lower temperatures and higher humidity in the montane zone provide favourable conditions for beech, accompanied by few plants beyond lady-fern, hepatica and the early flowering angel's-tears, although grassy glades sometimes turn up the diminutive pansy *Viola kitaibeliana* and elder-flowered orchids. Moving east, humidity decreases and the beech is replaced by sessile oak, accompanied by rowan, whitebeam, bilberry and red-berried elder.

Clearings in the forests provide the perfect habitat for parachuting tree pipits, while the depths of the beech forest itself are home to the secretive woodcock plus song thrush, nuthatch and short-toed treecreeper. Long-eared owl, goldcrest, crested tit, crossbill and citril finch, on the other hand, prefer the extensive pine plantations, which are also the favoured hunting territory of both honey buzzard and goshawk.

The Santuario de la Virgen del Moncayo (1610 m) commands marvellous views of the whole of the northern flank of El Moncayo, each forest type dressed in its own particular shade of green. Rock outcrops around the chapel sport clumps of the Spanish endemic saxifrage *Saxifraga moncayensis* (flowering in late May), as well as calcifuges such as parsley fern, *Silene ciliata*, *Saxifraga pentadactylis* subspecies *willkommiana*, rock lady's-mantle and the pansy-like *Viola montcaunica*, confined to the mountains of northern and central Spain.

Above 1600 m, the only plantations able to survive are those of mountain pine, with the intervening ridges carpeted with dwarf juniper and hedgehog broom, and dotted with a few twisted specimens of Phoenician juniper and yew. Peregrine, alpine swift, crag martin, chough and raven frequent the rocky outcrops, with rock bunting and, in winter, alpine accentor around the Santuario itself. Golden eagle, water pipit and rock thrush fly above the tree-line and, given the number of sightings in recent years, it is also worth looking out for lammergeier.

Mammals recorded in the park include pine and beech martens, Eurasian badger, wildcat, common genet, wild boar and roe deer, plus a whole range of micromammals. Reptiles are represented by ocellated lizard, large psammodromus, slow-worm, Montpellier and smooth snakes and Lataste's viper, while the most noteworthy amphibians are the fire salamander and marbled newt.

To date, 127 species of butterfly have been recorded in and around El Moncayo, with each of the different altitudinal zones having its specialities. Of particular note in the lower levels are mother-of-pearl, chequered and Iolas blues and Spanish fritillary in May, and southern hermit in summer. The montane zone provides a dazzling collection of fritillaries in June–July – notably Niobe, marbled, violet, meadow and Glanville – as well as an interesting array of coppers: scarce, purple-edged, purple-edged and sooty, the latter the brightly coloured subspecies *bleusei*. Above 1500 m the prize in July is the Moncayo endemic race of Apollo (*laufferi*), with distinctly grey-coloured females, flying in the company of Esper's marbled white.

Access and information: El Moncayo is located due south of Tarazona; head for San Martín de la Virgen del Moncayo, and keep winding upwards to the information centre (signposted; tel: 976 192125). Beyond here, a zigzag road leads to the Santuario (best to park and walk the last few hundred metres), with the summit accessible only on foot.

Valle de Echo

The quietest and most accessible of the four major north–south high Aragonese valleys to the west of Ordesa, with an excellent high-mountain flora and fauna; one of the easiest places in the Pyrenees to see wallcreeper.

As you follow the little-transited HU-2131 north from the village of Echo, a pleasant succession of habitats appears: first the narrow limestone gorge known as the Boca del Infierno, quickly followed by the superb forest of the Selva de Oza. The track ends a few kilometres short of Aguas Tuertas ('Twisted Waters'), from where it is an easy walk up to the French border.

The Boca del Infierno is a narrow defile cut by the Río Aragón Subordán between the limestone peaks of Atxar de Forca

Selva de Oza

(2391 m) and Peña Agüerri (2449 m). Stop just before the first tunnel and search the rock face for wallcreeper – here at one of its lowest breeding stations in the Pyrenees – while lammergeier, griffon vulture, golden eagle, alpine swift, crag martin and both choughs cruise the crags overhead and more terrestrial species include rock thrush and rock bunting.

European silver-fir, Scots pine, beech, Italian maple and large-leaved lime crowd right down to the water's edge here, but seemingly bare expanses of cliff should be examined for petrocoptis, tufted catchfly, Pyrenean saxifrage, rock snapdragon and ramonda. Wherever you can gain access to the steep woods, scout around for dark-red, broad-leaved, large white and sword-leaved helleborines, as well as bird's-nest orchid.

Further north, you enter the Reserva Nacional de Caza de los Valles (ZEPA; 28 757 ha) and the gorge gradually widens out into an area of pasture surrounded by the European silver-fir and beech forest of the Selva de Oza. Paths lead up into the Selva, where a few pairs of white-backed

woodpecker breed – their only Iberian site outside Navarra – along with the rather more abundant black woodpecker. Here, too, listen out for goldcrest, the very common marsh and crested tits and both treecreepers.

The understorey of these beech–fir woods is rather poor, although yellow anemone and pinnate coralroot create splashes of colour in spring, aconite-leaved buttercup blooms along the stream margins from May onwards and high summer brings purple lettuce into flower. One group of plants which does do well here, however, is the wintergreens; in the European silver-firs at around 1300 m

Alpine marmot *Marmota marmota*

you may find common, pale-green and serrated wintergreens and, perhaps slightly lower down, the delightful one-flowered. Keep an eye out, too, for the rather insignificant creeping lady's tresses.

Once out of the Selva, the road – now a track – continues northwards, but as it turns east a chain obliges you to park your vehicle down by the river and continue on foot. A summer exploration of the open pastures here should turn up Apollo, clouded Apollo, mountain clouded yellow, purple-edged and purple-shot coppers, Eros and large blues and shepherd's fritillary, as well as transparent and Scotch burnets, and the confusingly similar *Zygaena romeo*, *Z. nevadensis* and *Z. osterodensis*.

Throughout the upper reaches of the valley, keep an eye out for two-toothed golden-ringed dragonfly hawking over the pastures (easily mistaken for the more common-place golden-ringed dragonfly). Ring ouzels and citril finches forage among the open beech forest to the south, while both choughs feed on the invertebrates attracted by an abundance of cow-pats. After about 6 km, a couple of hairpin bends in the track take you up and over the moraine which guards the entrance to Aguas Tuertas – a flat

peatbog formed by the much-braided river – where siliceous boulders sport the Iberian endemic scented-leaved saxifrage and the pastures teem with trumpet gentians in early summer.

The limestone crags which surround the Valle de Echo are best reached via the GR-11, which runs west from the aforementioned car park. Botanical highlights include Thore's buttercup above 1500 m, mountain avens and dwarf buckthorn around 2000 m, Pyrenean columbine and Pyrenean vetch on screes and yellow and purple saxifrages and *Saxifraga hariotii* on summits. Likewise, keen bird and butterfly watchers get their just deserts in the form of ptarmigan and snow finch, always over 2000 m, plus peak white and a myriad ringlets, notably silky, Gavarnie, false dewy and Lefèbvre's.

Vertebrates of the Valle del Echo in general include Pyrenean desman and Pyrenean brook salamander in the main river, plus plenty of Alpine marmots and chamois at higher levels; asps are also abundant here, while at altitude the common wall lizard does justice to its name. The only surviving population of brown bear in the Pyrenees shares its time between the upper Echo and Ansó valleys and the Aspe valley in France.

SITE
41 San Juan de la Peña

A pine-clad plateau surrounded by sheer cliffs; good populations of breeding vultures, black woodpecker and citril finch, as well as typical pre-Pyrenean fissure plant communities.

Conveniently placed near Jaca, San Juan de la Peña (*monumento nacional*, 264 ha) is best known for its two monasteries: the recently restored Romanesque edifice that nestles under a cliff on the north side of the ridge, and the abandoned eighteenth-century abbey in the clearing on top of the mountain. Nevertheless, San Juan is also a delightful spot for the naturalist, providing excellent opportunities to see lammergeier, an interesting cliff-top flora and the best of the characteristic pre-Pyrenean butterflies.

Meleager's blue *Meleageria daphnis* (M.L.)

San Juan de la Peña

Taking the A-1603 south off the Jaca-Iruñea/Pamplona road through Santa Cruz de la Serós, you quickly pass from western holm oak with juniper and box scrub, through Lusitanian oaks and into a forest of Scots pine with beech, the latter once the dominant tree of the area but now relegated to gullies on the northern flanks. After passing the restored monastery under the cliff, you emerge onto a pine-ringed plateau; citril finch, black redstart and rock sparrow abound in open areas, while the forests harbour an abundance of great spotted woodpeckers, Bonelli's warblers, firecrests, crested tits and short-toed treecreepers. Crossbills sometimes begin nesting in November if there is a good crop of pine seeds, while black woodpeckers (10 pairs) breed throughout the area, especially in the area above the restored monastery.

Head north from the abandoned monastery for a short walk through the pines to the 'Balcón de los Pirineos', a fabulous viewpoint commanding the whole of the Aragonese Pyrenees. Griffon vultures (30–50 pairs) breed in the area; 200+ individuals in winter) float past the top of the conglomerate 'pudding' cliffs and, with a bit of luck, one of the local lammergeiers or goshawks may put in an appearance. Alpine swifts, crag martins and choughs abound, while other raptors breeding in the area include Egyptian vulture (2–4 pairs), golden (1–2 pairs) and booted eagles (2–3 pairs) and red kite (30 pairs). Shady crevices below the viewpoint harbour *Petrocoptis hispanica*, Pyrenean saxifrage, ramonda and *Valeriana longiflora*.

Back at the ruins, take the metalled track south then west for a walk of about 5 km to San Salbador (1547 m), for excellent views to the south. The Scots pine forest en route is

Information: A small information point run by the SEO/BirdLife on the top of San Juan is open every day in the summer and at weekends and on public holidays during the rest of the year (tel: 974 361476). The Romanesque monastery can be visited every day, but in winter only in the morning.

amply bedecked with mistletoe and enlivened by beech, snowy mespilus, whitebeam, holly and fly honeysuckle. In open areas the main ground cover consists of fearsome cushions of echinospartum and stunted box, with twisted thymelaea (subspecies *nivalis*) and bearberry in less-sheltered north-facing localities. On the thin, stony soil of the exposed ridge look out for tufted soapwort, livelong saxifrage, mountain onion and Pyrenean hyacinth, with sunny rock faces matted with white and thickleaved stonecrops and *Globularia repens*.

San Juan is also prime butterfly country. Carry on further east towards Bernués,

where late May to early June should turn up Spanish festoon, Duke of Burgundy fritillary, green-underside blue and pearlbordered fritillary, or the last week of July for safflower and carline skippers, Apollo (subspecies *aragonicus*, whiter and larger than the high Pyrenean race *pyrenaicus*) and a plethora of fritillaries, including lesser spotted and twin-spot. Among the summer blues, keep an eye out for Meleager's, Ripart's anomalous and Forster's furry blues, this last species being *Agrodiaetus ainsae* and not *A. dolus* which, contrary to some sources, does not actually fly in Spain.

Also in the area

Los Mallos de Riglos Dramatic orange conglomerate rock pinnacles or *mallos* towering over the village of Riglos. Just behind the village church, look up for wallcreeper in winter, plus alpine accentor, blue rock thrush and black wheatear. Griffon and Egyptian vultures breed west of the village, along with peregrine, eagle owl, alpine swift, crag martin, chough and jackdaw. The cliffs hold *Petrocoptis montserratii*, endemic to these *mallos* and a handful of other outcrops in the area, sarcocapnos, *Saxifraga fragilis* subspecies *fragilis*, Pyrenean saxifrage and

ramonda, with Pyrenean figwort in the enriched soils at the base of the cliffs.

Embalse de Sotonera Large reservoir south of Riglos: an important staging post February–March for cranes on northwards migration (maximum 20 000), visible from the dam off the A-1207, or from behind the village of Montmesa. To the south lies an interesting area of cereal pseudosteppes whose tracks can be driven in search of little bustard and black-bellied and pin-tailed sandgrouse.

42 Sierra de Guara

One of the most spectacular collections of canyons in Europe, harbouring the world's highest known density of lammergeier (nine pairs), a distinctive montane flora, including many local endemics, and 137 species of butterfly.

Until the 1980s, Guara was best known to speleologists, but with the declaration of the *parque natural* (47 450 ha; also a ZEPA of 81 350 ha) the whole area has become much

Edelweiss
Leontopodium alpinum

Boltaña
Ainsa
A-1604
Laguarta
Bara
Belsué
Nocito
Used
Arcusa
● Petreñales
mountain hut
▲
Tozal de Guara
2077 m
Rodellar
Sierra de Guara
Embalse
de Vadiello
Santa Cilia
de Panzano
Bárcabo
Vadiello
Bastarás
Panzano
i
Alquézar
Bierge
Loporzano
Huesca
Abiego
N-240
Barbastro

0   10 km

frequented by walkers, mountain-bikers and naturalists. Eastern Guara is sliced open by immense limestone gorges – approachable, for example, from the villages of Alquézar and Rodellar – home to a rich fissure plant community of *Petrocoptis guarensis*, sarcocapnos, lax potentilla, Pyrenean honeysuckle, *Globularia repens*, small cushions of *Valeriana longiflora* subspecies *paui* and a confusing collection of hawkweeds. Ramonda and Pyrenean figwort prefer the shadiest nooks, here or on the calcareous conglomerate cliffs to the west, while Pyrenean saxifrage chooses sunny expositions, almost exclusively on the conglomerate.

Another recommended entry point into Guara is the road linking Loporzano with the Embalse de Vadiello, where you have an excellent chance of seeing up to five adult lammergeiers at any time of year. Griffon vultures are in perpetual motion here (500 pairs in the area), Egyptian vultures fly in their curious tight circles and choughs appear in close-knit formations. Vadiello is also about the only place in Huesca province where you might just see Bonelli's eagle,

although as pasture and arable land is being invaded by scrub and pines, this eagle (four pairs in 1997, one pair in 2000) is losing the open habitats it prefers. More opportunistic species such as booted eagle and red kite are benefiting, however, and are now commoner than they were 20 years ago. As you walk across the dam at Vadiello, keep an eye out for golden and short-toed eagles, alpine swift, crag martin and rock thrush, as well as for wallcreeper and alpine accentor in winter.

Vadiello is also a fine spot for butterfly enthusiasts. The ever-scarce spring ringlet and Portuguese dappled white fly in the area in early spring: the former is the only ringlet on the wing so early in the year, while the lat-

Tufted soapwort *Saponaria caespitosa*

ter can be separated from the very similar dappled white by the more rounded upper edge to its hindwing. Scattered colonies of the scarce chequered blue appear in May, the three 'low-level' ringlets – autumn, de Prunner's and Piedmont – are all common in summer, while Apollos (subspecies *aragonicus*) fly above 1000 m. Throughout the area, there are particularly good populations of calcicolous species such as Duke of Burgundy fritillary and Forster's furry, Damon and Ripart's anomalous blues, while July sees Spanish, Provence and the 'normal' chalk-hill blues on the wing at the same time.

The only way to get to the roof of Guara (Tozal de Guara, 2077 m) is to ascend over 1000 m on foot. The route from Santa Cilia de Panzano in the south is probably the smoothest, although the northern routes are shorter and pass through more interesting mixed woodland, home to black woodpeckers, with European silver-fir forest above the Petreñales mountain refuge. On the southern flank, typical Mediterranean woodland and scrub occur up to 1400 m, above which lies a vast swathe of echinospartum: an attractive but spiny yellow-flowered shrub that flowers in June–July.

The summit flora includes tufted soapwort, white musky and purple saxifrages, *Potentilla nivalis* and edelweiss, while the scree slope on the northern side is worth examining for the presence of pink sandwort, *Aquilegia pyrenaica* subspecies *guarensis*, *Cochlearia aragonensis*, vitaliana, *Linaria alpina* subspecies *guarensis*, alpine honeysuckle and pygmy hawk's-beard. A few mountain pines cling to the northern slopes just below the summit, with an understorey of alpine pasque flowers in spring.

Vertebrates in the park include all the typical Mediterranean species – common genet, bee-eater, black wheatear, blue rock thrush and ocellated and Iberian wall lizards, for example – but also a healthy population of Aesculapian snake, with the rivers harbouring some of the peninsula's most southerly populations of Pyrenean brook salamander.

Information: The park information centre is in the village of Bierge, on the A-1227 (tel: 974 318121 or 974 318238). 'Boletas' – a birdwatching centre and guest-house in the village of Loporzano, northeast of Huesca – gives advice readily and acts as an unofficial information centre for walkers.

SITE 43 Ordesa y Monte Perdido

Fabulous glaciated limestone scenery, harbouring an incomparable array of the most charismatic Pyrenean flora and fauna, including 131 species of butterfly.

The Parque Nacional de Ordesa y Monte Perdido (15 608 ha; also a Biosphere Reserve and ZEPA) comprises four main valleys: the perfectly glaciated Ordesa and Pineta valleys and, sandwiched in between, the much narrower, river-eroded gorges of Añisclo

Alpine snowbell *Soldanella alpina*

and Escuaín. Forested areas range from thermophilic western holm oak formations low down, through incredibly varied woods in the Añisclo and Escuaín gorges, with beech in Ordesa and Pineta, to pure Scots pine, with mountain pines struggling up to about 2000 m.

The classic walk from the main car park in the Ordesa valley up to the Góriz mountain hut takes you through splendid mixed Scots pine, European silver-fir and beech woods, where you should see all the typical Pyrenean forest species: black and great spotted woodpeckers, firecrest, marsh and crested tits and treecreeper; Tengmalm's owls also breed here and can be heard calling on spring evenings. Once the beech thins out, to be replaced by mountain pine, look out for ring ouzel, crossbill and citril finch, plus rock thrush in boulder-strewn areas and on crags. Any of the high ridges should turn up lammergeier (try around the village of Escuaín if you miss it here), as well as griffon vulture, golden eagle, alpine chough and chough. The pastures and waterfalls of Soaso are a good place to track down water pipit and wheatear.

Pink form of common rockrose *Helianthemum nummalarium* in the Ordesa national park

From Soaso you can return to the car park via the Senda de los Cazadores along the Faja de Pelay: a stunning walk which contours high above the valley before dropping down very steeply (640 m) to your starting point. Not for the faint-hearted, this option is good for capercaillie (20 males in the park), Pyrenean lily, whorled Solomon's-seal and lily-of-the-valley, as well as boasting marvellous views over the Ordesa valley. By carrying on to Góriz, however, you increase your chances of seeing ptarmigan – roughly 20 pairs breed in the park, always above 2000 m – and snow finch: a small colony breeds just above the refuge. Alpine accentors are common at this altitude and you may also encounter wallcreeper in these rocky limestone wastes.

Trees or shrubs cover a mere 28% of the park, the remainder comprising either bare rock or pastures where cattle graze all summer long. Acid bedrock supports fairly uniform mat-grass pastures, dotted with Pyrenean buttercup, Pyrenean gentian, *Pedicularis mixta*, arnica and vanilla orchid, while pastures on base-rich soils are more diverse, housing pink sandwort, Samnitic milk-vetch, ashy cranesbill, spring gentian, alpine aster and edelweiss.

Rock faces lower down are home to Pyrenean saxifrage, ramonda and Pyrenean honeysuckle, while limestone screes host Pyrenean columbine, parnassus-leaved buttercup, Pyrenean poppy, cylindric rock-jasmine and pygmy hawk's-beard. The highest crags provide refuge for Pyrenean catchfly, Pyrenean whitlow-grass, alchemilla-leaved cinquefoil, mountain avens and a dazzling variety of saxifrages, including yellow and neglected. One speciality on rock walls is the Pyrenean yam – a member of the tropical Dioscoreaceae, with male and female flowers on separate plants – while shady, humid habitats are home to alpine snowbell and long-leaved butterwort. For those few who struggle right to the top of Monte Perdido (3355 m) the reward comes in the shape of hairy saxifrage (subspecies *iratiana*), purple saxifrage and *Androsace ciliata*.

Butterfly watchers will be amply rewarded at Ordesa; try the Pineta valley for the scarce

Ordesa valley, looking south

northern wall brown, which flies in open pine woods up to about 2000 m in June and July. Lower down, the meadows and waysides harbour white-letter hairstreak, Camberwell beauty and southern white admiral, with the higher pastures home to alpine grizzled skipper and Gavarnie and Glandon blues (feeding on *Androsace villosa* and vitaliana, respectively). At altitude the *Erebia* species are the most plentiful butterflies; large, Lefèbvre's, mountain, Spanish and common brassy, Gavarnie, autumn and false dewy ringlets have all been recorded from the park. The Tau emperor (the males day-flying), is abundant at around 1500 m in the fir and beech forests of Pineta in June.

Ordesa's most renowned mammal is no longer with us. The last *bucardo* – the Pyrenean subspecies (*pyrenaica*) of Spanish ibex – slipped and died in January 2000, thereby dashing any faint hopes of establishing a captive breeding programme. Chamois and Alpine marmots, however, are extremely common at altitude, while all the main rivers are inhabited by otter and Pyrenean desman.

The small, long-legged Pyrenean frog – endemic to fast-running streams in the central Pyrenees – was first described from Ordesa in 1990. Adults stay close to rivers all year round, lay relatively few eggs and often share habitat with Pyrenean brook salamanders, but never with common frogs,

Access and information: Certain restrictions have been imposed by the park authorities. You can go anywhere on foot, although freelance camping is not permitted. There is only one mountain hut in the park – Góriz – and you should make a reservation well in advance (tel: 974 341201). Access by car beyond Torla is restricted during Easter and from July to mid-October: a bus service then links Torla with the main car park and information centre (park offices: tel: 974 243361; fax: 974 242725; e-mail: ordesa@mma.es). However, the service is suspended when the park's hypothetical carrying capacity of 1800 people is reached (generally late July and August). The inviting minor road through Fanlo to the south of the park can only be driven *east to west* in the summer months.

which prefer eutrophic pools. Other herptiles of note include fire salamander, palmate newt and the endemic Pyrenean rock lizard, abundant around the Góriz mountain hut. Lower down, ocellated and green lizards thrive in sunny areas, while the commonest snakes are smooth snake and asp.

SITE

44 Valle de Benasque

A narrow glaciated valley squeezed between the granite bulks of Aneto (3404 m) and Posets (3369 m) – the two highest peaks in the Pyrenees – with a wide range of easily accessible subalpine and alpine habitats.

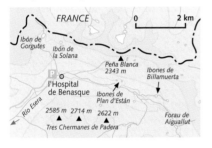

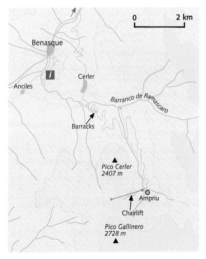

accessible – and often ignored – Ampriu valley to the southeast of Benasque, or the main valley to the east of l'Hospital de Benasque are obvious places to start. On the other hand, the 'hanging' side valleys of Estós and Ballibierna harbour some of the best forests and, for the fittest, are gateways to dozens of glacial lakes (known locally as *ibones*), the Aneto and Posets glaciers and most of the main peaks.

You can drive right up to the species-rich meadows at the head of the Ampriu valley (1912 m), where blues are provided by round-headed and Pyrenean rampions, *Campanula scheuchzeri*, clustered bellflower and English iris, and contrasting yellows by globeflower, great yellow gentian, *Gentiana burseri*, *Senecio adonidifolius*, spotted cat's-ear and golden-rod. Orchids here include elder-flowered, burnt-tip, greater butterfly and frog, all in flower by late June, before the sheets of fragrant, heath-spotted and early marsh, plus a few broad-leaved marsh orchids (subspecies *alpestris*), are at their best.

July brings impressive clumps of martagon lilies into bloom, with leafy lousewort, Pyrenean sneezewort, chives and white false helleborine occupying damp depressions. In really boggy areas, look out for yellow mountain saxifrage, Pyrenean angelica, *Pedicularis mixta*, marsh arrow-grass and Tofield's asphodel at this time of year, but the abundance of bird's-eye primroses here is best appreciated in mid-June. The verges of the road up from Cerler are packed with pale

The most pressing problem for the visiting naturalist in the Benasque valley (a *parque natural* of 33 267 ha known as Posets-Maladeta, also a ZEPA) lies in choosing which of the many well-preserved subalpine and alpine valleys to tackle first. The easily

yellow Pyrenean thistle, while drier pastures hereabouts teem with Pyrenean pink, Mt Cenis restharrow and Pyrenean golden drop.

A chair-lift operates from Ampriu in the summer (plenty of Alpine marmots on view during the ascent), depositing you at 2245 m, where late-June visitors will find Pyrenean pheasant's-eye and vanilla orchid in flower, along with moonwort, parnassus-leaved buttercup and snow gentian. A fairly intrepid descent down the slope beneath the chair-lift might reward you with the zigzag stems of streptopus on damp rocks, as well as Pyrenean brook salamander.

July is undoubtedly the best month for butterflies at Ampriu: Eros, Mazarine and Idas blues, along with the abundant scarce copper are on the wing then, together with Apollo, clouded Apollo, mountain dappled white and mountain clouded yellow. Higher slopes harbour the always elusive silky, Gavarnie, Spanish brassy, false dewy and Lefèbvre's ringlets, as well as Glandon blue and olive skipper.

The Ampriu basin is regularly hunted over by the local lammergeier trio, while the ridge to the east is frequented by cruising griffon vultures and golden eagles. The high pastures are full of water pipits, with hovering short-toed eagle, rock thrush, whinchat, red-backed shrike and ortolan bunting lower down around the barracks. The meadows between Cerler and Anciles hold mountain Alcon and large blues and western whip snake, while the birch and box woods along the trail which links the two villages are good for baneberry, herb-Paris, twayblade and bird's-nest orchid.

A contrast to Ampriu is the upper part of the Benasque valley above l'Hospital; from the hotel, follow the road eastwards through an open mountain pine forest populated by tansy-leaved rocket, Welsh poppy, straw foxglove, red-berried elder, hairless blue-sowthistle and purple lettuce. Black woodpecker, crested tit, treecreeper, citril finch and crossbill nest in the area, and this open wooded habitat is also ideal for shepherd's fritillary and large and bright-eyed ringlets, all three absent from Ampriu.

The road passes close to a shady limestone outcrop which will keep the botanists happy: examine the low cliffs for the creeping Pyrenean willow, *Aquilegia hirsutissima*, Thore's buttercup, narcissus-flowered anemone, Pyrenean saxifrage, round-leaved St John's-wort, the attractive rampion *Phyteuma charmelii* and leafless-stemmed globularia. Climb up to the south-facing limestone outcrop below Peña Blanca to the north for tufted soapwort, blue saxifrage, alchemilla-leaved cinquefoil and the handsome yellow betony.

Next you come to the Ibones de Plan d'Están: two small lagoons on the far side of a large boggy area. Mats of the pencil-like flowering spikes and floating leaves of amphibious bistort cover the lagoons, with the margins harbouring radish-leaved bittercress, water avens, marsh felwort and broad-leaved cottongrass. Mud-puddling butterflies abound on sunny days, including large concentrations of marbled skipper, while alpine grizzled skipper is also regularly recorded from this area. Few odonates other than large red damselfly, southern hawker and keeled skimmer have been recorded from these pools, but check all 'golden-ringed' individuals as two-toothed golden-ringed dragonfly is known to occur in the area.

For those who want to walk further, continue along the road to the Forau de Aiguallut, an impressive waterfall where melt-water from the Aneto glacier disappears down a sinkhole to reappear 5 km away in the Vall d'Aran on the north side of the main Pyrenean axis. Alternatively, climb the trail from l'Hospital to the Ibón de la Solana and Ibón de Gorgutes for fabulous views of Aneto and its glacier and a chance of lammergeier, alpine accentor and wall-

Lammergeier *Gypaetus barbatus*

Merendera *Merendera pyrenaica* in the Benasque valley

creeper. Look out, too, for pink rock- jasmine between the two *ibones*, as well as moss campion, Pyrenean buttercup, alpine bitter-cress, hairless lady's mantle, alpine bartsia and *Pedicularis mixta*.

The extensive beech, European silver-fir and mountain pine forests of the Estós and Ballibierna valleys are home to all the typical Pyrenean forest birds, including Tengmalm's owl. If entering Estós in July, check the flowery verges for large blue and great sooty satyr, keeping an eye open, too, for Moroccan orange tip, Camberwell beauty and large tortoiseshell at this time of year.

Those who tackle the real heights of the park – in excess of 3000 m – will have only ptarmigan and snow finch for company among the birds, but will be rewarded by a specialised flora which includes glacier crowfoot around the edge of ice-fields, as well as mossy, purple and hairy saxifrages and *Androsace ciliata*: the only flowering plants to reach the peak of Aneto.

Access and information: The park interpretation centre lies 1 km south of Benasque on the road to Anciles (tel: 974 552066). The Benasque tourist office also provides information on the network of waymarked footpaths, access restrictions beyond l'Hospital and the buses which run up the valleys; guidebooks and maps are widely available in Benasque itself.

Also in the area

To the south of Benasque looms the immense limestone massif of **Turbón** (2492 m), housing a pre-Pyrenean fauna and flora that includes snow finch on the summit, and wallcreeper and the locally endemic *Petrocoptis pseudoviscosa* in the Congosto de Ventamillo gorge to the west (the main road to Benasque). The quieter

Congosto de Obarra along the Isábena river to the east (visit the beautiful monastery at the gorge entrance to the south, near the turn-off to Ballabriga) is resplendent with sarcocapnos, Pyrenean saxifrage, lax potentilla, large-leaved lime, Pyrenean bellflower and *Phyteuma charmelii*.

45 Laguna de Sariñena

One of the most important wetlands in Aragón, home to important heron colonies and attracting wintering duck and passage migrants.

Once a moderate endorheic lagoon of some 100 ha, the Laguna de Sariñena (*refugio de fauna silvestre*, 605 ha) grew steadily throughout the 1970s as run-off from newly established irrigation projects began to drain into the lagoon basin. An outlet canal was dug to stabilise water levels, leaving a much larger but less saline waterbody, girded by a belt of *Tamarix canariensis* and with an impressive bed of common reed at its shallow southern end.

Up to 10 000 duck winter at Sariñena: mainly teal, shoveler and mallard, accompanied by rather fewer red-crested pochard, gadwall, pintail, wigeon, tufted duck, pochard, shelduck and up to 140 greylag geese. Other obvious winter visitors to look out for are black-necked grebe, cormorant, little gulls among the black-headed and yellow-legged gulls, both snipe and jack snipe and a few surprises: in 2000 Sariñena birdwatchers enjoyed rare views of red-necked grebe, spoonbill, greater flamingo and ruddy shelduck.

Cattle, little and great white egrets, bittern and grey heron can be seen all year round, but purple heron (19 pairs in 2000) and little bittern only in summer. Other breeding waterbirds include great-crested grebe, red-crested pochard (4 pairs), marsh harrier (4 pairs) and, for the first time in 2000, purple gallinule (2 pairs). Nesting

waders are limited to little ringed plover (36 pairs), black-winged stilt (20 pairs) and a few avocets. In the reedbeds, great reed, reed and Cetti's warblers are the commonest breeders, with stone curlew, great spotted cuckoo and scops owl occupying dry habitats around the lagoon.

Herptiles at Sariñena are represented by Iberian pool frog, common and natterjack toads, western spadefoot and ladder, grass and viperine snakes, while among the lizards, Iberian wall lizard is by far the commonest, but both Spanish and large psammodromus are present and you should also look for Moorish gecko on the buildings around the lagoon.

Purple heron *Ardea purpurea*

Access and information: A broad track circumnavigates the lagoon, with the best views from the southern end by the sluice gate. A small information centre, located to the northeast of Sariñena and signposted off the A-129 to Zaragoza, is usually open during weekends and public holidays. (See map on p. 142.)

Also in the area

Sierra de Alcubierre Forested ridge (Monte Oscuro, 822 m) southwest of Sariñena with deeply gullied northern flanks housing western holm and Lusitanian oaks, *Paeonia officinalis* subspecies *microcarpa*, blackthorn, Montpellier maple, box, strawberry-tree, bearberry, wild privet, wayfaring-tree, Pyrenean hawk's-beard, angular Solomon's-seal, large white helleborine and violet limodore; open areas teem with dull, early spider and woodcock ophrys, plus the striking milk-vetch *Astragalus alopecuroides* in spring. Good densities of Egyptian vulture, booted, short-toed and golden eagles, black and red kites, goshawk, peregrine, hobby and eagle owl, while south-facing pine forests host long-eared owl, red-necked nightjar, Bonelli's warbler, firecrest, crested tit and crossbill. Rock thrushes breed up high and crag martin, black wheatear and rock sparrow are common in the dry southern gullies. Cereal fields, scrub and orchards to the north are excellent for stone curlew, great spotted cuckoo, bee-eater, Thekla lark, woodchat shrike and black-eared wheatear. Best accessed via the minor road south from Lanaja (on the A-129 Zaragoza–Sariñena road) towards Monegrillo.

Arrozales de Sariñena North of Sariñena, the rice-paddies around the villages of San Lorenzo and Capdesaso are excellent for white storks (37 pairs in Sariñena itself), waders on spring passage and water pipit in winter.

Los Monegros

A vast expanse of pseudosteppe with a full complement of breeding steppe birds and an interesting gypsophilous flora.

The name 'Monegros' (*montes negros*) derives from the dark juniper forests that formerly clothed much of the huge arid area (some 3000 square kilometres) which straddles the middle reaches of the Ebro to the east of Zaragoza. Owing to centuries of felling, burning and overgrazing, the largest remaining forest enclave today, however, is Retuerta de Pina (south of the Hostal del Ciervo, 9.8 km west of Bujaraloz on the N-II): 1500 ha of sparse woodland in which – owing to frequent temperature inversions – Aleppo pines grow on the frost-free hilltops, leaving the hardy junipers to occupy the valley bottoms.

The birdlife of Retuerta is typical of dry Mediterranean scrublands, offering spectacled, subalpine and Orphean warblers, as

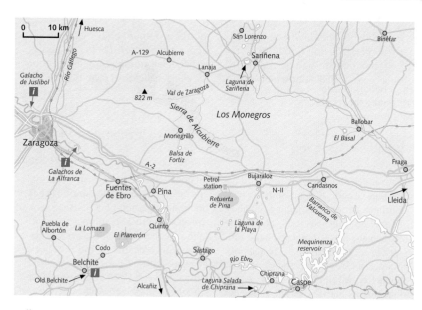

well as great spotted cuckoo, bee-eater, hoopoe and black-eared wheatear. Raptors are attracted by the abundance of rabbits and reptiles here, such that golden, short-toed and booted eagles and black and red kites are regularly seen hunting over the forest. In open areas large psammodromus and ocellated and spiny-footed lizards scurry underfoot, but less obvious are the Montpellier, southern smooth and ladder snakes which occur here. Apart from the rabbits, the only larger mammals are Iberian hare, red fox, western hedgehog and garden dormouse.

The soils of Los Monegros are predominantly saline and gypsum-based, originating from the evaporation of the huge lake which filled the Ebro Depression around 30 million years ago. The dominant shrubs of the Retuerta tend to be *Salsola vermiculata*, *Cistus clusii* and *Artemisia herba-alba*, along with *Ephedra nebrodensis*, *Genista scorpius*, *Rhamnus lycioides* and rosemary. Also frequent are the attractive member of the pink family *Gypsophila hispanica*, *Aizoon hispanicum*, the crucifer *Lepidium subulatum*, *Ononis tridentata* and the distinctive rockrose *Helianthemum squamatum*. Deeper soils, often disturbed, harbour *Euphorbia serrata*, peganum (a curious member of the Zygophyllaceae with greenish flowers), silvery-leaved pink convolvulus, henbane, dip-

cadi and the autumn-flowering slender sternbergia.

Confusingly, the majority of maps mark all the Monegros wetlands as permanent when, in fact, most are endorheic and hold water only in wet years. A particularly important complex of these saline lagoons (*saladas*) lies south of Bujaraloz, including the largest in the area – Laguna de la Playa – which, thanks to a small saline spring, usually contains at least some water, even in dry years. Macrophytes such as *Ruppia drepanensis* appear en masse in the *saladas* after a wet winter or spring, and – in years of generous rainfall – birds are not slow to follow.

Morrocan orange tip *Anthocharis belia* (Peter Wilson)

Shelduck, red-necked pochard, pintail, shoveler and wigeon turn up on passage to filter out the seeds of *Ruppia* or crustaceans of the genus *Artemia*, while waders such as little stint, ruff, lapwing, avocet and black-winged stilt (sometimes staying on to breed in the more permanent pools), feed on crustaceans stranded around the margins.

Artificial water supplies for domestic livestock, notably the good-sized Balsa de Fortiz (4 km due south of Monegrillo, accessible via a broad track), attract drinking pin-tailed and black-bellied sandgrouse, choughs and large flocks of rock sparrows, as well as spawning amphibians. Look out for the huge (up to 15 cm) tadpoles of the western spadefoot, which completely dwarf the more 'normal-sized' larvae of the natterjack toad. Any pond may hold interesting communities of odonates, notably southern emerald and common winter damselflies, scarlet and southern darters, *Sympetrum sinaiticum* and *Trithemis annulata*.

The minor road linking Candasnos with Caspe (A-2410) is also worth exploring. Just after leaving Candasnos, stop to check the lagoon to the right of the road, which attracts migrant herons, garganey, black-tailed godwit and terns, with breeding birds including black-necked grebe, red-crested pochard, black-headed gull and great reed warbler.

A few kilometres further south, you reach the Barranco de Valcuerna, the only permanent watercourse in the whole of the Monegros. 'Tumbleweeds' – in fact desiccated bushes of prickly saltwort – accumulate in the low-lying depressions, while the gypsophilous scrub is enlivened in early spring by the yellowish flowers of *Boleum asperum*, a woody crucifer covered in short, stiff hairs and endemic to the Monegros. Look out, too, for *Adonis microcarpa*, sad stock, the Afro-Iberian endemic *Genista fontanesii* subspecies *fontanesii*, the showy flowers of burning bush, Egyptian mallow, *Sideritis scordioides*, *Salvia lavandulifolia*, *Crupina vulgaris*, blue iris and *Fritillaria lusitanica* at this time of year.

Follow tracks down the Barranco, past unexpected stands of turpentine tree and wild jasmine, as far as the Mequinenza reservoir, where a few strawberry-trees are home

Great reed warbler *Acrocephalus arundinaceus* (Mike Lane)

to a small colony of two-tailed pashas. Keep your eyes peeled along the way for Egyptian vulture, Bonelli's and golden eagles and black kite, as well as red-necked nightjar, turtle dove, bee-eater, subalpine warbler, woodchat shrike, golden oriole and rock sparrow. Spring butterflies include Moroccan orange tip, Adonis blue, spotted fritillary, western marbled white, Spanish gatekeeper and southern marbled skipper, the latter best around the reservoir.

The outstanding characteristic of Los Monegros, however, is the seemingly endless arid plains, recently protected by four ZEPAs totalling more than 100 000 ha. The birdlife of these immense open spaces is very similar to that described for Belchite (see p. 145) with the addition of lesser kestrel (553 pairs recorded by SEO/BirdLife in 1998; about 15% of adults stay on for the winter) and great bustard, both found above all in the huge cereal pseudosteppes southwest of Bujaraloz.

The Monegros also houses exceptional invertebrate communities, including many endemic species, although the non-specialist should perhaps just look out for greenish black-tip and sooty orange tip in spring, the former feeding on stocks, rocket and mignonette, the latter on hoary and buckler mustards, with southern hermit emerging at the end of June in areas of rosemary and thyme scrub, as well as for the appropriately named ribbon-tailed lacewing.

Also in the area

Saladas de Alcañiz Comprising the Salada Grande (150 ha) and Embalse de la Estanca. Salada Grande is a true endorheic lagoon, with *Microcnemum coralloides*, *Aizoon hispanicum* and various species of sea-lavender in hyper-saline habitats, appealing to migratory black-winged stilt, avocet, dunlin, spotted redshank, ruff, little ringed plover and grey plover. La Estanca – formerly endorheic but now permanent – attracts both storks, osprey and crane on passage, plus red-crested pochard and short-eared owl in winter. The surrounding steppe supports little bustard, both sand-grouse and calandra, short-toed and Dupont's larks.

Saladas de Chiprana (Ramsar Site; 162 ha) High levels of salinity in the Laguna Salada permit few macrophytes other than beaked tasselweed and foxtail stonewort. Few wintering duck, although spring migration brings little stint, dunlin, curlew sandpiper and avocet; breeding shelduck, red-crested pochard, marsh harrier, black-winged stilt, Kentish plover, great reed warbler and, in some years, black-necked grebe, gadwall, black-headed gull and little ringed plover.

SITE

47 Galacho de Juslibol/ Galachos de La Alfranca

Two groups of ox-bow lakes (galachos) near Zaragoza, created by changes in the course of the river Ebro: breeding herons, riverine forest birds and easy access to the nearby gypsum steppe.

The Galacho de Juslibol is managed by Zaragoza city council more as a public park than a nature reserve, with the main interest for the visiting naturalist lying in the gypsum scarp – an ancient river terrace – which forms a backdrop to the ox-bow lake. Black wheatears nest in the soft cliffs, along with crag martin, bee-eater, rock sparrow and, occasionally, eagle owl, while black-eared wheatears occur along the cliff-top habitats at the edge of the steppe. Up on the plateau itself, numerous small tunnels are inhabited by the impressive, burrow-dwelling wolf-spider *Lycosa fasciventris*, while the scorpion *Buthus occitanus* and the enormous (12 cm) centipede *Scolopendra cingulatus* (both of

Night heron *Nycticorax nycticorax* (Peter Wilson)

which are venomous) live in darker, more humid habitats beneath piles of stones.

The flora of these eroded gypsum soils includes *Gypsophila hispanica*, the white-flowered crucifer *Lepidium subulatum*, *Ononis tridentata*, the bizarre, fleshy peganum, lavender-leaved rock-rose, *Helianthemum squamatum*, *Thymus vulgaris* and the shrubby composite *Launaea pumila*, endemic to eastern Spain. Look out, too, for the peculiar joint pine *Ephedra distachya*, sad stock, *Ruta angustifolia*, twisted thymelaea, shrubby globularia and the distinctive heads of *Scabiosa stellata*.

In contrast, the Galacho de La Alfranca (part of a larger ZEPA (777 ha) comprising three different *galachos*) is managed by SEO/BirdLife with the birds' interests at heart. The stars of the show here are undoubtedly the 90-odd pairs of night heron, 10 of little egrets, 100 of cattle egrets and 7 of purple heron (2000 figures), many easily observed from a hide strategically positioned 20 m from their ground-level nests. Paths through the reserve give access to an attractive *soto* (fluvial woodland), home to bee-eater, wryneck, nightingale, great reed, reed, melodious and Cetti's warblers, penduline tit and golden oriole.

The margin of the Río Ebro within the reserve is a good place to sit and watch the sand martins nesting in the river bank, or wait for purple heron, booted eagle, black kite, marsh harrier or little ringed plover to pass by. The corridor formed by the river is followed by many migrants, with osprey, a variety of migrant waders and whiskered tern passing through each year.

Access and information: Although most of the Alfranca reserve can be freely visited, the main hide can be entered only with a guide at weekends; contact the SEO/BirdLife interpretation centre (tel: 660 152878), which is signposted to the south of Puebla de Alfindén, on the N-II east of Zaragoza. To visit the Galacho de Juslibol, either drive west from the village of Juslibol, park where a chain blocks the track and walk the remaining 2 km along the foot of the scarp (a wooden staircase climbs to the plateau above just opposite the *galacho*); alternatively, take the 'train' which, at weekends, leaves from the car park of the Carrefour hypermarket in Calle María Zambrano in Zaragoza. More information and guided tours available from CEAM (tel: 976 284568; fax: 976 443332). (See map on p. 142.)

SITE
48 Belchite

The best-preserved steppe habitat in the Ebro Depression, with abundant sandgrouse, Dupont's lark and gypsophilous plant communities.

The best of Belchite is protected in the twin reserves of El Planerón (600 ha) and La Lomaza (961 ha, also a ZEPA), the former a broad plain centred on the endorheic lagoon of the same name, and the latter a long, raised terrace atop the soft gypsum cliffs that provide a very photogenic backdrop to the north of El Planerón and the main Belchite steppe.

Although frequently called 'steppe', this habitat is only superficially similar to the true *stepj* of the Cossacks and Mongol hordes. The central Asian steppe is characterised by fertile soils with rains during the brief continental summer promoting the growth of a dense carpet of grasses, whereas those of the Ebro typically suffer long, hot, dry summers and possess poor, thin soils, supporting a scanty cover of woody and herbaceous plants; they are thus better referred to as 'pseudosteppes'.

The flora of Belchite is more closely linked to the semi-arid regions of north Africa than to anywhere in Europe or Asia. The grasses *Stipa lagascae*, *S. parviflora* and albardine are among the most representative plants here, and although they once covered vast areas of the Ebro Depression, they require the deep limy soils preferred for cultivation, such that few true grasslands persist today.

More saline soils are dominated by *Salsola vermiculata*, shrubby orache, peganum, thyme-leaved sea heath and the wormwood *Artemisia herba-alba*, here parasitised by *Orobanche arenaria*; unlike the tough steppe grasses, they provide excellent grazing for sheep and cattle. Gypsum-loving communities cover large areas and include species such as *Gypsophila hispanica*, confined to central, southern and eastern Spain, and the pink-flowered restharrow *Ononis tridentata* and rock-rose *Helianthemum squamatum*, both of which are Afro-Iberian endemics.

In many gullies and endorheic areas, levels of salinity are so high that plants must be especially adapted to survive. A zonation of salt-tolerance sees purple glasswort, *Microcnemum coralloides* and shrubby sea-blite (whose ashes were once used for making bleach) in the most saline areas, grading into a belt of sea-lavenders, notably *Limonium latebracteatum*, and African tamarisk. Finally come communities of *Genista scorpius*, white flax, rosemary, sage and various thymes, all of which tend to avoid both gypsum and saline soils.

Belchite – particularly La Lomaza – is one of the best places in Spain to see the elusive Dupont's lark (800 pairs). Identify with care as short-toed, lesser short-toed and Thekla larks all nest in the same area; Dupont's will tend to run when approached, only flying at the last instant and popping back down to earth after a few metres. Both black-bellied (1000 pairs) and pin-tailed sandgrouse (800 pairs) also breed here, along with stone curlew (150 pairs), little bustard (80 pairs) and calandra lark which, unlike the other larks, prefers to feed in cultivated fields.

The Planerón lagoon is used by drinking sandgrouse in the mornings and – if water levels are sufficiently high – can hold black-winged stilt, other passage waders and wintering duck, with black-eared wheatear, spectacled warbler and southern grey shrike breeding in the environs. Golden eagle and Egyptian vulture nest on the cliffs that provide a backdrop to the area, and short-toed eagles – which breed in the pine forests further west – frequently hunt over the site.

Albardine
Lygeum spartum

Winter birdwatching is profitable: juvenile golden eagles use the area in dispersion, skylarks, lesser short-toed and calandra larks form large mixed flocks, and groups of sandgrouse feed in recently ploughed fields. Thekla and Dupont's larks also remain in the area in winter (but never form flocks), although by late October most little bustards have migrated to spend the winter in the warmer climes of central and western Spain.

Steppe environments are unsuitable for most amphibians, although the existence of a number of wells provides habitat for Iberian pool frog, natterjack toad and western spadefoot. Reptiles are much more in

Stone curlew *Burhinus oedicnemus* at nest (Peter Wilson)

El Planerón, Belchite (T.F.)

evidence, however, with Belchite renowned for its healthy populations of spiny-footed and ocellated lizards, large and Spanish psammodromus and southern smooth snake. Rabbits and Iberian hares are also abundant.

Access and information: La Lomaza abuts the A-222 Belchite–Mediana road to the east, about 9 km north of Belchite, where a small car park and information board marks the start of the recommended itinerary. The Planerón lagoon lies 2.9 km along the first of two tracks which head north 4.5 km and 5.4 km after the village of Codo, on the minor road northeast to Quinto. About 3.7 km beyond Codo, the road kinks past a small reedy pool which is good for penduline tit in winter (see map on p. 142). SEO/BirdLife runs an interpretation centre in the village of Belchite (tel: 976 830870, open at weekends and, if you phone ahead on 679 552090, midweek also). You are strongly recommended to visit this centre first for maps and detailed instructions on how best to explore Belchite's fragile habitats (permits are required for La Lomaza).

Also in the area

Old Belchite To the south of modern-day Belchite lies the old town, all but razed to the ground during the Spanish Civil War and untouched since. It can still be visited and is home to hoopoe, black wheatear, blue rock thrush, Sardinian and Dartford warblers and serin.

Limestone to the north of Puebla de Albortón The minor road which heads north to Valmadrid crosses a plant-rich area of limestone pavement, home to coris, *Phlomis lychnitis*, Spanish rusty foxglove, wild gladiolus, mirror ophrys and blue aphyllanthes in May, with Orphean warbler and woodchat shrike in the scattered junipers.

SITE 49 Laguna de Gallocanta

*Spain's largest natural waterbody – also the most extensive salt lake in Western Europe –
renowned as a winter staging post for migrating cranes.*

A dusk vigil on the shores of Gallocanta, waiting for as many as 60 000 cranes to fly in to roost, is a truly memorable wildlife experience. Crane numbers usually peak in the last week of November, but by mid-December the bulk have wandered off to southwest Spain for a couple of months of acorn-eating, leaving behind just a few thousand to endure the cruel Aragonese winter. By mid- to late February, numbers have swollen again, with the departure for breeding quarters in Scandinavia and Russia usually occurring before the end of the month.

Gallocanta (a *refugio de fauna silvestre*, Ramsar Site and ZEPA of 6720 ha) is a shallow lagoon lying 995 m above sea level in the midst of a 543 square-kilometre endorheic basin, subject to an arid continental climate that in many years fails to bring the rains needed to fill the lagoon. When the lake is full (1330 ha), bird numbers rocket; as in 1997 when 62 000 cranes (80% of the western European population) passed through Gallocanta, or in 1992 when 36 000 red-crested pochard and 72 000 pochard somehow crammed onto the open water.

The lagoon is ringed by a cordon of common reed, bulrush, lesser bulrush and common club-rush, while the patchwork grassland surrounding the lagoon boasts jointed rush and *Juncus fontanesii* in drier environments and purple glasswort, annual sea-blite and *Suaeda splendens* in more saline areas, along with extensive brackish beds of black bog-rush, sea rush and Borrer's saltmarsh-grass (subspecies *pungens*). The margins of the fresh streams that flow into the lagoon from the north harbour marshmallow, brooklime and yellow flag, with damp grasslands nearby coloured by the loosestrife *Lythrum thymifolia* and hoop-petticoat daffodil.

Underwater feeders such as pochard and coot predominate when the lagoon is full, feeding on submerged 'meadows' of *Potamogeton, Groenlandia, Zannichellia*

Laguna de Gallocanta

Crane *Grus grus*

and *Ruppia*, and the beds of the charophytes *Chara galioides* and foxtail stonewort which carpet the lake bottom. Otherwise, dabbling duck such as wigeon, shoveler, pintail, teal, gadwall and mallard are the commonest wildfowl.

In winter, the stubble of the cereal fields around the lagoon is alive with thousand-strong mixed flocks of tree and rock sparrows, chaffinch, serin, linnet, goldfinch and greenfinch. Meadow pipits and a few water pipits feed along the water's edge, reed buntings flit amongst the reeds and calandra larks form monospecific flocks of 100+ individuals. Amid this passerine profusion, keep your eyes peeled for chough and flocks of 30+ black-bellied sandgrouse, especially on the southwestern side of the lagoon. Inevitably such bounty attract predators; merlin, peregrine and the occasional short-eared owl or juvenile golden eagle hunt the fields, while marsh and hen harriers ply the lagoon's shores.

When water is present, wader passage in spring and autumn is significant, the principal species being snipe, dunlin, little stint, curlew and redshank. Avocet, black-winged stilt and gull-billed and whiskered terns will breed if the lagoon is full enough to create safe islands, but Kentish plovers, on the other hand, need large areas of exposed mud. Stone curlews and short-toed lark are common in the basin, although the 10 pairs or so of little bustards are harder to track down (try around the cross-roads of the A-211 and A-2506). The area is also attractive to great bustards (3–4 nests each year), with more arriving in late summer from neighbouring areas, although all have disappeared by mid-November.

In summer, the water's edge is teeming with Iberian pool frogs, and you might also encounter painted and parsley frogs, western spadefoot and viperine snake. Iberian wall lizards abound, especially around buildings, while ocellated lizard and large psammodromus lurk in scrubby habitats.

Access and information: Parties of cranes may be scattered all around the Gallocanta basin; the network of muddy tracks around the lagoon *can* be driven, but try to disturb foraging birds as little as possible; retreat if they stop feeding and look up. Some days, however, all the cranes leave the basin and disappear in straggly flocks to feed elsewhere, returning only at dusk. The SEO/BirdLife information centre at the southeastern end of the lagoon (tel: 978 725004) can inform you as to which end of the lagoon the cranes will enter at dusk. Night-time temperatures in winter can drop to a rather alarming –20°C! Be sure to visit the Allucant ornithological hostel in the village of Gallocanta for up-to-date information about the area (tel: 976 803137; fax: 976 803090; website: www.gallocanta.com).

Also in the area

Laguna de Guialguerrero A small permanent lagoon hidden away to the north-west of the main lagoon with garganey on passage and breeding black-necked grebe and red-crested pochard in some years. From the cross-roads of the A-211 and

A-2506, drive north towards Cubel and after 12.3 km take a track which cuts back right towards Guialguerrero in 1.8 km.

Also northwest of Gallocanta, you can walk from the village of Torralba de los Frailes down into the **gorge of the Río Piedra**, home to griffon vulture, peregrine, crag martin, rock thrush and rock bunting.

SEO/BirdLife has recently established a reserve at **Mas de Cirugeda** (ZEPA of 800 ha) about 45 km north of Teruel: an area harbouring one of the highest densities of Dupont's lark in the peninsula, also renowned botanically for the chenopod *Ceratoides latens*, in Spain confined to the Ebro Depression, and the crucifer *Vella pseudocytisus*, endemic to central and southern Spain. Includes a *páramo* covered in hedgehog broom, low calcareous cliffs and riverine forest along the Río Alfambra. Home to Egyptian vulture, Montagu's harrier, stone curlew, a few great bustards, black-bellied sandgrouse, eagle owl and blue rock and rock thrushes. Signposted east off the N-420 between Perales de Alfambra and the turn-off to Fuentes Calientes.

SITE 50 Sierra de Javalambre

One of Europe's most renowned botanical localities, as yet unprotected; around 50 000 ha of rolling calcareous and siliceous uplands harbouring many endemic plants and a rich butterfly fauna.

The upper slopes of the large domed massif of Javalambre boast a wonderfully diverse relict flora, stranded when the ice sheets retreated from the Iberian peninsula at the end of the Pleistocene. A number of plants such as *Sideritis javalambrensis* have evolved into true local endemics, while others, notably hairy stonecrop (*Sedum villosum* subspecies *nevadense*) and vitaliana (*Vitaliana primuliflora* subspecies *assoana*), survive as isolated populations, well separated from nuclei in other European mountain areas.

Plant-hunters and birdwatchers should visit in early June and wind lazily up the road towards the ski-station and then on to the spectacular cushion communities on the summit of Javalambre itself (2020 m). En route, the overgrazed stony hillsides boast only a sparse scrub of prickly and Phoenician junipers and stunted western holm oaks, coloured by *Thalictrum tuberosum*, *Euphorbia serrata*, beautiful flax, common lavender, blue aphyllanthes and common grape hyacinth. Conical orchids are scattered throughout at the beginning of the season, followed by woodcock ophrys and bug orchid (subspecies *fragrans*).

The typical birds of these open slopes are tawny pipit, stonechat, wheatear and black-eared wheatear, with subalpine warbler and cirl bunting in small patches of trees and rock sparrow around abandoned buildings. Flower-rich habitats hold many colourful spring butterflies, in particular swallowtail and scarce swallowtail, Spanish festoon, Moroccan orange tip, green hairstreak and black-eyed blue. Ocellated lizards are particularly common at lower altitudes, with smooth snake close to the southern edge of its range in higher terrain; Javalambre also hosts an isolated population of the painted frog *Discoglossus jeanneae*.

At length you enter the pine forests. Here *Pinus nigra* subspecies *salzmannii* gradually gives way with altitude to dense stands of

Scots pine, sheltering a plethora of sword-leaved and red helleborines. Apart from the usual birds of Spanish pinewoods – firecrest, crested and coal tits, short-toed treecreeper and crossbill – Javalambre hosts a good population of citril finch, which can often be seen feeding by the road in the quietest part of the forest. As the pines thin out, more flowers appear: hunt around under the smaller trees for *Paeonia officinalis* subspecies *microcarpa*, and out in the open for mats of mountain tragacanth plus perennial cornflower and wild tulip.

Above the ski-station the road leads gently up to a massive undulating plateau, where dark, straggling patches of savin dapple the terrain as far as the eye can see. These low mats provide refuge for less hardy plants such as *Geum heterocarpum*, *Erodium celtibericum* (endemic to southeastern Spain), alpine skullcap and several Javalambre endemics, notably *Oxytropis jabalambrensis*, *Sideritis javalambrensis* and *Veronica tenuifolia* subspecies *javalambrensis*. Pride of place, however, must go to the bright yellow cushions of vitaliana (subspecies *assoana*) which clothe the northern flank of the summit, just below the TV repeater station.

Fewer birds are found at these heights, with tawny pipit, wheatear and linnet the commonest species, although rock sparrows call insistently from the repeater station, and prominent outcrops should be examined for perching rock thrushes. Short-toed eagles hunt over any open area for the abundant common wall lizards, and golden eagles likewise are not an unusual sight at altitude.

Early July sees the greatest butterfly diversity on the wing, with marbled, lesser marbled and twin-spot fritillaries all flying in flowery areas over 1000 m; Oberthür's and Ripart's anomalous blues – thus called because both the males and females of these 'blues' are brown – and Damon, Amanda's and Zephyr blues are all a possibility. Zapater's ringlet, one of the few true Iberian endemic butterflies and – like much of the flora – an ice-age relict species, flies from late July into September in clearings in the pine forests up to 1650 m. The spring ringlet is on the wing by late March, with a distinct form of the Apollo (subspecies *hispanicus*) flying later in the year.

Access: The road up to the summit – initially the TEV-6006 to Camarena de la Sierra – turns southwest off the main N-234 Teruel–Sagunt road, 23 km southeast of Teruel.

Wild tulip *Tulipa sylvestris* subspecies *australis*

Also in the area

To the west, Javalambre overlooks the **Rincón de Ademuz**: an isolated mountainous enclave of the País Valencià sandwiched between Aragón and Castilla–La Mancha. Along the CV-478 between Ademuz and Negrón look for tawny pipit, all three Iberian wheatears, both rock thrushes and corn, rock, cirl and ortolan buntings. The gorge of the river Bohigas below Vallanca holds otter, wryneck, nightingale, Cetti's warbler and golden oriole, plus stripe-necked terrapin and white-clawed crayfish. The road from Ademuz to Puebla de San Miguel (CV-363) has glorious spring butterflies: scarce swallowtail, Berger's clouded yellow, green-underside and Zephyr blues, Provençal and marsh fritillaries and western marbled white. From Puebla de San Miguel the PR-131-6 footpath leads to Las Blancas – an area populated by enormous Spanish junipers – and then to a floral micro-reserve on Pico Calderón (1839 m), with savin, the delicate *Dianthus costae* (endemic to eastern Spain), *Paeonia officinalis* subspecies *microcarpa*, *Coronilla minima* and more vitaliana (subspecies *assoana*).

Catalunya

Catalunya

Introduction

In landscape terms, Catalunya is incredibly varied. Western, continental Catalunya is a natural continuation of neighbouring Aragón and so a north–south transect passes through a similar succession of 3000 m peaks, forests, limestone gorges and arid plains with comparable floral and faunal communities. Further east, however, as the influence of the Mediterranean becomes apparent, a diversity of coastal habitats confers on Catalunya (along with Andalucía) the distinction of possessing a greater variety of wildlife than anywhere else in the peninsula.

The high Catalan Pyrenees are almost exclusively composed of granites and shales, providing the perfect substratum for a mass of glacial lakes, especially well represented in Catalunya's only national park: Aigüestortes i Estany de Sant Maurici. European silver-fir forests predominate, particularly at the Mata de València, while notable calcifuge flowering plants include geranium-like, rough and water saxifrages, all Pyrenean endemics. As in Aragón, chamois and the introduced Alpine marmot are common at altitude, while Catalunya also holds the Iberian peninsula's only breeding dotterel and sand lizards. Pyrenean populations of the Iberian rock lizard are nowadays considered as three separate and endemic species: the Pyrenean rock lizard (*Lacerta bonnali*), found above 1800 m throughout much of Aragón and northwest Catalunya, and *L. aurelioi* and *L. aranica*, both confined to small areas in the eastern Pyrenees.

Further south, the pre-Pyrenean ridges – for example, the Montsec and the Cadí – closely resemble their Aragonese counterparts, above all in terms of breeding raptors and fissure-plant communities. The arid interior plains of the Central Catalan Depression lack the sheer vastness of the Aragonese Monegros and much habitat is being lost to large-scale irrigation projects. Nevertheless, the remaining areas of dry farmland around Lleida still support little bustard, both sandgrouse, roller and the world's most westerly lesser grey shrikes.

Maritime Catalunya – the coastal strip and inland areas influenced by moist sea breezes – is surprisingly well wooded, despite the ravages of the tourist industry. In the northeast, beech, deciduous oaks and cork oak forests thrive near the coast in the Albera massif, which is also home to Catalunya's greatest diversity of herptiles: Hermann's tortoises and painted frogs, found nowhere else in the peninsula, occur here in close proximity to Aesculapian and western whip snakes, whose Iberian distribution is limited to the extreme north.

Travelling south along the Serra Prelitoral – a discontinuous jumble of limestone and calcareous conglomerate ridges running roughly parallel to the coast – you eventually reach the Ports de Beseit: the easternmost outlier of the Sistema Ibérico and home to a healthy population of Spanish ibex. En route, you by-pass Montserrat, Sant Llorenç del Munt and many limestone escarpments in Tarragona: a classic habitat for Bonelli's eagle and blue rock thrush. Frequent forest fires have left many areas covered in open garrigue formations, rich in spring butterflies and orchids such as Bertoloni's ophrys. Thickly wooded exceptions are the Muntanyes de Prades in Tarragona province, home to Catalunya's only Pyrenean oak woodland, the 1706 m granite and gneiss massif of the Montseny, and the Iberian peninsula's most extensive volcanic landscape in the Garrotxa.

The coast itself exhibits a mixture of tourist sprawl around Barcelona and

Catalunya

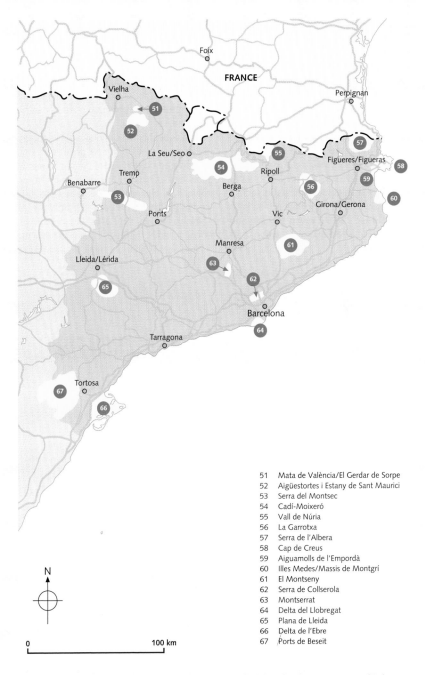

Foix

FRANCE

Vielha
Perpignan

51

52

La Seu/Seo
55
57
Figueres/Figueras
58

54
Ripoll
56
59

Tremp
Berga
60

Benabarre
53
Girona/Gerona

Ponts
Vic

Manresa
61

Lleida/Lérida
63

62

65
Barcelona

64

Tarragona

Tortosa
67

66

51	Mata de València/El Gerdar de Sorpe
52	Aigüestortes i Estany de Sant Maurici
53	Serra del Montsec
54	Cadí-Moixeró
55	Vall de Núria
56	La Garrotxa
57	Serra de l'Albera
58	Cap de Creus
59	Aiguamolls de l'Empordà
60	Illes Medes/Massis de Montgrí
61	El Montseny
62	Serra de Collserola
63	Montserrat
64	Delta del Llobregat
65	Plana de Lleida
66	Delta de l'Ebre
67	Ports de Beseit

N

0   100 km

Tarragona – with the Llobregat delta an honourable exception – and contrastingly well-preserved northern and southern extremes. To the north, the rugged Cap de Creus exemplifies the Costa Brava, and is home to such essentially Balearic plants as tree spurge and cneorum, while the low-lying Empordà plain comprises a pleasant mixture of marshland and dry-farmland, with pride of place going to the Aiguamolls wetland: a vitally important staging-post for birds migrating along the Mediterranean flyway. At the southern extreme lies the enormous, arrow-shaped Ebro delta: Spain's second most important wetland for birds, home to outstanding heron colonies plus breeding glossy ibis, Audouin's and slender-billed gulls and many terns.

Catalunya has seven *parcs naturals*, and a growing network of visitor centres; the official website – www.parcsdecatalunya.net – contains a wealth of information. The 1990s saw the birth of two Catalan NGOs whose aim, almost for the first time in the peninsu-

la, is to acquire land or land rights as a tool for nature conservation. The Fundació Natura is active in the Plana de Lleida and the conservation of the capercaillie in the Pyrenees, while the Fundació Territori i Paisatge runs a state-of-the-art sustainable development interpretation centre near the Aigüestortes national park.

Català is the first language of Catalunya (with dialects of this spoken in the País Valencià and the Balears), but most people also speak Castilian Spanish. Many major roads in Catalunya were renumbered in 2001 and may differ on the ground from those on the 2000 edition of the Michelin map; in the texts the old numbering appears in brackets.

SITE 51 Mata de València/ El Gerdar de Sorpe

The largest (around 1000 ha) and best-preserved European silver-fir forests on the southern flank of the Pyrenees, home to Tengmalm's owl and many saprophytic plants.

In the Catalan Pyrenees, European silver-fir forests develop mainly on north-facing slopes between 1400 and 1900 m, giving way to mountain pine at higher altitudes. La Mata de València is a mass of pure fir with a ground flora composed largely of mosses, but neighbouring El Gerdar has been repeatedly damaged by avalanches, opening large clearings which offer more light for pioneer plants and butterflies. A waymarked trail following the left bank of the river Cabanes takes you uphill through El Gerdar, and then back down through La Mata on the opposite bank.

The first plants to establish themselves in the clearings in El Gerdar are common nettle, raspberry (El Gerdar means 'the raspberry patch'), wild strawberry and woodruff. With time, shrubs such as rock redcurrant, bilberry and red-berried elder appear, to be

replaced gradually by a mixed deciduous woodland of aspen, goat willow and silver birch, which later gives way to the climax forest of European silver-fir. The margins of the river Cabanes are choked with megaforb communities of the robust umbellifers sweet cicely and hairy chervil, plus *Scrophularia alpestris*, Pyrenean valerian and adenostyles.

A dawn or dusk vigil at the edge of one of the clearings is the best way to track down the abundant wild boar which leave their calling-cards in the form of large areas of churned-up ground. Chamois also come down to feed here, with red, roe and fallow (introduced) deer also present in the forest, although in no great numbers. Another prize is the black woodpecker: a bird that you are sure to hear during the breeding season and which, with patience, should appear some-

Wild boar *Sus scrofa*

where along the route. Typical passerines of the clearings include tree pipit, wren, dunnock and robin, with firecrest, goldcrest, crested, marsh and coal tits and both treecreepers on the forest edge.

In high summer, El Gerdar's woodland glades are alive with butterflies. Camberwell beauties patrol up and down, mountain ringlets keep closer to the ground and basking male scarce coppers compete in showiness with a myriad fritillaries: Queen of Spain, shepherd's, lesser marbled, pearl-bordered, false heath and meadow. Other common species include clouded Apollo, Esper's marbled white, autumn ringlet, chestnut and pearly heaths and Idas and Mazarine blues.

Beyond the first major clearing, the path enters an open formation of mountain pine with an understorey of alpenrose and plenty of common and serrated wintergreens. Once over a jumbled boulder chaos, the path then enters another large clearing, crosses the river and divides, the right-hand branch continuing up the Cabanes valley, the left-hand option taking you back downhill and into the depth of La Mata. Take time

out here to look for raptors over the ridge: a pair of golden eagles breeds in the vicinity, while lammergeier and griffon vulture are regular visitors.

Before entering the gloom of La Mata, check the massive limestone boulders along the path for clumps of the calcicolous blue saxifrage. Here, too, more open areas are carpeted with alpine pasque flowers in spring, to be replaced later in the year by yellow monk's-hood, *Aconitum vulparia* subspecies *neapolitanum*, wood saxifrage and martagon lily. Once in La Mata proper, saprophytic plants come into their own; yellow bird's-nest is common, especially lower down around the river, although bird's-nest orchids are more sporadic, but the real prize here is the ghost orchid, recently found close to the path and only known from three other sites in the Iberian peninsula.

The path winds down gently through La Mata, where capercaillie and black woodpeckers show themselves occasionally, woodcock can be heard roding on summer evenings and Tengmalm's owls breed … somewhere. Once at the bottom of the path, a wooden bridge takes you back over the river and a short climb leads back to your starting point.

Access: Turn left to 'El Gerdar' about 8 km north of València d'Àneu on the C-28 (C-1412), and park on the right-hand hairpin bend just after the refuge. Follow wooden stakes with yellow paint up a steep track that narrows eventually into a pleasant path.

Also in the area

Val d'Aran A small part of Catalunya lying north of the main Pyrenean axis with an appropriately more Atlantic feel to its flora and fauna. The valley haymeadows and mixed pedunculate and sessile oak woods of the Toran valley (Canejan–Pradet) – all but in France – house

Catalunya's only middle spotted woodpeckers, and butterflies which include silvery argus, the only Catalan purple emperors, northern wall brown and large chequered skipper. The mixed beech and fir forests of the Artiga de Lin valley (south of Es Bòrdes) have creeping lady's tresses, while the peatbogs of the Tredòs valley – some of the most diverse in Europe – boast aconite-leaved and amplexicaule buttercups, round-leaved and great sundews, water avens, bogbean, lousewort, alpine bartsia, lesser bladderwort and Tofield's asphodel. The lizard *Lacerta aranica* is known only from here.

SITE 52 Aigüestortes i Estany de Sant Maurici

*Catalunya's only national park, comprising a vast area of rugged granite landscape dotted with glacial lakes (*estanys*) and boasting a splendid alpine flora and fauna.*

A walk up the Escrita valley from the village of Espot takes you through all the major habitats present in the Aigüestortes national park (14 119 ha, plus 26 733 ha buffer zone; part ZEPA), including the high-level rocky wilderness dotted by the greatest concentration of lakes anywhere in the Iberian peninsula: 272 in all.

Three kilometres above Espot the road into the park is closed to traffic (except taxis) and an information point signals the start of the *Ruta dels Isards*: a trail that follows the river Escrita up to the glacial lake known as the Estany de Sant Maurici (1929 m). At first the path traverses dense European silver-fir forest, harbouring black woodpecker, firecrest, crested and marsh tits, both treecreepers and bullfinch, plus, in higher areas, capercaillie, woodcock and Tengmalm's owl. In the oldest part of the forest, the firs drip with *Usnea* lichens, while large patches of the mosses *Hylocomium splendens* and *Mnium spinosum* sprawl across the forest floor.

On the north side of the river, clumps of Scots pine, silver birch and hazel form a mosaic with carpets of common juniper, Pyrenean broom and ling, interspersed with numerous haymeadows. Whinchat, red-backed shrike and rock bunting are the char-

acteristic birds here, plus a phenomenal diversity of butterflies including clouded Apollo and large blue, while the river harbours Pyrenean desman and dipper.

Once up at the Estany de Sant Maurici, where the twin calcareous rock spires of Els Encantats tower over the lake, the track continues northwest towards the delightful Estany Ratera (2100 m), passing through sparse mountain pine forest with an understorey of dwarf juniper, wild cotoneaster, bilberry and alpenrose, many plants of the latter decorated by white spherical galls caused by the fungus *Exobasidium rhododendri*. Apollos float lazily across clearings in summer, in the company of scarce, sooty, purple-shot and purple-edged coppers, silvery argus and Mazarine and Idas blues. Groups of crossbills 'chip-chip' overhead, siskins are present in varying numbers according to the year's pine-cone crop, and neither citril finches nor ring ouzels are uncommon. Keep an eye on the high ridges of Pui Pla to the north, which is one of the likeliest places for cruising lammergeier, griffon vulture or golden eagle.

Common wall lizards occur up to about 2000 m, but the extreme heights are undoubtedly the domain of the Pyrenean rock lizard, which sometimes attains altitudes of almost 3000 m. You may come

Estany de Sant Maurici

across green lizards in sunnier areas, or perhaps smooth and western whip snakes or asp, while viviparous lizards abound in more humid habitats.

Whereas the deep, high-level *estanys* are almost abiotic, the lower, shallower lakes such as Ratera – ringed by belts of bottle sedge and bladder-sedge and partially covered by the leaves of floating bur-reed – are far more hospitable environments. Male white-faced darters take up territories here in July, while Pyrenean brook salamander and common frog occupy the shallows. Boggy areas, often dominated by common cottongrass and Davall's and common sedges, are coloured by the pink-flowered hairy stonecrop, grass-of-Parnassus, marsh violet, marsh felwort, common and large-flowered butterworts, Tofield's asphodel and broad-leaved marsh orchid.

Well-grazed pastures are dotted with clumps of great yellow gentian, Pyrenean lily and English iris, all unpalatable to cattle, while typical megaforb communities in wetter areas include the highly toxic monk's-hood, yellow monk's-hood and *Aconitum vulparia* subspecies *neapoli-*

tanum, plus Pyrenean valerian, adenostyles and white false helleborine, with lush clumps of water saxifrage decorating the many rushing streams.

Once above Estany Ratera, the track continues up beyond the tree-line into a vast expanse of alpine pasture and bare rock. *Festuca eskia* – accompanied by Pyrenean buttercup, alpine clover, spignel and *Campanula scheuchzeri* – dominates the acid pastures around Estany Amitges and the Amitges mountain hut (2345 m), while woody plants are represented by stunted bushes of the pink-flowered false medlar and mats of bog bilberry (subspecies *microphyllum*). Tucked away in the extensive areas of rock chaos are holly-fern, parsley fern, mountain male-fern and alpine lady-fern, interspersed with lesser masterwort, *Gentiana burseri* and Tournefort's ragwort in more humid habitats.

Beyond the Amitges hut the landscape is characterised by glacial cirques, separated by spectacular *arêtes* (narrow crests) and *agulles* (rock needles). The Agulles d'Amitges is a good area for wallcreeper and almost any high-level walk should turn up chamois, alpine marmot, water pipit, alpine accentor, alpine chough and, just possibly, ptarmigan. Butterflies at this altitude include mountain clouded yellow, peak white and common brassy, Spanish brassy, Gavarnie and Piedmont ringlets. Make the effort to track down white musky, mossy and scented-leaved saxifrages and the delicate, rock-hugging cushions of the rock-jasmine *Androsace vandellii*, plus moss campion, alpine butter-cup, chamois cress and woolly clumps of *Potentilla nivalis*. Highest of all – for example on Tuc de Ratera (2857 m) – grow pink rock jasmine and southern gentian.

> *Access and information*: Park informa-tion centres exist in Espot (tel. and fax: 973 624036) and Boi (tel: 973 696189; fax: 973 696154); general e-mail enquiries to aiguestortes@mma.es) Visitor pressure is very high at week-ends and in July and August. From Espot many people take 4WD taxis as far as Sant Maurici and walk from there; these start at 9.00 am, departing when full; to leave earlier, make a pri-vate arrangement with a driver.

53 Serra del Montsec

A typically varied pre-Pyrenean ridge with an important population of otter, plus breeding vultures and a rich limestone fissure flora.

The Serra del Montsec (maximum 1684 m) in fact comprises three contiguous ridges run-ning from west to east – d'Estall, d'Ares and de Rúbies – all with dramatic, south-facing limestone cliffs. A good starting point for the visiting naturalist is the delightful Àger valley on the southern side of the Montsec d'Ares, where the gently sloping valley floor – filled with olive and almond groves and extensive

cereal cultivation – contrasts with the abrupt, wooded crags to the north. Scops owls breed around the village of Àger itself, while quail, bee-eater, southern grey and woodchat shrikes and golden oriole are common in the valley bottom.

From Àger take the broad track north off the road past the cemetery, turning left after 200 m to reach the high windswept crest. The

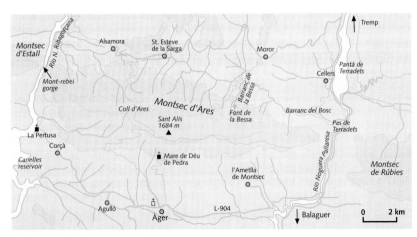

Catalunya

highest areas are carpeted with bristly cushions of hedgehog broom, accompanied by mountain kidney-vetch, white and hoary rock roses, common lavender and matted globularia. Of note here is an outlying population of the Pyrenean endemic tufted soapwort, accompanied by more commonplace species such as lesser meadow-rue, *Pulsatilla rubra*, *Narcissus palearensis* (recently separated from the common jonquil), star-of-Bethlehem, wild tulip and St Bernard's lily. Alternatively, a right turn after the cemetery leads to the Mare de Déu de Pedra: a white chapel set amid rocky slopes halfway up the main ridge, where a late May visit should turn up black wheatear and rock and blue rock thrushes, with mother-of-pearl blues – one of the peninsula's scarcer lycaenids – basking on the track.

The fabulous Mont-rebei gorge – declared a *reserva natural parcial* to protect one of Catalunya's best populations of otter – borders the Montsec d'Ares to the west and can be walked on a remarkable path, roughly hewn from the cliff face above the river Noguera Ribagorçana. To get there, follow the road from Àger to Corçà, from which village the track passes through olive groves interspersed with a sun-drenched garrigue of prickly and Phoenician junipers, holly oak, lentisc, wild jasmine and rosemary, interspersed with clumps of blue aphyllanthes. Further on, shady gullies harbour St Lucie's cherry, snowy mespilus, Montpellier maple, strawberry-tree (a relict population in the Montsec), *Phillyrea angustifolia* and laurustinus.

Each successive shady rock face is studded with ramonda, whereas sunny crags hold sarcocapnos and the delicately pale soft snapdragon, endemic to the pre-Pyrenees. Further along, *Petrocoptis montsicciana*, unique to the Montsec (best in April) and just one neighbouring ridge, appears under overhangs, along with smooth rock spleenwort, many splendid spikes of Pyrenean saxifrage and fairy foxglove. Keep an eye out for Moroccan orange tip and Provence chalk-hill and Adonis blues in spring, plus dusky heath and possibly Catalan furry blue (probably synonymous with Agenjo's anomalous blue) and

Mont-rebei (M.L.)

mountain small white in early summer. Birds include crag martin, subalpine and Sardinian warblers and rock bunting.

The trail eventually drops down (via an old farmhouse with a permanent spring) to the narrow jaws of the gorge itself. Two immense rock faces guard the entrance to Mont-rebei, the western wall home to around 15 pairs of griffon vulture, 2 of Egyptian vulture and the peninsula's most southerly pair of lammergeiers, as well as golden eagle, peregrine, eagle owl, alpine swift, blue rock thrush and chough. Booted eagles wander through from their breeding sites on the north side of the ridge, while wallcreepers are regular outside the breeding season; there are often a few alpine choughs mixed in with the clouds of 'red-billed' choughs.

Once through the gorge, you emerge onto the gentler northern slopes of the Montsec, thickly clothed with western holm oak and *Quercus cerrioides* up to about 1000 m, and then with downy oak and Scots pine to around 1400 m. Italian maple, whitebeam, large-leaved lime, beech and aspen appear in the moister gullies, along with eye-

Catalunya

Àger, Serra del Montsec

catching clumps of alpine pasque flower, *Aquilegia hirsutissima* (on screes), *Paeonia officinalis* subspecies *microcarpa*, *Saxifraga fragilis* subspecies *fragilis*, martagon lily and greater and lesser butterfly orchids. These forests also harbour one of the peninsula's most southerly populations of pine marten, living side-by-side with red squirrel, Eurasian badger, common genet, wildcat and wild boar.

The Terradets gorge borders the Montsec d'Ares to the east, secreting in its depths the Barranc del Bosc, a dramatic gully whose dry slopes are clothed with orlaya (a tall umbellifer), St Bernard's lily and yellow garlic in spring. The extra moisture trapped in the narrow defile maintains a veritable thicket of holm oak (as opposed to the *west-*

ern holm oak found in the rest of the area), strawberry-tree, *Phillyrea angustifolia* and laurustinus, while the base of the small cliffs is excellent for close-up views of all the fissure plants so often out of camera range in the Mont-rebei gorge.

Access: The northern slopes of the Montsec d'Ares can be reached off the minor road linking the C-13 (C-147) north of the Pas de Terradets with Alsamora. The Barranc del Bosc can be walked via a small path (signposted) just before the first tunnel (coming from Balaguer) on the C-13 (C-147).

Also in the area

Pantà de Terradets Reservoir to the east of Cellers, with a well-developed reedbed; home to otter and breeding great reed warbler and purple heron, plus osprey on passage. A small hide, set up by Fundació Natura, is situated just north of the large Hostal del Llac on the C-13 (C-147).

Pantà de Sant Llorenç de Montgai (*reserva natural de fauna salvatge*; 468 ha) Another reservoir, to the south of the Montsec; has breeding purple heron, while cliffs in the area are a regular haunt of Bonelli's eagle. Dragonflies include *Trithemis annulata* in late summer, a species which has spread into the Iberian peninsula from Africa since the 1980s.

54 Cadí–Moixeró

An imposing pre-Pyrenean limestone ridge peaking at 2647 m (Puig de la Canal Baridana/Cristal) with sheer north-facing cliffs and a rich flora and butterfly fauna.

A full month would barely be enough time to do justice to the Cadí–Moixeró (*parc natural* and ZEPA, 41 342 ha), so the following are just two of the many possible wildlife itineraries in the park. On the northern flank, the most satisfying route is a moderate two-hour walk from the village of Estana (1500 m) to the beautiful subalpine pasture of the Prat de Cadí (1820 m) at the base of the sheer cliffs and screes of the main Cadí ridge, while on the south side of the Moixeró ridge, a good metalled road leads from the village of Bagà to the Coll de Pal (2110 m), characterised by extensive grasslands and limestone outcrops.

Around Estana in summer, butterfly watchers will delight in a mosaic of habitats which boasts sloe hairstreak on the blackthorn just below the village, Apollo and Esper's marbled whites in and around the meadows, black satyr in clearings in the Scots pine forest, and lycaenids such as Amanda's, Chapman's, Adonis and Baton blues. In early July try to find a flowering bank of danewort, often by the side of a track, as this species acts as a magnet for nectaring white-letter hairstreaks and many coppers and fritillaries (especially marbled).

The final stretch of the walk up to the Prat de Cadí passes through dense mountain pine and European silver-fir woodland where the calls of black woodpecker resound in spring. Three pairs of Tengmalm's owls nest here and for a complete gamut of the forest's passerines – Bonelli's warbler, chiffchaff, firecrest, goldcrest, crested tit, short-toed treecreeper, crossbill, siskin and citril finch – continue to the *prat* itself and walk the perimeter of the pasture. Up towards the base of the cliffs to the south is the best area for woodcock and capercaillie, and the nearer the cliffs the better for wallcreeper or views of lammergeier, golden eagle and alpine chough cruising the ridge above.

In the drier forests around the Prat de Cadí, mountain pines shelter carpets of alpine pasque flower in early spring, while in

Ramonda *Ramonda myconi*

more humid gullies European silver-firs harbour an understorey of alpenrose and bilberry, four wintergreens – pale-green, common, serrated and one-flowered – plus purple lettuce and purple colt's-foot. The *prat* itself is ablaze with white crocus and spring bulbocodium by mid-April, followed by spring and trumpet gentians and Pyrenean snakeshead until the hungry cattle arrive in June. Look out for alpine snowbell around persistent snow patches, while globeflowers and early marsh orchids colour the damper parts of the meadow around the spring to the south.

Limestone fern, alpine buckthorn and dark-red helleborine grow on the consolidated screes at the back of the Prat de Cadí, while further up – in areas of greater gradient and smaller rock size – look out for powerfully rooted species such as *Aquilegia hirsutissima* and xatardia, an umbellifer endemic to the eastern Pyrenees with short, thick stems and very unequal rays. Higher still, parnassus-leaved buttercup, purple saxifrage, mountain avens and garland flower appear, while Pyrenean saxifrage, ramonda and Pyrenean honeysuckle cling to the cliffs (a small limestone outcrop hidden in the woods to the west of the scree saves a lot of climbing).

For the second itinerary, take the quiet road which winds up from Bagà in the eastern sector of the park, which leads to a charming area of subalpine grassland above the tree-line. As the first pastures appear, stop by a mountain hut on the right and check the ridge to the north for lammergeier, griffon vulture, golden eagle, peregrine and both choughs, with rock thrush, ring ouzel and citril finch often seen at the base of the cliffs. Escher's, Eros and turquoise blues fly over the pastures, where botanists will find cushions of the white-flowered alchemilla-leaved cinquefoil, mountain kidney-vetch, Pyrenean golden drop, the cream-flowered crested lousewort, spiked speedwell and stemless cotton-thistle. Limestone outcrops in the area should be examined for Pyrenean saxifrage and ramonda.

At the Coll de Pal, where Pyrenean thistles crowd the disturbed verges, walk west up the grassy slope to Coma Floriu for a wonderful view of the north face of the Moixeró ridge. Water pipits, wheatears and common brassy and mountain ringlets accompany you on the climb, through pastures dotted with mountain tragacanth (subspecies *catalaunicus*), alpine forget-me-not, mountain everlasting and vanilla and greater butterfly orchids. Rocky outcrops here have common houseleek, dark stonecrop, the rock-jasmine *Androsace ciliata*, alpine skullcap and *Globularia repens*.

From Coma Floriu, where Pyrenean gentians colour the close-cropped turf, walk 200 m south to low limestone outcrops for purple, livelong, hairy and the rare reddish saxifrage, as well as moss campion, mountain avens and *Potentilla nivalis*. Alternatively, pick up a narrow path which contours northwards, leading eventually to the cliffs below Tossa d'Alp (2536 m): an area frequented by chamois, alpine accentor, rock thrush and wallcreeper.

It is possible to walk to the top of Tossa d'Alp, although most visitors prefer to take the *telecabina* from the La Molina ski-station, which drops you just 100 m below the summit. Peak white, Glandon blue and Lefèbvre's ringlet await those who make the final ascent, as well as a rich limestone flora including parnassus-leaved buttercup, Pyrenean whitlow-grass, spoon-leaved candytuft, reddish saxifrage, mountain avens, yellow milk-vetch, alpine toadflax and the lovely yellow genipi.

Information: The park information centre is in Bagà, just west of the C-1411/E-9 Barcelona–Puigcerdà road (tel: 93 8244151; fax: 93 8244312; e-mail: cadi-moixero@mixmail.com). In summer, the La Molina *telecabina* normally runs only for part of July and August (tel: 972 892164 for exact dates).

Also in the area

Other nearby areas to explore include **Puigpedrós** (on the French border; 2914 m) for ptarmigan, dotterel (the only breeding locality in Spain) and screes studded with white musky and geranium-like saxifrages, plus the **Segre Valley near Prats de Cerdanya** (via Sanavastre) for otter, lesser purple emperor, map butterfly and odonates. Mountain Alcon blues and bright-eyed ringlets are not uncommon in abandoned meadows (with meadow clary and cross gentian) on the south side of the Segre above 1000 m, while Pyrenean brook salamanders abound in the mid-course of any of the gullies running north down from the Cadí. At the peaty **Clot de l'Orri**, above the Cap del Rec mountain hut (1980 m, north of Lles), botanists can expect carpets of Pyrenean gentian, as well as bog bilberry, alpine bartsia and common and large-flowered butterworts, with surrounding acid rock outcrops harbouring the yellow-flowered subspecies (*apiifolia*) of alpine pasque flower, mountain houseleek, the scarce rough saxifrage, tight pincushions of the rock-jasmine *Androsace vandelii* and Pyrenean lily.

SITE

55 Vall de Núria

An isolated eastern Pyrenean valley surrounded by peaks of over 2800 m, harbouring a rich flora of both acid and calcareous bedrock and typical high-level birds and butterflies.

For many years the delightful Vall de Núria – inaccessible by road – has been an obligatory destination for Catalan walkers. A rack-and-pinion railway deposits you at almost 2000 m by a small ski-complex and the not-so-small Santuari de Núria, from where you can either walk back down through the gorge of the river Núria to the village of Queralbs or head for the high surrounding peaks which culminate in Puigmal (2910 m).

Pyrenean lily
Lilium pyrenaicum

Especially recommended is the walk towards Puigmal via the large glacial cirque of Coma de l'Embut. Soon after leaving the Santuari, the last mountain pines – and with them the last ring ouzels, crossbills and citril finches – disappear, giving way to rocky pastures studded with alpine clover, pyramidal bugle, hyssop-leaved sideritis, alpine aster and vanilla orchid. South-facing slopes are ablaze with yellow Pyrenean broom and deep-pink alpenrose in summer, interspersed with robust clumps of the yellow-flowered molopospermum.

These slopes are home to a well-established population of around 300 mouflon, an ancestor of the domestic sheep introduced from Corsica to the French side of the eastern Pyrenees in the 1970s as a game species. Although mature males have heavy curled horns and a reddish-brown hide with a lighter flank patch, females are paler and lack horns, and so can be confused at a distance with the chamois which also abound

Catalunya

Small pearl-bordered fritillary *Clossiana selene* (Alec Harmer)

here. Alpine marmots are common above 2000 m, while a plethora of common and snow voles provides prey for stoats. The Iberian peninsula's only sand lizards inhabit the eastern Pyrenees between Andorra and Núria, always above 1400 m, and are particularly fond of this mosaic of subalpine pasture and pine forest.

Butterfly-wise, expect Apollo and shepherd's, small pearl-bordered and pearl-bordered fritillaries lower down, with increasing numbers of ringlets – Gavarnie, dewy, Lefèbvre's, mountain, silky and Spanish brassy – as you ascend, accompanied by peak white, mountain clouded yellow and, perhaps, mountain fritillary. Look out, too, for the small, almost melanic alpine fritillary, sometimes considered to be a subspecies of marsh fritillary, which here feeds on Pyrenean, snow and other gentians. Wonderfully tame alpine accentors will accompany you up to the large scree below Puigmal, where you may also catch a glimpse of ptarmigan, wallcreeper or snow finch. With luck, a lammergeier or golden eagle might just cruise along the ridge above you.

This high scree, composed of ice-shattered gneiss, is home to an interesting plant community dominated by large white patches of the ragwort *Senecio leucophyllus*, accompanied by *Cerastium pyrenaicum*, unique to the eastern Pyrenees, the yellow-flowered Pyrenean poppy, diverse-leaved violet, vitaliana and yellow genipi. The few calcareous screes in the area host the dense, almost spherical flower-heads of spoon-leaved candytuft and xatardia, a squat

umbellifer which is also confined to the eastern Pyrenees.

The path heading down to Queralbs from the Santuari is most rewarding in June, when the lemon-yellow alpine pasque flower (subspecies *apiifolia*) is in full bloom. By July, other attention-grabbing plants appear, in particular the yellow monk's-hood *Aconitum vulparia* subspecies *neapolitanum*, clumps of water saxifrage in the river Núria, crested and leafy louseworts, English iris and Pyrenean lily, rounded off with pastures teeming with St Bruno's lily and acid rockgardens full of hairy saxifrage, *Androsace vandellii* and the purple-flowered viscid primrose.

The uncommon geranium argus, flying in mid-July, is the main prize for lepidopterists; note that the adults use *Geranium* species, especially wood crane's-bill, both for egg-laying and nectaring. Look out, too, for Apollo, chestnut heath, Escher's and silver-studded blues and scarce and purple-edged coppers. Birds include alpine swift, crag martin, dipper, grey wagtail and, in recent years, black woodpecker in the least disturbed areas of pine forest, with just a possibility of wallcreeper on the cliffs in the gorge.

Hyssop-leaved sideritis *Sideritis hyssopifolia*

Access: The rack-and-pinion railway connects to the main Barcelona– Puigcerdà railway line in Ribes de Freser on the N-152 (14 km north of Ripoll) and runs approximately once an hour between 7.30 and 18.30, although not necessarily connecting with trains to and from Barcelona. Timetable information: tel: 93 2051515; website: www.valldenuria.com

SITE

56 La Garrotxa

The Iberian peninsula's most extensive volcanic landscape, today clothed with extensive beech and oak forests; interesting odonate communities plus 106 species of butterfly.

The oldest of the today dormant – but not extinct – volcanos in La Garrotxa date from around 350,000 years ago, although since Croscat erupted just 11,500 years ago, there have been no new additions to this, mainland Spain's youngest and largest volcanic landscape. The extinct cones and 20-odd lava flows that dot the countryside are today clothed with superb beech and oak forests that occupy almost 75% of the Parc Natural de la Zona Volcànica de la Garrotxa (11 908 ha, including 26 *reserves naturals* totalling 900 ha).

Garden dormouse *Eliomys quercinus*

The volcanos act as a barrier to warming winds from the Mediterranean and permit more Atlantic vegetation to appear at unusually low levels. The best-known example is La Fageda d'en Jordà, a lowland beech forest situated to the southeast of Olot that was spared the axe because the underlying lava flow was too uneven to cultivate. Although plant diversity is rather low here, more humid, high-level beechwoods off the lava flows are associated with sessile oak, Italian maple and box, with a ground flora of pinnate coralroot, narrow-leaved lungwort, the rather scarcer *Pulmonaria affinis* and Pyrenean squill.

Little remains of the pedunculate oak woodland which once covered most of the valley floor around Olot, although stands at La Moixina and Parc Nou have a rich spring herb layer that includes rue-leaved isopyrum, wood and yellow anemones, yellow archangel, snowdrop and Solomon's-seal, with nettle-leaved bellflower and twayblade appearing later in the season. The most humid soils support marsh marigold, the locally endemic subspecies (*olotensis*) of large bittercress, tuberous comfrey and yellow flag.

The moist oakwoods and marshes at La Moixina are gradually being restored following many previous attempts at drainage. Amphibians here are represented by fire salamander, marbled and palmate newts and stripeless tree frog, while odonates around the Estany d'en Broc – a small reed-fringed pool – include goblet-marked damselfly, emperor dragonfly and scarlet darter. Dragonfly buffs should also visit the river Fluvià, for example at the old mill of Molí de Collell, for Mediterranean and beautiful demoiselles (the latter the Iberian subspecies *meridionalis*), *Platycnemis acutipen-*

Damselfly *Platycnemis acutipennis*

nis, blue-eyed hooked-tailed dragonfly, crepuscular hawker and keeled skimmer, while lesser purple emperor and map butterfly fly here in August. The pools near Can Jordà, the park's resource centre (tel: 972 264666; fax: 972 265567 to visit), hold small emerald damselfly, while a Butterfly Monitoring Scheme transect in the same area has revealed wood white, violet and marsh fritillaries and sloe and false ilex hairstreaks as the commonest butterflies.

Other faunal communities differ little from one deciduous forest to another; typical birds include marsh tit (no confusing willow tits in Spain!), nuthatch and bullfinch. Winter is a good time for finding mixed flocks of passerines, with an influx of bram-

blings joining the resident firecrests, tits and short-toed treecreepers. Reptiles benefit from the many cavities in the lava flows, with green lizard and smooth snake being typical of forest edges, while the asp is common throughout the park. Of the mammals, wild boar are very abundant, as are red fox, beech marten, Eurasian badger and common genet, with smaller creatures including pygmy white-toothed, common and pygmy shrews, and both garden and edible dormice. Bats are also well represented, notably greater, lesser and Mediterranean horseshoes, Schreiber's, Geoffroy's, Leisler's, lesser mouse-eared and grey long-eared, plus common pipistrelle.

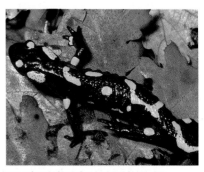

Fire salamander *Salamandra salamandra*

Access and information: The main park information centre is in the Casal dels Volcans, (tel: 972 266012; fax: 972 270455; e-mail: wpnzvg@correu.gencat.es), well signposted off the C-152 into Olot from the south. Other information points exist at Can Serra, on the edge of the Fageda d'en Jordà, 4 km southeast of Olot towards Santa Pau (GI-524), and at Can Passavent, 2 km further along the same road. La Moixina lies just to the east of Olot, while the Molí de Collell is on the river Fluvià to the south of Olot. Of the waymarked walks in the natural park, itineraries 1 and 12 are the most rewarding, for the volcanic landscape and flora respectively.

Also in the area

The limestone peaks and gorges surrounding the volcanic landscapes of La Garrotxa provide an interesting contrast: a footpath leading north from Coll de Bracons on the minor road between Joanetes and Torelló (southwest of Olot) leads up to the pastures and imposing crags of **Puigsacalm** (1515 m). Look out for golden and short-toed eagles, peregrine, hobby, alpine swift, crag martin, tree pipit, dunnock, red-backed shrike and chough; the pastures here are studded with spring and trumpet gentians in spring, and with great yellow and ciliate gentians in summer and autumn, respectively, while north-facing cliffs hold livelong saxifrage and common houseleek. The gorges north of **Oix** (north of Castellfollit de la Roca, on the N-260) have smooth rock spleenwort, Pyrenean saxifrage and ramonda, or you could explore the valley west of **Sant Privat d'en Bas** (west of Olot).

Estany de Banyoles Large permanent lake (118 ha), which sits on a massive fault-line and receives most of its water from subterranean upwellings originating in the limestone mountains of the Alta Garrotxa. Small strips of fluvial woodland along the western margin, while a number of satellite lagoons are worth examining for Mediterranean and banded demoiselles, *Platycnemis acutipennis*, goblet-marked damselfly, green-eyed hook-tailed dragonfly, Norfolk hawker, lesser emperor, orange-spotted emerald, scarce chaser, yellow-veined darter and *Trithemis annulata*. Owing to its great depth, few ducks or herons frequent the lake, but great reed warbler, penduline tit and golden oriole occur in the surrounding vegetation.

SITE
57 Serra de l'Albera

The last outliers of the Pyrenees before the Mediterranean coast, home to Iberia's only native Hermann's tortoises, plus Bonelli's and golden eagles and lesser grey shrike.

In a final generous flourish, the easternmost 25 km of the Pyrenees provides the setting for a transitional flora and fauna, replete with elements characteristic of both the high mountains and the Mediterranean region. The best-preserved forest formations lie in the central part of the acid Albera massif (*paratge natural*, 3428 ha) around the castle of Requesens: a glorious nineteenth-century folly to the northeast of Cantallops.

Below Requesens, dense cork oak forest harbours a typical understorey of sage-leaved cistus, tree heath, green heather and strawberry-tree. Two-tailed pashas are very common here in late summer, violet limodores sprout in the undergrowth and breeding birds include an abundance of Bonelli's warblers, firecrests and short-toed treecreepers. Above the castle, a mixed forest

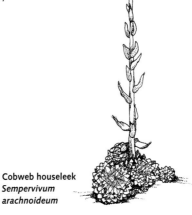

Cobweb houseleek
Sempervivum arachnoideum

of beech and deciduous oaks is interrupted by splendidly vegetated gullies housing wych elm, wild service-tree, Italian and Montpellier maples and narrow-leaved ash, home to garden and edible dormice, beech marten, common genet and wildcat. The beech forest has an incredibly diverse beetle fauna, with over 1200 species cited here, including the rare, steely-blue longhorn *Rosalia alpina.*

On the French border, Puig (Pic) Neulós – at 1256 m the highest point of L'Albera – is the best place to see golden eagle, with just a single pair breeding in the area, as well as harbouring goshawk, alpine swift, red-rumped swallow, crag martin, alpine accentor (in winter), rock thrush, red-backed shrike and raven. A pair of Bonelli's eagles also breeds in L'Albera, although these usually hunt over the lower, more open parts of the massif, as do the local short-toed eagles.

The main ridge here is well grazed, with a thin belt of scrub composed of common juniper, broom, Pyrenean broom, holly and ling grading into the mixed deciduous wood-

land below, part of which – at the headwaters of the river Orlina further east – is a *reserva natural parcial* (395 ha). On the granite outcrops look out for forked spleenwort, cobweb houseleek, alpine lady's-mantle and crested lousewort, all more reminiscent of the high Pyrenees, as are the occasional wintering wallcreeper and the groups of mouflon which have recently been sighted here.

L'Albera is home to Catalunya's richest assemblage of herptiles. Typical Mediterranean species enter into direct competition with congeners that are more frequent in upland habitats: Iberian wall versus common wall lizards, ocellated vs. green lizards, and ladder vs. Aesculapian snakes. Other characteristic lowland species include Montpellier snake, large psammodromus and the most northerly population of Spanish psammodromus in the peninsula,

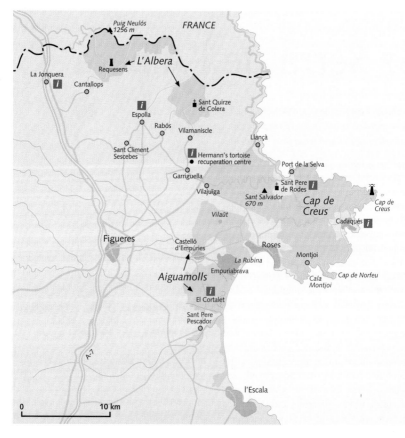

Looking towards Cap de Creus from l'Albera (M.L.)

here cohabiting with the typically upland western whip snake. Low-level streams harbour stripe-necked terrapin, while the garrigue – especially in the *reserva natural parcial* of Sant Quirze (580 ha), in the valley to the northeast of Rabós – is home to Hermann's tortoise.

At the lowest levels, the Albera massif is clothed with a mosaic of thorny broom, small-flowered gorse, narrow-leaved, sage-leaved and grey-leaved cistuses and tree heath, interspersed with stands of Aleppo pine and low-intensity vine, olive and cereal cultivation. The most renowned bird of this habitat is undoubtedly the lesser grey shrike, which nests around Sant Climent Sescebes in the company of short-toed, crested and Thekla larks and southern grey and woodchat shrikes. The low scrub houses abundant Dartford warblers, while the open cork oak forest is home to healthy populations of Orphean warbler. Lesser kestrels have been successfully reintroduced to the Sant Quirze Valley around Rabós.

Access and information: L'Albera is best entered along the tracks which lead up to the base of the main ridge from the villages of Cantallops, Espolla or Vilamaniscle; there is a small information centre in Espolla (tel: 972 545079; fax: 972 545139). For easy access to Puig Neulós follow the N-II into France and turn right onto the D-71 just past the border. For more information about the wildlife of the area, visit the Hermann's tortoise recuperation centre just north of Garriguella (tel: 972 552245).

SITE 58 Cap de Creus

Prominent headland in the northern Costa Brava, with interesting coastal plant communities and fine opportunities for sea-watching.

It is hard to believe that the forests of Cap de Creus (*parc natural*, 10 813 ha terrestrial plus 3073 ha marine) were once so thick that people from Cadaqués found it easier to travel by sea to Mallorca than overland to nearby Figueres. Charcoal-burning, grazing and the planting of vines – subsequently destroyed by the *Phylloxera* epidemic in the 1890s – all took their toll on the forests of the area and today the windswept slopes of Cap de Creus are characterised above all by abandoned terraces clothed with vast expanses of dense scrub, dominated by thorny broom, small-flowered gorse, narrow-leaved and sage-leaved cistuses, tree heath, green heather, French lavender and *Asparagus acutifolius*. Typical herbs sheltering within the scrub include birthwort, smearwort, narrow-leaved lupin, reichardia, friar's cowl and sword-leaved helleborine, with tongue, champagne and Provence orchids in more open areas.

The best-preserved floral communities, however, are confined to the narrow, rocky coastal strip, where prevailing northerly winds force shrubs such as prickly juniper, *Thymelaea hirsuta* and sage-leaved cistus to assume an unnaturally prostrate habit. An examination of the wild, northern headlands – for example, east of Port de la Selva – might turn up *Dianthus pungens*, unique to northeastern Spain, *Seseli farrenyi*, endemic to Cap de Creus, the sea-lavender *Limonium tremolsii*, found only in the province of Girona, and the thrift *Armeria ruscinonensis*, confined to southeast France and Catalunya, as well as yellow horned-poppy, spiny, white-flowered cushions of tragacanth, the woody *Plantago subulata* and silver ragwort.

In contrast to the prevailing acid bedrock, the calcareous headland of Cap de Norfeu is home to a disjunct population of cneorum, with fissure plants such as sarcocapnos and *Erodium crispum* on the north-

Cap de Creus

facing cliffs. Clumps of *Coronilla minima*, tree spurge and sea mallow plus *Narcissus dubius* and dull and sawfly ophrys bloom prolifically in March and April, with October bringing autumn narcissus and autumn squill into flower.

A fine assemblage of ferns will keep ardent botanists on their toes. Mediterranean elements such as scented and scaly cheilanthes, Jersey fern and the sub-Mediterranean least adder's-tongue (appearing in autumn), mix in with typical pan-European species such as scaly male-fern and soft shield-fern, plus essentially Atlantic taxa that include royal fern and lanceolate and (on sea-cliffs) sea spleenworts.

For the best of the area's birds, head for the evocative monastery of Sant Pere de Rodes, and from there up to Sant Salvador (670 m), the highest peak in the area. Thekla lark and blue rock thrush, present all year round, are joined by common, pallid and alpine swifts, rock thrush and black-eared wheatear in summer. Crag martins also breed here, while Bonelli's eagles wander over from time to time and winter brings a small group of alpine accentors down from the high mountains. Scrub formations harbour the typical Mediterranean *Sylvia* warblers – subalpine, Orphean, Dartford and Sardinian – although with an overwhelming preponderance of the latter two species.

Sea-watching is worthwhile from Cap de Creus, especially in spring and autumn when both Cory's and Yelkouan shearwater pass by in good numbers, and in winter when a surprising number of razorbills, gannets, Mediterranean gulls, kittiwakes and great and Arctic skuas enter the Mediterranean to winter. Among the cetaceans you are most likely to see striped or bottled-nosed dolphins, with just the possibility of a distant fin whale.

> *Information*: The information centre at Sant Pere de Rodes is open every day between 1 June and 31 September, but only at weekends and on public holidays during the rest of the year (tel: 972 193191; fax: 972 193192). Scuba-diving and sailing in the park are subject to restrictions. (See map on p. 170.)

SITE 59 Aiguamolls de l'Empordà

Extensive coastal marshland with abundant passage and breeding birds, plus drier habitats harbouring roller and lesser grey shrike.

Only a relatively small part of the vast maze of *aiguamolls* (marshes) that once covered the low-lying hinterland of the Bahia de Roses has survived the twin scourges of drainage and holiday complexes. Today protected as a *parc natural* (4729 ha), Ramsar Site and ZEPA, these *aiguamolls* can be easily visited along a series of well-marked trails leading to 15 strategically positioned hides.

The park exhibits a complex series of interrelated habitats, with pride of place – in terms of uniqueness – going to the *closes*: wet meadows cut for hay in spring and grazed in summer, traversed by freshwater ditches filled with marsh-mallow, purple loosestrife and yellow flag. Larger ditches, such as those on the Massona trail leading out from the Cortalet information centre, are fringed with galleries of white willow, white and black poplars, alder, downy oak, narrow-leaved ash and many dead small-leaved elms, with a shrub layer of hawthorn, blackthorn, Mediterranean buckthorn and Etruscan honeysuckle inhabited by nightingales and Cetti's warblers competing for sound-space.

The somewhat drier meadows in the Vilaüt sector of the park are dotted with small enclaves of downy and cork oaks and granite outcrops clothed with *Aristolochia longa*, golden clumps of *Euphorbia serrata*, Mediterranean mezereon, wild olive, French lavender, tassel hyacinth and the diminutive conical orchid; damper areas harbour ragged-robin and tree lavatera. This area is one of the best for great spotted cuckoo, hoopoe, roller (5+ pairs), Thekla lark and lesser grey shrike (6 pairs). The Vilaüt lagoon at the end of the trail is often carpeted with a fine crop of brackish water-crowfoot and fringed with banks of willowherbs which attract the scarce day-flying hawk-moth *Proserpinus proserpina*.

A further dry habitat lies to the north of the tower-blocks of the Empuriabrava holiday complex, where the once-cultivated sandy soils of La Rubina – dominated by *Plantago crassifolia* – sport a wealth of orchids: large groups of man, giant, tongue and bee orchids plus early spider and sawfly ophrys. Sea-lavenders abound here, notably *Limonium virgatum*, *L. ferulaceum* and *L. girardianum*, while the nearby dunes are home to the joint pine *Ephedra distachya*.

The most visited habitats of the Aiguamolls, however, are the wetlands. Two artificial freshwater lagoons – Estany de Cortalet and Estany d'Europa – provide some of the best 'armchair' birdwatching in Catalunya, with all the typical Mediterranean herons, *Tringa* (including regular marsh sandpiper) and *Calidris* waders and terns passing through on migration. The Estany d'Europa are the most permanent of the park's wetlands, regularly attracting greater flamingo, purple gallinule and whiskered terns in late summer, especially when the Cortalet lagoon is dry. White stork, fallow deer and otter have all been successfully reintroduced here, although the latter are rarely seen nowadays, having migrated away up the river Fluvià. Freshwater habitats hold European pond terrapin, palmate and mar-

Aiguamolls de l'Empordà

Black-winged stilt *Himantopus himantopus*

bled newts, western spadefoot and stripeless tree and painted frogs, the latter an essentially African species introduced to southern France at the end of the nineteenth century, which has since expanded into Catalunya.

The Massona trail brings you out at the Estanys del Matà, a large area of former rice-paddies in which the regeneration of the natural marsh vegetation is being encouraged. Camargue horses are grazed here to maintain a grassland–reedbed mosaic that is perfect for breeding black-winged stilts (154 pairs), the very ostentatious purple gallinule (30 pairs) and secretive crakes on passage. An unbelievable number of dragonflies appears in late summer, the commonest being scarlet and red-veined darters, but look out, too, for the smaller southern darter, poorly marked on the side of its thorax, and the powder-blue males of the southern skimmer.

The *llaunes* – an interconnected series of lagoons of varying salinity lying behind the beach – are the strictly 'no-access' heart of the Aiguamolls. Typical halophytes here are common and purple glassworts and sea-purslane, merging into stands of sea-rush and small cord-grass, with splashes of blue iris (subspecies *maritima*) at the edge of the saltmarsh. Winter brings a host of duck and waders to the *llaunes*, while the dense reedbeds in the less saline areas (viewable from hides along the Massona trail) harbour bittern (1 pair), little bittern (11+ pairs) and purple heron (48 pairs), along with marsh harrier (7 pairs) and moustached (20+ pairs) and Savi's warblers, the former breaking into song in mid-March, a good month before Savi's begins singing.

The *llaunes* can be also viewed from the beach path (closed between 1 April and 15 June to prevent disturbance to breeding Kentish plovers). The dunes here are fixed by marram, *Sporobolus pungens* and sand couch-grass, interspersed with sea spurge, echinophora, sea bindweed and sea daffodil, and are home to abundant large psammodromus and crested and short-toed larks.

> *Information*: El Cortalet information centre is signposted east off the road to Sant Pere Pescador, 3 km south of Castelló d'Empúries (tel: 972 454222; fax: 972 454474; e-mail: aiguamolls@ aiguamolls.org). (See map on p. 170.)

(See map on p. 170.)

SITE 60 Illes Medes/Massís de Montgrí

Seven small rocky islets surrounded by a dazzling marine flora and fauna, plus a mainland limestone plateau with a diverse community of spring monocots.

The Medes archipelago (22.6 ha), which lies about 1.5 km off the coast of Girona, is now fully protected by a *reserva marina* (418 ha), such that the abusive underwater hunting

Catalunya

Silene sedoides on coastal rocks

sea caves and tunnels which are also a noted refuge of spiny, black squat and little Cape Town lobsters. Congregations of the small shrimp *Hemimysis speluncola* provide food for leopard-spotted gobies and swallowtail seaperch.

On dry land, the combination of gull guano and sea spray provides for interesting floral communities which include *Silene sedoides* and tragacanth near the cliff edges, plus the nitrogen-loving shrubby orache, *Brassica fruticulosa*, tree mallow and slender thistle. Since landing on the Medes has been prohibited, a large heronry has formed in a small patch of olives, figs and carobs on the main island; in 1996, 49 pairs of little egret, 1081 of cattle egret, and 120 of night heron nested here. The sea-cliffs hold a few pairs of storm petrel, shag, pallid, alpine and common swifts and blue rock thrush, but these are completely overshadowed by almost 14 000 pairs of yellow-legged gulls.

The Medes are a physical continuation of the Massís de Montgrí: a karstified limestone plateau crowned by twin peaks (one topped by a castle) rising north of the town of Torroella de Montgrí. Aleppo, maritime and stone pines, planted in the nineteenth century to stabilise the vast inland dune, cover much of the northern part of the massif,

and coral collection which were threatening to lay waste to the islands' ecologically complex submarine habitats are now a thing of the past.

Around the Medes, the wave-break zone is clothed predominantly with the red calcareous alga *Lithophyllum lichenoides*. Various sponges cling to the rocks, notably the encrusting dull orange *Hymeniacidon sanguinea* in intertidal zones and the vivid-yellow *Verongia aerophoba* between 2 and 10 m, while in the near-darkness 20 m down, brightly coloured coral 'forests' are dominated by the fan-shaped *Paramuricea clavata* and the white *Eunicella singularis*. Large shoals of European pilchard, European anchovy and Mediterranean sand smelt fry swim near the shore, providing rich pickings for European seabass, European barracuda and Atlantic bonito.

Flat, sandy bottoms are carpeted with meadows of posidonia, much frequented by shoals of salema, while those covered in rock debris are home to small-spotted catshark, spotted torpedo, thornback ray and angler. Under and around fallen blocks of rock skulk comber, axillary wrasse, dusky perch, black scorpionfish and European conger, while cotton-spinners feed on the bottom of the

Stripeless tree frog *Hyla meridionalis* (T.F.)

which is elsewhere dominated by an at times impenetrable scrub of holly oak, lentisc, grey-leaved cistus and rosemary, with a supporting cast of osyris, Mediterranean spurge, turpentine tree, *Lavandula latifolia* and a few of Europe's most northerly dwarf fan palms. The whole area is excellent for orchids (27 species) and monocots in general: in early spring look out for giant and man orchids and yellow, sawfly and dull ophrys, as well as dipcadi, *Asphodelus ramosus*, hollow-stemmed asphodel, *Allium moschatum*, rosy garlic, round-headed leek, field gladiolus and carpets of *Iris lutescens* on the castleless summit of Montplà (317 m), by far the less transited of the two peaks. North-facing cliffs harbour tufted catchfly and an isolated population of the spiny cushions of *Hormathophylla spinosa*.

The pines are alive with Bonelli's warbler, crested tit, short-toed treecreeper and cross-bill, while more open areas hold blue rock thrush, black-eared wheatear and Sardinian and Dartford warblers. Check out the sea-cliffs for pallid and alpine swifts and black wheatear; eagle owl and Bonelli's eagle also breed locally. September sees the arrival of south-bound passage migrants, above all pied flycatcher and redstart, as well as a steady trickle of raptors, notably short-toed eagle, plus tawny pipit, ring ouzel and ortolan bunting.

The Montgrí is home to a diverse assemblage of butterflies. Early spring brings southern small white, Moroccan orange tip, wood white and black-eyed blue, with marsh and Provençal fritillaries, southern white admiral, western marbled white and sloe hairstreak on the wing by May. Summer satyrids include tree and striped graylings and southern and Spanish gatekeepers.

Information and access: L'Estartit's tourist office has information about cruises around the Medes and the strict regulations to be followed by divers and sailors approaching the islands (tel: 972 751910; fax: 972 751749; e-mail: ofestar@ddgi. es). For the best of the Montgrí massif, follow the GR-92 coastal footpath southwards from L'Escala then west to Torroella de Montgrí.

Also in the area

Aiguamolls del Baix Ter North and south of the mouth of the river Ter are similar habitats to the Aiguamolls de l'Empordà (see p. 173), best visited from the information centre and trail at Les Basses d'en Coll (*espai natural*, 60 ha; tel: 699 949289; fax: 972 668020; e-mail: info@bassesdencoll. com). Access east from Pals along the GIV-6502 and then north towards Platja El Grau and Càmping Playa Brava. Most of the herons breeding on the Illes Medes (plus squacco and purple) feed here in the summer; breeders include little bittern, bee-eater, Cetti's and great reed warblers, penduline tit and golden oriole. Rice-paddies are flooded from mid-April into the summer, attracting waders such as marsh, wood and curlew sandpipers and little stint; less frequent visitors include great white heron, osprey, whiskered tern, red-throated pipit and woodchat shrike. Three-toed skink, Spanish and large psammodromus and spiny-footed lizard on the beach, plus viperine and Montpellier snakes, Iberian pool and stripeless tree frogs and southern water vole in wetter habitats. Dunes near the river mouth harbour yellow horned-poppy, *Thymelaea hirsuta*, tragacanth, white rock-rose, *Fumana ericoides* and early spider ophrys, while the river mouth itself is good for good for idling gulls, terns and waders.

61 El Montseny

Granite massif displaying a well-preserved zonation of Mediterranean to subalpine plant communities, home to an amazing 142 species of butterfly.

As it lies barely 40 km from Barcelona, generations of Catalan naturalists have cut their teeth on El Montseny (*parc natural* and Biosphere Reserve; 17 372 ha, plus 12 748 ha buffer zone). Human pressure is intense across most of the massif, especially on the twin peaks of Turó de l'Home (1706 m) and Matagalls (1697 m), and elsewhere on autumn weekends when mushroom-pickers flood the forests in search of chanterelle, grey tricholoma and saffron milk cap.

Heading up into the Montseny, for example along the BV-5114 north from Sant Celoni, you pass quickly from holm oak woodland into commercially exploited cork oak forests with an understorey of thorny broom, strawberry-tree, tree heath, green heather and French lavender, then eventually into stands of sweet chestnut. By about 1000 m, the first beech trees appear, here accompanied by sessile oaks: a prelude to the uniform beech forest which dominates much of the upper reaches of the Montseny, where little breaks the monotony apart from some massive holly trees (up to 20 m) and alders in the gullies.

Vertebrate communities, while interesting in the context of the Iberian peninsula, differ little from those of central Europe; beech marten, wild boar, common wall and green lizards, fire salamander and common frog are reasonably abundant, while common moles reach their southernmost limit in the peninsula here. Breeding forest birds include crested tit, nuthatch and jay, joined by an autumn influx of chaffinches and bramblings to feed on the beech-mast.

The road to the radar-topped peak of Turó de l'Home passes close to a relict enclave of European silver-fir – the southernmost in the peninsula – and leaves you well placed to walk northeast from the summit along the rocky ridge known as Les Agudes. Here the best of the subalpine floral communities grow: a carpet of dwarf juniper, mountain currant, wild cotoneaster, bearberry and bilberry, with rock outcrops harbouring *Saxifraga vayredana* and *S. genesiana*, both

El Montseny

endemic to the Montseny (the latter having recently been split from geranium-like saxifrage), plus gems such as moonwort, orpine and creeping snapdragon.

Rock thrush and rock bunting nest at these heights, alpine swifts are often seen overhead and there is a good wintering population of alpine accentor, which formerly bred here. Butterfly numbers peak in July when by far the commonest species are small tortoiseshell, dark green fritillary and Piedmont ringlet; rock grayling and grayling are abundant throughout August. Queen of Spain fritillaries are on the wing from March onwards, while brimstones perform altitudinal migrations away from the parched lowlands in summer in search of fresh nectar sources.

Quieter all round is La Calma, a less-transited (except on Sundays) plateau on the western edge of the Montseny, covered by a mosaic of pasture and scrubby patches of broom, green heather and ling. Violet mountain pansy is one of the earliest plants to flower, followed by *Potentilla montana*, pheasant's eye daffodil, wild tulip and green-winged and greater butterfly orchids. The scattered shrubs provide perfect perching habitat for red-backed shrike, in one of its most southerly Iberian outposts, with Dartford warblers skulking among the foliage. Open areas host skylark, woodlark, tree pipit, wheatear and mistle thrush, and the local pair of short-toed eagles are commonly seen hovering with great, deep wing-beats.

Six Butterfly Monitoring Scheme transects have provided considerable information about the butterflies of the Montseny. The Sant Marçal transect, just north of Santa Fe, picks up around 70 species annually, with late May seeing lesser spotted fritillary – a scarce species whose caterpillars feed gregariously on hoary mullein – on the wing, and June best for marbled, violet and spotted fritillaries and purple-shot copper.

The transect on La Calma is equally productive, giving daily totals of up to almost 900 butterflies: July brings good numbers of false ilex hairstreak, brown argus and Mazarine and Escher's blues, with August turning up a few Camberwell beauties plus great banded grayling, the hermit and overwhelming numbers of gatekeepers. The western edge of La Calma and the valley below are limestone and, as such, are about the only places in the massif where you might find essentially calcicolous butterflies such as dingy skipper, Berger's clouded yellow, Duke of Burgundy fritillary and Adonis, Ripart's anomalous, Osiris, little and chalk-hill blues.

Information and access: The main park interpretation centre is at Can Casades, Santa Fe (tel: 93 8475113; fax: 93 8475368), which lies on the BV-5114 north of Sant Celoni. Subsidiary information points exist in the surrounding villages, including one at the railway station in El Figaró (on the N-152), run by English-speaking naturalists (tel: 93 8429361). The BV-5114 also leads all the way to the summit of Turó de l'Home, while La Calma is easily reached from Collformic (1145 m) on the BV-5301.

SITE
62 # Serra de Collserola

A wooded ridge abutting the city of Barcelona, encompassing surprisingly well-preserved forests and butterfly communities.

Rather unpromising when viewed from Barcelona, the dark slates and granites of Collserola (maximum Tibidabo, 512 m) are in fact splendidly verdant on the north-facing slopes hidden from the city. Although much frequented by local people at week-

Common smilax *Smilax aspera*

ereon, Mediterranean buckthorn and shrubby hare's-ear cover large areas of the south-facing slopes, with thinner soils characterised by a low garrigue dominated by holly oak, the winter-flowering small-flowered gorse, thorny broom, rosemary and several species of cistus, in particular sage-leaved and narrow-leaved. Giant orchids – in flower by late February – are found throughout, while Spanish broom and fennel grow on the southeastern flank of the ridge, together with the grass *Hyparrhenia hirta*, food-plant of the cone-head grasshopper *Brachycrotaphus tryxalicerus*: a plant–insect association which is best known from the African savannah.

The forests and scrub support healthy populations of red squirrel, stoat, beech marten, common genet and wild boar, plus a mixture of Mediterranean birds – hoopoe, subalpine and Sardinian warblers, woodchat shrike and serin – and typical Euro-Siberian species: robin, blackbird and blackcap. Listen out, too, for nightingale, Bonelli's warbler, firecrest and crested tit. Fire salamanders favour humid habitats such as Font Groga, while areas of low garrigue hold ocel-

ends, Collserola still harbours a rich and varied flora and fauna, best exemplified by a wealth of butterflies and the autumn migration of soaring birds along the ridge top.

The north face of Collserola supports dense stands of Aleppo and stone pines, interspersed with patches of holm oak, *Quercus cerrioides* (thought to be a hybrid between Lusitanian and downy oaks) and a few cork oaks (especially around the information centre). Stands of the semi-evergreen Algerian oak – an Afro-Iberian endemic with large, regularly serrated leaves, far from its Iberian stronghold in Andalucía and the Algarve – thrive in the humid woods of the Reserva Natural de la Font Groga, along with *Salix atrocinerea* subspecies *catalaunica*, alder, wild cherry, wild service-tree, large-leaved lime and many taxa from more northerly climes: soft shield-fern, wild strawberry, leopard's-bane and remote and pendulous sedges.

Elsewhere on Collserola, more open areas on the northern slopes harbour dense tracts of strawberry-tree, tree heath, *Phillyrea latifolia* and laurustinus, while humid gullies shelter hazel, traveller's-joy, *Cytisus villosus*, Mediterranean coriaria, wild madder, butcher's broom and common smilax, with ground cover characterised by black spleenwort and common ivy. Mediterranean mez-

Giant orchid *Barlia robertiana*

lated lizard, large psammodromus and Montpellier snake.

A Butterfly Monitoring Scheme transect has demonstrated the wealth of butterflies present in Collserola, above all on the calcareous outcrops at the southwestern end of the ridge above El Papiol. By early March, dappled white, Cleopatra, nettle-tree butterfly and black-eyed and Panoptes blues are on the wing, followed in early April by both green and Chapman's green hairstreaks (the larvae of the latter feeding on strawberry-tree) and, by the end of the month, by Moroccan orange tip, western marbled white and spotted, Provençal and marsh fritillaries. An explosion of species in June–July sees southern and Spanish gatekeepers, striped grayling, dusky heath and false ilex hairstreak on the wing, while late summer brings the abundant second generation of the two-tailed pasha and the greatest numbers of the introduced geranium bronze.

September also brings a constant southward migration of both black and white storks and raptors – particularly black kite and honey buzzard – along the coastal ridges, peaking mid-month. While numbers do not match those of the Pyrenean crossover points, the sight of a low-flying black stork or osprey with the city of Barcelona as a backdrop never fails to amaze.

Access and information: From the Baixador de Vallvidrera railway station, climb the steps (5 minutes) to the information centre (just off the BP-1418 Barcelona to Valldoreix road), open every morning (tel: 93 2803552; fax: 93 2803552; e-mail: cpcollserola@amb.es). Font Groga is north of the BP-1417 Barcelona to Sant Cugat road; access on foot just before the junction with the road which heads west to Molins de Rei.

Also in the area

Garraf (*parc natural*; 10 630 ha) Highly karstified landscape just south of Barcelona, supporting a low garrigue of holly oak, lentisc, Mediterranean mezereon, tree heath, rosemary, shrubby globularia and dwarf fan palm, plus spectacular tussocks of *Ampelodesmos mauritanica*. Spring-flowering bee orchid, dull, woodcock and yellow ophrys, rush-leaved jonquil and the low, yellow- or purple-flowered *Iris lutescens*. Pla de Campgràs harbours breeding Thekla lark, tawny pipit, black-eared wheatear, rock thrush, Dartford and Sardinian warblers, southern grey shrike and ortolan bunting. Roca Falconera cliff just south of the Garraf resort has peregrine, pallid swift, red-rumped swallow, crag martin, black redstart, black wheatear and blue rock thrush, with wallcreeper possible in winter. Migrating storks and raptors pass right over the Garraf in September: expect osprey, short-toed eagle, marsh harrier, honey buzzard, goshawk and possibly black stork to join the resident pairs of Bonelli's eagles. Butterflies include marbled and sage skippers, Spanish festoon, two-tailed pasha, black satyr, Chapman's green hairstreak and Provence chalk-hill, Escher's and chequered blues. Access from the C-32 (A-16) Barcelona–Sitges motorway at the Port Ginesta junction; turn right immediately towards the Rat Penat holiday-home complex. Signs to the park will take you up a very steep windy road to the information centre (tel. and fax: 93 5970892; e-mail: p.garraf@diba.es) at La Pleta, also leading to Pla de Campgràs.

^{SITE}
63 Montserrat

An extraordinary complex of finger-like rock pinnacles of interest for its well-preserved holm oak forests and fissure flora.

Instantly recognisable from afar by its implausible, stegosaurus-like silhouette, the Muntanya de Montserrat (a *parc natural* of 3630 ha) is composed of hard pudding conglomerates – well-rounded stones held together by a limy matrix – which have resisted erosion much better than the surrounding clays and marls. The renowned Monestir de Montserrat, perched halfway up the eastern end of the massif, houses a much-venerated black virgin that attracts many visitors at weekends, although with a little walking it is easy to leave the crowds behind.

The best way to tackle Montserrat is to catch the rack-and-pinion railway from the monastery up to the main ridge, from where a gentle path – about 3 km, equipped with steps and hand rails – leads to Sant Jeroni (1238 m):

the high point of the massif. The shelving, north-facing rocky slopes which accompany you are home to a wonderful fissure community of smooth rock spleenwort, *Saxifraga catalaunica* (endemic to Montserrat and neighbouring Sant Llorenç), lax potentilla, ramonda, *Globularia repens*, Pyrenean honeysuckle and Pyrenean bellflower. Sunny south-facing cliffs have a very different flora, however, composed largely of sarcocapnos, rock milkwort, snapdragon, Malling toadflax and *Jasonia glutinosa*.

In the thin soils of the ridge few trees or shrubs can survive, but an attractive spring flora includes *Paronychia kapela*, *Erodium rupestre*, the large umbellifer *Laserpitium gallicum*, the attractively furry *Convolvulus lanuginosus* and monocots such as wild

Muntanya de Montserrat

Catalunya

tulip, dipcadi, common grape hyacinth, mountain onion, *Fritillaria lusitanica* and rush-leaved jonquil.

Black redstart and Sardinian warbler are perhaps the commonest birds up on the ridge, but keep a look out, too, for the cliff-nesting Bonelli's eagle, peregrine, alpine swift, crag martin and raven, all breeding somewhere in the massif. Rock buntings abound here, while alpine accentors (especially around the *monestir*) and wallcreepers turn up out of the breeding season. Two further inhabitants of the cliffs are Moorish gecko and, surprisingly, beech marten, while in sunny rocky areas you may come across basking ocellated and Iberian wall lizards, large psammodromus and Lataste's viper; a few dozen introduced Spanish ibex inhabit the highest parts of the ridge.

To get a more complete picture of Montserrat, walk back down to the monastery along the main gully through the best of the holm oak woodland, here accompanied by snowy mespilus, whitebeam, scorpion-senna, the delicately trifoliate *Cytisus sessilifolius*, Italian maple, box, fly honeysuckle and martagon lily. Sunnier habitats further down are dominated by laurustinus, interspersed with turpentine tree, Mediterranean buckthorn, strawberry-tree,

Phillyrea latifolia, wild privet, *Lonicera implexa* and common smilax.

The basal zone of the massif, much transformed by agriculture and forest fires, is covered by thick secondary scrub formations. Shady habitats to the north are dominated by a dense maquis of Mediterranean coriaria, twisted thymelaea, the winter-flowering *Erica multiflora*, shrubby hare's-ear, rosemary and shrubby globularia, while holly oak, lentisc, *Rhamnus lycioides* and grey-leaved cistus carpet the more arid southern flanks, sheltering Bertoloni's, dull and yellow ophrys, fly orchid and *Ophrys dyris*. Spring butterflies here include Moroccan orange tip, Cleopatra and both green and Chapman's green hairstreaks.

Access and information: A road and rack-and-pinion railway lead up to the monastery from Monistrol de Montserrat (on the C-55 (C-1411)); a second rack-and-pinion railway runs every 20 minutes from 10.00 am to 6.00 pm (tel: 93 8777777) to the ridge top and interpretation centre.

Also in the area

Sant Llorenç del Munt i l'Obac (*parc natural*, 13 693 ha) Twin calcareous conglomerate ridges (maximum 1104 m) with well-preserved holm oak forest plus all the typical accompanying Mediterranean shrubs. Thin-soiled summits are home to *Arenaria conimbricensis*, Sequier's pink, grass-leaved buttercup, *Erodium glandulosum*, wild gladiolus, St Bernard's lily, *Fritillaria lusitanica* and Provence orchid, while shady rocky outcrops harbour *Saxifraga fragilis* subspecies *fragilis*, *S. catalaunica* and ramonda. Early spring sees Moroccan orange tip, dappled white

and the diminutive Panoptes blue on the wing, followed by marsh, spotted and Provençal fritillaries and little, Provence chalk-hill and Escher's blues in June and southern gatekeeper in July and August. Hibernating Schreiber's bats. The information centre at Coll d'Estenalles (tel. 93 8317300; fax: 93 4022493; e-mail: p.santllorenc.estena@diba.es) is on the BV-1221, 17 km north of Terrassa (Tarrasa) and is the starting point for highly recommended walks to La Mola and Castellsapera.

64 Delta del Llobregat

A small coastal wetland close to Barcelona, important for breeding waders and herons and migrant birds.

The Barcelona conurbation has swallowed up much of the alluvial plain of the Llobregat delta and left behind only about 3% of its once extensive marshes, today protected by two *reserves naturals* and a ZEPA (585 ha). A wealth of wildlife can still be seen in the delta's numerous different habitats, however, with obvious highlights being the migrant and breeding birds and the splendid orchid and dragonfly communities.

A cross-section through the Llobregat delta reveals the beach–dune–pinewood–marsh progression so common along the Spanish Mediterranean coast. Sand couch-grass and *Sporobolus pungens* form the first line of vegetation, backed up by echinophora, sea-holly and sea bindweed on the seaward side of the dunes, with *Thymelaea hirsuta*, felty germander, coastal crucianella and sea daffodil carpeting the lee.

Stone pines were planted in the seventeenth and eighteenth centuries to stabilise the dunes, such that today few patches of the native coastal scrub of prickly juniper, lentisc, *Phillyrea latifolia*, sage-leaved cistus and *Asparagus acutifolius* remain. Behind the pine cordon, the wetlands vary in salinity, with purple glasswort and *Sarcocornia fruticosa* merging indistinctly into a mosaic

of sea club-rush and sharp and sea rushes in moderately saline areas, and thence into more freshwater communities of common reed and bulrush.

Despite major transformation since the days when it was regarded as a malarial wasteland, the Ricarda–Ca l'Arana *reserva natural parcial* (177 ha), lying between the town of El Prat and the sea, still exhibits this succession of habitats. Coming from El Prat, you first pass through an area of market gardens, criss-crossed by drainage ditches frequented by *Ischnura graellsii*, emperor and lesser emperor dragonflies, black-tailed and southern skimmers and red-veined and scarlet darters, with a few Norfolk hawkers in June and *Orthetrum nitidinerve* in July.

Most local farmers flood their fields in April or early May to leach out excess salts, inadvertently creating a perfect habitat for waders and red-throated pipits on passage. Little stint, spotted redshank and wood sandpiper are common, while a few Temminck's stints and marsh sandpipers appear annually; local birders turn up a fine array of rarities, including broad-billed and semipalmated sandpipers in May 1998. Continuing towards the sea, short-toed larks breed in the dry fields and magpies harry great-spotted cuckoos in and around the pines, while the reedbeds are home to fan-tailed, Cetti's and great reed warblers.

Access to parts of the beach is restricted between 15 March and 31 July to protect Catalunya's second-largest breeding population of Kentish plover (80+ pairs in 2000), although there are paths leading southwest behind the beach (look out for both large and Spanish psammodromus here) which lead to the mouth of the Ricarda lagoon: a spot favoured by roosting Audouin's gulls in spring and Mediterranean gulls in winter. Sea-watching in autumn and winter can produce Yelkouan (mainly in autumn),

Short-toed lark *Calandrella brachydactyla* (Mike Lane)

Lesser emperor dragonfly *Anax parthenope*

Balearic (especially in winter) and Cory's (summer and autumn) shearwaters and great and Arctic skuas. The beach receives migrant plain tigers in late summer and autumn in invasion years, while Mediterranean skippers sit on sandy tracks in the area throughout the summer.

The other major protected area – the Remolar–Filipines *reserva natural parcial* (110 ha) – has recently undergone a serious facelift which has benefited the breeding birds. In 2000, grey and squacco herons nested for the first time and a male bittern called throughout February and March. Other breeders here in 2000 included purple heron (4+ pairs), little egret (1–3 pairs), little bittern (10–12 pairs), marsh harrier (1 pair), red-crested pochard (4 pairs) and black-winged stilt (162 pairs). Migrant waders and purple gallinules strut around in front of the hides, great white egrets are now regular in spring

and autumn, and black storks pass through in September. Winter brings black-necked grebe, booted eagle, jack snipe, water pipit and bluethroat, as well as over 3000 duck, mainly mallard, teal and shoveler.

This reserve can be explored by two short itineraries, both leading to hides overlooking the main area of marsh. The one to the right of the information centre takes you through sandy flats dominated by *Plantago crassifolia* and bellardia, packed with bug orchid, early spider, mirror and sawfly ophrys and small-flowered serapias in spring, plus autumn lady's tresses later in the year. The second walk passes under a scops owl nestbox, in a white poplar whose seeds are used by penduline tits to construct their domed nests, and leads to a hide which looks out over the marsh, where the males of the small red-eyed damselfly defend territories on patches of floating vegetation; monk parakeets make themselves noisily apparent in the poplars on the left.

> *Access and information*: The turn-off to the Remolar–Filipines *reserva* and information centre (tel: 93 6586761; fax: 93 6586783; e-mail: rndeltallobregat@hotmail.com) is east off the Barcelona–Castelldefels dual carriageway C-31 (C-246) at km 11, although coming from Barcelona you have to continue on to km 13 and then do a U-turn to be able to enter the access road.

SITE 65 Plana de Lleida

The remnants of a formerly much more extensive area of dry farmland, today housing Catalunya's only little bustards, sandgrouse and Dupont's larks.

Although neither in extent nor in numbers of breeding birds comparable with Los Monegros (see p. 141), the *secans* (areas of non-irrigated mixed farmland) scattered around the city of Lleida do still possess interesting pseudosteppe vegetation and associated fauna. Great efforts are being made, above all by local conservation groups, to safeguard the area's remaining populations of lesser kestrel, little

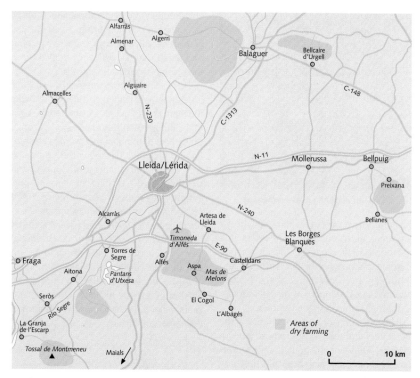

bustard and black-bellied and pin-tailed sandgrouse.

Bird-wise, Mas de Melons (*reserva natural parcial* of 1140 ha, also a ZEPA) is the richest part of the Lleida plains, largely due to its mosaic of habitats, ranging from stands of Aleppo pine through areas of mixed cereals, olive and almond cultivation to remnants of the holly oak, *Cistus clusii* and rosemary scrub which would have once covered much of the Plana de Lleida. Little bustard, stone curlew and pin-tailed sandgrouse feed in areas of fallow, crested, Thekla and lesser short-toed larks prefer more open areas, and scattered trees and bushes provide ideal habitat for great-spotted cuckoo, roller and woodchat and southern grey shrikes. Breeding raptors include short-toed eagle and hobby, while the abundance of rabbits, Iberian hares and red-legged partridges also attracts juvenile Bonelli's and golden eagles in dispersion during the winter. To visit Mas de Melons, take the C-233 west out of

Castelldans towards L'Albagés, bearing right along a broad track after about 800 m; continue west – stopping at will – through the main part of the reserve as far as the village of Aspa.

Two other good areas of *secans* with similar species lie north of Aspa. For the first, head north from Aspa towards Artesa de Lleida, turning left 50 m before the 2 km marker (300 m before the motorway bridge) along a track which traverses a mosaic of almond groves, cereals and fallow, home to lesser grey shrike and lesser kestrel. Continue along the track as it bears right then left, and immediately after crossing the motorway cut back sharp left and continue through cereal fields studded with *Hypecoum procumbens* in spring towards the Alfés aerodrome.

The second – the Timoneda d'Alfés, partially occupied by the aerodrome – is the Plana de Lleida's last remnant of a once much more widespread low scrub dominated by *Genista scorpius*, *Thymus vulgaris* and *Sideritis scordioides* subspecies *cavanillesii*,

and brightened by *Aizoon hispanicum,
Euphorbia isatidifolia* (with yellowish latex), *Helianthemum hirtum, Teucrium gnaphalodes, Centaurea linifolia* and the delicate upwards-pointing white flowers of *Narcissus dubius* (if there has been enough winter rain). Catalunya's only Dupont's larks (about 20 pairs) breed here, along with stone curlew, noisily obvious great spotted cuckoos and short-toed and calandra larks. Look out, too, for lesser grey shrikes around the poplars behind the aerodrome buildings.

To the southwest, the Tossal de Montmeneu (495 m) is the highest point in the Plana de Lleida and offers good views of the whole area (5 km southeast of La Granja de l'Escarp and obvious from the road/track to Maials). At the base, a lilac haze of moricandia clothes the waysides and the rich purple flowers of violet horned-poppy brighten areas of fallow. *Cistus clusii* and rosemary scrub dominates, grading into Aleppo pine as you climb the Tossal. Once on top, look out for *Moricandia moricandioides* (more robust than its much more abundant congener below), *Ononis tridentata, Genista fontanesii* subspecies *fontanesii* and the

Lesser grey shrike
Lanius minor

prostrate and very spiny caper, whose pickled flower buds are much appreciated in salads. Early spring butterflies include an abundance of dappled and Bath whites, with Moroccan and possibly sooty orange tips feeding on the abundant crucifers in fallow fields; swallowtail, scarce swallowtail and long-tailed blue hill-top on the Tossal itself. Choughs breed in disused farmsteads and golden eagles hunt in the area; if you continue along the track towards Maials there is a good chance of lesser kestrel, roller and woodchat shrike.

Two areas of *secans* to the north of Lleida are also worth a visit: immediately west of

Arid pseudosteppe near Lleida

Balaguer and south of the C-26 (C-148) for lesser kestrels and north of Bellcaire d'Urgell (east of Balaguer) on the C-53 (C-148) for little bustard. Try the area to the south of Preixana – in turn south of Bellpuig, close to junction 495 of the N-II east of Lleida – for roller, little bustard and Montagu's harrier.

> *Information*: Before visiting the Plana de Lleida it is worth contacting one of the local conservation groups, be it Fundació Natura (see Useful contacts) or EGRELL (e-mail: egrell@egrell.org).

Also in the area

Pantans d'Utxesa Reed-choked reservoirs harbouring breeding little bittern, purple, grey and night herons, cattle and little egrets, black kite, marsh harrier, great reed warbler, penduline tit and reed bunting. Wintering duck and spring passage of waders if water levels are low, plus garganey, osprey and whiskered and black terns. Surrounding halophytic vegetation contains the Spanish endemic sea-lavenders *Limonium catalaunicum* and *L. latebracteatum*, plus *Suaeda spicata* and *Frankenia pulverulenta*. Less saline areas have *Salsola vermiculata*, shrubby orache and *Artemisia herba-alba*, plus *Polygonum equisetiforme* and *Spergularia diandra*. Access is from Torres de Segre, south of Lleida; follow signs to Utxesa.

A colony of night herons and little and cattle egrets has formed in recent years at the confluence of the rivers Segre and Cinca at the **Aiguabarreig Segre–Cinca**, close to Granja d'Escarp. White stork, black kite, black-headed gull, kingfisher and penduline tit breed along the river banks, with crag martin, black and black-eared wheatears, blue rock thrush, spotless starling and rock sparrow nesting on and around the riverside cliffs.

SITE 66 Delta de l'Ebre

One of Europe's most important coastal wetlands, home to the world's largest colony of Audouin's gulls and nine breeding species of heron.

In late April, from the moment that its 150 square kilometres of paddy fields are flooded, the Delta de l'Ebre (*parc natural* of 7736 ha; also a Ramsar Site and ZEPA) is miraculously converted into a huge wetland, strategically placed on the Mediterranean flyway at the height of the northwards waterbird migration. This artificial habitat is complemented by large expanses of natural wetlands, saltpans and sand-dune systems, both north and south of the Ebro.

In the northern hemi-delta, just inland from the sandspit of El Fangar, migrant waders pack the flooded paddies in spring, but the real joy lies in finding scarcer species such as Temminck's stint and marsh sandpiper among the thousands of little stints, curlew sandpipers, black-tailed godwits and spotted redshanks. A multitude of herons and terns also appears at this time of year, many of which stay on to breed; squacco herons pop out of roadside ditches, little and cattle egrets stalk the fields and purple, grey and night herons move constantly between breeding and feeding areas, while little, common, gull-billed, and

Encanyissada lagoon, Delta de l'Ebre

whiskered terns fish the canals, oblivious to passing cars.

Nine species of heron breed in the delta, most abundantly cattle egrets (almost 6000 pairs), plus around 1000 pairs each of little bittern and little egret. Night, squacco and purple herons are also well represented here (382, 479 and 577 pairs, respectively, in 1998), with a few pairs of bittern, great white egret and grey heron completing the picture. Other notable wetland breeders include glossy ibis, greater flamingo (1600 pairs in 2000), red-crested pochard (several thousand), black-winged stilt (5000 pairs), avocet and Kentish plover, plus smaller numbers of oystercatcher and collared pratincole. Superb gull and tern colonies are headed by more than 10 000 pairs of Audouin's gull, 3000+ of common tern and almost 1000 pairs of Sandwich tern, as well as good numbers of slender-billed gull and gull-billed, little and whiskered terns; Mediterranean gull and Caspian and lesser crested terns also nest sporadically.

In winter, the shallow bay behind El Fangar teems with wildfowl, waders and gulls, notably great northern diver, black-necked grebe, Mediterranean gulls (30 000+ in the delta) and a plethora of mallard, shoveler, dunlin, little stint and black-tailed godwit; greater flamingos also congregate here at low tide in May. The recent trend of flooding paddy fields in winter has encouraged a greater dispersal of wintering aquatic birds and, seemingly, caused a proliferation of unusual records: spoonbill, squacco heron, osprey, booted eagle, black-winged stilt, Kentish plover, Temminck's stint, slender-billed gull and whiskered tern all wintered in 2001, along with good numbers of great white egret (95), glossy ibis (67) and night heron (188). In summer, El Fangar holds a large mixed tern colony, with the nest sites of common, Sandwich, little and a few gull-billed terns spilling over onto the track to the lighthouse. Also present are an abundance of clockwork-legged Kentish plovers and the two typical beach reptiles: large psammodromus and spiny-footed lizard.

Some of the Ebro delta's best sand-dune vegetation grows behind the Platja de La Marquesa, south of El Fangar. Widespread

Audouin's gull *Larus audouinii*

species here include shrubby sea-blite, salt-wort, yellow horned-poppy, sea rocket, sea spurge, sea-holly and hare's-foot, accompanied by typical southern European psammophiles such as *Thymelaea hirsuta*, the robust spiny umbellifer echinophora, the pink-flowered shrubby limoniastrum and coastal crucianella, as well as the bindweed-like stranglewort, the food-plant of the plain tiger butterfly which turns up here most autumns.

Saltmarshes throughout the delta are dominated by common and purple glasswort plus large expanses of sea-purslane, sharp and sea rushes and round-headed club-rush, with less saturated soils harbouring the white-flowered Saharan member of the Caltrop family *Zygophyllum album*, found only in the southern hemi-delta in the whole of Continental Europe, and the wormwood *Artemisia caerulescens* subspecies *gallica*; at least nine species of sea-lavender will keep the botanists on their toes. Unfortunately, the best-preserved area of coastal marsh – the Illa de Buda – is closed to the public, although a look-out point at L'Alfacada in the southern hemi-delta provides the delta's best views of great white egret, glossy ibis, purple gallinule and collared pratincole.

The southern hemi-delta has large reedy lagoons and two interesting areas of commercial saltpans. A number of observation points around the Encanyissada lagoon provide views of spectacular concentrations of red-crested pochard in March and April, and Savi's, Cetti's, reed and great reed warblers, singing in unison, although not necessarily in harmony. The road to the east of the neighbouring Tancada lagoon gives easy views of the group of greater flamingos that is almost always present and which returns to the Punta de la Banya at dusk to roost. On the other side of the road, the dry saltmarsh has breeding terns, crested, short-toed and lesser short-toed larks and, at dusk on the beach itself, groups of collared pratincoles.

The Sant Antoni saltpans south of La Tancada are excellent for lounging Caspian tern in September, plus shelduck, Kentish plover, avocet and slender-billed gull in spring and summer. The commercial Salines de la Trinitat at the end of the 5 km-long Trabucador sandspit are ideal for close views of breeding waders, Audouin's and slender-billed gulls and terns. From here the Punta de la Banya stretches away in the distance, closed off to the public but with an observation point that is good for waders, gulls and terns throughout the year, plus close-up views of red-necked phalaropes in September.

The delta is gastronomically famous for its European eels, while saltwater habitats harbour Spanish toothcarp and a small shrimp, *Palaemonetes zariquieyi*, which is endemic to the Catalan–Valencian coastline. Freshwater fish include three-spined stickleback, soiffe and *Barbus graellsii*, as well as Valencia toothcarp in some of the *ullals* (freshwater upwellings) located on a spring-line at the inland edge of the delta. These *ullals* also hold clover and water ferns, white water-lily and yellow flag, as well as odonates such as lesser emperor and small red-eyed, goblet-marked and southern damselflies.

Intensive cultivation has destroyed much of the delta's riverine forest, today only rep-

Information and access: The main information centre is in Deltebre (tel: 977 489679; fax: 977 481597). The Ebre can be crossed in three places by car via *transbordadors* (small, flat-bed ferries) which ply constantly back and forth across the river during daylight hours. Bicycles are widely available for hire and represent an excellent means of exploring the delta.

Catalunya

resented in any acceptable state of conservation on the Illa de Gràcia, dominated by white willow, black and white poplars, alder and small-leaved elm, and a refuge for the scarce Afro-Iberian endemic honeysuckle *Lonicera biflora*. Amphibians have been similarly affected, such that palmate and marbled newts, stripeless tree and painted frogs are now rather scarce, although Iberian pool frogs are still noisily abundant, as are western spadefoot and common toad. Both stripe-necked and European pond terrapins still occur, but are increasingly affected by the use of pesticides.

SITE
67 Ports de Beseit

The extremely rugged easternmost sector of the Sistema Ibérico, harbouring a large population of Spanish ibex, good numbers of the larger raptors and a rich calcicolous flora.

The limestone massif of the Ports de Beseit (a *parc natural* of 35 110 ha) is blessed with a diverse flora and fauna, where refugees from more northerly climes mix in with typical thermophilic Mediterranean species. A sinuous road leading up from sea level to the top of Caro (1442 m) – the highest peak in the area – provides easy access to all the principal habitats in the park.

To the southeast of the Ports lies a broad plain clothed with mature olive and carob groves that provide suitable habitat for scops owl, red-necked nightjar, bee-eater, hoopoe, black-eared wheatear, Orphean warbler and woodchat shrike. Late spring and early summer butterflies include Lulworth skipper, swallowtail, Berger's clouded yellow, Cleopatra, western marbled white, false ilex hairstreak and Lang's short-tailed blue. The extravagantly long-tailed large psammodromus is the commonest lizard, with Moorish gecko on buildings and sharp-ribbed salamanders in wells and irrigation ponds. Among the more eye-catching plants here are coris, lavender-cotton, *Antirrhinum barrelieri*, urospermum and *Tragopogon crocifolius*.

Where the olives and carobs fade out, a typical Mediterranean maquis appears, consisting of Phoenician and prickly junipers, holly oak, fragrant clematis, *Genista scorpius*, lentisc, Mediterranean buckthorn, *Rhamnus lycioides*, narrow-leaved cistus, *Erica multi-*

flora, *Phillyrea angustifolia*, shrubby globularia and dwarf fan palm. Areas of bare, karstified limestone are dotted with scores of *Iris lutescens* and nodding *Fritillaria lusitanica* in late March, with lavender-leaved rock-rose, dark swallow-wort, blue hound's-tongue, narrow-leaved valerian, the wasp-waisted 'knapweed' mantisalca and round-headed leek appearing as spring advances. Other herbaceous plants include the catchfly *Silene muscipula*, bladder-vetch, rough marshmallow, mallow-leaved bindweed, groundpine, weasel's-snout and a cornucopia of composites: andryala, *Tanacetum corymbosum*, *Anacyclus × valentinus*, (a hybrid between *A. homogamus* and *A. radiatus*) and cone knapweed.

The road up to Caro winds up through dense woods of *Pinus nigra* subspecies *salz-*

Tragopogon crocifolius (T.F.)

Catalunya

Mallow-leaved bindweed *Convolvulus althaeoides*

mannii, holm oak and box; when it flattens out after the last major set of hairpin bends, you should take time to ascend the imposing Tossa de la Reina (1113 m) to the north. The locally endemic fissure-loving willow *Salix tarraconensis* and *Knautia rupicola* flower here by the roadside, while the Tossa itself is clothed with a mosaic of the shrubby white-flowered crucifer *Hormathophylla spinosa*, prostrate cherry, snowy mespilus, *Genista scorpius*, hedgehog broom, mountain kidney-vetch and the cushion-forming umbellifer *Bupleurum fruticescens*, accompanied by patches of bright pink rock soapwort, white rock-rose, *Lavandula latifolia*, the lovely dusky-mauve labiate *Salvia lavandulifolia* and blue aphyllanthes.

Tossa de la Reina – with alpine swifts in constant movement all around – is a good place to wait for griffon vulture, short-toed eagle or black kite to float past, while Spanish ibex (subspecies *hispanica*) may appear profiled on a distant hillside. Butterflies hill-top from spring onwards, the commonest species being swallowtail, scarce swallowtail and wall brown, accompanied by de Prunner's ringlet and purple-edged copper. In July, look out for cardinal, lesser spotted fritillary, black satyr and false grayling.

On north-facing slopes over 1000 m, Euro-Siberian species such as moonwort, yew and pale-green and serrated wintergreens appear in the Scots pine forests. Follow the GR-7 long-distance footpath from Coll de Carrasqueta to Coll dels Pallers for some of the best high-level flora: grass-leaved buttercup, *Paeonia officinalis* subspecies *microcarpa*, sword-leaved helleborine and heath spotted (subspecies *meyeri*) and bird's-nest orchids, with lax potentilla, fairy foxglove, *Globularia repens* and Pyrenean honeysuckle on rocky outcrops. Other notable fissure-loving species in the Ports include tufted catchfly, Pyrenean saxifrage, *Antirrhinum sempervirens* subspecies *pertegasii* and Pyrenean bellflower, harder to track down, but possible on the walk from the village of Fredes along the PR-16 footpath down to the Ulldecona reservoir through the Portell de l'Infern (Hell's Gate), which also houses beautiful stands of *Acer granatense* and the butterwort *Pinguicula grandiflora* subspecies *dertosensis*, endemic to Beseit and the Ports de Morella (see p. 328).

Access: The road up to Caro continues straight on when the T-342 Roquetes to Alfara de Carles road bears right 3 km west of Roquetes. Near the top, the road splits, with the narrow left-hand fork leading to the peak (best to walk!); the GR-7 heading south from Coll de la Carrasqueta to Coll dels Pallers and then southwest along the main ridge can be picked up at a very sharp right-hand bend about 3 km after this turn-off. (See map on p. 329.)

Also in the area

Inland Tarragona province is littered with attractive limestone ridges. Try the 'lost world' plateau of **Mola de Colldejou** (919 m; accessed south of La Torre de Fontaubella (southwest of Falset) on the T-322 towards Mont-roig del Camp) for sarcocapnos, *Paeonia officinalis* subspecies *microcarpa, Saxifraga fragilis* subspecies *fragilis* and Pyrenean bellflower on north-facing slopes. The cliffs of the **Serra del Montsant** behind the village of La Morera de Montsant (west of Cornudella) have black wheatear, while across the valley, the area around the cliff-top village of **Siurana** holds Bonelli's and short-toed eagles, redrumped swallow and rock sparrow. The cliffs and woodland opposite the village of **Farena** (TV-7041/7044 east of Prades) have been acquired by the Fundació Territori i Paisatge to safeguard a wellestablished pair of Bonelli's eagles. The **Serra de Prades**, unlike the rest of this area, is capped by a layer of acid rocks supporting Catalunya's only Pyrenean oak forest, with an understorey of laurelleaved cistus and bearberry.

Balears

Introduction

For millions of years the Mediterranean Sea has been rising and falling, such that the Balearic archipelago – 5 main islands plus 189 islets, together covering over 5000 square kilometres – has at various times been left high-and-dry, completely submerged or somewhere in between. Intermittent land bridges permitted floral colonisation from neighbouring areas, which helps to explain the affinity of the flora of Eivissa and Formentera – the Illes Pitiüses – with that of the Dianic region of Alacant (around Dénia: Roman Dianium), a mere 85 km away, and the coincidence in the flora of Mallorca, Menorca and Cabrera – the Illes Gimnèsies – with the Tyrrhenian islands of Corsica, Sardinia and Sicily.

Since about 4 million years ago, however, the whole archipelago has been isolated from the mainland, leading to the evolution of a wealth of endemic taxa. All in all the Balears are home to around 1500 species of vascular plant, of which 65% are unique to the Mediterranean and about 124 are found only in the archipelago. For example, Mallorca boasts a long list of endemic plants, including *Ranunculus weyleri*, *Astragalus balearicus*, *Hippocrepis balearica*, Mallorcan violet, Balearic St John's-wort, *Naufraga balearica*, *Digitalis dubia*, *Sibthorpia africana*, *Senecio rodriguezii* and *Helichrysum ambiguum*, plus *Paeonia cambessedesii*, *Globularia cambessedesii* and *Crocus cambessedesii*, the last three named after Jacob Cambessèdes, a nineteenth-century botanist who, it is claimed, obtained specimens by shooting them off inaccessible ledges.

In general, bird diversity is poorer in the Balears than on the Iberian mainland, particularly on the smaller islands; no woodpeckers breed other than wryneck (of the North African race *mauretanica*), while

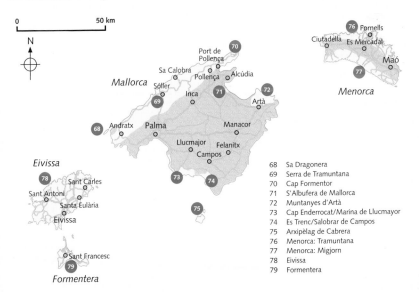

68 Sa Dragonera
69 Serra de Tramuntana
70 Cap Formentor
71 S'Albufera de Mallorca
72 Muntanyes d'Artà
73 Cap Enderrocat/Marina de Llucmayor
74 Es Trenc/Salobrar de Campos
75 Arxipèlag de Cabrera
76 Menorca: Tramuntana
77 Menorca: Migjorn
78 Eivissa
79 Formentera

Opposite page: **Typical almond orchard flora: gladioli and crown daisies** other notable absentees include tawny owl, woodlark, crested lark, Bonelli's warbler and black-eared wheatear. The relative isolation of the archipelago, however, has been sufficient to encourage speciation among the resident birds; the Marmora's warblers in the Balears are just about to be classified as a separate species – *Sylvia balearica* (Balearic warbler) – while endemic races of spotted flycatcher (*balearica*), blue tit (*balearicus*) and crossbill (*balearica*) have also been described.

The Serra de Tramuntana is home to the world's only island population of black vultures, with the Balears also harbouring resident populations of the elsewhere migratory osprey, booted eagle, red kite (seriously declining) and Egyptian vulture. Seabird colonies are exceptional throughout the archipelago – particularly at La Trapa and on Sa Dragonera and Cabrera – with pride of place going to the endemic Balearic shearwater; breeding has only been proven here (1750–2125 pairs recorded between 1999 and 2001; a disappointing figure which reflects the almost total disappearance of the once prolific Formentera colonies). Storm petrel (subspecies *melitensis*), Cory's shearwater (subspecies *diomedea*), shag (of the Mediterranean endemic subspecies *desmarestii*) and Audouin's gulls all maintain important colonies here, as does Eleonora's falcon. S'Albufera, in northern Mallorca, is the most important wetland in the Balears, harbouring significant colonies of herons and purple gallinule plus the western Mediterranean's largest population of moustached warbler, as well as attracting huge numbers of passage migrants. Other bird-rich wetlands include Salobrar de Campos (Mallorca), S'Albufera des Grau (Menorca) and Ses Salines (Eivissa–Formentera).

The outstanding Balearic amphibian is undoubtedly the Mallorcan midwife toad, first described in 1977 from fossil remains, with live specimens discovered in 1980 in the deep limestone canyons of the Serra de Tramuntana. Two endemic reptiles occur in the archipelago: Lilford's wall lizard, once common on Mallorca and Menorca but nowadays found only on Cabrera and the islets around Mallorca and Menorca, and the Ibiza wall lizard, still common on Eivissa and Formentera, with around 45 distinct races having been described from the offshore islets of the Pitiüses.

With the exception of a few bats, the remainder of the mammals, reptiles and amphibians which inhabit the archipelago today have been introduced, either by accident or by design, with species of note including green toad – introduced in the Bronze Age, probably as a religious totem – Hermann's tortoise, Moroccan rock and Italian wall lizards on Menorca, and mammals such as the garden dormouse, common genet and pine marten, all three of which have had time to evolve into distinct Balearic races.

The archipelago of Cabrera is the sole Balearic national park, while the whole island of Menorca has been declared a Biosphere Reserve. Aside from the *parcs naturals* of Sa Dragonera and S'Albufera in Mallorca and S'Albufera des Grau in Menorca, and the *reserva natural* of Ses Salines of Eivissa–Formentera (also a World Heritage Site), however, the most widely used conservation designation in the Balears is that of *àrea natural d'especial interès* (ANEI); there are 82 in total, including almost 90% of the coastline of Menorca and much of Mallorca's Serra de Tramuntana (itself a proposed *parc natural*). A useful website is the unofficial www.webverd.com/espais.htm

Mallorca

Mallorca is the largest and highest of the islands, peaking at Puig Major 1445 m, a kilometre higher than anywhere else in the archipelago. The dramatic northern coastline contrasts with the generally flatter lowlands which make up much of the southern part of the island. Although it is a very popular tourist destination, the varied landscape offers much to interest the naturalist.

SITE 68 Sa Dragonera

Sixth-largest island in the Balears, home to important colonies of Eleonora's falcon and seabirds, plus many endemic plants.

Less than a kilometre from the small fishing harbour of Sant Elm (San Telmo), the serrated profile of Sa Dragonera reclines in the cerulean Mediterranean, the intervening straight dotted with the islets of Es Pantaleu and Illa Mitjana. Although a westerly continuation of the jagged limestone Serra de Tramuntana (see p. 199), Sa Dragonera peaks at only 310 m (Na Pòpia), causing little interruption of the rain-laden winds from the northwest and giving rise to a semi-arid climate (average annual rainfall is just 370 mm). The main island is ellipsoid in shape – some 4 km long and 1 km wide – with a sheer scarp along the northwestern flank but descending gently to a fringe of sandy coves towards the mainland.

Sa Dragonera (a *parc natural* of 290 ha and ZEPA) is home to some 360 species of vascular plant, of which 20 are confined to the Balears. Several of these endemics can be found around the windswept coasts of the island, particularly on the sheer, northwest-facing cliffs, the most noteworthy of which is the sea-lavender *Limonium dragonericum*, unique to this locality. Here, too, grow *Scabiosa cretica, Helichrysum ambiguum, Launaea cervicornis*, yellow sea aster, rock and golden-samphires, the sprawling viper's-bugloss *Echium arenarium* and sea

stork's-bill, a north European species at its only Balearic station.

Other Balearic endemics – notably *Hippocrepis balearica, Teucrium cossonii, Sibthorpia africana, Globularia cambessedesii, Crocus cambessedesii* and *Allium antonii-bolosii* – thrive in Sa Dragonera's shady screes and rockgardens and on inland north-facing crags, growing together with *Buxus balearica, Micromeria filiformis, Bellium bellidioides* and *Cheirolophus intybaceus*, plus Mediterranean selaginella and ferns such as scaly cheilanthes and the spleenworts *Asplenium petrarchae* and *A. sagittatum*.

Much of the interior of Sa Dragonera was once clothed with Aleppo pines, but these were heavily exploited for timber in the 1930s, such that Mediterranean scrub com-

Moorish gecko *Tarentola mauritanica*

munities dominate today. Deeper soils host a shrubby garrigue of cneorum and wild olive, in association with joint pine, osyris, tree spurge, lentisc, *Rhamnus lycioides* subspecies *oleoides*, Balearic St John's-wort and *Phillyrea angustifolia*, laced together with Virgin's bower, wild madder and the related Balearic endemic *Rubia angustifolia*, and sheltering Balearic sowbread and autumn arum. More open formations on thin soils are dominated by *Erica multiflora* and rosemary, accompanied by *Anthyllis cytisoides*, shrubby violet, cone knapweed and a diverse assemblage of spring-flowering orchids – giant, pyramidal and bee orchids, small-flowered serapias and dull ophrys – as well as autumn narcissus later in the year.

More than 50 species of bird are recorded regularly on Sa Dragonera, of which some 32 are known to breed. Outstanding are the island's colonies of Eleonora's falcon – the largest colony in the Balears, at around 200 pairs – and the endemic Balearic shearwater (250 pairs), with other cliff-nesting species including Cory's shearwater (80 pairs on the main island and 100 pairs on Es Pantaleu), a handful of pairs of storm petrel on Es Pantaleu and a maximum of 25 pairs of shag. Over 200 pairs of Audouin's gulls nest here, as well as 500+ of yellow-legged gulls, numbers of the latter having been controlled since 1989 to reduce competition with other seabirds. Two or three pairs of peregrines

and a single pair of ospreys – which don't nest every year – complete the picture.

Other breeding birds of Sa Dragonera include kestrel, scops owl, rock dove, pallid swift, crag martin, nightingale, blue rock thrush and one of the highest densities of Marmora's warbler in the Balears, while the island is also an important landfall for migrating passerines, particularly in the autumn; over 80 species were ringed here between 1981 and 1992. By contrast, the only reptiles are Lilford's wall lizard (subspecies *giglioli*) and Moorish gecko, while native mammals are limited to grey long-eared, European free-tailed and Schreiber's bats and Savi's pipistrelle; Algerian hedgehogs, black rats, house mice and rabbits have been introduced.

Either of the capes – Tramuntana to the northeast or Es Llebeig to the southwest – provides a great vantage point for cetacean-watching, primarily for common, striped and bottle-nosed dolphins, although fin and sperm whales also turn up occasionally, as do loggerhead turtles. More than 110 species of marine invertebrate have been recorded from the coralline formations and undersea meadows around Sa Dragonera, with saddled and annular seabream, comber, painted comber, dusky perch, brown and Mediterranean rainbow and ornate wrasse among the more noteworthy of the hundred or so fish species cited here.

Access and information: Sa Dragonera is served by boats (Crucero Margarita; tel: 971 470449/757065) from Sant Elm (San Telmo); about 10 minutes, not Sundays. Other companies operate from Port d'Andratx. Permits are issued on arrival at the park centre in Cala Lledó (Lladó), along with details of the authorised itin-

eraries (several areas are strict reserves). Only 150 people are allowed on the island at any one time and it is forbidden to spend the night there. There is no access to Es Pantaleu or Illa Mitjana, to protect the vulnerable seabird colonies from disturbance. The park offices can be contacted on 971 180632.

Also in the area

La Trapa (together with Sa Dragonera and intervening marine habitats, a ZEPA of 975 ha) A 75 ha estate centred on the

Puig de Sa Trapa (472 m), acquired by GOB in 1980; best accessed from Sant Elm. Many Balearic endemic plants, with cushions of *Astragalus balearicus* and Balearic St John's-wort on exposed flanks of the *puig*, and *Brassica balearica*, *Hippocrepis balearica* and *Helichrysum ambiguum* on the sea-cliffs. Around 80 species of bird recorded, including breeding Eleonora's falcon and a notable colony of Balearic shearwater. Peregrines and crag martins on the inland cliffs, with Marmora's warbler common in the garrigue and scops owls and booted eagles in the pines. Also green toad, Moorish gecko, false smooth snake, Algerian hedgehog, beech marten and common genet. More information from gobtrapa@mallorcaweb.net.

SITE 69 Serra de Tramuntana

One of Mallorca's last wilderness areas, with many endemic plants and important raptor populations, including the only island-dwelling black vultures in the world.

A labyrinth of serrated limestone peaks and vertiginous gorges, the Serra de Tramuntana is a far cry from the Mallorca of the package-tour brochures. Although not of gargantuan proportions – Puig Major rises to just 1445 m – the terrain is wild and sparsely populated, harbouring a wealth of wildlife not commonly associated with the Mediterranean islands.

An easterly continuation of Andalucía's Sierras Béticas, the Serra de Tramuntana is about 80 km long and some 15 km wide, extending along the whole northwestern flank of the island. On the north face, the mountains plunge abruptly into an azure sea in a virtually unbroken line of cliffs – sometimes over 300 m high – stretching from Port

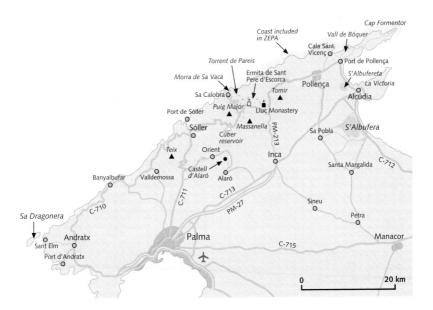

d'Andratx to Cap Formentor (see p. 203). Many peaks exceed 1000 m; apart from Puig Major, the most renowned are Teix (1062 m) Massanella (1352 m), and Tomir (1102 m).

The Serra protects the plains to the south from the *tramuntana* winds which originate in the northwest (hence the name) and thus has a noticeably wetter climate than the rest of the island. Precipitation here may be 1500 mm per year, allowing yew, the Afro-Iberian endemic maple *Acer granatense* and the shrubs *Buxus balearica* and *Rhamnus ludovici-salvatoris* to thrive in sheltered enclaves. In addition, more than 30 species of vascular plant are endemic to these mountains, particularly in the 'subalpine' zone above the tree-line – notably the buttercup *Ranunculus weyleri*, the crucifer *Brassica balearica* and the umbellifers *Bupleurum barceloi* and *Ligusticum lucidum* subspecies *huteri* – accompanied by species such as spring rock-cress, lax potentilla and fairy foxglove which are more commonly associated with montane habitats elsewhere in Europe.

Another interesting plant community occupies the sheer-sided gorges carved out by the seasonal *torrents*, where typical high-altitude species such as *Paeonia cambessedesii*, *Helleborus lividus*, the storks-bill *Erodium reichardii*, the shrubby St John's-wort *Hypericum hircinum* and the mullein *Verbascum boerhavii* have been washed down almost to sea level. These chasms are the only place in the world where you might encounter the Mallorcan midwife toad. Middle-altitude limestone rockgardens are also worth a look, harbouring an interesting spring-flowering community of polyanthus narcissus, the slender white bells of *Allium subhirsutum* and a wealth of orchids, including man, pyramidal, giant, naked man and milky, with September bringing a sprinkling of the delicate *Crocus cambessedesii*, the yellow-flowered common sternbergia and autumn lady's tresses into bloom.

The Serra de Tramuntana (48 000 ha of which are a ZEPA) is home to the only island population of black vultures in the world (some 70 individuals), with 8–12 breeding pairs rearing 3–4 chicks in 1996. This is also the only place on the island where red kites nest today (albeit only about six pairs), with other breeding raptors including good numbers of booted eagle and peregrine. Almost 200 pairs of Eleonora's falcons occupy the north coast of the Serra de Tramuntana, sharing their cliff-side habitat with 7 pairs of osprey and some 200 pairs of shag. Other breeding birds of note in the Serra are rock thrush, blue rock thrush and Marmora's warbler, with alpine accentor a regular winter visitor.

The best way to familiarise yourself with the Serra de Tramuntana is to drive the narrow, winding road (C-710) which links Andratx with Pollença – a journey of around 110 km – taking in some of the hot-spots described below; avoid weekends and the height of summer and make an early start.

Pantà de Cúber

Adjacent to the C-710 at km 34, the Cúber reservoir lies in a dry basin populated mainly by spiny or unpalatable plants such as *Astragalus balearicus*, thorny broom, Mediterranean spurge and *Euphorbia pithyusa*. Bird-wise, the stony margins harbour hoopoe, short-toed lark and tawny pipit, while subalpine and spectacled warblers and cirl buntings have been known to nest in the waterside scrub. This is also a classic breeding locality for rock thrush (rare on Mallorca), as well as for the Balearic race of blue tit (*balearicus*). Wrynecks (subspecies *mauretanica*, which is resident on Mallorca), also occur here, while red kites and black vultures are a regular feature of the skies. Ospreys are frequently seen fishing here, with Eleonora's falcons dropping in to bathe.

Sa Calobra/Torrent de Pareis

Superb limestone rockgardens line the road winding down to the cove of Sa Calobra, populated by the lovely winter-flowering polyanthus narcissus and many orchids; Balearic specialities include Balearic St John's-wort, the robust, fetid umbellifer *Pastinaca lucida* and *Phlomis italica*. Once at Sa Calobra, walk east through a series of

Mallorcan midwife toad *Alytes muletensis*

tunnels to reach the shingle beach at the mouth of the Torrent de Pareis, beneath shady cliffs studded with tree spurge, *Cymbalaria aequitriloba*, *Scabiosa cretica*, the related *Cephalaria squamiflora* subspecies *balearica*, three-cornered garlic and the Balearic endemics *Galium crespianum*, *Helichrysum ambiguum*, *Senecio rodriguezii* and *Crepis triasii*.

The setting at the mouth of the Torrent de Pareis – a small beach almost completely encircled by sheer limestone walls – is simply stunning. Summer snowflakes cluster in the shade of lentisc and chaste tree, and as you venture into the narrow defile of Pareis (8 km long and up to 200 m deep), you should find *Genista majorica*, *Buxus balearica* and laurustinus at the foot of the cliffs. Fissure plants here include Mallorcan violet, the yellow-flowered, creeping *Sibthorpia africana* and *Digitalis dubia*, all Balearic endemics. The Mallorcan midwife toad, unique to the island, has one of its strongholds here, with the defile also being home to breeding rock dove, alpine swift, crag martin, blue rock thrush, nightingale and Marmora's warbler. The headland to the east of the seaward end – Morra de Sa Vaca – harbours nesting pallid swifts and Eleonora's falcons.

The southern, topmost end of the Torrent de Pareis is not quite as accessible. A steep descent into the canyon is the order of the day, with ropes and wetsuits often required to complete the route to the sea, but almost anybody can descend the narrow, winding path through the holm oaks, limestone rock-gardens and *Ampelodesmos* garrigue as far as the Entreforc (where the Torrent de Pareis joins that of Sa Fosca); start from the Ermita de Sant Pere d'Escorca (at about km 25 on the C-710). The view across the Entreforc is

stunning – you could easily spot black vulture, booted eagle or peregrine from this vantage point – while botanical highlights include Balearic sowbread, the purple-flowered, white-woolly labiate *Phlomis italica* and the germander *Teucrium asiaticum*.

Massanella

The twins peaks of Massanella (1348 and 1352 m) are the second highest on Mallorca, boasting magnificent views of Menorca and Cabrera on a clear day. The lower slopes are clothed with lush forests of holm oak and Aleppo pine over an understorey of prickly juniper, thorny broom, the Spanish endemic buckthorn *Rhamnus ludovici-salvatoris* (also found in the province of València), narrow-leaved cistus, tree heath, *Erica multiflora* and rosemary. Look out for small-leaved, broad-leaved, large white and sword-leaved helleborines here, as well as violet limodore. Forest birds include scops owl, spotted flycatcher, firecrest and goldcrest, with garden dormouse, common genet and pine marten among the notable mammals.

Above the tree-line is a rich garrigue of *Ampelodesmos mauritanica* and a number of endemic dwarf shrubs: spiny 'hedgehogs' of *Teucrium subspinosum* and *Astragalus balearicus*, the crinkle-leaved Balearic St John's-wort, the lavender-cotton *Santolina chamaecyparissus* subspecies *magonica* and *Phlomis italica*. The seemingly bare rock above 1200 m harbours a number of specialist high-altitude Balearic endemics, such as the fleshy-leaved *Brassica balearica*, the spurge *Euphorbia maresii* and the white-flowered primrose *Primula vulgaris* subspecies *balearica*, with the screes home to *Paeonia cambessedesii*, *Pastinaca lucida*, *Linaria aeruginea* subspecies *pruinosa* and the scrambling pink-flowered skullcap *Scutellaria balearica*. Once above the trees, you might spot black vultures cruising above the surrounding peaks, with crag martin, blue rock thrush and possibly rock thrush closer at hand; alpine accentors regularly turn up during the winter.

Vall de Bóquer

This trail across the neck of the Formentor peninsula runs through the privately owned Bóquer estate, so please greet the residents politely! To get there, follow signs through Port de Pollença towards Cap Formentor and just before leaving town turn left opposite Avenida Bocchoris; follow this road north and park by the sign saying 'Predio Bóquer'.

The valley – flanked by knife-edged limestone ridges – is a renowned stopover for passage migrants. In the fig and olive groves around the farm look out for passage yellow wagtail (several subspecies), black-eared wheatear, pied flycatcher and warblers (mainly wood, Bonelli's and subalpine), as well as resident cirl buntings. Stone curlews are usually present, but often tricky to locate under the trees. The crags further along host resident peregrine, blue rock thrush and raven, while a pair of Egyptian vultures bred here as recently as 1996. Eleonora's falcons are often seen feeding in the skies above, while migrating raptors commonly include marsh harrier and, in early May, honey buzzard. Just as Cala Bóquer comes into view, dense low scrub harbours Marmora's warbler, with Audouin's gull and shag regular around the rocky cove.

Cala Bóquer

Also in the area

Fundació Jardí Botànic de Sóller Botanical gardens at km 30 on the Palma to Port de Sóller road (tel: 971 634014; fax: 971 634781; e-mail: fjbs@bitel.es).

Castell d'Alaró On the southern flank of the Serra de Tramuntana, accessible from Alaró or Orient. Sheer-walled plateau (822 m) reached via a zigzag trail through terraced almond, olive and carob groves teeming with orchids. Cuckoo, hoopoe, spotted flycatcher, Sardinian warbler, woodchat shrike, serin and corn bunting in farmed areas, nightingale in streamside thickets, crossbills in Aleppo pines and firecrests in evergreen oak copses, while cliff-breeders include blue rock thrush, crag martin, kestrel and raven. From Alaró, the trail is driveable up to Es Verger at the base of the cliff, but you must walk the last 2 km.

SITE 70 Cap Formentor

A precipitous limestone headland, home to many endemic plants and cliff-nesting birds and an exceptional locality for migrating raptors and passerines.

A northeasterly extension of the Serra de Tramuntana (included in the ZEPA of the same name), the blade-shaped Formentor peninsula offers superb views over sheer cliffs, tiny offshore islets and the azure Mediterranean in almost every direction. A narrow road (PM-221) takes you from Port de Pollença to the lighthouse at the tip of the peninsula (20 km), winding through shady Aleppo pine forests, *Ampelodesmos* garrigue and limestone rockgardens.

At the top of the first climb, the precipitous north-facing cliffs (some 230 m high) of the Mirador d'es Colomer provide a foothold for *Hippocrepis balearica* and *Anthyllis fulgurans*, both unique to the Balears, as well as for *Scabiosa cretica* and *Launaea cervicornis*. Examine the surrounding rockgardens for endemic cushions of *Astragalus balearicus* and *Teucrium subspinosum*, as well as rock milkwort, autumn arum and sea squill. Breeding birds here include rock dove, pallid swift, crag martin, blue rock thrush and Sardinian and Marmora's warblers, plus black redstart in winter, while a road up to the right (south) leads to an old signal tower which can be excellent for spotting raptors migrating north, especially when the cloud is low; buzzard, honey buzzard, black kite and marsh harrier are common, with an occasional red kite, Montagu's harrier, hobby or, rarely, short-toed eagle putting in an appearance.

Secreted in the heart of the pine forest, the fields around Cases Velles (Casas Veyas; at km 11 on the PM-221) have been much studied by generations of ornithologists. Resident species include Marmora's warbler, firecrest and crossbill, but it seems that almost anything might drop in on migration; among the

Cap Formentor

Paeonia cambessedesii

regular visitors are turtle dove, bee-eater, redstart, whinchat, ring ouzel, subalpine warbler, golden oriole and ortolan bunting. Rufous bush robin also occurs on occasion, while real rarities have included olive-backed pipit and yellow-browed warbler.

Nearing the lighthouse, the road passes through a tunnel, on the far side of which lies one of Mallorca's classic botanical localities. The screes here house the endemic peony

Paeonia cambessedesii, Balearic sowbread, the foxglove *Digitalis dubia*, polyanthus narcissus and dragon's mouth (a striking arum which is also found on Sardinia and Corsica), while the cliffs are smothered with the white-flowered endemic storksbill *Erodium reichardii*, trailing clumps of a deep-blue-flowered rosemary (subspecies *palaui*) and *Helichrysum ambiguum*.

Cap Formentor, its 300 metre-high cliffs topped by a lighthouse, is a great place for watching gannets (in winter) and shags fishing in the waters below, with Cory's and Balearic shearwaters out to sea and peregrines and Eleonora's falcons hawking overhead. Nearer at hand you might spot crag martin, blue rock thrush and Marmora's warbler, while the Balearic race of crossbill (*balearica*) can be seen in the pines at the furthest tip of the peninsula. Carpets of the white, papery flowers of *Paronychia argentea* sprawl over the cliffs, interspersed with the daisy-like Tyrrhenian endemic *Bellium bellidioides*, the diminutive *Senecio rodriguezii* and many species of sea-lavender.

Also in the area

S'Albufereta (ANEI; 506 ha) Small wetland in the Badia de Pollença with breeding marsh harrier, water rail, black-winged stilt, yellow wagtail, moustached warbler and probably little bittern and purple heron. Interesting passage records include great white egret, squacco heron, glossy ibis, black stork, red-footed falcon and red-throated pipit.

La Victoria (ANEI; 1198 ha) Limestone headland separating the bays of Pollença and Alcúdia. Military installation on the coastal cliffs at Cap des Pinar (ZEPA; 2500 ha) provides refuge for a pair of ospreys and breeding peregrine and shag (25 pairs). Trail from Ermita de La Victoria up to Atalaya d'Alcúdia (444 m) runs through mature Aleppo pine forest, with Balearic St

John's wort, Balearic sowbread and violet limodore, grading into *Ampelodesmos* garrigue above, with cushions of *Teucrium subspinosum* and *Astragalus balearicus*, plus giant orchid and mirror ophrys in early spring. Atalaya renowned for fissure community of *Silene mollissima*, *Galium crespianum*, *Digitalis dubia* and *Cheirolophus intybaceus*, while the sea-cliffs host *Hippocrepis balearica*, *Scabiosa cretica* and *Helichrysum ambiguum*. Birds include turtle dove, cuckoo, hoopoe, tawny pipit, Marmora's warbler and woodchat shrike.

Pollentia Ruins of a second-century Roman city with impressive theatre; museum; access off the C-712 between Alcúdia and Port d'Alcúdia (tel: 971 547004).

SITE
71 S'Albufera de Mallorca

Largest coastal wetland in the Balears, of superlative importance for its breeding, migratory and wintering birds; interesting odonates.

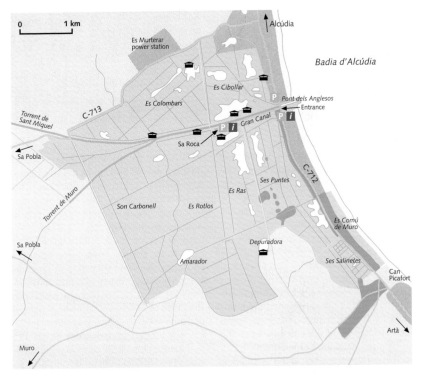

Considering the general lack of surface water in Mallorca, the Parc Natural de S'Albufera (1708 ha, also a Ramsar Site; ZEPA of 2584 ha) certainly seems to have more than its fair share. Approaching from the west, you are greeted by an enormous expanse of reedbeds – often over 3 m high – while the coast road between Alcúdia and Artà (C-712) reveals tantalising glimpses of shallow lagoons and *salines* through the pines.

Located in the northern reaches of the Badia d'Alcúdia, the Albufera wetland is cordoned off from the sea by a broad belt of sand dunes, although the network of dykes and drainage canals (relics of previous attempts to drain the area) which dissects the marshes maintains a saltwater connection via the Gran Canal (S'Oberta). Areas which are permanently inundated with freshwater (entering the marshes via the Torrents de Muro and Sant Miquel) harbour dense stands of common reed, great fen-sedge and bulrush, dotted with metre-high purple spikes of bog orchis and less conspicuous tongue orchids and small-flowered serapias in late spring. The canals themselves harbour soft horn-

S'Albufera de Mallorca

wort and fennel and horned pondweeds, and are lined with sparse gallery forests of white poplar, small-leaved elm and tamarisks (*Tamarix africana, T. gallica* and *T. canariensis*), home to breeding scops owl and the bulk of the night heron colonies.

More saline habitats closer to the sea are populated by common glasswort, shrubby sea-blite, sea-purslane, sea-lavenders, *Plantago crassifolia*, golden-samphire and *Artemisia caerulescens*, while towards the southern end of the site, fossil dune hummocks clothed with Aleppo pines rise above the general level of the marshes. In spring these pinewoods are carpeted with friar's cowl, *Asparagus stipularis* and *A. acutifolius*, common grape and tassel hyacinths, common asphodel and three-cornered garlic, plus a number of orchids: dull, bumble-bee, early spider and sawfly ophrys and *Ophrys dyris*. Just to the south of the pines is an expanse of dry pasture, inhabited by small numbers of stone curlew, short-toed lark and tawny pipit.

S'Albufera is undoubtedly the showpiece of nature conservation in Mallorca, with 230 bird species – almost 80% of those recorded from the Balears – having been observed here. Of the 61 breeding species, several have recently made spectacular recoveries; in 1999, 90–120 pairs of purple heron bred in the park, as well as 90 pairs of night heron, 25–30 pairs of little egret, 50–100 pairs of little bittern and 5 pairs of bittern. A few pairs of squacco heron and cattle egret have also nested in recent years.

Others have been reintroduced, with remarkable results. From just 28 purple gallinules released in 1991, the park now harbours a breeding nucleus of almost 300 pairs. Similarly, 45 red-crested pochard chicks from the Delta de l'Ebre were duly acclimatised and released in 1991, to give a resident population of around 35 pairs today. In order to maintain a genetically pure population of white-headed duck in Spain – given the problems of hybridisation with non-native ruddy duck on the mainland – 36 individuals were introduced from Doñana in 1993, although with limited breeding success to date.

S'Albufera is of international significance for its moustached warblers, the reedbeds housing around 1000 pairs: the largest population in the western Mediterranean, if not the world. Here, too, breed nightingale, fantailed, Cetti's, reed and great reed warblers and reed bunting (subspecies *witherbyi*, with a notably thicker bill), as well as water rail (maximum 250 pairs). In addition, some nine pairs of marsh harrier nest, ospreys fish

Balears

Squacco heron *Ardeola ralloides* (Mike Powles)

The network of canals and ditches is home to a number of fish, of which only the eastern mosquitofish, introduced from the New World to control mosquitoes, and three-spined stickleback occur in fresh waters. A further 27 species are essentially marine, using S'Albufera only as a feeding or nursery ground, including shore pipefish, European seabass, shi drum, rusty and peacock blennies, giant, black, common and rock gobies and several species of mullet and seabream.

These watercourses also provide refuge for the increasingly scarce European pond terrapin, which nowadays has to compete with the non-native red-eared slider. Other S'Albufera herptiles include Iberian pool and stripeless tree frogs, green toad, Moorish gecko and viperine and grass snakes. Algerian hedgehog, brown rat, rabbit and weasel are the commonest mammals here, but there is evidence that the pine marten population is on the increase, while common genets are also seen from time to time. Eight species of bat have been cited in the park, notably the barbastelle.

Odonates are probably the most eye-catching invertebrates of the marshes, particularly the hawkers (southern, migrant and Norfolk) and emperor and lesser emperor, while the rare *Selysiothemis nigra* is a threatened species in Europe, with a highly disjunct Mediterranean distribution. Look out, too, for smaller species such as common winter, small emerald, willow emerald, goblet-marked and dainty damselflies, as well as black-tailed and keeled skimmers and ruddy, scarlet and red-veined darters.

Butterflies abound in the relict dune communities, including mallow skipper,

here all year round and Eleonora's falcons – sometimes in phalanxes of over 100 individuals – feed over the marshes in May and June. The abandoned *salines* at the southern end of the park are a prime breeding site for 100+ pairs of black-winged stilt and significant numbers of Kentish and little ringed plovers.

Over 3500 coot and some 5000 wildfowl take refuge in the marshes in winter, particularly mallard, teal, wigeon and shoveler, as well as lesser numbers of gadwall, pintail, pochard and tufted duck, a handful of greylag geese and shelduck and two or three ferruginous duck. Wintering passerines include bluethroat, chiffchaff, penduline tit and the nominate race of reed bunting. Waders and marsh terns – whiskered and black in fair numbers – abound during the spring migration, while flocks of tens of thousands of swallows have been recorded here in the autumn and huge numbers of migrating starlings use the reedbeds on their way south in mid- to late November (sometimes more than a million birds!).

Apart from a long list of Iberian rarities (black-winged pratincole, lesser yellowlegs, lesser crested tern, citrine wagtail, etc.), scarce species in a Balearic context are surprisingly regular here, especially on passage, and have included both black and white storks, great white egret, spoonbill, glossy ibis, marbled teal (has also bred recently), red-footed falcon, merlin, collared pratincole, Temminck's stint, marsh sandpiper, Mediterranean, slender-billed and little gulls, gull-billed, Caspian and white-winged black terns, red-rumped swallow and red-throated pipit.

Purple gallinule *Porphyrio porphyrio*

swallowtail, Camberwell beauty, cardinal, striped grayling, two-tailed pasha, Spanish brown argus and long-tailed, Lang's short-tailed, Adonis and common blues, while migrant plain tigers occur sporadically. More than 300 species of moth have also been recorded at S'Albufera, including a number of hawk-moths – death's-head, convolvulus, silver-striped, striped and humming-bird – but perhaps the most notable is the arctiid *Pelosia plumosa*, very abundant here in the old reedbeds but extremely rare elsewhere; known from only a handful of Mediterranean sites, the Albufera population is of world significance.

To the south lies a small area of coastal sand dunes – Es Comú de Muro – whose primary communities comprise sea knotgrass, sea rocket, sea medick, southern birdsfoot-trefoil, sea-holly, coastal crucianella,

Helichrysum stoechas and sea daffodil, backed by a belt of prickly juniper (subspecies *macrocarpa*), here associated with *Halimium halimifolium*, found nowhere else in Mallorca, and the Balearic endemic *Thymelaea velutina*, known only from a handful of coastal sites and, curiously, the highest peaks of the Serra de Tramuntana.

The Aleppo pine forest behind the dunes shelters a rich understorey of lentisc, shrubby violet, myrtle, *Erica multiflora*, *Phillyrea angustifolia*, rosemary, felty germander, Sodom's apple and dwarf fan palm, festooned with climbing fragrant clematis, Virgin's bower and *Lonicera implexa*. Look out for orchids here, particularly mirror and bumble-bee ophrys in spring, bee orchid later on and autumn lady's tresses at the end of summer. Firecrest, serin, greenfinch, chaffinch and crossbill are the most typical birds of these pinewoods.

Access and information: The interpretation centre of Sa Roca (tel: 971 892250; fax: 971 892158; e-mail albufera@ wanadoo.es; website: www. oninet.es/ usuarios/salbufera) is signposted off the C-712 Alcúdia–Artà road, by the Pont dels Anglesos; park at the entrance to the reserve, opposite the Hotel Parc Natural, and walk (about 20 minutes). Sa Roca provides maps showing the location of the hides and waymarked trails (on foot or bicycle; open 24 hours a day). Mosquito repellent is a must!

Also in the area

Dunes de Son Real/Sa Canova d'Artà (ANEIs; 1048 and 1021 ha, respectively) Sand dunes, 80 m high, straddling the resort of Son Serra de la Marina. Seaward side dominated by rocky limestone shore and mobile dunes hosting yellow horned-poppy, rock samphire and *Senecio rodriguezii*. Inland Aleppo pine forest and rosemary garrigue home to pine marten and breeding Dartford and Marmora's warblers. Stone curlew, tawny pipit, Hermann's tortoise and Moorish gecko in dry habitats, with Kentish plover, kingfisher and green toad in small permanent lagoons at the mouths of the Torrents de Son Bauló, Son Real and Na Borgues; bee-eaters occasionally nest along the banks of the latter. Abundant two-tailed pasha at the end of the summer.

72 Muntanyes d'Artà

SITE

Extensive limestone massif harbouring many endemic plants and colonies of cliff-nesting seabirds.

The Muntanyes d'Artà (an ANEI of 7295 ha and proposed *parc natural*) forms a squarish peninsula in the northeastern corner of Mallorca, although to use the word 'mountain' is rather misleading, since Morey – despite being the highest peak in the Serres de Llevant – weighs in at just 561 m. The interior of the massif is dominated by garrigue and patches of Aleppo pine, presided over by impressive limestone crags and buttresses, especially to the west. Orchids abound here, with naked man, milky and autumn lady's tresses in open habitats, violet limodore amid the pines, and damp grasslands housing bug and tongue orchids and small-flowered serapias.

Black vultures sometimes stray here from their stronghold in the Serra de Tramuntana, the highest peaks are a renowned haunt of wintering alpine accentors and the coastal scrub on the track between the resort of Betlem and Cap Ferrutx is a good place to encounter warblers in spring – both the resident Marmora's and rarer migratory species such as icterine and melodious – with alpine swifts around the crags in summer.

A particularly scenic road leading to the Ermita de Betlem crosses the very heart of the massif. Just before the road drops down towards the chapel and the sea, the vegetation is highly typical of the peninsula as a whole: robust tussocks of *Ampelodesmos mauritanica* and a scattering of dwarf fan palms, here growing to a height of up to 2 m, with distinct trunks topped by tufts of foliage (a growth habit generated by the traditional harvesting of the leaves to make the artisan baskets and mats for which Artà is renowned). Common asphodel, sea squill and the thorny stems of *Asparagus stipularis* abound here, as well as spiny cushions of the white-flowered tragacanth *Astragalus balearicus* and the pink-flowered germander *Teucrium subspinosum*, both unique to the Balears. Thekla larks forage around the small

Naked man orchid
Orchis italica

lay-by here rather in the manner of sparrows hoping for crumbs.

The low cliffs to the east of the Ermita de Betlem are worth examining both for their birdlife and endemic plants; the path to the spring leads you through a grove of Aleppo pines and past walled orchards and vegetable gardens. Here you might turn up resident cirl bunting, crossbill, firecrest and hoopoe, plus woodchat shrike in summer, with migration periods bringing in good numbers of whinchats, redstarts, whitethroats, blackcaps, chiff-chaffs and garden, wood and willow warblers. Booted eagles are fairly common in the skies above the crags, with at least seven pairs breeding in the massif.

From the shrine at the spring, a path heads up to low cliffs studded with pink-flowered cushions of *Scabiosa cretica* and a number of Balearic endemics: *Hippocrepis balearica*, *Galium crespianum*, *Crepis triasii* and *Helichrysum ambiguum*. In particularly shady gullies look out for *Lotus tetraphyllus*, a Balearic endemic like a small four-leaved clover, the variegated leaves of Balearic sowbread, known only from these islands and one station in southern France, and the Tyrrhenian *Micromeria filiformis*, as well as maidenhair fern and Mediterranean selaginella. Ravens croak from their cliff-top perches and crag martins zoom overhead, while the huge boulder at the end of the path

Coastal hillside, Artà peninsula, with dwarf fan palms *Chamaerops humilis* and Aleppo pines *Pinus halepensis*

is home to blue rock thrushes and a pair of rock doves.

The small beaches on the northern shore of the Artà peninsula are among the least visited on the island, doubtless because of the 9 km of potholes separating them from civilisation. Take the Capdepera road east out of Artà (C-715), then turn left by the petrol station after only 500 m (signposted 'Cala Torta'). Unfortunately, much of the Aleppo pine forest and *Ampelodesmos* garrigue en route suffered an extensive forest fire in 1999, virtually wiping out the best-established breeding nucleus of Dartford warbler on the island.

At the end of the road, Cala Torta harbours a small dune system with similar psammophiles to Es Comú (see p. 208), while rocky shores adjacent to the sea are studded with spiny, yellow-flowered cushions of *Launaea cervicornis* and the diminutive, pink-flowered ragwort *Senecio rodriguezii*. The low cliffs a little further inland are clothed with *Astragalus baleari-cus, Anthyllis fulgurans*, felty germander, the lavender-cotton *Santolina chamaecyparissus* subspecies *magonica* and *Helichrysum stoechas*. With increasing distance from the sea, the coastal vegetation grades into a wind-pruned scrub of Aleppo pine, *Genista tricuspidata*, the shrubby, pink-flowered rock milkwort, lentisc, narrow-leaved cistus, wild olive, *Phillyrea angustifolia*, rosemary and dwarf fan palm. Man orchids and bumblebee and early spider ophrys abound here, while butterflies include Bath white, brimstone, wall brown (subspecies *paramegaera*), green hairstreak and small copper.

The sheer cliffs along this north coast – from Cap Ferrutx in the west to Cap des Freu in the east (an 80 ha ZEPA) – are renowned for their seabird colonies, including shag (around 100 pairs), storm petrel (25 pairs), yellow-legged gull (225 pairs) and peregrine (3 pairs). Although Audouin's gulls last bred here in 1992, they are still commonly seen at Cala Torta.

Also in the area

Cap Vermell (ZEPA; 80 ha) Limestone headland housing an important shag colony (75 pairs) plus several hundred pairs of yellow-legged gull, apparently unaffected by their close proximity to the tourist-ridden Coves d'Artà.

Punta de n'Amer (ANEI; 200 ha) Promontory between the resorts of Sa Coma and Son Moro. Eroded limestone coastal platform has rock samphire, yellow sea aster and *Launaea cervicornis*, with more sandy soils hosting sea spurge, sea daffodil and, more rarely, *Thymelaea velutina*. The interior of the plateau is clothed with stunted Aleppo pines, dense maquis, *Ampelodesmos* garrigue and dry cereal fields. Red-legged partridge, Thekla lark, tawny pipit and linnet favour open areas, with cuckoo, stonechat and Sardinian and Marmora's warblers inhabiting the scrub and pines; Audouin's gulls regularly feed along the rocky shore. False smooth snake and Algerian hedgehog.

73 Cap Enderrocat/ Marina de Llucmayor

Precipitous coastal cliffs with an important shag colony, topped by a mosaic of garrigue and cultivated land supporting good numbers of stone curlew and Marmora's warbler.

The contrast between the high-rise resorts of the Platja de Palma and the adjacent stretch of wild sea-cliffs on Mallorca's southwest coast could not be more striking. From Cap Enderrocat (an ANEI of 396 ha and ZEPA (150 ha) as far as Cap Blanc) southwards, the crumbling terraces of the pale limestone cliffs house one of the largest breeding colonies of shags (of the Mediterranean sub-species *desmarestii*) in the world (around 200 pairs). The cliff-top plateau is sparsely clothed with a garrigue of Aleppo pine, joint pine, lentisc, narrow-leaved cistus, wild olive and rosemary, home to Thekla lark, stonechat, black redstart, Marmora's warbler and linnet.

A little to the south, the cliffs lose altitude and have consequently gained a couple of busy resorts, but south from here there is little to disturb the seabirds until you reach Cala Pi: some 12 km of vertiginous precipices rising to a maximum of 120 m, haunt of nesting peregrine, rock dove and blue rock thrush. The lighthouse at Cap Blanc (in the heart of the Marina de Llucmayor ANEI; 3124 ha) is a prime example, the characteristic 'dip and scarp' shrub profiles indicating strong onshore winds. Even so, several species more typical of warmer climes occur here, notably the lovely lilac-flowered sea mallow and the fleshy-leaved *Lycium intricatum*. The protected area ends where the cliffs give out, at the town of S'Estanyol de Migjorn, only a few kilometres west of the superb sandy beach and dunes of Es Trenc

Marmora's warbler *Sylvia sarda*

Woodchat shrike *Lanius senator* **(Mike Lane)**

Away from the sea, this whole stretch of coast is clothed with a mosaic of garrigue, small plots dedicated to vines or cereals, and drystone-walled orchards of almond, carob and fig, most of which are in private ownership. This patchwork landscape houses some 140 pairs of Marmora's warblers and 220 pairs of stone curlew, along with a multitude of colourful southern European birds such as scops owl, bee-eater, hoopoe and woodchat shrike, as well as cuckoo, turtle dove and nightingale. Eleonora's falcons, kestrels and, occasionally, red kites can be seen hunting here, while mammalian predators include weasel and common genet. Other vertebrates recorded in the area are Algerian hedgehog, garden dormouse, rabbit, Iberian hare (the smaller Mallorcan race *solisi*), Hermann's tortoise and green toad.

(see below). A seasonal *torrent* discharges into a small gravelly cove here, populated by prickly saltwort, yellow horned-poppy, sea rocket, sea-lavenders and sea-holly, backed by a narrow belt of Aleppo pines accompanied by *Anthyllis cytisoides* and shrubby globularia.

Also in the area

Es Carnatge des Coll d'en Rabassa (ANEI; 4.75 ha) Last stretch of natural coast along the Platja de Palma, rich in fossil molluscs found only along tropical African coasts today. Interesting coastal plant communities of yellow horned-poppy, ice plant, tree-mallow, *Thymelaea hirsuta*, the Balearic endemic *T. velutina*, *Echium arenarium*, coastal crucianella, *Anthemis maritima*, yellow sea aster, the quasi-endemic *Launaea cervicornis* (only in the Balears and Sierra de Gádor in Almería) and sea daffodil. Inner reaches (along the PM-19) have sparse Aleppo pines with an understorey of *Cistus clusii* and *Helianthemum marifolium*. Hoopoe, Sardinian warbler, fan-tailed warbler, linnet and corn bunting; Audouin's gulls feed along the rocky shore.

74 Es Trenc/Salobrar de Campos

Saltpans and brackish lagoons of high ornithological significance, particularly during migration periods, lying behind one of Mallorca's best-preserved dune systems.

Until fairly recently, the Salobrar de Campos (otherwise known as the Salines de Llevant; an ANEI of 1493 ha, 200 ha of which is also a ZEPA) was regarded as one the prime birdwatching sites on the island, but the days of being able to stroll along the banks separating the *salines* are strictly a thing of the past; visitors arriving at the gates of these working saltpans today are confronted with large notices telling them to 'Keep Out' in five languages.

Salobrar de Campos lies to the west of the PM-604 which links Campos with Colònia de Sant Jordi; a couple of kilometres before Sant Jordi, take a small road on the right which is clearly signposted 'Platja d'Es Trenc'. It is only 2.5 km from here to the car park at the beach, the route taking you between the salt-pans on the right and a mosaic of arable land, orchards, scrub – mainly Phoenician juniper, joint pine and lentisc – and pockets of Aleppo pine forest on the left.

Along the margins of the *salines* the vegetation is markedly halophytic, comprising glassworts, shrubby sea-blite, golden-samphire and a few stunted tamarisks. On the other side of the road, however, the fields are a riot of colour in spring, studded with blue pimpernel, mallow-leaved bindweed, wild clary, crown daisies, field marigolds and sheets of common asphodels. Butterflies abound in spring, including scarce swallowtail, clouded yellow, Cleopatra, southern gatekeeper and common and holly blues. Both Sardinian and Marmora's warblers inhabit the scrub here,

with stone curlew, short-toed and Thekla larks and tawny pipit frequenting more open areas; hoopoes and woodchat shrikes are ten-a-penny in the fig orchards.

Good views across the largely disused northern *salines* – particularly of migrant terns and collared pratincoles in spring – are obtained from the track which heads west from the Balneari de Sant Joan. This is also the locality in which most of the site's major rarities have been recorded in recent years, including pectoral and Terek sandpipers and greater yellowlegs, as well as notewor-thy migrants such as greater flamingo, glossy ibis, great white egret, sanderling, knot, Temminck's stint, bar-tailed godwit, whimbrel, marsh sandpiper, turnstone, slender-billed gull and gull-billed and white-winged black terns.

The *salines* as a whole harbour the largest breeding population of black-winged stilts in the Balears, plus an important colony of Kentish plover, with lesser numbers of water rail, redshank and possibly marsh harrier also rearing their young here. Ospreys fish all year round and Audouin's gulls are often seen during the summer, while Kentish plover, lapwing and dunlin make up the bulk of the wintering waders.

Es Trenc is one of the largest and best-pre-served sand-dune systems remaining in Mallorca. The first wave of dunes behind the

Helichrysum stoechas

beach is colonised by sea medick and southern birdsfoot-trefoil, purple and sea spurges, sea-holly and tuberous hawk's-beard, growing amid sheets of sea daffodils. A little further inland, more robust plants are able to gain a foothold, forming a delightful mosaic of yellow restharrow, felty germander and *Helichrysum stoechas* between bushes of Phoenician juniper, joint pine, shrubby orache and lentisc.

The older dunes behind have been colonised by Aleppo pine and some magnificent Phoenician junipers, accompanied by *Anthyllis cytisoides*, *Cistus clusii*, *Phillyrea angustifolia* and *P. latifolia*, rosemary and *Asparagus stipularis*, with wetter hollows containing tamarisk, golden-samphire and black bog-rush. Firecrests, serins and crossbills are the most visible (and audible) avian inhabitants of these pinewoods, but long-

Kentish plover *Charadrius alexandrinus* on nest (Mike Lane)

eared and scops owls are also known to occur here. The sand-cliffs in the higher dunes occasionally host bee-eater colonies, with other vertebrates including Hermann's tortoise, false smooth snake and the Balearic subspecies (*balearicus*) of green toad.

Also in the area

Cap de Ses Salines (ANEI; 1786 ha) Southernmost tip of Mallorca. Eastern shore is a long stretch of 80 m-high cliffs, home to breeding shag and raven, while along the western shore cliffs alternate with sandy coves, with a sprinkling of offshore islets (Na Guardis, close to Colònia de Sant Jordi, has an endemic subspecies of Lilford's wall lizard (*jordansi*) which is almost completely black). Well-preserved sand dunes at nearby Es Carbó. Inland of the cape is Aleppo pine forest with Phoenician juniper and all four Mallorcan cistus species; Marmora's warblers in the scrub and red-legged partridge, stone curlew and Thekla lark in more open areas; rarities cited around the lighthouse include bar-tailed desert lark and trumpeter finch. Offshore, look out for shearwaters, Eleonora's falcon and Audouin's gull from the Cabrera colonies.

SITE 75 Arxipèlag de Cabrera

The only national park in the Balears, harbouring exceptional seabird colonies and many endemic plants and terrestrial invertebrates; diverse marine flora and fauna.

The Parc Nacional Marítim-Terrestre de l'Arxipèlag de Cabrera (10 021 ha, of which only 1318 ha are terrestrial; also a ZEPA), comprises 20 islands and islets and lies scarcely 10 km from the southern tip of Mallorca. The principal island is Cabrera Gran, its 1154 ha rising abruptly to the 172 m peak of Na Picamosques, the only other island of any size being Sa Conillera (137 ha). Formerly a military outpost, the archipelago is virtually uninhabited today.

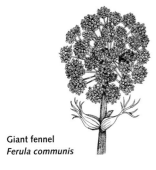

Giant fennel
Ferula communis

Geologically Cabrera is a continuation of Mallorca's Serres de Llevant, separated from the main island during a period of subsidence about 12 000 years ago. The predominant rock type is highly karstified Jurassic and Cretaceous limestone, sculpted into a series of high inland cliffs (over 100 m) overlooking small valleys. A semi-arid climate (334 mm of rain each year) means that the only tree able to survive is the Aleppo pine, typically associated with xerophytic scrub species such as Phoenician juniper, joint pine, tree spurge, cneorum, lentisc, *Rhamnus ludovici-salvatoris*, wild olive and *Phillyrea angustifolia*.

Where the pines have been removed and long-term goat-grazing has prevented their regeneration, a garrigue of *Erica multiflora* and rosemary has developed, accompanied by narrow-leaved cistus, felty germander (subspecies *pii-fontii*) and shrubby globularia, plus numerous eye-catching yellow umbels of giant fennel and an abundance of the Tyrrhenian endemic dragon's mouth. Windswept coastal habitats are dominated by hemispherical, spiny cushions of the legumes *Anthyllis fulgurans* and *Astragalus balearicus* and the labiate *Teucrium sub-*

spinosum. The accumulation of guano around the seabird colonies creates a nitrogen-rich habitat favouring shrubby sea-blite, tree mallow and the Afro-Iberian endemic *Withania frutescens*.

Almost 500 species of vascular plant have been recorded in the Cabrera archipelago, 17 of which are unique to the Balears, including the lovely *Paeonia cambessedesii*, *Helleborus lividus*, the sea-lavenders *Limonium pseudebusitanum* and *L. caprariense* and the wild onion *Allium antonii-bolosii*, with pinkish, trumpet-shaped flowers and wiry leaves. Similarly, Cabrera is home to 22 species of Balearic endemic invertebrate, 8 of which are found only here. Most are beetles and gastropods – the latter including members of the endemic genus *Iberellus*, the slug *Limax majoricensis* and the operculate snail *Tudorella ferruginea* – plus the spider *Nemesia brauni*. Nine endemic crustaceans occur in the small subterranean lakes, including the Cabrera endemic genus *Burrimysis*, recently discovered in Sa Cova des Burrí.

Among the reptiles, only Moorish and Turkish (rare) geckos and Lilford's wall lizard occur in the terrestrial habitats; about 80% of the world population of the latter is found here, pertaining to 10 distinct subspecies (*kuligae*, on Cabrera Gran, is a melanic form with a blue belly). In addition, the surrounding seas are often visited by loggerhead turtles – whose nearest occasional breeding grounds are in Sardinia (one successful nest in Almería in 2001) – and very rarely by leathery turtles.

The seabird colonies of the Cabrera archipelago are truly exceptional. Up to 500 pairs of Cory's and 120 of Balearic shearwaters breed here, along with 300–400 pairs of storm petrel, 85 of shag, some 1500 of yellow-legged gulls and almost 400 of Audouin's gulls (the largest colony in the Balears). These are accompanied by at least three pairs of osprey, a few pairs of peregrine and more than 50 pairs of Eleonora's falcon. Most of the seabirds can be observed on the crossing to the island during the summer months.

Apart from notable concentrations of Marmora's warbler (350+ pairs), other breeding birds of the archipelago include kestrel,

Helleborus lividus

stone curlew, wood pigeon, turtle dove, long-eared and barn owls, hoopoe, swift, blue rock thrush, Sardinian and subalpine (subspecies *moltonii*) warblers, spotted flycatcher, house sparrow, serin, goldfinch, greenfinch and linnet. During migration periods, the island can be alive with birds on passage – some 150 species have been recorded – particularly passerines. Scarce migrants include honey buzzard and golden oriole, with Cabrera renowned for attracting Balearic rarities such as red-necked nightjar, rufous bush robin, olivaceous warbler, collared flycatcher and red-backed shrike; yellow-breasted bunting and Radde's warbler have also been recorded in recent years.

Among the mammals, it would appear that all the land-dwelling representatives – Algerian hedgehog, common genet, feral cat, black rat, house mouse and rabbit – have been introduced, with the only indigenous species being grey long-eared and Schreiber's bats and Savi's pipistrelle. The sea caves on the southern side of Cabrera itself were the last breeding locality for the Mediterranean monk seal in the western Mediterranean, while bottle-nosed, striped and common dolphins still frequent the waters around the islands.

The underwater habitats are incredibly diverse, hence their inclusion in the national park; over 85% of the total protected area lies between sea level and a depth of 120 m. The marine catalogue to date includes no less than 162 species of alga, 87 sponges, 25

Yellow-legged gull *Larus cachinnans*

crustaceans, 22 molluscs and 34 echinoderms, with black and large-scaled scorpionfish, dusky perch, blacktip grouper, Mediterranean rainbow, ornate and pearly wrasse, damselfish, Atlantic stargazer, European barracuda, European conger and the aggressive Mediterranean moray among the 200+ species of fish recorded here.

The sandy and muddy flats down to a depth of 45 m have been colonised by posidonia meadows, which provide food and refuge for some 60 species of epiphytic algae, the enormous, quill-shaped fan mussel and rock sea-urchins. The rocky platforms and walls extending down to 90 m, on the other hand, are home to the yellow encrusting sea anemone, the blue sea-slug *Hypselodoris elegans*, common octopus, black sea-urchin, red and purple starfish and spiny and Norway lobsters.

Access and information: Tourist boats (*golondrinas*) are most frequent from Colònia de Sant Jordi (Excursions a Cabrera; tel: 971 649034) and Portopetro (Cruceros Llevant; tel: 971 657012), but only during Easter week and from the end of May to October; crossing time 40 minutes. Once on Cabrera Gran you can chose from several itineraries led by national park guides (no charge), but freelance access is restricted. For more information contact the main national park office (tel: 971 725010; fax: 971 725585; e-mail: cabrera@mma.es).

Balears

Menorca

The island of Menorca (a Biosphere Reserve of 70 200 ha; 43% of which lies within 19 ANEIs) is one of the best-preserved islands in the western Mediterranean. It can be conveniently divided geologically into the acid mountains of the northern Tramuntana, named after the fierce wind which sweeps down from the north in winter and spring, and the southern limestones of the Migjorn ('midday') region.

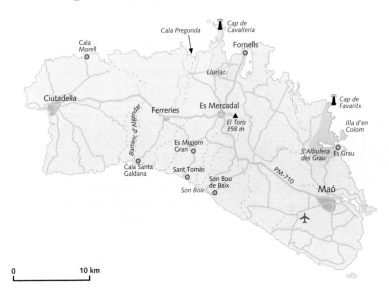

Cap de Cavalleria
Cala Pregonda
Cala Morell
Fornells
Lluriac
Ciutadella
Ferreries
Es Mercadal
Cap de Favaritx
Barranc d'Algendar
El Toro 358 m
Illa d'en Colom
Es Migjorn Gran
Cala Santa Galdana
Sant Tomàs
S'Albufera des Grau
Es Grau
Son Bou de Baix
Son Bou
PM-710
Maó

0   10 km

SITE 76 Menorca: Tramuntana

The northern sector of Menorca with a largely unspoilt coastline merging into low-intensity farming inland: important nuclei of the unique socarell *plant communities and abundant Egyptian vulture; Lilford's wall lizard on offshore islands.*

Menorca's Tramuntana comprises old, predominantly siliceous Devonian and Jurassic rocks which have been eroded into an undulating terrain of hills and gentle valleys. Low-lying coastal areas around Fornells and Cala Pregonda sport primary sand-dune systems harbouring sea rocket, sea-holly, sea bindweed, marram and sea daffodil, while older dunes inland are home to stunted Aleppo pines, Phoenician juniper (subspecies *turbinata*), clumps of lentisc and the endemic figwort *Scrophularia ramosissima* subspecies *minoricensis*. Further west the rocky coast harbours rock samphire and a whole range of sea-lavenders (12 species have been identified on the island, many of which are endemic to the Balears) including the cushion-forming *Limonium caprariense*.

Just inland lie the wind-sculpted cushions of the so-called *socarell* community, dominated by five species – *Astragalus balearicus, Anthyllis hermanniae, A. fulgurans, Launaea*

Cistus creticus

cervicornis and *Centaurea balearica* – which can look very similar when not in flower, as convergent evolution has produced spiny aerial parts designed to reduce desiccation and buffeting by the wind.

The next stop inland is the typical Menorcan coastal maquis – commonest in the north – of lentisc wild olive and *Phillyrea latifolia* subspecies *rodriguezii*, home to two members of the arum family: autumn arum and the spectacular dragon's mouth. Further inland, but still on sandy soils, appears *Cistus creticus*, a small pink-flowered species which, apart from one station in València, occurs here in its only western Mediterranean location. Denser areas of maquis are dominated by thorny broom, narrow-leaved cistus, tree and green heaths and, in the most degraded areas, the tall grass *Ampelodesmos mauritanica*.

The narrow promontory of Cap de Cavalleria which protrudes from the centre

of Menorca's north coast is one of the island's most accessible sea-watching localities. From March to September, Cory's and Balearic shearwaters are on the move around the coast, along with shags and yellow-legged and Audouin's gulls. At least six pairs of osprey breed along the north coast (a ZEPA of 900 ha), with good numbers of peregrines feeding on the rock doves here but, curiously, no Eleonora's falcons; these cliffs are also home to common and pallid swifts and blue rock thrush.

The inland mosaic of fields, scrub and woodland hosts stone curlew, short-toed lark and tawny pipit in open habitats, while bee-eater, hoopoe and woodchat shrike abound in areas with perching posts. Other common birds include Thekla lark (no crested larks to confuse you), stonechat and fantailed, Sardinian and Dartford warblers, the latter having colonised the island in the 1970s, possibly to the detriment of the once-common Marmora's warblers (now extinct here). The only lizards on the main island are also fairly recent arrivals, with both Moroccan rock and Italian wall lizards having established themselves in the niche left vacant by the disappearance of Lilford's wall lizard, now confined to offshore islets.

Extensive Aleppo pine and holm oak woodland appears northwest of the village of Es Mercadal. Passerine communities here are very impoverished: firecrest, yes, but no Bonelli's warbler, only great tit among the tits, and no woodpeckers or treecreepers. However, birdwatchers in Menorca will be compensated by the resident populations of Egyptian vulture, booted eagle and red kite, although numbers of the latter have plummeted in recent years, from 135 pairs in 1987 to a mere 10 in 2001. Blame for the almost inevitable extinction of this raptor in Menorca lies largely with the hunters (shooting and poisoned baits), although a decline in the rabbit population and collisions with overhead cables have also taken their toll.

Also in the area

Lluriac Damp meadows to the north-west of Es Mercadal which, when wet in spring and autumn, potentially hold almost any of the migrant birds using the western Mediterranean flyway. Recent records include black-necked grebe, bittern, great white egret, squacco heron, glossy ibis, garganey, marsh sandpiper and white-winged black tern. Black-winged stilts sometimes breed, with winter good for jack snipe.

S'Albufera des Grau (*parc natural* of 1947 ha, also a ZEPA) Shallow lagoon which is Menorca's largest wetland, harbouring a fair smattering of waterbirds, above all on passage and in winter. Winter brings black-necked grebe, grey heron, little and great white egrets, coot, mallard, shoveler, pochard and pintail, with purple heron, garganey, whiskered tern and 'blue-headed' wagtails on passage; breeding birds include water rail and great reed, Cetti's and fan-tailed warblers. Waters populated by leaping and thicklip grey mullet, common two-banded seabream, big-scale sand smelt, black goby and the introduced eastern mosquitofish. European pond terrapin and viperine snake along the water's edge, plus patrolling lesser emperor dragonflies and red-veined and scarlet darters. From Maó (Mahón) head north along the PM-710, then turn off right on the PMV-7102 to Es Grau.

Illa d'en Colom A rocky islet at the mouth of S'Albufera. Out of bounds to casual visitors, its typical Menorcan maquis is enriched by the pink-and-green flowers of *Daphne rodriguezii*, unique to here and Cala Mesquida. Breeding shag and yellow-legged gull, with Cory's and Balearic shearwaters and Audouin's gulls frequently seen offshore. Important nucleus of Lilford's wall lizard.

77 Menorca: Migjorn

The southern and central sectors of Menorca, with limestone coastal ravines harbouring a rich flora and cliff-breeding bird community.

The sheltered, southern half of Menorca consists of a fairly uniform plateau of base-rich bedrock, with deep limestone gorges carrying seasonal *torrents* down to the sea. Most of the island's population is concentrated here, with the age-old human influence evidenced by a plethora of remains of the Talaiot culture (1400 to 0 BC) and a bucolic landscape of small fields separated by many kilometres of drystone walls.

Much of the inland area is covered by a mosaic of dry farmland and scrub, the latter

Balearic sowbread
Cyclamen balearicum

dominated by tree spurge, lentisc, wild olive, *Phillyrea latifolia* and *Prasium majus*, enlivened by the creamy flowers of Virgin's bower in mid-winter, with areas of loose rock

Coastal limestone at Cala d'Alcaufa (Tony Bates)

housing the Balearic endemics *Paeonia cambessedesii* and *Pastinaca lucida*. El Toro (358 m), the high point of the island, is of interest for its community of *Teline linifolia*, Balearic St John's-wort and dwarf fan palm, plus a number of Balearic endemic fissure plants, notably *Sibthorpia africana*, *Crepis triasii* and *Helichrysum ambiguum*.

In the deeper soils at the bottom of the many limestone gorges and gullies that run down to the southern coast, the wild olive scrub communities are enriched by myrtle, chaste tree and *Lonicera implexa*, plus *Asparagus albus* and *A. stipularis*. More humid gullies, such as the Barranc d'Algendar, harbour fine stands of holm oak and strawberry-tree, with an understorey of Balearic sowbread, *Digitalis dubia* and autumn arum; here, too, you might encounter the Menorcan endemic race of pine marten (*minoricensis*). Cliffs here are studded with Irish spleenwort, *Hippocrepis balearica*, *Erodium reichardii*, *Cymbalaria aequitriloba* subspecies *fragilis* and *Scabiosa cretica*.

Those gorges with permanent watercourses attract stripeless tree frog, green toad, European pond terrapin and viperine snake, while more wooded areas are home to Algerian hedgehog, lesser white-toothed shrew (subspecies *balearica*), garden dormouse, stoat and pine marten. Cliff-breeding birds include peregrine, kestrel, rock dove, scops owl, the odd alpine swift, blue rock thrush and raven; among the larger raptors, Egyptian vulture and booted eagle are common, but red kites are increasingly rare.

Outside the gullies, areas not occupied by farmland are clothed with Aleppo pines and a scrub composed of grey-leaved cistus, the winter-flowering *Erica multiflora* and rosemary. *Merendera filifolia* and sea squill bloom in large swathes in autumn, while *Phlomis italica*, tassel hyacinth, polyanthus narcissus and a number of *Ophrys* species – yellow, Bertoloni's, bumble-bee and Iberian – are all at their best from March onwards.

Menorca's list of butterflies and moths is clearly dominated by long-distance migrants (crimson speckled moth, clouded yellow, Bath white, long-tailed and Lang's short-tailed blues, red admiral and painted lady), generalists with less specific ecological needs (small white, green hairstreak and common blue) and satyrids which feed on almost any species of grass (wall brown, speckled wood, small heath, southern gatekeeper and meadow brown). Other species include Cleopatra, two-tailed pasha, cardinal and Queen of Spain fritillary, plus the geranium bronze, which recently hitch-hiked to the Balears with *Pelargonium* cuttings from South Africa.

The essentially rocky southern coastline is interrupted by the large sandy beach of Son Bou, behind which lies a shallow, but permanent wetland maintained by underground springs, notable for its moustached warblers and purple gallinules, both recent colonists from Mallorca, as well as breeding water rail and great reed, Cetti's and fan-tailed warblers; winter brings marsh harrier and reed bunting, while herons, waders and other waterbirds drop in on passage.

Illes Pitiüses

The Pitiüses archipelago is dominated by two main islands – Eivissa (Ibiza) and Formentera – all but connected by a narrow isthmus: the remnants of a former land-bridge. The Iberian mainland is a mere 85 km away: a fact born out by the presence of several Dianic plant species such as *Silene hifacensis*, *Asperula paui* and *Carduncellus dianius*. Overall, the islands possess a typically impoverished insular fauna, albeit enlivened by the presence of the endemic Ibiza wall lizard and several 'giant' races of mammals, notably of garden dormouse (*ophiusae*, on Formentera) and wood mouse (*eivissensis* and *frumentariae*).

SITE 78 Eivissa

The largest of the Pitiüses, harbouring interesting saltpans in the south, a rich endemic flora on the northern cliffs and important seabird colonies on the offshore islets.

Eivissa (boasting nine ANEIs) is by far the most forested of all the Balearic islands; indeed, the name 'Pitiüses' comes from the Greek for 'island of the pines'. Groves of almond, carob, citrus fruits and fig occupy the lower levels, with the higher reaches dominated by extensive Aleppo pine forests interspersed with a calcicolous maquis of Phoenician and prickly junipers, holly oak, small-flowered gorse, yellow restharrow, grey-leaved and narrow-leaved cistuses, myrtle, strawberry-tree, tree heath, *Erica multiflora*, rosemary (parasitised by the reddish broomrape *Orobanche latisquama*), and, less commonly, *Osyris quadripartita*, chronanthus and cneorum. Dry gullies are brightened up by oleander, unknown elsewhere in the Balears, and chaste-tree, while more open areas of maquis harbour Balearic St John's-wort, *Helianthemum marifolium*, toothed lavender, Barbary nut, dipcadi, giant orchid and Bertoloni's, bumble-bee and Iberian ophrys.

Eleonora's falcon *Falco eleonorae*

Bumble-bee ophrys *Ophrys bombyliflora*

Breeding birds in inland areas lack the variety of the Iberian mainland or neighbouring Mallorca, but wooded areas hold scops owl (resident on Eivissa), hoopoe, firecrest, spotted flycatcher, woodchat shrike and serin, with an abundance of Marmora's and Sardinian warblers in the scrub. In more open habitats you might expect bee-eater, Thekla lark, wheatear (not black-eared), rock sparrow and corn bunting, while sea-cliffs and rocky outcrops hold blue rock thrush. Winter brings crag martin, black redstart and Dartford warbler to Eivissa, with black-eared wheatear and spectacled warbler not uncommon on passage.

Unfortunately many of the more interesting fissure-loving plants of Eivissa are confined to the abrupt northern and western cliffs and largely inaccessible offshore islets. Cala d'Aubarca (Albarca) is a particularly noted locality, harbouring *Silene hifacensis*, *Bupleurum barceloi*, *Asperula paui*, *Scabiosa cretica*, *Helichrysum rupestre*, *Carduncellus dianius*, the Eivissan endemic *Allium grosii* and dwarf fan palm.

Eivissa's offshore islets are also tailor-made for nesting seabirds and hold large colonies of Cory's and Balearic shearwaters, storm petrel (subspecies *melitensis*), shag (subspecies *desmarestii*), Eleonora's falcon and yellow-legged and Audouin's gulls. Outstanding are the 4000 pairs of storm petrels and 300 of Cory's and 100 of Balearic shearwaters on the Ses Bledes, Sa Conillera and S'Espartar group of islands off the west coast, and the 75 pairs of Eleonora's falcons on Es Vedrà (with Es

Vedranell, a 100 ha ZEPA); several pairs of peregrine still breed, but nesting ospreys are a thing of the past. These offshore islets are also renowned for harbouring genetically distinct races of the Ibiza wall lizard, endemic to the Pitiüses (including both the main islands): a classic case of divergent evolution, with some 45 races having been described. Boat trips to the islands are possible from Eivissa town harbour; contact the tourist office.

The Ses Salines saltpans (*reserva natural* of 1500 ha, also a Ramsar Site and ZEPA) in the south of the island attract greater flamingos all year round (maximum c. 500 birds) and waders on passage, in particular little ringed and grey plovers, avocet, dunlin, ruff and bar-tailed godwit. Purple heron, little egret, osprey and marsh harrier drop in on occasion, mainly on passage, while the principal breeding species are shelduck, black-winged stilt (100+ pairs) and Kentish plover (200+ pairs). The best area of *salines* lies behind the pebble beach of Platja d'Es Codolà, although access to the old saltpans behind Platja d'en Bossa is easier. The low halophytic vegetation around the *salines* is very attractive to migrant spectacled warblers in spring, while the scattered buildings harbour blue rock thrush and both Turkish and Moorish geckos, the former generally living at the base of walls, the latter towards the top.

The extensive sand dunes here are stabilised by Phoenician juniper (subspecies *turbinata*), with open areas populated by *Silene cambessedesii* and *Lotus halophilus*. Be sure also to climb one of the two small peaks in the area (Falcó, 141 m, or Coromarí, 159 m) for superb views and encounters with the cistus parasite *Cytinus hypocistis*, the Eivissan endemic greenweed *Genista dorycnifolia* and two-leaved gennaria. Marmora's warblers are common in the scrub, and you might also be lucky enough to spot a common genet, here the Eivissan endemic race *isabelae*, which is much smaller than the mainland individuals as a consequence of having evolved on an island where the main prey available is small lizards.

^{SITE}
79 Formentera

The southernmost island of the Balears, renowned for its transparent seas and marine fauna and flora; eight ANEIs cover almost the whole coastline.

Known to the Romans as 'Frumentari' owing to the bounteous crop of wheat the island once produced, Formentera is the least spoilt of the Balearic islands. Most tourists stick to the sandy beaches and crystalline waters, ignoring the *salines* and coastal lagoons which are essentially a continuation of southern Eivissa (part of the Ses Salines d'Eivissa-Formentera World Heritage Site; 8564 ha, also a *reserva natural*, ZEPA and Ramsar Site), while the twin headlands of Sa Mola and Cap de Barbaria in the east and southwest, respectively, are rocky and forbidding, and thus also remain relatively peaceful.

The once extensive holm oak and Phoenician juniper forests that covered most of Formentera have been largely replaced by farmland and opportunistic Aleppo pines. Wooded areas hold abundant Algerian hedgehog, the 'giant' Formentera garden dormouse (subspecies *ophiusae*), long-eared owl, turtle dove and Sardinian warbler, whereas Marmora's warbler is commonplace in the typical Mediterranean scrub of prickly juniper, lentisc, grey-leaved cistus, wild olive and rosemary. The island as a whole is well positioned to receive trans-Mediterranean migrants, notably bee-eaters, wheatears and warblers in spring and autumn.

The impressive sea-cliffs of Sa Mola hold breeding storm petrel, shag, peregrine and blue rock thrush, as well as a large yellow-legged gull colony. In the woods around Sa Talaiassa (192 m) – the highest point of the Mola peninsula – two-leaved gennaria is common, while the summit is home to *Asplenium sagittatum*, clusters of *Saxifraga corsica* subspecies *cossoniana* on rocky outcrops, *Lycium intricatum*, fan-lipped orchid and sawfly ophrys.

The many sea-caves of the Barbaria peninsula were once home to Mediterranean monk seals, now extinct in western European

waters, while the sea-cliffs, together with those of Sa Mola, were until recently home to the largest colonies of Balearic shearwater in the world (at least 1350 pairs in 1991). The inland scrub community is composed of *Anthyllis cytisoides*, Mediterranean mezereon, cneorum, *Helichrysum stoechas* and an abundance of labiates. Look out for least adder's-tongue and bumble-bee and sawfly ophrys here, as well as breeding stone curlew, Thekla lark and rock sparrow.

The northern part of the island is dominated by the large, circular Estany Pudent, literally the 'stinking lake': a shallow brackish lagoon which can hold winter concentrations of up to 4000 black-necked grebes (January 1996). The flora of the arid, saline soils here is reminiscent of the steppes of southeastern Spain and includes the bizarre cynomorium, fagonia and *Frankenia pulverulenta*, as well as ice plant, its congener *Mesembryanthemum nodiflorum* and the related *Aizoon hispanicum*. The dunes behind the beach are carpeted with southern birdsfoot-trefoil and also harbour the attrac-

Sawfly ophrys
Ophrys tenthredinifera

Balears

Mesembryanthemum nodiflorum (T.F.)

tive Afro-Iberian endemic *Linaria peduncu-lata*, here at its only Balearic locality.

The islets of Es Freus form an all but complete land-bridge to Eivissa and have a true Caribbean feel about them, so clear are the surrounding seas. One of the criteria for the declaration of the Ses Salines World Heritage Site was their superbly conserved posidonia meadows, said to support the greatest species diversity of any marine habitat in the Mediterranean. Of the two main islets, S'Espalmador – joined to Formentera in historical times – is low and sandy and hosts the area's best remaining stands of Phoenician juniper, while S'Espardell is rockier, with 30 m-high underwater cliffs, and is probably the best place in the western Mediterranean to see loggerhead turtles.

Castilla y León and Madrid

Castilla y León and Madrid

Introduction

The vast area encompassed by the autonomous community of Castilla y León is pretty well contiguous with the catchment area of the Río Duero in Spain, collecting waters from the Cordillera Cantábrica to the north, the Sistema Ibérico to the east and the Sistema Central – the Sierras de Gredos and Guadarrama – to the south, before heading into Portugal and out into the Atlantic at Porto. Lying within this horseshoe of mountains – some of which exceed 2500 m in height – is an extensive plateau known as the north Meseta, which rarely drops below 700 m. The autonomous community of Madrid, on the other hand, lies on the southern flanks of the Sierra de Guadarrama, with rivers rising here eventually joining the Tajo, which runs almost parallel to the Duero across the peninsula to Lisboa. Madrid itself is the highest capital city in Europe (655 m),

and the only one whose skies are wont to contain cruising griffon vultures.

The highest reaches of the Cordillera Cantábrica are home to a specialised 'alpine' avifauna that includes wallcreeper, alpine chough and snowfinch, as well as chamois (of the endemic race *parva*) and many plants unique to these mountains, most notably at Fuentes Carrionas, in northern Palencia. Well-preserved deciduous oak forests on the southern flanks contain important populations of capercaillie (particularly around Riaño, in the province of León) and black and middle spotted woodpeckers, with the bulk of the eastern nucleus of brown bear occupying the Fuentes Carrionas area. One of Spain's best remaining populations of partridge (of the Iberian endemic species *hispaniensis*) inhabits the mountains around the Lago de Sanabria, while wolves have one of their Iberian strongholds in the nearby Sierra de la Culebra. The Cordillera

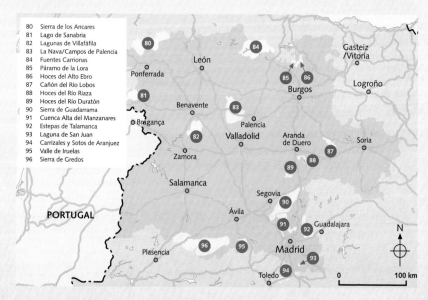

80   Sierra de los Ancares
81   Lago de Sanabria
82   Lagunas de Villafáfila
83   La Nava/Campos de Palencia
84   Fuentes Carrionas
85   Páramo de la Lora
86   Hoces del Alto Ebro
87   Cañón del Río Lobos
88   Hoces del Río Riaza
89   Hoces del Río Duratón
90   Sierra de Guadarrama
91   Cuenca Alta del Manzanares
92   Estepas de Talamanca
93   Laguna de San Juan
94   Carrizales y Sotos de Aranjuez
95   Valle de Iruelas
96   Sierra de Gredos

Previous page: **Limestone cliffs near Pesquera de Ebro, northern Burgos (T.F.)**

Cantábrica is also extremely rich in butter-flies – second only to the Pyrenees in Spain – with notable examples being Lefèbvre's and Chapman's ringlets, the latter endemic to these mountains, plus Apollo, mountain clouded yellow, mountain, bog and shepherd's fritillaries, dusky large blue and Spanish and mountain arguses.

On the other side of the north Meseta, the Sistema Central – sometimes referred to as the 'backbone of Spain' – is renowned for its enormous population of Spanish ibex (sub-species *victoriae*), breeding bluethroats and diverse herptile community (35 species, several of which are endemic races), with the extensive pine forests – both natural and planted – providing refuge for important populations of black vulture, particularly in the Valle de Iruelas. An incredibly rich flora – around 1600 species in the Sierra de Gredos alone – includes about a dozen endemic taxa, most of which occur in the montane zone. The southern flanks of the Sistema Central harbour some of the best-preserved lowland western holm oak forests in Spain – notably at El Pardo, just north of the capital – which are renowned for their Spanish imperial eagles (in 2001, 24 pairs bred in Madrid and 18 in Castilla y León, rearing a total of 49 chicks).

The interior of the north Meseta and the plains to the east of Madrid are variously given over to cereal cultivation and extensive pastures, but at such low intensity that arable 'weeds', nowadays scarce elsewhere in western Europe, are often more abundant than the crops themselves, colouring vast swathes of the countryside red, yellow and blue in early summer. Not surprisingly, great bustards are very much at home here, with a good proportion of the world population of this stately bird found in the plains of Castilla y León, and Villafáfila alone harbouring the largest nucleus in Europe. Other steppe birds with notable populations in the region are lesser kestrel, little bustard, stone curlew and black-bellied sandgrouse, with the plains also attracting large wintering concentrations of red kite. Black-winged kites and azure-winged magpies are expanding northwards from their southwest Iberian strongholds into the *dehesas* and pine plantations of southern Castilla y León.

Wetlands scattered across the north Meseta attract hordes of wintering wildfowl, notably greylag geese at Villafáfila, La Nava and Boada, as well as providing inland breeding grounds for waders such as avocet, black-winged stilt and lapwing, plus gull-billed tern. The windswept limestone *páramos* of eastern Castilla y León, home to healthy populations of Montagu's harrier and Dupont's lark and rich spring-flowering assemblages of monocots, are dissected by deep river gorges which shelter a wealth of cliff-breeding raptors: griffon and Egyptian vultures, golden and Bonelli's eagles, peregrine and eagle owl. The *hoces* of Riaza and Duratón, for example, harbour two of the largest griffon vulture colonies in Europe, while those of the Alto Ebro y Rudrón are notable for their nesting Bonelli's eagles and large post-breeding concentrations of Egyptian vulture, but perhaps the most exceptional bird populations are to be found in the chasms excavated by the rivers Duero and Tajo along the Spanish–Portuguese border (see pp. 432 and 436, respectively). These sheltered defiles are also home to a rich fissure vegetation with many Iberian endemics, plus well-preserved gallery forests which provide refuge for forest raptors, golden oriole and a wide range of amphibians.

The Junta de Castilla y León website (www.jcyl.es/jcyl/cmaot/dgmn/svenep/esp acios/index.htm) contains useful information about protected areas in the autonomous community.

80 Sierra de los Ancares

A little-visited mountain area straddling the Galicia–León border, harbouring extensive deciduous forests and subalpine habitats with a rich flora and butterfly fauna.

Lying at the extreme western end of the Cordillera Cantábrica, the Ancares (a proposed *parque natural* (67 280 ha) and a ZEPA of 55 582 ha in León) is very much a world apart, the rugged and inaccessible terrain sheltering a way of life which has changed little since pre-Roman times; typical vernacular architecture takes the form of *pallozas*: two-storey dwellings with an oval floor-plan, stone walls and roofs thatched with brooms and greenweeds.

A number of peaks approaching 2000 m dominate the Ancares, notably Miravalles (1969 m), situated close to the union of the provinces of Galicia, Asturias and León. Geologically speaking, the main ridge and northern sector are composed of granites, slates and quartzites, with a narrow belt of limestone and other calcareous rocks occurring to the south. The flanks of the main ridge are scalloped with cirques harbouring small glacial lakes and peatbogs: for example, the Lago de los Ancares at the head of the Burbia valley.

The north-facing slopes support relatively undisturbed forests of sessile and pedunculate oaks, accompanied by yew, rowan, whitebeam and ash, sustained by levels of precipitation which exceed 2000 mm, while downy birch (subspecies *celtiberica*) occurs at the highest altitudes; beech is found only on the thinnest, most lime-rich soils. More southerly aspects are the domain of Pyrenean, Lusitanian and western holm oak woods, although protracted felling and burning have converted large areas to secondary scrub today, with species-rich haymeadows – many harbouring drifts of *Narcissus pseudonarcissus* in spring – and groves of sweet chestnut commonplace around the villages.

The forest food chain of the Ancares is topped by breeding raptors such as booted eagle, honey buzzard, goshawk, sparrowhawk and tawny owl, with other nesting birds of note including short-toed eagle, woodcock (particularly above 1200 m) and black woodpecker (several dozen pairs),

Los Ancares

Brown long-eared bat *Plecotus auritus*
(Peter Wilson)

viviparous lizard in wet meadows and boggy areas, while golden-striped salamander, Bosca's newt, Iberian frog and Schreiber's green lizard cohabit along the watercourses.

Subalpine habitats support an interesting assemblage of parsley fern, forked spleenwort, alpine clover, the thrift *Armeria cantabrica*, confined to the mountains of northern Spain, great yellow gentian (here belonging to the subspecies *aurantica*, with reddish-orange flowers), the Iberian endemic bellflower *Campanula herminii*, mountain everlasting, the knapweed *Centaurea micrantha*, unique to northwestern Iberia and the diminutive *Narcissus asturiensis*.

The scrub and grassland habitats above the tree-line are favoured by partridge (subspecies *hispaniensis*, nowadays very scarce), water pipit, dunnock, rock thrush and red-backed shrike, as well as hen and Montagu's harriers and golden eagle. A few dozen chamois also make their home here – reintroduced following their extinction during the Civil War – while wolves are fairly abundant and one or two brown bears maintain a constant presence in the area. Look out, too, for Castroviejo's hare in the tall broom scrub, a species whose world distribution is confined to the high Cordillera Cantábrica, from the Ancares in the west to Peña Labra in Palencia in the east.

Many of the more interesting butterflies of the Ancares are also found in the high-level habitats, including Galicia's only Apollos. The peak of Mostallar (1935 m), on the border with León, is a good place to look, where you might also turn up mountain, de Prunner's and Chapman's ringlets and purple-edged and scarce coppers on the surrounding slopes, plus lesser marbled, marbled and violet fritillaries on woodland margins.

although the capercaillie is thought to have disappeared at the end of the twentieth century. A diverse woodland passerine community comprises spotted flycatcher, redstart, Bonelli's warbler, goldcrest, firecrest, long-tailed and marsh tits, nuthatch, short-toed treecreeper and bullfinch.

Typical forest mammals include roe deer, wild boar, red squirrel, edible dormouse, beech and pine martens (the latter very abundant and fairly easy to see in the wild here) and wildcat, as well as smaller creatures such as yellow-necked mouse, pygmy shrew and bank vole. Lesser mouse-eared, brown and grey long-eared and greater and lesser horseshoe bats have been cited here, while Pyrenean desmans occur in the many unpolluted watercourses of the high mountains. Among the noteworthy herptiles of the Ancares are Iberian rock lizard at altitude and

Access: The LU-723 which leaves the N-VI at Ambasmestas will take you through a number of extremely picturesque villages – Degrada, Robledo, Donís – before crossing the border into León (not marked on the Michelin map) and heading southeast towards Vega de Espinareda via Suarbol and Pereda de Ancares. Some of the best-preserved *pallozas* are located in Balouta, Piornedo and Campo del Agua.

Also in the area

Sierras de Gistreo y Coto (partly within the Alto Sil ZEPA; 43 752 ha) East–west-oriented ridges on the southern flank of the Cordillera Cantábrica, encompassing several peaks over 2000 m. A few capercaillie, plus partridge, peregrine, eagle owl, rock thrush and chough; also wintering wallcreeper. Forests harbour honey buzzard, short-toed and booted eagles, black kite, woodcock, black woodpecker and citril finch. Breeding Montagu's and hen harriers, plus Mediterranean species at the northern limits of their range: black-eared wheatear, blue rock thrush and Orphean warbler. Relict population of chamois, with brown bear regular in the middle-mountain habitats.

Montes Aquilanos (ZEPA of 33 280 ha, including the Sierra del Teleño) To the south of Ponferrada. Golden eagle (7–11 pairs), eagle owl, lesser spotted woodpecker and stone curlew, the latter breeding in fallow land at more than 1100 m.

Las Médulas (World Heritage Site and proposed *monumento natural* (1115 ha)

At the western end of the Aquilanos; fabulous pinnacles of clay-rich bedrock, the result of water-powered gold mining by the Romans during the first and second centuries AD. To the north, the **Lago de Carucedo** attracts wintering pochard, tufted duck, water rail and reedbed passerines, plus breeding little and great crested grebes and little bittern.

Palacios de Compludo (SEO/Asociación Tyto Alba reserve of 969 ha) Between the village of Bouzas and the peak of Becerril (1876 m). High-altitude scrub, enclaves of Pyrenean and western holm oak and mixed valley forests of sweet chestnut, alder, aspen and wild cherry. Breeding partridge, skylark, water pipit and rock thrush at altitude, dunnock, whitethroat, red-backed shrike and rock bunting in the broom/genista scrub and goshawk, sparrowhawk, honey buzzard, tawny owl, nuthatch and bullfinch in the forests. Pyrenean desman, abundant roe deer and presence of wolf and wildcat, plus ocellated lizard, Montpellier snake and Cantabrican viper. For more information contact SEO/BirdLife in Madrid.

---

81 Lago de Sanabria

Largest glacial lake in Iberia lying in a horseshoe of mountains rich in endemic plants and with an important population of partridge.

Sandwiched between the Sierra de la Cabrera and the Portuguese border, the Lago de Sanabria covers some 368 ha, its gelid waters lying at 997 m above sea level and descending to a depth of more than 50 m. The lake forms only a small part of the homonymous *parque natural* (22 365 ha, also a ZEPA of 30 155 ha), which also encompasses a large portion of the Sierra Segundera, peaking at Peña Trevinca (2124 m). Essentially a high granite plateau at around 1700 m, Segundera is sprinkled

Río Tera, Lago de Sanabria

with a score of glacial lakes of more modest dimensions and rift by several deep gorges, notably those occupied by the rivers Tera, Cárdena and Segundera.

Up to about 1500 m, the natural climax vegetation of the park is Pyrenean oak forest, best preserved in the southeastern sector of the park, where it is accompanied by sweet chestnut and harbours a diverse ground flora of columbine, wood bitter-vetch, pyramidal bugle, bastard balm, narrow-leaved lungwort, common cow-wheat, *Linaria triornithophora*, *Campanula lusitanica*, *Hispidella hispanica*, Spanish bluebell, spring squill, angular Solomon's-seal, St Bernard's lily and dog's-tooth-violet. Where secondary scrub communities have replaced the oakwoods, look out for cushions of *Echinospartum ibericum*, unique to the peninsula, between which grow the star-of-Bethlehem *Ornithogalum concinnum* and yellow-flowered toadflax *Linaria saxatilis*, both of which occur only in central Iberia.

Above the tree-line lies a dense carpet of *Chamaespartium tridentatum*, *Halimium lasianthum* subspecies *alyssoides*, Spanish heath, *Erica umbellata* and the wood-rush *Luzula lactea*, interspersed with acid pastures studded with *Narcissus asturiensis* and hoop-petticoat daffodils in spring. Wetter soils support petty whin, *Genista micrantha* and cross-leaved heath, as well as marsh gentian, lousewort and the Iberian endemic *Campanula herminii*, while small peatbogs should be examined for round-leaved sundew, grass-of-Parnassus, marsh cinquefoil and common butterwort.

The glacial lakes of the Segundera plateau support an interesting community of awlwort, lesser marshwort, marsh speedwell, water-plantain and *Baldellia alpestris* (endemic to northwestern Iberia), plus floating bur-reed and the grass *Antinoria agrostidea*. Sanabria itself is home to the quillwort *Isoetes velatum*, pond water-crowfoot, alternate-leaved water-milfoil, greater bladderwort, broad-leaved pondweed and lesser water-plantain, with whorled caraway, yellow loosestrife and *Lythrum borysthenicum* around the margins.

The park harbours a diverse vertebrate fauna, including 41 species of mammal and a score of herptiles, notably fire salamander, marbled and Bosca's newts, parsley frog, natterjack toad, Schreiber's, ocellated, viviparous and Iberian rock lizards, large psammodromus, ladder and Montpellier snakes and Lataste's and Cantabrican vipers: a real mixture of Euro-Siberian and Mediterranean species, with a few Iberian endemics thrown in for good measure. The myriad streams and rivers provide suitable habitat for Pyrenean desman, otter, kingfisher and brown trout, while the oakwoods harbour an abundant population of roe deer as well as wildcat, Eurasian badger, beech and pine martens and wild boar. Some 88 species of butterfly have been recorded in the park; in early June, look out for Spanish festoon, marsh fritillary, de Prunner's ringlet and black-eyed, green-underside and Amanda's blues.

Any visit to Sanabria should commence with a visit to the park interpretation centre in the twelfth-century monastery of San Martín de Castaneda (tel: 980 622063). From here you can follow the road to within a few metres of the delightful Laguna de los Peces (1707 m) at the foot of the slate and granite ridge of the Sierra de la Cabrera Baja. The undulating plateau here, traversed by numerous small streams and boggy depressions, is home to woodlark, water pipit, dunnock, rock thrush, bluethroat, Dartford warbler and ortolan bunting, as well as one of the real specialities of the region: the Iberian endemic subspecies (*hispaniensis*) of partridge, which is pretty much confined to the Pyrenees, Cordillera Cantábrica and Sistema Ibérico, just extending into northern Portugal.

Keep an eye on the skies for some of the larger raptors of the area, notably golden eagle (which breeds in the nearby Sierra de la Cabrera) and the griffon and Egyptian vultures (probably just a single pair of the latter) which hunt for carrion over the plateau in summer, when transhumant cattle roam the high-level pastures; Montagu's and hen harriers also breed in the area. From the Laguna de los Peces you can follow the trail down to Vigo de Sanabria via the impressive gorge of the Río Forcadura, where grey wagtail, dipper and crag martin abound.

Also from San Martín, a cobbled trail – the Senda de los Monjes – leads to the village of Ribadelago Viejo, through Pyrenean oak forest where you can hope to encounter a good range of raptors, namely short-toed and booted eagles, goshawk, sparrowhawk, honey buzzard and hobby, as well as wryneck, Bonelli's warbler, short-toed treecreeper, red-backed shrike, serin and bullfinch.

Once in Ribadelago Viejo (also accessible by road along the southern shore of the lake), a footpath leads into the canyon of the Río Tera, where granite outcrops along the early part of the trail support the lavender-cotton *Santolina rosmarinifolia*, round-headed leek and angel's-tears, plus *Armeria transmontana* and the silvery-leaved, daisy-like *Phalacrocarpum hoffmannseggii*, both of which are endemic to northwestern Iberia. Within the confines of the gorge, notable plants to look out for are *Asplenium billotii*, *Saxifraga fragosoi* and *Narcissus rupicola* on shady cliffs, with sunnier habitats harbouring *Cheilanthes hispanica* and *Sedum hirsutum*; look out, too, for the crane's-bill *Geranium bohemicum*, otherwise found only in the Pyrenees in Spain.

The higher watercourse is lined with galleries of downy birch (subspecies *celtiberica*) and *Salix atrocinerea*, sheltering *Aconitum vulparia* subspecies *neapolitanum*, white false helleborine, martagon lily and alpine leek. This is also the only place in the park where holly grows to any size, often associat-

Herb-Paris *Paris quadrifolia*

ed with hard shield-fern, broad buckler-fern, herb-Paris and bird's-nest orchid. Towards the top of the gorge, shady boulder chokes are populated by great yellow gentian, adenostyles, the leopard's-bane *Doronicum*

carpetanum, white false helleborine and streptopus, here on the western edge of its range. Among the characteristic birds of the gorge are eagle owl, black redstart and blue rock thrush.

Also in the area

Peña Trevinca Best-accessed from Porto (ZA-102) along the Río Bibey valley, or from Casaio (OR-122), via the Río de San Xil, the latter route taking you through the Teixeira de Casaio (the only true yew forest in the Iberian peninsula). Around Peña Trevinca, subspecies *aurantica* of great yellow gentian, the eryngo *Eryngium duriaei*, endemic to north-western Iberia and an abundance of chough and partridge. Butterflies (almost 100 species) include Chapman's ringlet, Spanish argus, large blue and purple-edged copper.

Sierra de la Cabrera (ZEPA; 19 992 ha) To the northeast of Sanabria, an immense, serrated slate and quartzite ridge (maximum Vizcodillo, 2124 m). Nesting golden eagle, peregrine, eagle owl and chough, plus important populations of partridge and rock thrush; black-winged kite and lesser kestrel are non-breeding visitors. Notable plants include parnassus-leaved buttercup (subspecies *cabrerensis*), *Teesdaliopsis*

conferta and *Genista sanabrensis*, all confined to the Cordillera Cantábrica. The northern flanks harbour two *monumentos naturales*: **Lago de la Baña** (731 ha) and **Lago de Truchillas** (1066 ha). These small glacial lakes – accessible only on foot from the homon-ymous villages (waymarked) – harbour interesting amphibians: fire salamander, marbled, Bosca's and palmate newts, natterjack toad and common tree, Iberian and common frogs. Surrounding rocky habitats have Iberian rock and Schreiber's green lizard and Cantabrican viper.

Sierra de la Culebra (proposed *paisaje protegido*; 65 891 ha) A 50 km-long ridge of moderate altitude (maximum Peña Mira, 1238 m) to the southeast of Sanabria. Although largely under pine plantations, it is home to one of the highest densities of wolves in the Iberian peninsula; groups of up to five individuals are commonplace. Also wildcat, otter, beech marten and common genet.

82 Lagunas de Villafáfila

Unprepossessing pseudosteppe landscape of supreme importance for great bustard and lesser kestrel, encompassing a series of endorheic lagoons which attracts thousands of wintering grey-lag geese plus breeding avocet and gull-billed tern.

Secreted within the flat, almost featureless landscape of the northern Meseta lie the shallow saline lagoons and gently rolling pseudosteppes of Villafáfila, which regularly harbour more than 30 000 greylag geese in

winter and one of the highest densities of great bustards in the world: certainly the largest European enclave of this species, with 2270 individuals recorded here in the spring of 1998.

Located in a semi-arid region (only 400 mm of rainfall per year), the endorheic Lagunas de Villafáfila are one of the last remaining wetlands in Castilla y León (a Ramsar Site (2854 ha), ZEPA (32 682 ha) and proposed *reserva natural*). Seasonal streams traverse an enclosed drainage basin lying on Quaternary clays, where water accumulates to form three main lagoons linked by the Arroyo del Salado – Barillos (118 ha), Grande (192 ha) and Las Salinas (83 ha) – plus a number of satellite pools. As with most endorheic systems, the lagoons suffer marked seasonal variation in water levels, with salinity increasing as they dry out; in wet winters the flooded area can exceed 600 ha, although nowhere is more than 60 cm deep.

At their wettest, the Villafáfila lagoons are typically occupied by large expanses of sea club-rush and the related *Scirpus littoralis*, although these practically disappear in times of drought. Typical hydrophytes include the quillwort *Isoetes velatum*, thread-leaved water-crowfoot, various-leaved and short-leaved water-starworts, spiral tasselweed, horned pondweed and common duckweed, with charophytes particularly characteristic, notably common, foxtail, bearded, fragile and bird's-nest stoneworts, *Tolypella hispanica*, *T. glomerata*, *Chara aspera* and *C. galioides*.

Halophytic vegetation around the lagoons includes purple glasswort, shrubby sea-blite, saltwort, lesser sea-spurrey, sand spurrey, *Frankenia pulverulenta*, thyme-leaved sea heath, sea plantain and sharp, sea and salt-marsh rushes, plus *Aeluropus littoralis*, *Sphenopus divaricatus*, Bermuda-grass and southern beard-grass. Some 30 000 ha of the proposed reserve is dedicated to cereal and alfalfa cultivation, but the headlands harbour small and slender hare's-ears, silvery-leaved pink convolvulus, chondrilla, cut-leaved viper's-grass and the stalkless pink stars of merendera from mid-summer onwards.

More than 260 species of bird have been recorded at Villafáfila, with the highest diversity coinciding with passage periods; notable visitors include spoonbill, crane and the occasional black stork, as well as a good variety of waders, albeit in small numbers, plus congregations of more than 500 white

Female great bustard *Otis tarda*

storks. Maximum biomass, however, occurs between November and February, when hordes of greylag geese are joined by good numbers of mallard, shoveler, teal, shelduck, wigeon, gadwall, pintail, pochard and tufted duck, plus thousands of lapwing and golden plover and several hundred snipe and curlew. The skies are rarely empty of the distinctive fork-tailed silhouettes of the many red kites, while other winter visitors include hen harrier, peregrine, merlin and short-eared owl; look out, too, for the occasional bean, barnacle, white-fronted and even bar-headed geese which sometimes turn up with the greylags.

Breeding birds in recent years include small numbers of gadwall, mallard, teal (1–2 pairs), shoveler, pochard and tufted duck, as well as at least one pair of black-tailed godwits in 1997 and 1998. By contrast, whiskered and black terns haven't bred since the late 1980s, the vacancy apparently having been filled by gull-billed terns – which first nested in 1990 – with 13 pairs in 1998. More established are the breeding populations of lapwing (around 100 pairs) and black-winged stilt (some 300 pairs), while Villafáfila is the only locality in Castilla y León where avocets nest regularly (almost 100 pairs). Breeding wetland passerines include yellow wagtail and fan-tailed, Cetti's (rare), great reed and reed warblers.

Despite being unusually favoured by great bustards, Villafáfila just doesn't incorporate enough rough, long-term fallow for many of the other classic Iberian steppe birds, with pin-tailed sandgrouse now apparently extinct and black-bellied declining fast (only 10–30 pairs remain). Little bustards (around 100 individuals), tawny pipits and short-toed larks breed only in small numbers, although quail and calandra larks abound, and several pairs of short-eared owl have bred here since 1994, ostensibly taking advantage of the explosion in the common vole population that dates from this time.

On the other hand, the many ruined dovecotes scattered across the reserve support the largest breeding population of lesser kestrel in Castilla y León (exceeding 200 pairs and particularly abundant around Otero de Sariegos), and are also the haunt of little and barn owls and spotless starling. Other breeding birds of Villafáfila include white stork (34 pairs), marsh (8 pairs) and Montagu's (around 40 pairs) harriers and hobby (10 pairs).

Sharp-ribbed salamanders are present in almost all the lagoons and marbled newts fequent water-troughs and wells, while small numbers of Iberian painted and parsley frogs and western spadefoots are vastly out-

Avocet *Recurvirostra avosetta* (Mike Powles)

numbered by the natterjack toads and Iberian pool frogs that inhabit the borders of the lagoons and other marshy areas. Suitable habitat for reptiles is sparse, however, with these limited to a few ocellated and Iberian wall lizards around the ruined dovecotes, three-toed skinks in the damper grasslands, and Montpellier and viperine snakes. Small mammals abound, providing food for both diurnal and nocturnal raptors, notably Iberian blind mole, greater white-toothed shrew, southern water and common voles, Iberian and Mediterranean pine voles, wood mouse and black and brown rats. Iberian hares are very common, with foxes and weasels the most common predators.

> *Information*: The interpretation centre of El Palomar is located at the northern end of the site (Carretera de Villafáfila–Tapioles, km 1.5; tel: 980 586046; fax: 980 586001 closed Mondays and Tuesdays). A telescope is required to get the best out of Villafáfila.

Gull-billed tern *Gelochelidon nilotica* (Mike Lane)

Also in the area

Embalse de Ricobayo Long, narrow reservoir on the Río Esla attracting wintering greylag goose, pochard, shoveler, wigeon, teal and pintail, but far better known as the last wintering locality for bean goose in the Iberian peninsula (6000 individuals in 1969, but none in 2000–01).

Riberas de Castronuño (*reserva natural* (8420 ha) and ZEPA of 4671 ha) Elbow in the Río Duero between Tordesillas and Toro, centred on the Embalse de San José. Extensive reedbeds and gallery forests harbour the best assemblage of breeding herons in Castilla y León: grey heron (several hundred pairs), night heron (50-odd pairs) and a few purple herons, little bitterns and cattle and little egrets. Breeding great crested and possibly black-necked grebes, white stork, marsh harrier (7–11 pairs; many more in winter), black kite, booted eagle, long-eared and tawny owls, kingfisher, Cetti's warbler, nightingale and penduline tit. To the north, along the road to San Román de Hornija, western holm oak *dehesa* is good for hobby, great spotted cuckoo, roller, hoopoe, black-eared wheatear, Sardinian warbler, southern grey shrike and azure-winged magpie.

Tierra de Campiñas (ZEPA; 150 059 ha) Immense tract of arable plains dotted with stands of western holm oak, planted pines and vineyards, at the junction of Valladolid, Salamanca and Ávila provinces. Of great significance for steppe birds, with resident great bustard (2500; particularly to the east of Madrigal de las Altas Torres), little bustard (1500), stone curlew, black-bellied sandgrouse (about 200 pairs) and lesser numbers of pin-tailed. Breeding Montagu's harrier (200 pairs), lesser kestrel (100 pairs in 1995; try the church at Nava del Rey), black-winged (3+ pairs), black and red kites, booted eagle, hobby and long-eared owl. Also calandra, short-toed, Thekla and crested larks, tawny pipit and wheatear, as well as azure-winged magpie around the pines and oaks. Wintering cranes, red kite, hen harrier, merlin and peregrine, plus roller and great spotted cuckoo in summer. A few seasonal lagoons – the largest is Los Lavajares (north of Rágama, on the C-610) – attract wintering greylag goose and passage black-winged stilt, ringed plover and curlew sandpiper.

SITE
83 La Nava/Campos de Palencia

Cultivated plains with good populations of steppe birds, in the heart of which lie the lagoons of La Nava and Boada, attracting large numbers of wintering greylag geese and breeding waders which are rare in northern Spain.

The Tierra de Campos (a ZEPA of 84 790 ha) is an enormous plateau of arable pseudosteppes lying at around 800 m and straddling the border between Palencia and Valladolid, the monotony of the terrain occasionally relieved by low calcareous ridges, small blocks of woodland – planted pines and relict enclaves of western holm oak – and crumbling adobe villages.

Secreted in the midst of this rather uninspiring landscape is the Laguna de la Nava, on the former site of the Mar de Campos, which once covered an immense 5000 ha and attracted vast numbers of wintering and breeding aquatic birds before being drained for agricultural purposes in the 1950s. In the early 1990s, the Fondo Patrimonio Natural Europeo (now Fundación Global Nature) launched an ambitious project to recuperate the lagoon, resulting in the inundation of around 300 ha of arable land south of Fuentes de Nava; some 210 species of bird, 16 mammals, 7 reptiles, 6 amphibians and 4 fish have been

Marsh harrier *Circus aeruginosus* (Mike Lane)

recorded here since the project commenced.

In January 2001, the census of greylag geese at La Nava was in the order of 5000 birds, along with some 3000 mallard, lesser numbers of gadwall, wigeon, teal, pintail, shoveler and coot, and about 1200 lapwing. Less commonplace species which turn up from time to time include white-fronted, lesser white-fronted, bean and barnacle geese. In 1998 the Laguna de Boada joined the recuperation project; although much smaller (about 60 ha flooded so far) it is apparently far more attractive to greylag geese, with the January 2001 census turning up 8500 individuals. Marsh harrier and peregrine are often seen hunting over both lagoons in winter, while red kite and hen harrier prefer the surrounding cultivated land; in the winter of 2000–01, La Nava supported a roost of some 180 marsh harriers. Not surprisingly, Ramsar status has been proposed.

Many birds stop off to feed and rest at La Nava and Boada on migration, notably little egret, spoonbill, garganey, grey plover, curlew sandpiper, little stint, ruff, snipe, black-tailed godwit, whimbrel, spotted redshank, greenshank, wood sandpiper and whiskered, black and gull-billed terns. Furthermore, 187 aquatic warblers were ringed at La Nava in the autumn of 2000: the first indication that this species is actually much more widespread on passage through the peninsula than was previously thought.

In terms of breeding waterbirds, however, regular nesting is seen only by little grebe, mallard, coot, black-winged stilt, lapwing, yellow wagtail and fan-tailed, Cetti's, Savi's, reed and great reed warblers. More sporadic breeders include marsh harrier, garganey, shoveler, little ringed plover, black-tailed godwit, redshank and whiskered and black terns, while in 1999 avocets returned to breed in Palencia for the first time since the Mar de Campos was drained, although none of the four pairs was successful. White storks breed in most of the villages of Tierra de Campos, with La Nava attracting post-breeding concentrations of up to 500 individuals.

A rich aquatic flora has gradually recolonised La Nava from the surrounding streams and feeder canals, with emergent plants of interest including flowering-rush, starfruit and narrow-leaved and lesser water-plantains, while the open water hosts many charophytes, notably *Chara oedophylla* (known from only four Spanish localities), plus pond and thread-leaved water-crowfoots, amphibious bistort and several species of *Zannichellia*. Among the herptiles to look out for are sharp-ribbed salamander, common tree, Iberian pool and parsley frogs and viperine snake, while Miller's water shrew and western polecat are the most notable of the mammalian colonists.

The cultivated plains of the Tierra de Campos are by no means devoid of wildlife, harbouring common vole, Iberian hare and predators such as weasel, stoat and red fox, while the field margins – and often the crops themselves – are coloured by corn-cockle, several members of the curious genus *Hypecoum*, common poppy, the eye-catching scarlet pheasant's-eye *Adonis aestivalis* subspecies *squarrosa*, corn mignonette, shepherd's-needle, annual androsace, henbit dead-nettle, field gromwell, cornflower and common grape hyacinth.

Perhaps more significantly, high densities of steppe birds occur here, particularly great bustard and calandra lark, as well as lesser numbers of Montagu's and hen harriers, black-winged kite, lesser kestrel, stone curlew, little bustard and black-bellied sandgrouse; short-eared owls (which also breed occasionally) occur in winter. Particularly good for steppe birds is the road (P-951) which links Frechilla with Guaza de Campos, to the northwest of Fuentes de Nava, best in winter when the bustards form large flocks and are much more visible. The more vegetated plateau to the west of Dueñas (just off the N-620 south of Palencia; junction 96), which is traversed by the P-903 en route to Santa Cecilia del Alcor, is known to support a few pairs of Dupont's lark and good numbers of Orphean, subalpine and spectacled warblers, plus great spotted cuckoo, black-eared wheatear and cirl bunting.

Access and information: La Nava is traversed by the P-940 (Mazariegos to Fuentes de Nava road), with a small parking area at the southwestern corner of the lagoon, from which a track leads east to a hide opposite the ruins of Casa de Don Marcelo (about 700 m). Boada can be reached by following a way-marked trail (1200 m) from the village of the same name (on the P-922) to the hide on the northern edge of the lake, which also gives good views of the surrounding cereal pseudosteppes. In both cases a telescope is almost essential. An information centre is located in Fuentes de Nava (c/Mayor 17; tel: 979 842500); Boada continues to be managed by the Fundación Global Nature (tel: 979 842398; fax: 979 842399; e-mail: lanava@teleline.es).

Also in the area

Laguna de la Toja Small reed-fringed lagoon north of Palencia; one of the best places to see marsh harriers at close quarters in northern Spain: 6–10 pairs breed but dozens winter here. Take the N-611 as far as km 24, then turn west towards San Cebrián de Campos (P-984). Just after the point where the road crosses the Canal de Castilla (km 5.6), park on the left by the series of locks on the canal and walk north until you reach a small hide overlooking the lake (300 m). Teal, pintail, red-crested pochard and pochard winter, while water rail, gadwall and great reed warbler breed and purple herons feed and roost. Well-preserved riverine forest where the canal joins the Río Carrión to the south: haunt of penduline tit and golden oriole.

SITE
84 Fuentes Carrionas

Fabulous mountain area harbouring many endemic plants, interesting butterfly and forest bird assemblages and the bulk of the Cordillera Cantábrica's eastern nucleus of brown bear.

The Parque Natural de Fuentes Carrionas y Fuente Cobre (78 360 ha, also a ZEPA) encompasses some of the most splendid scenery on the southern flanks of the Cordillera Cantábrica, as well as some of its highest peaks, with Curavacas – the summit of the park – rising to an impressive 2525 m. The northwestern corner of the park is a hulking mass of dark siliceous rocks (conglomerates, shales and quartzites), the peaks ice-sculpted to form sweeping cirques housing a number of glacial lakes, notably the Laguna de Fuentes Carrionas (2230 m). To the south, much of the bedrock is

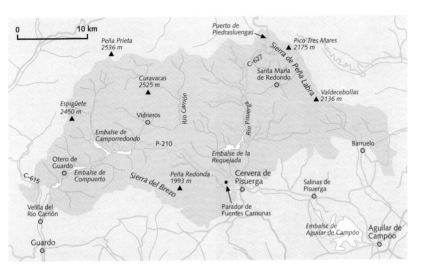

Carboniferous limestone, rising to such notable eminences as Espigüete (2450 m) and Peña Redonda (1993 m), while the extreme northeastern boundary is marked by the Sierra de Peña Labra: a complex mosaic of acid shales and calcareous limestones crowned by Valdecebollas (2136 m) and Pico Tres Mares (2175 m).

More than 1100 species of vascular plant have been recorded at Fuentes Carrionas, with three major botanical hot-spots. The first lies at the head of the Carrión valley, between the peaks of Peña Prieta (2536 m) and Curavacas, whose siliceous rocks harbour parnassus-leaved buttercup (subspecies *cabrerensis*), the pink-flowered rock jasmine *Androsace cantabrica*, unique to the Cordillera Cantábrica, and the Spanish endemic *Senecio boissieri*, distinguished by its close mats of silver-hairy leaves and curious reddish-orange heads of disc florets. Species found in other European mountains but rare in the Cordillera Cantábrica include the arctic-alpine starwort mouse-ear, the yellow-flowered stonecrop *Sedum alpestre*, hairless mossy saxifrage and Piedmont primrose.

Access to the Upper Carrión valley is possible along the track leading north from the village of Vidrieros, although the 5 km walk to the foot of Curavacas involves a climb of around 1000 m. Here you'll find two exquisite glacial lakes – Pozo Oscuro and Pozo de

Curavacas – and numerous peatbogs, home to round-leaved sundew, hairy stonecrop, grass-of-Parnassus, cross-leaved heath and bog asphodel, while the surrounding acid rocks and screes support parsley fern, mountain male-fern, the catchfly *Silene ciliata*, *Teesdaliopsis conferta*, *Linaria alpina* subspecies *filicaulis* and mountain everlasting.

The second enclave of botanical significance is the Sierra de Peña Labra, particularly on the south-facing limestone, where you might turn up Pyrenean pheasant's-eye, a rare plant indeed outside the Pyrenees, Samnitic milk-vetch, alpine skullcap, the Spanish endemic speedwell *Veronica mampodrensis*, found also on Espigüete, and *Artemisia cantabrica*, endemic to just two localities in the Cordillera Cantábrica, with lower slopes harbouring hyssop and the

Wolf *Canis lupus*

Saxifraga canaliculata

viper's-bugloss *Echium cantabricum*, known only from the Puerto de Piedrasluengas (1329 m) on the C-627.

The limestone outcrops to the east of Piedrasluengas are absolutely delightful in early summer, harbouring an abundance of the lovely blue-tinged anemone *Anemone pavoniana* and cushions of *Draba dedeana*, both confined to the Cordillera Cantábrica, plus masses of the Spanish endemic *Saxifraga canaliculata*, livelong saxifrage, wild cotoneaster, Pyrenean spurge and *Globularia repens*. Later in the year, look out for the houseleek *Sempervivum vicentei* subspecies *cantabricum*, again unique to the Cordillera Cantábrica.

Peña Redonda – at the eastern end of the Sierra del Brezo which extends between Guardo and Cervera de Pisuerga, in the southern part of the park – is the third botanical hot-spot. Beechwoods here harbour yellow anemone, with the limestone rock-gardens home to the cushion-forming, yellow-flowered crucifer *Draba hispanica* subspecies *lebrunii*, endemic to this peak, as well as being the only locality in the Cordillera Cantábrica for *Silene boryi*. The north face of this ridge secretes a stand of

millennial yew trees known as the Tejeda de Tosande – one of the best preserved in Spain – numbering several hundred individuals of truly gargantuan proportions.

Fuentes Carrionas lies at the cross-roads of the Euro-Siberian and Mediterranean bioclimatic zones, such that the climax vegetation of the park varies considerably from north to south. North-facing slopes at relatively high altitudes are the domain of beech and sessile oak which, on acid soils, support a ground flora of soft shield-fern, scaly male-fern and northern buckler-fern, green hellebore (subspecies *occidentalis*), wood anemone, wood-sorrel, spurge-laurel and broad-leaved helleborine. Try Piedrasluengas for truly diverse calcareous beechwoods; just to the south of the pass is a spectacular – albeit short – limestone gorge, on the north flank of which the beech shelters baneberry, Gouan's buttercup (endemic to northern Spain and the Pyrenees) and ramsons in early summer, with the yellow-flowered *Aconitum vulparia* subspecies *neapolitanum*, martagon lily and whorled Solomon's-seal in bloom from July onwards.

The most extensive forest community of Fuentes Carrionas, however, comprises Pyrenean oak, found on sunny slopes at height and north-facing ones at lower altitudes, but always on acid bedrock. Often associated with Plymouth pear and *Genista florida*, typical herbs include the Iberian endemic toadflax *Linaria triornithophora* and bladderseed. One of the best places to explore this habitat type is around the *parador* of Fuentes Carrionas on the P-210 which links Cervera de Pisuerga with Velilla del Río Carrión.

More Mediterranean vegetation in the lowest regions of the park, where the bedrock is mainly calcareous, is dominated by western holm oak, accompanied by Spanish and common junipers, Lusitanian oak, snowy mespilus, *Spiraea hypericifolia* subspecies *obovata*, *Genista scorpius*, Spanish gorse, Cornish heath and wayfaring-tree. The area to the north of Velilla del Río Carrión, along the C-615, is studded with Spanish junipers and creeping mats of savin and dwarf junipers, between which lizard orchids and early spider ophrys abound in

Snow finch *Montifringilla nivalis*

June, together with rock soapwort, mountain tragacanth, sheets of white flax, the curious *Centaurea lagascana*, with pale-yellow stemless flowers nestling in clusters in spiny leaf rosettes, and common grape hyacinth.

The fauna of Fuentes Carrionas is no less diverse, numbering 48 species of mammal, 190 birds (of which 135 breed), 18 reptiles and 11 amphibians. The most noteworthy mammalian inhabitant is indisputably the brown bear, the park harbouring the bulk of the population of the so-called eastern nucleus in the Cordillera Cantábrica, now numbering just 20–25 individuals. Among the Iberian endemic mammals, Pyrenean desmans occur in a few of the high-mountain watercourses, Castroviejo's hares occupy tall broom and genista scrub close to the tree-line and Iberian blind moles are typical of grasslands at lower altitudes.

The forest fauna includes a wide range of predatory mammals, notably wolf (three or four family groups live in the park), wildcat, common genet, beech and pine martens and western polecat, with large herbivores including roe and red deer (the latter reintroduced in 1968) and wild boar; garden and edible dormice and red squirrels occupy the canopy. Smaller mammals include Millet's shrew, bank vole and Iberian pine vole, all with Iberian ranges limited to the north of the peninsula. At the highest altitudes, snow voles are common, while chamois (here subspecies *parva*, confined to the Cordillera Cantábrica) are most abundant between Espigüete and Peña Prieta, with a small, isolated population on Peña Labra.

The highest peaks also harbour some of the more noteworthy birds of the park, par-

ticularly wallcreeper and snowfinch, nesting above 1800 m but often seen at much lower altitudes outside the breeding season. Other birds to watch out for at these heights are water pipit, alpine accentor, rock thrush, chough (200+ pairs) and alpine chough (100+ pairs), while scrubby habitats around the tree-line are the haunt of an important population of partridge, plus woodcock, bluethroat and red-backed shrike. Fuentes Carrionas is also home to small numbers of breeding golden eagle (5–6 pairs), Egyptian vulture (10 pairs) and griffon vulture (10–15 pairs), with other cliff-nesting species including a handful of peregrines and possibly eagle owl; try the area between Velilla del Río Carrión and Otero de Guardo, to the north of the P-210.

Also of interest are the Atlantic forest birds, with Fuentes Carrionas harbouring about a dozen pairs of black woodpecker, notably in beechwoods on both sides of Piedrasluengas, and an abundance of middle spotted woodpeckers in mature oak forests (sessile and Pyrenean). Woodland passerines include tree pipit, goldcrest, marsh tit, nuthatch, treecreeper, citril finch and bullfinch, while among the raptors are large numbers of breeding goshawks, sparrowhawks, black kites, honey buzzards and booted and short-toed eagles.

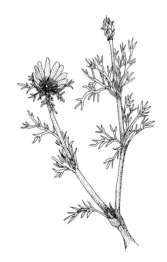

Pyrenean pheasant's eye *Adonis pyrenaica*

Iberian endemic reptiles to watch out for in the park are Bocage's wall lizard in damp Pyrenean oak woods, Schreiber's green lizard, never far from water, Iberian rock lizard in the highest rockgardens, Bedriaga's skink and Cantabrican viper. The high-level damp grasslands and peatbogs are home to viviparous lizard and common frog, both at the southern edge of their European range here, while alpine and palmate newts can be found in the glacial lakes. Interestingly, the park is one of the few places where the distributions of asp and Cantabrican viper overlap.

Fuentes Carrionas is one of the best butterfly localities in the whole of the Cordillera Cantábrica. June is an excellent time to visit, when fritillaries abound – notably bog, small pearl-bordered, pearl-bordered, marbled, lesser marbled, dark green, Queen of Spain, Glanville, knapweed, Provençal, meadow, heath and spotted – as do ringlets, with species to look out for including de Prunner's, large, Piedmont and Chapman's, the latter unique to the Cordillera Cantábrica. Also abundant at this time of year are swallowtail, Moroccan orange tip, Berger's clouded yellow, Duke of Burgundy fritillary and turquoise, Adonis and Mazarine blues, while come July Apollos are on the wing by the score, with other noteworthy species including high brown and silver-washed fritillaries, chestnut heath, rock and great banded graylings, Esper's marbled white, chalk-hill blue and a profusion of coppers: scarce, purple-edged, purple-shot and sooty. In mid-July, Peña Prieta is home to hill-topping large tortoiseshell, shepherd's fritillary and Lefèbvre's and common brassy ringlets, while the Sierra del Brezo is home to an isolated colony of mountain small white.

Information: Take heed of signs indicating '*zonas de reserva*'. Not only have these been designated to protect rare and vulnerable plant populations, but also to safeguard the most sensitive brown bear breeding and wintering areas. A visitor centre is planned for Cervera de Pisuerga; a useful website is www.altocarrionacade.es

Also in the area

Embalse de Aguilar de Campóo Large reservoir hosting breeding little and great crested grebes and gadwall plus passage waders. Surrounding pine plantations and enclaves of Pyrenean, Lusitanian and western holm oaks harbour black kite, nightjar, wryneck, Bonelli's warbler and crossbill, with stone curlew and great spotted cuckoo in more open areas. Access via the roads linking Aguilar with Salinas de Pisuerga to both north and south of the reservoir.

Las Tuerces (proposed *monumento natural*; 782 ha) Limestone plateau to the south of Aguilar de Campóo topped by eroded limestone pinnacles. Orchids abound – early purple, green-winged and lady, plus early spider, yellow, dull and woodcock ophrys – with cereal fields to the south rich in arable weeds: corn buttercup, dragon's teeth, shepherd's-needle, blue woodruff and cornflower. Small gorge carved out by the Pisuerga to the west – Cañón de la Horadada – is a known locality for eagle owl, alpine swift (in one of its few Palencian localities) and rock thrush, while the buttresses of Las Tuerces proper harbour breeding griffon and Egyptian vultures, peregrine, a single pair of golden eagles and chough. Wolves are frequently seen in the area and otters and Miller's water shrews occur along the river. Access from Villaescusa de las Torres; turn off the N-611 at Valoria de Aguilar.

Peña Amaya (ZEPA; 39 854 ha) Spectacular two-tiered limestone buttresses in northwestern Burgos topped by a flat plateau rising to 1362 m, with a diverse flora resembling that of the Páramo de la Lora (see below). Similar cliff-nesting birds to Las Tuerces, with a griffon vulture colony of more than 100 pairs; surrounding cereals support breeding Montagu's and hen harriers and stone curlew. Access to the plateau from the village of Amaya, with best views of breeding raptors from the road to Villamartín de Villadiego.

SITE 85 Páramo de la Lora

Limestone plateau on the Cantabria–Burgos border, home to a rich flora – including 22 species of orchid and 20 members of the Liliaceae – plus a diverse butterfly fauna.

Lying between the village of Sargentes de la Lora in the south and the buttresses which drop abruptly to the Río Ebro in the north, the vast, karstified limestone plateau known as the Páramo de la Lora (part of the Hoces del Alto Ebro y Rudrón ZEPA; see p. 245) is characterised by low winter temperatures (often below freezing), a pronounced summer drought, relatively low precipitation (725 mm per year) and almost perpetual winds. Nevertheless, a diverse flora thrives here, combining both Euro-Siberian and Mediterranean elements, for which reason Lora is sometimes referred to as the 'Spanish Burren'.

Centuries of felling, grazing and burning have virtually destroyed the original western holm and Lusitanian oak forests, such that today the dominant vegetation of the plateau is a low mosaic of common juniper, snowy mespilus, *Spiraea hypericifolia* subspecies *obovata*, Spanish gorse, *Genista scorpius*, bearberry, Cornish heath, *Lavandula latifolia* and blue aphyllanthes. The thin soils overlaying the limestone support a tremendous diversity of geophytes, which flourish in the absence of competition from more aggressive plants.

In May, close to the trig point of Muñata (1181 m) on the northern edge of the plateau, drifts of green-winged, Provence and elder-flowered orchids are interspersed with clusters of man, dense-flowered, Barton's, burnt and lady orchids, while early spider, yellow, dull and sawfly ophrys are more typical of the slightly deeper soils near Sargentes de la Lora (1019 m). At this time of year any route between these two points (some 6 km) should also turn up Pyrenean snakeshead, wild tulip, spring squill and common grape and tassel hyacinths, as well as hoop-petticoat daffodils, angel's-tears and the sand crocus *Romulea bulbocodium*. Other floristic delights of the *páramo* include a profusion of the Spanish endemic stork's-bill *Erodium daucoides* near Muñata, scarlet-flowered clumps of common peonies in sheltered ravines near Sargentes, and an abundance of Deptford pink, *Thalictrum tuberosum*, grass-leaved buttercup, *Iberis carnosa*, dropwort, white flax and common globularia throughout.

Elder-flowered orchid *Dactylorhiza sambucina*

Bird-wise, the cereal fields and marginal hedgerows around Sargentes are the haunt of quail, skylark, short-toed lark, tawny pipit and yellowhammer, with rougher ground harbouring black redstart, wheatear, rock thrush and rock sparrow. Black kites and both hen and Montagu's harriers can be seen quartering the plateau in spring, while the north-facing buttress below Muñata is occupied by nesting kestrel and chough, as well as being used as a vantage point by large congregations of griffon vultures from the nearby Rudrón colony.

The most notable early-flying butterfly here is undoubtedly the spring ringlet, an extremely scarce species confined to southeastern France and Spain, but look out, too, for marbled skipper, swallowtail, scarce swallowtail, Moroccan orange tip and Cleopatra. Later in the year butterfly diversity increases considerably, with species on the wing in July and August including mallow, olive and silver-spotted skippers, Apollo, chestnut heath, great banded, rock and tree graylings, the hermit, black satyr, Esper's marbled white, dusky meadow brown, silver-studded, Chapman's, turquoise, Spanish chalk-hill, Forster's furry and Ripart's anomalous blues and Spanish argus.

Access: Sargentes de la Lora is reached either from the N-623 Burgos–Torrelavega road (turn west at San Felices), or from the N-627 which links Burgos with Aguilar de Campóo (turning off at Basconcillos del Tozo). Another possibility is the minor road (S-620) which climbs the face of the buttress from Polientes (Valderredible) on the Ebro; footpaths ascend the buttress from San Martín de Elines and Villota.

Also in the area

Páramo de Masa Around the junction of the BU-629 with the BU-503/502 (to the north of the village of Cernégula and east of the Puerto de Páramo de Masa (1050 m) on the N-623). Rather more vegetated limestone plateau with resident little bustard, stone curlew, long-eared and little owls and calandra lark, plus whinchat and spectacled and Orphean warblers in summer. Similar rich butterfly fauna to the Páramo de la Lora.

SITE
86 Hoces del Alto Ebro

Superb limestone river gorges – carved out by the infant Ebro and its tributary the Rudrón – harbouring an important assemblage of cliff-breeding birds, well-preserved gallery forest and a diverse limestone flora.

Whether you are perched on the lip of the Hoces del Alto Ebro y Rudrón (a ZEPA of 59 754 ha and proposed *parque natural*) or ensconced deep within the defile, the scenery cannot fail to impress; spectacular limestone precipices drop almost perpendicularly for over 200 m, with the floor of the gorge often less than 100 m wide.

The Ebro and Rudrón gorges are best known for their cliff-breeding birds, notably more than 200 pairs of griffon vulture, a couple of dozen pairs of Egyptian vulture and a handful of pairs of golden and Bonelli's eagles. Here, too, nest peregrine and eagle owl (a dozen pairs of each), plus some 20 pairs of alpine chough at the extreme southern edge of their European range. Other typical cliff-nesters include alpine swift, crag martin, black wheatear, rock thrush and chough, while post-breeding concentrations of Egyptian vultures number close to a hundred individuals. Also keep an eye out for

black vultures soaring over the gorge; there have been several sightings here in recent years, despite the fact that their nearest known breeding territories lie several hundred kilometres to the southwest.

A very different assemblage of birds occupies the gallery forests in the depths of the gorges, headed by black kite, goshawk, sparrowhawk and hobby, but also including kingfisher, wryneck, redstart, nightingale, Iberian chiffchaff, Cetti's, Bonelli's and garden warblers, long-tailed tit and golden oriole; the river itself is home to a healthy population of otters. The surrounding plateau is clothed with a mosaic of degraded Lusitanian and western holm oak forest, juniper scrub, small meadows and pockets of cereals, supporting breeding booted and short-toed eagles, hen harrier, cuckoo, nightjar, woodlark, tawny pipit and red-backed shrike.

The riverine forests are dominated by black and white poplars, alder, wych elm and

Hoces del Alto Ebro (T.F.)

narrow-leaved ash, with a wide range of shrubs occupying the shady nether regions, notably *Salix elaeagnos* subspecies *angustifolia*, spindle, dogwood, wild privet, wayfaring-tree and guelder-rose. Look out for purple toothwort parasitising the roots of the poplars, with other characteristic herbs including columbine, purple gromwell, bastard balm, Pyrenean valerian and hempagrimony. Red squirrels are fairly abundant, while Iberian pool frogs produce a noisy chorus from the margins of the river.

The flanks of the gorge are dotted with enclaves of western holm and Lusitanian oaks, typically associated with prickly and common junipers, snowy mespilus, St Lucie's cherry, Mediterranean buckthorn, strawberry-tree and wild jasmine. Where more light penetrates, the understorey comprises Spanish gorse, *Genista scorpius*, *Dorycnium pentaphyllum*, *Spiraea hypericifolia* subspecies *obovata*, the white-flowered *Halimium umbellatum*, round-headed thyme and *Lavandula latifolia*, although this latter species does not flower until late summer, while the bulk of the flora is at its best in May and early June.

More open areas on the screes at the foot of the cliffs harbour a colourful assemblage of pink-flowered cushions of rock soapwort, the delicate, cream-flowered *Thalictrum tuberosum*, white and beautiful flaxes, hoary rock-rose, bearberry, ground-pine, perennial yellow-woundwort, *Digitalis parviflora*, with cylindrical spikes of small, coppery flowers, *Helichrysum stoechas* and blue aphyllanthes, while the shady overhangs of the lower precipices provide shelter for blue-leaved petrocoptis, sarcocapnos, thick-leaved stonecrop, the Iberian endemic saxifrage *Saxifraga cuneata* and fairy foxglove.

Orchids abound in the bottom of the gorge, particularly man, green-winged, military and lady, plus violet limodore, with drier habitats harbouring a number of insect-imitating members of the genus *Ophrys*, namely yellow, woodcock and early spider. The cereal fields in the surrounding *páramo* are rich in arable weeds such as corn buttercup, violet horned-poppy, common poppy, scorpion senna, perfoliate alexanders, thorow-wax, cornflower and even bulbs such as hoop-petticoat daffodil, rosy garlic and common grape and tassel hyacinths.

In fine weather a number of butterflies can be found here, of which the most typical are swallowtail, scarce swallowtail, Moroccan orange tip, Cleopatra, black-veined and wood whites and Adonis, common, black-eyed, Panoptes and small blues early in the year, with July seeing dark green fritillary, cardinal, the hermit and rock grayling on the wing.

Access: One of the most stunning reaches of the Ebro and Rudrón gorges lies between Valdelateja (on the N-623 Santander–Burgos road) and Pesquera de Ebro (see p. 225) to the east; a circular route ascends the limestone cliff at Valdelateja and leads you to Pesquera via the ruined hamlet of Cortiguera, accompanied by fabulous views over the *hoces* from above, returning along the Ebro deep in the heart of the defile. A second, much less visited section of the Ebro lies to the north, between Tubilleja (accessible by road from Pesquera) and Cidad de Ebro.

Also in the area

Sierras de Oña y de la Tesla (part ZEPA) Series of limestone ridges (maximum 1332 m) along the N-232 between Incinillas and Solduengo. Many cliffs and numerous small gorges harbour breeding griffon and Egyptian (15 pairs) vultures, golden eagle, peregrine, eagle owl, rock thrush, alpine chough and large numbers of choughs (325 pairs). The surrounding *páramos* support small numbers of nesting hen harriers.

Ojo Guareña (*monumento natural*; 13 850 ha) Centred on the cave system of the same name, south of the C-6318 between Soncillo (on the N-232) and Espinosa de los Monteros. Subterranean galleries extend over almost 90 km and are considered to be the most important karstic formation in Spain. Significant bat colonies and a diverse community of cave-dwelling invertebrates, with six taxa endemic to the system. Access only with a guide; visits can be organised through the information centre in the town hall in Cornejo (tel: 947 138614).

SITE 87 Cañón del Río Lobos

Sinuous limestone canyon, with a rich flora and important populations of cliff-nesting birds.

From the viewpoint known as Alto de La Galiana (1143 m), the Cañón del Río Lobos yawns vertiginously at your feet, the impressive limestone cliffs plunging almost vertically into a narrow river valley. The sheer walls of this spectacular chasm (a *parque natural* of 9580 ha, also a ZEPA) – often more than 60 m high – are riddled with numerous cavities, horizontal ledges and overhangs, occupied by legions of cliff-nesting birds.

The 2000 breeding bird census in this 14-km gorge revealed the presence of no less than 159 pairs of griffon vulture, 5 of Egyptian vulture, 2 of golden eagle, 6 of peregrine, 4 of eagle owl and around 90 pairs of chough. Other cliff-nesting species include kestrel, stock dove, alpine swift (a small colony most years near the Ermita de San Bartolomé), crag martin, black redstart, black wheatear, both rock thrushes and rock sparrow; it is not unheard of for mammals such as red fox, common genet, garden dormouse and even red squirrel to use the many orifices as bolt-holes.

The Río Lobos canyon is also of considerable botanical interest, with more than 1000 species of vascular plant having been recorded here. With the advent of May the monocots start to flower, notably woodcock and

Blue cupidone
Catananche caerulea

early spider ophrys, blue aphyllanthes, star-of-Bethlehem, round-headed leek, *Allium paniculatum*, *Asphodelus ramosus* and St Bernard's lily, with large white helleborine and merendera appearing later in the year.

The cliffs themselves harbour a notable assemblage of calcareous fissure plants, including a number of Iberian endemics: *Dianthus subacaulis* subspecies *brachyanthus*, *Draba dedeana*, *Alyssum lapeyrousianum*, *Saxifraga cuneata*, *Erodium daucoides* and *Antirrhinum meonanthum*.

Wall germander *Teucrium chamaedrys*

Here, too, are the more widespread sarco-capnos, burnt-candytuft, dwarf buckthorn, Malling toadflax, Spanish bellflower and *Jasonia glutinosa*. The unstable habitat represented by the screes at the base of these cliffs is equally interesting, supporting lesser meadow-rue (subspecies *pubescens*), the Spanish endemic crucifer *Biscutella valentina*, *Ononis aragonensis*, prostrate toadflax and peach-leaved bellflower.

A fragrant carpet of labiates clothes the less vertiginous limestone rockgardens in early summer, particularly the pinkish-mauve-flowered horehound *Marrubium supinum*, *Phlomis lychnitis*, ground-pine, *Lavandula latifolia*, *Salvia lavandulifolia*, *Satureja cuneifolia*, perennial yellow-woundwort, *Stachys heraclea*, lesser catmint, *Sideritis hirsuta*, *S. incana* and *S. montana* (whose flowers range from white through yellow to pink), cut-leaved and wall germanders and *Thymus zygis*. Here, too, you can find *Thalictrum tuberosum*, *Paeonia officinalis* subspecies *microcarpa*, dropwort, coris, Spanish rusty foxglove, the blood-red toadflax *Linaria aeruginea*, common globularia, round-headed rampion, blue cupidone and *Inula montana*, as well as the prostrate Iberian endemic greenweed *Genista pumila*

and cushions of *Hormathophylla spinosa* and *Bupleurum rigidum*.

These dry, sunny habitats are home to a wealth of reptiles, notably spiny-footed, Iberian wall and ocellated lizards, large and Spanish psammodromus, Montpellier, ladder and southern smooth snakes and Lataste's viper, while more humid, sandy soils harbour amphisbaenian, slow-worm and three-toed skink.

Gallery forests in the upper part of the valley are dominated by crack willow, black poplar, wych elm and narrow-leaved ash, sheltering thick stands of *Salix atrocinerea*, the Iberian endemic *S. salvifolia* and purple, almond and olive willows. The river margins also support a colourful array of marsh mallow, yellow and purple loosestrifes, parsley water-dropwort, lesser water-parsnip, gypsywort, round-leaved, water and horse mints, skullcap, trifid bur-marigold, water-plantain, narrow-leaved water-plantain and yellow flag, while some of the backwaters house amphibious bistort, yellow water-lily, spiked water-milfoil and curled pondweed.

The watercourse itself is the haunt of brown trout, the loaches *Cobitis paludica* and lamprehuela, Iberian nase, bermejuela and the Iberian endemic barbel *Barbus bocagei*, with amphibians including fire salamander, marbled newt, Iberian pool, common tree, parsley and Iberian frogs, natterjack and midwife toads and western spadefoot. Among the waterside mammals are Iberian blind mole, greater white-toothed shrew and southern water vole, while typical birds of the less-disturbed sections of riverine forest include lesser spotted woodpecker, kingfisher, nightingale, Cetti's and melodious warblers and golden oriole, as well as goshawk and tawny and long-eared owls.

The western reaches of the park lie on more acid, siliceous soils and are largely clothed with mature plantations of Scots pine and small enclaves of Lusitanian oak, particularly attractive to sparrowhawk and goshawk, booted and short-toed eagles, hobby, crested and long-tailed tits, nuthatch, short-toed treecreeper, serin, hawfinch and crossbill, and also providing refuge for the park's larger mammals, notably roe deer,

San Bartolomé, in the Cañón del Río Lobos (T.F.)

wild boar, red fox, wildcat, Eurasian badger and common genet. The Spanish junipers and laurel-leaved cistus scrub on the more lime-rich plateau to the south of Hontoria del Pinar are favoured by black-eared wheatear, subalpine warbler, woodchat shrike, azure-winged magpie and rock and ortolan buntings.

Several car parks are located between the entrance to the park on the SO-920 and the area known as Valdecea, from which it is just a short stroll to the Romanesque chapel of San Bartolomé. This – the deepest and most spectacular – section of gorge is by far the most visited, but even so harbours

numerous griffon vulture nests. The viewpoint of La Galiana lies a few kilometres further north on the road towards San Leonardo; from here you can walk along the rim of the gorge and descend to San Bartolomé.

> *Information*: The park interpretation centre is located in the former trout-farm on the SO-920 to the north of Ucero (tel: 975 363564; open from mid-March to the end of October); avoid weekends, Easter and high summer.

Also in the area

Sabinares del Arlanza (proposed *parque natural*; 26 055 ha, also a ZEPA; 37 404 ha) Limestone gorges formed by the Ríos Arlanza and Mataviejas harbouring some 240 pairs of griffon and 17 pairs of Egyptian vulture, golden eagle, peregrine

and eagle owl. Nearby **Garganta de la Yecla** is an incredibly narrow defile accessed via a suspended walkway about 200 m long, south of the Romanesque monastery of Santo Domingo de Silos. Flora includes the Afro-Iberian endemic catchfly *Silene boryi*, mountain alyssum, sad stock, *Hormathophylla spinosa* and *Saxifraga cuneata*. Other cliff-breeders of the area include alpine swift, crag martin, blue rock thrush, chough and rock sparrow, with alpine accentor and wall-creeper among the winter visitors. Mediterranean forest and scrub contain redstart, Dartford, subalpine and Orphean warblers, azure-winged magpie and rock and ortolan buntings.

Sabinar de Calatañazor (*monumento natural*; 30 ha) One of the most important Spanish juniper forests in Iberia,

with a typical avifauna of black-eared wheatear and *Sylvia* warblers, plus goldcrest and citril finch in winter. Dissected by numerous river gorges with many cliff-breeding birds; more open areas harbour short-toed and Dupont's larks and tawny pipit. Try the Avión river valley between Aldehuela and Calatañazor, just north of the N-122. Some 5 km to the northwest of Calatañazor lies the village of Muriel de la Fuente, from which you can visit **La Fuentona** (*monumento natural*; 215 ha): a classic resurgence of an underground river.

88 Hoces del Río Riaza

Spectacular limestone river gorge – a ZEPA of 6540 ha and proposed parque natural – harbouring the Iberian peninsula's largest colony of griffon vultures and a rich calcicolous flora.

The Refugio de Rapaces de Montejo de la Vega (2415 ha) – one of the first of Spain's now considerable network of protected areas – was declared in 1974 to protect cliff-breeding birds in the Hoces del Río Riaza. Since this time the colony of griffon vultures has increased more than fourfold and is now the largest breeding concentration in Iberia, numbering some 390 pairs in 2000.

Around 300 species of vertebrate have been cited at Montejo de la Vega, including 111 breeding birds. Other cliff-nesters include Egyptian vulture (18–19 territories), a single pair of golden eagles (which has recolonised the gorge since 1974), peregrine, and 7–8 pairs of eagle owl, as well as a multitude of smaller birds: alpine swift, crag martin, rock dove, black wheatear, both rock thrushes, chough and rock sparrow. Notable among the herptiles are Iberian painted, Iberian pool and parsley frogs, midwife and natterjack toads, large psammodromus,

ocellated lizard, amphisbaenian and ladder, viperine and southern smooth snakes, with fish including brown trout, *Barbus bocagei*, Iberian nase and bermejuela.

The surrounding plains are a different world entirely. Although much of this rolling *páramo* is dedicated to dry cereal cultivation, small hummocks are often left unploughed and retain a carpet of low thyme scrub dotted with near-spherical western holm oaks, the whole mosaic providing suitable habitat for Iberian hare, black-bellied sandgrouse, Dupont's and Thekla larks and tawny pipit, with small pine plantations hosting nesting short-toed eagle and hobby. Look out, too, for hoopoe, black-eared wheatear, spectacled and subalpine warblers, southern grey and woodchat shrikes, spotless starling and azure-winged magpie.

The cultivated areas are not short on botanical interest either, with low levels of fertilisers and pesticides permitting a wide range of arable 'weeds' to flourish. Many are extremely colourful – common and rough poppies, *Hypecoum imberbe* and *H. pendulum*, large blue alkanet and undulate anchusa – tinting the landscape with broad swathes of reds, yellows and blues in early summer. Less conspicuous are the pheasant's-eye *Adonis aestivalis*, the yellow-flowered *Ceratocephalus falcatus*, corn buttercup, spiked fumitory, violet horned-poppy, sand catchfly, rough marsh-mallow, corn mignonette, annual androsace, small caltrops (with distinctive star-shaped fruits), the lemon-flowered toadflax *Linaria simplex* and Venus's-looking-glass.

The whole 11.5 km of the Riaza gorge can be explored via a riverside trail, with the eastern end, close to the Linares del Arroyo reservoir, considerably more rugged, where almost every ledge holds a griffon vulture crouching atop an untidy nest in spring. The rocky slopes beneath the buttresses harbour a diverse scrub community of the joint pine *Ephedra nebrodensis*, prickly and Spanish junipers, snowy mespilus, the horribly spiny *Genista scorpius*, hairy thymelaea, the Iberian endemic hare's-ear *Bupleurum fruticescens*, *Lavandula latifolia*, *Thymus zygis*, *Phlomis lychnitis*, shrubby gromwell, the lavender-cotton *Santolina chamaecyparissus* subspecies *squarrosa*, Spanish rusty foxglove and blue aphyllanthes.

Chough *Pyrrhocorax pyrrhocorax* (Mike Lane)

Spring comes late to the north Meseta, even within the confines of gorges such as this, although March sees drifts of rush-leaved jonquil and a few early-flowering clumps of the silver-leaved crucifer *Alyssum lapeyrousianum*. By May or June, however, the consolidated screes will be teeming with *Thalictrum tuberosum*, *Saxifraga carpetana*, beautiful flax, mountain rue, coris, the thrift *Armeria alliacea* subspecies *matritensis* (endemic to central-eastern Spain), lesser catmint, cut-leaved germander, *Salvia lavandulifolia*, the robust snapdragon *Antirrhinum hispanicum* subspecies *graniticum*, the Iberian endemic toadflaxes *Linaria aeruginea* and *L. badalii*, the pink-flowered *Allium pallens*, *Fritillaria lusitanica* and tall spikes of *Asphodelus ramosus*.

Shady overhangs on the lower buttresses harbour clumps of hart's-tongue and maidenhair fern, sarcocapnos, the crucifer *Biscutella valentina*, endemic to central, southern and eastern Spain, *Saxifraga cuneata*, dwarf buckthorn, wall germander, Malling toadflax (subspecies *segoviense*), the related *Chaenorhinum villosum*, Spanish bellflower and *Jasonia glutinosa*.

Most of the river Riaza is fringed by a thick belt of spiny shrubs – hawthorn, blackthorn, small-leaved sweet-briar and the wild roses *Rosa nitidula* and *R. corymbifera* – adorned with hop, berry catchfly, wild liquorice and marsh-mallow; damp grasslands here are home to common grape hyacinth, robust marsh orchid, large white helleborine and early spider ophrys. Emergent vegetation includes marsh horsetail, branched bur-reed, common and

Viperine snakes *Natrix maura* hunting fish in a river (Michael Woods)

round-headed club-rushes, galingale and greater pond-sedge, coloured by purple and yellow loosestrifes, blue water-speedwell and yellow flag in summer. Typical inhabitants of the riverine habitats include scops owl, kingfisher, great spotted woodpecker, nightingale and golden oriole, as well as mammals such as Miller's water shrew, southern water vole, beech marten and otter.

Access and information: Montejo de la Vega lies at the western end of the Hoces del Río Riaza; approaching from the north, just before the river, a track off left (signposted Refugio de Rapaces) leads to an information panel with waymarked routes. The eastern end of the gorge is reached by taking the C-114 east from Fuentelcésped as far as km 135, then turning right onto a small road marked 'Pie de Presa'. For more information contact WWF/Adena in Madrid.

SITE 89 Hoces del Río Duratón

Magnificent canyon housing a rich cliff-breeding avifauna, with the surrounding plateau good for Dupont's lark.

The 10-minute drive across the featureless stony plateau to the west of Villaseca does nothing to prepare you for the stunning panorama which unfolds when you finally reach the defile carved out by the Río Duratón. The Romanesque chapel of the

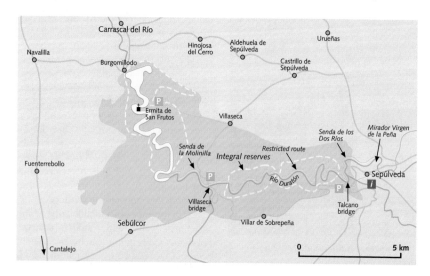

Ermita de San Frutos perches atop a knife-edged spur which protrudes into a sheer-walled, ochre meander of almost 270°; dozens of griffon vultures spiral overhead, peregrines cruise the canyon below and the rifle-shot calls of choughs echo from the cliffs.

The Duratón rises at the eastern end of the Sierra de Guadarrama, running for just over 100 km before discharging into the Duero at Peñafiel. Where it encounters limestones and dolomites around Sepúlveda it has carved out a spectacular 25 km chasm – up to 100 m deep in places – known as the Hoces del Río Duratón (a *parque natural* of 5037 ha, also a ZEPA).

The margins of the river responsible for such a feat of erosion are today almost invisible beneath thick fringes of gallery forest, home to a myriad nightingales, Cetti's warblers, golden orioles and serins. Amid enormous clumps of yellow flag thrive Iberian pool frog, midwife toad, ocellated lizard, viperine snake and southern water vole, while the brown trout, Iberian barbels and soiffe which inhabit the aquatic environment provide food for a handful of otters.

Away from the river, sunny slopes are studded with stunted western holm oaks, *Rhamnus lycioides* and grey-leaved cistus, while the more humid, north-facing inclines support a luxuriant tangle of snowy mespilus, whitebeam, Montpellier maple, fly honeysuckle and wayfaring-tree. Crevices in the walls of the gorge proper provide a foothold for delicate clumps of maidenhair fern, sarcocapnos and Spanish bellflower, growing together with contorted mats of dwarf buckthorn and the sticky, yellow-flowered composite *Jasonia glutinosa*. A late-spring visit to the steps of crumbling limestone which flank the road between Sepúlveda and Villar de Sobrepeña should turn up sad stock, white and beautiful flaxes, hairy thymelaea, *Phlomis lychnitis*, the white-felted composite *Andryala ragusina*, common grape and tassel hyacinths and blue aphyllanthes, as well as yellow and early spider ophrys, with butterflies on the wing including clouded yellow, Adonis, common and Panoptes blues, Spanish brown argus and small copper.

Clouded yellows *Colias croceus*

The exposed *páramo* at around 1000 m surrounding the gorge receives the brunt of the highly continental climate which typifies the northern Castilian Meseta, such that the only trees that can survive are a few stunted junipers (prickly, common and Spanish), scattered across a stony plain clothed with a low, fragrant garrigue of round-headed thyme, *Salvia lavandulifolia* and *Lavandula latifolia*. The 4 km of track between Villaseca and the San Frutos chapel is a good place to track down the elusive Dupont's lark (some 280 pairs here), best located when singing in March and April (before dawn, when vocal competition from other larks is minimal), as well as for quail, short-toed, calandra and Thekla larks, tawny pipit, wheatear and black-eared wheatear. Montagu's harriers and stone curlews also favour this habitat, as do large psammodromus and Montpellier and ladder snakes.

Early spider ophrys *Ophrys sphegodes* (T.F.)

Black-eared wheatear *Oenanthe hispanica*
(Mike Lane)

roller, southern grey shrike and azure-winged magpie.

The gorge itself houses one of the largest colonies of griffon vulture in Europe (386 pairs), while a more careful examination of the skies should turn up Egyptian vulture (8 pairs), peregrine (5 pairs) and – with a bit of luck – golden eagle (a single pair). Other cliff-nesting birds include kestrel (23 pairs), eagle owl (at least 2 pairs), crag martin, black redstart, rock thrush (a dozen or so pairs), blue rock thrush (30+ pairs), chough (300–400 pairs) and rock sparrow.

Of the 130+ species of bird that have been recorded in the park, the real stars of the show are the raptors, with 13 diurnal and 5 nocturnal species breeding here; look out for short-toed and booted eagles, red and black kites, goshawk and hobby, which breed in the gallery forests here and in the pines on the sands around Cantalejo, to the south. The cliff-side scrub is home to Dartford and spectacled warblers and rock bunting, while the more mature juniper copses on the *páramo* might turn up great spotted cuckoo,

Access and information: The park interpretation centre is in the restored church of Santiago de Sepúlveda (tel: 921 540586). Three restricted-access integral reserves protect the main griffon vulture colonies; between 1 January and 31 July a permit is required to walk the 12 km of gorge between the Talcano and Villaseca bridges (maximum 75 people per day).

Also in the area

Lagunas de Cantalejo (ZEPA of 12 302 ha) Series of endorheic lagoons on wind-blown sands amid maritime pines. Marsh harrier, water rail and azure-winged magpie all year round, with roller and an occasional black stork in the summer. Pines important for forest raptors, also harbouring large numbers of white storks' nests. Otter and American mink. Access from the C-112 to the northwest of the village of Cantalejo.

Pedraza Medieval castle overlooking another deep gorge, good for red kite, blue rock thrush, Cetti's and melodious warblers, golden oriole and rock sparrow.

Juniper forest around Pradena On both sides of the N-110 between Arcones and Casla. Stony limestone plateau studded with ancient Spanish junipers, some truly gargantuan; similar flora to the Duratón *páramo*.

Segovia (World Heritage Site) Roman aqueduct, one of the best preserved of its kind, is home to thousands of nesting swifts plus black redstart. Large white stork population (60–70 pairs), with nocturnal roost on the cathedral, which also harbours breeding chough and rock sparrow. Two small colonies of lesser kestrel, plus large post-breeding concentrations of black and red kites on the rubbish tip.

SITE 90 Sierra de Guadarrama

Extensive acid mountain chain to the north of Madrid, harbouring Spain's most extensive Scots pine forests and an important enclave of black vulture, as well as an interesting high-level endemic flora.

The Sierra de Guadarrama (a proposed national park) is a northeast–southwest-oriented granite and gneiss ridge almost 100 km long, which forms the watershed between the Duero and Tajo rivers at the eastern end of the Sistema Central. Often referred to as the 'Gable of Madrid', the Guadarrama peaks at Peñalara (2429 m) – focal point of the Cumbre y las Lagunas de Peñalara *parque natural* (768 ha) – with other protected areas including the ZEPAs of Alto Lozoya (5500 ha) on the southern flank and the Sierra de Guadarrama (109 265 ha), which covers the whole of the Segovian north face.

More than 1500 species of vascular plant have been recorded in the Sierra de Guadarrama. Relict enclaves of Mediterranean forest, plantations of maritime and stone pines and large tracts of secondary scrub occur up to about 1200 m, above which lies a narrow band of Pyrenean oak, typically associated with laurel-leaved cistus and the Afro-Iberian endemic grass *Stipa gigantea*. Between 1600 and 2000 m lie the best-preserved natural Scots pine forests in Spain, accompanied by yew, aspen, rowan and holly, and with an understorey composed primarily of common juniper, bearberry, tree heath and a range of yellow-flowered leguminous shrubs: *Adenocarpus telonensis*, broom, Pyrenean broom and *Genista florida*. In the ground layer, look out for several toad-flaxes with restricted distributions: *Linaria nivea*, unique to central Spain, the unmistakable *L. triornithophora*, found only in western Iberia, and the Afro-Iberian endemic *L. incarnata*.

Above the forest lies a bleak landscape of granite rockgardens, nevertheless home to the tuft-forming pink *Dianthus subacaulis*

subspecies *gredensis*, unique to the Gredos and Guadarrama, plus Iberian endemics such as *Ranunculus gregarius*, *Saxifraga pentadactylis* subspecies *willkommiana*, *Armeria caespitosa*, *Leucanthemopsis pallida* and *Crocus carpetanus*. Look out, too, for *Narcissus rupicola* and the autumn-flowering *Crocus serotinus* subspecies *salzmannii*, both Afro-Iberian endemics. Of particular note is the storksbill *Erodium paularense*, confined to localised calcareous deposits at around 1100 m in the upper part of the Lozoya valley; an area which also harbours a renowned population of dusky large blue.

Despite the ever-increasing human presence in the Sierra de Guadarrama, many birds of prey maintain important populations here, notably black vulture (around 100 pairs), plus griffon vulture, Spanish imperial, golden, short-toed and booted eagles, red and black kites, honey buzzard, goshawk, peregrine and eagle owl. The

Crested tit *Parus cristatus* (Mike Lane)

forests are home to great spotted woodpecker, pied flycatcher (subspecies *iberiae*), goldcrest, crested tit, nuthatch, short-toed treecreeper, crossbill and citril finch, while Mediterranean scrub provides suitable habitat for hoopoe, southern grey shrike and ortolan bunting. The most common mammals are the forest-dwelling red squirrel, garden dormouse, roe deer, wild boar, red fox, western polecat and wildcat, while the streams are said to house otters and introduced American mink, the latter probably responsible for the disappearance of the Pyrenean desman here in recent years.

Any exploration of the *sierra* should start with a visit to the **Peñalara** *parque natural*, characterised by a glacial topography of cirques, moraines and a rosary of ice-cold, aquamarine lakes. The most popular trail starts at the Puerto de los Cotos (1830 m) visitor centre and links three small glacial lakes occupying the main cirques on the south face of Peñalara: Laguna Grande de Peñalara, Laguna Claveles and Laguna de los Pájaros. Aquatic plants in these lagoons include pedunculate water-starwort and the grass *Antinoria agrostidea*, with marsh violet and large-flowered butterwort in the peaty surrounds. Fire salamander and Iberian and Iberian pool frogs are common in and around these glacial lakes, where you might also encounter alpine newts, almost undoubtedly introduced from the Cordillera Cantábrica.

The start of the lakes trail takes you through Scots pine forest – teeming with

Narcissus rupicola in May – and out into the granite rockgardens above. Amid the mats of dwarf juniper and clumps of Pyrenean broom, look out for *Ranunculus gregarius*, the lemon-flowered *Leucanthemopsis pallida* and the tiny yellow stars of Pyrenean gagea in spring, plus tall spikes of great yellow gentian in late summer. Black and griffon vultures frequently fly over the area and scattered pines are the haunt of woodlark, coal tit and rock bunting, while at ground level you will be serenaded by a dunnock on every bush; keep your eyes peeled for bluethroats, too.

The wet, peaty grasslands below Laguna Grande – riddled with the semicircular tunnels of snow voles – harbour blinks, lousewort and hoop-petticoat daffodil, with parsley fern in the screes around the lake. Rocky outcrops are a prime habitat for Iberian rock lizards, the robust males a distinctive, black-mottled lichen green, which serves to distinguish them from the smaller, brownish common wall lizards which also abound. Here, at over 2000 m, the most typical birds are water pipit, alpine accentor, wheatear, rock thrush and raven, with crag martins and choughs wheeling around the cliffs at the back of the cirque. Spring butterflies include clouded yellow, Queen of Spain fritillary, painted lady and small copper, with Apollo (subspecies *escaleri*) and mother-of-pearl blue appearing later in the year (81 species have been recorded in the park). The real lepidopteran gem of the Guadarrama, however, is the Spanish moon moth – a relative of the tropical silk moths – whose larvae feed on pines.

From the nearby Puerto de Navacerrada (1860 m), the CL-601 runs north through the **Montes de Valsaín** – the setting for Hemingway's *For whom the bell tolls* – where a narrow footpath along the left bank of the river Eresma passes through some of the most splendid Scots pine forest in the Guadarrama. Red squirrels and dippers abound, while the spring ground flora includes drifts of angel's tears plus hard-fern, meadow saxifrage, bitter vetch, wood-sorrel, sanicle and bluebells galore.

Returning to the Puerto de los Cotos, if you head east along the M-604 you eventual-

Spanish moon moth *Graellsia isabelae*

ly arrive at Rascafría, from which the M-611 leads south over the **Puerto de la Morcuera** (1796 m), winding up through Pyrenean oak forest and dry, acid grasslands containing narrow-leaved lupin and the pale-pink *Lupinus hispanicus*, yellow and tufted vetches, false sainfoin, white rock-rose and the superficially similar *Halimium umbellatum* subspecies *viscosum*, southern red bartsia, *Valeriana tuberosa*, *Santolina rosmarinifolia*, the green-tinged trumpets of *Narcissus graellsii*, star-of-Bethlehem, tassel hyacinth and green-winged and early purple orchids. Great spotted woodpecker, woodlark, tree pipit, Bonelli's warbler and ortolan bunting are very much in evidence here in spring, while the Pyrenean broom scrub around the pass itself is a renowned haunt of water pipit, bluethroat and rock bunting.

Once you reach Miraflores de la Sierra, the M-629 heads north again to the **Puerto de Canencia** (1524 m), where granite boulders house the cushion-forming *Armeria caespitosa*, unique to the Sistema Central, the Iberian endemic toadflax *Linaria elegans*, the blood-red *L. aeruginea*, *Centaurea tri-*

umfetti and *Narcissus rupicola*. Look out for Mazarine and turquoise blues here in late June and Lang's short-tailed blue at the end of August. Once back on the M-604, turn left towards Lozoya. Approaching Rascafría, you suddenly enter a region of calcareous soils with a rich flora; in May, look out for horseshoe vetch, annual scorpion-vetch, white flax, hoary rock-rose, viper's-bugloss, felty germander, wild clary, large speedwell, common globularia, xeranthemum, early spider ophrys and tongue orchid, with high-summer butterflies including ilex and blue-spot hairstreaks, scarce copper and Adonis and Spanish chalk-hill blues.

> *Access and information*: You can reach the Puerto de los Cotos on the *Tren de la Naturaleza* (train) which starts in Cercedilla. The information centre for the Lozoya valley (Puente del Perdón) lies at km 28 on the M-604 (close to El Paular; tel: 91 8691757). A useful website is www.sierranorte.com

Also in the area

Pinar de Abantos y Zona de la Herrería (*paisaje pintoresco*; 1171 ha) Around the Monasterio de El Escorial. To the south, **La Herrería** is primarily Pyrenean oak and narrow-leaved ash forest, harbouring red squirrel, roe deer, wild boar, beech marten, Eurasian badger, red fox and a few wildcats, plus sharp-ribbed and fire salamanders, natterjack toad, amphisbaenian and Montpellier and ladder snakes. Many raptors feed and/or breed: golden eagle, red and black kites and tawny, little, scops and barn owls. Access from the M-505, which bisects the estate. The **Pinar de Abantos**, to the north, is a mature plantation of maritime, stone and black pines; similar fauna to La Herrería, plus crossbill and Spanish moon moth.

Río Guadarrama (*parque regional*; 22 253 ha) Tributary of the Tajo which rises in the Sierra de Guadarrama. Well-preserved gallery forest of narrow-leaved ash is home to common tree frog, stripe-necked terrapin, nightingale, great reed, Cetti's and melodious warblers, penduline tit and golden oriole, while relict enclaves of western holm oak harbour breeding Spanish imperial eagle. From the M-501, follow the track along the right bank of the river through rough grassland – haunt of Montagu's harrier, red-necked nightjar, great spotted cuckoo, roller and woodchat shrike – for about 2.5 km until you reach a small tributary whose low banks host a large bee-eater colony.

SITE 91 Cuenca Alta del Manzanares

The southern flank of the Sierra de Guadarrama, incorporating a wide range of habitats and diverse assemblages of birds and butterflies.

The Cuenca Alta del Manzanares (a *parque regional* of 46 728 ha, also a Biosphere Reserve), straggles down the southern slopes of the Sierra de Guadarrama to embrace the royal estate of Monte de El Pardo. Centred on the upper reaches of the Río Manzanares, the park encompasses three distinct landscape units: the granite 'boulder-city' of La Pedriza, lying in the bowl of the semicircular crest of the Cuerda Larga (maximum 2383 m); the rolling grasslands of the Sierra del Hoyo de Manzanares, studded with western holm oak *dehesa* and copses of Spanish juniper; and the Embalse de Santillana, sur-rounded by groves of narrow-leaved ash – pollarded over many years to form a distinc-tive *cabeza de gato* ('cat's head') silhouette – stands of Pyrenean oak and extensive stony pastures.

La Pedriza (a *reserva natural integral*) is one of the most spectacular examples of granite geomorphology in the peninsula and the undoubted showpiece of nature conser-vation in Madrid. The road up to Canto Cochino – the car park in the heart of La Pedriza – winds through planted stone, mar-itime and black pines over an aromatic understorey of prickly juniper, Pyrenean

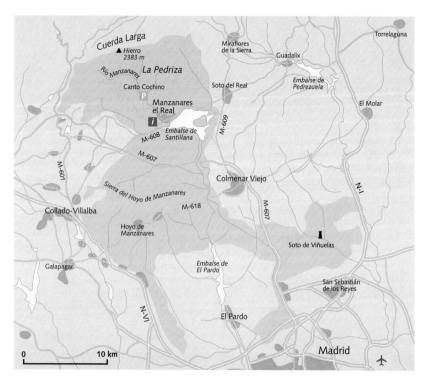

broom, gum and laurel-leaved cistuses, rosemary, French lavender and *Santolina rosmarinifolia*. Amid the scrub grow *Ranunculus gregarius*, western peony, *Linaria spartea*, common and white asphodels, star-of-Bethlehem, bluebell and early purple orchid, while the granite outcrops host *Dianthus subacaulis* subspecies *gredensis*, bearberry and *Digitalis thapsi*.

Birds of these lower levels include hoopoe, red-rumped swallow, black-eared wheatear, blue rock thrush, firecrest, crested tit, woodchat shrike, azure-winged magpie and ortolan and rock buntings, plus *Sylvia* warblers in abundance, notably Dartford, Sardinian and subalpine; raptors include resident golden eagle, peregrine and eagle owl, which are joined by black kite, booted eagle and hobby in summer. Schreiber's green and Iberian wall lizards are often spotted sunning themselves in the vicinity of rock outcrops.

Walking north from Canto Cochino, native Scots pine forest eventually gives way to the windswept rockgardens beneath the **Cuerda Larga**, dominated by dwarf juniper and Pyrenean broom and haunt of snow vole, Iberian rock lizard and butterflies galore in high summer (85 species in the park), including olive skipper, Queen of Spain fritillary, Piedmont and de Prunner's ringlets, black satyr, purple-shot copper and, if you're lucky, the Guadarrama endemic subspecies (*escalerae*) of Apollo. The largest griffon vulture colony in Madrid is found here, numbering some 50–70 pairs, with other species that favour these rocky environs including rock dove, crag martin, skylark, water pipit, wheatear, rock thrush and chough, with bluethroat possible in the Pyrenean broom scrub. Spanish ibex, which disappeared from the area at the beginning of the nineteenth century, were successfully reintroduced in the 1990s.

From the *mirador* at the tail-end of the **Embalse de Santillana** (signposted off the M-608 just west of Manzanares el Real), the view of La Pedriza to the north is stunning. If you rummage around at the edge of the water here you could well find marbled newt and Iberian pool frog, while the rough pas-

Marbled newt *Triturus marmoratus*

tures and scrub are favoured by Spanish festoon and Bath white in spring plus large tortoiseshell, lesser spotted fritillary, great banded grayling and Iberian marbled white later in the year.

Good views over the reservoir can also be had from the M-608, which runs along the northern shore. In summer, look out for little egrets and yellow wagtails along the margins, while winter brings in black-necked grebe, wigeon, teal, pintail and the occasional red-crested pochard, as well as waders such as little ringed plover and snipe. Passage visitors in recent years include purple and night herons, black stork, osprey, avocet, both godwits, greenshank and black and whiskered terns, while autumn sees the influx of large post-breeding concentrations of white stork.

The outflow of the Santillana reservoir can be accessed from the M-609 between Soto del Real and Colmenar Viejo. A turn-off at km 2.25 (signposted 'Embalse de Manzanares el Real' from the south only) leads you through stone-walled pastures studded with small ponds, the latter home to adder's-tongue spearwort, water-starworts, Iberian pool frog and little ringed plover. Scattered trees provide the focal point for a rich avifauna, particularly great spotted cuckoo, cuckoo,

Spanish festoon *Zerynthia rumina*

bee-eater, woodchat and southern grey shrikes, golden oriole and azure-winged magpie, with patches of Mediterranean scrub deserving of attention for their *Sylvia* warblers: Dartford, Sardinian and subalpine. Birds of the open fields include little bustard, stone curlew, hoopoe, short-toed, Thekla and crested larks, corn bunting and flights of spotless starlings, plus Montagu's harrier and hobby on passage.

Finally, you can traverse the extensive *dehesas* and rolling, flower-filled grasslands of the **Sierra del Hoyo** by taking the little-transited M-618 between Colmenar Viejo – where the church hosts breeding white storks and lesser kestrels – and Hoyo de Manzanares. Particularly worth a look is the small gorge carved out by the river Manzanares between the reservoirs of Santillana and El Pardo. A trail leads both north and south along the left bank, where the rocky bluffs should turn up red-rumped swallow, crag martin and both rock thrushes. *Dehesa* butterflies include scarce swallowtail, Spanish festoon, Bath white, Niobe and marsh fritillaries, Iberian marbled white, tree grayling, all three Iberian gatekeepers, purple and false ilex hairstreaks and Spanish brown argus.

Access and information: To get to La Pedriza, turn north off the M-608 just west of Manzanares el Real; an impressive interpretation centre lies close to the junction (tel. and fax: 91 8539978). Guided walks (no charge) must be booked in advance; avoid weekends, public holidays, Easter and the summer months, when the car park at Canto Cochino will probably be full and the access road closed.

Also in the area

Soto de Viñuelas (ZEPA; 4252 ha) Private estate surrounding the castle of the same name in the southeastern corner of the park. Sandy soils clad with a *dehesa* of western holm oaks and pollarded willows and narrow-leaved ashes, home to breeding Spanish imperial eagle, plus red and fallow deer, common genet, wildcat, beech marten and Eurasian badger.

Monte de El Pardo (ZEPA; 14 774 ha) Some 15 000 ha of western holm oak *dehesa*, much inaccessible as the estate houses the royal residence in Madrid. One of Spain's best-preserved Mediterranean forest habitats, with an exceptional vertebrate fauna: wild boar, red and fallow deer abound, plus western polecat, beech marten, common genet and wildcat. Breeding black stork (2 pairs), Spanish imperial eagle (7–8 pairs), black vulture (5–6 pairs) and eagle owl (15–20 pairs), with nocturnal roosts of some 500 black kites. Very abundant red-necked nightjar, plus black wheatear and blue rock thrush in open rocky habitats. Excellent riverine habitats along the Manzanares, harbouring little bittern, kingfisher, reed, great reed, Cetti's and melodious warblers, golden oriole and hawfinch. Large reservoir attracts post-breeding concentrations of black and white storks; passage spoonbill, night heron, greylag goose, osprey and crane. Access via the M-601 off the N-VI.

SITE
92 Estepas de Talamanca

Mosaic of small-scale cereal cultivation and fallow land, with a classic steppe-bird fauna.

The area around Talamanca, to the northeast of Madrid, is dedicated primarily to the extensive cultivation of cereals, generally with little application of fertilisers or pesticides, allowing a diverse community of steppe birds to thrive, for which reason it has been declared a ZEPA (33 520 ha).

This is not the endless arable monoculture so frequent in Europe today, however. Here the plots are small, with much left fallow each year for the poor soils to recover, providing grazing for sheep and often colonised by colourful assemblages of narrow-leaved crimson clover, the distinctive mauve flowers and serrated seedpods of *Biserrula pelecinus*, bellardia, *Linaria spartea*, French figwort, *Andryala ragusina* and the Spanish endemic composite *Hispidella hispanica*. Unploughed hummocks often support a few stunted western holm oaks, accompanied by lygos, *Genista hirsuta*, French lavender and round-headed thyme.

Perhaps the best place to track down steppe birds – in particular great bustards – is the area enclosed by the M-103, between Valdetorres de Jarama and Talamanca de Jarama, and the N-320 directly to the east. A rough track links these two roads, passing close to a ruined castle (from the N-320, turn off at km 320.7, just north of where the road crosses a stone bridge, or from the M-103, pass the roundabout to the north of Valdetorres then take the first track on the right, signposted 'Vía Pecuaria'). Another good place to look is the track immediately opposite the one leaving the N-320 described above, which heads east along the line of a small stream, bordered by cliffs to the south.

The curious seed-pods of *Biserrula pelecinus*

Whichever option you chose, a spring visit will be characterised by a plethora of little bustards 'blowing raspberries' in the surrounding fields, while a careful scan with binoculars should pick out one or more great bustards stalking regally across the plain, seemingly oblivious to your presence. Other breeding birds include an abundance of Montagu's harriers plus hen and marsh harriers, lesser kestrel, stone curlew, black-bellied sandgrouse and a wealth of larks, particularly the robust calandra, with its distinctive white trailing edge to the wing.

The presence of the small stream on both sides of the N-320 adds to the wildlife interest of the site, providing a 'watering-hole' for white storks and steppe birds, while the line of tamarisks and sallows attracts roosting passerines on migration. Short-eared owls sometimes hunt here in winter and the area is also known as a feeding ground for raptors breeding elsewhere in the area, so keep your eyes peeled for golden and Spanish imperial eagles and black vultures.

SITE 93 Laguna de San Juan

Small wetland harbouring the basic waterbirds of central Spain, with an interesting gypsum flora on the adjacent river terrace.

The result of past gravel extraction, the Laguna de San Juan (a *refugio de fauna* of 47 ha) comprises three lagoons and two reedbeds associated with the lower reaches of the Río Tajuña. The main area of open water – roughly triangular in shape – extends over some 5 ha and is fed primarily by a subterranean aquifer, with lesser contributions via filtration from the nearby river and rainwater run-off, such that the lagoon never dries out completely.

A thick belt of fringing vegetation is dominated by common reed and bulrush, with the edges of the canals hosting marsh-mallow, yellow flag, round-headed club-rush and giant reed, and drier marginal habitats supporting planted tamarisks and white willows plus a few small-leaved elms. True aquatics here include the charophyte *Chara hispida* and common water-crowfoot.

At any time of year you might encounter little and great crested grebes, mallard, pochard, marsh harrier, water rail, stock dove, kingfisher, and Cetti's, fan-tailed and Dartford warblers, with the list augmented in summer by little bittern, white stork, cuckoo, bee-eater, hoopoe, nightingale, reed and great reed warblers and woodchat

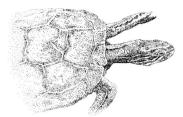

Stripe-necked terrapin *Mauremys leprosa*

shrike. Passage periods regularly turn up purple heron, little ringed plover, sand martin, yellow wagtail and sedge warbler, while winter sees an influx of grey heron, gadwall, teal, shoveler, red-crested pochard (has also bred in the past), penduline tit and reed bunting, as well as nocturnal roosts of up to 20000 starlings (both 'spotted' and spotless).

The adjacent river terrace – a gypsum scarp which rises to 588 m – provides a niche for the lime-loving, delicate pink flowers of *Gypsophila struthium*, unique to central and southeastern Spain, sad stock and a number of Afro-Iberian endemics: the white-flowered crucifer *Lepidium subulatum*, the rock-rose *Helianthemum squamatum* and clumps of the tough grass known as false esparto. Here, too, you should find less obligate calcicoles such as dragon's teeth, field eryngo, wild clary and tassel hyacinth, as well as many species typical of disturbed soils: *Silene colorata*, sand catchfly, *Euphorbia serrata*, large blue alkanet and red star-thistle. Butterflies on the wing around these flowery banks in May include scarce swallowtail and common and Adonis blues. Look out, too, for quail and red-legged partridges in these drier habitats, as well as for black wheatear near the top of the cliff.

The Laguna de San Juan and its surrounds are also home to a diverse assemblage of herptiles, including midwife toad, parsley frog, stripe-necked terrapin, three-toed skink, large psammodromus, ocellated, Iberian wall and spiny-footed lizards and

Water rail *Rallus aquaticus* (Mike Lane)

ladder, Montpellier, grass and viperine snakes. Among the mammals cited here are Mediterranean pine vole, greater white-toothed shrew, wood mouse, brown rat, weasel, beech marten and red fox.

Access: Take the M-404 from Titulcia to Chinchón; about 1 km after crossing the Río Tajuña, turn right along an unmade road (signposted 'Refugio de Fauna de la Laguna de San Juan') and continue for about 2 km. Very little of the lagoon is visible through the thick fringing vegetation, except from two small hides, but this can be rectified by a short scramble up the adjacent gypsum cliffs. Insect repellent advisable.

Also in the area

Parque Regional del Sureste Madrileño (also a ZEPA; 31 550 ha) The lower reaches of the rivers Manzanares and Jarama, also encompassing more than 120 lagoons (mostly abandoned gravel workings) as well as gypsum river terraces, cereal fields and limestone plateaux clothed with western holm and holly oaks. Incredibly diverse assemblage of breeding birds, including little bittern, night and purple herons, gadwall, red-crested pochard, pochard, black kite, marsh harrier, lesser kestrel, peregrine, purple gallinule, great and little bustards, black-winged stilt, eagle owl, sand mar-

tin, bee-eater, black wheatear, blue rock thrush, bearded and penduline tits, chough and rock sparrow. Abundance of wintering and passage waterbirds, including such notables as squacco heron, spoonbill, ferruginous and white-headed ducks, osprey, crane, green sandpiper and little gull. Gravel pit herptiles include marbled newt, western spadefoot and stripe-necked terrapin. Good starting point is **Laguna de Campillo** (off the N-III at km 19 to Rivas-Vaciamadrid; tel: 600 508638). Nature trail up the gypsum river terrace near Titulcia. A useful website is www.elsoto.org

SITE 94 Carrizales y Sotos de Aranjuez

Gallery forests and reedbeds along the Río Tajo, also encompassing the freshwater wetland and gypsum scrub of the Mar de Ontígola.

To the south of Madrid, the provincial boundary protrudes narrowly towards Toledo along the margins of the Río Tajo, almost the whole of the spur lying within the ZEPA of Carrizales y Sotos de Aranjuez (15 520 ha). The margins of the river are flanked by relatively well-preserved gallery forests, with abandoned meanders containing stands of common reed, important for its otters and breeding night herons and marsh harriers (although in small numbers); access is via the CM-4001 or M-416, leading west off junctions 44 and 47 of the N-IV, respectively, or where the CM-4004 and CM-4006 cross the river.

Red horned-poppy *Glaucium corniculatum*

At the heel of the spur lies the Mar de Ontígola (part of a 635 ha *reserva natural* with El Regajal), lying adjacent to the minor road which links Aranjuez with the village of Ontígola (in Toledo). Today a reed-choked permanent lagoon, it was originally an artificial reservoir constructed between 1565 and 1572 by order of Felipe II to supply the Royal Gardens in Aranjuez. Common reed is the dominant plant in and around the lake, accompanied here and there by stands of marsh mallow, tamarisk, bulrush and giant reed.

The dense vegetation means that little can be seen of the open water from the path around the lagoon, but from the observation tower you might spot grey heron, little or great crested grebes, teal, wigeon, pintail, shoveler, pochard or red-crested pochard, depending on the time of year. In spring, the cacophony of nightingales and fan-tailed, Cetti's, great reed and reed warblers is all but deafening, with other notable breeding birds including little bittern and marsh harrier. Amphibians include sharp-ribbed salaman-

der and natterjack toad, but you are far more likely to notice the vociferous Iberian pool frogs, whose chorus continues day and night during their breeding season.

The surrounding low gypsum hills – a favoured haunt of quail, red-legged partridge, subalpine warbler and rabbit – are clothed with *Salsola vermiculata*, shrubby orache, *Lepidium subulatum*, lygos, *Thymus zygis*, rosemary, *Artemisia herba-alba*, *Helichrysum stoechas* and false esparto, with open areas studded with sad stock, the tall, white-flowered *Reseda suffruticosa*, spherical umbels of *Thapsia villosa*, ground-pine germander and candelabra-spikes of *Asphodelus ramosus*. Disturbed soils host red horned-poppy, peganum, annual bellflower and a number of composites: *Urospermum picroides*, *Atractylis cancellata*, *Asteriscus aquaticus*, downy safflower, rough cocklebur and red star-thistle. Typical reptiles include spiny-footed and ocellated lizards, large and Spanish psammodromus and ladder, Montpellier and false smooth snakes.

Towards the toe of the spur lies the Carrizal de Villamejor, a small wetland straddling the

N-400 between Aranjuez and Toledo. To the north of the road, thick reedbeds surround the Arroyo Cedrón, with a dense belt of tamarisk marking the stream itself. Nightingales and Cetti's warbler abound here, while several pairs of marsh harrier breed and night herons drop in to feed from their colonies on the nearby Tajo. In winter the reedbed houses a noisy roost of starlings and corn buntings, with passage birds including little bittern, teal and pochard.

By contrast, several tracks lead south from the N-400 up onto a gravelly plateau – a mosaic of dry cereal cultivations and lygos and *Artemisia herba-alba* scrub – where a little patience should turn up little bustard, stone curlew, calandra lark and, possibly,

Otter *Lutra lutra*

great bustard or pin-tailed sandgrouse; try the one at km 14.9, just to the west of a ruined farm.

Also in the area

El Regajal Just west of the Mar de Ontígola, this 570 ha private estate is one of central Spain's foremost butterfly reserves, home to some 65 species. Early April sees false Baton and Baton blues, Provence hairstreak, sooty and Moroccan orange tips, Spanish festoon (here subspecies *minima*, the smallest papilionid in the world) and Portuguese dappled and green-striped whites on the wing, with May bringing Zephyr (subspecies *pardoi*), Iolas, Chapman's, black-eyed and green-underside blues and Spanish and western marbled whites. Look out, too, for nettle-tree butterfly and isolated colonies of Mediterranean skipper and southern small white. Unfortunately there is no public access, but surrounding areas of holly and thyme scrub on gypsum-rich soils should turn up similar species.

SITE 95 Valle de Iruelas

Extreme eastern end of the Sierra de Gredos, with a significant breeding population of black vulture and many Iberian endemic plants.

The Valle de Iruelas (a *reserva natural* of 8828 ha, also a ZEPA) is situated on the northern flanks of the Gredos, sandwiched between the Embalse de Burguillo to the north and the Puerto de Casillas (1477 m) to the south. The reserve is split in two by the northbound Río Iruelas, such that vegetation typical of both the *solana* and *umbría* can be found here, although little of the mixed climax forest of yew, Scots pine, *Pinus nigra* subspecies *salzmannii* (at the western limit of its natural distribution in Iberia), Pyrenean oak and holly remains today, mostly having been replaced with plantations of maritime pine. Nevertheless, the reserve harbours some 235 species of vertebrate,

French lavender *Lavandula stoechas*

notably an important population of black vulture (around 70 pairs), as well as at least one pair of Spanish imperial eagle, plus Eurasian badger, common genet and wildcat.

To the west of El Tiemblo, on the N-403, turn off on a narrow road which runs along the southern shore of the Burguillo reservoir (signposted Las Cruceras), which will take you into the heart of the reserve. En route, huge granite boulders are shaded by a scattering of enormous pines, interspersed with prickly juniper, stunted western holm oaks, lygos, gum cistus, French lavender and rosemary, with clumps of western peonies and the Iberian endemic foxglove *Digitalis thapsi* adding colour to the scene. Bee-eater, red-rumped swallow, black and black-eared wheatears, nightingale, melodious, Dartford and subalpine warblers, rock sparrow and cirl and rock buntings are birds to watch out for here, with scops and little owls also present. At Las Cruceras there is an information point (tel: 91 865059; fax: 91 8625395; www.valledeiruelas.com), which gives details of waymarked routes in the reserve.

A small road follows the Río Iruelas south to the Puerto de Casillas. As you gain altitude the riverine forest becomes increasingly

diverse, harbouring yew, black poplar, Pyrenean oak, sweet chestnut, alder, hazel, wych elm, wild cherry, alder buckthorn and Montpellier maple; otters are often seen here, with Schreiber's green lizards inhabiting the marginal vegetation. Sunny glades along the way are studded with white asphodel and star-of-Bethlehem and attract a wealth of butterflies in May: Spanish festoon, Moroccan orange tip, wood white, marsh fritillary and a myriad blues.

The pines which stretch away on all sides shelter western peonies, white Spanish broom, *Genista florida* and bluebells, plus an abundance of red squirrels and vociferous Bonelli's warblers, nuthatches and serins. When the road veers away from the river, the rocky margins of the pine forests are clothed with large-flowered sandwort, meadow saxifrage, French lavender, the Iberian endemic toadflax *Linaria elegans*, with deep-purple flowers, the yellow-flowered variant of the Iberian endemic, daisy-like *Leucanthemopsis pallida*, angel's-tears and green-winged orchids.

All too soon the asphalt comes to an end, and from this point onward you will have to employ shanks's pony, but the climb is well worth the effort, and you could continue over the pass and down to the village of Casillas. Approaching the Puerto de Casillas, the pines disappear and the views to the north are simply fabulous: the perfect place to sit back and wait for raptors to drift across the sky. Apart from the much-vaunted black vulture and Spanish imperial eagle, you might also turn up griffon vulture, honey buzzard, black and red kites and golden, short-toed and booted eagles. The low scrub here is dominated by dwarf juniper, Pyrenean broom, the western Iberian endemic *Echinospartum barnadesii*, green heather, tree heath and the lavender-cotton *Santolina oblongifolia*, unique to the Sierra de Gredos, with numerous boggy streams harbouring blinks, marsh violet and lousewort, the banks speckled with the diminutive trumpets of *Narcissus graellsii* in May.

From the Puerto de Casillas a waymarked footpath leads west to the peak of Escusa (1959 m), through high-altitude scrublands

Leucanthemopsis pallida (T.F.)

which are a renowned haunt of breeding water pipit, whitethroat, rock thrush, bluethroat and rock bunting. The crystal-clear mountain streams are home to Pyrenean desman, while granite outcrops at these altitudes harbour Iberian rock lizard. The highest grasslands – dominated by *Festuca indigesta*, *Koeleria crassipes* and the sandwort *Arenaria querioides* (the latter two endemic to the peninsula) – support a thriving population of snow voles: here subspecies *abulensis*, which is confined to the Sistema Central.

Once on the southern side of the pass, look out for the Afro-Iberian endemic *Narcissus rupicola* and the eye-catching pink-purple crucifer *Erysimum lagascae*, unique to southwestern Iberia. Thick maritime pine plantations accompany your descent almost as far as Casillas, although the final section traverses an area of sweet chestnut wood–pasture, the grassland thick with the pink-flowered *Lupinus hispanicus*, tassel hyacinths and Lange's orchids.

Also in the area

Encinares de los Ríos Alberche y Cofio (ZEPA; 75 600 ha) Huge, rolling expanse of western holm oak *dehesa* studded with abrupt granite outcrops, linking the Sierras de Gredos and Guadarrama. The only remaining locality for pardel lynx in the province of Madrid, plus significant populations of wildcat, otter and Spanish imperial eagle, plus breeding griffon and black vultures, golden, booted and short-toed eagles, black and red kites, peregrine and eagle owl. Several pairs of black stork, with notable post-breeding concentrations. Little bustard in more open areas, abundant red-necked nightjar, and black wheatear around the rock outcrops.

^{SITE}
96 Sierra de Gredos

Magnificent range of glaciated granite mountains, with a rich endemic flora, diverse community of forest raptors and large population of Spanish ibex.

The 250 km-long ridge of the Sierra de Gredos comprises the lion's share of Iberia's granitic Sistema Central – often referred to as the backbone of Spain – which divides the north and south Mesetas and effectively separates the animals and plants living on either side. The two faces of the Gredos present very different aspects, with the northern one gently sloping down to about a thousand metres around Hoyos del Espino, while the southern flank descends abruptly for over 2000 m, from Almanzor – the highest peak in the range, at 2592 m – down to Candeleda, in the space of just 10 km as the crow flies. The Parque Regional de la Sierra de Gredos (87 160 ha, also a ZEPA), encompasses the central sector of the ridge, including the majority of its spectacular glacial cirques, lakes, moraines and U-shaped valleys, as well as most of the plants and animals unique to this mountain chain.

Four altitude-dependent vegetation zones occur in the Gredos, which can be described briefly as western holm oak up to 550 m, Pyrenean oak from 550 to 1800 m, Pyrenean broom from 1800 to 2300 m and subalpine pastures and rockgardens above 2300 m, although their distribution is also affected by aspect. Within the western holm oak zone you might also encounter prickly juniper, cork oak, white Spanish broom, strawberry-tree, tree and Spanish heaths and a variety of cistuses, primarily gum, sage-leaved, poplar-leaved and *Cistus psilosepalus*, interspersed with tracts of French lavender, round-headed thyme and *Thymus zygis*, with eye-catching herbs here including palmate anemone, western peony, *Campanula lusitanica* and Spanish bluebell.

The Pyrenean oak zone has suffered most in the past, today largely replaced by extensive Scots and maritime pine plantations and vast secondary tracts of adenocarpus,

hairy-fruited broom, *Genista cinerascens, G. florida, G. falcata* and laurel-leaved cistus. Nevertheless, the typical Pyrenean oak ground flora persists, with characteristic species including *Aquilegia dichroa, Paeonia officinalis* subspecies *microcarpa*, toadflax-leaved St John's-wort, wood and bloody crane's-bills, oxlip, the viper's-bugloss *Echium flavum*, bastard balm, rampion bellflower, *Centaurea triumfetti* subspecies *lingulata, Santolina rosmarinifolia*, St Bernard's and martagon lilies, white asphodel, angular Solomon's-seal, Spanish iris and angel's-tears, as well as a smattering of red helleborines and bird's-nest orchids.

Here, too, you might come across a number of Iberian endemics, notably the yellow-flowered crucifer *Erysimum merxmuelleri* and its purple-bloomed relative *E. lagascae*, the slender toadflax *Linaria elegans*, the star-of-Bethlehem *Ornithogalum concinnum* and *Paradisea lusitanica*. Particularly splendid displays of the lemon-flowered pasque flower *Pulsatilla alpina* subspecies *apiifolia* can be seen in the Pinar de Hoyocasero (a proposed *reserva natural* of 370 ha, to the east of the N-502) in early June, accompanied by the eye-catching papery flower-

Spanish ibex *Capra pyrenaica*

Pulsatilla alpina subspecies *apiifolia*

The high rockgardens are also of great botanical interest, harbouring such notable species as *Saxifraga pentadactylis* subspecies *almanzorii*, the thrift *Armeria bigerrensis* subspecies *bigerrensis* and the lovely *Antirrhinum grosii*, all of which are endemic to the Gredos, plus the crucifer *Murbeckiella boryi*, the houseleek *Sempervivum vicentei* and rock lady's-mantle.

Not to be outdone, the dry screes also host species unique to the mountains of central Iberia, including *Reseda gredensis*, the fig-wort *Scrophularia grandiflora* subspecies *reuteri* and the lavender-cotton *Santolina oblongifolia*, with more widespread species including alpine toadflax, *Linaria saxatilis*, Tournefort's ragwort and *Senecio adonidi-folius*. Particularly shady, damp habitats associated with boulder chokes are home to leafy megaforb communities of *Aconitum vulparia* subspecies *neapolitanum*, aconite-leaved buttercup, the western Iberian endemic *Angelica major*, great yellow gentian, Pyrenean rampion, adenostyles, *Doronicum carpetanum*, streptopus and white false helleborine.

The same degree of evolutionary specialisation applies, to a lesser degree, to the animal life of the Sistema Central. The fire

heads of *Leuzea rhaponticoides*, endemic to the Sistema Central.

Above the tree-line lie extensive tracts of low-growing Pyrenean broom scrub, often accompanied by dwarf juniper and cushions of *Echinospartum ibericum* and *E. barnadesii*. Notable herbaceous species here include the yellow-flowered violet *Viola langeana*, unique to the mountains of central Iberia, the Spanish endemic toadflax *Linaria nivea* and the lousewort *Pedicularis schizocalyx*, found only in western Iberia. Rocky outcrops harbour *Antirrhinum meonanthum* and *Narcissus rupicola*, while high-level streams and springs are coloured by marsh violet, starry saxifrage, yellow loosestrife and ivy-leaved bellflower, and peatbogs support *Sedum lagascae*, unique to the Gredos, hairy stonecrop, grass-of-Parnassus, marsh cinquefoil and bogbean.

The highest peaks house only sparse, acid grasslands and species adapted to growing in rock fissures and screes. The subalpine pastures are home to the Iberian endemic pink-flowered mucizonia and tight cushions of *Armeria caespitosa*, as well as to starwort mouse-ear, *Silene ciliata*, alpine plantain, globe-headed rampion and dwarf cudweed.

White false helleborine *Veratrum album* (T.F.)

salamanders (subspecies *almanzoris*) of these high peaks are relatively small and almost completely black, irregularly speckled with small yellow spots, the common toads (subspecies *gredosicola*) have larger paratoid glands and a more mottled appearance, and the Iberian rock lizards in the Gredos and Guadarrama (subspecies *cyreni*) are completely isolated from the northwest Iberian population (subspecies *cantabrica*). In point of fact, the Sierra de Gredos is considered to be one of Europe's most significant herpetological enclaves, not just for the presence of these endemic taxa, but also because of the high diversity of species found here (23 reptiles and 12 amphibians), including the Iberian endemic Bedriaga's skink, Schreiber's green lizard, Iberian frog, Iberian painted frog and Bosca's newt.

Similarly, the Gredos' isolated population of snow voles has been assigned taxonomic autonomy (subspecies *abulensis*), while subspecies *victoriae* of the Spanish ibex is native only to the Sierra de Gredos, having recuperated spectacularly from just a couple of dozen individuals in 1905 to a five-figure population today. Also here are Iberian blind moles and Cabrera's voles, both endemic to the peninsula, as well as the Pyrenean desman, mostly in small

mountain streams on the northern flanks, although its population has been much reduced by predation from escaped and naturalised American mink. Forest habitats provide refuge for red squirrel and garden dormouse, plus roe deer, wild boar, common genet, wildcat, beech marten, western polecat, Eurasian badger and the majority of the 16 species of bat cited here, notably Leisler's, greater mouse-eared, brown long-eared, greater horseshoe, Daubenton's, European free-tailed and greater noctule.

Bird-wise, the Gredos houses small breeding nuclei of black stork (some five pairs), Egyptian vulture, black vulture, Spanish imperial eagle and peregrine, as well as rather better populations of griffon vulture, golden eagle and eagle owl (25–30 pairs of each). Raptors associated with more vegetated habitats abound, notably honey buzzard, black and red kites, short-toed and booted eagles and goshawk.

Almost 100 species of butterfly have been recorded in the Gredos, with those flying at altitude including Niobe fritillary, Piedmont ringlet, black satyr, scarce and purple-shot coppers, brown argus and Adonis and common blues, although, curiously, *not* Apollo, despite its occurrence in the nearby Sierra de Guadarrama. Flowery grasslands and scrub

Sierra de Gredos (Peter Wilson)

Adonis blue *Lysandra bellargus* (T.F.)

at lower levels might turn up carline, rosy and large grizzled, mallow, southern and tufted marbled skippers, black-veined, Bath and western dappled whites, a wealth of fritillaries – high brown, Queen of Spain, meadow, heath, Provençal, spotted, knapweed, marsh and cardinal – Spanish purple hairstreak, Spanish brown argus and long-tailed, Lang's short-tailed, silver-studded and black-eyed blues.

Probably the best place to encounter the five endemic vertebrate taxa mentioned above is around the Laguna Grande de Gredos (1950 m), also one of the most emblematic landscapes in the park, nestling in the ice-scoured basin of the Circo de Gredos and surrounded by a jagged ring of peaks in excess of 2500 m. This is also one of the easiest high-mountain habitats to access, as you can drive as far as the natural terrace known as La Plataforma from Hoyos del Espino (12 km, along the AV-931), from there following a well-marked trail on foot as far as the lake (about two hours' walk).

In addition to some incredibly confiding Spanish ibex around La Plataforma, the scrub here is worth examining for bluethroat – the Gredos harbours what is probably the best breeding nucleus in Spain – as well as dunnock, whitethroat, Dartford warbler, linnet and rock and ortolan buntings. Many of the more notable upland birds of the Gredos are relatively easy to see on the trek up to the lake, particularly water pipit, alpine accentor, wheatear, rock thrush and chough, with the skies above the cirque often inhabited by golden eagle and griffon vulture. These rugged rockgardens and screes are also home to many of the unique high-level plants of the Gredos described earlier.

The central massif of the Gredos is otherwise inaccessible except on foot, with a well-developed network of high mountain trails and refuges at the disposition of more determined backpackers. If this is not your idea of fun then you will be limited to the few roads which cross other parts of the *sierra*. One major traverse is the N-502, which ascends to 1352 m at the Puerto del Pico, where you can again encounter bluethroat, rock thrush and ortolan bunting, plus the Iberian endemic Spanish argus, with the steep slopes to the east a favoured haunt of Spanish ibex. Further south, around Mombeltrán, a more Mediterranean landscape populated with olive groves, vineyards and sweet chestnut copses is a good place to track down great spotted cuckoo, spectacled warbler, woodchat and southern grey shrikes, azure-winged magpie and hawfinch.

The Sierra de Candelario (a proposed *parque natural* of 10 737 ha and ZEPA) to the west also combines reasonable access with good birdwatching, especially along the road which leads south out of the town up to around 2000 m, through pine plantations housing firecrest, crested tit, crossbill and citril finch. From the end of the road, a path leads up to the 2425 m peak of Calvitero, with bluethroat again possible on the way, plus the principal high-altitude birds at the top.

Information: There is no interpretation centre for the *parque regional*, but the Parador de Gredos (on the C-500 to the east of Hoyos del Espino; tel: 920 348048) acts as an unofficial information point.

There are also tourist offices in Candeleda, Hoyos del Espino and Arenas de San Pedro, the latter the start of many walking routes into the high central massif.

Extremadura and Castilla–La Mancha

Introduction

The two autonomous communities of Extremadura and Castilla–La Mancha together cover a vast swathe in the centre of the Iberian peninsula, encompassing the whole of Spain's southern Meseta. Except to the west, bordering Portugal, the region is ringed by mountains, separated from Castilla y León to the north by the rugged granite and gneiss *sierras* of Gata, Gredos and Ayllón, from the País Valencià to the east by the limestones of the Serranía de Cuenca, and Andalucía to the south by the rounded acid hills of the Sierra Morena and the karstified ridges of Alcaraz. As a result, the two major rivers draining the area – the Tajo and Guadiana – are forced to flow west into the Atlantic, while southwesterly weather systems have a more or less unrestricted path into western Extremadura, allowing animal and plant communities requiring more humid conditions to thrive here.

The northern uplands of the region are home to several animals with a marked westerly distribution in the Iberian peninsula, including Bosca's newt, Schreiber's green lizard and bluethroat. The Garganta de los Infiernos, at the western end of the Sierra de Gredos, peaks at almost 2300 m and is home to the most diverse floral communities in the west of the region, including the Iberian endemics *Antirrhinum grosii* and *Gentiana boryi*, while the humid valleys of Las Villuercas, in central Extremadura, provide a refuge for the Tertiary relict Portugal laurel; both sites host an extremely rich butterfly fauna.

Much of the lower reaches of Extremadura and Castilla–La Mancha was once covered by western holm oak forests, with cork and

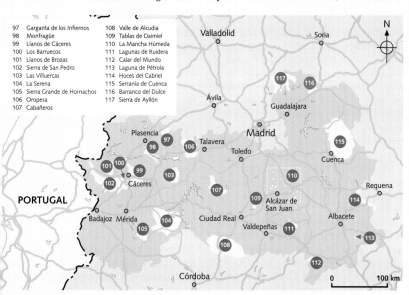

97 Garganta de los Infiernos	108 Valle de Alcudia
98 Monfragüe	109 Tablas de Daimiel
99 Llanos de Cáceres	110 La Mancha Húmeda
100 Los Barruecos	111 Lagunas de Ruidera
101 Llanos de Brozas	112 Calar del Mundo
102 Sierra de San Pedro	113 Laguna de Pétrola
103 Las Villuercas	114 Hoces del Cabriel
104 La Serena	115 Serranía de Cuenca
105 Sierra Grande de Hornachos	116 Barranco del Dulce
106 Oropesa	117 Sierra de Ayllón
107 Cabañeros	

Opposite page: **Western holm oak *dehesa***

Lusitanian oaks on north-facing slopes or in areas with deeper soils. Today, however, much of lowland Extremadura and western Castilla–La Mancha is clothed with wood–pasture known as *dehesa* – partially cleared, lowland forest – and only in certain privileged areas do primeval Mediterranean woodlands survive (for example, on north-facing slopes in the showpiece protected areas of Monfragüe and Cabañeros).

Land-use in the *dehesas* is extensive and balanced, permitting the survival of a largely intact ecological pyramid which is topped by three of the world's most threatened vertebrates: black vulture, Spanish imperial eagle and pardel lynx; these habitats are understandably well represented in this chapter, with notable examples found in Monfragüe, the Sierra de San Pedro and Oropesa. *Dehesas* are also home to birds such as black winged kite and azure-winged magpie, virtually unknown in mainland Europe outside Spain and Portugal, and some of the best Iberian assemblages of herptiles, notably large and Spanish psammodromus, Iberian midwife toad, sharp-ribbed salamander and common and stripeless tree frogs, while the southern Meseta as a whole harbours the peninsula's healthiest populations of European pond and stripe-necked terrapins.

Vast areas of the primeval evergreen forest have been cleared completely for cereal cultivation and pasture, today harbouring important assemblages of steppe birds. The Llanos de Cáceres and La Serena in Extremadura, plus the cross-border site of Badajoz–Elvas (see p. 438), harbour up to half the Iberian peninsula's great bustards, the best European population of lesser kestrel and high densities of Montagu's harrier and pin-tailed and black-bellied sandgrouse. Further east, the flat eternity of the plains of Castilla–La Mancha, world famous as the setting for Don Quixote's adventures, are home to the most important European nuclei of little bustard, stone curlew and short-toes larks.

This sweeping open terrain is enlivened sporadically by a series of natural wetlands known as La Mancha Húmeda, which encompasses freshwater *tablas* (riverine floodplains, notably the Tablas de Daimiel national park), karstic lakes (Lagunas de Ruidera) and a rash of endorheic lagoons (for example, the Laguna de Pétrola, where greater flamingos bred for the first time in 1999). These wetlands harbour internationally important breeding populations of red-crested pochard, white-headed duck, black-winged stilt, avocet and gull-billed tern.

Little remains of the original western holm oak forests of upland Albacete in the south, or in Cuenca and Guadalajara to the north. In the Serranía de Cuenca and El Calar del Mundo, pine forests are dominant today, albeit leaving plenty of room for a diverse calcicolous flora with fascinating cushion communities, while above 1000 m, on the treeless *páramos* to the northeast, Dupont's larks reach high densities. These limestone plateaux are sliced by numerous limestone gorges – for example, the Serranía de Cuenca's Hoces de Beteta and Priego, the Hoces del Cabriel and the Barranco del Dulce – which provide nest sites for cliff-breeding bird communities of world significance, notably of Egyptian and griffon vultures, golden and Bonelli's eagles, peregrine and eagle owl, as well as refuge for fissure-plant communities that include the Iberian endemic saxifrage *Saxifraga latepetiolata* and bellflower *Campanula betetae*.

This eastern sector of Castilla–La Mancha is home to a rich selection of butterflies – best experienced in late June and early July – including sandy grizzled skipper, the Iberian endemic Zapater's ringlet and Andalusian anomalous blue. Also unique to southeastern Spain are the Spanish algyroides, a delicate, svelte lizard which is confined to the *sierras* of Alcaraz and neighbouring Cazorla y Segura, and the diminutive midwife toad *Alytes dickhilleni*, only described in 1995, whose world distribution is limited to the Sierras Béticas. The tail-end of the far-reaching Sistema Central just creeps into northern Guadalajara, where the beech forests and high pastures of the Sierra de Ayllón provide a stark contrast to the rest of Castilla–La Mancha.

The Junta de Extremadura web page gives detailed information about each of its protected areas, including waymarked routes: www.juntaex.es/consejerias/aym/espacios/home.html

SITE
97 Garganta de los Infiernos

Spectacular river gorges plus scrub and alpine pastures above the tree-line, hosting a flora and fauna unlike any other in Extremadura; superb summer butterflies.

Although much of Extremadura comprises rolling plains – partly clad with *dehesa* and teeming with raptors, the remainder treeless and populated by stately great bustards and whirring flocks of sandgrouse – its northern edge is bordered by the outliers of the Sistema Central, arching westwards from the extremities of the Gredos to the Sierra de Gata, close to the Portuguese border.

White false helleborine
Veratrum album

The Garganta de los Infiernos (a *reserva natural* of 6800 ha), which lies just to the southwest of the Puerto de Tornavacas (1277 m) on the N-110, is thus unique among Extremadura's protected areas in encompassing peaks of almost 2300 m and an essentially high-mountain flora and fauna. The focal point of the reserve is a series of sheer-walled gorges, home to spectacular waterfalls and cascades, where the erosive power of the river has scoured huge cauldrons from the granite bedrock.

The riverine forests in the shelter of the gorge are dominated by a mixture of alder, *Salix atrocinerea* and narrow-leaved ash, accompanied by a scattering of yew, silver birch, southern nettle tree and holly. This lush vegetation supports melodious and Bonelli's warblers and golden oriole in summer, while the river harbours dipper, Pyrenean desman and otter. Brown trout are common here, with the river's edge home to fire salamander, Bosca's and marbled newts and stripe-necked terrapin. The cliffs which enclose the gorge are occupied by small numbers of breeding griffon vulture, golden and Bonelli's eagles, peregrine and eagle owl, and are also a classic locality for the Gredos endemic snapdragon *Antirrhinum grosii*.

Away from the water, the forest is monopolised by Pyrenean oak and planted groves of sweet chestnut, associated with rowan, wild cherry and strawberry-tree, with an understorey dominated by hairy-fruited and white Spanish brooms. Late spring brings sword-leaved helleborine and early purple and bird's-nest orchids into bloom, with the eye-catching *Linaria triornithophora* producing swathes of pinkish-purple in summer.

A curious mixture of northern and Mediterranean birds is to be found in and around these broad-leaved forests, including sparrowhawk, goshawk, short-toed and booted eagles, black kite, honey buzzard, scops owl, nightjar, lesser spotted woodpecker, firecrest, spotted and pied flycatchers, jay, azure-winged magpie and hawfinch; in winter you might come across bullfinch and siskin. The most characteristic of the larger forest mammals are wild boar, red deer, Eurasian badger, wildcat and common genet, but don't expect to see them and you won't be disappointed.

Above the tree-line, granite and gneiss outcrops are carpeted with dwarf juniper, Pyrenean broom, *Adenocarpus hispanicus* subspecies *gredensis* and *Echinospartum barnadesii*, the latter endemic to western Iberia. From March onwards, as the snows melt, sheets of hoop-petticoat daffodils and *Crocus carpetanus* clothe the grasslands, with marsh gentian and *Gentiana boryi* –

Marsh gentian *Gentiana pneumonanthe* (T.F.)

Iberian frog and viperine snake in the vicinity of the small, snow-fed streams that abound here.

The Garganta de los Infiernos is also one of Extremadura's most renowned butterfly localities, harbouring several species which occur only here in the region: Camberwell beauty, small pearl-bordered fritillary, large wall brown, pearly heath, Piedmont ringlet, black satyr, false grayling, scarce copper and Mazarine blue. Others are shared with the nearby Sierra de Gata, notably olive skipper, silver-washed, dark green and meadow fritillaries, dusky heath, dusky meadow brown, Esper's marbled white, mountain argus and silver-studded blue. In late June and July, look out for yellow-banded skippers – a particularly distinctive member of the genus *Pyrgus*, with two broad orange-yellow stripes on each hindwing – which occur only in the western Gredos in Spain. Green-striped

whose pale-blue, ten-toothed flowers are found only in the Sierra de Gredos, the Cordillera Cantábrica and the Sierra Nevada – appearing later in the year.

In high summer, the boulders, screes and drier pastures above 1700 m support a number of plants which are unique to the Sistema Central, including the thrifts *Armeria arenaria* subspecies *vestita* (a large, tussock-forming species of acid pastures) and *A. bigerrensis* subspecies *bigerrensis* (small and favouring fissures), and the pink *Dianthus subacaulis* subspecies *gredensis*. More humid areas host Tournefort's ragwort, the Iberian endemic leopard's-bane *Doronicum carpetanum* and white false helleborine.

These treeless high plateaux are home to a breeding bird community which has much in common with the rest of the Sistema Central, typically of water pipit, dunnock, wheatear, rock thrush, bluethroat, Dartford warbler and ortolan bunting. Look out, too, for Spanish ibex (belonging to the Gredos subspecies *victoriae*), as well as Schreiber's green lizard and three-toed skink, with

Mating silver-studded blues *Plebejus argus* (T.F.)

Access and information: Most of the reserve's waymarked walks commence in the village of Jerte or from the Puerto de Tornavacas; this latter is a good locality to explore 'freelance', as you can wander at will from the car park on the col. For more information phone the reserve authorities on 924 386278.

Esper's marbled white *Melanargia russiae*

white, Moroccan orange tip, Cleopatra, Spanish festoon, nettle-tree butterfly, Spanish purple and ilex hairstreaks and Lang's short-tailed blue are more typical of Mediterranean habitats, with other species of note here including silver-spotted skipper, swallowtail and scarce swallowtail, large tortoiseshell, southern white admiral, cardinal, Niobe, lesser spotted and marsh fritillaries, oriental meadow brown, purple hairstreak and purple-shot and sooty coppers (the latter pertaining to the subspecies *bleusei*).

Also in the area

Sierra de Gata Slate and granite mountains (maximum 1500 m) riddled with sheer-walled gullies. Almost 1200 species of vascular plant, including endemics such as *Bufonia macropetala*, *Sedum pedicellatum* subspecies *lusitanicum*, *Thymelaea procumbens* and *Omphalodes brassicifolia*. Last refuge for wolf in the Spanish Sistema Central and Iberia's northernmost outpost of Egyptian mongoose. Good raptor populations – black vulture (40 pairs), honey buzzard, booted, golden and Bonelli's eagles and a single pair of Spanish imperial eagles – plus breeding black stork. More information from ADENEX (see Useful contacts).

Embalse de Borbollón Reservoir with large island heronry (an ADENEX reserve) dominated by little and cattle egrets and grey heron, plus a few night herons and up to 50 pairs of black kite. Wintering greylag goose, black-tailed godwit and crane, with important post-breeding concentrations of black stork. Surrounding western holm oak *dehesa* and open plains harbour Montagu's harrier, black-winged kite, stone curlew, little bustard, a few great bustards and pin-tailed sandgrouse, plus an abundance of quail, bee-eater and calandra lark.

Las Batuecas–Sierra de Francia: (*parque natural*; 32 300 ha, also ZEPA) Quartzite mountains peaking at 1732 m (Peña de Francia). Pyrenean and western holm oaks, enclaves of cork oak, sweet chestnut groves and maritime and Scots pine plantations, with large expanses of secondary scrub. Two large colonies of black vulture, plus breeding griffon and Egyptian vultures, black kite, golden and short-toed eagles, lesser kestrel and peregrine; 3+ pairs of black stork. Also great spotted cuckoo, alpine swift, lesser spotted woodpecker, Thekla lark, red-rumped swallow, black and black-eared wheatears, both rock thrushes, chough and ortolan bunting. Pardel lynx, abundant Spanish ibex and Iberian endemic herptiles: Schreiber's green, Iberian rock and Bocage's wall lizards, Iberian midwife toad, Iberian painted and Iberian frogs and Bosca's newt. Try the road which links Las Mestas with the Peña de Francia via La Alberca or the trail along the Arroyo de las Batuecas, northeast of the San José de las Batuecas monastery.

SITE 98 Monfragüe

Magnificent dehesas, relict Mediterranean forests and riverine habitats with precipitous rocky outcrops house what is probably the world's largest breeding nuclei of black vulture and Spanish imperial eagle.

A few hours' spring vigil at the altar of the massive quartzite monolith of Peñafalcón is without a doubt one of the most rewarding wildlife experiences on offer in the Iberian peninsula today. As the thermals start to rise, the skies fill with griffon vultures, circling ever higher to gain sufficient altitude to cruise off over the surrounding plains in search of carrion, while others – as yet undecided – squat in an ungainly fashion on rock outcrops flanking the road.

About 80 pairs of these magnificent birds breed on the sheer, inaccessible rock face of Peñafalcón, separated from the viewing area alongside the EX-208 by the mighty river Tajo which – once powerful enough to carve this strait though the Sierra de las Corchuelas, backbone of the park – has long since been pacified by a series of dams. The undeniable security of these crags is also exploited by at least two pairs of black stork, single pairs of Egyptian vulture, eagle owl and peregrine and numerous choughs.

Red-rumped swallows and crag martins swoop low over the water, white-rumped swifts fly high over Peñafalcón and blue rock thrushes sing their hearts out from the crags behind the viewpoint, while the western holm oaks below harbour short-toed treecreeper, serin and rock bunting; black wheatear is also a possibility here. Outstanding amid the surrounding vegeta-

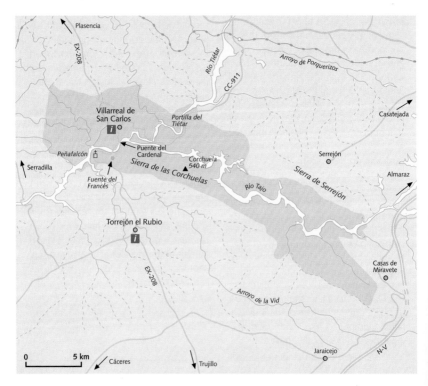

Peñafalcón

tion are silver-leaved bushes of the Afro-Iberian endemic legume *Adenocarpus hispanicus* subspecies *argyrophyllus*, while an examination of the shady cliffs should turn up *Digitalis thapsi* and dwarf sheep's-bit (subspecies *sessiliflora*, unique to central Iberia), with Spanish seakale and the pungent *Ballota hirsuta* growing along the base.

A couple of kilometres to the north, just before the newish bridge across the Tajo – look out for alpine swifts here in spring – lies a small spring called the Fuente del Francés: haunt of marsh fritillary, nettle-tree butterfly, small red damselfly and *Ischnura graell-*

sii. From here a narrow trail winds up to the Castillo de Monfragüe through the thick Mediterranean forest that clothes the *umbría* of the Sierra de las Corchuelas: gloomy cork and Lusitanian oak woods, accompanied by Montpellier maple, turpentine tree, sage-leaved and gum cistuses, myrtle, strawberry-tree, Lusitanian and tree heaths, wild jasmine, *Phillyrea angustifolia*, wild olive and laurustinus.

Small clearings along the way often harbour spring-flowering hoop-petticoat daffodil, wild tulip, bluebell, star-of-Bethlehem, common and white asphodels, tassel hyacinth and Lange's and dense-flowered orchids, as well as palmate anemone and the diminutive dwarf pansy. Near the top of the climb lies a small pool, home to both Bosca's and marbled newts, while the surrounding shady, humid outcrops host Mediterranean selaginella, maidenhair fern, meadow saxifrage, spring rock-cress and the birthwort *Aristolochia longa*: principal food-plant of the Spanish festoon butterflies that are so common in Monfragüe. Once at the castle you stand virtually eye-to-eye with the vultures, and although griffons make up the bulk of the birds cruising past, black and Egyptian are also frequently seen, along with all five of the park's breeding eagles, black kite and alpine and white-rumped swifts; look out, too, for chough, black redstart and rock sparrow.

The trail continues down the sunny southern flank (*solana*) of the ridge, through scattered western holm oaks with their feet buried in clumps of lygos, *Genista hirsuta*, round-headed thyme and French lavender, with spotted rock-rose, blue pimpernel, mallow-leaved bindweed, *Phlomis lychnitis*, *Linaria spartea*, *Pallenis spinosa* and wild

gladiolus providing additional patches of colour. Reptiles abound here, particularly large psammodromus, while butterflies on the wing in April and May include western dappled white, Lang's short-tailed and black-eyed blues, Spanish brown argus and small copper. This is a noted locality for hawfinch, and you might also add Thekla lark, Orphean warbler, woodchat shrike, azure-winged magpie and cirl bunting to your list here.

Following the EX-208 across the new bridge over the Tajo, the road follows the river north towards Villarreal de San Carlos. Between the river and the road runs a stretch of ancient drover's-road – the Cañada Trujillana – which originally crossed the Tajo via the Puente del Cardenal, these days generally submerged beneath the waters of the dam except in high summer. Granite rock-gardens here are studded with the Afro-Iberian endemic pink *Dianthus lusitanus*, with black wheatear often seen around the bridge. If you follow the *cañada* from here up to Villarreal, you pass a delightful wet flush, teeming with *Silene laeta*, the curious coral-necklace, pale flax, yellow bartsia and

Reservoir on the Río Tajo, Monfragüe

tongue orchids in spring, while the surrounding low scrub harbours dipcadi, Barbary nut and the Afro-Iberian endemic bellflower *Campanula lusitanica*; look out for summer lady's tresses later in the year.

To the north of Villarreal, a right turn onto the CC-911 will eventually lead you to another sheer outcrop of rock known as the Portilla del Tiétar, again on the far side of the river. About 20 pairs of griffon vulture nest here, plus black stork and Egyptian vulture on nearby outcrops, but the main interest is the pair of eagle owls that rears its young here each year. The extremely acid soils of this area support a mixture of pink-flowered *Erica umbellata*, Spanish heath and ling, white-flowered tree heath and greenish-yellow-flowered green heather, as well as rosemary and narrow-leaved cistus, the latter abundantly parasitised by *Cytinus hypocistis*.

Information: The park information centre is located in Villarreal de San Carlos (tel. and fax: 927 199134); where you can pick up maps and details of waymarked walks. A private exhibition and information centre (La Dehesa), run by the Fundación Global Nature (tel: 927 455178; fax: 927 455096: e-mail: fondotorrejon@sinix. net) is located in Torrejón el Rubio, to the south of the park.

Wildlife significance of Monfragüe

Monfragüe (*parque natural* and ZEPA; 17 852 ha) is the undisputed flagship of wildlife conservation in Extremadura, harbouring 276 species of vertebrate. Outstanding among the birds are black vulture (224–255 pairs) and Spanish imperial eagle (10 pairs), most of which nest in a strictly protected *reserva integral* to which there is no access, as well as more than 30 pairs of black stork in some of the most visible nests in Iberia. Add to this several hundred pairs of griffon vulture, 20-odd pairs each of Egyptian vulture and eagle owl and 7–8 pairs of both golden and Bonelli's eagles, plus numerous short-toed and booted eagles, black-winged, black and red kites, goshawk, hobby and peregrine – to say nothing of the smaller owls – and you have one of the best assemblages of breeding raptors in Europe.

Mediterranean birds are also well represented and include great spotted cuckoo, scops owl, hoopoe, red-necked nightjar, black-eared wheatear, Orphean, subalpine and Sardinian warblers and woodchat shrike, plus high densities of blue rock thrush and azure-winged magpie. The more remote forests probably still harbour pardel lynx, although wild boar, wildcat, common genet, beech marten and garden dormouse are much more abundant; otters thrive along the margins of the multiple rivers feeding the dams, with red deer sometimes seen in the more open *dehesa*.

Excellent herptile populations, including the Iberian endemic Bosca's newt, Iberian midwife toad, Iberian painted and Iberian frogs and Bedriaga's skink, plus more widespread sharp-ribbed and fire salamanders, marbled newt, midwife toad, western spadefoot, parsley frog, natterjack toad, both common and stripeless tree frogs, European pond and stripe-necked terrapins, Moorish gecko, spiny-footed, Iberian wall and ocellated lizards, large and Spanish psammodromus, three-toed skink, amphisbaenian, horseshoe whip, southern smooth, ladder, false smooth and Montpellier snakes and Lataste's viper.

Introduction of largemouth bass, common carp and northern pike to the reservoirs has not done the autochthonous fish any favours, but the park's rivers are still home to Iberian nase, calandino and Iberian barbel, all endemic to Spain and Portugal. Among the dragonflies, look out for species with a marked southerly distribution: *Platycnemis acutipennis*, *Ischnura graellsii* and the extremely rare orange-spotted emerald.

Also in the area

Small reservoir to the east of Torrejón el Rubio Great for dusk excursions in spring, when mole crickets are almost deafening and surrounding small pools turn up marbled newts and sharp-ribbed salamanders galore. Natterjack toads common in the streets of the village itself after dark.

Río Almonte, where it crosses the EX-208 Upstream is good for kingfisher and otter, with abundant Iberian pool and stripeless tree frogs; drier areas host Moorish gecko and large psam-modromus. All five Iberian hirundines hawk over the water.

Sierra de Almaraz Low limestone out-crops harbouring a wealth of orchids: giant, fan-lipped, conical, naked man and bee, plus yellow, Iberian and woodcock ophrys and *Ophrys dyris*. Try the minor roads linking Valdecañas del Tajo and Belvís de Monroy with Almaraz, in the area to the south of the N-V (exit 197).

99 Llanos de Cáceres

An enormous expanse of rolling plains of supreme significance for steppe birds and hunting raptors.

Although the Llanos de Cáceres extend over more than 100 000 ha (some 48 000 ha of which is a ZEPA), its steppe-bird populations are so prolific that the proverbial 'needle-in-a-haystack' scenario just doesn't apply here. Around 3000 little bustards, 1300 great bustards, 220 pairs of stone curlew and about 100 pairs each of black-bellied and pin-tailed sandgrouse are present all year round, joined by 140 pairs of Montagu's harrier and 150 pairs of roller in summer, as well as some 450 pairs of lesser kestrel, most of which nest in Cáceres itself but disperse across the plains to hunt.

On a sunny morning in late April, the N-521 – which runs roughly across the centre of the ZEPA, linking the cities of Cáceres and

Black-bellied sandgrouse *Pterocles orientalis*

Trujillo – is chock-a-block with Montagu's harriers quartering the plains, while excursions along the minor roads and tracks which lead off north and south provide virtually effortless encounters with little and great bustards. About 10 km west of Trujillo, turn north off the N-521 at km 10.4 towards Santa

Marta de Magasca. After passing the *dehesa*, a springtime stroll along this little-used thoroughfare will find you surrounded by dozens of raspberry-blowing male little bustards, while small enclaves of western holm oak and abundant lygos scrub provide suitable habitat for great spotted cuckoo, Thekla lark, azure-winged magpie and Iberian hare, with Montagu's harrier, tawny pipit and calandra lark abundant in more open areas.

Once past Santa Marta, head back towards the N-521 in a southwesterly direction. Having crossed the Río Tamuja – with abundant red-rumped swallows and crag martins – you enter a seemingly endless expanse of treeless arable land and pastures: an excellent locality for great bustard, especially around the junction with a pot-holed road leading off to the north. Roller nest-boxes adorn the telegraph poles, flocks of Spanish sparrows feed in the cereals, black-eared wheatears abound and you also stand a reasonable chance of seeing lesser kestrel,

stone curlew and both sandgrouse. Don't forget to keep one eye on the sky, as black and griffon vultures, all the Iberian eagles (including juvenile Spanish imperial) and red kites regularly cruise over the area.

By contrast, the Sierra de Fuentes, to the southeast of Cáceres, is a low granite massif clothed in a mosaic of western holm and cork oaks and stone pines, where booted eagles are particularly abundant, while the Embalse del Salor to the south hosts breeding black-winged stilt and yellow wagtail and wintering greylag goose, gadwall, wigeon, teal, shoveler, pochard and tufted duck, as well as passage avocet, collared pratincole, ruff, snipe, green sandpiper and marsh terns, depending on water levels; cranes are present in winter. Both El Salor and the Embalse de Guadiloba (to the north of the N-521) are renowned for their post-breeding concentrations of black stork, with the steppes surrounding the latter a good locality for black-bellied sandgrouse.

Also in the area

Embalse de Talaván Small reservoir which hosts a variety of wildfowl plus little egret, avocet and roosting cranes in winter; black-necked grebe and sedge and reed warblers on spring passage. Breeding birds include black-winged stilt, little ringed plover, kingfisher, red-rumped swallow, sand martin and fan-tailed warbler. A grove of eucalypts near the road which crosses the tail end of the dam has breeding black kite and a winter roost of red kites. In spring the surrounding scrub and dry pastures harbour great spotted cuckoo, bee-eater, hoopoe, rufous bush robin, southern grey and woodchat shrikes and Spanish sparrow. Also European pond terrapin and Moorish gecko. Streamside flora includes yellow bartsia, rampion bellflower, hoop-petticoat daffodil, rosy garlic, star-of-Bethlehem and tongue orchid.

Stone pines on CC-912 (the Torrejón el Rubio to Cáceres road) About 1.5 km east

of the junction with the road south to Monroy, a stand of massive stone pines houses a colony of white stork and innumerable pendulous nests of Spanish sparrows. Olive groves and rough grassland north of the road are carpeted with *Silene colorata*, small-flowered catchfly, strawberry and starry clovers, Iberian milk-vetch, narrow-leaved lupin, purple vetch, purple viper's-bugloss, bellardia, weasel's-snout, sheep's-bit, andryala, galactites, dipcadi and tongue orchid in spring. Also quail, little bustard, great spotted cuckoo, bee-eater, hoopoe, woodlark, Thekla and crested larks, red-rumped swallow, fan-tailed and Sardinian warblers and azure-winged magpie, but the real star is the black-winged kite, often seen towards the end of the track around a few scattered Lusitanian oaks. Overhead look out for black vulture, booted eagle, Montagu's harrier, black kite and, rarely, Spanish imperial eagle.

SITE
100 Los Barruecos

An assemblage of huge granite monoliths and artificial lagoons, renowned for being the only place in Spain where white storks nest on terra firma.

Although the focal point of Los Barruecos (a *monumento natural* of 319 ha) is undoubtedly the outcrop of barn-sized, granite blocks of batholithic origin (Las Peñas del Tesoro) – in particular the colony of some 30-odd pairs of white storks whose nests perch precariously on their summits – the three shallow reservoirs, originally created for wool-washing, add considerably to the diversity of the site. Both elements are set in a typically Extremaduran matrix of scattered western holm oaks, scrub of white Spanish broom, adenocarpus and Mediterranean mezereon and flower-rich grassland which positively glows with colour from March to May.

A springtime stroll around the largest lake – the Charca del Barrueco de Abajo, closest to the car park and also to the 'boulder-city' – takes you through ankle-deep yellow-vetch, *Biserrula pelecinus*, purple viper's-bugloss, wild clary, bellardia, *Linaria spartea*, yellow bartsia and tassel hyacinths. Butterflies on the wing at this time of year include Spanish festoon, swallowtail, scarce swallowtail, green-striped and black-veined whites, small copper and black-eyed blue, but look out, too, for the distinctive ribbon-tailed lacewing, with its trailing, streamer-like hindwings, and the ant-lion *Palpares libelluloides*.

Crevices in the boulders support glaucous tufts of the pink-flowered *Dianthus lusitanus* (an Afro-Iberian endemic), clumps of the figwort *Scrophularia schousboei*, found only in central Iberia, and *Digitalis thapsi*. In good weather spiny-footed lizards stalk small invertebrates across the grainy veneer, while large psammodromus and ocellated lizards skulk in the undergrowth.

The margins of the lake are fringed with round-headed club-rush, cushions of blinks and white-flowered carpets of common water-crowfoot, while the water itself is

Los Barruecos

sprinkled, confetti-like, with the delicate fronds of water fern (a naturalised tropical American species) and common duckweed. Dragonflies abound here, particularly towards the end of May, when robust species such as emperor, lesser and vagrant emperors, black-tailed skimmer, four-spotted and broad-bodied chasers and scarlet and red-veined darter can be seen, as well as the delicate goblet-marked damselfly and the Afro-Iberian species *Ischnura graellsii*. These reservoirs are also the haunt of sharp-ribbed salamander, Bosca's newt, Iberian pool frog, stripe-necked terrapin and grass snake.

Bird-wise, the lakes support resident great crested and little grebes and gadwall, and feeding cattle and little egrets and grey herons, with black-winged stilts and little ringed plovers arriving in summer to breed. Whiskered tern, bee-eater and black stork drop in on passage, while large numbers of cormorants spend the winter here. Red-rumped swallows hawk the lakes, while the granite monoliths provide an ideal vantage point for resident little owl, hoopoe, Thekla lark and stonechat.

Keep one eye on the skies, as the black and red kites and short-toed and booted eagles which breed in more wooded areas in the Sierra de San Pedro regularly head this way to hunt, while Montagu's harrier, little bustard, stone curlew and both sandgrouse are known to occur in the surrounding cereal fields and pastures. On the mammal front, southern water vole, Iberian hare, Eurasian badger and otter have been recorded here.

Access: Los Barruecos is signposted from the centre of the town of Malpartida de Cáceres (on the N-521 to the west of Cáceres); approximately 4 km of asphalted road takes you to the car park next to the Museo Vostell-Malpartida. Three waymarked trails take in the various lagoons and the Peñas del Tesoro.

Also in the area

Cáceres (World Heritage Site) The old part of the city boasts some 30 towers dating from the Moorish occupation of Spain and the single largest concentration of lesser kestrel in Spain (around 450 pairs); abundant white storks' nests and breeding pallid swift.

Cáceres city rubbish tip In winter visited by thousands of white storks, hundreds of red kites and cattle egrets, plus buzzard, lesser black-backed and black-headed gulls, jackdaw and raven. From Cáceres take the EX-100 towards Badajoz and turn right onto a narrow asphalt road at km 4 (signposted 'Vertedero Controlado'). After 2 km, follow the track to the left of the tip into the pastures beyond for the best views of sentinel storks and wheeling kites.

Lagunas de Petit Small fourteenth-century reservoirs to the northeast of Arroyo de la Luz with an enormous colony of cattle egrets (maximum 2000 pairs). Fringing vegetation harbours water rail, kingfisher, reed and great reed warblers, penduline tit, golden oriole and Spanish sparrow, with passage visitors including spoonbill, purple and night herons, black stork, greylag goose, garganey and green sandpiper. Wintering wigeon, teal, red-crested pochard, tufted duck and crane. Nearby mature Mediterranean forest ideal for booted eagle, great spotted cuckoo, scops owl, red-necked nightjar and azure-winged magpie. Take the EX-207 north off the N-521, just west of Malpartida, go through Arroyo de la Luz and turn right on the track by a metal silo about 2.5 km after the village. The reservoirs lie within a private estate, so permission should be requested from anyone you meet.

SITE
101 Llanos de Brozas

A proposed Natura 2000 site of 52 954 ha encompassing extensive pastures and dry cereal cultivations, primarily of interest for its steppe-bird community.

To the north of the Cáceres–Portugal road (N-521), sandwiched between the Río Tajo and the Sierra de San Pedro (see p. 287) lie the Estepas de Brozas: a sweeping landscape of treeless plains dotted with countless seasonal endorheic lagoons, the vista interrupted only by a few low slate walls, small herds of the native *retinta* cattle and close-packed flocks of cream-coloured sheep. This is probably one of the best places in Spain in which to encounter great bustards in winter (a maximum of 800 individuals here), with groups of up to 80 birds standing out like proverbial sore thumbs from the harvested fields only metres from the road. Add to this healthy populations of little bustard (1000 individuals), stone curlew (500 pairs) and both black-bellied and pin-tailed sandgrouse (500 pairs of each), plus several thousand wintering cranes, and you have all the necessary ingredients for a prime birdwatching site.

The simplest strategy for exploring the area is to drive the triangle of roads (EX-302, EX-324 and N-521) immediately to the south of Brozas, stopping frequently to scan with binoculars and listen for sandgrouse, generally located by their distinctive flight calls. Early morning is undoubtedly the best time, before the heat-haze so typical of these sun-baked plains has developed, with the area around the Rivera de Jumadiel (km 41 on the EX-302) particularly good.

Montagu's harriers are very common in summer, as are black-eared wheatear and southern grey shrike, while winter sees the arrival of characteristic open-habitat raptors such as hen harrier, red kite and an occasional merlin, as well as large numbers of cranes, golden plover and lapwing. Calandra lark and Spanish sparrow are present all year round, with notable post-breeding concentrations of black storks occurring in late summer.

In the southern part of the triangle, where the two minor roads cross the Río Salor, the steppes give way to western holm oak *dehesa*, here associated with lygos, French lavender and swathes of colourful forbs in spring. Black storks are known to breed here (some five pairs), as well as black and red kites and short-toed and booted eagles, while griffon and black vultures often hunt over less densely vegetated habitats. On the EX-302, park by the new bridge (km 53.4) and follow the old road down to the west where the original stone bridge crosses the river, where you might turn up kingfisher, crag martin, Thekla lark, black redstart, blue rock thrush, great reed warbler, rock sparrow and hawfinch.

Azure-winged magpie *Cyanopica cyanus* (Mike Lane)

Also in the area

Charca de Brozas Small lagoon to the northeast of Brozas, accessed from the EX-207 from the bar called Merendero La Isla at km 33.7. Water levels vary, with expanses of mud around the margin good for waders (little stint, redshank, greenshank) and egrets in winter, and as feeding grounds for the town's 40-odd pairs of white stork. Little and great crested grebes, pintail, wigeon and shoveler on the open water in winter, with migrants including greylag goose, garganey and little tern. Eucalypts support a mixed winter roost of red kite, raven, jackdaw and both starlings.

Mata de Alcántara – Vilar del Rey road
Turn north off the EX-207 at km 40 and follow the minor road through traditionally managed *dehesa* around small pools among curvaceous granite topography. In summer good for black kite, booted eagle, Egyptian vulture, great spotted cuckoo, bee-eater, roller and woodchat shrike, with wintering red kites and cranes. The **Charca de la Mata** lies about 6 km north of the junction with the EX-207, with access from a small roadside picnic area on the left. Resident little and great crested grebes, gadwall and little ringed plover, plus breeding black-winged stilt and red-rumped swallow; black storks congregate in late summer; passage spoonbill plus wintering wildfowl.

102 Sierra de San Pedro

Well-preserved expanse of dehesa *of supreme importance for breeding raptors, particularly Spanish imperial eagle and black vulture, with a rich assemblage of orchids.*

Extending for almost 70 km along the Cáceres–Badajoz border, the series of low parallel ridges which makes up the Sierra de San Pedro (a ZEPA of 83 217 ha) forms a link between the Montes de Toledo to the east and Portugal's Serra de São Mamede to the west. Although the high point of the range – Torrico de San Pedro – rises to just 703 m, numerous razor-backed quartzite bluffs protrude through a mantle of primeval Mediterranean forest, separating wide valleys brimming with old-established cork and western holm oak *dehesa*.

The Sierra de San Pedro is renowned for its healthy raptor populations (both forest- and cliff-breeding), notably such Iberian specialities as black vulture, Spanish imperial eagle (21 pairs) and black-winged kite. Other resident raptors include griffon vulture, golden and Bonelli's eagles, goshawk, sparrowhawk, red kite, peregrine and eagle owl, joined in summer by Egyptian vulture, short-toed and booted eagles, black kite, honey buzzard,

Spanish imperial eagle *Aquila adalberti*

Naked man orchid *Orchis italica*

the typical avian inhabitants of the region. As well as scanning the skies for raptors, don't forget that almost any patch of *dehesa* might host great spotted cuckoo, hoopoe, wryneck, Sardinian, Orphean and subalpine warblers, firecrest, crested tit, nuthatch, short-toed treecreeper, woodchat shrike, azure-winged magpie and Spanish and rock sparrows, while the roadside telegraph wires in more open areas are often frequented by bee-eaters, rollers, black-eared wheatears and southern grey shrikes.

More open, rocky areas should be examined for blue rock thrush, rock bunting and chough, while the numerous river crossings (for example, the Río Zapatón and Rivera de Albarragena) provide an opportunity to add kingfisher, crag martin, red-rumped swallow, great reed warbler and golden oriole to the list. These watercourses are also the place to track down sharp-ribbed salamander, Bosca's newt, Iberian midwife toad, parsley frog and stripe-necked terrapin. Ocellated lizard, horseshoe whip and Montpellier snakes and Lataste's viper occur in drier habitats.

The road running southeast from Aliseda to the EX-100 passes through unfenced cork oak *dehesa*, where you can wander at will. Amid colourful displays of *Genista hirsuta*, gum and narrow-leaved cistuses, the crimson-flowered *Cistus crispus*, French lavender, tree germander and daisy-leaved toadflax, look out for western peonies, dipcadi, loose-flowered and tongue orchids, broad-leaved helleborine and woodcock, sawfly and Iberian ophrys, as well as the yellow-flowered cistus parasite *Cytinus hypocistis*. Other, less common, orchids cited from the *sierra* include green-winged (subspecies *picta*), champagne, conical, naked man, bug (subspecies *martrinii*), robust marsh, dense-flowered and bee orchids, dark ophrys and summer lady's tresses.

lesser kestrel and hobby. Black storks also breed here – with post-nuptial concentrations of up to 100 individuals recorded – and small bands of cranes occur in winter; the arable plains to the south of the *sierra* are home to great and little bustards. The forested habitats also support a rich assemblage of predatory mammals, including wildcat, common genet and Egyptian mongoose, with pardel lynx having recolonised the area from the Sierra de Gata to the north, ostensibly along the corridor of the river Erjas/Erges. Other mammalian inhabitants include otter, wild boar and red deer, but roe deer were hunted out in the 1930s.

Much of the Sierra de San Pedro comprises private estates, but a drive along any of the smaller roads which traverse the ridges and valleys from north to south (particularly the EX-303 and EX-324) should turn up most of

Also in the area

Cornalvo y Sierra Bermeja (*parque natural*; 10 570 ha; also a ZEPA) Expanse of rolling cork and western holm oak *dehesa* on slates and quartzites, littered with outcrops of huge, rounded granite boulders. Includes a Roman dam on the Embalse de Cornalvo (44 ha), with many orchids in the surrounds: champagne, loose-flowered, bug, conical and tongue, plus small-flowered serapias and sawfly and Iberian ophrys. Rivers, notably the Aljúcen, harbour many Iberian endemic fish: jarabugo, pardilla, calandino, Iberian nase, Iberian barbel and *Cobitis paludica*. Breeding black and white storks, plus similar assemblages of raptors (although not all breed) and Mediterranean birds to San Pedro. More open country along the road from Trujillanos has breeding Montagu's harrier, little bustard and stone curlew, plus wintering crane and great bustard. Vehicle access only as far as the dam, via exits 331 and 334 off the N-V.

Mérida Roman city of Augusta Emerita, founded in 25 BC and the ancient capital of Lusitania; now a World Heritage Site. Impressive bridge over the Guadiana has breeding alpine and pallid swifts. Also nesting white stork and lesser kestrel (some 50 pairs). Immediately to the west lies the **Embalse de Montijo**, a narrow, dammed stretch of the Guadiana whose wooded islets host a large mixed colony of cattle and little egrets and night heron. Marginal vegetation harbours breeding little bittern, waxbill and red avadavat, with little, whiskered and gull-billed terns on passage and wintering water rail, bluethroat and penduline tit.

103 Las Villuercas

An unprotected series of parallel quartzite ridges separated by deeply incised river valleys harbouring excellent populations of breeding raptors and Iberia's best stands of Portugal laurel.

A quick glance at a relief map of Extremadura will reveal a curious group of narrow ridges in southeastern Cáceres, curled like the fingers of a thin, gnarled hand. Including the *sierras* of Viejas and Altamira, but known collectively as Las Villuercas (maximum 1601 m), this abrupt terrain conceals a series of precipitous river valleys which are moist enough to provide refuge for several species belonging to more Atlantic floral and faunal communities, here well separated from their main ranges. By contrast, the sunnier lower slopes of the ridges harbour all the typical Mediterranean bird species you would expect to find in Extremadura.

Las Villuercas still possess large tracts of forest, essentially dominated by western holm, cork and Pyrenean oaks, the exact composition varying with aspect and altitude. The summits of the ridges harbour a stunted western holm oak community, accompanied by prickly juniper, *Genista cinerascens*, the eye-catching *Adenocarpus hispanicus* subspecies *argyrophyllus* and Spanish heath, the latter also appearing in the extensive secondary scrub which clothes deforested areas, in association with *Genista hirsuta*, lygos and gum and laurel-leaved cistuses. Clearings in the oak forests are often populated by the large, yellow-flowered *Iris lusitanica*, Sicilian orchid and violet limodore, as well as the Iberian endemic composites *Centaurea toletana* and *Carduus platypus*.

More interesting vegetation occurs in the moist gullies. Alder and narrow-leaved ash line the stream banks, along with a few

Southern white admiral *Limenitis reducta*

Lusitanian oaks, Montpellier maple, holly, alder buckthorn, strawberry-tree, Lusitanian heath, green heather, laurustinus and butcher's broom. The jewel in the crown, however, is the Portugal laurel: a relic from the cloud forests of the Tertiary which survives by capturing moisture from the frequent mists that hang around in the valley bottoms, notably that of the Río Viejas. These humid habitats also harbour Irish spleenwort, soft shield-fern, broad buckler-fern and royal and Jersey ferns, as well as stinking hellebore, sword-leaved helleborine and white hoop-petticoat daffodil, which flowers in January and February. Las Villuercas also boasts a number of interesting *Sphagnum* bogs, likewise home to a flora with clear Atlantic influences; look out for the insectivorous pale butterwort and round-leaved sundew, as well as cross-leaved heath and robust marsh orchid (subspecies *sesquipedalis*).

The best way to see the area's raptors is to tour the minor roads north of Berzocana. The long ridge to the east of the road up through Solana is excellent for Bonelli's eagle, with booted and short-toed eagles over the *dehesa* further north. A good stopping place is on a bridge over a stream 1 km before the turn off to Roturas. The cliffs here hold griffon vulture, red-rumped swallow and blue rock thrush, while a small path leading along the stream is lined with western peonies in spring. Continue the tour up through Roturas, keeping an eye on the ridge tops for golden eagle and being alert for the overhead presence of black stork, black and Egyptian vultures and red and black kites, with just a chance of Spanish imperial eagle.

The mosaic of chestnut groves, open fields and orchards around Navezuelas supports a good range of typical Mediterranean birds such as hoopoe, Sardinian warbler and woodchat shrike, along with the more far-ranging woodlark, nuthatch and jay. Dartford warblers abound in the cistus scrub and more wooded areas are home to vociferous groups of the elegant azure-winged magpie, while characteristic species of the Pyrenean oaks include great spotted woodpecker, pied flycatcher, firecrest and short-toed treecreeper.

The sheer variety of habitats on offer also makes Las Villuercas one of the richest areas for butterflies in Extremadura, with species more reminiscent of the central or northern Iberian mountains – high brown and twin-spot fritillaries, brown hairstreak, sooty copper and Amanda's blue, for example – mixing with more southerly elements such as nettle-tree butterfly, two-tailed pasha, southern white admiral and Chapman's green hairstreak. Look out, too, for Spanish, spotted and Glanville fritillaries, great banded and rock graylings, Spanish purple hairstreak, purple-shot copper and green-underside and Osiris blues.

It is thought that a handful of pardel lynxes still roam Las Villuercas, feeding largely on rabbits and Iberian hares, while a few otters survive in the least-disturbed rivers. Red deer are common in the area; unlike many Spanish populations, which have been rein-

---

Access: From Guadalupe with its impressive Monasterio de Santa María (a World Heritage Site, with breeding white storks and lesser kestrels) take the EX-118 north towards Castañar de Ibor, and after 6 km turn left up a 10 km road towards the disused radar station on the peak of Villuercas (1601 m). After about 5 km, you pass over the headwaters of the river Viejas; turn north down a track leading into the valley to Navezuelas, or alternatively head south to Guadalupe.

troduced, the nucleus here is autochthonous. Other vertebrates of note include Iberian frog and Schreiber's green lizard, both unique to the peninsula and represented here by isolated populations, and European pond terrapin.

Also in the area

Embalse de Cíjara (*reserva regional de caza*; 24 999 ha) Vast reservoir on the Río Guadiana straddling the borders of Extremadura and Castilla–La Mancha. Surrounding rocky hills (maximum 856 m) are planted with maritime and stone pines and eucalypts, with a few enclaves of cork, western holm, Lusitanian and Pyrenean oaks associated with strawberry-tree, lentisc and *Phillyrea angustifolia*. Also extensive tracts of gum cistus, *Erica* species and rosemary; quartzite scarps abound, plus several rocky islets in mid-stream. Breeding birds include black stork, griffon, black and Egyptian vultures, golden eagle (10–12 pairs), Bonelli's eagle (5 pairs) and eagle owl, plus stock dove, southern grey shrike, azure-winged magpie and rock sparrow. Among the forest mammals are red deer, wild boar, common genet, beech marten, wildcat and pardel lynx, with otter along the watercourses. Stripe-necked terrapins abound.

---

104 La Serena

Vast area of practically treeless xerophytic pastures and cereals, considered to be the most important area for steppe birds in Spain.

In February, if you arrive at Puerto Mejoral just before dawn, you can be assured of an unforgettable wildlife experience: wave after wave of cranes cruising low overhead, as they commute from their overnight roosts along the margins of the Zújar reservoir to richer feeding grounds in the *dehesa* to the south. Mejoral is the obvious low point in the quartzite ridges of Castuera and Tiros which mark the southern edge of La Serena, such that almost all the cranes – up to 3000 birds – of the morning's rush-hour aim for this gap before dispersing in a wide arc.

The Sierras de Castuera y Tiros, which extend for more than 25 km from east to west and peak at 957 m, provide suitable nesting habitat for small numbers of black stork, golden and Bonelli's eagles, griffon and Egyptian vultures and eagle owl, as well as for alpine swift, crag martin, blue rock thrush and black wheatear, usually visible around the castles at Benquerencia de la Serena and Almorchón; white-rumped swifts also probably breed here. Puerto Mejoral, like most of the northern flank of the *sierra*, is clothed with a dense mosaic of secondary Mediterranean scrub, the haunt of Dartford and Sardinian warblers, azure-winged magpie and rock bunting all year round, which are joined by great spotted cuckoo, red-necked nightjar, black-eared wheatear, spectacled warbler and woodchat shrike in spring.

To the north, however, lies La Serena: an immense rolling plain of tawny pastures inhabited by vast flocks of merino sheep and some of the healthiest populations of steppe birds in Europe. Pockets of deeper soils are

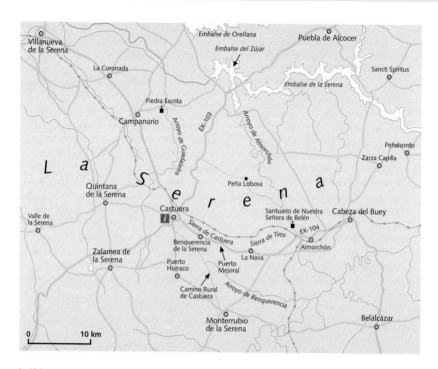

half-heartedly planted with cereals, with the fallow indicated by sheets of bright-yellow crucifers and field marigolds in spring. The whole area is traversed by a network of temporary streams – which eventually mature into permanent, albeit insignificant, rivers such as the Guadalefra and Almorchón – and is littered with small, artificial watering-holes, often carpeted with water-crowfoots and attracting drinking sandgrouse, especially in summer.

The ornithological significance of La Serena (a proposed Natura 2000 site of 74 950 ha) cannot be overstated. Despite the fact that its populations of steppe birds have declined alarmingly since the mid-1980s, this is still one of the most important enclaves in Spain for sandgrouse, and supports one of the highest densities of nesting Montagu's harrier, stone curlew, little bustard and calandra lark in Iberia, as well as housing a breeding nucleus of some 800 great bustards.

If you possess a reasonably robust vehicle or don't mind walking all day, then the following itinerary is a must. Take the EX-103

from Castuera north towards Puebla de Alcocer and turn right onto a rough track at km 76.8; after about 10 km you arrive at the abandoned mine of Peña Lobosa – complete with nesting white storks and jackdaws – and from there can continue to the Santuario de Nuestra Señora de Belén, to the west of Almorchón, (a further 15 km or so).

The many small rises along the way give excellent views over these pseudosteppes, providing all but continual sightings of small flocks of great bustard and numerous little bustards and stone curlews; black-bellied sandgrouse are usually more closely associated with the ploughed fields to the south-east of the mine, however, which are also patronised by large numbers of wintering golden plover and lapwing. Crested larks and southern grey shrikes are ten-a-penny here in winter, when you might also turn up red and black-winged kites and hen harrier.

Another interesting excursion is along the winding EX-349 – recently asphalted – which runs east from Campanario to join the EX-103 (signposted Piedra Escrita). The terrain is more abrupt here, dropping sharply down to a small reservoir on the Arroyo de Guadalefra (and the Piedra Escrita chapel) after 5 km. In early spring the pastures on either side of the stream are studded with *Romulea ramiflora*, with the slaty outcrops above hosting later-flowering narrow-leaved lupin, *Digitalis thapsi* and *Phlomis lychnitis*. Flocks of Spanish sparrows frequent the oleanders along the water's edge, particularly in winter, while bee-eaters and red-rumped swallows zoom overhead from April onwards.

The Arroyo de Guadalefra – a tributary of the Zújar – is also noted for its populations of Iberian endemic fish, including calandino and pardilla, with haphazard piles of stripe-necked terrapins common in the river downstream of the small dam; you might also investigate pools in the river for Bosca's newt and sharp-ribbed salamander. In the Zújar itself thrive Iberian barbel and the related *Barbus microcephalus*, again unique to the peninsula, as well as a few otters.

To the south of the Sierras de Castuera and Tiros lies another expanse of rolling plain, although here granite replaces the slates, the deeper soils clothed with western holm oak *dehesa*, interspersed with olive groves and cereals. This area – sometimes called the Dehesas de Benquerencia – is the favoured feeding area of the cranes which pass over Puerto Mejoral twice a day; as good a route as any to locate them is to take the Camino Rural de Castuera, a narrow surfaced road which runs northwest from Monterrubio de la Serena (signposted from the western end of the village). Once across the Arroyo de Benquerencia – a small temporary stream teeming with Iberian pool frogs – you enter open *dehesa* planted with cereals, where numerous small family groups of cranes can be seen foraging for the acorns which make up the bulk of their winter diet.

In late spring, La Serena is a different world, the pastures flushed with green and the cereals almost knee high, which makes observing steppe birds more difficult, although compensation is at hand in the form of Montagu's harrier, black kite, lesser kestrel, collared pratincole (especially around the small pools along the EX-103), bee-eater and short-toed lark, with rollers very visible along the EX-103, where the telegraph poles have been fitted with nest-boxes. The many reptiles which make their home here are also easier to see when the ambient temperature increases: ocellated lizard and ladder and Montpellier snakes are particularly abundant.

La Serena

Also in the area

Embalse de Orellana y Sierra de Pela (ZEPA of 25 000 ha, with the reservoir also a Ramsar Site; 5500 ha) Narrow reservoir 35 km long with well-preserved riverine forest and several small islands, sandwiched between the quartzite bluffs of the Sierra de Pela and undulating plains dotted with western holm oak *dehesa*. Superlative importance for wintering cranes (up to 24 000 birds), plus breeding black-winged stilt (140 pairs), collared pratincole (maximum 120 pairs) and gull-billed tern (around 450 pairs). Enormous cattle egret colony (6000 nests), plus breeding little egret, night heron, red-crested pochard, little tern, bee-eater, red-rumped swallow and golden oriole. Around 30 000 wintering waterbirds, plus passage osprey and marsh terns and large post-breeding concentrations of black stork. Sierra de Pela hosts nesting black stork, golden and Bonelli's eagles, eagle owl, crag martin, blue rock thrush and black wheatear. Southern pseudosteppes are good for Montagu's harrier, both bustards, pin-tailed sandgrouse and lesser kestrels (which breed in Puebla de Alcocer), with *dehesa* harbouring nesting black-winged, black and red kites, short-toed eagle and roller.

Rice-fields along the N-340 Particularly good between Obando and Hernán Cortés, harbouring thousands of white storks, cattle and little egrets, black-tailed godwits and lapwing in January and February, plus a few cranes and hunting hen harriers and black-winged kites. The steppe area to the north of Obando is excellent for feeding cranes.

105 Sierra Grande de Hornachos

SITE

One of Extremadura's mountain 'islands', home to a diverse community of cliff-breeding birds and a rich Mediterranean forest and dehesa *fauna.*

Rising to a maximum of 951 m (Peñón de Marín) above gently undulating plains clothed in traditionally managed *dehesa* and dry cereal cultivation in southeastern Badajoz, the Sierra Grande de Hornachos (a ZEPA of 6000 ha and a 2600 ha *reserva biológica* created by ADENEX) comprises an abrupt quartzite ridge oriented approximately northwest–southeast. The shady *umbría* harbours well-developed Mediterranean vegetation while the *solana* presents a sun-scorched rock-and-scree façade to the world.

The prevalent tree of Hornachos is without a doubt the western holm oak, notably in the *dehesa* of the foothills but also forming small enclaves of unadulterated Mediterranean forest on the lower slopes of the *solana*, here accompanied by holly oak, lygos, *Genista hirsuta, Cistus crispus,* wild olive and French lavender. Deeper soils in the more humid conditions of the *umbría* harbour tracts of cork oak, with an understorey of lentisc, gum cistus, strawberry-tree, *Phillyrea angustifolia* and laurustinus.

The highest crags are virtually bare of vegetation, but are noteworthy for the Afro-Iberian endemic stork's-bill *Erodium mourettii*, in Spain found only in the province of Badajoz. Riverine vegetation is pretty well limited to scattered copses of narrow-leaved ash and belts of the drought- and flood-tolerant *Securinega tinctoria* and oleander, but look out for champagne, fan-lipped and loose-flowered orchids and sawfly ophrys here in the spring.

Cliff-breeding birds are of particular note, with the plethora of nooks and crannies in the quartzite ridge providing suitable nest sites for a few pairs of Egyptian vulture, golden and Bonelli's eagles, peregrine and eagle owl, as well as for passerines such as crag martin, blue rock thrush, black redstart and chough. More forested habitats harbour breeding booted and short-toed eagles, sparrowhawk, red and black kites and long-eared and barn owls, as well as all the colourful Mediterranean birds which so typify the Extremaduran *dehesa*: hoopoe, Sardinian, subalpine and Orphean warblers, woodchat and southern grey shrikes, azure-winged magpie and cirl bunting. Spanish imperial eagles and black vultures can often be seen flying over the area, although neither breed in the *sierra*.

Predatory mammals also find these *dehesas* and forests to their liking, particularly Egyptian mongoose, common genet, beech marten and wildcat, which share their domain with Eurasian badger, wild boar and Iberian hare. Among the most characteristic reptiles are Moorish and Turkish geckos, Iberian wall lizard, large psammodromus, ocellated and Schreiber's green lizards, Bedriaga's skink, horseshoe whip, ladder and Montpellier snakes and Lataste's viper, while the amphibians are also well represented, including the Iberian endemic Bosca's newt and Iberian midwife toad, as well as the more widespread sharp-ribbed salamander, marbled newt and both tree frogs.

Embalse de los Molinos

Access and information: The ADENEX Reserve Biológica de Sierra Grande maintains an interpretation centre at km 8 on the EX-344 which links the village of Hornachos with Puebla de la Reina (tel: 924 381402); waymarked walks explore both *solana* and *umbría*, mostly commencing in the village of Hornachos. Good views of the Sierra Grande and the area's raptors can be obtained from Puerto Llano (590 m), also on the EX-344.

Also in the area

Embalse de los Molinos A frequent haunt of black storks in late summer, also harbouring a winter crane roost. The mosaic of cereals and *dehesa* around **Campillo de Llerena** to the east is good for open-country birds such as black-winged kite, great and little bustards and stone curlew all year round and Montagu's harrier and roller in summer.

Alange Enormous reservoir on the Río Matachel close to its confluence with the Guadiana. The castle of the same name lies atop a crag immediately east of the dam and is the haunt of alpine swift, crag martin, black wheatear, blue rock thrush and rock sparrow. Bee-eaters and red-rumped swallows hawk over the water and cranes roost in winter. The Matachel itself is noted for its community of Iberian endemic fish: jarabugo, calandino, pardilla and Iberian nase.

SITE
106 Oropesa

One of Spain's finest dehesas, *home to pardel lynx and a superb assemblage of breeding raptors; associated reservoirs and pseudosteppes harbour an interesting winter avifauna.*

The extreme northwestern reaches of Castilla–La Mancha boast what has been described as 'the best-preserved lowland forest in western Europe': a vast *dehesa* extending south from the Río Tiétar, uninterrupted apart from a couple of minor roads and the two large reservoirs of Rosarito y Navalcán (a ZEPA of 53 167 ha).

Access to this mixed cork and western holm oak *dehesa* is, for once, fairly simple: 4 km west of the N-502, the Cañada Real Leonesa Occidental (royal drover's road) crosses the minor road to Parrillas and heads off south into the *dehesa*, bridging the tail-end of the Navalcán reservoir before entering the rolling pastures around Oropesa. This stretch of the *cañada* can be walked or cycled – in total a distance of around 19 km – and is undoubtedly the best way to track down the special birds of the area, although the chances of seeing one of the few surviving pardel lynxes are obviously very small.

Local birdwatchers recommend a visit in winter. Groups of 35+ black storks winter around Rosarito, while some 6000 cranes roost on both Rosarito and neighbouring Navalcán. Once the breeding season is over, red kite, hen harrier and merlin arrive from the north to replace their congeners – black kite, Montagu's harrier and hobby – which

Black-winged kite *Elanus caeruleus* (Mike Lane)

have departed for Africa by September. Resident Bonelli's eagles still breed in the area (2 pairs), as well as golden (10 pairs) and Spanish imperial (1 pair) eagles, but you won't see summer visitors such as booted or short-toed eagles until early spring. Black-winged kites are also resident here and black and griffon vultures are easily seen throughout the year, while Egyptian vulture and lesser kestrel return by March.

Winter also brings great crested grebe, tufted duck, gadwall, shoveler, pintail, wigeon and mallard to the two reservoirs, along with thousands of cormorants, black-headed and lesser black-backed gulls and the occasional over-wintering spoonbill or osprey. Cattle egrets are abundant in pastures throughout the area, roosting along the Tajo, while passerines present in winter include crested lark, southern grey shrike, azure-winged magpie, spotless starling, Spanish sparrow and cirl and rock buntings.

In the rolling pasture and cereal pseudosteppes to the south of Oropesa (a ZEPA of 14948 ha), winter brings huge groups of little bustard (more than 3000 in total) as well as small flocks of great bustard and pin-tailed and black-bellied sandgrouse; look out, too, for golden plover, lapwing, calandra lark and mixed groups of linnet, goldfinch and tree and rock sparrows. Needless to say, spring and summer also have their obvious charms, in the form of red-necked nightjar, roller, bee-eater, red-rumped swallow, black-eared wheatear and woodchat shrike, for example.

Access and information: The best steppe area lies either side of the CM-4101 between Calera y Chozas and Alcolea del Tajo. View both reservoirs from their respective dams. Rosarito can also be visited from **El Vado de los Fresnos**, a privately run environmental education centre with a trail through a diverse selection of Mediterranean habitats, pools with sharp-ribbed salamanders and marbled and Bosca's newts and good views over the reservoir. It lies south of the C-501, 2 km west of Candeleda (tel. and fax: 920 377223).

Also in the area

Embalse de Azután (*refugio de fauna* and ZEPA) One of a number of interesting reservoirs along the middle reaches of the Tajo, holding breeding little bittern, night, purple and grey herons, little and cattle egrets, purple gallinule, scops owl, great reed and Cetti's warblers, penduline tit and golden oriole. Head south on the CM-4160 from Calera y Chozas and turn left after about 5 km along Camino General N°4 to the Tajo. Alternatively, view from the CM-4160, 3 km beyond the Tajo in and around the attractive narrow-leaved ash *dehesa* on the banks of the Río Gévalo (Gébalo).

Río Tajo at Valdeverdeja Further west, tracks lead south of Valdeverdeja to a narrow, cliff-lined section of the Tajo for breeding black stork, Bonelli's eagle, eagle owl, red-rumped swallow, Thekla lark and hawfinch; Bosca's newt in small streams and pools.

¹⁰⁷ Cabañeros

A showpiece national park of Mediterranean ecosystems in the heart of the Montes de Toledo, harbouring largely intact animal and plant communities.

Incredible as it may seem, in the 1980s Cabañeros was almost converted into Europe's largest military bombing range. It was only the opportune decision taken by the regional government to declare 25 000 ha of prime *dehesa*, Mediterranean montane forest and grassland a *parque natural* in 1988 that saved this wonderful area from an ignominious fate. In 1995, Cabañeros was upgraded to national park status (39 000 ha, also part of the Montes de Toledo ZEPA of 117 191 ha), and its survival was assured.

Cabañeros is sometimes known as the 'Spanish Serengeti', although this epithet is really only applicable to the Raña, a broad plain dominating the southern and eastern part of the park whose lowland forests were ploughed up in the 1950s to create sparse *dehesa*, pasture and arable land. By contrast, the surrounding upland areas of the park – the ancient quartzites of the Sierra del Chorito to the north and the Cuerda de Miraflores to the south – are still clad with extensive western holm, cork, Lusitanian and Pyrenean oak woodland, interspersed with steep, alder-lined gullies harbouring stands of silver birch (subspecies *fontqueri*) and large areas of cistus and *Erica* scrub; the highest and largely out-of-bounds ridgetops are carpeted with Pyrenean broom and *Genista cinerascens* scrub.

Owing to the fragility of many of its habitats, most of the park can only be visited in small, pre-booked groups which enter in

Western holm oak *Quercus ilex* subspecies *ballota*, with Cabañeros beyond

4WD vehicles along set itineraries. The first of three possible excursions (starting in Alcoba de los Montes) takes you into the heart of the Raña. Great-spotted cuckoo, roller, hoopoe, southern grey and woodchat shrikes, azure-winged magpie and corn bunting nest here in the scattered oaks of the *dehesa*, which also provide suitable perches for the omnipresent bee-eaters and stable bases for voluminous white stork nests (unwitting hosts to colonies of jackdaws and Spanish sparrows). The open grasslands of the Raña, on the other hand, are the domain of great (1–2 breeding females) and little bustards (40 pairs), stone curlew, Thekla lark and black-eared wheatear, while areas of cereal cultivation with scattered trees attract hovering black-winged kites. Mid-summer explosions of grasshoppers and crickets attract hundreds of Montagu's harriers, black kites, kestrels and a few lesser kestrels, which gorge themselves on the invertebrate bounty.

Red deer rut in the Raña in September – Cabañeros is one of the few places in the mountains of central Spain where the seasonal migration of red deer is not barricaded by high estate fences – and can be seen out in the open until they return to the forests and scrub in March. November sees a few thousand cranes stopping off on their way to the *dehesas* of Extremadura – a few hundred also winter here – as well as an influx of great bustard, red kite, merlin, flocks of calandra larks and skylarks and the odd juvenile Spanish imperial eagle.

The impermeable soils of the Raña often flood in wet seasons to provide suitable habitat for vast hordes of natterjack toads and lesser numbers of sharp-ribbed salamander, Bosca's and marbled newts, western spadefoot and parsley, Iberian pool and Iberian painted frogs. Most of the more thermophilic reptiles also turn up in the Raña: look out for ocellated and spiny-footed lizards in sandy habitats, and false smooth, Montpellier, horseshoe whip and ladder snakes basking in almost any open area in the park.

This itinerary also covers part of the south-facing slopes of the Sierra del Chorito, including an interesting area of *trampales* (sphagnum bogs) whose sodden soils are

Western peony *Paeonia broteri* (T.F.)

crowded with bog-myrtle, *Genista ancistrocarpa*, dyer's greenweed, cross-leaved heath, star and long-stalked yellow sedges, black bog-rush and heath-spotted orchids; green and Lusitanian heaths take refuge on the drier margins. On close examination, the sphagnum (here *Sphagnum palustre*, *S. subnitens* and *S. auriculatum*) holds two small insectivorous plants: the delicate round-leaved sundew and pink-flowered pale butterwort. These bogs are also worth checking out for fire salamander and Iberian midwife toad, as well as for Schreiber's green lizard: a northwest-Iberian endemic, here in an isolated southeastern outpost.

The second of the 4WD routes (starting in Horcajo de los Montes) concentrates on the forests of the Cuerda de Miraflores, on the southern edge of the park. Superb stands of cork oak form a mosaic with western holm oaks (south-facing slopes) or Lusitanian oaks (north-facing slopes), both formations being accompanied by wild service-tree, Montpellier maple, turpentine tree, myrtle, strawberry-tree, *Phillyrea angustifolia*, *Lonicera implexa* and laurustinus in the shadiest nooks, and by wild olive and *Pyrus bourgaeana* in sunnier corners. Stands of Pyrenean oak on cooler north-facing slopes tend to be monospecific, with a ground flora all but limited to western peony.

Secondary communities abound where years of felling and burning have laid waste to the original forests. Commonest in higher areas are shoulder-high tracts of gum cistus and Spanish heath, mixed in with low-growing communities of *Chamaespartium tridentatum*, *Halimium ocymoides* and

H. umbellatum subspecies *viscosum*, *Erica umbellata* and French lavender. Species diversity increases on lower, sunnier slopes, where true Mediterranean scrub elements such as poplar-leaved, laurel-leaved and sage-leaved cistuses, *Halimium atriplicifolium* and tree heath appear, side-by-side with holly oak, osyris, *Genista hirsuta*, *Adenocarpus telonensis* and lentisc. Firebreaks are enlivened in spring by palmate anemone, *Scilla ramburei*, wild tulip, *Fritillaria lusitanica* and champagne orchid.

This itinerary also takes you to the marvellous Laguna de los Cuatro Cerros, a hidden lagoon carpeted with pond water-crowfoot and fringed with lesser water-plantain, where black storks (3 breeding pairs plus 20 birds in post-breeding dispersion) come to feast on the abundance of sharp-ribbed salamanders, Bosca's newts and both stripeless and common tree frogs. The surrounding area harbours woodlark, subalpine, Dartford and melodious warblers and hawfinch, the latter relatively abundant here.

The third of the 4WD excursions (starting in Retuerta del Bullaque) enters the park from the north and takes in part of the Raña and forest and scrub formations which are the typical habitat of carnivores such as beech marten, Egyptian mongoose, common genet and wildcat. The pardel lynx, however, is now rarely recorded in the park, the lack of rabbits being one of the main reasons for its decline. Iberian hares are still common, though, in the low scrub bordering the Raña, sharing their habitat with Iberian blind mole, pygmy white-tailed shrew, Mediterranean pine vole, Algerian mouse, wild boar and roe deer. The Cabañeros bat

fauna includes all four Iberian horseshoes, both mouse-eareds, Savi's and Kuhl's pipistrelles and Schreiber's and free-tailed bats.

Any one of the itineraries provides opportunities for seeing raptors: February is a good month for displaying Spanish imperial eagles (2 pairs and 6–7 juveniles), although you will have to wait until mid-March and early April, respectively, for the much commoner short-toed (8 pairs) and booted eagles (15 pairs). Cabañeros also supports a large colony of black vultures (140 pairs plus large numbers of non-breeders) which usually build their nests atop tall, isolated trees next to open screes, in order to be able to detect the approach of potential predators. The absence of large cliff-faces prevents griffon vultures from nesting in the park, although they are often seen mixed in with groups of black vultures, while golden eagle (five pairs) and Egyptian vulture make do with the few rocky outcrops the area has to offer.

Three walking routes are possible: two obligatorily accompanied by guide and a third without. The latter is the most interesting and follows the river Estena – one of the area's cleanest – southwest from the village of Naves de Estena through a gorge known as the Boquerón del Estena. The river is lined with alder, *Salix atrocinerea* and *S. salvifolia* and narrow-leaved ash, while the extra humidity of the narrow valley also provides an appropriate environment for yew, hazel, Portugal laurel, whitebeam, Montpellier maple, holly and alder buckthorn, providing shelter for hard-, lady-, scaly male- and royal ferns. Rock fissures here host Irish spleenwort, *Cheilanthes tinaei* and *C. hispanica* and the stonecrops *Sedum brevifolium* and *S. hirsutum*, as well as the Afro-Iberian endemic pink *Dianthus lusitanus* and the white-flowered snapdragon *Antirrhinum hispanicum* subspecies *graniticum*, unique to the peninsula.

These quiet waters hold otter – which largely feed on the introduced American crayfish *Procambarus clarkii* here – and both European pond and stripe-necked terrapins, as well as a series of Iberian endemic fish: jarabugo (one of the most endangered of all Iberian freshwater fish), cacho, pardilla, calandino, Iberian barbel and *Barbus micro-*

European pond terrapin *Emys orbicularis*

cephalus. Birdwatchers should be on the alert for black stork, kingfisher, red-rumped swallow, dipper, nightingale, blue rock thrush, golden oriole and rock bunting, while butterfly enthusiasts will enjoy a feast of scarce swallowtail, Spanish festoon, wood white, Cleopatra, large tortoiseshell, Queen of Spain fritillary, cardinal and black-eyed blue in spring. June brings out Spanish purple hairstreak and late-summer visitors will find two-tailed pasha anywhere there are strawberry-trees.

Access and information: 4WD itineraries can be booked by phoning or faxing 926 775384; for guided walks, phone 926 783297 or fax 926 783484. For general information, the national park's e-mail is cabaneros@mma.es The main interpretation centre (Casa de Palillos) lies between El Bullaque and Santa Quiteria; there are also small reception points in Alcoba, Retuerta and Horcajo. Two roads traverse the park: the CM-4017 and the tortuous CM-4157, the latter taking you up to 1129 m and providing stunning views, although few opportunities for walking. Interesting non-official website: http://perso. wanadoo.es/monroy/

Also in the area

Around Cabañeros Many of the species mentioned above can be seen without entering the national park. Immediately to the east, dry fields hold little bustard and short-toed and calandra larks, while great bustards are often seen on the Raña southeast of the Casa de Palillos. The braided Río Bullaque has fine riverine woodland festooned with *Clematis campaniflora* and *Lonicera implexa*; yellow water-lily, hoop-petticoat daffodil and bug and loose-flowered orchids along the banks. Birds include booted eagle, bee-eater, wryneck, red-rumped swallow, Orphean, subalpine and Cetti's warblers, azure-winged magpie, golden oriole, rock and Spanish sparrows and hawfinch. Also otter, stripe-necked terrapin and odonates such as willow emerald and goblet-marked damselflies. The laguna Grande, north of Alcoba, is also good for amphibians and dragonflies.

---

^{SITE}
108 Valle de Alcudia

A broad pastoral valley sandwiched between wooded quartzite ridges; many forest carnivores, steppe birds and a rich butterfly fauna.

The Valle de Alcudia (15 km wide and 90 km long; part of the much larger Sierra Morena ZEPA of 97 528 ha) harbours a range of habitats very similar to those of Cabañeros (see p. 298), but with greatly improved freelance access. From Puerto Pulido (850 m) on the N-420, the flat expanses of the valley-bottom grasslands of Alcudia – partially covered by mature western holm oak *dehesa* – unfold majestically at your feet, with closer views provided by the CM-4202 which runs west to Bienvenida.

The winter destination of the cattle that formerly trekked south along the Real Soriana and Real Segoviana drover's roads every autumn (today they arrive by train!), these rolling pastures harbour healthy breeding populations of Montagu's harrier, stone curlew and little bustard, as well as a few great bustards and both black-bellied and pin-tailed sandgrouse. Lesser kestrel, roller, calandra and short-toed larks, black-eared wheatear, southern grey shrike and corn bunting frequent open areas, while the *dehesas* typically support black-winged kite and azure-winged magpie all year round, woodchat shrike in summer, and merlin, lapwing and 50+ cranes in winter.

To the south, Alcudia is hemmed in by a parallel series of wooded, siliceous ridges which, albeit modest in height (Bañuela, 1323 m, is the highest peak in the whole of the Sierra Morena), are still high enough to trap humid air masses emanating from the distant Atlantic. North-facing slopes show a theoretical altitudinal zonation from western holm oak (to around 700–800 m), through cork oak (to around 900 m) and then Pyrenean oak, although many *umbrías* have been partially cleared and nowadays are clothed with mature strawberry-trees and just a few isolated stands of cork oak, Montpellier maple and turpentine tree. The secondary scrub consists of tree and Spanish heaths, ling and *Erica umbellata*, enlivened by the yellow blooms of *Chamaespartium tridentatum*, *Halimium ocymoides* and *H. halimifolium* and the white flowers of *H. umbellatum* subspecies *viscosum*.

The chained-off road leading west from the Puerto de Niefla (902 m; again on the N-420) to the radio masts on Chorreras (1095 m) is a good example of a cleared

Halimium halimifolium (T.F.)

umbría. Gum and poplar-leaved cistuses flank the road, while rocky outcrops house Irish and maidenhair spleenworts, *Asplenium billotii*, *Dianthus lusitanus*, the Iberian endemic *D. toletanus*, *Digitalis thapsi* and dwarf sheep's-bit (subspecies *mariana*, unique to the Sierra Morena and Montes de Toledo). Bird-wise, look out for alpine swift, crag martin, Dartford and sub-alpine warblers and rock bunting, while griffon vultures float overhead, as often as not accompanied by one of the local black or Egyptian vultures, or any of the five species of eagle which breed around the valley.

A better-preserved *umbría* is that of Puerto Viejo (about 8 km south of the Puerto de Niefla, take a track leading west through a group of mature Lusitanian oaks surrounding a small chapel), where Pyrenean oak dominates but is accompanied by more northerly elements such as whitebeam, true service-tree and wild cherry; typical birds here include robin, Bonelli's warbler, nuthatch and short-toed treecreeper. Western peonies and perfoliate alexanders are common in the understorey, with the March-flowering *Narcissus muñozii-garmendiae* – endemic to the Sierra Morena in southern Ciudad Real – occurring sporadically.

Two other habitats worth exploring are the peatbogs along the Río Montoro valley, which harbour cross-leaved heath, bog-myrtle, round-leaved sundew and pale butterwort; and the summit communities, for example, that of Bañuela, which sports prickly cushions of *Echinospartum ibericum* (in Fuencaliente ask for directions to 'Camino del Ejeño').

In terms of the large mammals, a few pardel lynx still roam the forests to the south of the valley, as do other carnivores – notably wildcat, common genet and Egyptian mongoose – and plenty of red and roe deer and wild boar, the main prey of big-game hunters, also locally abundant. Schreiber's, grey long-eared and serotine bats have been detected in the area. The rivers still hold good populations of otter; try along the unfenced banks of the Río Montoro 21 km southeast of Mestanza, heading west from

Pardel lynx *Lynx pardina*

the bridge. Here you might also encounter European pond and stripe-necked terrapins, black stork, red-rumped swallow, blue rock thrush, black wheatear and Spanish and rock sparrows.

The waters of the Montoro are the domain of many Iberian endemic fish, notably cacho, pardilla, Iberian nase, *Barbus microcephalus* and jarabugo, while sharp-ribbed salamander and Bosca's newt are common in pools along the tributary streams. Reptiles on the surrounding sunny slopes include spiny-footed and ocellated lizards, large and Spanish psammodromus, horseshoe whip,

false smooth and Montpellier snakes and Lataste's viper.

The extra humidity provided by altitude provides for a considerable diversity of butterflies in the montane areas of Alcudia. Of special interest are isolated nuclei of southern white admiral, purple-shot and sooty coppers and Amanda's blue, while more widespread species on the wing throughout much of Alcudia include marbled skipper, Spanish festoon, Cleopatra, sooty and Moroccan orange tips, two-tailed pasha, large tortoiseshell, high brown and twin-spot fritillaries, western and Spanish marbled whites, oriental meadow brown, southern and Spanish gatekeepers and Provence and Spanish purple hairstreaks.

> *Information*: The Centro de Desarrollo Rural del Valle de Alcudia in Almodóvar del Campo (7 km west of Puertollano) has information on footpaths and the area's many cave paintings (tel: 926 483400).

Also in the area

Sierra de Andújar (*parque natural*; 73 976 ha) Head south from Mestanza until you reach the Collado de Hontanar, on the Andalucían border, then enter the park. Home to around 100 pardel lynx, the last remaining viable population in the world of this endangered feline. The endless tracts of scrub and *dehesa* also harbour some of the last Andalucían wolves, as well as Spanish imperial eagle and black vulture. The information centre is at Viñas de Peña Plana (tel: 953 012400; fax: 953 272191; e-mail: PN.SAndujar@ cma. junta-andalucia.es).

SITE 109 Tablas de Daimiel

One of the most valuable inland wetlands in the Iberian peninsula, home to important populations of breeding waterbirds and attracting many migrants.

Back in the 1980s, it was said that the Tablas de Daimiel had more history than future. The shallow, wildfowl-rich waters of this *par-* *que nacional* (1928 ha, encompassing a *reserva integral* of 318 ha, plus a buffer zone of 5419 ha; also a Ramsar Site and ZEPA) had

Tablas de Daimiel

provided centuries of hunting for Spanish kings and dictators, but in 1986 – for the first time ever – the springs nourishing the park dried up, leaving its raised boardwalks embarrassingly high and dry. Although the root of the problem – the over-exploitation of the huge underground freshwater reservoir known as Aquifer 23 – has only subsequently been partially remedied, water diverted from the Tajo–Segura canal and a series of wetter winters have together enabled the Tablas de Daimiel to recover some of their former splendour.

Around 40 years ago, the Tablas de Daimiel covered 150 square kilometres and were the largest of the many *tablas* (mid-course floodplains of the rivers of the southern Meseta) that were once such a feature of La Mancha. Today, at best, the *tablas* cover just 20 square kilometres, since little water now enters from either of the twin mother rivers: the brackish Cigüela (Gigüela) and the fresh Guadiana. Western Europe's largest expanses of great fen-sedge once covered much of the area, but diminishing water lev-

els have allowed the invasion of common reed and *Typha domingensis*, while seasonally flooded areas are being colonised by black bog-rush, sea rush and sea club-rush.

Today species diversity among the hydrophytes is poor – the yellow and white water-lilies having disappeared along with the fresh water from the Guadiana – although charophytes and water-crowfoots are still well represented. The flora of the brackish waters of the Cigüela is largely limited to beaked tasselweed, while salt-tolerant communities are composed of *Suaeda fruticosa* and *Salsola vermiculata*, along with clumps of the sea-lavender *Limonium longebracteatum*, unique to the saline lagoons of La Mancha, and thick stands of tamarisks.

Nevertheless, Daimiel is still a very important wetland for birds. In 1996 the purple heron colony re-established itself, while bittern, squacco heron (for the first time ever), white-headed duck, purple gallinule and over a thousand pairs of red-crested pochard also bred. Other breeders in 2000 included night heron (65+ pairs), little bittern (8–10 pairs), marsh harrier (9–10 pairs), collared pratincole (24+ pairs), whiskered tern (8–10 pairs), bearded tit, Savi's and great reed warblers and reed bunting. Look out, too, for black-winged stilts (85–90 pairs) in areas of shallow water, penduline tits in the tamarisks and black-necked and great-crested grebes in the deeper reaches of the *tablas*.

Daimiel is also well positioned to receive cross-peninsula passage migrants, many en route between northern Europe and Extremadura or Doñana. Greylag goose, glossy ibis, black stork, crane (1400 wintered in 2000) and waders such as avocet, ruff, black-winged godwit and greenshank are some of the most obvious autumn migrants, a prelude to the wintering duck – mainly red-crested pochard (5365 birds in 1996), pintail, teal, shoveler, mallard and wigeon – that start to arrive in October.

Other aquatic vertebrates have also been badly affected by the receding water levels and recent (1997) pollution episodes. Just a handful of otters frequent the park today, while the number of fish species present has dropped from 16 in 1956 to just 5 in 1997, the most abundant today being common carp and eastern mosquitofish, both introduced. Amphibians have likewise suffered, although good populations of common tree, stripeless tree and Iberian pool frogs still occur, plus lesser numbers of midwife toad and Iberian painted frog. Rather surprisingly, European pond and stripe-necked terrapins maintain healthy populations, as do both 'water' snakes: grass and viperine. On dry land, keep an eye out for three-toed skink, Iberian wall and ocellated lizards and ladder and Montpellier snakes. Despite representing an ideal habitat for odonates, few studies have been carried out in the Tablas de Daimiel, with published records limited to the observation of Mediterranean hawker, emperor and vagrant emperor dragonflies and scarlet darter on a single day in September.

Access and information: Various itineraries head out from the interpretation centre, open every day until dusk and signposted northwest off the N-340 Daimiel ring-road (tel: 926 693118); more information available from the park offices (tel: 926 851097; fax: 926 851176; e-mail: daimiel@mma.es). In the town of Daimiel itself, the Centro de Interpretación del Agua (tel: 926 260633) provides an alternative view of the ecology of the area.

Also in the area

Campo de Calatava Area of undulating dry farmland south-southeast of Ciudad Real, declared a ZEPA (6545 ha) for its breeding populations of lesser kestrel, great and little bustards, stone curlew and pin-tailed sandgrouse. Also remarkable for its 100+ volcanos exhibiting many different types of vulcanism: crater lakes, lava flows and pyroclastic, lava and gassy volcanic cones.

Puerto de los Santos (970 m) The minor road (CM-4169) north of Daimiel linking Villarrubia de los Ojos and Urda crosses western holm and Lusitanian oak woodland with an interesting selection of butterflies: Spanish festoon, Moroccan orange tip, Glanville and twin-spot fritillaries, western and Spanish marbled whites, tree grayling, oriental meadow brown and Mediterranean skipper.

SITE
110 La Mancha Húmeda

A complex of semi-endorheic lagoons (a ZEPA of 11 520 ha) harbouring the best range of aquatic birds in central Spain.

The Biosphere Reserve of La Mancha Húmeda (25 000 ha) encompasses three types of wetland: *tablas* (see Daimiel; p. 303), karstic lakes (see Ruidera; p. 308) and the shallow endorheic basins to the north and east of Alcázar de San Juan that we are concerned with here. All three serve to break the monotony of kilometre after kilometre of vineyards which dominates the treeless plains of La Mancha (from the Arab *ma'ancha* or 'dry land'), and are essential feeding stations for tens of thousands of cross-peninsula migrants, also providing safe refuge for wintering and breeding waterbirds.

Although inherent differences between the various endorheic lagoons were once very noticeable, today – as natural inputs dry up and are replaced by treated sewage water – these waterbodies are losing their individuality. Halophytic plant communities have suffered badly, although many lagoons have gained in depth and permanence, with a consequent spectacular growth in reedbeds and macrophyte communities which has benefited birds such as black-necked grebe, white-headed duck and bearded tit.

In no one lagoon will you see all that La Mancha Húmeda has to offer, and the following itinerary takes you around the most diverse and accessible sites.

Begin in the north at the shallow Laguna de Lillo, to the west of the CM-3001, which typically holds pintail in winter, crane on passage and breeding shelduck, Kentish plover, avocet and gull-billed tern. Also notable is the well-preserved albardine steppe that separates the lagoon from the village, home to breeding stone curlew,

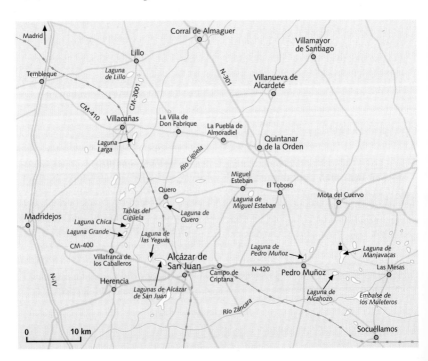

Collared pratincole *Glareola pratincola*
(Peter Wilson)

skylark and calandra, short-toed and, it is said, Dupont's larks.

Further south lies the Laguna Larga, accessed from the Villacañas ring-road (CM-410) along a track next to a *punto blanco* recycling point. Esparvel – the local conservation group – has built a number of hides around the lagoon, which give excellent views of the breeding collared pratincoles and the as-yet unsuccessful nesting attempts of greater flamingos.

Next stop is the Laguna de Miguel Esteban, a SEO/BirdLife reserve signposted south off the CM-3162 east of Miguel Esteban, which has received an artificial kiss-of-life from treated wastewater. Close-up views of black-necked grebe, white-headed duck and red-crested pochard are almost guaranteed from the hides in spring. Black-winged stilt, lapwing and whiskered tern nest, while pintailed sandgrouse regularly come to drink in the morning, either around the main lagoon or in the flooded area to the south, which is also excellent for waders in spring (little stint, ruff, spotted redshank and wood sandpiper, for example).

From Miguel Esteban, head west on the CM-3158 to the hyper-saline but rather disturbed Laguna de Quero (breeding Kentish plover) and then on towards Villafranca de los Caballeros, passing through the Tablas del Cigüela, these days rarely flooded and so

a good area for lesser kestrel, Spanish sparrow and steppe birds, including great bustard to the east of the road.

Just before Villafranca, the interconnected Lagunas Grande y Chica de Villafranca are visible to the west. The extensive reedbeds of the Laguna Chica support breeding purple heron, little bittern, marsh harrier, Savi's, reed, great reed and Cetti's warblers and bearded tit. Whiskered and gull-billed terns (the latter feeding on the introduced crayfish *Procambarus clarkii*) usually breed, while the deeper waters also provide for great crested grebe and osprey on passage. The Villafranca complex is home to a few otters, while parsley frogs are particularly well adapted to the poorly vegetated, often saline environments of many of these lagoons, but non-avian vertebrate communities are generally unexceptional.

From Villafranca de los Caballeros, head east along the CM-400, from which the Lagunas de Alcázar de San Juan (Ramsar Site, 240 ha) are visible to the north. This complex (also known as the Lagunas del Camino de Villafranca) harbours a large gull-billed tern colony and well-developed halophytic vegetation (purple glasswort, saltwort, *Suaeda spicata* and *S. splendens*) in the hyper-saline Laguna de las Yeguas at the western end of the group.

The Laguna de Pedro Muñoz (Ramsar Site, 34 ha; also called Laguna de la Vega o del Pueblo), 200 m north of the town of the same name, has 'evolved' from endorheic and saline to permanent and eutrophic and as such exemplifies the fate of many of the lagoons in the area: common reed and sea club-rush have spread to the detriment of purple glasswort and cressa. A track along the eastern shore provides excellent views of breeding black-necked grebe, white-headed duck, gadwall, little ringed plover and whiskered tern. Spanish sparrows winter around the lagoon, white-winged black tern are regular in spring and many waders frequent the shallower northern sector on passage.

From Pedro Muñoz, take the road towards Las Mesas (off the N-420 just east of the town), passing the hyper-saline Laguna de Alcahozo on the right, ringed by belts of

Extremadura and Castilla–La Mancha

purple glasswort, the sea-blight *Suaeda spicata* and formations of Borrer's salt-marsh-grass with the Iberian endemic sea-lavenders *Limonium tournefortii* and *L. longebracteatum*.

Alternatively, from Pedro Muñoz head southeast towards Socuéllamos (CM-3111) and, 1 km after the bridge over the river Záncara, turn left next to a white hut down towards the Embalse de los Muleteros: a large expanse of reeds which – if flooded – can be as equally productive as any of the lagoons. The nearby poplars hold a pair of rollers and the whole area is good for little bustard (flocks in alfalfa fields in autumn), stone curlew and pin-tailed sandgrouse, while a walk along the reed-choked bed of the Záncara in winter will turn up water pipit, bluethroat, bearded and penduline tits and reed bunting.

And so finally to the Laguna de Manjavacas (Ramsar Site, 231 ha and *reserva natural*), a personal favourite and easily accessible from the minor road which links Mota del Cuervo with Las Mesas. This is one of the largest lagoons and possesses a wide range of freshwater and saline habitats where all and any of the birds already mentioned can turn up, plus stone curlew and black-eared wheatear in the surrounding vineyards.

Access and information: Unless indicated, all the lagoons are visible from roads and can be reached via tracks (very muddy at times); take care not to block farmers' access. For more information (water levels, bicycle hire and local SEO/BirdLife group), contact the ornithological guest house Salicor in Pedro Muñoz (tel: 926 586603; e-mail: salicor@yahoo.es).

---

111 Lagunas de Ruidera

A 28-km chain of unique karstic lakes with breeding red-crested pochard and marsh harrier; marginal Mediterranean habitats and crags add faunal and floral diversity.

The Lagunas de Ruidera (a *parque natural* of 3722 ha) are the product of the dissolution of the limestone strata of the surrounding Campo de Montiel by the river Guadiana, and the subsequent gradual precipitation of the dissolved carbonates to form a series of tufa barriers that dam the river, forming a chain of 15 lakes.

The three lower lakes, downstream (northwest) of the village of Ruidera, are shallow and almost completely choked by common reed, bulrush and *Typha domingensis*, while the 12 upper lakes are much deeper and generally support emergent vegetation only on their southern shores. Here the inner circle of reeds and bulrushes grades first into cordons of great fen-sedge, accompanied by *Sonchus maritimus*, grey club-rush, *Scirpus littoralis* and black bog-rush, and then gives way to stands of *Carex hispida* and round-headed club-rush, coloured by purple-loosestrife, *Lysimachia ephemerum*, blue water-speedwell and bog orchis.

Macrophytes with floating leaves include yellow water-lily, amphibious bistort, whorled water-milfoil and fennel and horned pondweeds, as well as carpets of pond and thread-leaved water-crowfoots

Lagunas de Ruidera

and common water-starwort. In the *lagunas* of Cueva Morenilla and Concejo, the insectivorous bladderwort is common. Fish include freshwater blenny and three barbels endemic to the peninsula: Iberian barbel, *Barbus bocagei* and *B. microcephalus*.

Great crested grebe, pochard, red-crested pochard and marsh harrier are the most obvious birds in and around the upper lakes, with the lower lakes better for purple gallinule (a pair nested in 1999), water rail, nightingale and Cetti's and great reed warblers, with bearded tits breeding some years. Spring passage can turn up black stork, purple and night herons, garganey, osprey, booted eagle, crakes, a few waders and common and whiskered terns. Large concentrations of hirundines pass through on both spring and autumn passage, and you can expect to see crag and house martins, swallow and red-rumped swallow hawking the lakes in summer.

Little work has been done on the dragonflies of the lakes, although there are early August records of *Platycnemis latipes*, *Ischnura graellsii*, common blue, goblet-marked and small red damselflies, lesser

emperor, southern, black-tailed and keeled skimmers, *Trithemis annulata* and – most interestingly of all – *Selysiothemis nigra*, rare on the Spanish mainland.

Amphibian communities are unexceptional, with Iberian pool frog and common and natterjack toads the only abundant species. A few otters survive here and there, stripe-necked terrapins are fairly common in the least-disturbed terminal lakes of Tomilla and Conceja, and grass and viperine snakes abound. On dry land, look out for Iberian wall, ocellated and spiny-footed lizards, large psammodromus and Montpellier and ladder snakes.

Dense patches of western holm oak woodland with an understorey enlivened by western peony and sword-leaved helleborine cling to the hillsides on the southern side of Laguna Colgada, while a few lollipop-shaped Spanish junipers stand out around Conceja and Tomilla. In general the lakes are surrounded by scrub formations of *Ephedra nebrodensis*, osyris, bladder-senna, Mediterranean mezereon, wild jasmine and *Lonicera implexa*, alternating with a stunted garrigue of holly oak, *Genista scorpius, Rhamnus lycioides, Cistus clusii* (often parasitised by *Cytinus hypocistis*) and rosemary. Additional splashes of colour are provided by beautiful flax, *Euphorbia serrata, Helianthemum cinereum, H. hirtum,* annual omphalodes, undulate anchusa, dyer's alkanet, *Salvia lavandulifolia, Phlomis herba-venti, Ornithogalum narbonense* and blue aphyllanthes.

In these drier Mediterranean habitats, look out for hoopoe, bee-eater, woodlark, Dartford and subalpine warblers, southern grey and woodchat shrikes and rock bunting, while of the larger raptors, both short-toed eagles and a solitary pair of Bonelli's eagles breed in the area and occasionally hunt around the lagoons. Scops owl and golden oriole nest in the lakeside poplars, a few azure-winged magpies hang around the rather built-up Laguna de San Pedro looking for picnic scraps, and the low cliffs have breeding eagle owl, stock dove, blue rock thrush and black wheatear.

Information and access: The park information centre is in the village of Ruidera on the N-430 Manzanares–Albacete road (tel. and fax: 926 528116; website: www.lagunasderuidera.net). A track along the southern shores provides the best access to the lakes.

Also in the area

Campo de Montiel (combined disjunct ZEPAs of 27 283 ha) A huge area of low-intensity cereal cultivation, western holm oak thickets, almond groves and stony plains with good populations of Montagu's harrier, around 150 great bustards, stone curlew, black-bellied sandgrouse and roller; post-breeding dispersal area for Spanish imperial eagle. Try the road from El Bonillo to Villanueva de la Fuente via Viveros. Winter visitors will find stony uncultivated areas carpeted with the delightful *Iris planifolia*.

---

112 Calar del Mundo

A dramatic karst landscape concealing one of the peninsula's most spectacular waterfalls and a fascinating high-level Mediterranean limestone flora.

Crowds or otherwise, Los Chorros – a waterfall 80 m high bursting from a sheer 200 m cliff – is not to be missed. Few of the many visitors, however, realise that hidden away high above the cascade (otherwise known as El Nacimiento del Río Mundo) is the heavily karstified plateau of El Calar del Mundo, plant-wise one the richest areas in the peninsula, harbouring no less than 51 Iberian endemic taxa.

The short walk from the car park takes you up to the base of the main waterfall, from where two narrow paths approach smoothly rounded tufa deposits to the right of the

Echium boissieri

nuthatches, short-toed treecreepers and crossbills. Be alert, too, for griffon vulture, golden eagle, goshawk, crag martin and chough around the high cliffs, while Egyptian vulture, Bonelli's and booted eagles and alpine swift are all possible where the valley opens out somewhat.

The quietest sections of the river support otter and stripe-necked terrapin, with wild-cats plentiful throughout, although most of the Spanish ibex, red deer and mouflon keep to the higher crags; the Iberian endemic Cabrera's vole is typically found in damp meadows here. Among the herptiles you are most likely to come across ocellated and Iberian wall lizards and large psammodromus, as well as strong populations of fire salamander, Iberian pool frog and natterjack and common toads. Most notable, however, are the Spanish algyroides and the diminutive midwife toad *Alytes dickhilleni*, both confined to southeastern Spain.

Recent work on the butterflies along the upper course of the Mundo has revealed a previously unsuspected diversity. As an example, 29 species of lycaenid have been recorded here, including Oberthür's anomalous, Amanda's, Chapman's, Escher's, mother-of-pearl, Carswell's little and green- underside blues. The peak period to visit is late June or early July, although April sees Provence hair-streak, false Baton, Chapman's, Panoptes and African grass blues on the wing, while August is good for satyrids such as south-ern gatekeeper and rock grayling.

The bare, windswept and sometimes even snow-covered plateau of El Calar, which exceeds 1600 m in places, is carpeted with common juniper (subspecies *hemisphaerica*) and spiny cushions of hedgehog broom and *Echinospartum boissieri*, the latter endemic to the Sierras Béticas, interspersed with clumps of imbricate sandwort, *Convolvulus boissieri* and the nodding bells of *Fritillaria lusitanica*. Summit communi-ties are accompanied by *Arenaria armerina*, *Cerastium boissieri*, *Genista pseudopilosa*, *Lonicera arborea*, *Jurinea humilis*, Pyrenean hawk's-beard and a large contingent of labi-ates: *Thymus orospedanus*, *T. granatensis*,

main amphitheatre that are studded with clumps of the butterwort *Pinguicula vallis-neriifolia* (tentatively separated recently as *P. mundi*). The tufa also harbours maiden-hair fern, lax potentilla, *Hypericum tomento-sum* and *Campanula velutina* subspecies *velutina*, while drier parts of the main cliff support sweet violet, *Jasione foliosa* sub-species *minuta* and round-headed rampion, as well as the southeast Iberian endemics *Linaria lilacina* and *Globularia spinosa*.

Alternatively, approach Los Chorros on a track along the right bank of the river Mundo (starting from the CM-3204 just south of the CM-412), thereby getting a good view of the region's splendid mixed pine forests: Aleppo, maritime and *Pinus nigra* subspecies *salz-mannii*. Look out, too, for the 2 m-high, salmon pink-flowered *Echium boissieri* on roadside verges around Riópar. Up towards Los Chorros, stately Lusitanian oaks mix in with the pines, accompanied by *Berberis his-panica*, western peony, wild service-tree, *Acer granatense*, holly and spurge-laurel.

Throughout the whole upper valley of the Río Mundo, from Los Chorros as far as the cliff-top village of Liétor, the pines are alive with firecrests, crested tits,

Sideritis incana, felty germander (sub-species *aureum*) and *Satureja cuneifolia* subspecies *obovata*. This is also a good place to track down some of the Iberian endemic taxa for which the area is renowned, notably *Moehringia intricata*, *Pterocephalus spathulatus*, *Scorzonera albicans* and *Centaurea boissieri*.

Access: Los Chorros is well signposted off the CM-412, 1 km east of Fábricas de Riópar. The lower reaches of the Río Mundo further east are accessible from the minor road passing through La Alfera. Access to El Calar is more complex; beware caves, sinkholes and the possibility of low clouds. One possible route heads south along a path marked 'Cañada de los Mojones' from the Puerto del Arenal (1180 m) on the CM-3204, 1 km beyond the turn-off to Los Chorros.

Also in the area

Sierra de Alcaraz Holds many similar species to El Calar, plus *Saxifraga camposii* on the high peaks. Butterflies (100+ species) include Osiris, Amanda's, mother-of-pearl and Andalusian anomalous blues. Access is more straightforward, however. A track runs southwest from Puerto del Barrancazo on the CM-3216 and skirts the northern base of Almenaras (1798 m) or, from the same place, take the drover's road which, remarkably, follows the summit of the whole ridge. Alternatively, 4 km further east, at the junction of the road to Paterna del Madera, another good track heads southwest to Fuente del Pino de los Muchachos (8 km), at the base of the southern flank of Almenaras; from here a path leads to the summit.

113 Laguna de Pétrola
SITE

The most important wetland in Albacete, harbouring a successful breeding colony of greater flamingo.

Pétrola is one of the few endorheic lagoons in Castilla–La Mancha that is not being totally swamped by treated wastewater, such that the hyper-saline conditions required by greater flamingos have remained largely intact. The lagoon – 1.5 km across and with an average depth of only 0.5 m – is large enough for human disturbance to be kept to a minimum, while water levels have been ideal in recent years: neither too high to

Greater flamingo *Phoenicopterus ruber*

Shoveler *Anas clypeata*

flood their nests, nor too low to permit access to predatory mammals.

In the last 30 years, the greater flamingo has successfully bred in just six sites in the Iberian peninsula, the most recent colonisation occurring at Pétrola in 1998. The first young did not fly, however, until 1999, when around 70 fledged, followed by 170 more in 2000. Shelduck also nest here, preferring – like the flamingos – the more saline areas of the lagoon furthest from the village of Pétrola. More freshwater reaches are ideal for wintering duck (up to 5000 individuals in some years) – red-crested pochard, shoveler, teal, wigeon and pintail – as well as for breeding white-headed duck (since 1998); marbled teal are also observed sporadically, having bred once in 1998.

Good numbers of avocet, black-winged stilt, lapwing and Kentish plover also breed at Pétrola, as well as colonies of black-headed gull and gull-billed tern, and the odd pair of marsh harriers. Great reed and Cetti's warblers nest in the rather thin reedbeds, while the fields and orchards around the lagoon hold great spotted cuckoo, crested lark, black-eared wheatear and corn bunting. Passage, best in late April and September, brings a plethora of additional species: above all expect ruff and *Tringa* and *Calidris* waders, plus a smattering of herons and terns.

Pétrola is set in an area of rolling cereal pseudosteppes which harbour reasonable populations of both bustards, stone curlew and both sandgrouse. The tracks heading southeast off the CM-3211 between Pétrola and Las Anorias are worth a try, while further northeast, great bustards can be seen east of the CM-3209 between Bonete and the abandoned Estación de Bonete.

Access and information: The lagoon can be easily explored along tracks heading north off the CM-3255 just west of Pétrola. For more information, contact the Sociedad Albacetense de Ornitología, Apartado de Correos 18, 02080 Albacete.

Also in the area

Saladar de Cordovilla Although unprotected, considered floristically to be the best inland *saladar* (salt-steppe) in the peninsula, the botanical star being the small *Helianthemum polygonoides*, endemic to the Tobarra–Cordovilla area, which flowers in June and July. Other plants include cynomorium, *Arthrocnemum macrostachyum, Microcnemum coralloides, Limonium caesium* and *L. cossonianum* and the viper's-grass *Scorzonera parviflora*. The Saladar lies about 1 km due south of the village of Cordovilla (on the CM-412 Hellín–Almansa road).

SITE 114 Hoces del Cabriel

A long chain of limestone defiles on the Albacete–València border, home to one of the highest breeding densities of Bonelli's and golden eagles in eastern Spain.

South of the huge Embalse de Contreras, the river Cabriel begins an extraordinary meandering journey through a 60 km stretch of limestone *hoces* (gorges), whose northern entrance is presided over by a group of stunning 200 m-high limestone pinnacles known as Los Cuchillos (literally 'the knives'). An easy 3 km walk south from the reception centre of the Reserva Natural de las Hoces del Cabriel (1662 ha; also part of a ZEPA of 56 136 ha) along the right bank of the Cabriel takes you through much of the best habitat and right up to the base of the Los Cuchillos themselves, although access beyond this point is forbidden.

Dipper *Cinclus cinclus* **at nest with chicks (Robert Dickson)**

Upstream of Los Cuchillos, the gradually narrowing valley of the Cabriel is covered by Aleppo pine woodland, alternating with almond and olive groves and a splendidly diverse jungle of Phoenician juniper, osyris, lentisc, turpentine tree, box, Mediterranean buckthorn, Mediterranean mezereon, strawberry-tree, *Erica multiflora*, wild jasmine, laurustinus and Etruscan honeysuckle. More open waysides harbour a xerophytic scrub of sturdy bushes of joint pine, *Dorycnium pentaphyllum*, shrubby scorpion-vetch, grey-leaved cistus, *Cistus clusii* and shrubby globularia. The most degraded areas are covered by communities of false esparto

Black wheatear *Oenanthe leucura*

and Mediterranean false-brome, harbouring an abundance of fragrant labiates such as *Thymus vulgaris*, winter savory and *Lavandula latifolia*, plus attractive clumps of white flax and *Helianthemum cinereum*.

Once at the base of Los Cuchillos, stop to consider the erosive history of the site: a period of severe uplift folded a series of horizontally stratified deposits – limestones alternating with softer clays and marls – into an inverted U-shape and, once the 'cap' had been eroded away, weathering then made short shrift of the softer intermediate strata and exposed the limestone pinnacles which today tower over the river Cabriel. Phoenician junipers and a few western holm oaks spring from the bare limestone, accompanied by the glandular-hairy *Asplenium petrarchae*, maidenhair fern, sarcocapnos, *Saxifraga latepetiolata*, endemic to eastern Spain, *Globularia repens* and *Jasione foliosa*.

These cliffs (and others which line the river) provide a wealth of niches for cliff-nesting raptors such as golden and Bonelli's eagles, peregrine and eagle owl, as well as for alpine swift, crag martin, rock thrush, raven and chough. Booted and short-toed eagles and goshawk breed in the pine forests, along with Bonelli's warbler, firecrest, crested tit, short-toed treecreeper and crossbill, while black wheatear, black redstart and blue rock thrush frequent the many sunny, boulder-strewn slopes.

As the Cabriel often all but dries up in summer, the gallery woodland is not particularly well developed: a few stands of black and white poplars, *Salix elaeagnos* subspecies *angustifolia*, *S. atrocinerea*, purple willow, tamarisk and narrow-leaved ash. Golden orioles are particularly abundant here, although birds such as kingfisher, dipper, grey wagtail and Cetti's warbler, as well as the few otters that still frequent the river, are all suffering from the retention of water upstream by the Contreras dam. Other vertebrates linked to humid habitats here include natterjack and midwife toads, Iberian painted and common tree frogs, stripe-necked terrapin and viperine snake, while drier habitats away from the river are home to Moorish gecko, both large and Spanish psammodromus, ocellated lizard and Lataste's viper.

Wildcats are especially common in the *hoces*, accompanied by Eurasian badger, beech marten, common genet and wild boar. Spanish ibex are very confiding and you might just get a glimpse of a mouflon, introduced as a game species. Spring butterflies are abundant – look out for wood white, Moroccan orange tip, Cleopatra and black-eyed blue, among others – although no full survey has ever been carried out and surprises are sure to turn up.

Access and information: Las Hoces are signposted south off the *old* and now practically deserted N-III just to the west of the Contreras reservoir. Wind down the hairpin bends past the Venta de Contreras and the campsite and, as you approach the river Cabriel, turn right down a narrow road which takes you to the reserve information centre (1.5 km). Only 100 people per day are permitted to walk to Los Cuchillos; phone 969 178300 to guarantee a place. This said, same-day permits can almost always be obtained from 10.00 am onwards at the information centre, as the limit is only ever reached on summer weekends and public holidays. More information from the Requena–Utiel branch of SEO/BirdLife (e-mail: svorequeutiel@yahoo.es).

SITE 115 Serranía de Cuenca

A vast, predominantly limestone, pine-clad upland boasting a superb flora and an incredibly diverse assemblage of butterflies.

It is hard, if not impossible, to define the Serranía de Cuenca exactly (a ZEPA of 128 345 ha). Some claim that its essence lies in its vast, uninterrupted pine forests, while others opt for the fabulous erosive processes on both 'macro' and 'micro' scales, which have sliced the massif into a landscape beloved of cliff-breeding raptors, fissure plants and day-trippers alike.

On the 'macro' scale, the two major landscape features of the Serranía are the high limestone plateaux – known as *parameras* and *muelas* – and the river gorges that separate them. *Parameras*, such as the evocatively named Paramera de Tierra Muerta ('Dead Land') south of Uña, form on Jurassic limestone and are distinguished by their poor soils, a complete absence of surface water and sparse forests composed mainly of Spanish juniper, with an understorey of common juniper (subspecies *hemisphaerica*) and *Genista scorpius*, decorated by

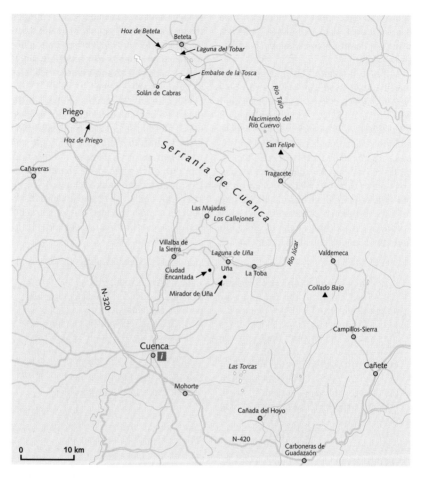

clumps of proliferous pink, beautiful flax, *Armeria alliacea*, *Phlomis lychnitis* and *Lavandula latifolia*.

Muelas, on the other hand, form on the Cretaceous limestone, have slightly better-developed soils and tend to be pine-clad. Overgrazing, however, has impoverished the understorey, leaving sparse formations composed of laurel-leaved cistus at lower levels, replaced by common juniper, barberry, *Genista scorpius*, holly and box with altitude. The impressive Muela de San Felipe (1839 m) harbours *Arenaria aggregata*, grass-leaved buttercup, *Thalictrum tuberosum*, *Saxifraga carpetana*, chalk milkwort, *Armeria trachyphylla* (endemic to south-eastern Spain) and silvery-leaved pink convolvulus, as well as a number of species which have a definite northern feel about them: globeflower, monk's-hood, bird's-eye primrose and cross gentian.

Pine woodland throughout most of the area holds long-eared owl, nightjar, great spotted woodpecker, Bonelli's warbler, firecrest, crested tit, short-toed treecreeper, citril finch and crossbill, as well as goshawk (principal food ocellated lizards, red squirrels and jays) and sparrowhawk. Garden dormouse, Eurasian badger, beech marten, wildcat and common genet are widespread, while micromammals include house and wood mice, greater white-toothed shrew and Mediterranean pine vole; large ungulates are represented by wild boar, Spanish ibex, a few introduced mouflon and red and roe deer.

Separating the high plateaux are the typical gorges or *hoces* of limestone regions, resplendent with a diversity of deciduous trees and shrubs that the higher pine forests lack. A good starting place is the Hoz de Beteta, where a botanical trail winds between sturdy pines (*Pinus nigra* subspecies *salzmannii*), yews and large-leaved limes up to the cliff-face, giving access to camera-height clumps of sarcocapnos, lax potentilla, the pale yellow flowers of rock snapdragon (subspecies *pulverulentum*, endemic to the southeastern quadrant of the peninsula) and *Globularia repens* (subspecies *borjae*). Other fissure plants here include smooth rock spleenwort, wall-rue, *Draba dedeana* subspecies *zapaterii*, in flower by mid-March, dwarf buckthorn and the locally endemic bellflower *Campanula betetae*.

The nearby Hoz de Priego is much broader, with roadside verges full of grey-leaved cistus and shrubby scorpion-vetch, plus Cetti's warblers and nightingales singing from the riverbanks. All the area's cliff-nesting diurnal raptors breed here – griffon (250 pairs; all figures for the whole area) and Egyptian vultures (20 pairs), golden (35

pairs) and Bonelli's eagles (11 pairs) and peregrine – sharing air-space with alpine swift, crag martin, raven and chough.

A good example of erosion on a 'micro' level is the Ciudad Encantada, where the extreme erosion of a network of faults crisscrossing the flat surface of a *muela* has produced a labyrinth of deep intersecting gullies of varying width. The fissure vegetation bears certain similarities to that of Beteta, with the addition of an abundance of the hairy-leaved *Saxifraga latepetiolata* in the shadiest corners; ferns include rustyback, hart's-tongue, maidenhair spleenwort and *Asplenium seelosii*. An alternative karstified 'city' at Los Callejones de las Majadas to the north is much less visited and not quite so dramatic, but does harbour the attractive *Arenaria vitoriana*, which has a disjunct distribution in limestone mountains in eastern Spain.

Other 'micro' erosive features include the lagoon complexes that have formed in the *torcas*: deep, vertical-sided dolines which are either dry – with yew, wych elm, St Lucie's cherry and Montpellier maple growing out of the sheer flanks – or are filled with sparkling water if the bottom of the *torca* comes into

Laguna del Tobar (M.L.)

contact with the aquifer. Amphibians here and elsewhere in the Serranía include sharp-ribbed salamander, marbled newt, common tree and Iberian pool frogs, Iberian painted frog and western spadefoot, while a recent study of the area's reptiles came up with the following list: Bedriaga's skink, ocellated lizard, southern smooth, ladder, Montpellier, grass and viperine snakes and Lataste's viper, plus smooth snake at the southern edge of its range.

The Serranía is one of the most renowned European sites for butterflies and moths; essentially Atlantic species such as large blue reach their southern limit here, and it is also one of the strongholds of the Spanish moon moth. The Ciudad Encantada, for example, has spring ringlet on the wing by April and Zapater's ringlet in July and August. Nearby Uña is renowned for its isolated population of sandy grizzled skipper – far from its main range in the Balkans and Turkey – on the wing in late summer, plus geranium argus in June and July. The Serranía is also a good place to get to grips with the differences between Esper's, Spanish, western and Iberian marbled whites, marsh and Spanish fritillaries, or Oberthür's anomalous, Ripart's anomalous, Escher's, Chapman's, Amanda's and mother-of-pearl blues.

For a completely different flora head southeast to the red sandstones and con-

Limestone 'sculpture', Ciudad Encantada

glomerates of Collado Bajo (1833 m), south-west of the village of Valdemeca. The maritime pine – native here – comes into its own, while more degraded areas are covered by typical Mediterranean montane calcifuge communities of Spanish and tree heaths and bell heather, interspersed with acid pastures of mat-grass. Some of the deeper, moister gullies contain stands of pedunculate oak, silver birch (subspecies *fontqueri*) and aspen, as well as herb-Paris.

The list of additional sites of wildlife interest in the Serranía is virtually endless, with notable highlights being the waterfalls and tufa formations of the Nacimiento del Río Cuervo, the Mirador de Uña – a stunning viewpoint opposite the Ciudad Encantada looking down to the Laguna de Uña and Hoz del Júcar – and the peaceful Laguna del Tobar south of Beteta, surrounded by commercial osier beds. Others include the gorge leading to the Embalse de la Tosca, east of the Solan de Cabras spa, the Spanish juniper *dehesa* at Campillos Sierra, south of Valdemeca, and the historic walled city of Cuenca itself (a World Heritage Site).

Access and information: The botanical walk along the Hoz de Beteta is signposted 'Fuente de los Tilos' and is located at km 46 on the CM-210 between Beteta and Vadillos; the Hoz de Priego lies 16 km southwest on the same road. Los Callejones de Las Majadas are 2.6 km southeast of Las Majadas along the narrow road to Uña. The best *torcas* are southeast of Cuenca near the villages of Mohorte and Cañada del Hoyo. For general information, try the Cuenca tourist office (tel: 969 232119).

Also in the area

Sierra de Albarracín A pine-clad upland similar to the Serranía, lying over the border in Aragón. Equally renowned for its butterflies, the type specimens of Zapater's ringlet, Oberthür's anomalous blue and the very turquoise-blue *caelestissima* race of the chalk-hill blue (sometimes considered a separate species) are all from this area.

Pinares de Rodeno (*paisaje protegido*; 3335 ha) Southwest of the town of Albarracín; comprises a large expanse of maritime and Scots pines on sandstones, plus numerous Palaeolithic cave paintings, including schematic representations of human figures, bulls and other animals.

The Río Tajo rises in the north of the Serranía and arcs westwards in a long gorge within the **Parque Natural del Alto Tajo** (32 375 ha, also a ZEPA of 125 998 ha). Many similar species to the Serranía, but with excellent opportunities to observe griffon and Egyptian vultures and Bonelli's and golden eagles from Puente de San Pedro, near the confluence of the rivers Tajo and Gallo, on the CM-2015 between Zaorejas and Torrecilla del Pinar.

SITE
116 Barranco del Dulce

Highly scenic limestone ravines carved out by the Río Dulce, home to important cliff-breeding bird communities and a rich calcicolous flora.

The chain of small defiles excavated by the Río Dulce (a ZEPA of 6361 ha) is a somewhat unexpected landscape feature, given the ironing-board flatness of the surrounding *páramos*. From the Mirador Félix Rodríguez de la Fuente, at the eastern end of the most spectacular ravine, the soft, fluting whistle of the golden oriole drifts up from the verdant gallery forest below, in absolute contrast with the sun-scorched plateau all around. Around the viewpoint the vegetation is dominated by Spanish juniper, gnarled western holm oaks, *Genista scorpius*, hedgehog broom, white flax (subspecies *apressum*), rock-roses galore, particularly white and hoary, *Lavandula latifolia*, *Thymus mastigophorus*, endemic to central Spain, *Artemisia pedemontana* and blue aphyllanthes.

The gorge itself is best accessed (on foot only) from nearby Pelegrina; on approaching the village, take the first left turn after the tarmac ends and follow the track upstream –

back towards the viewpoint – at river level. The gallery forest here is a curious mixture of planted – hybrid poplars, wild cherry, apple and walnut – and wild trees, the latter including white, crack and purple willows, *Salix atrocinerea*, black and white poplars, small-leaved elm and narrow-leaved ash; look out for large white helleborine and star-of-Bethlehem here early in the year. Along the margins of the river itself grow fool's-water-cress and blue water-speedwell, while submerged plants include spiked water-milfoil and opposite-leaved pondweed.

Away from the river, shady slopes support a few Lusitanian oaks and Montpellier maples, sheltering a dense tangle of St Lucie's cherry, snowy mespilus, sweet-briar, laurel-leaved cistus, dogwood, wild privet, guelder-rose and Etruscan honeysuckle, while trees are almost absent from south-facing inclines. The sun-baked rock instead supports a stunted scrub of Phoenician juniper, western

Blue aphyllanthes *Aphyllanthes monspeliensis*

holm oak, turpentine tree, Mediterranean buckthorn, *Rhamnus lycioides*, grey-leaved cistus and wild jasmine. The sheer walls of the gorge proper harbour a delightful assemblage of fissure plants, including maidenhair fern, sarcocapnos, dwarf buckthorn, the white-flowered rock snapdragon, endemic to Spain, and the yellow-flowered composite *Jasonia glutinosa*, as well as *Saxifraga moncayensis*, otherwise known only from El Moncayo (see p. 127).

If you walk upstream as far as the screes below the *mirador*, these true rock communities gradually merge with those of the limestone steppes above, in a colourful assemblage of sad stock, beautiful flax, the Afro-Iberian endemic horehound *Marrubium supinum*, *Phlomis lychnitis*, Spanish rusty foxglove and the handsome, blood-red *Linaria aeruginea*. Butterflies nectaring here in late May include Moroccan orange tip, Spanish festoon, painted lady, Queen of Spain fritillary, large wall brown, Spanish purple hairstreak and Panoptes and Escher's blues.

Both griffon and Egyptian vultures breed in the Barranco del Dulce (20+ and 4 pairs, respectively), as do golden and Bonelli's eagles, peregrine and eagle owl (at least 1 pair apiece) and 50+ pairs of chough; smaller cliff-nesting birds include alpine swift, crag martin, blue rock thrush, black redstart and rock sparrow. The riverine forest and stands of emergent vegetation are home to goshawk, sparrowhawk, hobby, scops and tawny owls, cuckoo, great spotted woodpecker, nightingale, Cetti's, reed, Bonelli's and melodious warblers, short-toed treecreeper, golden oriole and hawfinch, with kingfisher, dipper and grey wagtail on the river itself. An examination of the stunted junipers of the surrounding *páramo* should turn up little owl, black-eared wheatear, Dartford and spectacled warblers, southern grey and woodchat shrikes, tree

sparrow and rock, ortolan and cirl buntings, with open areas harbouring Montagu's harrier, quail, little bustard, stone curlew, black-bellied sandgrouse, tawny pipit and larks galore: calandra, Thekla, crested, short-toed and skylark.

Among the mammals, Iberian blind mole, beech marten (relatively common), western polecat, Eurasian badger, common genet, wildcat, Iberian hare, roe deer and wild boar have all been recorded here, with otters very scarce nowadays; a rich assemblage of micromammals includes greater and pygmy white-toothed shrews, Miller's water shrew and Mediterranean pine and southern water voles. As is usual with limestone terrain, numerous caves provide suitable habitat for roosting bats, particularly greater, lesser and Mediterranean horseshoe, greater mouse-eared, Geoffroy's and Schreiber's.

The herptiles are also well represented, with notable species including sharp-ribbed salamander, Iberian painted and parsley frogs, western spadefoot, natterjack toad, Moorish gecko, ocellated lizard, large and Spanish psammodromus, amphisbaenian, southern smooth, ladder, Montpellier and viperine snakes and Lataste's viper. The Río Dulce itself harbours a healthy population of brown trout plus several Iberian endemics: the barbel *Barbus bocagei*, cacho and bermejuela.

Access: Turn north off the N-II at km 118 towards Sigüenza. The Mirador Félix Rodríguez de la Fuente lies a few hundred metres beyond the river Dulce, with the left turn to Pelegrina shortly after. For La Cabrera and Aragosa further along the gorge take the CM-1101 out of Sigüenza to the southwest.

Also in the area

Río Salado (ZEPA; 11 585 ha) Saline steppes and small gorges along this small river to the northwest of Sigüenza, the former home to breeding little bustard, black-bellied sandgrouse and Dupont's lark, and the latter to griffon and Egyptian vultures, peregrine, eagle owl, chough and jackdaw. Inland saltpans near **Imón** and **La Olmeda de Jadraque** are still in use and attract passage waders.

Altos de Barahona (ZEPA; 42 974 ha) Rocky limestone *páramos* to the north of the Río Salado in southern Soria, much of which lies under dry cereal cultivation today. Largest population of Dupont's lark in Spain (2200 pairs), plus little and great bustards, stone curlew, black-bellied sandgrouse and calandra, short-toed, Thekla and crested larks, as well as skylark and wheatear. Try the Baraona–Rello road, to the west of the C-101. Similar habitats and birds on the **Páramos de Layna**, on the Soria–Guadalajara border to the east of Sigüenza and the N-II.

SITE 117 Sierra de Ayllón

A northeasterly outlier of the Sierra de Guadarrama, harbouring some of the southernmost beechwoods in Europe.

Dividing the river basins of the Tajo and Duero and the provinces of Guadalajara and Segovia, the Sierra de Ayllón (a ZEPA of 91 357 ha) is a Palaeozoic slate and quartzite ridge which peaks at 2273 m (Pico del Lobo). Its most outstanding ecological component is the relict beechwood encompassed within the Hayedo de Tejera Negra (*parque natural*; 1641 ha): the most extensive of all those persisting in the Sistema Central.

The main watercourses draining the Hayedo de Tejera Negra are the Lillas and Zarzas rivers – later combining as the Río Sorbe – which rise at the head of the glacial valley of La Buitrera (2046 m). Both are steep-sided and dissected by a multitude of small gullies which provide the necessary shade and humidity for the survival of beech forest in such southerly climes, generally on the coolest, north-facing slopes between 1300 and 1800 m, where winter frosts are rare and summer drought unheard of. Much of the remainder of the park is clothed with Pyrenean oak forest and secondary scrub.

Even where beech is dominant, the forest also harbours yew (some individuals calcu-

Astrantia
Astrantia major

lated to be more than 600 years old), downy birch (subspecies *celtiberica*), aspen, hazel, rowan, whitebeam, holly and ash. The calcifuge ground flora includes the penny-cress *Thlaspi stenopterum*, *Viola montcaunica* and the pignut *Conopodium bourgaei*, all of which are confined to central and northern Iberia, as well as the more widespread hollowroot, climbing corydalis, sanicle, bilberry, *Scrophularia alpestris*, woodruff, *Galium rotundifolium* and martagon lily.

The Pyrenean oak forests – found mainly on slopes with a more southerly aspect, between 1000 and 1700 m – have been much exploited for fuelwood and charcoal in the past, today harbouring a thick understorey of ling and tree and Spanish heaths; look out for large-flowered sandwort, wood bittervetch and southern wood-rush here. Above

Rock bunting *Emberiza cia* (Mike Lane)

the tree-line are acid pastures of sheep's-fescue, mat-grass and grey hair-grass, interspersed with tracts of dwarf juniper, bearberry and Spanish heath.

Among the most characteristic mammals of the extensive forests of Tejera Negra are roe deer, wild boar, wildcat, beech marten and badger, plus micromammals such as Mediterranean pine vole, wood mouse and common shrew, which provide food for long-eared, tawny and little owls. The commonest diurnal raptors are honey buzzard, booted eagle, sparrowhawk and goshawk, with other species regularly seen flying over the park including griffon vulture, shorttoed, golden and Bonelli's eagles and red kite; the Sierra de Ayllón as a whole is said to harbour one of the densest populations of golden eagle in Spain (16–19 pairs).

Less predatory woodland birds include great and lesser spotted woodpeckers, wryneck, pied flycatcher, Bonelli's warbler,

goldcrest, nuthatch, short-toed treecreeper and jay, while the tracts of laurel-leaved cistus at the south-eastern edge of the park attract more Mediterranean species such as great spotted cuckoo, red-necked nightjar, hoopoe, woodlark, Orphean warbler, southern grey and woodchat shrikes and rock bunting.

The crystal-clear rivers and streams of Tejera Negra are a renowned haunt of Pyrenean desman and otter, with reptiles such as Schreiber's green lizard and grass snake favouring the margins; look out, too, for common tree frog, natterjack and midwife toads and the curious amphisbaenian here. Drier areas in the lower reaches of the park are home to common and Iberian wall lizards, ocellated lizard and Lataste's viper. The Sierra de Ayllón also houses one of the last viable populations of Apollo in the Sistema Central.

Small fragments of beech forest are also found on the northern slopes of the Sierra de Ayllón, with the Hayedo de Riofrío de Riaza (a proposed *reserva natural* of 1930 ha) located along the SG-112, which winds its way up from Riaza to the Collado de la Quesera (1737 m). At the pass itself an interesting spring flora includes *Viola montcaunica, Leucanthemopsis pallida* and Pyrenean gagea, with the open terrain the haunt of water pipit, wheatear, rock thrush, whinchat, whitethroat and Dartford warbler.

Access and information: An autumn visit to Tejera Negra requires that you first stop at the information post – located about 3 km west of Cantalojas – to collect a permit (not necessary the rest of the year). Between here and the car park at the entrance to the park lies 5–6 km of muddy track, which may be impassable to non-4WD vehicles. A sign in the car park gives details of waymarked trails if the information centre is closed; for more information call the park offices on 949 885300 (885386 in autumn).

Also in the area

Hayedo de Montejo de la Sierra (*sitio natural de interés nacional*; 250 ha) Isolated beechwood to the west of Ayllón, on the shady right bank of the infant Río Jarama (in Madrid). Flora includes monk's-hood, astrantia, martagon lily and *Crocus carpetanus*, plus many fungi: slimy beech cap, slimy milk cap, *Echinoderma asperum* and *Tricholoma sulphureum*. Similar vertebrates to Tejera Negra. Visits (no charge) only possible with a guide from the Centro de Recursos de Montejo (in Montejo de la Sierra; tel: 91 8697058). Access from junction 76 of the N-I, then along the M-137 via Gandullas.

Villacádima To the northeast of Cantalojas, between the villages of Villacádima and Galve de Sorbe, the CM-1006 traverses a limestone plateau studded with junipers and thymes. Spring-flowering rock soapwort, Pyrenean vetch, hoary rock-rose, common grape hyacinth and early spider ophrys, with sparse Scots pines sheltering sheets of the deep purple pasque flower *Pulsatilla rubra*, columbine, grass-leaved buttercup and beautiful flax. Birds include cuckoo, hoopoe, Dupont's lark, wheatear, southern grey shrike, rock sparrow and rock bunting. Wetter meadows further south harbour great burnet, felted vetch, *Pedicularis schizocalyx*, green-winged orchid and *Fritillaria lusitanica*. Notable butter-flies in the Pyrenean oak forests around Condemios de Arriba to the east include purple-shot and scarce coppers, silver-washed and dark green fritillaries and the Guadarrama endemic subspecies of Apollo (*escalerae*) in late July.

Beautiful flax *Linum narbonense* (T.F.)

Ruinas de Tiermes Roman ruins to the northeast of Villacádima located close to a line of reddish sandstone and con-glomerate cliffs, the latter home to a large colony of griffon vultures plus breeding Egyptian vulture, golden eagle, peregrine, eagle owl, both rock thrushes, raven and chough.

Puebla de Beleña (*reserva natural*) Two shallow lagoons surrounded by cereals and seasonally flooded grasslands to the west of the village of Puebla de Beleña. An important stopover point for cranes on migration between Extremadura and Gallocanta (maxi-mum around 3000 individuals); also black stork, garganey and ferruginous duck on passage.

País Valencià and Murcia

Introduction

Much of the coastline of Murcia and the País Valencià was once characterised by a long series of large shallow lagoons (*albuferes*) separated from the Mediterranean by dune cordons. Despite the tourist infrastructure which has sprouted along the dunes, and the sacrifice of marshes to intensive horticultural projects, many vitally important wetlands for breeding and migratory birds remain, a fact reflected in the region's seven (six in València, one in Murcia) coastal Ramsar Sites. Many of the original *albuferes* have silted-up – L'Albufera de València is a notable exception – and have evolved into reedy marshes or *marjals* (for example, the Marjal del Moro) or, in even more advanced stages of sedimentation, into grazing pastures or *prats*, well represented at Prat de Cabanes in the north of the region.

Freshwater wetlands such as El Hondo and the Marjal del Moro are home to Europe's healthiest populations of marbled teal, with a supporting cast of white-headed duck, purple gallinule and reintroduced crested coot, while more saline habitats – the *salines* of Santa Pola, La Mata y Torrevieja and Mar Menor – harbour breeding slender-billed gulls and in some years greater flamingos. These same wetlands also support important populations of the endangered Valencia and Spanish toothcarps, the former a freshwater species unique to this region, the latter much more salt-tolerant and also found along the coasts of southern Iberia and Algeria.

The region's mountain chains are situated at the tail-ends of two major orogenic belts, with the substratum throughout almost exclusively limestone; the only major exceptions are the siliceous sandstones of the Desert de les Palmes, Calderona and Espadà regions in València and Castelló. The interior mountains of Castelló represent the eastern extreme of the Sistema Ibérico and are the southernmost strongholds of such Euro-Siberian plants such as cross gentian and twayblade (Penyagolosa), as well as harbouring large herds of Spanish ibex (Ports de Morella). At the other extreme of the region, the uplands of Murcia are an eastern continuation of the essentially Andalucían Sierras Béticas, sharing similar high-level cushion communities of *Hormathophylla spinosa*, hedgehog broom and *Genista longipes*. The introduced Barbary sheep has made itself very much at home here, above all in the Sierra Espuña. Inland cliffs in general support healthy breeding populations of golden and Bonelli's eagles, eagle owl and peregrine, plus stock dove, black wheatear, blue rock thrush and chough.

Along the southern coasts of the region, a frost-free climate has permitted the development of unique Mediterranean scrub communities, dominated by shrubs such as maytenus, *Zizyphus lotus*, *Periploca laevigata* subspecies *angustifolia*, *Lycium intricatum*, *Withania frutescens* and *Launaea arborescens*. Saline scrub assemblages all along the coast encompass a good selection of sea-lavenders, including southeastern Spanish endemics such as *Limonium carthaginense*, *L. angustebracteatum*, *L. caesium*, *L. dufourii*, *L. santapolense* and *L. insigne*.

Scrub habitats in coastal Murcia hold the Iberian peninsula's only native populations of spur-thighed tortoise, notably at Cabo Tiñoso, while the Illes Columbretes boast their own endemic wall lizard – *Podarcis atrata* – as well as breeding Eleonora's falcons. Trumpeter finches are increasingly common along the coast of Murcia, with densely vegetated *ramblas* here also home to

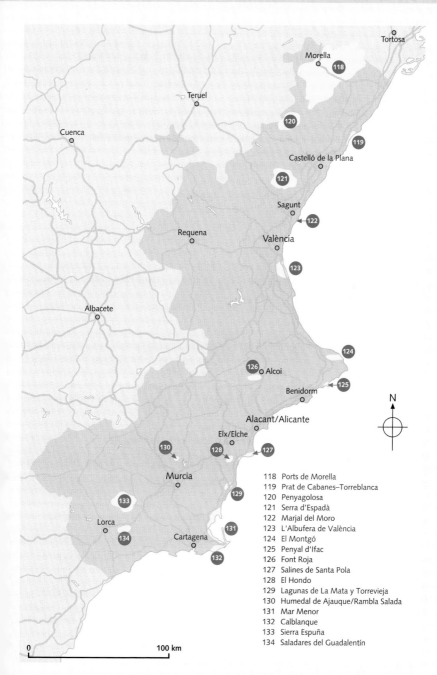

Tortosa

Morella
118

Teruel

120

Cuenca

119

Castelló de la Plana

121

Sagunt

122

Requena

València

123

Albacete

124

126 Alcoi

125

Benidorm

N

Alacant/Alicante

Elx/Elche

130   128   127

Murcia

129

133

Lorca

134

Cartagena   131

132

118 Ports de Morella
119 Prat de Cabanes–Torreblanca
120 Penyagolosa
121 Serra d'Espadà
122 Marjal del Moro
123 L'Albufera de València
124 El Montgó
125 Penyal d'Ifac
126 Font Roja
127 Salines de Santa Pola
128 El Hondo
129 Lagunas de La Mata y Torrevieja
130 Humedal de Ajauque/Rambla Salada
131 Mar Menor
132 Calblanque
133 Sierra Espuña
134 Saladares del Guadalentín

0   100 km

rufous bush robin. Murcia contains the region's only extensive areas of dry cereal cultivations – around the Saladares del Guadalentín and north of Yecla – which supports small populations of little bustard, black-bellied sandgrouse and calandra lark.

The botanical diversity of the region is considerable. The País Valencià alone is reckoned to have 338 endemic plant taxa, many of which are now being protected by *microreserves de flora*, a pioneering initiative that has established a network of over 140 floral micro-reserves – normally no more than 1–2 ha – with a high concentration of endemic, rare or threatened plants. For more information contact the Serveis Territorials del Medi Ambient (tel: 964 358750; e-mail: floracastello@cma.m400. gva.es). Of particular interest is the Dianic floral region of northern Alacant (El Montgó, Penyal d'Ifac and Font Roja, for example) where plant migration along the geologically continuous Sierras Béticas– Balears axis has left isolated pockets of endemic taxa such as *Silene hifacensis*, *Centaurea rouyi* and *Carduncellus dianius*.

As might be expected, the greatest variety of butterflies is found in upland areas: Apollo and Zapater's and spring ringlets all fly in Penyagolosa in northern Castelló, while Carswell's little blue – unique to the southeast of the peninsula, with its type-specimen from Espuña – is but one of a fine collection of lycaenids flying in the region. A recently discovered colony of spring ringlet in northern Murcia rather implies that there is still much to be learnt about the lepidoptera of the area.

The official Valencian website (www. gva.es/_Planificacion_Gestion_del_Medio/ esp_prin.htm) contains much information about the protected areas of the region, while 1:10 000 maps of the whole of the País Valencià can be downloaded from http:// turia.cap.gva.es/icv/pags/comu_1.asp For Murcia, you could try www.carm.es/cma/ dgmn/esquema/indice.htm

---

SITE 118 Ports de Morella

The southerly continuation of the Ports de Beseit, with a similarly diverse limestone flora, strong populations of breeding raptors and Spanish ibex.

You would need a full week to do justice to all the different habitats present in the complex series of thickly forested valleys and limestone ridges that comprises the Ports ('mountains') de Morella. Spanish ibex and red deer are common and such is the abruptness of the area that even wolves, far from their nearest known breeding areas in northern central Spain, are said to be occasional visitors. The four sites described below offer an excellent variety of habitats, but by no means exhaust the possibilities for finding wildlife in the Ports.

La Mola de la Garumba (1144 m) is a large limestone promontory west of Morella which can be climbed from the CV-125 between Cinctorres and Morella; head southwest from the junction with the CV-14 for 3.6 km, then follow the yellow-and-white

Spanish rusty foxglove
Digitalis obscura

markers heading northwest from the pass. The open landscape here provides good habitat for stock dove, woodlark, tawny pipit, wheatear and black-eared wheatear, as

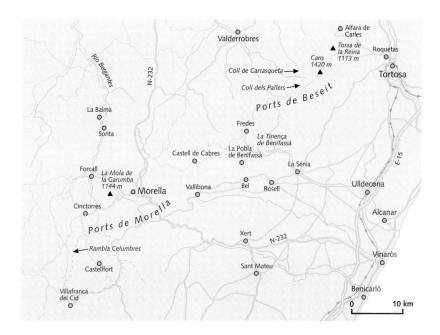

Valderrobres

Río Bergantes

N-232

Alfara de Carles

Tossa de la Reina 1113 m

Roquetas

Caro 1420 m

Coll de Carrasqueta →

Coll dels Pallers →

Ports de Beseit

Tortosa

E-15

La Balma

Sorita

Fredes

La Tinença de Benifassà

La Pobla de Benifassà

Castell de Cabres

La Sénia

Forcall

La Mola de la Garumba 1144 m

Morella

Vallibona

Bel

Rosell

Ulldecona

Cinctorres

Ports de Morella

Alcanar

Rambla Celumbres

Xert

N-232

Vinaròs

Castellfort

Sant Mateu

Villafranca del Cid

Benicarló

0   10 km

well as plenty of early-morning thermals for griffon vultures and other raptors.

Initially the vegetation is rather sparse: a blue haze of common globularia in the dry pastures mixes with cushions of Phoenician juniper, hedgehog broom, *Genista scorpius* and *Dorycnium pentaphyllum*. Check out the small cattle drinking pool near the first major junction of tracks for sharp-ribbed salamanders. Up towards the base of the cliffs the path steepens and enters sparse Spanish juniper and western holm oak woodland holding Dartford and Bonelli's warblers and firecrest, with the cliffs above harbouring rock buckthorn and noisy groups of rock sparrows. Once on top, a fine forest of *Pinus nigra* subspecies *salzmannii* appears, with early purple orchid (sub-species *olbiensis*) in the abandoned terraces and common lavender, *Asphodelus ramosus* and Solomon's-seal (hidden away under the holm oaks) on the flat plateau leading up to the triangulation point. Rest awhile and enjoy the hill-topping swallow-tails and scarce swallowtails in spring, flying together with Moroccan orange tip, knapweed and Glanville fritillaries and Spanish marbled white.

Rambla Celumbres is a normally dry river bed lying 4.4 km south of Cinctorres on the road (CV-124) to Castellfort, along which you can walk south for excellent views of the twin

Violet limodore *Limodorum abortivum*

Ports de Morella, with the monastery of Benifassà in the foreground

cliffs which hold the largest griffon vulture colony in the País Valencià and a single pair of Egyptian vultures. Thick pine forest (with many trees infested by mistletoe) crowds down to the edge of the boulder-filled *rambla*, enlivened by snowy mespilus, scorpion senna, bladder-senna and violet limodore. The few remaining pools in the river bed provide watering-holes for Spanish ibex and moisture for mud-puddling spring butterflies, notably Chapman's and turquoise blues and heath and knapweed fritillaries, while the boulders sprout clumps of Malling toadflax and shelter large psammodromus and Iberian wall lizard.

After about a kilometre, the pair of large cliffs – one on either side of the *rambla* – comes into view. The bulk of the vultures breed on the left-hand cliff, with the birds clearly visible on their nesting ledges. Golden eagles are occasional visitors, dwarfing the goshawks, alpine swifts, crag martins and choughs that also frequent the cliffs, while in the forest crested tit, short-toed treecreeper and crossbill are not uncommon.

You can stop almost anywhere north of Sorita (Zorita) along the CV-14 to explore the **Río Bergantes**, the cleanest watercourse in the Ports and the only one to hold otter. Look out too, for odonates such as *Calopteryx xanthostoma*, willow emerald damselfly, *Coenagrion caerulescens*, southern damselfly, green-eyed hook-tailed dragonfly, crepuscular hawker and southern skimmer. The riverside poplars are alive with golden orioles, with nightingales in endless song throughout the spring. The cliffs 8 km north of Sorita overlooking the western bank of the river harbour a few pairs of griffon vultures, with Egyptian vulture and Bonelli's and booted eagles also breeding in the area.

The curious cave church at La Balma, 2 km north of Sorita, would be worth visiting even if curtains of *Petrocoptis pardoi* – endemic to the Bergantes valley – did not brush your head as you walk in. Other fissure plants here include sarcocapnos, thick-leaved stonecrop and *Jasonia glutinosa* while *Cytinus hypocistis* is particularly common, parasitising the roots of *Cistus clusii* along the road further north, just after the boundary with Teruel.

La Tinença de Benifassà is a large tract of land – once owned by the Monestir de Santa María de Benifassà – which has remained all but unaltered for centuries. Drive the CV-105 Castell de Cabres to La Sénia road or the new road between Vallibona and Rosell linking the CV-111 and CV-100 (not marked on the Michelin map) for access to splendidly wild scenery and some of the area's best mixed woodland, in particular fine stands of Scots pine and huge Lusitanian oaks; the roadside verges are packed with Spanish rusty foxglove and Spanish ibex abound.

No less than five botanical micro-reserves have been created in La Tinença to protect the rich limestone flora, notably *Salix tarraconensis*, prostate cherry, *Armeria fontqueri*, *Antirrhinum sempervirens* subspecies *pertegasii*, the butterwort *Pinguicula grandiflora* subspecies *dertosensis* and *Knautia rupicola*, plus isolated stations for *Asplenium seelosii* and *A. sagittatum*, holly-fern and hard shield-fern.

Information: The walled medieval town of Morella is a good base and also has nesting scops owl, hoopoe, blue rock thrush and chough, with clumps of *Hormathophylla spinosa* on the north-facing slopes of the castle rock. Tourist office tel. and fax: 964 173032; email:touristinfo.morella@turisme.m400.gva.es

---

119 Prat de Cabanes–Torreblanca

An undeveloped stretch of beach backed by well-preserved grazing marshes, home to breeding collared pratincole and Montagu's harrier and an interesting shingle flora.

Prat de Cabanes–Torreblanca (a *parc natural* and Ramsar Site of 812 ha; also a ZEPA) is the longest continuous stretch of undeveloped beach along the much-abused Valencian coastline, if not in the whole Spanish Mediterranean. The shallow bays and lagoons so typical of this coastline (for example, L'Albufera; see p. 339) have here been transformed into marshy pastures (*prats*) by centuries of sedimentation, while in the northern sector of the park there is also a contrasting area of deep freshwater pools, left behind by industrial peat extraction.

Two micro-reserves have been established on the beach to protect floral communities largely untouched by exotic invaders (aside from a little Hottentot fig). The first lies between Torrenostra and Torre de la Sal and protects a stable shingle environment populated by *Ephedra distachya*, birthwort, the Afro-Iberian endemic *Silene ramosissima*, yellow horned-poppy, purple and sea spurges, cottonweed and golden-samphire.

The other micro-reserve is centred on 18 prickly junipers of the coastal subspecies *macrocarpa* growing on the fossil dunes around Torre de la Sal at the southern end of the park, where they are accompanied by *Cistus clusii* and *C. crispus* (the latter in an isolated eastern outpost), dwarf fan palm, sea squill and, for those who poke around under the shrubs, sawfly ophrys.

Behind the beach lies the nigh-on impenetrable mass of sharp and sea rushes of the Prat de Cabanes. Numerous ditches lined by stands of common reed, lesser bulrush and great fen-sedge criss-cross the *prat*, while in

Cattle egrets *Bubulcus ibis* in the Prat de Cabanes – Torreblanca park

the half-way house between beach and saltmarsh look out for the meadow-rue *Thalictrum morisonii*, blue iris, black bog-rush and Somerset rush. True halophyte communities are dominated by *Arthrocnemum macrostachyum* and purple and common glassworts.

Prat de Cabanes is graced by internationally important breeding colonies of collared pratincole and Montagu's harrier. Of the former, 76 pairs bred in 2000 in two separate nuclei; they can be seen hawking for insects over the peat pools from April onwards. At least 38 pairs of Montagu's harrier bred in 2000, hunting over the whole of the Prat for rodents, lizards and the introduced American crayfish *Procambarus clarkii*. The harriers start to arrive in mid-March, and for a couple of weeks in early spring the airspace over the marsh is filled by the wonderful sight of displaying harriers; the last two weeks in August see the equally spectacular first flights of the year's brood.

The permanent reedbeds harbour significant numbers of breeding moustached, great reed and reed warblers and reed bunting, with a single pair of marsh harriers nesting in 2000 (for the first time in 15 years). Other breeding birds include little bittern, Kentish plover on the beach, black-winged stilt if water-levels are right (14 pairs in 2000), red-crested pochard (80 pairs) in the peat pits, plus Cetti's and fan-tailed warblers. Hoopoe, crested lark, Sardinian warbler and woodchat shrike frequent the orange groves and market gardens behind the marsh.

Outside the breeding season there is a constant turnover of birds. In winter the deep peat-extraction pools attract occasional black-necked grebes and tufted duck, while the marshes might turn up the odd bittern, grey heron, cattle or little egret or bluethroat; Audouin's gulls fly offshore. Passage brings few waders as there is little exposed mud, but garganey and yellow wag-

Access: For the northern end of the park and the peat-extraction pools, enter Torreblanca on the N-340 and head for the beach (*platja/playa*) at Torrenostra. Alternatively, approach the southern part of the park via Torre de la Sal (signposted off the N-340 about 10 km south of Torreblanca). Part of the area behind the beach is closed off during the breeding season to protect the pratincole colonies; avoid the hunting season (12 October to the end of January).

tail are regular in March, and in April–May you can hope for purple heron, osprey, ferruginous duck and both whiskered and white-winged black terns. Other vertebrates to look out for in the park include an abundance of European pond terrapins plus ladder, Montpellier, viperine and grass snakes, Iberian pool frog and western spadefoot.

Also in the area

Illes Columbretes 18 ha archipelago (in a ZEPA of 2500 ha) of volcanic origin lying 56 km off the coast of Castelló, covered in shrubby sea-blight, an endemic subspecies of sweet Alison (*columbretensis*), tree mallow and *Lavatera mauritanica* (outnumbered by hybrids between the two). Other flora includes rock samphire, *Lycium intricatum* and *Withania frutescens* in the wave splash-zone and *Mesembryanthemum nodiflorum* in areas nitrified by bird guano. Breeding birds include yellow-legged gull – in loose colonies – and Audouin's gulls in tightly packed groups, plus Cory's shearwater, storm petrel, shag, peregrine and Eleonora's falcon (some 30 pairs). Also *Podarcis atrata*, the endemic Columbretes version of the Iberian wall lizard. Information from the Planetari located at Passeig Marítim 1, Castelló de la Plana (tel: 964 282968; fax: 964 285161; e-mail: planetari@ ayuncas.es).

Desert de les Palmes (*paratge protegit*; 3200 ha) Predominantly siliceous ridges running parallel to the coast, harbouring relict cork oak forest. Walk up Pico Bartolo (728 m) for Bonelli's eagle, Thekla lark, red-rumped swallow, rock and blue rock thrushes, black and black-eared wheatears, rock bunting and, from late summer to autumn, migrating storks and raptors. The contrastingly verdant Font de Miravet on the CV-146 to the north of the *paratge* is the haunt of Iolas and green-underside blues, large tortoiseshell and two-tailed pasha in May. The information centre is situated on the CV-147 which winds up into the *paratge* off the N-340 as it by-passes Benicàssim (tel: 96 4760727).

120 Penyagolosa
SITE

A unique yet unprotected massif with well-preserved pine forests, an interesting high-level limestone flora and Iberian endemic butterflies: Spanish argus and Zapater's ringlet.

The view from the heights of the spectacular south-facing, orange-striped cliffs of Penyagolosa (1814 m) takes in two very different worlds; to the south and east, the Mediterranean is plainly visible on a clear day, but to the north lies a broad expanse of pine forest, in which many essentially

Fritillaria lusitanica

Atlantic and central European plants such as lady-fern, wood anemone, cross gentian and twayblade, while reptiles such as smooth snake and common wall lizard, reach the southern edge of their ranges.

The obvious way to visit Penyagolosa is to walk south to the peak from the Santuari de Sant Joan de Penyagolosa (southwest of Vistabella del Maestrat, on the CV-170, close to the border with Teruel). Around the Santuari, Spanish gorse carpets the ground beneath the pines (*Pinus nigra* subspecies *salzmannii*), interspersed with Spanish catchfly, willow-leaved and white rock-roses and *Phlomis lychnitis*. Rock soapwort, blue aphyllanthes, tassel hyacinth and conical orchids bloom profusely in clearings among the pines in spring, with less conspicuous plants including slender vetch, *Euphorbia nicaeensis* and violet limodore. Spring-flying butterflies include Moroccan orange tip, turquoise blue, marsh, Queen of Spain and knapweed fritillaries and de Prunner's ringlet.

The route to the summit follows a broad track which heads south from just before the Santuari; at the first tight left-hand bend, continue south along a marked path into the Barranc de la Pegunta; a gully which harbours a micro-reserve containing yew, holly, field maple, bird cherry and white-

beam: an unusual assemblage for such a Mediterranean locality. As you climb, Scots pine begins to take over from *Pinus nigra* subspecies *salzmannii* and the forest thickens, supporting a community of hepatica, *Geum sylvaticum*, burnet rose, large self-heal and fly honeysuckle. The birdlife of the forest, however, changes little with altitude: dunnock, robin, coal tit and chaffinch mixed in with Bonelli's warbler, firecrest and short-toed treecreeper.

After the steepest part of the gully, you enter an area of younger pines, where the common yellow and scarcer red forms of the elder-flowered orchid occur side by side. The gully then divides, although whichever route you choose will lead you up to meet the original track and from there to La Banyadera: a pass from where the onward route to the summit is obvious. This much-eroded, steep and rocky path leads through increasingly stunted Scots pine forest which is the only location in the País Valencià for citril finch. The thinner soils here support grass-leaved buttercup, perennial cornflower, St Bernard's lily, wild tulip and *Fritillaria lusitanica*. Griffon vultures from the colony near Benassal, 25 km northeast of Penyagolosa, regularly fly overhead, and this is the best place to see the golden eagles and peregrines which breed in the area (4 pairs of each). Short-toed eagles (5+ pairs) are also possible, hovering hugely over almost any open area, but booted eagles are best looked for lower down.

Once at the top of Penyagolosa, the ascent pales into insignificance beside the immensity of the 300 m-high sheer cliffs that suddenly appear at your feet. Alpine swifts and choughs perform aerial acrobatics almost in front of your nose, while tawny pipits perform their song flights high above the summit. Take time out from the stupendous view to scout around for black redstart, wheatear and rock thrush, the latter breeding in good numbers throughout the massif (estimated 35 pairs).

Low-growing cushion and creeping plants dominate the windswept summit, notably *Alyssum lapeyrousianum*, *Draba hispanica*, grey cinquefoil, dwarf buckthorn, prostrate

Artiga de Garrido 1606 m

Pla d'Amunt & Vistabella de Maestrat

La Bertrana

El Rebollar

Sant Joan de Penyagolosa

Moleta de Mor 1440 m

Barranc de la Pegunta

Lloma Belart 1550 m

Roca de l'Aguila 1469 m

La Banyadera

Penyagolosa 1814 m

La Golosilla 1584 m

0   1 km

cherry, hedgehog broom and *Helianthemum marifolium*. Unfortunately the many feet which pass this way are severely damaging the few remaining plants of *Erodium celtibericum*, endemic to the limestone ridges of the eastern Sistema Ibérico and first described from Penyagolosa; this low-growing stork's-bill is also the food-plant of the Spanish argus here. Butterfly communities in general resemble those of Javalambre (see p. 150), and likewise include Apollo (subspecies *hispanicus*), Ripart's anomalous and Damon blues, black satyr, Esper's marbled white and Zapater's and spring ringlets.

Many other parts of the Penyagolosa massif are also worth a visit. The dry limestone pastures of the Pla d'Amunt – a broad plain stretching from Sant Joan to the village of Vistabella – teem with early spider ophrys in mid-May; at dusk listen out for stone curlew and try to avoid running over the nightjars that sit in the middle of the road.

Female black redstart *Phoenicurus ochruros* (Mike Lane)

To the north of Sant Joan, head for La Bertrana, an acid sandstone ridge harbouring Pyrenean oak woodland (good for red helleborine) at El Rebollar. Much of the original forest, however, has been replaced by maritime pines, with a calcifuge understorey of ling, tree heath and green heather; more degraded areas are carpeted with sage-leaved, poplar-leaved and laurel-leaved cistuses.

121 Serra d'Espadà
SITE

A much-incised acid massif harbouring the only sizeable cork oak forests in the País Valencià, with excellent populations of the larger raptors and predatory mammals.

So linked is the cork oak in people's minds to Extremadura that it is often forgotten that other areas of Spain also provide appropriate environmental conditions for the species. Moist northwesterlies douse the Serra d'Espadà (a *parc natural* and ZEPA of 32 000 ha) with plenty of rain, while the predominant rock-type – reddish, siliceous Triassic sandstones, found within the País Valencià only here, in the neighbouring Serra Calderona and Desert de les Palmes – are just right for the calcifuge cork oak.

About 70% of Espadà's original cork oak forest has survived replanting with maritime and Aleppo pines, with associated natural forest types including holm and Pyrenean oaks. The deeper, shadier gullies support a number of species more typical of cooler

climes, such as yew, holly, sweet chestnut, Lusitanian oak, wild service-tree and *Acer granatense*. The cork oaks themselves boast a lush understorey of prickly juniper, *Cytisus villosus*, turpentine tree, Mediterranean mezereon, strawberry-tree and tree heath.

Two-tailed pasha *Charaxes jasius*

Juvenile ocellated lizard *Lacerta lepida*

Secondary communities are dominated by thorny broom, green heather and the winter-flowering *Erica multiflora*, while cistuses – mainly grey-leaved, laurel-leaved and narrow-leaved – appear most commonly in burnt areas.

These thick woodlands and scrub provide cover and food for the most complete community of vertebrate predators in the País Valencià. At the top of the pyramid, wildcats are plentiful, while western polecats and common genets are more abundant here than anywhere else in the region. Eagle owls (15–20 pairs) and Bonelli's eagle (9 pairs) nest on the rocky outcrops, whereas short-toed (6–7 pairs) and booted (4 pairs) eagles build nests in tree-tops in the thickest forests. Curiously, the booted eagle's main prey in Espadà is the ocellated lizard, extremely abundant here, as are other typically Mediterranean reptiles such as large psammodromus, ladder and Montpellier snakes and Lataste's viper (above all in high, rocky areas).

The cork oaks are also home to wryneck, Bonelli's warbler, crested tit, short-toed treecreeper and golden oriole, while more open areas have both nightjar and red-necked nightjar, Thekla (not crested) lark, black-eared wheatear, *Sylvia* warblers and

rock bunting. The main crags harbour alpine swift, black wheatear and chough, red-rumped swallows are common throughout and there is a good autumn passage of soaring birds which always includes a number of black storks. Woodcock winter in the most humid forests and alpine accentors do so on the ridge-tops; there are even a few winter records of wallcreeper. Not surprisingly, two-tailed pashas abound in late summer, with other butterflies present including Moroccan orange tip, Provence hairstreak and large tortoiseshell, the latter emerging from hibernation in March–April.

Two micro-reserves encompass the crests of the highest points of the massif: Espadà (1083 m) and Pic de la Ràpita (1106 m). Both are accessible from the CV-215 between Algimia de Almonacid and Alcúdia de Veo, the former south from Collado de Algimia (waymarked), and la Ràpita northwest along the Riu Veo from Alcúdia. On the red sandstones of the former grow the Espadà endemic *Centaurea paui*, the Valencian endemic *Minuartia verna* subspecies *valentina* and a bewildering variety of naturally hybridising *Hieracium* species. An isolated nucleus of Mediterranean ferns also takes refuge at these heights, notably scented cheilanthes, *Cheilanthes hispanica*, *C. marantae* and *C. tinaei*.

Access and information: Eslida is the centre of the cork industry, with the best-preserved area of cork oaks in the Barranc de la Mosquera (3 km northeast of Almedíjar on the road (CV-200) to Aín; park in the lay-by on the left and go up the track to the right). Contact the local naturalist's association, GECEN, for more information (see Useful contacts).

Also in the area

Serra Calderona (*parc natural*, 44 000 ha) A fire-ravaged area lying southwest of Espadà across the valley of the Riu Palància. Characterised by a mixture of limestone and red Triassic sandstone substrata, the former covered by large tracts of holly oak, *Anthyllis cytisoides*, lentisc, *Erica multiflora*, rosemary and dwarf fan palm garrigue, and the latter harbouring a few patches of cork oak and scrub dominated by small-flowered gorse and narrow-leaved and sage-leaved cistuses. Good densities of Bonelli's (8 pairs) and short-toed eagles; also breeding peregrine, scops, long-eared and eagle owls, bee-eater, red-rumped swallow, crested and Thekla larks, blue rock thrush, black-eared and black wheatears, spectacled and sub-alpine warblers and rock sparrow. Important for herptiles (22 species), notably sharp-ribbed salamander, western spadefoot, parsley frog, stripe-necked terrapin, Turkish gecko, Bedriaga's skink, ocellated lizard, both psammodromus and horseshoe whip snake. Access via the CV-245 Segorbe–Casinos or CV-25 Segorbe–Olocau.

SITE 122 Marjal del Moro

A small, but bird-rich coastal wetland just north of València, with breeding collared pratincole, marbled teal and crested coot.

The Marjal del Moro (a ZEPA of 350 ha and proposed Ramsar Site) has few rivals in Spain when it comes to packing a lot into a small area. Marbled teal and collared pratincole are easy to observe here, with the overall diversity of breeding herons, waders and warblers – as well as the numbers of migrant and wintering birds – hard to better.

Nevertheless, it was only a happy twist of fate that saved the Marjal del Moro from joining the sorry list of drained Mediterranean wetlands. The closure of the Sagunt steelworks to the north meant that the coastal marshes – earmarked in the 1970s for a new plant – could be purchased by the Valencian Government and set aside as a future *paratge natural* (300 ha). Public ownership means that hunting is being completely phased out, while greater control of agricultural activities within the area is also possible; for example, farmers are offered alternative land if collared pratincoles choose to breed on their freshly ploughed fields.

Directly behind the beach, where Kentish plovers scuttle between clumps of sea-holly, echinophora and sea daffodil, lies a narrow strip of saltmarsh boasting a micro-reserve that protects the bulk of the known population of *Limonium dufourii*. In the same area, yellow horned-poppies appear on bare gravelly areas and blue irises brighten up the rush-beds as they merge into the less saline areas of the *marjals* (marshes) proper.

Despite over-exploitation of the aquifer which, if halted, would double the surface water of the Marjal, nowhere else on the Valencian coast is there so much relatively unpolluted fresh water. The communities of macrophytes are varied and well established, European pond terrapins abound and the Marjal is considered to be the best place in València for herbivorous fish such as Spanish and Valencia toothcarps, both listed

Crested coot *Fulica cristata*

País Valencià and Murcia

Black-tailed skimmer *Orthetrum cancellatum*

on Annex II of the Habitats Directive. Dragonflies are incredibly abundant in late summer with clouds of scarlet and red-veined darters swarming over the pools and ditches, while spring odonates include *Ischnura graellsii*, Norfolk hawker and black-tailed skimmer.

Until it is declared a *paratge natural*, the Marjal del Moro cannot join the Ramsar list, despite fulfilling criteria for five breeding species in 2000: marbled teal (3 pairs, with up to 24 birds), collared pratincole (45 pairs), black-winged stilt (121 pairs), purple gallinule (93 territories) and whiskered tern (37 pairs maximum). Marbled teal can be seen regularly from one of the observation platforms, along with plenty of red-crested pochard (68 pairs) and breeding black-necked grebes, avocets and common terns.

Other notable wetland birds include crested coot (40 birds released with identity collars in 2000) and ferruginous duck, both of which bred for the first time in 2001, as well as little, spotted and Baillon's crakes (breeding

of all three suspected), and the only colony of Montagu's harriers in València province. The only real absentee is the white-headed duck which may well breed once the aquifer problem is resolved and the deeper pools in the southern half of the marsh fill up to provide the habitat required by this species.

The reedbeds of the Marjal are equally alive with birds. Savi's, great reed, reed, Cetti's and moustached warblers (50 pairs) vie to dominate your eardrums, while herons pop up from the vegetation or flap lazily overhead. The summer of 2000 saw 7 pairs of purple heron, 2 of grey heron and 17 of little bittern nesting here, while male bitterns are heard often enough in spring and summer to suggest that they, too, might breed.

Water levels fluctuate throughout the year, but generally the Marjal fills up with migrants and then wintering birds as the autumn rains begin to fall. Purple gallinules form flocks of 50+, often parading in front of the hide, and over 4000 cattle egrets roost in winter, while duck numbers peak in March with groups of up to 800 red-crested pochard. Glossy ibis, greater flamingo, great white egret and bluethroat are regular wintering birds, with the spring migration bringing spoonbills and many waders, notably marsh sandpiper and Temminck's stint. At the end of summer, Eleonora's falcons feed on dragonflies as they kill time on the mainland before the first autumnal flux of migrating passerines arrives. Aquatic warblers pass through in small numbers in spring and autumn (8 birds ringed in April 1999), along with many pipits, flycatchers and warblers.

Access and information: The reception centre – Centro de Educación (tel: 96 2136671/72; fax: 96 2136673) – can be reached by taking the A-7 motorway north from València and then, after 18 km, following signs to El Port de Sagunt (Puerto de Sagunto); the centre is signposted off to the right after a further 2 km. Up-to-date information can be obtained from the excellent webpage www. terra.es/personal3/birder/

SITE 123 L'Albufera de València

A large shallow lagoon just south of the city of València; the third most important wetland for wintering waterbirds in Spain, with important breeding colonies of herons, purple gallinule and terns.

L'Albufera de València (a *parc natural* of 21 120 ha, also a Ramsar Site and ZEPA,) is the largest of the long line of *albuferes* (shallow coastal lagoons) that once stretched almost continuously down the Mediterranean seaboard of the País Valencià. Formerly a large bay, today the lagoon is considerably smaller – much land having been reclaimed over the centuries for rice cultivation – and is separated from the sea by a 1 km-wide *restinga* or sandspit, 30 km long and harbouring dunes, scrub and Aleppo pine woods. Water enters via run-off from the rice-paddies and rainfall, draining thereafter directly into the sea along three narrow canals with one-way sluice gates.

The obvious place to start is the Gola de Pujol: the drainage channel just north of the Platja de la Devesa. The psammophilic vegetation is well preserved, particularly in the micro-reserve just to the north of the Gola, and resembles that of the Ebro and Llobregat deltas, with the addition of southern birds-foot-trefoil, an abundance of *Halimium halimifolium*, with its yellow flowers and distinctive grey felty leaves, dyer's alkanet and cottonweed. Walk south along the beach from the Gola de Pujol away from the sun-bathers for the best dune slacks, populated by western spadefoots. Further inland, Aleppo pines and scrub communities clothe the fixed dunes; you can wander freely amid

L'Albufera de València

the prickly junipers (subspecies *macrocarpa*), lentisc, Mediterranean buckthorn, sage-leaved cistus, myrtle, *Lonicera implexa* and dwarf fan palm, coloured by *Anthyllis cytisoides* and rush-like scorpion-vetch. Spiny-footed lizards abound in open sandy habitats, while Iberian wall lizard, large psammodromus and Moorish gecko are commoner around buildings or in the pines.

Many pairs of Kentish plover nest on the beaches of the Devesa, with hoopoe, crested lark, Sardinian warbler and serin exceptionally common in and around the pines. Spring and autumn passage brings stone curlew, black-eared wheatear, spectacled warbler, pied flycatcher and southern grey shrike, with Eleonora's falcons regular in summer and booted eagles in winter. The Laguna de Pujol, just south of the Gola, is particularly good for black-necked grebe in winter.

Next, head for the information centre at Racó de l'Olla. Here a tower gives views over the reedy island of the Mata de Fang within the Albufera itself, home to all the park's breeding herons – little bittern (75+ pairs), little (1819 pairs) and cattle (4125 pairs) egrets, purple (47 pairs), grey (1095 pairs), squacco (157 pairs) and night (181 pairs) herons – as well as the bulk of the Albufera's purple gallinules (100 pairs), great reed, moustached and Savi's warblers and bearded tits. A didactic itinerary takes you around an artificially created area of pools next to the centre which, with a bit of luck, may hold some of the birds that breed in the neighbouring but unfortunately strictly no-access *reserva integral*: red-crested pochard (45 pairs), marbled teal (4 pairs), collared pratincole (28 pairs), black-winged stilt (444 pairs), avocet (93 pairs), slender-billed gull (56 pairs) and common, Sandwich, little and gull-billed terns (over 4000 pairs of terns in total).

Luckily, however, almost all the waterbirds of the area feed in the surrounding rice-paddies rather than in the somewhat polluted and eutrophic lagoon, so there is a constant transit of birds to and from the Mata de Fang and *reserva integral*. There is good freelance access to the paddies, with the best areas for feeding birds usually being El Tancat de Zacarés – an area of abandoned paddy fields on the southern shores of the Albufera which has more or less been given over to the birds – and the rice fields near the town of Silla, owned by the Valencian regional government, which are not cultivated but are kept flooded throughout the year. El Tancat de Zacarés also holds important heron colonies and a number of pairs of purple gallinule.

February is a good month to visit; the hunting season is over and some water remains in the paddies. Large groups of lapwing, golden plover and black-tailed godwit winter, and you should also turn up glossy ibis, great white egret, greater flamingo, spoonbill and, occasionally, black stork.

Purple gallinule *Porphyrio porphyrio* (Mike Lane)

Once the paddies are re-flooded in late April, they immediately become attractive to spring passage migrants, with the bulk of the non-breeding herons, ducks, waders, gulls and terns passing through quickly in a period of about four weeks. Post-breeding migration begins in the second half of July and lasts until the paddies have dried up (early October). Similar species are seen as in the Delta de l'Ebre, with the many rarities including sharp-tailed and Terek sandpipers and American golden plover (all September 2001).

L'Albufera also attracts many hunters at weekends (and full moons!) during the duck-shooting season, which lasts from the beginning of October to the end of January. Furthermore, from mid-November to mid-January in certain areas of paddies – known as *vedats* – food is provided to attract duck for the weekend shoots. The areas are thus especially worth visiting midweek (ask the information centre which *vedats* are currently the best), although once the shooting starts, many duck move to the safety of the Mata de Fang area.

Access and information: Coming from València, the CV-500 passes over la Gola del Pujol, 1 km before the right-turn to El Palmar and the Racó de l'Olla information centre (on the left after 50 m; closed Mondays and weekend afternoons; tel. and fax: 96 1627345; e-mail: raco.olla@terra.es). Two very informative websites are www.terra.es/personal7/jidies and www.albufera.com

124 _{SITE} El Montgó

A towering limestone peak and undeveloped coastal promontory with a rich Mediterranean flora and notable assemblages of endemic fissure plants.

The morning mist at its base often seems to accentuate the magnificent dimensions of El Montgó (Mongo). Sheer 100 m-high limestone crags loom over the town of Dénia, while concealed behind the 753 m peak, a karstified spur runs seawards to the spectacular 167 m sea-cliffs, topped off by the Sant Antoni lighthouse. A wealth of endemic plants is to be found throughout the *parc natural* (2200 ha) which is centred on the peak, with outstanding assemblages on the shadier north-facing cliffs.

The north side of El Montgó and the Cova de l'Aigua micro-reserve can be reached on foot from Dénia. From the palm-filled square (Plaça Jaume I) near the information centre, follow the signposted PR V-152 footpath along Avinguda del Montgó to an

Palmate anemone *Anemone palmata*

El Montgó

information panel (2.3 km distant), just beyond the last house. At this point, a broad track zigzags up to join another which contours across the whole north face of the mountain.

This second track was built in the 1920s to encourage the planting of vines and other crops, but since then the painstakingly built terraces have been abandoned and subsequently invaded by a thick, 2 m-high maquis of prickly juniper, joint pine, holly oak, *Osyris quadripartita*, lentisc, Mediterranean buckthorn, laurustinus and dwarf fan palm. Almonds, carobs and figs remind us, however, that these slopes were once cultivated.

In fire-damaged areas, a lower, more penetrable garrigue appears, dominated by small-leaved gorse, *Erica multiflora*, rosemary and toothed lavender, which shelters early-flowering giant orchids and *Ophrys* species – woodcock, yellow and sawfly ophrys and bee orchid – followed by pyramidal orchids in mid-May. Rush-leaved jonquil, wild tulip, dipcadi and common grape and tassel hyacinths are all in flower by April and the conical spikes of the very prickly *Asparagus stipularis* appear in May, with late summer bringing the delicate white petals and yellow coronas of autumn narcissus into bloom.

Not long after picking up the contouring track, take a narrow, well-signposted path up towards the Cova de l'Aigua, a cave hidden away at the base of the main cliff. An interesting scrub community here comprises *Hippocrepis valentina*, *Euphorbia squamigera* and the germander *Teucrium flavum* subspecies *glaucum*, as well as harbouring the large-leaved, creamy white *Carduncellus dianius*, a Dianic–Pityusan endemic once much appreciated by chefs, and shaggy clumps of *Centaurea rouyi*, a true Dianic endemic (i.e. unique to the Dénia area). On the rocks around the cave look for sarcocapnos and *Scabiosa saxatilis*, the latter confined to eastern Spain, as well as for Pyrenean saxifrage, *Sanguisorba ancistroides*, the toadflax *Linaria cavanillesii* and *Helichrysum rupestre*. Rummage around in the more humid and inaccessible corners for a unique community of box and Spanish butcher's broom.

Sardinian and Dartford warblers are the most frequent birds in the scrub, while crag martin, blue rock thrush and rock bunting can often be seen in the vicinity of the cave. Keep your ears open for choughs calling from on high and eyes peeled for the alpine, pallid and common swifts which scream along in front of the cliff face. Butterflies are at their best in May, before the vegetation dries up; look for both swallowtails, chequered blue, knapweed fritillary, Spanish and western marbled whites, Spanish gatekeeper, dusky heath and sage skipper.

Heading out towards Sant Antoni, the CV-736 from Dénia crosses the garrigue-covered plateau before reaching the lighthouse and sea-cliffs, where peregrine, yellow-legged gull, black wheatear and blue rock thrush nest and another micro-reserve protects similar plant communities to those found at the Cova de l'Aigua. Seawatching can be rewarding from the cape, with a good passage of Cory's shearwater in summer plus Balearic shearwater, gannet, great and Arctic skuas, Mediterranean gull and razorbill in winter.

The single pair of Bonelli's eagles that nests on the south side of the massif can sometimes be seen hunting over the Sant Antoni area, although it is equally wont to head south, to feed on the large numbers of racing pigeons in the Gata de Gorgos area. The other large raptor known to frequent the area – the eagle owl – is rarely seen, although its deep call can often be heard in February and March.

The whole of the Montgó ridge-top can be walked, although the wildlife differs little from that of the lower slopes. Western holm oaks find refuge in the highest gullies, while palmate anemone, *Helianthemum marifolium* and *Fritillaria lusitanica* appear on the windswept summits. Thekla larks prefer the higher, least disturbed areas, while crested larks are more abundant lower down, sharing their habitat with black-eared wheatear, stonechat and woodchat shrike. Most of the other vertebrates in the park also inhabit these lower levels: garden dormouse and common genet, above all in the taller scrub, Iberian wall lizard, large psammodromus and ocellated lizard in almost all habitats, and Montpellier and horseshoe whip snakes in the Aleppo pines.

Information: The park information centre is located in the Jardí Públic Torrecremada in the centre of Dénia (open weekday mornings only; tel. and fax: 96 6423205).

Also in the area

Marjal de Pego–Oliva (Ramsar Site and ZEPA; 1290 ha) Lying just to the north of Dénia, this is another of the many partially silted-up *albuferes* along the coast of the País Valencià. The relatively constant and unpolluted waters of the Marjal hold excellent macrophyte communities, in particular white water-lily, as well as breeding little bittern, purple heron, marbled teal, red-crested pochard, purple gallinule, black-winged stilt and Cetti's, great reed, Savi's and moustached warblers. Open areas are flooded once the breeding season is over and provide excellent habitat for passage waders such as marsh sandpiper and other *Tringa* waders, curlew sandpiper and little and Temminck's stints, as well as for osprey, marsh harrier and various terns. Turn right off the N-332 6 km south of Oliva (along the VV-1066, following signs to Pego). The best time to visit is September, with the hunting season starting on 12 October (until the end of January); information: tel: 96 6400251 or fax: 96 5561486.

125 Penyal d'Ifac

SITE

A dramatic 332-m limestone massif rising directly from the sea, harbouring an important botanical micro-reserve and a small area of salines at its base.

The Penyal d'Ifac (*parc natural*; 45 ha) dwarfs the tower-block hotels of nearby Calp and, despite its imposing vertical cliffs, can be climbed fairly easily along a path – tunnel included – leading up from the visitor centre at its base. Pass through a turnstile behind the centre and then up through small patches of Aleppo pine interspersed with *Osyris quadripartita*, lentisc and the eye-catching *Anthyllis cytisoides*, rush-like scorpion-vetch and *Cheirolophus intybaceus*. Look out, too, for the long-fringed petals of *Dianthus broteri*, sea mallow, the felty, sparsely flowered cat's-head rock-rose and abundant clumps of yellow sea aster.

At the base of the cliff you come to the Penyal's botanical micro-reserve: a small, roped-off cliff-face studded with the Dianic endemics *Hippocrepis valentina*, *Scabiosa saxatilis*, *Centaurea rouyi*, and *Teucrium buxifolium* subspecies *hifacense*. However, the real floral rarity of the park is the pink, fis-sure-loving *Silene hifacensis*, known only from Eivissa and four sites (20 plants in total) along this small section of the Valencian coast; artificial seeding of the Penyal has been successful and hopes are high for the species' recovery.

The basal scrub communities provide excellent habitat for *Sylvia* warblers: spectacled often in the salt-tolerant vegetation nearer the coast, subalpine in the taller scrub, Dartford in the lowest garrigue and Sardinian warblers almost anywhere, even in gardens. Other birds in the park include a single pair of peregrines, hawking Eleonora's falcons in early summer before their breeding season gets under way, pallid swift, crag martin and black wheatear.

Before heading through the short tunnel which takes you from the north face to a more southeasterly sector of the Penyal, take in the view seawards, where large, dark patches indicate the presence of extensive

Penyal d'Ifac

banks of posidonia. On the far side of the tunnel, higher levels of insolation do not favour the vegetation, such that the scrub is reduced mainly to joint pine, rosemary, dwarf fan palm and false esparto, along with a few stunted prickly junipers and wild olives. The rocks around the path here are a favoured spot for lizards: ocellated lizards give themselves away by panicking and disappearing noisily into the scrub, while the smaller lizards – here Spanish and large psammodromus and Iberian wall lizard – can be approached with stealth; both Turkish and Moorish geckos are also present. At the first junction, the left-hand path takes you along to the eastern limit of the Penyal (closed April–June to avoid disturbance to the yellow-legged gull colonies), while the right-hand option leads to the summit.

The small area of *salines* at the base of the Penyal can be easily viewed from the Calp road and often hold small, non-breeding groups of greater flamingos, while black-winged stilt, avocet and Kentish plover all nest here. Strategically located on the main Mediterranean flyway, good numbers of waders pop in briefly on migration, and Audouin's gulls can regularly be seen loafing around outside the breeding season.

> *Information*: The park information centre can be contacted on tel: 965 972015; fax: 965 972356. Get there early as daily limits on visitors are sometimes enforced, especially over Easter and during the main summer months.

Also in the area

Serra Gelada A 438 m coastal ridge which can be easily visited from neighbouring Benidorm along the road (closed to vehicles) between Platja de l'Albir and the lighthouse at Punta Bombarda. The scrub here includes lavender-leaved rock-rose, while the road is lined in many places by the 2-m high yellow thistle *Carthamus arborescens*, an Afro-Iberian endemic. Look out, too, for *Centaurium linariifolium* and *Teucrium buxifolium* subspecies *hifacense* on rocky outcrops; birds include pallid swift, black wheatear and blue rock thrush.

SITE 126 Font Roja

The last remaining western holm oak forest of any size in the region: a veritable oasis in an otherwise degraded labyrinth of limestone ridges.

The Carrascar de la Font Roja (*parc natural*, 2450 ha) is a supremely important forest enclave which gives us an excellent idea of how the multiple east–west-oriented limestone ridges in northern Alacant must have looked many centuries ago; it was saved from destruction by its importance as a sustainable source of charcoal and firewood for nearby Alcoi (Alcoy). The main ridge (El Menejador; 1352 m) catches the wettish winter winds from the northwest and provides an oasis for deciduous trees in the gullies which drain the western holm oak forest (or *carrascar*) on the steep north-facing slope.

On the other hand, the gentler southern flank lies in the rain shadow, its higher levels of insolation indicated by large tracts of xerophytic scrub.

Font Roja is best visited on a circular route, starting at the information centre, that takes you gently uphill along a broad track to the summit of the ridge. In the denser, more humid parts of the western holm oak forest species diversity is high, with hawthorn, strawberry-tree, laurustinus, Etruscan honeysuckle and *Lonicera implexa* in the shrub layer, and rush-like scorpion-vetch, *Ononis aragonensis* and grey-leaved cistus flowering along the verges. Limestone boulders beside the track sport clumps of *Saxifraga corsica* subspecies *cossoniana*, similar to meadow saxifrage but with well-divided leaves, while in the shady woods *Geum sylvaticum*, red helleborine and violet limodore provide sparks of colour. Take time out here to listen for Bonelli's warbler, firecrest, crested tit and short-toed treecreeper in the woods, with slightly more open areas harbouring good densities of nightingale and subalpine and melodious warblers.

Once atop the ridge, you can look down over the contrasting south-facing slopes, dominated by extensive scrublands of small-flowered gorse, *Genista scorpius*, *Cistus clusii* and many fragrant labiates, notably *Salvia lavandulifolia*. Wild tulips are wonderfully common in clearings in the scrub, while drifts of the Spanish endemic candytuft *Iberis hegelmaieri* appear on both sides of the track. This more open terrain, with its abundance of ocellated lizard, Montpellier snake and Lataste's viper, is favoured by hunting short-toed eagles, as well as by woodlark, skylark, black-eared wheatear and Dartford warbler.

The butterflies follow the typical western Mediterranean pattern of a spring rush in March and April (Berger's clouded yellow, wood white and Cleopatra, for example), followed by a lull and then the main population explosions in May and June (sloe hairstreak, cardinal, knapweed fritillary and western and Spanish marbled whites), with a third peak in September (two-tailed pasha and Lang's short-tailed and long-tailed blues). In late May, it is worth searching for Spanish fritillary on any abandoned terraces with either *Scabiosa* species or *Cephalaria* species: this butterfly's typical food-plants in Mediterranean Spain.

Below the TV repeater station the track divides; head up to the top for hill-topping butterflies, including swallowtail and purple-shot copper, although once on top the ridge-path is closed off to avoid disturbance to the single breeding pair of Bonelli's eagles,

Font Roja

diligently protected by closed-circuit television cameras.

Heading down from the junction, pick up a narrow path that descends steeply through the thick north-facing forest of the Carrascar and into a botanical micro-reserve. A rocky outcrop just below the ridge is decorated with clumps of *Hormathophylla spinosa*, and once in the forest yew, Lusitanian oak and whitebeam begin to appear, with scree slopes harbouring snowy mespilus, *Acer granatense* and flowering ash. Herbaceous species to look out for are rock soapwort, grass-leaved buttercup and Solomon's-seal.

> *Access and information*: Head south from Alcoi on the N-340 and turn right to the park half a kilometre after the new bridge, following signs to the Font Roja information centre (tel. and fax: 96 5337620; email:eefontroja @yahoo.es).

Also in the area

Serra d'Aitana The highest point (1558 m) in the mountains of northern Alacant, its summit harbours isolated enclaves of many plants – *Vella spinosa*, *Genista longipes*, *Cotoneaster granatensis* and *Daphne oleoides* – more characteristic of the Sierras Béticas. Spiny cushion communities dominated by hedgehog broom and *Hormathophylla spinosa* thrive here, while the north-facing cliffs and screes hold smooth rock spleenwort, *Draba hispanica*, *Alyssum lapeyrousianum*, Pyrenean saxifrage, *Saxifraga corsica* subspecies *cossoniana*, lax potentilla, *Linaria cavanillesii*, fairy foxglove, *Jasione foliosa* and *Scabiosa saxatilis*. Bonelli's eagle (8–9 pairs) breed in the mountains of northern Alacant and can be seen hunting almost anywhere over open areas of scrub. Golden eagle, peregrine, eagle owl, crag martin and chough nest on the cliffs of Aitana, with bee-eater, black wheatear, both rock thrushes, woodchat and southern grey shrikes, rock sparrow and rock bunting in the environs. *Access*: to the east of the Port (Puerto) de Tudons on the CV-770 between Alcoi and La Vila Joiosa.

1²7 Salines de Santa Pola

A large expanse of privately owned saltpans and freshwater marsh flanked by a well-preserved dune cordon; breeding marbled teal, herons, waders, gulls and terns, plus rich halophytic vegetation.

High levels of insolation, even in winter, enable the Mediterranean saltpans to remain in production all year round, thereby providing a relatively constant environment for birds such as the greater flamingo, present at Santa Pola (*parc natural*, Ramsar Site and ZEPA of 2496 ha) throughout much of the year.

Coastal habitats are best seen in the vicinity of the small Salines del Pinet, in the southern sector of the park. These saltpans are protected from the sea by mobile dunes, scantily vegetated with sea-holly, marram and sea daffodil, in the lee of which lie fixed dunes, clothed with stone pines over an understorey of yellow restharrow,

Salines de Santa Pola

Thymelaea hirsuta, Periploca laevigata subspecies *angustifolia* and *Helichrysum stoechas*. Crested lark, spiny-footed lizard and Spanish psammodromus frequent the sands, while stonechat, Sardinian warbler and southern grey shrike watch from their perches on surrounding bushes.

Immediately around the *salines* the vegetation is dominated by halophytes: the low-growing ice plant (flat leaves) and its congener *Mesembryanthemum nodiflorum* (fleshy, cylindrical leaves), the succulent chenopods *Arthrocnemum macrostachyum*, common glasswort and *Halocnemum strobilaceum*, an abundance of the pale-

Collared pratincole *Glareola pratincola*

pink-flowered sea heath *Frankenia corymbosa*, and sea and Somerset rushes. Many sea-lavenders are represented on the saline steppes, including the local endemics *Limonium santapolense* and *L. caesium*.

Most of the birds which breed around the saltpans can be seen at close quarters here. Slender-billed gulls swim tipping forward in shallow water, avocets dive-bomb any yellow-legged gull that strays too near their nests and there is a constant transit of whiskered and little terns coming to fish before returning to their nests elsewhere in the park. The endangered Spanish toothcarp thrives in this saline environment; you can see this delightful little fish in the information centre aquarium.

To the north of Pinet, the largest area of saltpans can be viewed from the main N-332, although the only feasible stopping point is next to the Torre del Tamarit: an old watchtower 4 km southwest of Santa Pola. From here, an extensive pink haze turns out to consist of hundreds, if not thousands, of greater flamingos (breeding is attempted unsuccessfully each year, with 5000+ sometimes present during post-breeding dispersal). Look out, too, for large numbers of passage waders, wintering cormorant and avocet (1600 over-wintering in 1997) and breeding black-winged stilt and Kentish plover.

Fresh water from the river Vinalopó enters the northern and western area of the *salines* and provides a greater diversity of habitats. Reedbeds here are alive with the comings and goings of the numerous breeding little bitterns, squacco and purple herons, cattle and little egrets, reed, great reed and moustached warblers and bearded tits. Marbled teal nest on the small freshwater pools, collared pratincoles hawk over the marsh in summer and red-crested pochard and black-necked grebes can be seen on larger expanses of open water all year round.

Information and access: The park information centre is located south of the N-332 just after the bridge over the first area of saltpans as you head southwest from Santa Pola (tel. and fax: 96 6693546). Advance permission is required to visit the private areas of freshwater marsh; write or fax the Parc Natural de les Salines de Santa Pola, Museu de la Sal, Avda. Zaragoza, 45, 03130 Santa Pola, Alacant. The Salines del Pinet lie to the east of the N-332, just south of two petrol stations.

Also in the area

From Pinet, walk south along the beach through stone pine-clad dunes as far as the **mouth of the river Segura**, where herons, waders and terns turn up on passage. The beach has an important breeding population of Kentish plover. Also try the scrub-covered **Cap de Santa Pola** to the north of the town, where the elusive rufous bush robin is known to have bred and pallid swift, black and black-eared wheatears and southern grey shrike are common.

128 El Hondo

One of the most important Iberian wetlands, housing up to 80% of the European population of marbled teal and attracting massive post-breeding concentrations of white-headed duck.

The enormous *albufera* that once stretched from the city of Elx (Elche) as far as the sea has been transformed by a mixture of human and natural forces into arguably the best wetland complex in Mediterranean Spain. Intimately linked to the neighbouring Santa Pola *salines*, El Hondo, or El Fondo as it is sometimes known (*parc natural*, Ramsar Site (2387 ha) and ZEPA), consists of two large and well-vegetated freshwater reservoirs and a number of canals which irrigate and help desalinate the land that has emerged since the silting-up of the original *albufera*. The reservoirs are fringed by a series of smaller lagoons of varying degrees of salinity, fed mainly by water from the Riu Vinalopó.

The four well-constructed hides on the main itinerary provide wonderful views over large expanses of open water and reedbeds. On a spring morning, Savi's, great reed and moustached warblers reel, caterwaul and chatter respectively from the thick curtains of common reed. Purple herons (45 pairs

White-headed duck *Oxyura leucocephala*

breed) appear suddenly from the reedbeds and fly off to feed, while little bitterns (55 pairs) shimmy up and down the tallest reeds. Squacco herons (40 pairs), often feeding along the main canal, and night heron and cattle (900 pairs) and little (40 pairs) egrets complete the range of nesting herons, although bitterns are heard often enough for breeding to be suspected. Other nesting birds include the whiskered terns (200 pairs) which nest on floating platforms, purple gallinule (probably) and the rarely stationary bearded tits.

On the open water, black-necked grebes (300 pairs) and red-crested pochard (110 pairs) are very much in evidence, but must take a back seat to the white-headed ducks (4035 birds in August 2000: 90% of the total European population) and marbled teal (60 pairs). Winter brings huge concentrations of duck from the north – over 10 000 shoveler in 1997, for example – as well as a few unwanted ruddy duck and more marbled teal, plus good numbers of bluethroats and water pipits.

A totally different assemblage of birds breeds in the more saline habitats on the fringes of the park. Avocet (40 pairs), black-winged stilt (200 pairs), Kentish plover, collared pratincole (50 pairs), little tern (15 pairs) and, in some years, greater flamingo all nest or feed in and among the halophytic vegetation, which is very similar to that of Santa Pola (see p. 347) but interspersed with the curious parasitic cynomorium and a number of sea-lavenders, notably *Limonium caesium* and *L. cossonianum*.

Among the non-avian fauna of the park, the commonest reptiles are stripe-necked terrapin, spiny-footed lizard and abundant grass and viperine snakes, with Spanish toothcarp and the ubiquitous Iberian pool frog in the canals and reservoirs themselves. Lesser emperors patrol up and down the main canal, but studies of the Odonata have yet to be undertaken; all records are welcome. The butterfly communities are unremarkable, with the exception of the abundant African grass blue along the main track, here feeding on medicks and other legumes and flying in overlapping generations from early spring onwards.

Cynomorium (T.F.)

Access: To reach El Hondo, leave the toll-free A-7 at junction 77 and head south towards Torrevieja. Follow signs to Sant Felip Neri and continue north and then northwest around the edge of the park to the main entrance on the right, just after you cross the main canal. There is no information centre, and visits – only between 8.00 and 11.15 am – have to be arranged by telephone beforehand (96 6678515) as the gates to this private estate are normally kept locked. The minor roads to the south of the park provide good views of the more saline habitats.

SITE 129 Lagunas de La Mata y Torrevieja

Two vast endorheic lagoons, renowned for their year-round greater flamingos and breeding slender-billed gulls and terns.

The two hyper-saline lagoons of La Mata and Torrevieja (a *parque natural* of 3755 ha; also a Ramsar Site and ZEPA) lie side by side barely a kilometre from the sea and are exploited as part of the world's fourth-largest commercial saltpan complex. Sea water flows first into La Mata and is then pumped along a connecting canal into Torrevieja as and when required, with both lagoons suffering sudden changes in water level, even during the bird breeding season.

Torrevieja often shimmers pink when population explosions of the diminutive red-dish crustaceans of the genus *Artemia* – the principal food of the greater flamingo – occur: the more they eat, the pinker they become. La Mata, on the other hand, is rather less saline and has a correspondingly greater floral and faunal diversity, much of which is concentrated around five hides, strategically placed opposite small artificial islands in the southeastern corner of the lagoon. Black-winged stilt, avocet and the here-resident Kentish plover all breed regularly, although gulls and terns are more at the mercy of external factors; in 1995, 63 pairs of

Laguna de La Mata

slender-billed gulls lost their nests to foxes, having chosen to nest on an island connected to the mainland, although 98 pairs did breed successfully in 2000. Common (230 pairs in 2000) and little (180 pairs in the same year) terns are usually more successful, but whiskered terns breed mainly when water levels are high, as in 1990 and 1991.

Shelduck also breed in small numbers, while Montagu's harrier (5 pairs) hunt over the reedbeds in the northwestern sector of the lagoon, where there is a freshwater influx. Stone curlews frequent the surrounding albardine steppe, with lesser short-toed larks occupying the areas of shortest vegetation. A highly specialised collection of chenopods occurs aroud the lagoons, although non-specialists would be better off looking out for yellow centaury in disturbed areas, growing together with ice plant, its fleshy leaves covered in hoarfrost-like crystals, and the parasitic cynomorium and bright yellow *Cistanche phelypaea*.

In winter, hunting in neighbouring wetlands causes a large-scale movement of waterbirds into La Mata, although less markedly since hunting has been reduced in nearby El Hondo. Black-necked grebes can peak at 2000+ individuals, shoveler and red-necked pochard are particularly common and as many as 2000 greater flamingos congregate on Torrevieja when the nearby Santa Pola *salines* are being hunted. A few Audouin's gulls can be seen all year round, with up to 2000 in winter in some years. The commonest winter waders are dunlin, little stint and redshank, their numbers reinforced in spring by oystercatcher, greenshank, curlew sandpiper, sanderling, bar-tailed godwit and turnstone. Late summer and autumn bring more of the same waders, along with regular red-necked phalarope.

Non-avian fauna tends to take a bit of back seat, although it is worth noting the presence of Iberian wall lizard, Spanish psammodromus, both Turkish and Moorish geckos and spiny-footed lizard among the reptiles, plus natterjack toad and Algerian hedgehog. Butterfly populations are unremarkable, although migrant plain tigers are regular in late summer, with the first Iberian records originating from this area in 1980.

Information: The excellent information centre is open every morning and Tuesday and Thursday afternoons (tel. and fax: 96 6920404). Coming from the north on the main N-332, the centre is 200m along a signposted track on the right opposite the first buildings of the town of La Mata.

Also in the area

Sierra de Escalona On the border between Murcia and Alacant; one of the most important areas for post-breeding dispersal of juvenile Bonelli's (up to 50 birds) and golden (up to 25 birds) eagles in the Spanish Mediterranean. Explore the CV-954 between Torremendo and Cabezo de la Plata, which runs along the northern side of the ridge where, between September and December, most of the eagles roost.

SITE
130 Humedal de Ajauque/Rambla Salada

An inland wetland consisting of two ramblas: the hyper-saline Rambla Salada, with breeding avocet and black-winged stilt, and the less saline and more reed-choked Humedal de Ajauque.

A surprising find in arid inland Murcia, this *paisaje protegido* and ZEPA (1632 ha) encompasses two *ramblas* (seasonal watercourses) – fed by saline springs – that converge on the large Santomera reservoir. In the Rambla Salada, the more saline of the two, only a handful of halophytes are able to gain a foothold: *Arthrocnemum macrostachyum* and common glasswort dominate in the hyper-saline areas, while *Anabasis articulata*, *Hammada scoparia*, *Limonium caesium* and the lilac-flowered *Lycium intricatum* only appear in less saline habitats away from the water's edge.

Eye-catching in early spring are the golden spikes of the broomrape *Cistanche phely-paea*, particularly common around the abandoned saltpans next to the interpretation centre. Away from the water, shrubby orache and *Atriplex glauca* compete for space with shrubby sea-blight, *Thymelaea hirsuta* and the sea heath *Frankenia corymbosa*, while undisturbed reaches of the surrounding gypsum steppe are coloured by *Ononis tridentata*, *Helianthemum squamatum* and *Thymus membranaceus*. Scattered copses of planted Aleppo pines shelter an understorey of *Periploca laevigata* subspecies *angustifolia* and dwarf fan palm.

Up to 40 pairs of black-winged stilts nest in the Rambla Salada, together with avocet (8 pairs) and Kentish plover (15 pairs). Migrant

Embalse de Santomera

waders such as dunlin and little stint pass through and a regular group of up to 100 greater flamingos frequents the area in winter. The soft clayey walls of the *rambla* provide nesting sites for rollers and bee-eaters, while the taller halophytic scrub is good habitat for Sardinian and spectacled warblers. Blue rock thrush and black wheatear are common in rocky areas, where Thekla larks pose in full view on large boulders and bushes. In early spring, great spotted cuckoos are very much in evidence in and around the pine plantations, which are also favoured by nesting short-toed eagles.

The Humedal de Ajauque is broader but less saline than Salada over much of its course, partly due to freshwater infiltration from the predominantly underground Tajo–Segura canal. Dense reedbeds have colonised much of Ajauque, providing breeding habitat for reed and great reed war-

blers; there is a large cattle egret roost in winter (700 birds) which has included, on occasion, glossy ibis and little egret. The peripheral halophytic scrub, dominated almost completely by common glasswort, is home to breeding Montagu's harrier (2 pairs in 2000), stone curlew (around 20 pairs), lesser short-toed lark, black-eared wheatear and fan-tailed warbler, also attracting bluethroats in winter.

Spiny-footed lizards scuttle across sandy areas in both *ramblas*, while natterjack toad and western spadefoot occur in the less saline reaches of the Humedal de Ajauque. Iberian hares are the most obvious mammals in the protected area, although red foxes and common genets use cavities in the soft gypsum cliffs as dens. Coleopterists should look out for *Ochthebius glaber*, a species of water-beetle endemic to the Rambla Salada.

Access and information: The protected area boasts an interpretation centre (open mornings only at weekends and on public holidays) next to the Rambla Salada, located west of the C-3223 to Fortuna (exit 83 north off the A-7 motorway) after 10 km. Look for a metalled track just after a blue and white bus-shelter leading up to a pair of red metal gates. The Humedal de Ajauque is harder to access; tracks lead east from the C-3223 towards the *rambla* as it enters the tail-end of the reservoir.

SITE 131 Mar Menor

Spain's largest coastal lagoon, associated with a wide range of habitats; important colonies of breeding gulls and waders and an Afro-Iberian relict flora.

Although much of the Mar Menor (a Ramsar Site of 14 933 ha) has been sacrificed at the altar of mass tourism, the remaining natural areas are still worth a visit. A 24 km-long sandspit – La Manga – virtually separates the lagoon from the Mediterranean and the area as a whole boasts interesting sand-dune, saltpan and saltmarsh habitats, complemented by a series of volcanic outcrops: three inland and five forming islands within the Mar Menor.

The Parque Regional de Salinas y Arenales de San Pedro del Pinatar (856 ha, also a ZEPA) to the north of the Mar Menor contains the best of the area's saltpans and halophytic and psammophilic vegetation. Southern birds-foot-trefoil, *Frankenia corymbosa*, sea-holly and sea daffodil populate the primary dunes, whereas the more stable secondary systems are better vegetated, harbouring a handful of Phoenician junipers (subspecies *turbinata*), plus clumps of lentisc, *Rhamnus lycioides*

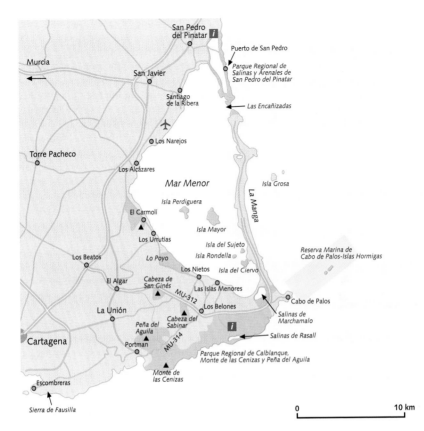

subspecies *oleoides* and *Lycium intricatum*. Without trampling too much, investigate the thyme scrub nearby for felty germander (subspecies *vincentinum*) and the locally endemic rock-rose *Helianthemum marminorense*, recently described by local botanists. Shelduck, stone curlew and lesser short-toed lark breed in the dunes, while Kentish plover and little tern make their rudimentary nests on the open beach.

A large part of the regional park is taken up by a complex of working saltpans (460 ha) which can be viewed from the road leading to the port of San Pedro (on the sandspit itself). Avocets, black-winged stilts and common terns are the commonest breeding birds in these *salinas*, while slender-billed gulls (182 in September 2001) and greater flamingos (1000+ in June 2001) occur all year round; Audouin's gulls are often present in small numbers, above all in August (96 in

2001). Unsurprisingly, the long-fingered bat – in Spain a markedly eastern species, which generally hunts over shallow water – has been recorded from the Mar Menor; less expected are the Schreiber's, greater mouse-eared and Mediterranean and greater horseshoe bats, usually thought of as forest species, that also occur in the area.

Continuing along the road to the port, you come to a hide overlooking a lagoon – recently created from an area of abandoned saltpans – which is being used in a reintroduction programme for the Spanish toothcarp. Since 1995, gull-billed terns have bred on the islands in the lagoon, favoured by the project to promote sustainable fishing techniques in the third of the major habitats in the park: the saltmarshes at Las Encañizadas. Since the project was launched, breeding tern numbers have increased as many birds now fish in and

Osyris quadripartita

ple, the saline steppes (teeming with *Limonium caesium*) northwest of El Carmolí are particularly good for spectacled warbler, while the area of abandoned saltpans northwest of Los Nietos – known as Lo Poyo – can be interesting for waders when flooded. A few passage waders also pass through the working Marchamalo *salinas* at the southern extreme of the Mar Menor. Three volcanic 'islands' emerge from the coastal plain. The 'peak' (just 117 m) adjacent to the village of El Carmolí is renowned for its wind-eroded calcareous volcanic rock formations, while the Cabeza de San Ginés is worth a climb to search for alpine swift, black wheatear and blue rock thrush; Cabeza del Sabinar harbours relict Barbary arbor-vitae formations.

Within the Mar Menor, the Isla del Ciervo is connected to the southern part of La Manga by a sandy tombolo and boasts a scrub of *Periploca laevigata* subspecies *angustifolia* and *Withania frutescens*, as well as monocots such as *Lapiedra martinezii* in late summer and sea and autumn squills and autumn narcissus in autumn; the island also harbours a notable population of natterjack toad. The neighbouring islands of El Sujeto and Rondella have breeding yellow-legged gulls, while Isla Mayor – or Isla del Barón – is covered by an exuberant Mediterranean scrub of holly oak, *Osyris quadripartita*, lentisc, maytenus, wild olive and dwarf fan palm. On the seaward side of La Manga, an important colony of 250+ Audouin's gulls breeds on Isla Grosa (ZEPA; 18 ha), with some 30 pairs of storm petrel inhabiting the small islets in the Cabo de Palos–Islas Hormigas *reserva marina*.

around the *encañizadas* (reed screens placed to trap fish moving between the sea and the Mar Menor).

This transitional area between the sea and the Mar Menor (reached by following the road along the dyke which separates the Mar Menor from the saltpans) is dotted with islands, sandbanks and mudflats and, unlike most of the Mediterranean, is subject to quite considerable oscillations in water level. The pseudo-tidal movement exposes large areas of mud and consequently attracts considerable numbers of waterbirds; grey plover, bar-tailed godwit, curlew, whimbrel and turnstone are common on passage in spring and autumn, while cormorant, spoonbill, greater flamingo, black-winged stilt, avocet, dunlin and little stint all winter. Look out for black-necked grebe and red-breasted merganser in the intervening channels and offshore.

The *paraje natural* known as Espacios Abiertos e Islas del Mar Menor (1154 ha) includes a number of contrasting habitats in and around the main lagoon. For exam-

---

Information: The park interpretation centre is located within the Centro de Conservación e Investigación de Humedales, adjacent to the roundabout giving access to the Puerto de San Pedro on the eastern outskirts of San Pedro del Pinatar (tel. and fax: 968 181116).

Also in the area

El Majal Blanco A largely pine-clad sector of the Parque Regional de Carrascoy y El Valle (16 725 ha), lying just south of the city of Murcia. Aleppo and stone pines shelter a rich understorey of prickly juniper, holly oak, turpentine tree, lentisc, *Rhamnus lycioides*, wild olive and dwarf fan palm, plus plenty of good-sized strawberry-trees and carobs. A trail to Las Cuevas del Buitre leads to a limestone outcrop with scaly cheilanthes, thick-leaved stonecrop, the navelwort *Umbilicus horizontalis*, *Teucrium buxifolium*, Malling toadflax and *Lapiedra* *martinezii*. Breeding raptors include short-toed and booted eagles, goshawk, peregrine and eagle owl. Pine forests harbour firecrest, crested and coal tits, short-toed treecreeper, crossbill and serin; expect red-necked nightjar on the tracks on warm summer evenings. Also hoopoe, bee-eater, nightingale, subalpine and melodious warblers, woodchat shrike and golden oriole. Lesser mouse-eared and long-fingered bats have been recorded. Head south off the MU-603 Murcia–Mazarrón road just after Sangonera la Verde.

SITE 132 Calblanque

A relatively unspoilt, arid coastal area harbouring important coastal scrub communities and the rare Barbary arbor-vitae.

After the tourist sprawl that surrounds most of the Mar Menor, the undeveloped rocky ridges of the easternmost part of the Sierra de Cartagena (linking the city with Cabo de Palos) and the Calblanque (a *parque regional* of 2453 ha) coastal plain come not only as a surprise, but also as a relief. Two roughly parallel, coast-hugging ridges form the backbone of the park and, where they retreat from the coast, there is room for a coastal plain with rich scrub communities and a small area of working saltpans (see map on p. 355).

The coastal scrub is separated from the sea by a series of fossil and mobile dunes where Bedriaga's skinks – their five toes separating them from the three-toed skink – and spiny-footed lizards scurry amid rock samphire, yellow sea aster and *Helichrysum stoechas* on more stable substrata, and *Silene ramosissima*, yellow restharrow, echinophora and sea daffodil on the mobile sands.

Pink butterfly orchid
Orchis papilionacea

Behind the dunes, two small hides on the north side of the Salinas de Rasall provide a chance to see breeding shelduck, Kentish plover, avocet and black-winged stilt at close quarters. Outside the breeding season, greater flamingos and Audouin's gulls winter, while a smattering of waders turns up on passage, along with the odd osprey. Around the saltpans, the halophytic vegetation consists largely of *Arthrocnemum macrostachyum*, common glasswort, *Thymelaea hirsuta* and

Juvenile spiny-footed lizard *Acanthodactylus erythrurus*

Limonium angustebracteatum, with the white-flowered *Limonium cossonianum* on drier hummocks.

Important scrub formations of *Zizyphus lotus* (check for common tiger blue) and *Periploca laevigata* subspecies *angustifolia* occur along the arid, frost-free coasts of southeast Spain; at Calblanque these assemblages also include maytenus, *Launaea arborescens* and dwarf fan palm. Sardinian warblers are the commonest birds in this habitat, while black-eared wheatears use prominent bushes as look-out points; around the scattered buildings it seems that each centuryplant harbours a perching Thekla lark, and each fig a skulking little owl.

The slight, but sufficient, increase in humidity in the normally dry *ramblas* running down to the sea provides habitat for rush-like scorpion-vetch, oleander and woody fleabane. Likewise, invertebrate communities benefit from these sheltered conditions, such that sooty orange tip, southern gatekeeper and mallow skipper, as well as the appropriately named ribbon-tailed lacewing, are on the wing on sunny spring afternoons. With a touch of patience and luck you might also encounter the scarce and secretive rufous bush robin which loiters in the densest vegetation of these *ramblas*.

The ridges behind the coastal plain are dominated by Aleppo pines, with a few patches of western holm oak providing some habitat diversity. Rocky outcrops harbour the curious, cactus-like *Caralluma*

europaea, while more open areas are clothed with a similar shrub assemblage to that of the coastal plain, with the addition of *Anthyllis cytisoides, Calicotome intermedia, Rhamnus lycioides*, narrow-leaved-cistus and toothed lavender. Also notable here is the juniper-like Barbary arbor-vitae which, despite being common in the foothills of the Atlas, is confined in mainland Europe to sunny limestone slopes in the easternmost part of the Sierra de Cartagena, plus a recently discovered relict enclave in Málaga. Small stands can be seen on the Peña del Águila north of Portman, along with a few strawberry-trees and – bar one plant in València – Europe's only *Cistus heterophyllus* subspecies *carthaginensis*.

To see the best of these forests, take the road from Los Belones towards Portman (MU-314) and stop at the small pass where a solitary Barbary arbor-vitae stands to the south. Tracks to the north lead towards Peña del Aguila, while to the south a chained-off road leads up to Monte de las Cenizas (337 m) and an abandoned gun emplacement with curious Aztec-style decoration. Along the road to Cenizas look out for caper, *Dorycnium pentaphyllum*, wild olive and the Spanish endemic viper's-grass *Scorzonera graminifolia*, with the pines harbouring mirror ophrys and pink butterfly orchid, crossbill and beech marten. The summit provides excellent views of the rocky coastline below, and might also turn up alpine swift, red-rumped swallow, black wheatear and blue rock thrush. Bonelli's eagles hunt over the scrub, while spring butterflies are plentiful and include scarce swallowtail, blue-spot hairstreak and southern marbled skipper, with dusky heath and southern gatekeeper appearing later in the year.

> *Information*: The park information centre (tel: 902 113792) can be reached 2 km along a dirt track running southeast from Los Belones (signposted).

Also in the area

From the port of Escombreras, dominated by a huge chemical complex to the east, a track leads up to the **Sierra de Fausilla** (ZEPA; 791 ha): a coastal ridge dominated by *Periploca angustifolia* and thyme scrub, associated with *Anabasis articulata*, maytenus and *Caralluma europaea*, plus a number of species unique to southeastern Spain: *Salsola papillosa*, the sea-lavenders *Limonium carthaginense* and *L. insigne*, *Sideritis marminorensis* and *Teucrium carthaginense*. Bird-wise, look out for Bonelli's eagle, peregrine, eagle owl, blue rock thrush and trumpeter finch.

West of Cartagena, the dry **Rambla del Cañar** supports similar scrub species to Calblanque, plus Syrian bean-caper, toothed and cut-leaved lavenders, *Thymus membranaceus*, *Centaurea ornata* subspecies *saxicola*, *Andryala ragusina* and reichardia. Around the spring in the middle of the *rambla*, look out for turtle dove, bee-eater, nightingale, spotted flycatcher and golden oriole, plus black and black-eared wheatears and rock sparrow. *Access*: turn south off the N-332 in Tallante opposite the 'Venta el Buen Descanso' along a metalled road signposted 'Rincón de Sumiedo'; continue past the village on a track along the *rambla*. **Peñas Blancas** (629 m), a limestone outcrop to the southeast, supports breeding Bonelli's eagle, peregrine, eagle owl, alpine swift, crag martin and chough.

Cabo Tiñoso Harbours interesting labiate communities including *Satureja cuneifolia* subspecies *obovata* and the germanders *Teucrium carthaginense*, *T. gnaphalodes* and *T. freynii*. Also Bonelli's eagle, pallid swift, red-rumped swallow and trumpeter finch, as well as spur-thighed tortoise, Spanish psammodromus, Iberian wall lizard, horseshoe whip, southern smooth and false smooth snakes and Lataste's viper. Accessed via the E-16 Cartagena to La Azohía road.

133 Sierra Espuña

Extensive pine-clad limestone mountains harbouring breeding golden eagle and eagle owl; rich high-level flora, a diverse assemblage of butterflies and large flocks of Barbary sheep.

Contrary to appearances, the Sierra Espuña (*parque regional* and ZEPA, 17 804 ha) is in fact one large, excellently planned forestry plantation. By the end of the nineteenth century, deforestation had left Espuña bare, erosion was rife and flash-floods were common in the villages below. Thus, in 1891 an ambitious reforestation project commenced, with Aleppo pines planted up to 500 m, followed by a mixture of Aleppo and maritime pines to 1300 m, and finally *Pinus nigra* subspecies *salzmannii* to 1500 m. In total, 5000 ha of pines were planted over a period of 12 years and such was the success of the project that in 1931 the area was declared a *sitio de interés nacional*.

Today, the mature Espuña pine forests are anything but sterile conifer plantations. Vertebrates abound: lesser horseshoe and Geoffroy's bats are known to fly here and red squirrels – recognised as subspecies *hoffmanni*, endemic to Espuña, with more white fur on their snout and shoulders – are common, as are pygmy white-toothed shrew,

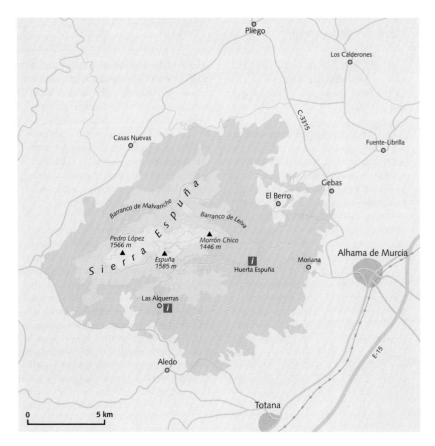

beech marten, weasel, common genet and wild boar. Ocellated lizard, large psammodromus and the Iberian peninsula's largest reptile, the Montpellier snake, prefer more open pine woodland, whereas fire salamander and natterjack toad are more at home in the damper gullies. Firecrest, crested and coal tits and short-toed treecreeper move around in the crowns of the trees, groups of crossbills pass overhead, woodlark and rock bunting feed on the ground in the firebreaks and, with luck, a goshawk might appear, like a large, dark arrow.

The original understorey of the long-gone western holm oak forest still thrives in many areas, dominated by prickly juniper, holly oak, lentisc, *Phillyrea angustifolia* and laurustinus. More open areas are populated by typical Mediterranean scrub communities of *Rhamnus lycioides*, rosemary, thymes and tough clumps of *Stipa tenacissima*. Roadside verges on the way up to the radar station on the summit of Espuña (signposted EVA-13) provide a good introduction to other common plants of the area. Lower down, look out for rush-like scorpion-vetch with its dangling, bean-like seedpods, *Anthyllis cytisoides*, *Dorycnium pentaphyllum*, grey-leaved cistus, *Cistus clusii*, *Phlomis lychnitis* and the woody *Thymus membranaceus*, with large tracts of *Genista valentina* appearing as you climb above 800 m.

On the shadier northern flanks of Espuña, the moist Barranco de Leiva provides a refuge for small stands of Montpellier maple, as well as a few mature western holm oaks, *Cotoneaster granatensis*, prostrate cherry, turpentine tree and sea mallow. Also on the north side, a number of large Lusitanian oaks survive in the more acid Barranco de

Common genet *Genetta genetta*

Malvariche, together with laurel-leaved cistus and strawberry-tree.

The windswept summits of Espuña (1585 m) and Morrón Chico (1446 m) – often snow-capped in winter – are clothe with spiny cushion communities of *Hormathophylla spinosa* (a dense, white-flowered crucifer), hedgehog broom and the greenweed *Genista longipes*, the latter not to be confused with the less dense and more irregular cushions of *Genista pumila* subspecies *pumila*. Herbs such as grass-leaved buttercup, *Salvia lavandulifolia* and *Linaria aeruginea* take refuge in crevices in the limestone pavement, together with *Thymelaea pubescens* subspecies *elliptica* and the stork's-bill *Erodium valentinum*, both of which are endemic to southeastern Spain, while fissures in the many small rock faces are home to the reddish-stemmed fern *Cheilanthes acrostica*, rock buckthorn, *Saxifraga camposii* and *Lonicera splendida*, the latter two again unique to southeast Spain.

These summits are also frequented by large herds of Barbary sheep. A group of 36 animals from zoos in Casablanca and Frankfurt was released in 1970 as part of a project to save this elegant wild ancestor of the sheep from extinction. Today flocks of more than 150 are common at altitude, the mountainside rippling with movement as a group moves off, the young animals calling to their mothers. Males form separate flocks and only join the females to breed in the autumn. Look out, too, for Thekla lark, tawny pipit, both wheatear and black-eared wheatear, rock thrush and rock bunting on the high-level plateaux, while golden eagle, peregrine, crag martin and chough sail along the cliff edges. Short-toed eagles hunt over open areas throughout Espuña, unlike the booted eagle, which prefers forest margins at low levels; eagle owls are also known to breed in the park.

Espuña harbours a wealth of butterflies, especially lycaenids; Carswell's little blue, recently separated from the little blue on the basis of larval colouration, flies during May, while the irregularly distributed Spanish argus, whose type-specimen is from Espuña, does so in high summer on the summits. Lower down a panoply of blues – chequered, Mazarine, mother-of-pearl and green-underside – is on the wing in spring, with July and August bringing out the scarce southern hermit, endemic to Spain and North Africa.

Access and information: The park lies to the west of the Alhama de Murcia to Pliego road (C-3315), from which a confusing labyrinth of narrow metalled tracks permits access; plenty of marked paths allow all major habitats to be visited; the summit can be reached by following signs to EVA-13. The information centre (Centro Ricardo Codorníu; well signposted) is at Huerta Espuña (tel. and fax: 968 431430).

Also in the area

Sierra María–Los Vélez (*parque natural*; 22 611 ha) In northeastern Almería in neighbouring Andalucía, comprising an island of karstified limestone mountains rising to 2045 m (María) surrounded by arid plains. Dense forests of *Pinus nigra* subspecies *salzmannii* on north-facing slopes, with diverse community of cushion plants on windswept crests: *Hormathophylla spinosa*, *Vella spinosa*,

Genista longipes, hedgehog broom and spiny hare's-ear. *Colchicum triphyllum* around melting snow patches in spring. Around 1200 taxa of vascular plant including seven endemics, of which the most notable are *Centaurea mariana* and *Sideritis stachydioides*, both on cliffs, where they are accompanied by *Hormathophylla cadevalliana*, *Draba hispanica* and *Linaria verticillata*, all unique to the peninsula. Wild tulip, *Fritillaria lusitanica*, *Crocus nevadensis*, *Iris lutescens* subspecies *subbiflora*, violet limodore, dark red, red and large white helleborines and Spitzel's orchid in spring plus *Lapiedra martinezii* in autumn. Good populations of short-toed, booted and golden eagles, goshawk, peregrine, hobby and long-eared, scops and eagle owls, plus little bustard and stone curlew in the surrounding steppes. Spur-thighed tortoise, Montpellier and ladder snakes, Lataste's viper, red squirrel, garden dormouse, wildcat, common genet and a small introduced population of Barbary sheep from the nearby Sierra Espuña. Butterflies (63 species) include ilex hairstreak, Iolas and mother-of-pearl blues, Spanish and geranium arguses, nettle-tree butterfly, Nevada grayling (subspecies *aislada*) and Apollo (subspecies *mariae*). Two visitor centres: one on the A-317 about 3 km east of María (tel. and fax: 950 527005) and another in Vélez-Blanco (tel: 950 614802).

134 Saladares del Guadalentín

An inland mosaic of dry cereals, orchards and halophytic scrub harbouring Murcia's most important assemblage of steppe birds.

This low-lying section of the Guadalentín valley is, theoretically, classed as a wetland, since groundwater levels in the past were high enough to give rise to a series of natural springs that would regularly flood the poorly drained soils of the area. Today, however, with the over-exploited aquifer far too low to flood, these *saladares* are anything but a wetland and are characterised instead by a mixture of intensive and extensive agriculture interspersed with patches of saline steppe exhibiting well-developed halophytic plant communities. Despite the human abuse of the area, however, Murcia's best collection of steppe birds can still be found here.

The Saladares del Guadalentín (a *reserva natural* of 2210 ha) have been described as semi-endorheic; most of the temporary streams that enter the area fail to reach the river, the water instead soaking into the soil, giving rise to sub-surface humidity. Intense summer evaporation dries out the soils and brings salts to the surface, thereby forming the area's characteristic *saladares*. The most saline areas support halophytic chenopods such as shrubby sea-blight, common glasswort, *Arthrocnemum macrostachyum*, *Halocnemum strobilaceum* and sea-purslane, coloured by golden-samphire in summer.

In more disturbed habitats – often once cultivated and then abandoned, and usually nitrogen-enriched – shrubby sea-blight continues to be abundant, but is instead accompanied by *Atriplex glauca*, *Suaeda pruinosa*

País Valencià and Murcia

Golden-samphire *Inula crithmoides*

balance here, there are still many birds to be enjoyed. Lesser short-toed, short-toed and calandra larks soar in song-flight above the halophytic scrub, while the resident Dartford and spectacled warblers flit from one bush to another. Stone curlews and black-bellied sandgrouse (both 20–30 pairs) only give away their presence if flushed, while the other typical steppe bird of the area – the little bustard – is best looked for in the winter (50+) in the alfalfa fields, although a handful do still breed. Up to nine pairs of Montagu's harriers once nested here, but today they are only seen on passage. Other characteristic vertebrates of the *saladares* are the spiny-footed lizard, Spanish psammodromus and Montpellier snake, with one of the commonest mammals being the Algerian hedgehog; the area is also important for its populations of greater and Mehely's horseshoe bats.

Away from the saline habitats and into the more humanised agricultural areas, black-eared wheatear and southern grey and woodchat shrikes perch on any suitable vantage point, while roller and bee-eater are common in and around the orchards. The many large, permanent irrigation ponds provide breeding habitat for the occasional marbled teal, little-ringed plover and black-winged stilt.

and *Mesembryanthemum nodiflorum*. Less saline areas are dominated by the sea heath *Frankenia corymbosa*, studded with attractive clumps of *Limonium caesium* (also present are *L. cossonianum* and *L. delicatulum*).

Less saline soils are characterised by an assemblage dominated by *Thymelaea hirsuta*, growing together with more *Frankenia corymbosa*, *Artemisia herba-alba* and albardine. Other shrubs scattered throughout include *Anabasis articulata*, *Lycium intricatum* and *Artemisia barrelieri*, the latter unique to the southeastern quadrant of the peninsula. Look out, too, for the lovely musk-scented lavatera and horribly spiny, black-berried *Asparagus stipularis*, while stands of the Afro-Iberian *Tamarix boveana* indicate the location of usually dry watercourses.

Although the trend towards intensive agriculture is upsetting the delicate ecological

Access: The *saladares* lie to the west of the MU-603 which links Alhama de Murcia with Mazarrón and can be accessed along the tracks that criss-cross the area, entering opposite the petrol station south of the junction of the MU-603 with the MU-602 (Alhama–Cartagena road).

Andalucía

Introduction

Andalucía is undoubtedly one of the richest Iberian regions in terms of both habitats and species diversity, with a vascular flora approaching 5000 taxa, of which some 10% is endemic. Separated from the rest of Spain by the 400 km ridge of the Sierra Morena, but from Morocco by just 14 km of open water across the Strait of Gibraltar, it is hardly surprising that the region's flora and fauna contains many Afro-Iberian elements: Algerian hedgehog, Andalusian hemipode, cream-coloured courser, Mediterranean chameleon, false mallow and Zeller's skippers, desert orange tip, Aetherie fritillary, Lorquin's and common tiger blues and, of course, the Barbary apes and Barbary partridges on Gibraltar, plus Afro-Iberian endemic plants too numerous to mention.

The Punta de Tarifa – the southernmost point of mainland Europe – divides the Mediterranean from the Atlantic, to the west of which strong onshore winds and currents have produced impressive dune systems. Intertidal saltmarshes are well represented at the Marismas del Odiel, renowned for its ground-nesting spoonbills, while the combined protected areas of Doñana – whose extensive marshes are independent of the sea today – are home to a magnificent array of birdlife: more than 1 200 000 wintering waterbirds, the largest colony of spoonbills in Europe (here nesting in ancient cork oaks), Iberia's most numerous breeding nuclei of black kite and purple gallinule, important populations of little bittern, glossy ibis and marbled teal, plus the endangered pardel lynx, Spanish imperial eagle and spur-thighed tortoise.

East of Tarifa, the more sheltered Costa del Sol was unfortunately fated to become one of Europe's prime sun-seeking destinations

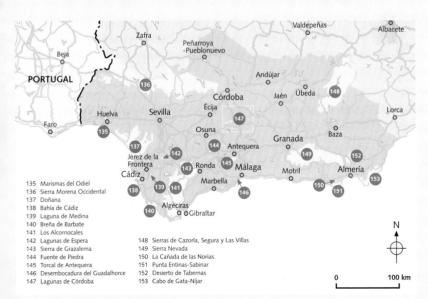

135 Marismas del Odiel
136 Sierra Morena Occidental
137 Doñana
138 Bahía de Cádiz
139 Laguna de Medina
140 Breña de Barbate
141 Los Alcornocales
142 Lagunas de Espera
143 Sierra de Grazalema
144 Fuente de Piedra
145 Torcal de Antequera
146 Desembocadura del Guadalhorce
147 Lagunas de Córdoba
148 Sierras de Cazorla, Segura y Las Villas
149 Sierra Nevada
150 La Cañada de las Norias
151 Punta Entinas-Sabinar
152 Desierto de Tabernas
153 Cabo de Gata-Níjar

Opposite page: **Torcal de Antequera**

Andalucía

Great spotted cuckoo *Clamator glandarius*

in the 1960s, such that untamed coastal habitats are rare today, with the notable exception of the isolated wetland at the mouth of the Guadalhorce, much visited by migrant birds, and the volcanic cliffs of Cabo de Gata, home to several endemic plants and breeding storm petrels.

The climate of Andalucía varies enormously from west to east. Atlantic weather systems sweep in unhindered from the southwest until they reach the limestone peaks of the Sierra de Grazalema, one of the rainiest places in Spain (an average of 2200 mm annually) and home to some of the last Spanish fir forests on the planet. The high temperatures and extreme humidity of the nearby Alcornocales support one of the largest cork oak forests in the world, with sheltered gullies harbouring a relict assemblage of ferns more typical of Macaronesia than Europe. By contrast, Almería is one of Europe's most arid regions, where precipitation rarely exceeds 200 mm. The semi-desert habitats of Tabernas, the Hoyas de Guadix y Baza and Cabo de Gata are the haunt of typically African species such as trumpeter finch and greenish black-tip, as well as significant numbers of stone curlew, black-bellied sandgrouse, lesser short-toed and Thekla larks and black wheatear.

Climate apart, Andalucía can be divided into four broad geographical regions running more or less parallel across the region from east to west. To the north lies the slaty, *dehesa*-clad ridge of the Sierra Morena, whose western reaches are renowned for their breeding black vultures and such emblematic Iberian birds as black stork, white-rumped swift and rufous bush robin. The Sierra de Andújar to the east harbours a significant enclave of Spanish imperial eagle and what is probably the sole remaining genetically viable population of pardel lynx in the world.

The southern flanks of the Sierra Morena descend to the broad depression of the Río Guadalquivir – christened '*wadi Al'Kabir*' by the Moors, literally 'big river' – which rises in the Sierra de Cazorla (home to a plethora of endemic calcicolous fissure plants and the bulk of the world population of Spanish algyroides) and discharges into the Atlantic at Doñana 655 km later. The left-bank tributaries of this mighty river originate in the limestone labyrinth of the Sierras Subbéticas, which in turn give way to the Sierras Béticas along the south coast, whose crags and defiles harbour Europe's best breeding nucleus of Bonelli's eagle, accompanied by important populations of chough and blue rock thrush.

The most impressive element of the Sierras Béticas is undoubtedly the metamorphic hulk of the Sierra Nevada, culminating in the highest peak in the peninsula: Mulhacén (3482 m). This is one of Europe's botanical hot-spots, harbouring more than 2100 species of vascular plant, including almost 80 taxa found nowhere else in the world. Many endemic races of butterfly occur here, with more than 15 000 Spanish ibex gracing the higher levels, accompanied by the southernmost nucleus of alpine accentor in Iberia and the most meridional population of snow vole in the world.

Andalucía is also home to a number of inland wetlands of international ornithological significance, most of which are lagoons of endorheic origin. Fuente de Piedra is renowned for its breeding greater flamingos – the second-most important colony in western Europe – and gull-billed terns, while the rosary of small lagoons in the hinterland of the Bahía de Cádiz, notably those of Medina and Espera, support significant breeding populations of white-headed duck, crested coot and purple gallinule. The more permanent Lagunas de Córdoba, the Albufera de Adra and Cañada de las Norias also harbour important enclaves of white-headed duck, with a few pairs of marbled teal nesting in the latter. The *salinas* at Punta Entinas–Sabinar, Cabo de Gata and the Bahía de Cádiz, are favoured by breeding collared pratincole, black-winged stilt, avocet and Kentish plover, all of which can be seen in even greater numbers at Doñana. The autumn passage of storks and raptors across the Strait of Gibraltar is exceptional.

Andalucía boasts more than 80 protected areas covering around 20% of the region, of which two are national parks, seven are Biosphere Reserves and eight are Ramsar Sites. Check out www.cma.junta-andalucia.es/espacios_naturales/indespacios.html for more information.

135 Marismas del Odiel
SITE

Some of the most extensive and best-preserved intertidal saltmarshes in Spain, with important spoonbill and heron colonies plus a healthy nucleus of little terns.

The Marismas del Odiel (a *paraje natural* of 6825 ha, also a Ramsar Site, Biosphere Reserve and ZEPA) is undoubtedly the most important tidal wetland on the Andalucían coast, with more than 300 species of bird recorded here, despite lying within a stone's throw of the industrial port of Huelva. A large proportion of the protected area is carpeted with intertidal saltmarshes of spirit-level flatness dissected by deep channels known as *esteros*, with other habitats present including large expanses of *salinas* (about 1000 ha), permanent brackish lagoons and sand dunes, the latter best developed along the spit known as El Espigón which extends right to the mouth of the estuary.

The lower tidal reaches are dominated by small cord-grass and purple, perennial and common glassworts, with dwarf eelgrass forming permanently submerged meadows. As tidal influence decreases, these give way to well-consolidated beds of the South American invader *Spartina densiflora* plus *Arthrocnemum macrostachyum*, shrubby sea-blite and sea-purslane, coloured by *Limonium ferulaceum*, resplendent spikes of *Cistanche phelypaea* and golden-samphire. Where marshes and sand dunes meet, belts of the lovely pink-flowered limoniastrum and mats of greater sea-spurrey and sea heath appear.

The avian star of Odiel is undoubtedly the spoonbill, more than 400 pairs of which breed on the Isla de Enmedio (*reserva natural*; 479 ha) which lies roughly in the centre of the site, here nesting in rush-beds rather than in trees as at Doñana. Also significant is the little tern colony on the Espigón – the largest in Spain – where 400 pairs reared more than 500 chicks in 2000. Other breeding waterbirds include several hundred pairs of little egret and grey heron, as well as lesser numbers of purple and night herons, little bittern, marsh harrier, purple gallinule, black-winged stilt and Kentish plover.

In winter, the marshes and *salinas* teem with aquatic birds, regularly attracting up to 30 000 waders and 10 000 duck, including

Map labels:
0 5 km
Gibraleón
Trigueros
Marismas del Burro
Aljaraque
Calatilla Huelva
Moguer
Laguna de El Portil
Isla de Enmedio
Palos de la Frontera
El Portil
Monasterio de la Rábida
Isla de Bacuta
Estero de Domingo Rubio
Enebrales de Punta Umbría
Punta Umbría
Laguna de Palos y las Madres
Marismas del Odiel
El Espigón
Mazagón

Limoniastrum *Limoniastrum monopetalum* (T.F.)

hundreds (if not thousands) of black-necked grebe, shoveler, dunlin, black-tailed godwit, redshank and lesser black-backed and black-headed gulls, as well as considerable numbers of cormorant, teal, wigeon, red-crested pochard, shelduck and grey plover. A dozen or more ospreys take advantage of the rich fishing grounds here at this time of year, while Sandwich and Caspian terns are also regular winter visitors. Greater flamingos are present all year round – and have even bred in small numbers in recent years – although they are most numerous in late summer, when post-breeding concentrations can number 2000 individuals, while avocets are usually most abundant on passage. Look out, too, for interesting casual visitors such as black stork, glossy ibis, red-breasted merganser, marsh sandpiper and

Audouin's and little gulls; in July 2000 three royal terns were observed.

The main freelance access to the Marismas del Odiel is the road which runs to the very end of El Espigón (about 26 km), along which you can sample all the main habitats present in the *paraje*. The northern part of the spit, around the visitor centre at Calatilla, is dedicated mainly to saltpans, populated by small groups of greater flamingos, spoonbills and little egrets at any time of year. Further south the verges are lined with white broom, gum and narrow-leaved cistuses, squirting cucumber and French lavender. A small bridge takes you onto the Isla de Bacuta, dominated by low-lying saltmarsh dotted with posts which are much favoured as perches by the wintering ospreys, and the only known locality for the lasiocampid moth *Malacosoma laurae*, discovered here in 1977, whose larvae feed on the abundant limoniastrum.

After Bacuta, the road passes over a high bridge; park just beforehand and walk over for the best views of the Isla de Enmedio and its ground-nesting spoonbills and grey herons (to the northwest). Continuing south, the road now traverses rather more solid terrain, punctuated by copses of stone pine and Phoenician juniper (subspecies *turbinata*) with a lush understorey of *Osyris quadripartita*, lentisc, *Rhamnus lycioides* subspecies *oleoides*, *Halimium halimifolium*, *H. calycinum*, rosemary, Sodom's apple and hollow-stemmed asphodel: a great place to track down reptiles, particularly large and Spanish psammodromus and spiny-footed and ocellated lizards.

As the spit narrows, you traverse an area of sparsely vegetated sand dunes, hosting sand stock, sea rocket, sea medick, sea spurge,

Information and access: The Calatilla interpretation centre is located on the Espigón, 2 km south of the A-497 which links Huelva with Punta Umbría (tel. and fax: 959 500236; e-mail:PN.MarismasOdiel@cma.junta-andalucia.es). If you want to get into the heart of the Marismas del Odiel you must book a guided tour with a company called Erebea (tel. and fax: 959 500512; e-mail: erebea@teleline.es), whose offices are behind the visitor centre; they offer boat-trips around the Isla de Enmedio in April–May and September–October, as well as 4WD trips and guided walks (weekends only).

sea-holly, *Echium gaditanum*, coastal cru-cianella, cottonweed, sea daffodil and *Cyperus capitatus*, while offshore a number of small islets provide high-tide roosts for wintering cormorants and waders, particularly curlew, grey plover, redshank, dunlin and turnstone. The road continues for about 6 km beyond the natural lie of the land out into the open sea, much frequented by Sandwich terns: a good place to watch for migrating seabirds, particularly Cory's and Balearic shearwaters.

Also in the area

Laguna de El Portil (*reserva natural*; 11 ha) Small seasonal lagoon west of Odiel, surrounded by a 1300 ha buffer zone of stone pines and massive Phoenician junipers. Hoop-petticoat daffodil and Barbary nut in spring and sea squill in autumn; open sands have sand stock, sea medick, *Echium gaditanum*, *Helichrysum italicum* subspecies *serotinum* and sea daffodil. Sharp-ribbed salamander, marbled newt, western spadefoot, stripeless tree frog and stripe-necked terrapin, plus wintering waders: black-winged stilt, little stint, black-tailed godwit and curlew. Black-necked grebe, glossy ibis and purple heron are regular passage visitors, while spoonbills from the Odiel and Doñana colonies often feed here. Breeding goshawk, great spotted woodpecker and crested tit. Mediterranean chameleons in the ancient white brooms around the hide at the eastern end of El Portil village.

Enebrales de Punta Umbría (*paraje natural*; 178 ha) Well-developed juniper forests – Phoenician (subspecies *turbinata*) and prickly (subspecies *macrocarpa*) – on coastal sand dunes. Resident azure-winged magpie and migrant passerines. Open dunes towards the sea have spiny thrift, coastal crucianella and sea daffodil, and are a noted haunt of stone curlew. Many reptiles, particularly Mediterranean chameleon, Moorish gecko, large and Spanish psammodromus, spiny-footed and ocellated lizards and Montpellier and horseshoe whip snakes. Look out, too, for Mediterranean skippers.

Estero de Domingo Rubio (*paraje natural*; 346 ha) Small tidal inlet at the foot of the Monasterio de la Rábida, with saltmarsh vegetation and many wintering and passage waders towards the mouth, plus extensive reed- and bulrush-beds around freshwater lakes further east (access via the A-494 between Palos de la Frontera and Mazagón), harbouring little bittern, red-crested pochard, purple gallinule and marsh harrier. Pinewoods around the monastery have spring-flowering three-leaved snowflake and *Narcissus gaditanus*.

Lagunas de Palos y las Madres (*paraje natural*; 635 ha) Two permanent endorheic lagoons plus several smaller, seasonal ones to the north of the N-442 just west of Mazagón, surrounded by ancient dunes clothed with mature stone pines. Thick stands of common reed, great fen-sedge, sea club-rush, *Typha domingensis*, African tamarisk and *Tamarix canariensis*. Important feeding ground for Doñana birds at the end of summer, notably spoonbill, white-headed duck, purple gallinule and water rail, plus greylag geese in winter. Otters regular. Exceptional odonates, including southern European *Orthetrum trinacria*, *Diplacodes lefebvrii*, *Brachythemis leucosticta* and *Trithemis annulata*, plus small red-eyed damselfly, western club-tailed dragonfly and vagrant emperor. Butterflies include Portuguese dappled white and African grass and silver-studded blues.

Marismas de Isla Cristina (*paraje natural* of 2525 ha; proposed Ramsar Site) Coastal saltmarsh, *salinas* and stone pine-clad dunes on the Spanish side of the Guadiana estuary. Breeding spoonbill (55–60 pairs) and Kentish plover (300–350 pairs), plus little terns (150 pairs) nesting in mixed colonies with black-winged stilt (some 300) pairs and avocet (maximum 220) pairs. Purple heron, cattle egret, stone curlew, collared pratincole, Caspian tern and small numbers of Montagu's and marsh harriers also breed. Many wintering waders, plus bee-eaters and whiskered terns on passage. Good *salinas* on the H-412 between Pozo del Camino and Isla Cristina, with extensive saltmarshes between Ayamonte and Isla Canela/Punta Moral.

136 Sierra Morena Occidental

SITE

The western sector of the Sierra Morena, housing one of the most important colonies of black vulture in the peninsula and good raptor populations in general.

The dark slaty ridge of the Sierra Morena extends east from the Portuguese border for more than 400 km, essentially separating Andalucía from Extremadura and Castilla–La Mancha. The bulk of the ridge, which rarely exceeds 900 m, is clothed with *dehesa* interspersed with huge secondary tracts of gum, narrow-leaved and poplar-leaved cistuses, *Cistus crispus*, Spanish heath and French lavender which, although monotonous, is home to some of the best populations of raptors and mammalian carnivores in Iberia. In Andalucía, virtually the whole of the Sierra Morena lies within one or another of a contiguous chain of protected areas.

At the extreme western end lie the Sierra de Aracena (a *parque natural* of 186 909 ha, also a ZEPA) and the *parajes naturales* of Peñas de Aroche (723 ha) and Sierra Pelada y Rivera del Aserrador (12 226 ha and ZEPA). The Atlantic influence on the flora here is palpable; Pyrenean oak woodland and groves of sweet chestnut litter the north-facing slopes, teeming with western peonies in May. More humid habitats harbour enclaves of cork oak, accompanied by *Pyrus bourgaeana*, white Spanish broom, *Genista hirsuta*, *Adenocarpus telonensis*, Iberian milk-vetch, myrtle, Lusitanian heath, tree germander and the Afro-Iberian endemic *Lavandula viridis*. Those forest formations which survive on south-facing slopes are dominated by Lusitanian and western holm oaks, here associated with lentisc, turpentine tree, strawberry-tree, tree heath, *Phillyrea angustifolia*, wild olive and laurustinus.

Black vulture *Aegypius monachus*

Orange-spotted emerald *Oxygastra curtisii*

The western Sierra Morena's most emblematic vertebrate is undoubtedly the black vulture, with the Sierra Pelada y Rivera del Aserrador housing some 70–80 pairs, here nesting in the crowns of isolated cork oaks. Golden eagle, a single pair of Bonelli's eagles and a plethora of short-toed and booted eagles also breed, with juvenile Spanish imperial eagles regularly dispersing over the area. Among the mammalian carnivores of note are a few pardel lynx and abundant beech marten, otter, Egyptian mongoose, common genet and wildcat.

The Rivera del Aserrador, a tributary of the Guadiana, harbours fine gallery forests of white poplar, alder and a range of willows, with drought-resistant oleander and *Securinega tinctoria* appearing in seasonal tributaries. Odonates of this and other rivers in the area include the endangered orange-spotted emerald, plus Mediterranean demoiselle, common winter, willow emerald and dainty damselflies, green-eyed hook-tailed dragonfly, crepuscular hawker, southern skimmer, scarlet darter and *Trithemis annulata*.

Further east, in northern Sevilla, the Sierra de Aracena merges imperceptibly into the Sierra Norte (a *parque natural* of 167 439 ha, also a ZEPA), whose impermeable substrata are riddled with small wetlands harbouring sharp-ribbed and fire salamanders, Bosca's and marbled newts, western spadefoot, Iberian midwife, natterjack and common toads and Iberian pool, Iberian painted and parsley frogs. European pond and stripe-necked terrapins occur in the rivers, with drier habitats hosting an abundance of large psammodromus, spiny-footed, ocellated and Iberian wall lizards and southern smooth snake.

On entering Córdoba, you find yourself in the Sierra de Hornachuelos (*parque natural*, 59 873 ha and ZEPA): one of the best-preserved sectors of the whole Sierra Morena, which boasts fine riverine forest along the Guadalora, almost pure stands of strawberry-tree and some 20 000 ha of prime lowland *dehesa*. The village of Hornachuelos itself lies on a small limestone outcrop harbouring wild olive and dwarf fan palm garrigue, while one of the region's few endemic flowers – *Centaurea cordubensis* – occurs in more acid, disturbed habitats, often accompanied by Childing pink, narrow-leaved crimson clover, daisy-leaved toadflax, *Linaria amethystea*, andryala and galactites.

The highlight of the park is the narrow valley of the river Bembézar, accessed via a trail extending for 11 km from the dam just below Hornachuelos upstream to the Embalse de Bembézar. In early spring the waysides are packed with friar's cowl and paper-white narcissus, while tufa outcrops harbour the lilac-blue flowers of throatwort later in the year and more acid rocks are decorated with scaly cheilanthes and rustyback. After 3 km, just past the ruins of the Santuario de Los Ángeles, a series of striking crags comes into view, where circling raptors consist mainly of the resident griffon vultures, but are often joined by black and Egyptian vultures, as well as any (or all!) of the five Iberian breeding eagles. Other birds associated with these rocky crags are black stork, pallid and alpine swifts, crag martin, red-rumped swallow, black wheatear, blue rock thrush, chough, raven and rock sparrow.

Elsewhere in the park, tracts of *dehesa* harbour little owl, hoopoe, crested lark, short-toed treecreeper, woodchat shrike, azure-winged magpie, spotless starling and serin, with more thickly vegetated habitats home to scops owl, golden oriole, wryneck, nightingale and melodious warbler. Open terrain should turn up red-necked nightjar, roller, black-eared wheatear and rock bunting, while white-rumped swift and rufous bush robin, both southern Iberian specialities, have also been cited in the park.

The Sierra Morena as a whole hosts a rich assemblage of spring butterflies but is rather poor later on in the year. Early spring in Hornachuelos brings out Spanish festoon, dappled white, nettle-tree butterfly, Provence hairstreak and African grass and black-eyed blues, followed a little later by cardinal, marsh fritillary, Spanish gatekeeper, false ilex hairstreak and long-tailed blue. Less commonplace species include sage, small, Lulworth and Essex skippers, scarce swallowtail, Cleopatra, twin-spot and Queen of Spain fritillaries, two-tailed pasha and Iolas blue.

Access and information: Most of the Sierra Morena comprises large private estates, so freelance access is limited; visit the various interpre-tation centres for further information. In the Sierra de Aracena, the principal interpretation centre (Cabildo Viejo) is in Aracena itself (tel. and fax: 959 128825; e-mail: PN.SAracena.PAroche@cma.junta-andalucia.es), while that of the Sierra Norte (El Robledo) is in Constantina (tel. and fax: 95 5881597; e-mail: PN.SNorte@cma.junta-andalucia.es). The Hornachuelos centre (Huerta del Rey) is in the village of the same name (tel. and fax: 957 641140; e-mail: PN. SHornachuelos@cma.junta-andalucia.es), and can provide you with on-the-spot permits for walks along the Guadalora and Bembézar rivers.

The three parks (Aracena, Sierra Norte and Hornachuelos) have recently been declared a Biosphere Reserve: Las Dehesas de Sierra Morena.

Also in the area

São Leonardo lagoon Shallow, endorheic waterbody north of the EX-107 (Villanueva del Fresno to Mourão road); from the Spanish–Portuguese border, head east and take the first asphalted left turn. Surrounding cereal fields are renowned for both bustards, black-bellied sandgrouse, stone curlew and calandra lark all year round, plus black kite, lesser kestrel and roller in summer and black-winged kite, crane and southern grey shrike in winter. Wintering herons and waders.

---

137 Doñana

The showpiece of Spanish nature conservation, without a doubt the most important wetland in the country and one of western Europe's prime birdwatching destinations; an important refuge for the pardel lynx, also of interest for its herptiles.

Although Doñana is the epithet widely recognised throughout Europe by birdwatchers and nature lovers alike, this vast wilderness of coastal marshes is more accurately referred to as the Marismas del Guadalquivir. The national park (56 544 ha), together with most of the surrounding natural park (55 099 ha), lies on the right bank of this mighty river, with the Brazo del Este (*paraje natural*; 1362 ha) encompassing the Isla Menor, on the left-hand margin.

Three-leaved snowflake *Leucojum trichophyllum* (Peter Wilson)

Unlike most Atlantic coastal wetlands, the Doñana marshes (also a ZEPA, Ramsar Site, Biosphere Reserve and World Heritage Site) are virtually independent of both sea and river. Rising sea levels at the end of the last glaciation resulted in the deposition of huge quantities of river-borne sediments in the former Guadalquivir estuary, thus isolating the marshes from the sea. The river carved out a new, narrow channel to the Atlantic, today leaving the *marismas* untouched by the tide.

Of the 200 000 ha of wetland documened in Roman times, however, barely 30 000 ha remain, nibbled away by schemes to convert pestilential, mosquito-ridden marshes into productive agricultural land. What survives is increasingly threatened by water extraction from the underlying aquifer to produce early strawberries, or by ecological disasters such as that of the Aznalcóllar mines in 1998, when more than 5 million cubic metres of toxic slag slid into the Río Guadiamar, poisoning the whole delicate food-web in the area surrounding the park. Today the marshes are maintained almost entirely by rainfall and often dry out before the end of the breeding season, such that many birds are forced to dis-perse to surrounding wetlands to feed in late summer.

These problems notwithstanding, it is estimated that around 8 million birds use the Guadalquivir marshes at some time during the year. No less than 378 species of bird have been recorded here, of which 136 breed regularly, while annual censuses of wintering individuals regularly exceed 1 200 000. The bulk of the wintering avifauna is made up of tens of thousands of greater flamingos, greylag geese, wigeon, teal, mallard, pintail, shoveler, coot, avocet, lapwing, ringed and Kentish plovers, little stint, dunlin, snipe, redshank, black-tailed godwit and black-headed and lesser black-backed gulls, although numbers vary from year to year according to the extent of the flooded area. In addition, black-necked grebe, cattle and little egrets, grey heron, white stork, shelduck, gadwall, pochard, red-crested pochard, common scoter, purple gallinule, black-winged stilt, little ringed, golden and grey plovers, sanderling, ruff, curlew, spotted redshank and green, wood and common sandpipers turn up by the thousand. Amid these hordes it is all but impossible to pick out the marbled teal and ferruginous and white-headed duck which spend the winter here in small numbers, although the cranes (up to 7000 individuals) and black storks are somewhat more conspicuous.

Notable among the breeding waterbirds are large concentrations of little and black-necked grebes, little bittern (2000 pairs), grey and purple herons, white stork, spoonbill (1400 pairs, the largest colony in Europe), purple gallinule (more than 5000 pairs, Iberia's principle nucleus), black-winged stilt (20 000 pairs), avocet, collared pratincole, Kentish plover, redshank and gull-billed and

Spur-thighed tortoise *Testudo graeca*

Andalucía

Doñana: coastal dunes

whiskered terns. These are accompanied by lesser numbers of squacco and night herons, gadwall, marbled teal, pochard, red-crested pochard, white-headed duck, stone curlew, slender-billed gull and little tern. Glossy ibis have bred – in a mixed colony with squacco herons – on the lagoon by the José Antonio Valverde visitor centre since 1996 (70+ pairs in 2000). Although greater flamingos nest from time to time (rearing 3800 chicks in 1984), the majority of those present in the marshes in summer are on nocturnal feeding forays from the colony at Fuente de Piedra (see p. 395).

Eleven pairs of the endangered Spanish imperial eagle (of only 152 pairs in the world in 2001) occupy territories in the Marismas del Guadalquivir, with other nesting raptors including short-toed and booted eagles, red and black kites (the 2000-odd pairs of the latter representing the most important breeding nucleus in Spain), marsh harrier, goshawk and hobby. Red kites are frequent winter visitors, along with a small but regular presence of black-winged kite and spotted eagle (5–10 individuals).

The outstanding mammal of Doñana is the pardel lynx, with some 40 individuals

inhabiting the area, plus large numbers of red and fallow deer and wild boar. Wildcat, Eurasian badger, western polecat, otter, common genet and Egyptian mongoose abound here, as do Iberian hare and southern water and Mediterranean pine voles, although rabbit populations have declined alarmingly in recent years. Among the 12 bats recorded are scarce species such as Mehely's and greater horseshoe, lesser mouse-eared, Geoffroy's and Schreiber's.

A long list of herptiles (21 reptiles and 11 amphibians) is headed by the increasingly rare spur-thighed tortoise, while spiny-footed lizard, large psammodromus, both Iberian skinks, Montpellier, ladder, horseshoe whip and false smooth snakes and Lataste's viper abound in the drier habitats. An exploration of the dune slacks might turn up sharp-ribbed salamander, Bosca's newt, western spadefoot, and stripeless tree frog, with European pond and stripe-necked terrapins thriving in the network of small streams. Doñana's most notable fish are *Barbus sclateri*, cacho, pardilla, *Cobitis paludica* and Spanish toothcarp, all Iberian endemics. Butterflies, on the other hand, are rather poorly represented here, with the

Andalucía

most emblematic species being Moroccan orange tip, African grass, Mazarine and silver-studded blues and Provence hairstreak.

The immense dune system which separates Doñana from the sea extends westwards from the mouth of the Guadalquivir almost as far as Mazagón. Much of the most westerly sector takes the form of a crumbling sandy cliff clothed in a rich psammophilic scrub, as can be seen at the Cuesta de Maneli (km 39 on the A-494). Many of the shrubs which clothe the leeward ascent are Afro-Iberian endemics, notably *Osyris quadripartita*, *Cytisus grandiflorus*, *Stauracanthus genistoides*, *Halimium calycinum*, *Corema album* and *Scrophularia frutescens*, accompanied by the more widespread Phoenician juniper (subspecies *turbinata*), *Halimium halimifolium*, myrtle and rosemary; spiny thrift and *Helichrysum italicum* subspecies *serotinum* appear at the crest.

The best embryo and primary dune vegetation occurs around Matalascañas, where swathes of cottonweed are interspersed with sea knotgrass, sea and sand stocks, sea medick, sea-holly, *Echium gaditanum*, coastal crucianella, sea daffodil and *Cyperus capitatus*, as well as the toadflax *Linaria tursica*, endemic to southwestern Iberia. The stabilised dunes behind are home to relict enclaves of prickly juniper (subspecies *macrocarpa*), while the seasonally inundated

dune slacks harbour green heather, *Corema album*, bog pimpernel, pennyroyal and heath lobelia. Kentish plover and stone curlew are the most typical breeding birds of these sparsely vegetated dunes, with spiny-footed lizards ten-a-penny; you might even encounter the endangered spur-thighed tortoise here.

The parallel waves of older dunes which are marching relentlessly inland are largely clothed with semi-natural stone pine forest, home to breeding booted eagle, red and black kites, hobby, great spotted cuckoo and azure-winged magpie. More significant, however, are the small enclaves of mature Mediterranean forest, dominated by cork oaks, some of which have a canopy more than 20 m in diameter, providing the main nesting habitat for Doñana's Spanish imperial eagles, as well as housing black kites and most of the mammalian predators of the park.

Most of this natural forest, however, has long since disappeared, resulting in the formation of fire-maintained scrub communities whose composition varies according to its position on the ancient dunes. The crests are generally characterised by *Halimium calycinum*, *Cistus libanotis*, unique to southwest Spain and Portugal, rosemary and round-headed thyme, studded with the nodding bells of three-leaved snowflake in

Doñana: feeding spoonbills in a freshwater lagoon

Andalucía

Doñana: Las Marismas de El Rocío

spring, while the middle slopes are clothed with the so-called *monte blanco* of Iberian endemic gorses – *Ulex australis* and *U. argenteus* subspecies *subsericeus* – plus *Cytisus grandiflorus, Halimium halimifolium* and *Cistus crispus*, often sheltering drifts of *Fritillaria lusitanica* early in the year. By contrast, the *monte negro* of the lowest slopes, where the water table is closer to the surface, is composed mainly of *Cistus psilosepalus*, ling, *Erica umbellata*, green heather, Dorset heath, the thrift *Armeria gaditana*, endemic to southwestern Iberia, purple moor-grass and huge white-flowered spikes of the grass *Imperata cylindrica*,

The narrow strip of grassland which marks the boundary between marsh and dry land – known as *la vera* – is inhabited by species of both terrestrial and aquatic ecosystems. Bee-eaters excavate their nests in low sandy banks and quail and yellow wagtails abound in summer; this is also one of the best places to track down red and fallow deer and wild boar. The scattered cork oaks in this belt harbour Doñana's world-famous colonies of spoonbill, grey and night herons, little and cattle egrets and white stork.

The heart of the national park harbours a number of more or less permanent lagoons which are maintained by the aquifer for most of the year, plus shallow, seasonal, brackish and freshwater pools known as *lucios*. These fairly well-defined waterbodies are surrounded by broad expanses of marshland, much of which is also inundated during very wet periods, forming a huge wetland which plays host to the majority of Doñana's wintering waterbirds. Among the belts of lesser bulrush, *Typha domingensis* and common reed which fringe the permanent lagoons, look out for marsh pennywort and narrow-leaved water-plantain, as well as odonates with a marked southern European distribution such as *Orthetrum trinacria, O. nitidinerve, Brachythemis leucosticta* and *Diplacodes lefebvrii*.

The only way to visit the interior of the national park is by joining one of the guided excursions (see box below), but a wealth of wildlife can also be encountered in the free-access marginal areas, not least in the Brazo del Este or around the village of El Rocío, which lies on the north bank of the wide watercourse known as the Madre de las Marismas de El Rocío. In early spring, the shallow pools here teem with feeding duck and flamingos, while the exposed mudflats harbour fidgety flocks of little stint and dunlin, large numbers of black-winged stilt, avocet, ruff and black-tailed godwit, and marsh sandpiper and Temminck's stint if you're lucky; this is also one of the best places to see crested coot in Doñana. The hides accessed from the La Rocina visitor centre to the west overlook a reed-fringed stream, boasting excellent views of purple gallinule, glossy ibis, little bittern and squacco heron early in the year, while the boardwalk to the western-most hides traverses a wide expanse of *monte blanco*, excellent for Thekla lark, red-necked nightjars after dusk on warm summer nights and scrub warblers in spring.

Doñana is best visited in autumn, winter or spring, but in the summer head for the working *salinas* in the natural park on the left bank of the Guadalquivir, where water is present all year round. The 40 000 ha or so of rice-paddies which border the park (access along tracks from Villamanrique and Villafranco) teem with birds at the end of summer, when the marshes themselves are often dry, as does the huge fish-farm known as Veta de Palma, adjacent to the Guadalquivir in the *parque natural*. It is here that the principal breeding nuclei of marbled teal, avocet, Kentish plover, slender-billed gull and little tern occur; although private, guided visits are planned for the near future.

Visiting Doñana

Five visitor centres in the national park and one in the *parque natural*:

La Rocina (tel: 959 442340) To the west of the A-483, 1 km south of the village of El Rocío (km 16). Interesting nature trail – Charco de la Boca (3.5 km) – takes in five hides overlooking the Arroyo de la Rocina.

El Acebrón Continue west past La Rocina for another 7 km. Nature trail (1.5 km) through mature cork oaks and stone pines and well-conserved gallery forest.

El Acebuche (tel: 959 448711) Principal visitor centre for the national park; from Matalascañas take the A-483 north for about 3 km, then turn left on the H-612. Nearby endorheic lagoon has eight hides, linked by a 1.5 km nature trail.

José Antonio Valverde Also known as Cerrado Garrido; accessible via a series of muddy tracks from Villafranco del Guadalquivir or Villamanrique de la Condesa (both about 30 km; pick up a map from El Acebuche).

Fábrica de Hielo In Sanlúcar de Barrameda, Cádiz (tel: 956 381635). The only visitor centre for the *parque natural* – **Bajo de Guía** – is also in Sanlúcar (tel: 956 360715).

e-mail contact for the national park is info@parquenacionaldonana.com

Brazo del Este No visitor centre but good freelance access (from the N-IV, signpost-ed 'Carretera de Isla Menor'); for more information contact the Seville branch of SEO/BirdLife (tel. and fax: 95 46442942; e-mail: andalucia@seo.org).

SEO/BirdLife also operates a small visitor centre and bird observatory on the north side of the Marismas de El Rocío; closed on Mondays (tel: 959 406093).

Cooperativa Marismas del Rocío (tel: 959 430432; fax: 959 430451) Offers 4WD trips departing from El Acebuche visitor cen-tre, taking 4 hours (at 8.30 am and 5.00 pm in summer (except Sundays), and at 8.30 am and 3.00 pm in winter (not Mondays); only 258 visitors permitted per day. Seven-hour trips also possible, but you must reserve the whole vehicle.

Cristóbal Anillo (tel: 956 363813; fax: 956 362916) Runs boat-trips up the Río Guadalquivir, incorporating two short walks in the national and natural parks, departing from close to the Fábrica de Hielo visitor centre in Sanlúcar de Barrameda (not Mondays); maximum 94 passengers per trip.

Discovering Doñana Runs 4WD excur-sions in both parks, with a maximum of eight passengers (tel: 959 442466; e-mail: donana@sistelnet.es). Best option for birdwatchers!

Andalucía

^{SITE}
138 Bahía de Cádiz

One of southern Europe's principal coastal wetlands, of interest for its breeding, migratory and wintering waterbirds, as well as for the superb stone pine forest of La Algaida.

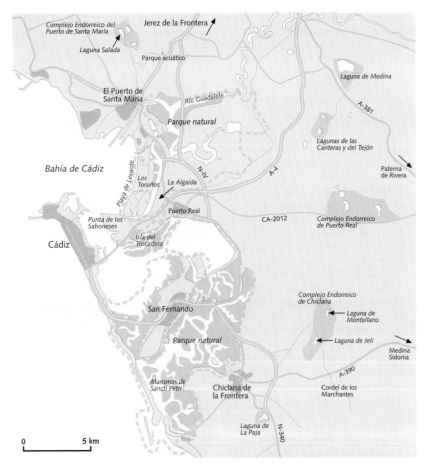

The city of Cádiz is located at the end of a tombolo which embraces a huge area of intertidal saltmarsh, more than 5000 ha of which was converted into a geometric grid of *salinas* by the Phoenicians. Despite the fact that the so-called Bahía de Cádiz (a *parque natural* of 10 453 ha; also a ZEPA and a proposed Ramsar Site) is surrounded by industrial development and urban nuclei, it is still harbours a wide range of wildlife.

The bay is effectively split in two by the Punta de los Saboneses; in the more northerly, outer bay the park encompasses the mouth of the Río Guadalete, the saltmarshes of Los Toruños and the fabulous sand dunes and stone pine forests of La Algaida, while the sheltered southerly sector encloses a vast maze of *salinas* and the more stringently protected *parajes naturales* of the Isla del Trocadero (290 ha) and Marismas de Sancti Petri (174 ha).

Andalucía

The intertidal saltmarsh flora – best preserved at Los Toruños and in the two *parajes naturales* – is dominated by dwarf eelgrass below the low-tide mark and purple and perennial glassworts and small cord-grass in the lower reaches, giving way to a diverse community of *Arthrocnemum macrostachyum*, common glasswort, annual sea-blite, *Suaeda splendens, Salsola vermiculata*, sea-purslane (parasitised by *Cistanche phelypaea*), limoniastrum, the sea-lavenders *Limonium algarvense, L. virgatum* and *L. ferulaceum*, golden-samphire and sea aster as the tidal influence diminishes. Damp pastures further inland are worth examining for three-leaved snowflake, Portuguese squill and *Allium pallens* in spring.

The embryo dunes of the Bahía de Cádiz, particularly along the Playa de Levante in the northern sector, are colonised by prickly saltwort and sea rocket, with the primary dunes stabilised by sand stock, southern birdsfoot-trefoil, sea spurge, sea-holly, *Anthemis maritima*, sea daffodil and marram. Moving inland, the secondary dunes support a mosaic of prickly juniper (subspecies *macrocarpa*), white broom, *Genista florida, Thymelaea hirsuta, Helichrysum italicum* subspecies *serotinum* and sea wormwood. In the dune slacks and areas where sandy ecosystems and saltmarshes meet, look out for the Afro-Iberian endemic sea heath *Frankenia boissieri* and the thrift *Armeria gaditana*, unique to southwestern Iberia.

At La Algaida, to the east of the Playa de Levante, the older dunes harbour mature stone pine forest which, although planted, shelters a rich understorey of Phoenician juniper, holly oak, *Osyris quadripartita, Cytisus villosus, Rhamnus lycioides, Corema album, Phillyrea angustifolia, Lonicera implexa* and dwarf fan palm, plus palmate anemone, wild gladiolus, *Romulea clusiana* and woodcock ophrys. Among the more notable plants of these sandy pinewoods are the thrift *Armeria macrophylla*, the chamomile-like *Hymenostemma pseudanthemis* and the fragrant *Scilla odorata*, all of which are endemic to the southern Iberian coast.

Most of the park's mammals occur at La Algaida, including Iberian blind mole,

weasel, garden dormouse and Iberian hare, with otters occupying both fresh and saline waters. Seasonal pools in the pine woods harbour many amphibians, notably sharp-ribbed salamander, Iberian painted, Iberian pool and parsley frogs, western spadefoot and natterjack toad, while both open dunes and the pine forests are home to an interesting assemblage of reptiles: a large population of Mediterranean chameleon, as well as spiny-footed and ocellated lizards, large psammodromus, three-toed skink and horseshoe whip, ladder and Montpellier snakes.

La Algaida is also home to nesting booted and short-toed eagles, black kite, long-eared, little and barn owls, red-necked nightjar and hoopoe, with the breeding passerine community including black-eared wheatear, Dartford and Sardinian warblers, woodchat shrike and serin. More open dunes are the haunt of stone curlew all year round and short-eared owl in winter. Butterflies in the park as a whole include sage and mallow skippers, scarce swallowtail, Spanish festoon, Spanish marbled white, dusky heath, Provence hairstreak, Spanish brown argus and long-tailed, African grass and Adonis blues.

Up to 50 000 waterbirds frequent the Bahía de Cádiz during the winter months, around half of which are waders. The lion's share of these are dunlin (12 000+ individuals), but you should also encounter smaller numbers of oystercatcher, black-winged stilt, avocet,

Portuguese squill *Scilla peruviana*

golden, grey, Kentish, little ringed and ringed plovers, sanderling, little stint, ruff, jack snipe, black-tailed and bar-tailed godwits, whimbrel, curlew, spotted redshank and greenshank. Since the 1980s, the gradual conversion of non-productive *salinas* to fish-farms means that wader numbers are declining, but the deeper waters find favour with wintering and passage spoonbills, herons and egrets and greater flamingos.

Outstanding among the bay's wintering duck are the 5000-odd wigeon present at any one time, with deeper waters in the outer reaches of the bay attracting divers, black-necked grebe and red-breasted merganser; gannet, Arctic and great skuas and razorbills patrol offshore at this time of year. Wintering gulls are predominantly lesser black-backed and yellow-legged, but look out, too, for Mediterranean and little gulls as well as kitti-wake and Caspian and Sandwich terns.

Osprey, peregrine, hen and marsh harriers and bluethroat also turn up regularly in and around the marshes in winter, while proximity to the Strait of Gibraltar means that the Bahía de Cádiz also attracts a wide variety of passage migrants, including black stork, garganey, marsh terns and innumerable waders and passerines.

In summer, the park supports notable concentrations of black-winged stilt (around 2000 pairs), avocet (1000 pairs), Kentish plover (several hundred pairs) and collared pratincole (140 pairs), as well as some sand-dune colonies of little tern, increasingly compromised by uncontrolled tourism. Spoonbills have also recently started breeding in the abandoned *salinas* – 28 pairs in 1997 – while short-toed larks nest in the drier marshes. Post-breeding concentrations of greater flamingo can exceed 1200 individuals.

Access and information: The park headquarters are in San Fernando (tel: 956 590405; fax: 956 880259; e-mail: PN.BahiaCadiz@cma.junta-andalucia.es). Many roads traverse the bay and several waymarked footpaths take in the saltmarshes, sand dunes and pinewoods, but access to the privately owned *salinas* is prohibited; permits are required to visit the Isla del Trocadero and Marismas de Sancti Petri.

---

139 Laguna de Medina

An endorheic lagoon to the northeast of the Bahía de Cádiz, with breeding white-headed duck, purple gallinule and crested coot and wintering marbled teal.

The rosary of shallow, often seasonal lagoons strung across the hinterland of the Bahía de Cádiz is but a remnant of a once far more extensive network of natural lakes, many of which were drained in the second half of the twentieth century. The largest and perhaps most important of these is the Laguna de Medina (*reserva natural* of 123 ha, also a ZEPA and Ramsar Site); despite covering some 120 ha when full, it often dries out completely by late summer (see map on p. 378).

Extensive reedbeds, stands of *Typha domingensis*, sea club-rush and sea rush, and peripheral tamarisk scrub provide breeding habitat for a few pairs of little bittern, increasing numbers of purple gallinule and an abundance of Cetti's, fan-tailed, reed and great reed warblers, as well as attracting sedge warbler on passage and penduline tit and bluethroat in winter. White-headed duck and a few pairs of crested coot regularly breed here, with other nesting waterbirds

Mandrake *Mandragora autumnalis*

including red-crested pochard, pochard, black-winged stilt and Kentish and little ringed plovers. Look out, too, for purple heron and collared pratincole at this time of year, plus a summer roost of some 300 cattle egrets. Greater flamingos occur all year round, as do hunting marsh harriers.

Providing the rains have refilled the lagoon, late summer and autumn habitually see congregations of some 25 000 coot and flocks of up to 110 marbled teal here, mostly from nearby Doñana, while the reedbeds provide cover for hundreds of thousands of roosting swallows and other hirundines prior to the autumn migration. Regular winter denizens include black-necked grebe, gadwall, pochard and red-crested pochard, white-headed duck (around 220 individuals in February 2001), up to 350 Mediterranean gulls, the occasional ferruginous duck and rarities such as scaup and goldeneye. When water levels are low, the muddy margins of the lagoon attract small numbers of migrating waders, primarily little stint, curlew sandpiper, spotted redshank and, more rarely, Temminck's stint and marsh sandpiper. Spoonbill, squacco and night herons, greylag goose, shelduck, garganey and black and whiskered terns also occur on passage.

The Laguna de Medina is surrounded by a peripheral protection zone of dry pastures and cereal fields interspersed with patches of Mediterranean scrub dominated by holly oak, lentisc, cistuses, wild olive, rosemary, *Phlomis purpurea* and dwarf fan palm; spring brings a flush of insect-imitating sawfly, mirror, yellow and bumble-bee ophrys into bloom here, with mandrakes flowering in autumn. The area is an important hunting ground for juvenile Spanish imperial eagles dispersing from Doñana at the end of the summer and also harbours typical open-country birds such as

Laguna de Medina

Montagu's harrier, quail, black-eared wheatear and woodchat shrike, as well as numerous red kites and an occasional hen harrier in winter. Among the most character- istic reptiles of the lagoon itself are European pond terrapin and viperine snake, with amphibians including sharp-ribbed sala- mander and Iberian pool frog.

Access: Medina is reached from the A-381 which links Jerez de la Frontera with Medina Sidonia (at km 10); you can no longer walk right round the lake, but a track along the southern shore gives good views over the reedbeds and open water. Follow the track which leads southwest from Medina for 3 km to get to the small, seasonal and highly saline **Lagunas de las Canteras y del Tejón** (*reserva natural*; 15 ha).

Also in the area

The Medina Ramsar Site also encom- passes the **Laguna Salada**, the largest and most permanent waterbody of the **Complejo Endorreico del Puerto de Santa María** (*reserva natural*; 53 ha, also a ZEPA), about 4 km to the north of the port. Breeding little bittern, white- headed duck, crested coot, water rail, purple gallinule, black-winged stilt, and moustached warbler; collared pratin- coles and bee-eaters breed nearby and often feed here. Passage night and purple herons, avocet, ruff, both god- wits, green and wood sandpipers and marsh terns, with marbled teal fairly abundant in winter, along with golden plover, snipe, bluethroat and penduline tit. Access off the N-IV, at the junction signposted 'Aquasherry Parque Acuático'; follow the track west.

About 8 km south of Medina lies the **Complejo Endorreico de Puerto Real** (*reserva natural*; 107 ha, also a ZEPA), to the north of the CA-2012 linking Puerto Real with Paterna de Rivera. Permanent Laguna de San Antonio has breeding little bittern, purple heron and purple gallinule, with white-headed duck and crested coot visible at any time of year; black-winged kite and large concentra- tions of white storks common in autumn (more than 3000 in September 2000).

The **Complejo Endorreico de Chiclana** (*reserva natural*; 56 ha, also a ZEPA) lies several kilometres north of the A-390 (Chiclana de la Frontera to Medina Sidonia road). Where an old drover's road – the Cordel de los Marchantes – crosses the A-390 (about 7 km from Chiclana) walk north to the Jeli lagoon (about an hour) and that of Montellano some 45 minutes later. Deeper, with better-developed submerged macro- phytes: horned pondweed, *Zannichellia peltata*, beaked tasselweed and fennel pondweed. Black-necked grebe, spoon- bill, marbled teal, white-headed duck, marsh harrier, purple gallinule, crested coot and spotted crake. The last of the Lagunas de Cádiz is that of **La Paja** (*reserva natural concertada*; 40 ha), located immediately west of the N-340 to the south of Chiclana.

SITE
140 Breña de Barbate

Extensive cliff-top stone pine forest with cliff-breeding cattle egrets and many plants restricted to southern Iberia.

In contrast to the low-lying coastline of most of Spain's southern Atlantic shore, the area to the west of Barbate is dominated by a 10 km stretch of impressive sandstone escarpment, rising sheer from the sea to a height of over 100 m, its western end marked by Cabo de Trafalgar, the site of Nelson's famous naval victory in 1805.

The lower layers of this rugged, golden precipice are thought to correspond to a fossilised sand-dune system, while the upper section is composed mainly of coarse limestones. Fierce onshore winds have created a series of highly mobile dunes at the top of the cliff, which were planted with stone pines at the beginning of the twentieth century to prevent their inland advance. Today this mature forest – the *breña* – is probably the best conserved of its kind in Andalucía. The drier sections support a sparse understorey of Phoenician juniper, the Afro-Iberian endemic, semi-parasitic *Osyris quadripartita*, Spanish broom, mountain rue, lentisc, *Rhamnus lycioides* subspecies *oleoides*, *Thymelaea hirsuta*, wild olive and

rosemary, with more humid hollows harbouring a luxuriant tangle of holly oak, white broom, rush-like scorpion-vetch, the sticky-leaved, white-flowered *Cistus libanotis*, found only in southwestern Iberia, strawberry-tree and shrubby pimpernel.

The most interesting vegetation of the *breña* is found close to the cliff top, however, where the stone pines are replaced by a narrow belt of wind-pruned Aleppo pines, whose meagre canopy allows more light to reach the forest floor. Here the dominant shrubs are the coastal subspecies of prickly juniper (*macrocarpa*), spectacular yellow-flowered bushes of *Halimium halimifolium* and *H. calycinum* and tree germander, draped with Virgin's bower and *Aristolochia baetica*, while open sands are decorated with showy clumps of *Romulea ramiflora* subspecies *gaditana* in spring and *Crocus serotinus* subspecies *clusii* in late autumn. This is also a good area in which to track down the Afro-Iberian endemic restharrow *Ononis subspicata*, shrubby violet, the thrift *Armeria macrophylla*, unique to Cádiz and the Algarve, the delicate, white-flowered annual omphalodes and the diminutive, yellow *Linaria oblongifolia* subspecies *haenseleri*, known only from southern Iberia.

These sun-baked, sandy habitats are particularly favoured by reptiles, notably Moorish gecko, ocellated lizard, large psammodromus, three-toed skink, horseshoe whip and Montpellier snakes and Lataste's viper, while the more mature white broom scrub is a renowned haunt of Mediterranean chameleon. Where seasonal pools form in hollows further inland you might turn up marbled newt, stripeless tree and parsley frogs and western spadefoot. Two-tailed pasha and migrant monarchs and plain tigers are the most noteworthy butterflies here.

Among the mammals are Iberian blind mole, greater white-toothed shrew, garden

Aristolochia baetica

dormouse, Eurasian badger, red fox and rabbit, while breeding birds include buzzard, booted eagle, red and black kites and scops, little and tawny owls at the top of the food chain, plus passerines such as spotted flycatcher, Bonelli's and melodious warblers and woodchat shrike. During the autumn passage period, particularly when onward migration across the Mediterranean is held up by poor weather, the pines are often crammed with small birds and roosting raptors.

The main ornithological highlight of this *parque natural* (4817 ha), however, is the assemblage of cliff-breeding birds beneath the sixteenth-century watch-tower of the Torre del Tajo (positioned at roughly the midpoint of the scarp), dominated by 400–700 pairs of cattle egret, nesting precariously on narrow, inaccessible ledges where the cliff is at its highest, accompanied by small numbers of little egret (around 50 pairs), a burgeoning colony of yellow-legged gulls, swifts and pallid swifts and large numbers of vociferous jackdaws and spotless starlings, as well as a few pairs of kestrel, peregrine, rock dove, blue rock thrush and raven.

This cliff-top vantage point is a prime locality from which to watch the twice-yearly bird migration across the Strait of Gibraltar, particularly if the wind is in the east, while marine mammals – notably common and bottle-nosed dolphins – and loggerhead, leathery and green turtles can sometimes be spotted offshore. Cabo de Trafalgar, to the west, is a renowned site among sea-watching enthusiasts, turning up great and sooty shearwaters, pomarine skua, Audouin's gull and gull-billed tern during passage periods and Leach's storm-petrel, Sandwich and Caspian terns, kittiwake and auks in winter.

The park also encompasses the intricate network of braided channels formed by the Río Barbate as it spreads across the low-lying basin behind the coast to the east. This ancient estuary, filled with river-borne sediments as the result of rising sea levels at the end of the last glaciation, is a veritable labyrinth of saltmarshes, *salinas* and intertidal mudflats, closed to the sea by a pincer-like pair of low sandspits. Although seemingly little visited by ornithologists, given the paucity of records for the area, typical breeding birds of the drier saltmarshes are known to include quail and lesser short-toed and short-toed larks, with collared pratincoles and yellow wagtails around the saltpans. During the winter fair numbers of lapwing and golden plover congregate in the brackish marshes, while avocets and black-winged stilts stalk through the *salinas* and small numbers of duck frequent the sheltered open water behind the spits.

Access and information: There is no visitor centre, but more information can be obtained from the headquarters of the Bahía de Cádiz *parque natural* (see p. 380). A route along the cliff top to the Torre del Tajo departs from just west of Barbate and a trail through the marshes, along the right bank of the main river channel, links Barbate with Vejer de la Frontera.

Also in the area

La Janda Formerly an enormous lagoon but drained to form a vast, this-tle-clad plain dissected by permanent channels and ditches to the north of the N-340 between Tahivilla and Vejer. Still an important staging post for migrants, sometimes harbouring more than 85 000 birds in autumn. In winter the area attracts small bands of greylag geese, cranes, lapwing and golden plover. Breeding steppe birds include little bustard, stone curlew and

Montagu's harrier, plus the only great bustards left in the province of Cádiz (a handful); white stork and collared pratincole (about 100 pairs) also breed. Foraging griffon vultures and Bonelli's eagles from their nesting areas in Los Alcornocales (see below). Juvenile Spanish imperial eagles from Doñana hunt here in autumn, with hen harrier, red and black-winged kites, booted eagle and short-eared owl occurring in winter. Cliffs to the north have nesting Egyptian vulture and peregrine. Much is private, but limited access at the southeastern end of the site; opposite the CA-2221 which leads south to Zahara de los Atunes, take the track north as far as the canalised Río Almodóvar (just over 1 km) and follow the watercourse in either direction.

SITE 141 Los Alcornocales

Ancient, humid cork oak forests harbouring 264 species of vertebrate – including 14 breeding raptors – and 40-odd species of fern.

Sometimes referred to as the 'Mediterranean Jungle', Los Alcornocales (a *parque natural* of 168 661 ha; also a ZEPA) is probably the largest cork oak forest in the world, maintained by high-humidity weather systems originating in the nearby Atlantic. The labyrinth of low sandstone ridges is clothed with an impenetrable mass of woodland from which only the highest peaks emerge, while secreted within its depths are a number of narrow, V-shaped river valleys known as *canutos*, which conceal relict enclaves of semitropical vegetation.

Although the core of the forest is dominated by cork oak, Algerian oak occurs in damp, shady areas and Lusitanian and western holm oaks abound on base-rich outcrops to the north and south. On the cooler, north-facing slopes of the Sierra del Aljibe (maximum 1092 m) stands of Pyrenean oak persist up to about 900 m, but above the tree-line the semi-evergreen *Quercus lusitanica* prevails: a suckering shrub found only in Iberia and North Africa which rarely exceeds 2 m in height.

The cork oak forests shelter a thick tangle of turpentine tree, poplar-leaved cistus, Mediterranean buckthorn, strawberry-tree, myrtle, wild olive, *Phillyrea angustifolia* and laurustinus. Particularly humid habitats harbour Dorset, Irish and Spanish heaths, green heather and *Erica umbellata*, as well as the curious, insectivorous yellow sundew. The richest flora, however, occurs in the *canutos*, particularly those in the southern part of the park – along the Río de la Miel, for example, accessible via a waymarked trail from Los Barrios – where the microclimate is characterised by 90% humidity, constant temperatures of 20°C and permanent shade, giving rise to Tertiary relict cloud forests. Here alder and bay are associated with alder buckthorn (subspecies *baetica*), holly, the amazingly floriferous *Rhododendron ponticum* subspecies *baeticum* and Spanish butcher's broom. The rich fern flora includes maiden-

White-rumped swift *Apus caffer*

hair, royal and lady ferns, but of far greater interest is the assemblage of Afro-Iberian endemic species – *Culcita macrocarpa*, *Diplazium caudatum*, *Psilotum nudum* and *Pteris incompleta*, the latter two in their only Continental European localities here – plus the essentially Atlantic Killarney fern and the diminutive, tropical *Thelypteris dentata*.

These forests harbour the southernmost population of roe deer in Europe – rather scarce today – as well as red deer, reintroduced in the 1950s. Pardel lynx are reputed to be present in the area, but far more characteristic predators are wildcat, common genet, beech marten, Eurasian badger and western polecat, as well as one of Europe's largest populations of Egyptian mongoose. No less than 20 species of bat have been cited here, including all four horseshoes, greater mouse-eared, Schreiber's, Bechstein's and Leisler's. Forest-breeding raptors include large numbers of booted and short-toed eagles, goshawk, sparrowhawk and scops and tawny owls, sharing their habitat with great spotted woodpecker, Bonelli's warbler, firecrest, crested tit, nuthatch and short-toed treecreeper.

More open river valleys are fringed with gallery forests of Mediterranean willow, small-leaved elm and narrow-leaved ash, with spring-lines home to the cream-flowered pimpernel *Anagallis crassifolia* and ivy-leaved bellflower. Otters are still fairly common along the park's multitudinous rivers, while typical birds of these habitats include kingfisher, yellow wagtail, dipper, nightingale, golden oriole and hawfinch; look out, too, for rufous bush robin. A number of reptiles and amphibians inhabit the slower-flowing watercourses, notably stripe-necked terrapin, sharp-ribbed and fire salamanders, Bosca's and marbled newts, Iberian painted frog – with the related Iberian endemic *Discoglossus jeanneae* in lime-rich areas – both midwife and Iberian midwife toads, stripeless tree and parsley frogs and western spadefoot.

The rocky sandstones of the Sierra del Aljibe harbour a rather different flora, including the western Iberian endemics *Polygala microphylla*, *Senecio lopezii* and the yellow-flowered *Allium scorzonerifolium*, as well as the shrubby legumes *Ulex borgiae* (confined to the provinces of Cádiz and

Semi-evergreen oaks, Los Alcornocales

Playa de los Lances

Málaga) and *Teline tribracteolata*, known only from the Aljibe ridge. Shady fissures are populated by the ferns *Cheilanthes guanchica* and *Davallia canariensis*, also hosting *Scilla monophyllos* and both hoop-petticoat daffodil and white hoop-petticoat daffodils in early spring. In sunny weather these rock-gardens are worth examining for basking Moorish gecko, large psammodromus and Iberian wall and ocellated lizards, as well as horseshoe whip and ladder snakes and Lataste's vipers. Among Aljibe's notable butterflies are sage skipper, Spanish festoon, large tortoiseshell, cardinal, two-tailed pasha, tree grayling, Provence hairstreak and Spanish brown argus. A trail to the top of the *sierra* departs from La Sauceda (on the CA-3331, south of the Puerto de Galis).

The best cliff-breeding raptor colonies are found in the parks' southern limestone *sierras*, which harbour almost 400 pairs of griffon vulture, Egyptian vulture (25 pairs in the park), Bonelli's eagles (20-odd pairs) and large numbers of peregrines and eagle owls, as well as alpine swift, black wheatear and blue rock thrush; to the west, Alcalá de los Gazules has a colony of lesser kestrels. Rocky outcrops near water should turn up the characteristic nests of red-rumped swallows (like upside down igloos, complete with entry tunnel), also used by white-rumped swifts, which mark their territory with a few white feathers at the entrance. White-rumped swifts were first discovered breeding in the Iberian peninsula in 1964 near Zahara de los Atunes (on the coast to the west of the park); a good place to search them out is along the extremely potholed road which follows the Ojén valley between Facindas and Los Barrios, but they are also found around Jimena and Castellar de la Frontera.

Access and information: Many extremely scenic roads traverse the park, while the visitor centres will be able to give you details of waymarked walks. The principal one is located in Algeciras (Huerta Grande, Barriada El Pelayo, N-340 km 72; tel: 956 679161), with subsidiary information points in Cortes de la Frontera, Algar, Los Barrios, Castellar de la Frontera and Jimena. Queries by e-mail to: PN.Alcornocales @cma.junta-andalucia.es, with www. alcornocales.org an interesting website.

Andalucía

Also in the area

Sierra de la Plata Limestone ridge between Barbate and Tarifa harbouring breeding griffon and Egyptian vultures and white-rumped and little swifts. Spring-flowering palmate anemone, Spanish iris, Portuguese squill and wild tulip, plus Cleopatra, Moroccan orange tip, Spanish festoon and long-tailed blue.

Playa de los Lances (*paraje natural*; 256 ha) A 5 km-long beach just west of Tarifa, backed by low dunes, saltmarsh and stone pines. Breeding short-toed larks and Kentish plover (80 pairs) and much used by migratory birds prior to passage across the Strait in autumn. Wintering waders and large numbers of Sandwich terns, with many Audouin's gulls in late summer and an occasional lesser crested tern in autumn.

Marismas del Río Palmones (*paraje natural*; 81 ha) Small estuary in the heart of the heavily industrialised Bahía de Algeciras, attracting passage greater flamingo, spoonbill, squacco heron, marbled teal, shelduck and short-eared owl and wintering garganey, marsh harrier, osprey, little gull, bluethroat, penduline tit and reed bunting. Resident water rail and little ringed and Kentish plovers, plus yellow wagtail and short-toed lark in summer. Open-topped observatory on the right bank of the river Palmones.

Gibraltar (British dependent territory covering 586 ha) Jurassic limestones form a sheer cliff on the eastern side (maximum 423 m), hosting locally endemic *Silene tomentosa* and Gibraltan candytuft plus the Afro-Iberian endemic sea-lavender *Limonium emarginatum*. Spring-flowering hollow-stemmed asphodel, dipcadi, three-cornered garlic, paper-white daffodil, mirror and bumble-bee ophrys, Barbary nut and the sand-crocus *Romulea clusiana*, known only from here and the province of Cádiz. Zeller's skipper and two-tailed pasha (larval food-plant *Osyris quadripartita* here), plus ocellated lizard and horseshoe whip snake. Around 230 birds cited, mostly on migration, but including the only European mainland population of Barbary partridge (also in Sardinia and Canarias), probably introduced from Africa in ancient times. Also a small free-living population of Barbary ape.

Estuario del Río Guadiaro (*paraje natural*; 33 ha) Small estuary surrounded by the luxury resort of Sotogrande with breeding reedbed warblers. Passage little bittern, night and purple herons, spotted crake and gull-billed, Caspian, little, common, whiskered and black terns (plus occasional royal and lesser crested). Wintering black-necked grebe, common scoter, red-breasted merganser and Mediterranean and little gulls.

Lagunas de Espera

Three endorheic lagoons of great importance for their wintering and migratory birds and breeding white-headed duck, purple gallinule and crested coot.

The Lagunas de Espera (*reserva natural* of 47 ha and ZEPA of 438 ha) are one of Spain's best-kept wildlife secrets, although to appre-

ciate this you must visit in April or May, before the water has evaporated and the rich assemblage of calcicolous annuals has shrivelled to nothing under the scorching summer sun.

The smallest lagoon is Hondilla, adjacent to the road and surrounded by a belt of sea rush, sea club-rush, *Typha domingensis* and common reed. Most years it is incredibly easy to see purple gallinule here in late April, with other habitual denizens including little and black-necked grebes, purple heron, black-winged stilt and yellow wagtail, the air echoing with the harsh calls of Iberian pool frogs and great reed warblers.

The trail south towards the second lagoon – Laguna Salada de Zorrilla, the largest of the three – runs through a colourful display of love-in-a-mist, fennel flower, tiny scarlet pheasant's-eye, bladder vetch, squirting cucumber, blue pimpernel, mallow-leaved bindweed, borage, large blue alkanet, yellow gromwell, *Stachys ocymastrum*, fedia, annual bellflower, *Asteriscus aquaticus*, yellow cupidone and the purplish, pencil-like spadices of the Afro-Iberian endemic *Biarum arundanum*.

The wealth of nectar on offer attracts swarms of insects, with butterflies including green-striped, dappled and Bath whites, clouded yellow, Cleopatra, painted lady, red admiral, Spanish gatekeeper and small copper, while towards the marshy margins of Salada you should look out for odonates such as scarlet and red-veined darters, goblet-marked damselfly and lesser emperor drag-onfly, as well as for large numbers of sizeable red-striped oil beetles – *Berbermeloe majalis* – trundling across the path.

Zorrilla supports salt-tolerant submerged macrophytes such as fennel and horned pondweeds and is fringed with African tamarisks. In spring, the surface is dotted with gadwall, red-crested pochard and pochard, plus good numbers of black-necked grebe and white-headed duck, with black-winged stilts and avocets stalking the margins; you might even encounter small groups of greater flamingos at this time of year. Thick reed and bulrush beds are the haunt of Cetti's, great reed and fan-tailed warblers, while the bushy wild olives along the trail are home to nesting turtle dove, nightingale and melodious warbler.

Continuing south, you enter a wide expanse of dry grassland, studded with clumps of dwarf fan palm and coloured by *Malva cretica*, tree lavatera, malope, bellardia, *Nonea vesicaria* and *Cleonia lusitanica* in early spring, which later give way to an attractive, if spiny, mass of *Cynara humilis*, cardoon, *Carduncellus caeruleus*, Syrian and milk thistles, red star-thistle and Spanish oyster plant. This area often turns up stone curlew and red-legged partridge, as well as rabbit and Iberian hare, while raptors float overhead in search of prey; as well as expected species such as Montagu's and marsh harriers, look out for booted and short-toed eagles, black kite, griffon vulture and just possibly Spanish imperial eagle. Reptiles include spiny-footed and ocellated lizards, three-toed skink and Montpellier snake, while a small well to the right of the track usually hosts a European pond terrapin or two.

The third lagoon – Dulce de Zorrilla – lies just out of sight behind the brow of a hill. Deeper than the others, it usually contains water throughout the year and is one of the easiest places in Spain to track down crested coot (15 pairs bred in 2001). These tend to skulk nearer the shore, with most of the individuals here having been tagged with conspicuous numbered necklaces as part of an ongoing monitoring programme. Purple gallinules are also ten-a-penny, particularly amid the dead bulrush tussocks along the

Fennel flower *Nigella hispanica*

Laguna Dulce de Zorrilla (T.F.)

northern edge of the lagoon, with purple herons often turning up on migration.

To the west of the lagoons, the main track continues through patchy Mediterranean forest, where you might turn up roller and golden oriole as well as little owl, black-eared wheatear, Sardinian warbler and woodchat and southern grey shrikes in late spring. Turn right onto the tarmac at the end to return to the Espera to Cabezas de San Juan road, passing the diminutive Laguna del Pilón en route.

Access: From the village of Espera, just to the north of which you turn west towards Las Cabezas de San Juan (labelled CA-4412 on the Michelin map and CA-P-4413 on the ground). After 1 km, turn left at a cross-roads onto a wide track and follow it down the hill and round to the right until you reach Hondilla on the left, by a gate-way bearing a *reserva natural* sign (which leads to the other two lagoons).

Also in the area

Embalse de Bornos (*paraje natural*; 692 ha) The tail-end – where the Río Guadalete enters the reservoir – harbours extensive tamarisk thickets, home to oli-vaceous warbler and an important mixed colony of cattle and little egrets and night and purple herons, easily visible to the north of the A-382 (between Villamartín and the A-371 turn-off) when water levels are high.

---

143 Sierra de Grazalema

Superb limestone landscape harbouring an important enclave of Spanish fir, sizeable griffon vulture colonies, abundant Spanish ibex and a rich flora including many endemic species.

The spectacular limestone massif of the Sierra de Grazalema (a *parque natural* of 53 439 ha; also a ZEPA and Biosphere Reserve) is yet another of Andalucía's prime destinations for nature-lovers. Reaching a maximum height of 1654 m (Torreón),

Grazalema is the westernmost of the Sierras Béticas, separated from the Atlantic only by a low-lying coastal plain and thus intercepting the lion's share of the region's rainfall (some 2230 mm per year).

As a result of long-term karstification, the terrain is distinctly rugged, characterised by sheer cliffs, precipitous gorges and a complex network of subterranean galleries; one of these, the Hundidero–Gata complex, is more than 5 km long and harbours one of Europe's largest winter bat roosts – principally Schreiber's – in excess of 100 000 individuals. Around the edges of this rocky core lie more fertile plains clothed with sweeping expanses of cork, western holm and Lusitanian oak *dehesa*.

Almost 1400 taxa of vascular plant have been recorded within the park, including 6 narcissi, 7 irises and 27 orchids. Of the total, around 150 are Afro-Iberian endemics and 13 are confined to the Serranía de Ronda and the Sierra de Grazalema, with several unique to Grazalema itself, notably *Papaver rupifragum*, *Echinospartum algibicum*,

Erodium recoderi and *Phlomis* × *margaritae*. Of greatest botanical significance, however, is the 420 ha relict Spanish fir forest – the *pinsapar* – on the shady north-facing slope of the Sierra del Pinar.

Grazalema's floristic diversity is matched by a rich vertebrate fauna, notably one of the largest concentrations of griffon vultures in Spain, breeding mainly in the deep ravines of the Garganta Seca and Garganta Verde in the northern reaches of the park. Other cliff-nesting raptors include a dozen or so pairs each of Egyptian vulture and Bonelli's eagle, plus eagle owl and peregrine, sharing this habitat with chough and alpine swift.

Among the mammals, pride of place must go to the Spanish ibex, with stable populations in the Sierra de Líbar and around the peaks of the Sierra del Pinar. Roe deer have recently colonised from Los Alcornocales (see p. 385) to the south, while red and fallow deer have both been introduced as game species. Most of the typical Mediterranean forest predators are also present, including western polecat, beech marten, Eurasian

Andalucía

Spanish fir *Abies pinsapo*

badger, wildcat, common genet and Egyptian mongoose; Bechstein's bat – one of Europe's rarest – has also been cited. Amphibians include sharp-ribbed and fire salamanders, Iberian painted, stripeless tree and parsley frogs and western spadefoot, while noteworthy among the reptiles are Moorish gecko, large and Spanish psammodromus, Bedriaga's and three-toed skinks, amphisbaenian, horseshoe whip, false smooth and Montpellier snakes and Lataste's viper.

The butterflies (75 species) are also of interest, with the 1103 m Puerto del Boyar (on the A-372) a prime locality. Notable records for the park include mallow, southern marbled, sage and safflower skippers, both swallowtails, Spanish festoon, black-veined white, large tortoiseshell (often on the wing from February onwards), cardinal, many fritillaries – Niobe, Queen of Spain, Provençal, knapweed, Aetherie, Spanish and marsh – two-tailed pasha, dusky heath, dusky meadow brown, Spanish and southern gatekeepers, rock, tree and striped graylings, nettle-tree butterfly, Spanish purple, blue-spot and Provence hairstreaks, purple-shot copper (subspecies *boyarensis*) and long-tailed, African grass, Osiris, Lorquin's, green-underside, Iolas, Panoptes, false Baton and Spanish chalk-hill blues.

Roosting black kites *Milvus migrans*

The road leading west out of Grazalema towards El Bosque and Zahara is shaded by tall limestone cliffs that harbour an interesting collection of plants which thrive in humid conditions, notably *Saxifraga bourgeana* and the white-flowered *Omphalodes commutata*, both of which are found only here and in the Serranía de Ronda, the cream-flowered catchfly *Silene andryalifolia*, unique to southern Spain, and the Afro-Iberian endemics *Mucizonia hispida* and *Ornithogalum reverchonii*. Heading up to the statue of Christ which overlooks the town, the pinewoods and rocky pastures harbour Spanish bluebell and man, dense-flowered, pyramidal and lizard orchids in early summer, while typical birds include black redstart, Bonelli's warbler, firecrest, long-tailed tit, short-toed treecreeper and serin.

The *mirador* in Grazalema's main car park provides splendid views to the east, while closer at hand the precipitous cliffs below are adorned with frothy clusters of the Afro-Iberian endemic crucifer *Biscutella frutescens*. In early May the air is filled with wheeling crag and house martins, swallows, swifts and pallid swifts, while the song of a myriad nightingales drifts up from the vegetation along the small stream below. The narrow cobbled trail that zigzags down the cliffs (from behind the church) traverses limestone rockgardens populated by the silvery-leaved hound's-tongue *Cynoglossum cheirifolium*, the yellow-flowered toadflax *Linaria platycalyx*, found only here and in the neighbouring Serranía de Ronda, and the Afro-Iberian endemic valerian *Centranthus macrosiphon*.

Once at the foot of the cliff, look out for the woundwort *Stachys circinata* and silver-leaved clumps of the yellow-flowered *Centaurea clementei* (unique to southwest Spain) on the sheer limestone above you, while the rubbly pastures support robust leafy spikes of licebane and one of the most beautiful of all viper's-buglosses – *Echium albicans* – whose silvery leaves and blue-and-pink flowers are confined to southern Spain. Choughs and griffon vultures are usually present overhead, the base of the cliff often houses a black wheatear nest and

Andalucía

Puente Nuevo and the Tajo gorge, Ronda

blue rock thrushes forage amid the limestone outcrops.

Taking the A-374 towards Ubrique, you soon come to an unfenced area of damp pastures on the left known as La Rana: one of the best areas for orchids and other late-spring monocots in the park. Look out for tongue orchid, small-flowered serapias, bumble-bee, sawfly, yellow and woodcock ophrys, *Ophrys dyris* and Lange's and champagne orchids, with dense-flowered orchids in the pine copses to the east. The pastures are studded with paper-white daffodils from January onwards, with May bringing a colourful assemblage of Spanish iris, the low-growing star-of-Bethlehem *Ornithogalum orthophyllum*, white asphodel, the Spanish endemic *Anthericum baeticum* and the magnificent Portuguese squill. Here, too, you can find the vermilion-flowered elder-leaved figwort and the crucifer *Crambe filiformis*, with sprays of tiny white flowers.

Hoopoe, bee-eater and woodchat shrike frequent the surrounding western holm oaks while the telegraph wires are often utilised by woodlark and rock sparrow, but the southerly continuation of this road – between the village of Villaluenga del Rosario and Benaocaz – is much more rewarding for birds, the scrubby pastures and limestone outcrops hosting a diverse community of Thekla lark, black-eared wheatear, both rock thrushes, melodious warbler, southern grey shrike and rock bunting. This long, narrow valley, backed by cliffs on either side, is also a good place to observe peregrine and alpine swift, as well as some of the larger raptors of Grazalema, notably golden and Bonelli's eagles.

The almost obligatory visit to the *pinsapar* starts on the CA-531 (Grazalema–Zahara road), a couple of kilometres north of the turn-off to El Bosque (A-372). The early part of the path harbours drifts of the white-flowered *Cerastium boissieri*, cushions of spiny hare's-ear, shrubby gromwell, *Chaenorhinum villosum*, the occasional diminutive spike of the Afro-Iberian endemic *Anarrhinum laxiflorum*, blue aphyllanthes and pink-flowered mats of putoria. Crested tits are common in the planted Aleppo and maritime pines which clothe the middle section of the ascent.

From the high point – Puerto de las Cumbres – the onward path contours through limestone rockgardens at around 1300 m, in May populated by the diminutive rush-leaved jonquil (subspecies *praelongus*) and *Romulea bulbocodium*, plus the candytuft-like *Ionopsidium prolongoi*, the tiny yellow *Viola demetria* and *Senecio minutus*, all of which are Afro-Iberian endemics. Look out, too, for *Saxifraga haenseleri*, found only in the Sierras Béticas, and *S. globulifera*, which also occurs in North Africa.

Information: Visitor centres are located in El Bosque (tel: 956 727029; e-mail: PN.SGrazalema@cma.junta-andalucia. es) and Zahara de la Sierra (tel. and fax: 956 123114). Permits are required to visit the *pinsapar*, Torreón and the 400 m-deep Garganta Verde (from El Bosque only). The tourist office in Grazalema's main square can also give you information.

Sierra de las Nieves

Cushions of the white-flowered crucifer *Hormathophylla spinosa* and hedgehog broom line the path, while the crags up to the left harbour the yellow-flowered *Draba hispanica*, unique to limestone mountains in southern and eastern Spain. In spring you might also turn up a few Barton's and dense-flowered orchids and nodding purplish-green bells of the snakeshead *Fritillaria lusitanica*, with the delicate, brick-red poppy *Papaver rupifragum* out in force later in the year. Scrub warblers abound here, notably Dartford, Sardinian and subalpine, while the limestone crags on both sides of the path often harbour small groups of Spanish ibex.

Once within the gloomy confines of the fir forest, the flora is reduced to stinking hellebore, spurge-laurel, shrubby hare's-ear, Etruscan honeysuckle and stinking iris, coloured by red and sword-leaved helleborines along the sides of the path and sheets of *Paeonia coriacea* from late May onwards. Few birds seem to appreciate the dense coniferous foliage; only wren, robin, Bonelli's warbler, Iberian chiffchaff and coal tit are present in any numbers. Continuing down to Benamahoma, look out for western peony, shrubby scorpion-vetch, the evil-smelling bean trefoil, tree germander and the red-flowered *Cytinus ruber*, parasitic on grey-leaved cistus here. Spanish ibex forage at the foot of the sheer cliffs up to the left and griffon vultures cruise almost constantly overhead.

Also in the area

Ronda Historic town situated on the edge of a sheer bluff and straddling the impressive Tajo gorge. From the Puente Nuevo look out for lesser kestrel, peregrine, alpine swift, blue rock thrush, black redstart, chough and rock sparrow; a trail down to the bottom of the gorge starts near the Palacio de Mondragón. The Roman ruins of old Ronda – **Acinipo** – lie to the northwest, accessed via the MA-449.

Sierra de las Nieves (*parque natural*; 20 172 ha and Biosphere Reserve;

Andalucía

93 930 ha) Karst landscape (maximum Torrecilla, 1919 m) to the east of Ronda with extensive Spanish fir forests on higher, north-facing slopes and abundant Spanish ibex, plus otter, Egyptian mongoose, Leisler's bat and introduced mouflon. Scrub hosts Orphean, subalpine and spectacled warblers, while high plateaux support breeding rock thrush, tawny pipit, skylark and all three wheatears, with alpine accentor and ring ouzel habitual in winter. Fir and pine forests good for raptors, plus eagle owl and Bonelli's eagle on the cliffs. Southern Spanish endemic plants include *Silene mariana, Galium viridiflorum, Ptilostemon hispanicus* and *Centaurea prolongoi,* with Lorquin's and green-underside blues, Spanish fritillary and western marbled white among the butterflies.

Los Reales de Sierra Bermeja (*paraje natural;* 1210 ha) Peridotite ridge of intrusive volcanic origin behind Estepona (maximum 1450 m); stunning views of the coast from the Puerto de Peñas Blancas (1010 m): a good place to watch for migrating storks and raptors. Small enclaves of cork oaks lower down and a small *pinsapar* on the north-facing crest. Iron-rich rocks host 17 endemic plants, including *Arenaria capillipes, Armeria colorata, Centaurea lainzii* and *Staehelina baetica.* Booted eagle, peregrine, eagle owl, Spanish ibex, common genet, Egyptian mongoose and wildcat.

SITE 144 Fuente de Piedra

The largest natural inland lake in Andalucía (1300 ha), housing Iberia's biggest colony of greater flamingo, which in wet years rivals that of the French Camargue.

A vast, shallow, typically endorheic lagoon, Fuente de Piedra (a *reserva natural* of 1476 ha, also a Ramsar Site and ZEPA) lies in a basin of impermeable gypsum-rich Triassic marls and is fed by small streams, rainfall and to some extent maintained by the underlying aquifer, but has no drainage outlet. Evaporation can reach phenomenal levels in hot, windy conditions, such that the lake generally dries out completely by late summer.

Not surprisingly, the waters are markedly saline, supporting an important community of submerged macrophytes, notably horned pondweed, *Althenia filiformis,* fennel pondweed and beaked tasselweed, although as water levels drop and salinity increases these are generally replaced by charophytes: common and bearded stoneworts, *Tolypella hispanica* and *Chara aspera.* The margins are fringed with halophytic chenopods such as *Suaeda splendens,* annual and shrubby sea-blites, *Arthrocnemum macrostachyum,* purple and common glassworts, sea-purslane and *Halopeplis amplexicaulis,* grading into drier habitats

Western spadefoot *Pelobates cultripes*

Greater flamingo *Phoenicopterus ruber* (Mike Lane)

carpeted with lesser sea-spurrey, *Spergularia nicaeensis, Frankenia pulverulenta,* false grass-poly, cressa and curved hard-grass. Less saline areas where the streams enter the lake harbour stands of common reed and bulrushes, occasionally accompanied by African tamarisk, *Tamarix canariensis,* oleander and giant reed.

Brackish and freshwater habitats accommodate stripe-necked terrapin, sharp-ribbed salamander, western spadefoot and stripeless tree and parsley frogs, as well as the Iberian painted frog, unique to Spain and Portugal, while natterjack toads and Iberian pool frogs can even breed in the main lagoon itself, providing salinity is less than about 10%. The margins of the lagoon also support large numbers of southern water voles, providing abundant prey for western polecats. A diverse community of odonates is headed by *Trithemis annulata,* an essentially Mediterranean species which is confined to the southern third of the Iberian peninsula, and dark emerald damselfly, which is restricted to highly saline waterbodies and known only from a handful of sites in the peninsula. More common-place species include southern emerald damselfly, *Ischnura graellsii,* emperor dragonfly, red-veined, common and scarlet darters and black-tailed skimmer.

The undulating hills which enclose the lagoon are dedicated mainly to the cultivation of olives, cereals and sunflowers, although some degraded stands of western holm oak persist, associated with holly oak scrub interspersed with tracts of yellow-flowered legumes – *Genista umbellata* (an Afro-Iberian endemic), *Ulex baeticus* subspecies *baeticus* (known only from southern Spain) and hairy thorny broom – plus a wide range of calcicolous labiates: felty germander, *Ajuga iva, Phlomis purpurea,* the thymes *Thymus zygis* and *T. capitatus, Sideritis hirsuta* and *Micromeria graeca.* Here, too, you should encounter *Helianthe-mum hirtum, Tuberaria lignosa, Asparagus albus* and the horribly spiny *A. stipularis,* as well as climbers such as fragrant clematis and the Afro-Iberian birthwort *Aristolochia baetica.* Reptiles abound here, notably Moorish gecko, ocellated and Iberian wall lizards, large and Spanish psammodromus, three-toed skinks and Montpellier, ladder and horseshoe whip snakes, while Fuente de Piedra's more terrestrial mammals include Iberian blind mole, pygmy and greater white-toothed shrews, Mediterranean pine vole, Algerian mouse, garden dormouse, Iberian hare, rabbit, red fox, weasel and Eurasian badger.

Andalucía

Fuente de Piedra is best known for its birds, however, although only 22 species of the 170+ cited here regularly breed in the aquatic habitats. Pride of place goes to what is usually considered to be the second-largest colony of greater flamingo in Europe, although some years the Andalucían population is more successful than that of the Camargue; in 1998, for example, some 22 000 pairs reared 15 387 chicks here: about two-thirds of all those fledged in the western Mediterranean breeding nuclei that year. It seems that the greater flamingos are particularly attracted to Fuente de Piedra's unique latticework of dykes and spits which crisscrosses the lagoon, testimony to the saltpans which were in operation here from Roman times to the 1950s.

Other birds which nest on this island grid include gull-billed tern (250–400 pairs), avocet and black-winged stilt (some 50 pairs of each), Kentish plover (around 100 pairs), and – for the first time in 30 years in 1997 – collared pratincole. Small numbers of pochard, red-crested pochard, white-headed duck (since 1990) and purple gallinule also breed in the reserve, favouring rather more vegetated areas, while 1998 saw the first ever breeding attempts of shelduck and crested coot in the reserve.

In winter, several thousand greater flamingos are present from December onwards, accompanied by hoards of lesser black-backed and black-headed gulls, lesser numbers of greylag goose, shelduck, red-crested pochard, white-headed duck, and the odd black-necked grebe, marbled teal and hen harrier. The commonest wintering waders are dunlin, little stint, bar-tailed godwit and redshank, augmented during passage periods by small groups of ringed and little-ringed plovers, curlew sandpiper, ruff, greenshank and green sandpiper. Several hundred white storks and large concentrations of both whiskered and black terns also turn up on migration, while more unusual passage migrants include little bittern, spoonbill, glossy ibis and osprey.

The surrounding olive groves, Mediterranean scrub and cereal pseudosteppes harbour a small breeding nucleus of stone curlew and around 20 pairs of Montagu's harriers, with black kite and lesser kestrel also using the area in summer. Among the nesting passerines are short-toed, crested and Thekla larks, black-eared wheatear, Sardinian and spectacled warblers and southern grey and woodchat shrikes. The area to the west of the lake harbours an isolated wintering population of crane between October and March (average 500 individuals, but sometimes exceeding 2000), as well as being favoured by concentrations of little bustards at this time of year.

Access and information: The Cerro del Palo interpretation centre (tel. and fax: 952 111715) is located at the northern end of the lagoon (signposted off the MA-454). May is a good time to visit, when high water levels disperse the birds across the lagoon, otherwise all will be huddled in the centre and a telescope essential. Small freshwater scrapes to the east of the centre host nesting black-winged stilt and black-headed gull plus hawking gull-billed tern and red-rumped swallow.

Also in the area

Fuente de Piedra is girdled by a number of much smaller, mostly seasonal lagoons, used as complementary feeding and roosting areas by many of the birds which have their main base at Fuente de Piedra, particularly the greater flamingos.

Lagunas de Campillos (*reserva natural*; 85 ha) Four protected lagoons – Dulce, Salada, de Capacete and del Cerero – plus two in private ownership. Dulce is pretty well permanent, hosting breeding reed and great reed warblers and occasionally white-headed duck. Wintering shelduck, shoveler, teal, pochard and Kentish plover, plus garganey on spring migration. Dulce is easily visible from the A-382 to the east of Campillos; the others lie along the minor road leading southeast of the town towards the reservoir of Guadalteba-Guadalhorce.

Laguna de la Ratosa (*reserva natural of* 24 ha) Good for purple gallinule plus shoveler, wigeon and avocet in winter. Access from the MA-705 between the villages of Los Pérez and Alameda (close to the border with Sevilla).

Lagunas de Archidona (*reserva natural*; 7 ha) Two lagoons – Grande and Chica – close to the Granada border which attract wintering black-necked grebes. Access via the MA-233 which links Estación de Salinas with Villanueva del Trabuco.

Laguna del Gosque (*reserva natural of* 42 ha) In the province of Sevilla; wintering and passage birds include pintail, shoveler, Kentish plover and dunlin; whiskered terns occasionally breed. Access via the A-353 which links Martín de la Jara with Pedrera.

SITE 145 Torcal de Antequera

A surreal limestone landscape, home to a wealth of Iberian endemic fissure plants, many orchids and abundant cliff-breeding birds.

One of Spain's most stunning karst landscapes, the Torcal de Antequera (a *paraje natural* of 2008 ha, also a ZEPA) displays almost all the water-eroded features classically associated with this type of geomorphology: limestone pavement, dolines, uvalas, sculpted pillars and balancing stones, as well as subterranean caverns and galleries. Relatively high rainfall for southern Spain, often exceeding 1200 mm at the highest altitudes (maximum 1337 m: Mástil de los Montañeros), means that the karstification of the limestone continues even today, millimetre by infinitesimal millimetre.

Little remains of the western holm oak forests that once clothed the bulk of the Torcal, with the exterior of the massif today hosting a dwarf scrub of chronanthus (a yellow-flowered Afro-Iberian endemic legume) and *Thymus capitatus* at the lowest levels, which above 500 m grades into an impenetrable tangle of holly oak, *Genista cinerea*, *G. umbellata*, *Ulex baeticus* subspecies *baeticus* (endemic to the provinces of Cádiz and Málaga), lygos, *Phlomis purpurea*, rose-

mary and dwarf fan palm, with more open areas supporting clumps of the Afro-Iberian endemic *Dianthus anticarius*, eye-catching western peonies and lilac spikes of lesser catmint. The highest levels of the Torcal – for example, the windswept limestone pavement of the Sierra Pelada, at the eastern end – are carpeted with low hummocks of hedgehog broom.

More than 25 species of orchid have been recorded in the protected area, including the early-flowering fan-lipped, naked man and pink butterfly orchids, as well as the Atlas ophrys, known only from the province of Málaga and North Africa (one of seven *Ophrys* species here). Later in the year look out for two-leaved gennaria, heart-flowered serapias, dark-red helleborine and bug and lizard orchids.

The rich calcicolous flora can be examined by following the so-called Ruta Verde (circular, 1.5 km) which starts from the upper car park and traverses a labyrinth of narrow limestone galleries flanked by crenate cliffs. In May, the sides of the trail are studded with the deep violet flowers of *Iris lutescens* sub-species *subbiflora*, stinking iris, Spanish bluebell, tassel hyacinth, rosy garlic, Portuguese squill and *Ornithogalum narbonense*, plus the yellow-flowered *Phlomis lychnitis*, the deep-red-flowered *Cynoglossum cheirifolium* and yellow bee and sawfly ophrys galore.

A careful examination of the humid cliffs and rock outcrops along the way will reveal several of the Torcal's most noteworthy fissure plants: the local endemic *Saxifraga biternata*, whose large white flowers bloom in profusion in early June, *Linaria anticaria* (originally described from here) and the related *L. oblongifolia*, both toadflaxes being unique to limestone mountains in southern Spain. The diminutive yellow-flowered violet *Viola demetria* (another southern Iberian endemic) is found only in the shadiest

Desfiladero de los Gaitanes

localities, often accompanied by spring rock-cress and the glossy yellow cups of *Ranunculus rupestris*. Here, too, you should encounter the robust, cream-flowered *Silene andryalifolia*, also unique to southern Spain, the fleshy Afro-Iberian endemic *Mucizonia hispida*, cymbalaria-leaved speedwell and *Hyoseris radiata*, with dandelion-like flowers and deeply divided leaves.

The Ruta Verde will also bring you face to face with some of the more typical cliff-nesting birds of Antequera, most commonly kestrel, alpine swift, crag martin, black redstart, blue rock thrush, jackdaw and chough. Abundant shrubby vegetation provides suitable habitat for black-eared wheatear, the occasional subalpine warbler, melodious warbler, serin and rock and cirl buntings, while the skies above are rarely lacking the huge silhouette of a griffon vulture or two, although these ceased to breed here in the mid-twentieth century. The Torcal does, however, still provide refuge for resident eagle, barn and tawny owls, as well as for scops owls in summer, with a single pair of peregrines hanging on by the skin of their teeth, so to speak.

Notable among the mammals is the Spanish ibex, with the prohibition on hunting in 1990 tempting a small group to put down roots here. Perhaps more surprising are the fairly abundant populations of wild-cat, Eurasian badger and beech marten, although common genets are rather scarce today, with greater horseshoe bat, garden dormouse and greater white-tooted shrew among the other mammals recorded. On a sunny day, the most conspicuous vertebrates will be the reptiles, with large and Spanish psammodromus and Iberian wall lizard extremely common, and ladder, Montpellier and horseshoe whip snakes and Lataste's viper all present in some numbers; tracking down Moorish gecko, ocellated lizard, three-toed skink and the secretive amphisbaenian, however, will require a more determined effort on your part. The amber-coloured scorpion *Buthus occitanus*, so common in limestone areas in southern Spain, can be located by turning over likely stones.

Access and information: The Torcal de Antequera is signposted off the A-343 from Antequera, a narrow road which climbs steeply up the southeast face leading you to the interpretation centre (Torcal Alto; tel. and fax: 952 031389), where you can hire a guide to take you into the restricted-access area of Las Vilaneras, in the western part of the *paraje*.

Also in the area

Desfiladero de los Gaitanes (*paraje natural*; 2177 ha) Also known as the Garganta del Chorro, a limestone chasm carved out by the Guadalhorce, 7 km long and up to 400 m deep, the walls in places just 10 m apart. The northern part of the gorge, accessed from the reservoir of Gaitanejo (on the MA-444), can be explored via a spectacular pathway known as the Caminito del Rey (3 km); from the south, approach the gorge via the road which links Alora with the station and village of El Chorro. Cliff-breeding birds include black redstart, black wheatear and blue rock thrush, while choughs, alpine swifts, crag martins and red-rumped swallows zoom between the walls at eye-level. Stunted pines harbour Bonelli's warbler, firecrest and crested tit, with olivaceous warbler and golden oriole in the riverine vegetation in summer. Typical raptors include peregrine, golden and Bonelli's eagles and griffon vultures, although the latter two breed further east, on the impressive cliffs to the north of the MA-226 which links El Chorro with Valle de Abdalajís. Lesser kestrel and the occasional Egyptian vulture in summer.

146 SITE Desembocadura del Guadalhorce

Small wetland at the mouth of the Río Guadalhorce, of exceptional importance for birds migrating along the Mediterranean coastal route.

The mouth of the Guadalhorce lies just 120 km – as the crow flies – from the Strait of Gibraltar, the latter selected by hundreds of thousands of migratory birds as the shortest route to Africa's winter sunshine. Despite its rather degraded aspect, more than 250 species of bird have been recorded from this coastal wetland (a *paraje natural* of 83 ha), such ornithological significance thought to be due partly to the change in direction of the Spanish shore at this point – from east–west to north–south – and partly to the paucity of other wetlands in the area.

The *paraje* encompasses the alluvial plain between the main outlet of the Río Guadalhorce, canalised along much of its length, and an abandoned 'arm' – the Cauce Viejo – to the northeast. The coastal reaches comprise a low sand-dune system and salt-marsh, while the interior harbours one large, more or less central lagoon and a number of smaller pools near the Cauce Viejo – the result of sand and gravel extraction – some of which are fringed with African tamarisk, common club-rush and common reed. Exotic, naturalised species abound, particularly castor-oil-plant and shrub tobacco, but in May the interior supports a colourful display of squirting cucumber, mallow-leaved bindweed, purple viper's-bugloss, crown daisies, andryala, galactites and milk and Syrian thistles.

Among the more notable breeding birds are a few pairs of little bittern and purple heron on the smaller pools, sometimes joined by black-winged stilts, with 20+ pairs of Kentish plover attempting to breed each year in the drier saltmarshes and dunes, although with limited success. The emergent vegetation should be examined for resident

Squirting cucumber
Ecballium elaterium

water rail and Cetti's and fan-tailed warblers, large numbers of sedge, reed and great reed warblers on migration and the odd penduline tit in winter. Bluethroats and marsh harriers are also fairly abundant in winter, with short-eared owls sometimes putting in an appearance. Among the more unusual species cited are a number of Nearctic vagrants – blue-winged teal, spotted sandpiper, sooty tern and laughing, ring-billed and Franklin's gulls – with other accidentals from far-away places including Bulwer's petrel and little shearwater; in the spring of 2001 no less than five cream-coloured coursers were observed here.

Although the majority of the wintering gulls are either yellow-legged or lesser black-backed, Audouin's and Mediterranean also turn up regularly, ostensibly on passage but usually hanging around for a while. The commonest migratory terns are little, common, black and whiskered, but look out, too, for white-winged black, Caspian and lesser crested. Sea-watchers are amply rewarded during passage periods, when Cory's, Manx and Balearic shearwaters, gannet, great, Arctic and pomarine skuas and razorbill abound, with Slavonian grebe and grey phalarope occasionally occurring around the mouth of the main river in autumn.

The inland pools also attract a wealth of aquatic birds in winter and on passage, ranging from black-necked grebe and all the usual duck – plus an occasional red-crested pochard, garganey, marbled teal, ferruginous and white-headed duck or crested coot – to small numbers of squacco and night herons, black stork, spoonbill and greater

Wood sandpiper *Tringa glareola*

flamingo. More commonplace waders include avocet, little stint, curlew sandpiper and greenshank, but keep an eye open for rarities such as Temminck's stint and marsh and wood sandpipers in spring, when collared pratincoles are also most likely.

Access: You cannot reach the *paraje* from the new Autovía del Mediterráneo but must follow the dual carriageway which links Málaga with the airport, taking the first exit to the east of the Río Guadalhorce and heading south – under the motorway – until you come to the car park at the northern end of the site.

Also in the area

Montes de Málaga (*parque natural of* 4956 ha) Small range of schistose mountains lying parallel to the coast (maximum 1031 m, Viento) to the north of Málaga. Planted with Aleppo and stone pines in the 1930s, but western holm, cork and Lusitanian oaks recuperating today. Red squirrel, wild boar, Egyptian mongoose common genet, beech marten, Eurasian badger and western polecat, plus a stable enclave of Mediterranean chameleon. Breeding goshawk, short-toed eagle and tawny and scops owls, with booted eagle, black kite and honey buzzard on autumn passage. Abundant azure-winged magpies plus crested and coal tits, crossbill, serin and rock bunting. Best accessed along the C-345 north from Málaga to just south of the Puerto del León, then turn left (following signs to Fuente de la Reina) to the environmental education centre of Las Contadoras (tel. and fax: 952 110255). General e-mail enquiries to PN. MontesMalaga@cma.junta-andalucia.es

SITE 147 Lagunas de Córdoba

A group of six small lagoons with breeding white-headed duck and interesting odonate communities.

In one of the recent success stories in Spanish wildlife conservation, the white-headed duck has come back from the brink, having been reduced to just 22 birds in 1977, all in the Laguna de Zóñar: one of the six lagoons collectively known as the Lagunas de Córdoba (all are *reservas naturales*, included within a ZEPA of 1107 ha, with the permanent lagoons of Zóñar, Rincón and Amarga also comprising a Ramsar Site of 86 ha). Greater protection of wetlands and a captive breeding programme based on the Zóñar population enabled this emblematic species to make a quantitative leap forward in the early 1980s, with strong breeding and wintering nuclei since established in La Mancha Húmeda, Almería and the wetlands of Alacant. Evidence of the white-headed duck's spectacular recovery was the 4035 birds which crowded into El Hondo (see p. 349) in August 2000.

Once Iberian populations had picked up, however, the unthinkable happened and the white-headed duck actually ceased to breed at Zóñar, largely because introduced common carp were muddying the lagoon, severely affecting the submerged plant populations on which these diving ducks depend. Despite attempts to remedy the situation, white-headed ducks have not bred at Zóñar since 1989, although the other permanent, freshwater lagoons – Amarga and El Rincón – have seen limited breeding success

every year since 1992, with 2000 seeing three females rear six chicks at Amarga and two females eight chicks at Rincón.

The three permanent lagoons also harbour nesting great crested grebe, purple heron, little bittern, red-crested pochard, marsh harrier, purple gallinule and great reed warbler. Less aquatic species are also abundant, with nightingale and melodious warbler occupying the lush marginal vegetation, while drier habitats are home to breeding bee-eater, short-toed lark, woodchat shrike and, above all at Zóñar, rufous bush robin: a species with an uncanny ability to skulk just out of sight.

Passage periods bring a few waders such as black-winged stilt and little ringed plover, as well as harriers, terns and large numbers of swifts and hirundines, with winter also a good time to visit, when larger numbers of white-headed duck are usually visible, accompanied by black-necked grebe, wigeon, teal, shoveler and tufted duck, plus regular ferruginous duck.

Herptile communities are unexceptional in these three lagoons – viperine snake and natterjack toad are the commonest species – while among the fish it is worth highlighting colmilleja, unique to Iberia, and big-scale sand smelt: a nationally rare species more typically found in coastal waters. To date 14 species of odonate have been recorded here, notably common winter damselfly in very early spring, vagrant and lesser emperors in March and April, respectively, Norfolk hawker in late spring, *Selysiothemis nigra* in May and June, *Trithemis annulata* throughout the summer and autumn and *Diplacodes lefebvrei* in September.

Unlike the well-developed reedy fringes surrounding Zóñar, Amarga and El Rincón, the three nearby endorheic lagoons of Tíscar, Los Jarales and Salobral are bordered by

Whiskered tern *Chlidonias hybridus*

Andalucía

Laguna de Zóñar

expanses of halophytic vegetation, primarily purple glasswort and the sea heath *Frankenia pulverulenta*. The highly saline waters of these seasonal lagoons regularly attract feeding greater flamingos, especially at Tíscar, while the less densely vegetated margins provide better habitat for breeding waders, typically black-winged stilt, avocet and little ringed plover, according to water levels.

A string of wet winters from 1998–2001 freshened up these endorheic lagoons to such an extent that white-headed duck have also begun to breed here. In 2000, two females raised seven chicks at Salobral and successful breeding also occurred at Los Jarales in 1999; gull-billed terns nest sporadically, with 13 pairs at Tíscar in 1993. The list of wintering wildfowl is similar to that of the permanent lagoons, but includes greater numbers of pintail, shelduck and shoveler and fewer diving ducks. When water is present, amphibians appear en masse in these endorheic waterbodies, notably at Los Jarales; look out for Iberian pool and Iberian painted frogs, natterjack toad and western spadefoot.

Information and access: The Zóñar visitor centre at km 77.6 on the A-309 southeast of Aguilar provides maps for all the lagoons in the area (tel: 957 335252; e-mail: RN.ZHumedas.SCordoba@cma.junta-andalucia.es), or try the tourist office in Aguilar (mornings). For more information, contact Oxyura, a group specialising in the conservation of the white-headed duck (Apartado de Correos 3059, 14080 Córdoba; e-mail: oxyura@teleline.es).

Also in the area

Embalses de Cordobilla y Malpasillo (Ramsar Site (1972 ha) and *parajes naturales* of 1470 and 519 ha, respectively) Twin reservoirs in the south of Córdoba province, where constant water levels provide suitable habitat for breeding purple heron, marsh harrier and purple gallinule and wintering white-headed duck. Cordobilla is additionally known for its small winter flock of cranes and regular greater flamingo; both sites are good for raptors, including Bonelli's and golden eagles, Montagu's harrier, lesser kestrel and eagle owl.

Sierras Subbéticas (*parque natural of* 32 070 ha) A series of medium-height, abrupt limestone ridges with secondary scrub, olive groves, enclaves of Lusitanian oak and Montpellier maple and summit cushion communities of hedgehog broom and *Echinospartum boissieri*. Breeding griffon vulture, golden, Bonelli's (10 pairs), booted and short-toed eagles, peregrine, eagle owl, alpine swift, crag martin, dipper, black and black-eared wheatears, both rock thrushes, *Sylvia* warblers, chough and rock bunting. Diverse amphibians: fire and sharp-ribbed salamanders, western spadefoot, Iberian painted and stripeless tree frogs and natterjack toad. Also stripe-necked terrapin, ocellated lizard and Lataste's viper, plus 17 species of bat, garden dormouse, wildcat, wild boar and Spanish ibex. Butterflies of note are sage skipper, Spanish festoon, Spanish marbled white, southern and Spanish gatekeepers, dusky heath, blue-spot hairstreak and false Baton and Lorquin's blues. The interpretation centre (Santa Rita) is at km 57 on the A-340 between Cabra and Priego (tel. and fax: 957 334034; email:PN.SSubbeticas@cma.junta-andalucia.es).

148 Sierras de Cazorla, Segura y Las Villas

SITE

Superb limestone mountains with a diverse endemic flora and home to a rich community of cliff-nesting birds; Spanish moon moth, Spanish algyroides and Spanish ibex.

The vast Parque Natural de las Sierras de Cazorla, Segura y Las Villas (209 945 ha, also a ZEPA and Biosphere Reserve) is the largest protected area in Spain, such that you really need a week or more to do justice to its knife-edged limestone peaks, upland plateaux and deep shady valleys. Occupying the whole northeastern corner of the province of Jaén, the park consists of a series of highly karstified ridges running northeast–southwest, on several occasions topping 2000 m; the range also extends north into Albacete as the Sierra de Alcaraz and south into Granada as the Sierra de Castril (*parque natural*; 12 682 ha).

More than 1500 m separates the tallest peaks – the most emblematic of which is Cabañas (2028 m) – from the lowest valleys, with sheer cliffs a major feature of the park.

On account of the relatively high levels of precipitation here (1800 mm), Cazorla formerly housed one of Spain's principal enclaves of Lusitanian oak forest, estimated to have covered some 50% of the park area, although the figure today is closer to 5%. The pines (*Pinus nigra* subspecies *salzmannii*) which occur naturally at higher levels in Cazorla, have expanded to fill the gaps, aided and abetted by the wholesale planting of maritime and Aleppo pines and other fast-growing conifers. Above the tree-line, however, the whole complexion of the park changes, and the landscape is dominated by stunning vistas of pale limestone peaks and pavements.

Broadly speaking, the park can be divided into three biogeographical zones: mesomediterranean up to 1200 m, supra-mediterranean from 1200 to 1800 m and oromediterranean above 1800 m. The lowest levels are those which have suffered most from felling and replanting, although humid enclaves of Lusitanian oak persist, accompanied by western holm and cork oaks, true and wild service-trees, turpentine tree, Montpellier maple, strawberry-tree, *Phillyrea latifolia*, narrow-leaved ash and laurustinus. These forests harbour a diverse ground flora, typified by hepatica, stinking hellebore, *Paeonia officinalis* subspecies *microcarpa*, yellow bird's-nest, angular Solomon's-seal and sword-leaved helleborine. As altitude increases, *Berberis hispanica*, whitebeam, St Lucie's cherry, *Acer granatense*, spurge-laurel and the Spanish endemic honeysuckle *Lonicera splendida* appear, while relict stands of box occur on middle-altitude, north-facing rocky inclines.

Deeper soils along the larger rivers and around the reservoirs in the park are occupied by thick gallery forests interspersed with patches of common reed, common club-rush and *Typha domingensis* which are coloured by purple and yellow loosestrifes, false grass-poly, *Lythrum ephemerum*, gypsywort and hemp-agrimony. Damp clearings in these woods are the best place to locate the metre-high clumps of *Narcissus longispathus*, endemic to the Cazorla area, which flower from April onwards.

The real botanical riches of Cazorla, however, are encountered at higher levels. Above 1800 m, the only trees present are a few contorted individuals of *Pinus nigra* subspecies *salzmannii*, interspersed with stunted bushes of common juniper (subspecies *hemisphaerica*) and *Daphne oleoides* plus mats of savin and prostrate cherry. This superb landscape is best appreciated in summer, when the cushions of *Hormathophylla spinosa*, hedgehog broom, *Genista longipes*, *G. pseudopilosa*, *Astragalus giennensis*, *Ononis aragonensis* and *Vella spinosa* are in full bloom. Scattered amid these 'vegetable sheep' are low-growing clumps of the Afro-Iberian endemic milkwort *Polygala boissieri*, the silver-leaved, pink-flowered *Convolvulus boissieri* and the scabious-like *Pterocephalus spathulatus*, confined to the southeastern corner of the peninsula, plus several species

Viola cazorlensis

found only in the park, notably the crucifer *Hormathophylla baetica* and the stork's-bill *Erodium cazorlanum*.

In total more than 1700 taxa of vascular plant have been recorded here, including almost 130 Iberian endemics, of which 24 are found exclusively here. The cliffs which are so much a feature of Cazorla's landscape are a prime site for many regional and national endemics, notably the exquisite yellow-flowered *Draba hispanica*, the saxifrages *Saxifraga rigoi* and *S. camposii*, the fluorescent-pink *Viola cazorlensis* and the toadflaxes *Linaria anticaria* and *L. lilacina*, all of which are unique to southern or eastern Spain. Look out, too, for the Afro-Iberian endemics *Potentilla petrophila*, *Teucrium rotundifolium* and *Campanula velutina* subspecies *velutina*, as well as more widespread species such as brittle bladder-fern, tufted catchfly and fairy foxglove.

Overhangs shelter more reclusive Spanish endemics such as *Moehringia intricata*, *Sarcocapnos baetica* and rock snapdragon (subspecies *pulverulentum*), while at the base of the cliffs – for example, below the summit of Cabañas – you might find the columbine *Aquilegia pyrenaica* subspecies *cazorlensis* and the crane's-bill *Geranium cinereum* subspecies *cazorlense*, both scarce plants which are unique to the park, as well as the diminutive *Narcissus hedraeanthus*, endemic to southeastern Spain. Under even more humid conditions, look out for the St John's-wort *Hypericum caprifolium* and the insectivorous *Pinguicula vallisneriifolia*, again both confined to the southeastern corner of the peninsula, as well as the eye-catching throatwort.

Among the mammals the *pièce de résistance* was formerly the Spanish ibex (subspecies *hispanica*), but an epidemic of mange between 1987 and 1989 reduced the 10 000-strong population by 95%. Emergency action plans have enabled this wild goat to recover somewhat, but competition from domestic livestock and introduced mouflon (from Sardinia) and fallow deer is undoubtedly hindering the process. Cazorla's other large herbivores are red deer, reintroduced in 1952, roe deer (also affected by the mange epidemic and had to be rein-

Sierra de Cazorla: Río Guadalquivir

troduced) and wild boar, with forest predators including wildcat, common genet, western polecat and beech marten as well as the more omnivorous Eurasian badger. Otters and southern water voles frequent the numerous watercourses, while garden dormouse and red squirrel (subspecies *baeticus*) abound in the forests; barbastelle and Bechstein's bats and Kuhl's and Savi's pipistrelles are also cited here.

Cazorla is particularly renowned for its cliff-breeding birds, notably griffon (around 200 pairs in Spain's southeasternmost colony) and Egyptian vultures, golden eagle, peregrine (some 40 pairs) and eagle owl, as well as rock dove, alpine swift, crag martin, red-rumped swallow and passerines such as black wheatear, both rock thrushes, black redstart, raven and chough. Forested habitats harbour healthy breeding populations of booted eagle, as well as nesting goshawk, sparrowhawk, short-toed eagle, black and red kites and hobby, plus long-eared, scops and tawny owls. Here, too, you should find great spotted woodpecker, wryneck, Bonelli's warbler, firecrest, long-tailed and crested tits, nuthatch, short-toed treecreeper, serin and crossbill.

More open habitats are the haunt of hoopoe, woodlark, Sardinian warbler, azure-winged magpie, rock sparrow and cirl and rock buntings all year round, which are joined by typical Mediterranean species such as great spotted cuckoo, black-eared wheatear, spectacled, subalpine and Orphean warblers and woodchat shrike in summer. Above the tree-line, look out for wheatear, whitethroat and Dartford warbler, with the possibility of wallcreeper and alpine accentor in winter, while the riverine habitats are home to lesser spotted woodpecker, nightingale, reed and Cetti's warblers and golden oriole.

The outstanding reptilian inhabitant of the park is without a doubt the Spanish algyroides, discovered here in 1958 and confined to Cazorla, Segura and Alcaraz, where it inhabits shady rockgardens between 1000 and 1500 m. Most of the other reptiles here –

Moorish gecko, Iberian wall and ocellated lizards, Bedriaga's and three-toed skinks, ladder, Montpellier and horseshoe whip snakes, southern and false smooth snakes and Lataste's viper – prefer drier, sunnier habitats, with the margins of the many small reservoirs and watercourses the best place to track down stripe-necked terrapin, fire salamander, western spadefoot, Iberian pool and parsley frogs and natterjack toad, as well as *Alytes dickhilleni*, endemic to southern Iberia.

Notable among the park's 103 species of butterfly are silver-washed, twin-spot and Niobe fritillaries, southern white admiral, purple-shot copper, Spanish argus and mother-of-pearl, Idas and Provence chalk-hill blues, but perhaps of greatest renown is the Andalusian anomalous blue, unique to southeastern Spain, while the exquisite Spanish moon moth (subspecies *ceballosi*) is a noted denizen of Cazorla's extensive pine forests.

Access and information: The park's main interpretation centre – Torre del Vinagre – is located at km 18 on the road (A-319) between Cazorla and Tranco (closed Mondays; tel: 953 720115; fax: 953 710068; e-mail: PN.Cazorla.SyV@cma.junta-andalucia.es), but there is also an information point in Cazorla. Several companies run guided walking and 4WD trips, while two botanical gardens housing the majority of Cazorla's most emblematic plants are located at Torre del Vinagre and in Siles.

Also in the area

Alto Guadalquivir (*paraje natural of* 331 ha) Three narrow, increasingly sediment-filled reservoirs – Puente de la Cerrada, Doña Aldonza and Pedro Marín – on the Río Guadalquivir to the southeast of Cazorla. Important breeding populations of little bittern, purple heron, gadwall, pochard, purple gallinule, black-winged stilt, avocet and marsh harrier, with wintering birds including wigeon, teal, pintail, red-crested pochard, jack snipe and black-tailed godwit. Marginal vegetation has nesting reed, great reed and Savi's warblers and penduline tit plus wintering bluethroat. Osprey and many waders on passage, with unusual records including ruddy shelduck, ferruginous duck and slender-billed gull.

Sierra Mágina (*parque natural of* 19 985 ha) Spectacular limestone landscape encompassing the highest summit in Jaén (Mágina, 2167 m). *Viola cazorlensis*, *Saxifraga erioblasta* and local endemics *Lithodora nitida* and *Jurinea fontqueri*. Eighteen raptors, notably cliff-nesting griffon vulture, Bonelli's and golden eagles and eagle owl, plus black wheatear, blue rock thrush and chough. Spanish ibex. The park information office is in Jódar (tel: 953 787656).

SITE
149 Sierra Nevada

Acid massif boasting the highest peak in mainland Spain (Mulhacén, 3482 m), 2100+ vascular plants, including many endemics, 124 species of butterfly and abundant Spanish ibex.

Spain's largest national park (86 208 ha, lying within a *parque natural* of 171 985 ha; also a Biosphere Reserve), the Sierra Nevada is undoubtedly one of the natural history hotspots of the Iberian peninsula. Due to the combination of extreme altitude and proximity to Spain's southern shore, all five Iberian bioclimatic vegetation zones occur here, from Mediterranean (up to 1200 m and rich in Afro-Iberian endemics), to Alpine (here known as *crioromediterráneo*, above 2600 m), harbouring a host of cryophilic endemic plants and invertebrates: the descendants of species isolated here when the Pleistocene ice sheets retreated north for the last time.

The Sierra Nevada extends for over 80 km from east to west, the whole range – including the valleys of Las Alpujarras to the south – covering around 200 000 ha. The bulk of the *sierra* – including all of the 15 peaks which

exceed 3000 m – lies in the province of Granada, with the A-337 over the Puerto de la Ragua defining the boundary with Almería to the east. The core area comprises acid, impermeable mica schists, amphibolites and gneisses, studded with peatbogs and marshy grasslands known as *borreguiles* at the highest levels. Although once covered with younger limestone deposits, repeated glacial erosion has scoured these from the higher levels such that they are relegated to the flanks today.

This is Europe's southernmost ice-sculpted landscape, the upper plateau traversed by moraines and the peaks riddled with cirques holding exquisite glacial lakes (some 50 in all). Although the last permanent glaciers succumbed to increasing global temperatures at the end of the twentieth century, even today about 95% of precipitation falling on the highest peaks takes the form of snow,

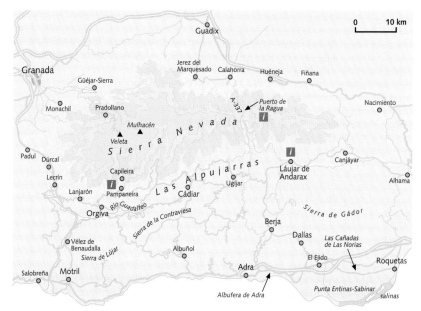

Crocus nevadensis

sometimes persisting for nine months of the year. This said, don't expect the jagged spires of the Central Pyrenees here; on the whole the terrain is fairly gentle, although the north face is pretty steep and the southern slopes – especially on the limestone – are traversed by numerous cliff-lined gullies: the product of centuries of water erosion.

Very little natural forest remains in the Sierra Nevada today, although extensive plantations of Scots, maritime and Aleppo pines occur at middle altitudes, interspersed with secondary scrub communities and relict enclaves of broad-leaved woodland. On the north flank you might find a few groves of Lusitanian oak, Montpellier maple and *Acer granatense* in the shadiest valleys, with western holm oak woodlands more widespread, occurring up to about 1700 m and variously accompanied by prickly juniper, lentisc, wild olive, Etruscan honey-suckle and the Afro-Iberian endemics *Berberis hispanica*, *Genista umbellata* and *Aristolochia baetica*.

The real botanical interest, however, occurs above the tree-line. Between 1900 and 2800 m, calcareous areas are dominated by savin, common juniper (subspecies *hemisphaerica*) and *Prunus ramburii*

(endemic to the Sierras Béticas), inter-spersed with compact cushions of *Hormathophylla spinosa*, hedgehog broom, *Vella spinosa* and spiny hare's-ear, with pink, lilac, creamy-yellow and greenish flowers, respectively. Under more acid conditions the dominant species are dwarf juniper and Pyrenean broom, accompanied by the yel-low-flowered cinquefoil *Potentilla nevaden-sis* and the prostrate greenweed *Genista versicolor*, both of which are confined to the Sierras Béticas.

Above 2800 m, around 40% of the 200 or so species present in the alpine pastures, rock-gardens and screes are found nowhere else in the world (see box below). These habitats harbour some of the most emblematic Nevada specialities, many of which are herbaceous perennials adapted to spend many months of the year under a carpet of snow, then bloom and set seed in the all-too-short summer (late July and August). Siliceous pastures are dominated by the fes-cue *Festuca clementei*, studded with eye-catching clumps of *Alyssum purpureum*, spiny flowers of the Afro-Iberian endemic *Eryngium glaciale*, a scattering of southern gentians and *Erigeron frigidus* in high sum-mer; if you're lucky you might also come across the endangered *Artemisia granatensis* here, which has suffered enormously from over-collecting to make a type of absinthe in the past.

Of greatest botanical significance, however, are the alpine scree and fissure communities, which support a host of showy Nevada endemics – *Saxifraga nevadensis, Viola crassiuscula, Chaenorhinum glareosum* and *Linaria glacialis* – accompanied by ice age relics such as glacier crowfoot, the glorious, orange-flowered Pyrenean poppy, purple saxifrage and *Androsace vandellii*, all hundreds of kilometres south of their Pyrenean stronghold in Spain.

In late summer, the margins of the glacial lakes harbour a lush community of *Ranunculus acetosellifolius* (arrow-shaped leaves), the thrift *Armeria splendens* and the silver-hairy 'stars' of *Plantago nivalis*, all of which are endemic to the Sierra Nevada, while peatbogs and *borreguiles* host the insectivorous butterwort *Pinguicula nevadensis*, whose lilac flowers bloom only here, and the Iberian endemic gentian *Gentiana boryi*, distinguished by its pale blue, apparently ten-lobed flowers. Small streams at this level support verdant cushions of starry saxifrage and the endemic speedwell *Veronica turbicola*.

Bird-wise, the Sierra Nevada is the only breeding locality for alpine accentor in southern Iberia, also the haunt of some 150 pairs of chough and providing refuge for a dozen or so pairs of golden eagle. Skylarks, tawny pipits, wheatears and black redstarts abound on the upland plateaux, with breeding records for grey wagtail and common sandpiper at more than 3000 m; you might also come across a rock thrush or two. The broom scrub hosts an isolated population of ortolan bunting in summer, plus wintering ring ouzel and hen harrier, while the forests at lower levels are the haunt of nesting goshawk and booted eagle, with resident pinewood passerines including coal tit, serin, crossbill and rock bunting, plus firecrest in summer and siskin in winter.

The cliffs along the southern valleys are occupied by a few pairs of Bonelli's eagle, peregrine and eagle owl, as well as numerous black wheatears and blue rock thrushes. The evergreen vegetation at lower levels, particularly in the Alpujarras, is also worth checking out for typically Mediterranean birds such as bee-eater, black-eared wheatear, subalpine, Orphean and spectacled warblers and southern grey shrike, as well as an occasional roller. Riverine vegetation along the margins of the Río Guadalfeo near Orgiva is a noted haunt of the secretive rufous bush robin and olivaceous warbler.

The high mountain habitats also provide refuge for snow voles – the southernmost

Endemic and endangered flora of the Sierra Nevada

The Sierra Nevada is a botanical enclave of supreme importance. More than 2100 taxa of vascular plant have been recorded here – almost one-third of the total flora of mainland Spain – of which more than 10% are unique to the Iberian peninsula. Of these latter, 53 species and a further 25 subspecies are found only in the Sierra Nevada.

Many of the sierra's most charismatic endemics – *Viola crassiuscula, Saxifraga nevadensis, Pinguicula nevadensis, Plantago nivalis, Linaria glacialis, Chaenorhinum glareosum* and *Artemisia*

granatensis – are found only above 2600 m and have suffered enormously at the hands of unscrupulous collectors, such that their very existence is in jeopardy. Around 18 species are threatened with extinction, while 8 have already disappeared. Many are listed on Annex II of the Habitats Directive: *Narcissus nevadensis, Arenaria nevadensis, Artemisia granatensis, Centaurea pulvinata, Erigeron frigidus, Leontodon microcephalus, Senecio elodes, S. nevadensis, Erodium rupicola, Pinguicula nevadensis* and *Odontites granatensis*.

Andalucía

population in the world – and more than 15 000 Spanish ibex (subspecies *hispanica*), despite the fact that mange and over-hunting had reduced the population to just 500 individuals at the beginning of the early 1960s; Mediterranean pine voles have been recorded at over 3000 m here. Forests at lower levels provide refuge for garden dormice and a few wild boar, plus common genet, Eurasian badger, beech marten and the increasingly scarce wildcat. Among the reptiles to look out for here are ocellated lizard, large psammodromus, Montpellier, ladder and southern smooth snakes and Lataste's viper. Amphibians are, curiously, rather uncommon in the Sierra Nevada, despite the wealth of aquatic habitats present, with only natterjack toad present in any numbers, with the most noteworthy denizen being the Iberian endemic midwife toad *Alytes dickhilleni*.

More than 80 endemic invertebrates have been discovered in the Sierra Nevada, usually melanic and often flightless. Of these, around half are beetles, 23 are moths or butterflies and 8 are members of the Orthoptera (grasshoppers and crickets), including the extremely scarce *Baetica ustulata*, a small, flightless bush-cricket confined to just seven 10 × 10 km squares, *Ephippigerida paulinoi*, another bush-cricket which occurs in *Genista* scrub, the tiny, plant-eating grasshopper *Omocestus bolivari*, which

inhabits montane grasslands between 2000 and 2900 m and the flightless *Eumigus rubioi* and *Pycnogaster inermis*.

Notable among the 124 species of butterflies cited in the Sierra Nevada are the Nevada blue – with the type race (*golgus*) confined to the Sierra Nevada and the recently described *sagratox* known only from the Sierra de la Sagra (Granada) to the north – as well as the Nevada grayling (subspecies *williamsi*), also known from the nearby *sierras* of Los Filabres, Gádor and María, although the nearest locality for the type subspecies is in the Urals, some 5000 km distant.

In addition, a whole suite of endemic races of more widespread species have been described from the Sierra Nevada (see box), of which the most distinctive is subspecies *nevadensis* of the Apollo, distinguished by its yellow-orange – rather than typically red – ocelli, while the extremely scarce subspecies *zullichi* of Glandon blue is often considered to be a species in its own right. Between June and August you might also come across the Spanish brassy ringlet, originally described from these mountains in 1862 but otherwise known only from the Pyrenees. Other interesting species to look out for are southern small white, Spanish, high brown and Niobe fritillaries, black satyr, ilex hairstreak, Spanish argus and Osiris, Lorquin's, Idas, green-underside, Zephyr, Escher's and Spanish chalk-hill blues.

Iberian endemic races of butterflies in the Sierra Nevada

Lycaena alciphron granadensis	purple-shot copper	500–2500 m; June–July
Lycaeides idas nevadensis	Idas blue	Above 1800 m; June–August
Aricia morronensis ramburi	Spanish argus	2050–3000 m; June–July
Agriades glandon zullichi	Glandon blue	2400–2700 m; July–August
Cyaniris semiargus montana	Mazarine blue	500–2000 m; May, July–August
Agrodiaetus thersites tova	Chapman's blue	Above 1000 m; June–August
Plebicula nivescens pascuali	mother-of-pearl blue	1000–2500 m; April, June
Plebicula golgus golgus	Nevada blue	Above 2300 m; July
Melitaea athalia nevadensis	heath fritillary	800–2300 m; May, August
Pseudochazara hippolyte williamsi	Nevada grayling	1400–2750 m; July–August
Parnassius apollo nevadensis	Apollo	700–3000 m; July–August

Sources: Moreno Durán, M.D. (1991) *Mariposas diurnas a proteger en Andalucía*. Agencia de Medio Ambiente, Junta de Andalucía; Tolman, T. and Lewington, R. (1997) *Collins field guide to the butterflies of Britain and Europe*. HarperCollins, London.

The Sierra Nevada is huge, such that any attempt to explore it in detail could well take you the rest of your life, but there are three main focal points for any more cursory investigation. The best option is to follow the road (A-395) from Granada to the *parador* and ski station of Pradollano, whose 50 km take you through four of the five bioclimatic vegetation zones present here, although the fifth – above 2600 m – will have to be tackled on foot; only authorised vehicles are now permitted to cross the heart of the Sierra Nevada to the village of Capileira, in the Alpujarras, owing to the severe impact of uncontrolled tourism on the fragile cold-desert habitats around Veleta and Mulhacén. Alternatively, cross the centre of the massif on the A-337 via the Puerto de la Ragua (2000 m) – rather less interesting, botanically, as pine plantations cover much of the landscape between 1700 and 2000 m, but Spanish ibex are relatively easy to see here – or explore the labyrinth of Alpujarran villages on the southern flank.

Andalucía

Information: The Granada interpretation centre is El Dornajo, at km 23 on the road to Pradollano (tel. and fax: 958 340625; e-mail:alhori@imfe.es), with the Almerían sector served by the centre in Láujar de Andarax (tel. and fax: 950 513548); the Puerto de la Ragua information point (tel. and fax: 950 524020) is open only from Friday to Sunday and public holidays. Las Alpujarras are served by a centre in the village of Pampaneira (tel: 958 763127; fax: 958 763301; e-mail: nevadensis@ arrakis.es). General e-mail enquiries should be directed to PN.SNevada@cma. junta-andalucia.es

Sierra Nevada in spring

SITE 150 La Cañada de Las Norias

Flooded clay pits of importance primarily for their aquatic birds, harbouring an important nucleus of white-headed duck and breeding marbled teal.

Sometimes known as Las Norias de Daza, this small wetland reserve is an extraordinary place: a veritable oasis amid a sea of plastic-clad greenhouses. In the early 1980s, the extraction of the rich red-clay subsoil to provide a suitable growth medium for the burgeoning market-garden industry resulted in the perforation of the underlying aquifer; water flooded the pits and made further excavation in the central area unfeasible. Once abandoned, swathes of emergent vegetation – mainly common reed and tamarisks – soon took over. The whole complex is of such recent origin that its aquatic plant and animal community is clearly still evolving, but what is certain is that as a wetland oasis in a region of Spain otherwise known for its extreme aridity, its wildlife significance is incomparable.

The strategic location of La Cañada de Las Norias (a SEO/BirdLife reserve of 130 ha) on the Mediterranean coast migration route meant that it was soon discovered by a multitude of birds as a convenient stopover point. Some 27 species of wader have been recorded here, including nesting black-winged stilt (more than 50 pairs), avocet (2 pairs in 1995), little ringed plover (22 pairs in 1995) and the occasional pair of Kentish plover. White-headed ducks started breeding in 1992, rearing no less than 33 young that year, and today Las Norias is one of the prime breeding localities for this endangered species in Europe (134 chicks in 1994), with many individuals resident.

The reserve is also renowned for its breeding marbled teal, with at least five pairs rearing 18 chicks in 1997; many more turn up regularly during the autumn passage. Here, too, breed a couple of dozen

pairs of little grebe, whose 'whinnying' calls are perhaps the most characteristic audible feature of the site in spring, as well as a few red-crested pochard and pochard, plus large numbers of fan-tailed, reed and great reed warblers. In winter, small numbers of dunlin, little stint and black-tailed godwit utilise the marginal mudflats, while bluethroat, penduline tit and reed bunting often take refuge in the emergent vegetation and marsh harriers and even the odd osprey occasionally hunt here.

During passage periods anything might turn up, with more unusual records including ruddy shelduck, ferruginous duck, Temminck's stint and jack snipe, plus night and purple herons and gull-billed tern. Although little bitterns are sometimes seen at Las Norias both on passage and during the summer, they are not thought to be breeding (yet!). In late March 2000, the breeding waterbirds were accompanied by black-necked grebe, teal and shoveler, while the air above the lagoons was alive with swifts and alpine and pallid swifts, crag, house and

Little ringed plover *Charadrius dubius* **at nest**

Albufera de Adra

sand martins, swallows, bee-eaters and a group of a dozen or so whiskered terns. Muddy areas around the shallower northern margins of the clay pits hosted foraging ruff, snipe and wood and green sandpipers, plus cattle egrets and yellow wagtails. On arrival, a purple gallinule was also glimpsed briefly as it scrambled for the safety of the reedbed, while the emergent vegetation was teeming with small passerines on migration, mostly chiffchaffs and willow warblers, but also a few sedge warblers.

Access: La Cañada de Las Norias lies to the east of the town of El Ejido, to the north of the A-358 between Las Norias and La Mojonera. Greenhouses extend right to the margins, but a narrow road to the east of Desguaces Baena (a scrap-yard) divides the two main pits; another small road runs along the eastern edge of the reserve (see map on p. 409).

Also in the area

Albufera de Adra (*reserva natural;* 47 ha and Ramsar Site of 75 ha) Two deep, slightly saline lagoons – Honda and Nueva – surrounded by thick belts of marginal vegetation, with spiked water-milfoil, holly-leaved naiad, fennel pondweed, beaked tasselweed and horned pondweed in the open water. Home to the endangered Spanish toothcarp, stripe-necked terrapin, natterjack toad and stripeless tree frog. Another good breeding locality for white-headed duck, apparently on the increase here, with other nesting birds including little bittern, pochard, red-crested pochard, nightingale and Cetti's, fan-tailed, reed and great reed warblers. Several hundred non-breeding Audouin's gulls present all year. Within a fenced compound, but views over the reedbed possible from the main entrance gate off the old coast road which links Adra with Balanegra.

Sierra de Gádor Sandwiched between the coastal plain around El Ejido and the eastern Sierra Nevada (maximum 2236 m, Morrón). Virtual wilderness area, with no road access except at the extreme western and eastern ends; deforested today, with many sheer cliffs on the northern face. Locally endemic plants include *Coronopus navasii, Astragalus tremolsianus, Seseli intricatum* and *Centaurea gadorensis*. Endemic subspecies of Apollo (*gadorensis*) has yellow-orange ocelli, like that of the Sierra Nevada, with Nevada grayling occurring as subspecies *augustinus* here. Spanish ibex, wildcat and one of the best breeding nuclei of Bonelli's eagle in Almería (maximum 12 pairs), plus good numbers of eagle owl, a few pairs of golden eagle and peregrine, both rock thrushes and Dupont's lark at 1600 m.

151 Punta Entinas–Sabinar

SITE

Salinas and endorheic lagoons with diverse waterbird assemblages, plus a well-developed sand-dune system and stony plateau with breeding stone curlew and lesser short-toed lark.

Between the burgeoning resorts of Almerimar and Roquetas del Mar, some 16 km of pristine Mediterranean coast have somehow escaped the ravages of the tourist industry. The protected area (*paraje natural* of 1948 ha encompassing a *reserva natural* of 595 ha, both within a ZEPA of 2745 ha) is only a couple of kilometres wide, sandwiched between swathes of plastic greenhouses and the sea, but is nevertheless home to a rich coastal flora and fauna (see map on p. 409).

Behind the magnificent white-sand beach lies a broad cordon of dunes, best preserved at the western end of the site. Here, between the headlands of Entinas and Sabinar, lie two

Wild gladiolus
Gladiolus illyricus

sizeable endorheic lagoons (together extending over some 180 ha, making them the largest natural wetland in the province of

Coastal lagoon, Punta Entinas–Sabinar

Almería), bordered to the north by a stony plateau backed by the low cliff of Los Alcores. To the east of Punta Sabinar lie two enormous abandoned saltpan complexes: the Salinas de Cerillos and Salinas Viejas, together covering around 740 ha. To the south of Cerillos lies the narrow lagoon known as the Charcón del Flamenco which, as its name suggests, usually hosts several hundred greater flamingos for much of the year, although they do not breed here.

Starting at the eastern end of the site, accessible from Urbanización Roquetas del Mar, you can drive along the southern edge of the *salinas*, using the vehicle as a hide. In March, the open water of the Salinas Viejas is dotted with black-necked grebe, shelduck, red-crested pochard and white-headed duck (a dozen or so pairs of the latter regularly breed here). Small groups of greater flamingos also hang out here in spring, although they are much more abundant at the end of summer, when post-breeding concentrations often exceed 3000 individuals.

In contrast, the shallower, mud-flanked pools further west attract a wealth of waders both during the winter and on passage,

notably black-winged stilt, avocet, grey, Kentish and little ringed plovers, sanderling, little stint, curlew sandpiper, dunlin, ruff, black-tailed godwit, spotted redshank, greenshank and wood sandpiper. Of these, only avocet (around 75 pairs in 1997), black-winged stilt (40+ pairs) and Kentish plover (some 65 pairs) stay on to breed. Among the rarer migrants which turn up from time to time are Temminck's stint and marsh sandpiper, while odonates here include lesser emperor dragonfly and *Selysiothemis nigra*, the latter with an extremely disjunct distribution around the Mediterranean basin.

A careful examination of the reedbeds and stands of the Afro-Iberian endemic *Tamarix boveana* around the margins of the *salinas* during passage periods might turn up a skulking purple or squacco heron, while collared pratincoles and marsh harriers occur regularly at this time of year and there are even records of cream-coloured courser for the area. Among the gulls and terns alternately at roost or wheeling above the saltpans, look out for Audouin's gull all year round and Sandwich, gull-billed, white-winged black, whiskered and black terns on passage, with small numbers of little and common terns breeding most years.

Continuing south and west, the Charcón del Flamenco is surrounded by an area of low secondary dunes, sparsely vegetated with Phoenician juniper, shrubby orache, *Silene littoralis*, southern birdsfoot-trefoil, *Frankenia corymbosa*, winged sea-lavender, French figwort, *Plantago lagopus*, *Senecio gallicus*, *Helichrysum stoechas*, *Asparagus stipularis* and the distinctive thick-stemmed *Cyperus capitatus*; look out for spectacled and Dartford warblers flitting around the taller bushes here. The coarse sands of the primary dunes behind the beach host typical pioneer species such as sea rocket, sea spurge, sea medick, sea knotgrass, sea-holly, cottonweed and – more rarely – sea daffodil.

Returning to Roquetas, take the minor road west towards Almerimar (which runs between the north side of the *salinas* and an immense sea of plastic greenhouses) until it turns abruptly north, at which point, follow the track that continues straight ahead, leaving the greenhouses on your right. The piles of rubble alongside the greenhouses are a noted haunt of some gargantuan ocellated lizards; in arid areas in southeastern Spain these belong to the subspecies *nevadensis*,

usually greyish-brown in colour rather than bright green like the northern Iberian subspecies (*lepida*).

Any of the tracks off to the left will take you into the best-preserved section of mature dunes, through a dense scrub of Phoenician juniper, joint pine, lentisc, *Cistus clusii* and *Thymelaea hirsuta*, with the slacks hosting almost impenetrable thickets of sharp rush, accompanied by *Arthrocnemum macrostachyum*, various sea-lavenders and golden-samphire. Notable mammals here include garden dormouse and Mediterranean pine vole.

If you head straight on, however, you'll emerge onto a stony plain with the Alcores cliff up to the right, where you must park and walk, as you are now entering the *reserva natural*. This is a prime site for stone curlew (more than 100 pairs breed in the *paraje*), as well as for lesser short-toed (200-odd pairs), calandra and Thekla larks, while in winter you might encounter little bustard, golden plover and black-bellied sandgrouse.

The Alcores cliff is dissected by small gullies housing a thick scrub of *Maytenus senegalensis*, *Zizyphus lotus* (accompanied by common tiger blue butterflies in March) and *Withania frutescens*, which attracts migrant

Punta Entinas–Sabinar: salt-steppe

passerines such as ring ouzel and redstart in spring and breeding black-eared wheatear from March onwards. An examination of the friable terraces at the top of the cliff should turn up mirror ophrys, hollow-stemmed asphodel, dipcadi, Barbary nut and wild gladiolus, amid clumps of *Genista umbellata*, fringed rue and *Thymus vulgaris*.

The avifauna of the endorheic lagoons which lie at the extreme western end of the *reserva natural* is at first sight rather disappointing when compared to that of the *salinas*, with the most characteristic spring denizens being little egrets galore and greater flamingo, with water rail in the marginal reedbeds. These shallow lakes dry out almost completely in late summer, but black-winged stilt (60 pairs), avocet (30 pairs) and Kentish plover (40 pairs) breed, and large numbers of Audouin's gulls hang out all year round.

SITE 152 Desierto de Tabernas

A pale lunar landscape of gullied tablelands and sheer ridges, of interest for its endemic flora and cliff-breeding and steppe birds, particularly trumpeter finch.

A desolate labyrinth of eroded plateaux and steep-sided arid mountains, the Desierto de Tabernas (a *paraje natural* of 11 475 ha, also a ZEPA) lies to the northeast of the Sierra Nevada, sandwiched between the Sierra de los Filabres and the Sierra Alhamilla. Rainfall rarely exceeds 200 mm per year – often in just a few fierce deluges – while more than 3100 hours of sunlight annually are responsible for an average annual temperature of 18°C, with extremes of 5 and 48°C. Pale, soft Miocene marls and sandstones have been eroded by torrential rainstorms into a spectacular maze of deep gullies separated by flat plateaux often known as badlands, while more durable conglomerates cap the mountains.

One of the most emblematic corners of the *paraje* is the Arroyo del Verdelecho: a cliff-lined gully or *rambla* accessible from the junction of the A-370 and C-3326 (this latter in the process of being converted into the Almería–Guadix motorway). In spring the bed of the lower watercourse houses a narrow rivulet, the margins of which are populated with tamarisk, oleander, giant and common reeds and salt-tolerant species such as shrubby orache, succulent clumps of *Salsola vermiculata*, *S. genistoides*, *S. longifolia*, *Arthrocnemum macrostachyum* and *Anabasis articulata*, golden-samphire and woody fleabane.

Sandy soils in the drier parts of the *rambla* host islands of lygos and *Ballota hirsuta* surrounded by deep-rooted clumps of Mediterranean needle-grass. Many endemic plants thrive amid these shady, relatively stable islands, notably the lilac-flowered toadflax *Linaria nigricans*, confined to the province of Almería, and the related *Chaenorhinum grandiflorum*, unique to southeastern Spain, as well as the spiny *Eryngium ilicifolium* and the feathery-flowered annual *Pteranthus dichotomus*, both of which are Afro-Iberian endemics. Keep an eye open, too, for the deep-purple cylinders of cynomorium and fabulous golden-yellow spikes of *Cistanche phelypaea* (the inland subspecies *lutea*), both of which are parasitic on the roots of the shrubby chenopods mentioned above, as well as the sea-lavenders *Limonium insigne* (endemic to southeast Spain) and *L. lobatum*.

The sides of the gully harbour clumps of the bristly, cream-flowered crucifer *Euzomo-*

Andalucía

Rambla in the Desierto de Tabernas

dendron bourgaeanum – a monospecific genus which is known only from Tabernas and the nearby *sierras* of Alhamilla, Gádor and Los Filabres – as well as the white-flowered *Moricandia foetida*, with large amplexicaule leaves, also confined to extremely arid habitats in southeastern Spain.

The majority of the Tabernas vertebrates take refuge in *ramblas* such as Verdelecho, as the parched plateaux are virtually inimical to life (although the stone curlews and short-toed larks which abound in the area seem to like it). Here you could well find such obligate wetland creatures as stripe-necked terrapin, viperine snake, Iberian pool frog and natterjack toad, as well as spiny-footed and ocellated lizards, ladder snake and even a rabbit or two. The birdlife of these cliff-lined gullies is of particular interest, with many species nesting in the abundance of small cavities which line the walls. Kestrel, rock dove, alpine swift, crag martin, black wheatear, blue rock thrush, black redstart,

jackdaw, spotless starling and rock sparrow are among the most typical denizens, but – in the absence of trees here – you might also come across hoopoes and even rollers using this habitat to rear their young. Trumpeter finches – typical of arid regions in North Africa and the Near East – have one of their European strongholds here, with some 20 pairs breeding in the Tabernas area.

A wander along the Arroyo del Verdelecho in spring will turn up large numbers of migrating passerines in the tamarisk and oleander scrub, including Orphean, sub-alpine, Bonelli's and willow warblers, while bee-eater, pallid swift and red-rumped swallow occupy the airspace above. The small stream in the southern sector attracts black-bellied sandgrouse early in the day, while Bonelli's eagles (two pairs here) are often seen floating over these gullies, using the thermals to gain height; eagle owl and peregrine also breed in the more inaccessible ravines.

Also in the area

Sierra Alhamilla (*paraje natural* and ZEPA of 8392 ha) 25 km-long ridge (maximum 1387 m, Colativí) housing the area's only remaining western holm oak forest and extensive pine plantations, home to common genet, Eurasian badger and wild boar, plus sparrowhawk, goshawk, booted eagle, crossbill and rock bunting. Bare hilltop ridges harbour breeding Bonelli's eagle (seven pairs), with deep ravines the haunt of peregrine, eagle owl, alpine swift, black wheatear and blue rock thrush. Sheltered gullies around the oasis of Baños de Sierra Alhamilla contain enclaves of *Maytenus senegalensis*, *Rhamnus lycioides* and *Withania frutescens*, while rocky areas here host Spanish rusty foxglove, *Aristolochia baetica* and the Afro-Iberian endemic *Lapiedra martinezii*; scops owls frequent the palm trees. Dry, open areas, sparsely clothed with Afro-Iberian endemics such as false esparto, *Genista spartioides*, *G. valentina*, *Phlomis purpurea*, round-headed thyme and *Thymus hyemalis*, are home to stone curlew, black-bellied sandgrouse, Dupont's, crested and Thekla larks and a few little bustards, plus spiny-footed, Iberian wall

and ocellated lizards, both psammodromus and ladder, Montpellier and horseshoe whip snakes. The dry farmland along the road up to Cuevas de los Úbedas is one of the best places in Europe for trumpeter finch.

Hoyas de Baza y Guadix Arid depressions of immense significance for their steppe bird communities: large numbers of stone curlew, black-bellied sandgrouse, roller and calandra, short-toed, lesser short-toed, crested, Thekla and Dupont's larks, as well as a handful of Montagu's harriers and a declining population of little bustard. Ravines in the Hoya de Guadix support huge numbers of black wheatear and rock sparrow, around 100 pairs of chough and a few pairs of golden and Bonelli's eagles and eagle owls. One of only two known Spanish – and indeed European – localities for greenish black-tip.

153 Cabo de Gata–Níjar

SITE

An arid, volcanic landscape, unique in Europe, harbouring several endemic plants, an important steppe bird community and a diverse avifauna associated with the salinas.

The Parque Natural Marítimo-Terrestre de Cabo de Gata–Níjar (49 618 ha, also a ZEPA (26 000 ha) and Biosphere Reserve) encompasses four distinct geographical units: the off-shore marine habitats; around 40 km of coastal cliffs (up to 100 m high) in the eastern reaches of the park; the coastal plain of the Bahía de Almería in the western sector (about 500 m wide and encompassing important dune systems, xerophytic scrub, *ramblas* housing small coastal lagoons and *salinas*); and the Sierra del Cabo de Gata of the hinterland, a labyrinth of raw, reddish volcanic rock which peaks at just 493 m (Cerro de los Frailes).

This is one of the most arid regions of Europe, with a climate similar to that of Tabernas (see p. 419). Trees are naturally scarce here, while much of the unique climax scrub of *Ulex canescens*, *Genista spartioides*, *Maytenus senegalensis*, *Zizyphus lotus*, *Periploca laevigata* subspecies *angustifolia* and dwarf fan palm has succumbed to felling, overgrazing and fire in historical times. Today the most characteristic landscape elements are prickly pears, introduced to provide food for the coccid bug *Dactylopius coccus*, from which cochineal is obtained, and sisals (*Agave fourcroydes* and *A. sisalana*), cultivated to make rope.

Andalucía

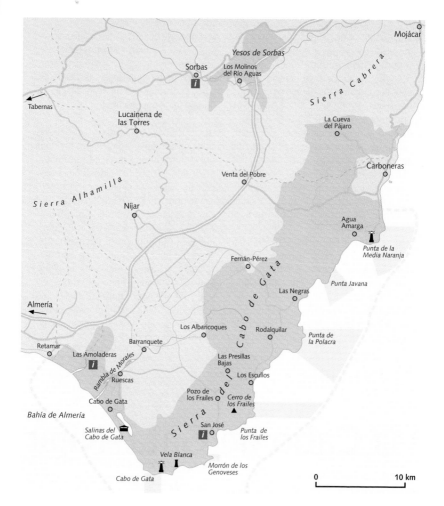

Despite – or perhaps because of – the high temperatures and extremely low levels of precipitation, Cabo de Gata is home to around 1000 species of vascular plant, about 12% of which are unique to Iberia. Several species are found only in the Cabo de Gata area: the pink *Dianthus charidemi*, the gorse *Ulex canescens*, the germander *Teucrium charidemi*, the mullein *Verbascum charidemi*, the snapdragon *Antirrhinum charidemi* and the lily *Androcymbium europaeum*.

Cabo de Gata's coastal waters are some of the least polluted in the western Mediterranean. Within the protected off-shore area – which covers 12 000 ha of the park and extends down to a depth of around 50 m – more than 1400 species of marine animals and plants have been recorded, the high biodiversity of this stretch of coast due in the main to the convergence of Atlantic and Mediterranean currents here. Sandy substrata in the Bahía de Almería harbour extensive undersea meadows of posidonia, eelgrass and *Cymodocea nodosa* down to a depth of around 20 m, and are also home to the enormous fan mussel: the Mediterranean's largest bivalve (up to 80 cm long). Rocky habitats to the northeast, by comparison, are carpeted with 'seaweeds' such as the delicate mermaid's cup, calcareous green alga and *Udotea petiolata*, and inhabited by thousands of runner crabs.

Andalucía

Your first port of call should be the SEO/BirdLife visitor centre at Las Amoladeras, at km 7 on the road (AL-P-202) between Retamar and Ruescas (tel. and fax: 950 160435). The surrounding stony plain harbours an abundance of the delightful, low-growing lily *Androcymbium europaeum*, whose clusters of violet-streaked white flowers flower in mid- winter, as well as the annual sea-lavender *Limonium lobatum*, with distinctive ice-blue calices and yellow flowers, field gladiolus, Barbary nut, hollowstemmed asphodel and dipcadi.

Heading south from here through the ancient dunes, the margins of the path are coloured by *Ononis ramosissima*, fagonia, mallow-leaved bindweed, *Andryala ragusina* and reichardia in early spring. Less disturbed areas are clothed with *Zizyphus lotus*, clumps of albardine and false esparto and a bewildering array of shrubby, succulent chenopods – *Salsola vermiculata*, *S. longifolia* and *S. genistoides*, the latter endemic to southeast Spain – parasitised by the frankly phallic cynomorium. Birds which perch atop the tall sisal inflorescences here to spy out

their prey include little owl, bee-eater, hoopoe, black-eared wheatear and woodchat and southern grey shrikes, while the dense scrub is home to Sardinian, Dartford and spectacled warblers, and pallid swifts and red-rumped swallows scythe through the air overhead. Spiny-footed and ocellated lizards and Iberian hares also frequent these ancient dunes, while the tiny but very lovely common tiger blue butterfly is often seen flying round the spiny, zigzagged stems of *Zizyphus lotus*, its larval food-plant.

To the northeast of Las Amoladeras lies an abandoned sisal plantation traversed by a road leading to a small radar tower for the nearby airport, set on a hill overlooking a vast stony plateau to the north. This is renowned as being one of the best places for Dupont's lark at Cabo de Gata (more than 130 pairs breed in the park), as well as housing one of the highest breeding densities of lesser short-toed and Thekla larks in Spain, and is also the haunt of stone curlew, blackbellied sandgrouse, short-toed lark and an occasional trumpeter finch or little bustard, with Richard's pipit habitual in winter.

Following the road further east (past the hamlet of Ruescas, where you keep right towards the coast), a track leading south to a campsite will eventually take you to the mouth of the Rambla de Morales. A small seasonal lagoon here attracts all manner of waterbirds on migration; several trips in late March 2000 turned up garganey, spotted redshank, collared pratincole (a group of 27 birds), Audouin's and Mediterranean gulls and gull-billed tern, among more commonplace species such as little egret, blackwinged stilt, avocet, Kentish and ringed plovers, sanderling, little stint, both godwits, Sandwich and whiskered terns, sand martin and yellow wagtail.

The coastal dunes here are clothed with a succession (from the shore inland) of sea medick, coastal crucianella, cottonweed, the sea heath *Frankenia corymbosa*, winged sealavender, with its distinctive undulate leaves, *Thymelaea hirsuta*, *Helichrysum stoechas*, *Cyperus capitatus*, the silvery stems of *Atriplex glauca* and succulent, purple-tinged carpets of *Mesembryanthemum nodiflorum*,

Tertiary dunes, Cabo de Gata

Salinas del Cabo de Gata, with the volcanic *sierra* in the background

decorated at intervals with small white flowers. The quicksilver Bedriaga's skink is very much at home here, as are short-toed larks in summer, while the marshy edges of the lagoon are the haunt of *Ischnura graellsii* and southern darter.

Once past the village of Cabo de Gata itself, you reach an area of *salinas* just to the north of the coast road (a Ramsar Site of 300 ha and *reserva integral*). Entry is forbidden, but you can walk around the edge and a

small hide about halfway along the south side will furnish you with excellent views of greater flamingo; present in small numbers during much of the year (late summer concentrations often exceed 2000 individuals), various breeding attempts have been noted in recent years. Habitually more successful are nesting avocet (193 pairs), Kentish plover (35 pairs), little tern (35 pairs) and a few pairs of common tern, as well as Cetti's, reed and great reed warblers in the reedbeds.

Winter brings shelduck, wigeon, shoveler, osprey and even Caspian tern, while spring usually turns up most of the waders, terns and gulls mentioned for the Rambla de Morales, with non-breeding Audouin's present all year; among the more interesting passage records are black stork, purple heron, white-headed duck, red-breasted merganser and slender-billed gull. Montagu's harrier and red-necked nightjar breed in the scrubby steppes to the north of the *salinas*.

The halophytic flora of these working salt-pans is dominated by a multitude of succulent chenopods, the Spanish endemic sea-lavender *Limonium cossonianum* and the grasses *Aeluropus littoralis*, *Crypsis aculeata*, *Cutandia memphitica* and *Sporobolus pungens*, as well as fringing stands of giant and common reeds and the Afro-Iberian endemic tamarisk *Tamarix boveana*. Much the same dune species as at Rambla Morales occur in the surrounding sandflats, with the addition of some spectacular fluorescent-pink clumps of *Silene littorea* and flower-studded cushions of yellow sea aster.

From here it is only a short distance to the lighthouse, where you can continue on foot up to the Vela Blanca watch-tower and down towards San José via an impressive stretch of volcanic cliffs, populated by the majority of Cabo de Gata's most interesting plants: untidy masses of the pink-flowered *Antirrhinum charidemi*, woolly clumps of *Teucrium charidemi* and sprawling, thorny bushes of *Periploca laevigata* subspecies *angustifolia*. Along the margins of the path grow yellow horned-poppy, sea mallow, the bushy sea-lavender *Limonium insigne* and urospermum, together with a multitude of aromatic Mediterranean shrubs: fringed rue, *Thymus vulgaris*, *T. hyemalis*, cut-leaved, toothed and French lavenders, *Phlomis purpurea* (subspecies *almeriensis*) and *P. lychnitis*. This is also as good a place as any to search for the cactus-like *Caralluma europaea*: a square-stemmed, succulent member of the Asclepiadaceae whose star-shaped, purple-striped yellow flowers appear between March and June.

Typical cliff-breeding birds here are peregrine, black wheatear, blue rock thrush and jackdaw, while scrubby habitats host Sardinian and spectacled warblers. Offshore, gannets and Audouin's gulls float by at regular intervals, while scattered colonies of storm petrel occur along the more remote cliff-lined coast to the north, possibly accompanied by small numbers of shag. The area around the lighthouse regularly turns up rock sparrow and trumpeter finch, but although around 50 pairs of these distinctive orange-billed finches breed in the park, they are notoriously hard to track down.

An interesting excursion into the heart of the Sierra de Cabo de Gata leads you from the hamlet of Las Presillas Bajas north and east to the caldera of Majada Redonda, the first part of the trail following a sandy *rambla*. The sides of this gully and the surrounding cultivated plots are home to the purple-flowered stock *Matthiola lunata*, red horned-poppy, *Anthyllis cytisoides*, bladder-vetch, *Lathyrus clymenum*, grey-leaved cistus, the enormous yellow-flowered umbellifer *Ferula tingitana* (an Afro-Iberian endemic), large blue alkanet, ground-pine germander, fan-lipped orchid and mirror ophrys.

Among the reptiles, look out for large and Spanish psammodromus, ladder and Montpellier snakes and Lataste's viper, while Bonelli's eagles are sometimes seen floating above the crater (a handful of pairs breed in these interior ranges, together with about 20 pairs of eagle owl). Closer at hand you might encounter red-legged partridge, alpine swift, crag martin, Thekla lark, black redstart, black and black-eared wheatears, blue rock thrush, woodchat shrike and scores of corn buntings, while spring butterflies include mallow skipper, Bath, dappled and green-striped whites, clouded yellow, painted lady, Spanish marbled white, small copper and Lang's short-tailed blue.

Information: There is a second park information centre in San José (tel: 950 380299; fax: 950 611055); e-mail enquiries should be directed to PN.CaboGata-Nijar@cma.junta-andalucia.es

Yesos de Sorbas

Also in the area

Yesos de Sorbas (*paraje natural*; 2432 ha) Largest area of karstified gypsum in Spain. Below the village of Los Molinos del Río Aguas (on the AL-140), a narrow path along the river houses the Almerían endemic rock-roses *Helianthemum alypoides* and *H. almeriense*, plus *Guiraoa arvensis*, *Teucrium turredanum*, *T. freynii* and *Santolina viscosa*, all confined to southeastern Spain. Other gypsum specialists include *Gypsophila struthium*, *Ononis tridentata* and *Anthyllis cytisoides*, plus many spring-flowering monocots and *Cistanche phelypaea* subspecies *lutea*. Bonelli's eagles often fly over, with cliffs housing black wheatear, blue rock thrush, rock sparrow and possibly eagle owl. Iberian pool and parsley frogs, stripe-necked terrapin and ladder snake. Visitor centre (Los Yesares) in Sorbas (tel: 950 364563).

Cross-border sites

Introduction

While we hope that the preceding pages have shown that Spain harbours a magnificient array of habitats and species, we cannot ignore the fact that several of the country's most emblematic wildlife refuges are shared with neighbouring Portugal. Our selection of cross-border sites for the most part concentrates on the various rivers which form a natual boundary between the two nations, but also includes an area of bird-rich pseudo- steppe centred on the cities of Badajoz and Elvas.

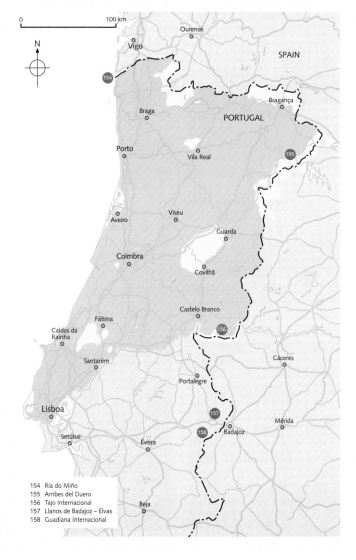

154 Ría do Miño
155 Arribes del Duero
156 Tajo Internacional
157 Llanos de Badajoz – Elvas
158 Guadiana Internacional

SITE 154 Ría do Miño

Rich assemblage of alluvial forest, reedbeds and marshland with a diverse avifauna, the river itself housing healthy fish populations.

The river Miño – Minho to the Portuguese – marks the border between Galicia and northwestern Portugal for some 74 km, terminating in a broad estuary harbouring intertidal sandbanks, mudflats and salt-marsh, plus large vegetated islands and rocky and sandy beaches, the latter often backed by low dune systems.

Further upstream, gallery forests of alder and willows appear, often associated with stands of pedunculate oak and narrow-leaved ash, particularly along the Coura, which joins the Minho to the north of Caminha (the focal point of Portugal's 3393 ha ZPE). These gallery forests, interspersed with reedbeds and brackish pastures, provide suitable breeding habitat for many aquatic birds, notably little bittern, marsh harrier, water rail, kingfisher, yellow wagtail, fan-tailed, Savi's, melodious, reed and great reed warblers, golden oriole, common waxbill and reed bunting.

On the Spanish shore, it is worth exploring the windswept Santa Tegra (Tecla) headland, haunt of oystercatcher, purple sandpiper, turnstone and kingfisher in winter. The southern extremity of the cape – opposite the island fort of A Insua – is a good sea-watching locality during migration periods, often turning up gannets, guillemots and razorbills, as well as Cory's shearwater, great and Arctic skuas and kittiwake.

The shallow, sheltered bays to the east are carpeted with intertidal saltmarsh, views over which are provided by two open-plan hides located on the narrow coast road to the north of the Pasaxe docks. The southernmost hide overlooks shallow pools which attract wintering grey plover, lapwing, dunlin, snipe and greenshank, with spoonbill, marsh harrier, bar-tailed godwit and whimbrel dropping in on pas-

sage. The more northerly hide commands views of Isla Canosa and a sheltered arm of the main river: a noted refuge of wintering red-breasted merganser, although teal, wigeon, mallard and tufted duck are typically the order of the day. In recent years, great northern and red-throated divers, black-necked grebe, osprey, shelduck, velvet scoter, scaup, eider, long-tailed duck and Mediterranean, little and Sabine's gulls have also turned up in the estuary.

On the Portuguese margin, head for the Mata Nacional do Camarido, about 1 km south of Caminha. Despite consisting mainly of planted pines and acacias, this forest harbours a sparse understorey of the Afro-Iberian endemic shrub *Corema album* (with white, mistletoe-like berries) and is a renowned staging-post for migrating passerines, with great spotted woodpecker, firecrest, crested tit, short-toed treecreeper and cirl bunting present all year round. A stroll through the *mata* will take you to the sandspit of the Ponta de Caminha, populated by a diverse assemblage of typical Atlantic dune plants and breeding Kentish plover, with Iberian hares skulking among the thickets of acacia.

Kingfisher *Alcedo atthis* (Mike Lane)

Today the Miño/Minho is one of only two Portuguese rivers which still harbour viable populations of Atlantic salmon, also providing breeding grounds for other migratory fish such as European eel, brown trout, sea lamprey and Twaite and Allis shad, and supporting healthy resident populations of Iberian nase, *Barbus bocagei* and bermejuela, all of which are found only in Spain and Portugal.

Accesss: To cross the Miño estuary take the flat-bed car ferry (*transbordador*) – operational all year – which links A Guarda (Pasaxe/Pasaje docks) with Caminha, saving a longwinded roundabout trip by road via Tui.

Río Miño

Also in the area

As Ribeiras do Louro Riverine forest, permanent and seasonal lagoons, peatbogs and damp pastures on the floodplain of the Río Louro close to its confluence with the Miño in Galicia, sometimes called As Gándaras de Budiño. Breeding little bittern, water rail, Savi's warbler (not every year) and the only regular nesting site for teal in Iberia. Passage crakes, marsh terns, bluethroat and, occasionally, purple heron and marsh harrier, plus Pyrenean desman, otter, European pond terrapin, Schreiber's green lizard and golden-striped salamander. Iberian endemic flora includes *Genista berberidea* and *Ulex micranthus*; Alcon blue butterfly feeds on marsh gentians here, plus a wealth of small odonates. Access via the As Gándaras industrial estate (junctions 163/164, west off the N-550/N-120).

Río Tea Tributary of the Miño in Galicia with an exceptional community of freshwater and migratory fish, including Atlantic salmon, sea lamprey, Iberian nase, bermejuela and bordallo. Also Pyrenean desman, otter, Iberian painted frog and the endangered splendid emerald dragonfly.

SITE 155 Arribes del Duero

Fabulous river canyons harbouring important populations of cliff-breeding birds and an interesting calcifuge flora.

The 120-odd kilometres of the river Duero/Douro which mark the boundary between Spain and Portugal represent the spine of what is probably the largest complex of river gorges – known locally as *arribes* – in the Iberian peninsula. Add to this the tributary 'ribs' and you're talking about more than 300 km of river-excavated ravines in some of the wildest and least inhabited terrain in Europe: a 85 146 ha *parque natural* in Portugal and a massive proposed natural park of around 170 000 ha in Spain (also protected by a ZPE of 50 744 ha and ZEPA of 123 876 ha, respectively).

The main gorge – gouged for the most part from an essentially siliceous bedrock of granite, gneiss, slate and quartzite – is up to 400 m deep in places, resulting in the formation of spectacular waterfalls and cascades where tributaries descend suddenly to the level of the main river, although the Duero itself has long since been tamed by the construction of five immense hydroelectric dams.

Away from the river lies an irregular mosaic of agricultural land and more natural vegetation, the latter dominated by stands of western holm oak, usually associated with prickly juniper, bristly greenweed, turpentine tree and *Asparagus acutifolius*, although small expanses of *dehesa/montado* also occur. The most notable stand of cork oak lies at the foot of Penedo Durão, growing together with white-flowered and hairy-fruited brooms, strawberry-tree and *Phillyrea angustifolia*. Pyrenean oak characterises the windswept plateaux which flank the gorge, sometimes accompanied by Lusitanian oak and Montpellier maple in more sheltered localities.

Most characteristic of the continental climate and very thin soils of the upper gorge, however, are large, almost mono-specific stands of prickly juniper, where you might also turn up noted thermophiles such as scaly cheilanthes, *Asparagus albus* and *A. aphyllus*, with spring scattering clumps of the delightful common jonquil across the rock outcrops. Down below, the succession of dams means that gallery forests are scarce here, with just a few remnants – dominated by alder, *Salix salvifolia*, small-leaved elm and narrow-leaved ash – confined to less adulterated tributaries. In between, the cliffs – for the most part inaccessible to grazing animals and unaffected by fire – are home to the Iberian endemic pink *Dianthus laricifolius*, the Afro-Iberian endemic catchfly *Silene boryi*, here represented by the subspecies *durensis*, practically confined to these canyons, the robust, woad-like crucifer *Isatis platyloba*, unique to central Spain and northeastern Portugal, and the western Iberian endemic toadflax *Linaria coutinhoi*.

Among the birds, pride of place undoubtedly goes to the cliff-breeding communities. Griffon vultures (325 pairs) can be seen all year round and just about anywhere along the length of the Arribes

Black stork *Ciconia nigra*

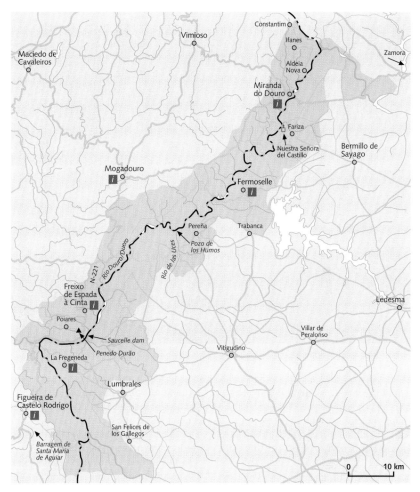

del Duero, while the summering black storks (16 pairs) and Egyptian vultures (129 pairs) and resident eagle owls (10–20 pairs) are commonest in the deeper, northern gorges. Bonelli's eagles (14 pairs) and golden eagles (18 pairs) are pretty evenly distributed throughout, as are peregrine (some 20 pairs), alpine swift (50+ pairs), blue rock thrush and chough, although black wheatears are very localised and found mainly in dry, rocky habitats in the southern reaches.

The surrounding plateaux support birds more typically associated with forest and scrub habitats, including goshawk, short-toed and booted eagles, red and black kites, Dartford, subalpine, spectacled and Orphean warblers, azure-winged magpie, hawfinch and rock bunting, as well as those linked more specifically to open, agricultural land-scapes: black-winged kite, Montagu's harrier, little bustard, stone curlew, roller, Thekla and calandra larks, tawny pipit, black-eared wheatear and woodchat shrike. Hen harriers, red kites, lapwings and redwings are common in open coun-try during the winter, with wooded areas attracting large numbers of siskins.

The mammalian inhabitants of the combined parks are also predominantly associated with the plateaux, notably

Arribes del Duero near Miranda

Cabrera's vole, wildcat and roe deer, with a handful of wolves inhabiting the northern Portuguese sector of the park. The more natural watercourses support a thriving population of otters and the area is also important for bats, hosting both breeding and hibernating colonies of Schreiber's and greater mouse-eared, with the extremely rare Geoffroy's bat turning up on migration.

As one might expect, fish are also well represented here, with 14 species having been recorded in recent years, including Iberian nase, calandino and bermejuela, all of which are endemic to the peninsula. Look out, too, for European pond terrapins which, although widespread in Iberia, have an extremely disjunct distribution, as well as Bedriaga's skink, Bosca's newt, Iberian midwife toad and Iberian painted frog, all confined to the peninsula.

This is not an easy terrain to explore, as there are no roads running along the lip of the gorge and only a few places where you can cross from one side to the other,

most of which are linked to the large dam installations and thus not wildly scenic. There are, however, many small roads which lead to ancient chapels, forts and such-like, located strategically so as to overlook the international border.

In **Miranda do Douro**, the river valley houses nightingale and golden oriole, with alpine swifts and crag martins wheeling over the water and blue rock thrushes on the rocky flanks of the gorge; scops owls and red-necked nightjars are commonly heard at dusk. Bear north through the town on a minor road signposted Ifanes and Constantim and after about 3 km turn right towards Vale de Águia and Aldeia Nova. Once in the latter hamlet, follow signs to the Castro de São João das Arribas, a small chapel on the lip of a spectacular section of gorge. Egyptian vulture, golden eagle, red kite, alpine swift, crag martin, red-rumped swallow and chough are relatively easy to see here, while the scrub around the chapel hosts Dartford and subalpine warblers and hawfinch. Europarques runs guided one-hour boat-trips up-river all year round from Miranda (tels: 980 557557 (Spain) and 273 432396 (Portugal); www.europarques.com).

On the Spanish side it is well worth visiting the **Pozo de los Humos**, a seething cauldron at the foot of a powerful waterfall on the Río de las Uces, close to its confluence with the Duero. Follow the C-525 south from Fermoselle to the village of Trabanca, then turn right and head for Pereña. Enter the village then follow signs to the Pozo along 5 km of unsurfaced track through open countryside populated by a few sentinel southern grey shrikes, vociferous flocks of azure-winged magpies and cirl buntings. Near the end of the track, you will see the spray rising from the 50 m-high waterfall over to your left; an easy five-minute walk takes you to a suitable vantage point. At the foot of the waterfall lies a handsome grove of southern nettle trees, with otter, black stork and Egyptian vulture all found nearby.

Around the Saucelle dam, the broad river valley is dominated by the hulking buttress of **Penedo Durão** (727 m) on the Portuguese margin. From below you can pick out the guano-stained rocks which identify griffon vulture roosts and nests, as well as the enclave of thick cork oak forest at the foot of the buttress. The top of this impressive cliff is accessed by turning north towards Freixo de Espada à Cinta (N-221) and winding up out of the valley to a left turn (N-325–1) signposted Poiares/Penedo Durão. This minor road peters out only metres from the lip of the buttress: a superb viewpoint overlooking rocky outcrops populated by crag martin, black wheatear, blue rock thrush and chough. Egyptian vulture, alpine swift and red-rumped swallow are all easily seen from here in summer, with golden eagle a distinct possibility at any time of year.

Information: Spanish information centres are planned for Fermoselle and La Fregeneda; contact the Servicio de Medio Ambiente in Salamanca (tel: 923 296026) or Zamora (tel: 980 559600) for more information. The Portuguese park headquarters is in Mogadouro (tel: 279 340030; fax: 279 341596; e-mail: pndi@icn.pt), with subsidiary offices in Miranda do Douro, Freixo de Espada à Cinta and Figueira de Castelo Rodrigo (all weekdays only).

SITE
156 Tajo Internacional

Superb assemblage of cliff-breeding birds along a 40 km-long dammed stretch of the river Tajo where it forms the border between Spain and Portugal.

From whichever direction you approach the international Tajo/Tejo, the rolling *dehesa/montado* completely masks the prodigious cleft in the bedrock until you are right on top of it. A mantle of evergreen shrubs clothes the sides of the valley, frequently interrupted by rugged bluffs of slates, schists and granites which provide ideal habitat for cliff-nesting birds. Of outstanding importance in the Tajo defile (a ZPE of 24 406 ha in Portugal) are 24 pairs of black stork, 130 of griffon vulture, 11 of Egyptian vulture, 6–10 of eagle owl, 7 of Bonelli's eagle and 5 of golden eagle, while good numbers of booted eagle and a handful of pairs of black kite and short-toed eagle breed in the surrounding wood–pasture. Ospreys occur on passage and black vultures are regularly spotted throughout the year, on forays from their breeding area in the vast expanses of cork and western holm oak *dehesa* to the south.

Among the smaller cliff-breeding birds of the Tajo valley are pallid and alpine swifts, crag and house martins, black wheatear and blue rock thrush, while an examination of the sparse riverine forests – of alder, southern nettle tree and narrow-leaved ash – along the tributaries should turn up kingfisher, nightingale, melodious warbler and golden oriole. In winter hundreds of cormorants descend on the valley, the river's surface is dotted with small groups of mallard, shoveler and tufted duck, and red kites are ten-a-penny in the skies above.

Sometimes referred to as the Embalse/ Barragem de Cedillo, the Tajo was dammed for hydroelectric power at the western end of its international section in 1972, which resulted in the extinction of Spain's only nucleus of the migratory European river lamprey. Fortunately the resident fish have not suffered the same fate, with the Tajo Internacional still harbouring residual populations of the

Black wheatear *Oenanthe leucura* (Mike Lane)

Iberian endemic barbel *Barbus micro-cephalus* and, curiously, the big-scale sand smelt, a predominantly intertidal species of the Mediterranean basin which nevertheless occurs in a few inland freshwater localities in Iberia.

Much of the land surrounding the Tajo is privately owned, such that access to the river is limited, but surfaced roads lead to the river at Cedillo and to the north of Herrera de Alcántara on the Spanish side. The Cedillo dam area is liberally sprinkled with electricity substations and huge pylons, but there are numerous waymarked walks through the cork oaks, small slate-walled meadows – known as *lameiros* in Portugal – and patches of Mediterranean scrub around the village itself, where orchids abound in spring, particularly heart-flowered and small-flowered serapias. The narrow road (EX-377) which zigzags down to the river near Herrera is much more attractive, providing excellent views over the Tajo in both directions: a good place to sit and watch for black stork, griffon and Egyptian vultures and Bonelli's eagle, often accompanied by alpine swift, bee-eater and red-rumped swallow. Look out, too, for black-winged kites and Montagu's harriers venturing over the area from more open habitats nearby.

From Portugal, access to river can be gained from Rosmaninhal and Malpica do Tejo. Two other interesting localities nearby are Segura (where the N-355 crosses the Erges: a tributary of the Tajo) and Salvaterra do Extremo, both of which are likely to turn up similar species to

Herrera, plus booted and short-toed eagles and black wheatear.

On both margins, the surrounding Mediterranean scrub and forest is a rich mosaic of western holm, Lusitanian and cork oaks, lentisc, turpentine tree, *Rhamnus lycioides* subspecies *oleoides*, Mediterranean buckthorn, laurel-leaved and gum cistuses, strawberry-tree, wild olive, *Phillyrea angustifolia* and *P. latifolia* and laurustinus. Azure-winged magpies are extremely common in these evergreen habitats, accompanied by woodlark, subalpine, Dartford and Orphean warblers, black-eared wheatear, woodchat shrike and hawfinch, with the onset of dusk heralded by the piping calls of scops owls and bringing out dozens of red-necked nightjars. Among the forest mammals here are wildcat, common genet and Egyptian mongoose, while otters are a fairly frequent sight along the margins of the river.

Information: Offices of the recently declared Parque Natural do Tejo Internacional in Portugal are located in Castelo Branco (tel: 272 321445) and Idanha-a-Nova (tel. and fax: 277 202087). The Portuguese NGO Quercus owns and manages two estates in the area and has published an excellent guide (in Portuguese) to the wildlife of the area which details interesting routes on the northern margin; Quercus also provides guided tours (further details from their Rosmaninhal office; tel: 277 477196/277 477463).

Also in the area

Puente de Alcántara Fabulous Roman bridge (106 AD) over the Tajo to the north of Alcántara (194 m long with a 70 m-high central arch). Crag martins galore at any time of year, joined by alpine swift and red-rumped swallow in summer. Older buildings in the town of Alcántara itself

host breeding white stork and lesser kestrel. The area around the nearby **Embalse de Alcántara** harbours important breeding nuclei of black stork, Egyptian vulture, Spanish imperial eagle and lesser kestrel, as well as concentrations of great and little bustards.

SITE 157 Llanos de Badajoz–Elvas

Vast expanse of pseudosteppes straddling the Spanish–Portuguese border around the cities of Badajoz and Elvas, of interest for its open-country birds.

On the Spanish side of the border, the vast tract of open country to the north of Badajoz – between the rivers Gévora and Zapatón, tributaries of the Guadiana – boasts healthy populations of steppe birds, including great (300+ individuals) and little bustards (some 500 birds) and both sandgrouse, as well as two small winter roosts of cranes. Try the EX-110 towards Alburquerque for Montagu's harrier, great spotted cuckoo, red-necked nightjar and roller in summer, with black-winged kite, stone curlew and azure-winged magpie abundant at any time of year; Spanish imperial eagles are sometimes seen hunting here in winter. Also in the winter, many small temporary lagoons form in the *dehesa* around Botoa and El Zangallón, attracting small numbers of

wigeon, gadwall, teal, pintail, shoveler, pochard and tufted duck, plus golden plover, lapwing, snipe, black-tailed godwit and spotted redshank.

To the south of Badajoz, the EX-310 to Valverde de Leganés and the BA-V-2001 running east of Valverde towards La Albuera traverse extensive pastures and arable land, the habitat diversity increased by olive groves, vineyards and pockets of western holm oak. In spring, these rather more calcareous soils host giant and fan-lipped orchids, with the area also housing the only Extremaduran colony of Aetherie fritillary: a species pretty well confined to Andalucía and the Algarve in Iberia. Bird-wise, look out for Montagu's harrier, black-winged kite, stone curlew, collared pratincole and both sandgrouse, with cranes

Llanos de Badajoz–Elvas

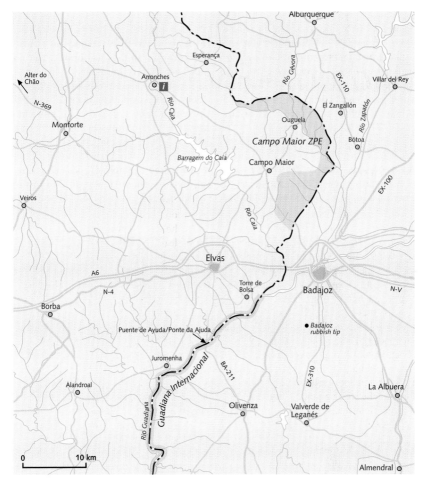

from November onwards. A recent census estimated the presence of at least 1500 great bustards and 200 pairs of little bustards (increasing to around 3000 birds in winter) in this area; lesser kestrels are a common sight hunting over the plains in early summer and Iberian hares are particularly abundant.

Despite considerable agricultural intensification and the recent construction of the Madrid–Lisboa motorway, the Campo Maior ZPE (9576 ha) to the northeast of Elvas is still one of Portugal's most important sites for steppe birds. Great bustard (now just a few individuals, following a dramatic decline in recent years), little bustard (up to 250 birds), stone curlew (some 30 pairs) and Thekla, short-toed and calandra larks are typical denizens, with black-winged and black kites, Montagu's harriers and lesser kestrels all breeding in small numbers; look out, too, for wintering cranes (maximum 1000 birds).

An exploration of the sparse western holm oak *montado* around Campo Maior should turn up great spotted cuckoo, scops owl, red-necked nightjar, roller, hoopoe, black-eared wheatear, woodchat and southern grey shrikes, azure-winged magpie and Spanish and rock sparrows, with more dense vegetation hosting subalpine and Orphean warblers. Calcareous soils here are carpeted with the broad leaves and sweet-scented flowers of *Iris planifolia* in spring.

Along the margins of the Rio Xévora (the Spanish Gévora) fringed with white willow, alder, tamarisks and oleander, you can expect breeding little ringed plover, kingfisher, bee-eater, red-rumped swallow, sand martin, nightingale, melodious, fantailed and Cetti's warblers and golden oriole, as well as great reed warbler and waders on passage.

The Rio Caia – another tributary of the Guadiana, which crosses the rolling plains between Campo Maior and Elvas – is also worth a visit in the hope of seeing otters or the rare aquatic fern *Marsilea batardae*, which grows along seasonally flooded margins, but you'll probably have to make do with a plethora of stripe-necked terrapins. Common waxbill and red avadavat also occur here, while the extensive Caia reservoir is a known haunt of osprey and red-crested pochard in winter. The Caia's Iberian endemic piscine community includes Iberian nase, the related *Chondrostoma willkommii*, calandino, pardilla and the endangered jarabugo: a schooling, minnow-like fish known only from the Guadiana and Guadalquivir river basins.

Iris planifolia

Also in the area

Rubbish tip to south of Badajoz From Badajoz take the EX-310 towards Valverde de Leganés, then turn right at around km 9.5 (signposted Centro de Tratamiento de Residuos) and follow the road for 4.5 km. Just before the entrance to the tip, a slight rise gives views across the dump, haunt of hordes of cattle egrets, white storks and red and black kites in winter; alternatively, go past the entrance and take the first track on the right. Before the sun comes up, the cork oaks along the entry road are topped by dozens of roosting white storks.

SITE 158 Guadiana Internacional

One of the longest stretches of 'wild' river remaining in southern Europe today, with mature gallery forests and adjacent rice-fields housing interesting bird communities.

The so-called Guadiana Internacional separates Spain from Portugal for more than 60 km, extending from the Badajoz–Elvas area southwards to just east of Monsaraz (see map on p. 440), although the imminent flooding of the Alqueva dam in Portugal will eventually inundate most of the meridional section, along with large tracts of pristine riverine forest.

For much of its international reaches the Guadiana is wide, shallow and slow-moving, flowing over a slaty substratum and often braiding when it encounters outcrops of harder rock. Thick riverine forests occur where alluvial sediments have accumulated, but otherwise the marginal vegetation is scarce, consisting mainly of belts of the Iberian endemic *Securinega tinctoria*. The Guadiana Internacional houses good populations of the small Iberian roaches calandino and pardilla, plus Iberian barbel and Iberian nase, all of which provide food for the otters that are also fairly common here.

The bridge at Ayuda/Ajuda, due south of Elvas, is a good place to start your exploration of the Guadiana. Here the rocky pastures flanking the river are dominated by spiny plants which can survive the regular incursions of sheep and goats – cotton-thistles, Spanish oyster plant, field eryngo and the Afro-Iberian endemic cardoon *Cynara humilis* – although autumn rains generate a delightful profusion of merendera, autumn squill and the delicate, white-flowered autumn narcissus, as well as the much rarer, yellow-flowered tapeinanthus, in its only known Portuguese locality. In spring, look out for the insect-imitating Iberian ophrys,

endemic to the peninsula, as well as for butterflies such as African grass blue and Mediterranean skipper, both of which are more usually found near the Mediterranean coast.

Upstream, in the area around Torre de Bolsa, close to where the Guadiana commences its international trajectory, the margins of the river support a narrow belt of thick riverine forest composed of black poplar, alder and narrow-leaved ash, with clumps of common and giant reeds along the water's edge, home to nightingale, Cetti's, great reed and melodious warblers, golden oriole, common waxbill, red

Autumn narcissus *Narcissus serotinus*

avadavat and, occasionally, penduline tit. Many birds also make use of the open fields on the fertile floodplain here, especially wintering marsh and hen harriers, red and black-winged kites, little bustard and southern grey shrike, plus Montagu's harrier, bee-eater, roller and short-toed lark in summer. Look out for cattle and little egrets, stone curlew and fan-tailed warbler all year round. Slightly to the northeast of Torre de Bolsa, rice-fields close to the river attract a wealth of birds at all times of year, but are of particular note for their breeding collared pratincoles, black-winged stilts and little ringed plovers. Many waders drop in on migration, including ruff, black-tailed godwit and green sandpiper.

Access: Torre de Bolsa lies south of the N-4 to the east of Elvas (signposted), also accessible via a small road running south from the frontier village of Caia. Puente de Ayuda (Ponte da Ajuda) is on the recently upgraded road (BA-211) which links Olivenza with Elvas.

Glossary

acidophilic: literally 'acid-loving', referring to organisms which thrive best in acidic habitats.

alluvial: alluvial sediments are those deposited by slow-flowing rivers, often forming a floodplain on either side of the watercourse, or filling shallow basins in estuarine conditions. The term alluvial can also be applied to plant communities growing in such habitats, such as forests or grasslands.

anthropogenic: refers to habitats which have been shaped by man rather than occurring naturally, such as the haymeadows of the Picos de Europa, or the extensive 'pseudosteppes' of central Iberia.

autochthonous: species which are indigenous (native) to a certain area.

benthic: literally, 'bottom-dwelling' in a marine or freshwater context. It derives from the term **benthos**, which describes the community of animals and plants attached to, resting on or living near the bottom sediments.

boulder chokes: a jumble of large rocks, often in a valley bottom, generally deriving from chunks of rock split off from the peaks above which have arrived under their own momentum.

brackish: a term referring to water which is saline, but less so than sea-water, as occurs in estuaries with a strong input of freshwater from rivers and streams. It can also be applied to moderately saline vegetation communities, such as the Atlantic **polders**, or communities surrounding **endorheic** lagoons.

calcareous: soils or bedrock that contain large quantities of calcium carbonate and can be regarded as basic or alkaline in character.

calcicole: a plant which grows exclusively or preferentially on **calcareous** soils or bedrock (many such species together form calcicolous communities).

calcifuge: plant species which normally avoids **calcareous** soils, being more characteristic of acidic habitats such as granite rocks or peatbogs. See also **acidophilic**.

Carboniferous limestone: calcareous rock, mainly originating from marine sediments, which was laid down in the Carboniferous period (between 345 and 280 million years ago).

carr: a wet habitat, often with some peat development, but neutral rather than acidic waters. In this book we have used the term to refer to waterlogged woodlands such as the alder and willow carr at Valdoviño (Galicia).

cetacean: a member of the Order Cetacea (whales and dolphins); large aquatic (predominantly marine), air-breathing mammals, in which the forelimbs are modified to form paddles, the hindlimbs are absent; and the tail-fluke is horizontal and used for propulsion.

chenopod: a member of the Chenopodiaceae (Goosefoot) family of higher plants, including succulent, salt-tolerant species such as glassworts, sea-blites and saltworts.

cirque: a steep-sided hollow in a high mountain area, generally circular in plan but open to one side (rather like an armchair), created (or being created by) by glacial activity. Often contains a small lake.

continental climate: one which is characterised by its remoteness from **oceanic** weather systems, generally displaying extremes of temperature in winter and summer, and also typified by low precipitation in many cases. Such is the case in the centre of the Iberian peninsula.

climax community: the theoretical final stage of a plant succession in which the vegetation reaches a state of equilibrium with the environment, at which point it is more or less self-perpetuating. Imagine that a bare surface becomes available for colonisation by plants: the initial stages are typified by simple communities, usually short-lived, which give way to increasingly complex ones, until reaching climax. In many cases in lowland Europe, the climax vegetation is forest, although under certain conditions – low temperatures (at altitude, for example), high aridity, repeated burning and/or grazing, etc. – the communities never reach this stage.

crystalline: usually applied to metamorphic or igneous rocks formed by the process of crystallisation from solid or liquid precursors, although some sedimentary limestones may also be crystalline in nature.

doline: a steep-sided, enclosed depression in a limestone region, also variously known as a swallow-hole or sink-hole, created by the process of **karstification**.

embryo dune: the first stage in the sand-dune vegetation succession, occurring immediately behind the strand-line and formed by sands blown inshore or thrown up by the sea, usually sparsely populated by plants with long root-stocks which are tolerant of shifting sands. Once stabilised, other species are able to colonise, giving way successively to primary, secondary and tertiary dunes.

endemic species: one which is restricted naturally to a particular geographic region, due to factors such as evolutionary isolation or response to physical conditions (soil-type, climate, etc.).

endorheic lagoons can only become established in flat-bottomed basins lined with impermeable soils. Small, rainwater-fed streams rising in the surrounding hills flow into the basin, creating shallow lagoons in the absence of an outlet to the sea. An important feature of many of these lakes is their seasonality, given that they usually occur in southern regions with very low summer precipitation and high levels of evaporation. Substrata rich in mineral salts often confer a marked salinity on the water, such that marginal and aquatic vegetation is generally of a halophytic nature and most fish and amphibians are unable to survive here. The abundance of salt-tolerant aquatic invertebrates, however, means that endorheic lagoons often support diverse and abundant bird communities.

ericaceous: referring to plants, usually shrubs, belonging to the Ericaceae (Heather) family.

fluvial: pertaining to a river.

gallery forest: that which extends, ribbon-like, along the banks of a watercourse, also known as riverine or fluvial forest.

garrigue: low-growing (less than 1m high) secondary vegetation which is widespread in the Mediterranean basin, derived from the original forest and dominated by aromatic and/or prickly dwarf shrubs which are usually **xerophytic** by nature.

gneiss: a coarse-grained, banded metamorphic rock.

grike: see **limestone pavement**

gypsophilous: referring to plants which thrive best on gypsum-rich soils or bedrock.

halophyte: plant adapted morphologically and/or physiologically to grow in saline habitats, especially **chenopods**.

herptile: a term which includes both amphibians and reptiles.

hill-topping: a phenomenon observed among butterflies with low population densities whereby both males and females converge on the highest landform in their territories to increase their chances of finding a mate.

hydrophyte: a plant that displays morphological and/or physiological adaptations that enable it to grow in water or very wet soils.

insolation: the amount of incoming solar radiation that is received per unit area of the earth's surface, which tends to increase with altitude and closer to the equator.

karstification: a chemical weathering process involving a reaction between dilute carbonic acid (the solution in water of free atmospheric and soil carbon dioxide) and calcareous rocks, typically limestone. The resultant **karst** landforms include **dolines**, **uvalas** and **limestone pavement**.

limestone pavement: forms where limestone is horizontally-bedded, or almost so, by the process of karstification. Flat sections (**clints**), between one and two metres wide, are separated by narrow crevices called **grikes**.

Macaronesia: a floral region incorporating the Madeira archipelago, the Illas Salvagens, the Açores, the Islas Canarias and the Cabo Verde islands, some of whose elements are also found in mainland Spain.

maquis: term used to describe drought-resistant Mediterranean secondary scrub (1-3m high) which is taller than **garrigue** and composed mainly of evergreen shrubs with thick, leathery leaves or spiny foliage. It generally develops where the original Mediterranean forest has been burnt or grazed.

megaforb: a very robust, non-grassy herbaceous species.

meridional: characteristic of, or located in, the south.

metamorphic rocks: pre-existing rocks which have undergone changes within the earth's crust as a result of the application of pressure or temperature, or the action of chemically active fluids.

microclimate: very local climatic conditions.

monocot: an abbreviation of monocotyledon, referring to plants pertaining to the Monocotyledonaceae. This is one of the two great divisions of the angiosperms (flowering plants), in which the embryo characteristically has but a single cotyledon and the leaves are parallel-veined. Examples are orchids, lilies and grasses.

mud-puddling: a phenomenon observed particularly in butterflies. In warm weather, they often congregate around shallow, evaporating waterbodies, where the abundance of particular minerals act as a sort of butterfly 'salt-lick'.

mustelid: an abbreviation of Mustelidae: a family of small mammals (in the order Carnivora) which in Spain includes stoat, weasel, European and American mink, western polecat, pine and beech martens, Eurasian badger and otter.

oceanic climate: one characterised by maritime influences.

odonates: dragonflies and damselflies belonging to the Odonata, a primitive order of predatory insects with two pairs of large, transparent wings and prominent eyes; the nymphs are aquatic. Some 75 species occur in Spain today.

orogeny: mountain building, especially where an area of the earth's crust is compressed over many millions of years by lateral forces to create mountain chains, or orogenic belts.

peridotite: a coarse-grained, **ultrabasic**, igneous rock consisting predominantly of olivine.

polder: a low-lying, flat area reclaimed from the sea and protected by embankments or dykes. In Spain these are usually brackish grasslands used for grazing livestock and occur only on the Atlantic coast.

psammophile: a plant which typically grows in sandy environments such as coastal dune systems.

relict: a term applied to animals and plants which have survived a widespread change in conditions by retreating to small areas known as refugia, as for example the arctic-alpine plants of the Sierra Nevada, which 'outwitted' the retreat of the ice-sheets northwards by withdrawing to the highest peaks.

ria: a drowned river valley in an area of high relief, resulting from the post-glacial rise in sea-level, abundant along the Galician coast. In Spanish, the term *ría* also refers to a shallow estuary.

siliceous: referring to rocks or soils containing silica, often in the form of quartz.

tectonic (valley): a valley formed by the faulting of the earth's crust rather than by the action of rivers or glaciers.

Tertiary (relic): a plant which was formerly widespread during the Tertiary period (65-63 million years ago), when much of Europe was covered with semitropical forest, but now occurs very locally.

thermophilic: referring to an organism which thrives best in warm conditions.

tombolo: a spit of land linking an island to the mainland or to another island.

transhumance: the movement of livestock from one area to another to take advantage of grazing available at different times of year, either horizontally or vertically. For example, the sheep which travel from the winter pastures in Extremadura to the mountains of northern Spain at the beginning of summer, traditionally along drover's roads known as **cañadas**, or the cattle which ascend from their winter quarters in the valleys to the high pastures of the Picos de Europa in the summer.

ultrabasic: referring to igneous rocks which consist almost entirely of ferromagnesian minerals to the virtual exclusion of quartz and feldspar.

uvala: the coalescence of two or more **dolines**.

xerophyte/xerophytic: a plant that can grow in very dry conditions and displays morphological adaptations – reduced and/or waxy leaves, underground storage organs, etc. – to enable it to withstand periods of drought.

Useful contacts

National

Ministerio de Medio Ambiente
Dirección General de Conservación de la
Naturaleza
Gran Vía de San Francisco, 4
28005 MADRID
Tel: 91 5975400
Fax: 91 5975566
www.mma.es

Instituto Geográfico Nacional
Centro Nacional de Información
Geográfica
c/ General Ibáñez de Ibero, 3
28003 MADRID
Tel: 91 5979514
Fax: 91 5352913
www.mfom.es/ign/top_geografico.html

Servicio Geográfico del Ejército
Centro de Publicaciones del Ministerio
de Defensa
c/ Juan Ignacio de Tena, 30
28071 MADRID
Tel: 91 2054202
Fax: 91 2054025
e-mail: publicaciones@mde.es

WWF/Adena
Gran Vía de San Francisco, 8 (esc. D)
28005 MADRID
Tel: 91 3540578
Fax: 91 3656336
e-mail: info@wwf.es
www.wwf.es

Sociedad Española para la Conservación
y Estudio de los Mamíferos (SECEM)
Apartado de Correos 15450
29080 MÁLAGA
www.secem.es/primera.htm

Sociedad Española de Ornitología (SEO)
(Spanish BirdLife partner designate)
c/ Melquíades Biencinto, 34
28053 MADRID
Tel: 91 4340910
Fax: 91 4340911
e-mail: seo@seo.org
www.seo.org

Rare Birds in Spain
www.rarebirdspain.net

Asociación Herpetológica Española
Apartado de Correos 191
28911 LEGANÉS
http://elebo.fbiolo.uv.es/zoologia/AHE/
frame.htm

SHILAP (Sociedad Hispano-Luso-
Americana de Lepidopterología)
Apartado de Correos 331
28080 MADRID
http://members.es.tripod.de/SHILAP/
indice.htm

Sociedad para el Estudio y Conservación
de las Arañas (SECA)
Villafranca, 24, 1°C
28028 MADRID
Tel: 636 068322
e-mail: seca_es@yahoo.es

Federación Española de Deportes de
Montaña y Escalada
Floridablanca, 75, entlo. 2°
08015 BARCELONA
Tel: 93 4264267
Fax: 93 4263387
www.fedme.es

Galicia and Asturias

Galicia

Dirección Xeral de Montes e Medio Ambiente Natural
c/ San Lázaro, s/n
15704 SANTIAGO DE COMPOSTELA
Tel: 981 546050
Fax: 981 546102
e-mail: juan.porto.rodriguez@xunta.es
www.xunta.es/conselle/cma/CMA05e/p05e01.htm

Asociación para a Defensa Ecolóxica de Galiza (ADEGA)
Rúa de Touro, 21–1°
15704 SANTIAGO DE COMPOSTELA
Tel. and fax: 981 570099
e-mail: adeganacional@adega.org
www.adegagaliza.org

Asturias

Consejería de Medio Ambiente
c/ Coronel Aranda n° 2, planta tercera, izq.
33005 OVIEDO
Tel: 985 105500
Fax: 985 105538
www.princast.es/mediambi/siapa/inicio.htm

Fondo para la Protección de los Animales Salvajes (FAPAS)
La Pereda s/n
33509 LA PEREDA-LLANES
Tel: 985 401264
Fax: 985 402794
e-mail: fapas.asturias@terra.es
www.netcom.es/fapas

Cantabria, Euskadi and La Rioja

Cantabria

Consejería de Ganadería, Agricultura y Pesca
c/ Rodríguez, 5, 1°
39002 SANTANDER
Tel: 942 207851
Fax: 942 207034
www.medioambientecantabria.org/a6_2_espacios_protegidos.html

Fundación Naturaleza y Hombre
18 de julio, 25-Entresuelo
39610 EL ASTILLERO
Tel: 942 559119/558709
Fax: 942 559119
e-mail: fundacion@fundacionnaturalezayhombre.es
www.fundacionnaturalezayhombre.es

Asociación para la Defensa de los Recursos Naturales de Cantabria (ARCA)
Apartado de Correos 421
39080 SANTANDER
Tel. and fax: 942 362966
e-mail: arca@ctv.es
www.ctv.es/USERS/arca

Euskadi

Parks are run by the three Diputaciones but with an overall website: www.nekanet.net/naturaleza/renp/frameprincipal.htm

Diputación Foral de Bizkaia
Departamento de Medio Ambiente y Acción Territorial
Alameda de Rekalde, 30, 4°
48009 BILBO/BILBAO
Tel: 94 4206849
Fax: 94 4206899
e-mail: ingurugiroa@bizkaia.net
www.bizkaia.net

Diputación Foral de Araba
Servicio de Conservación de la Naturaleza
Plaza de la Provincia, s/n
01001 GASTEIZ/VITORIA

Diputación Foral de Gipuzkoa
Departamento de Agricultura y Medio Ambiente
Plaza de Gipuzkoa, s/n
20004 DONOSTIA/SAN SEBASTIAN
Tel: 943 482070
Fax: 943 431154

La Rioja

Area de Educación Ambiental
c/ Prado Viejo 62 bis.
Edificio SOS Rioja
26071 LOGROÑO
Tel: 94 1291360
Fax: 94 1291356
e-mail: informacion.ambiental@
larioja.org
www.larioja.org/ma

Navarra and Aragón

Navarra

Dirección General de Medio Ambiente
c/ Alhóndiga, 1, 1°
31002 IRUÑEA/PAMPLONA
Tel: 948 427638
Fax: 948 421495
e-mail: sian@cfnavarra.es
www.cfnavarra.es/Medioambiente/
biodiversidad/RNat2000/ParqNatu/
index.htm

**Gestíon Ambiental, Viveros y
Repoblaciones de Navarra**
c/ Padre Adoain, 219, planta baja
31015 IRUÑEA/PAMPLONA
Tel: 948 382438 or 902 076076
Fax: 948 382391
e-mail: gavr.gestcin@sarenet.es

**Gurelur (Fondo Navarro para la
Protección del Medio Natural)**
Manuel de Falla, 8
31005 IRUÑEA/PAMPLONA
Tel. and fax: 948 151077
e-mail: gurelur@bme.es
www.gurelur.org

Aragón

Dirección General del Medio Natural
Edificio Pignatelli
Paseo Maria Agustín, 36
50004 ZARAGOZA
Tel: 976 714812
Fax: 976 714817
e-mail: info.medioambiente@aragob.es
www.aragob.es/ambiente/index.htm

ANSAR (Asociación Naturista de Aragón)
Armisén 10
50007 ZARAGOZA
Tel. and fax: 976 251742
e-mail: ansar@arrakis.es
www.aragonesasi.com/ansar

Sociedad Entomológica Aragonesa (SEA)
Avda. Radio Juventud, 6
50012 ZARAGOZA
Tel: 976 324415
Fax: 976 535697
e-mail: amelic@retemail
http://entomologia.rediris.es/sea

Federación Aragonesa de Montañismo
c/ Albareda, 7 4°-4ª
50004 ZARAGOZA
Tel: 976 227971
Fax: 976 212459
e-mail: fam@fam.es
www.fam.es/index.htm

Catalunya

**Direcció General de Patrimoni Natural
i del Medi Físic**
Dr. Roux, 80
08017 BARCELONA
Tel: 93 5674200
Fax: 93 2803320
e-mail: wmadgpn@correu.gencat.es
www.parcsdecatalunya.net/

Institut Cartogràfic de Catalunya
Parc de Montjuïc
08038 BARCELONA
Tel: 93 5671500
Fax: 93 5671567
www.icc.es

Fundació Natura
Rambla de Catalunya, 121, 6è, 9a
08008 BARCELONA
Tel: 93 2373802
Fax: 93 2370181
e-mail: info@fundacionatura.org
www.fundacionatura.org

Fundació Territori i Paisatge
c/ Provença 261-265, 2n, 2a
08008 BARCELONA
Tel: 93 4847367
Fax: 93 4847364
e-mail: fundtip@fundtip.com

DEPANA
c/ Sant Salvador, 97
08024 BARCELONA
Tel: 93 2104679
Fax: 93 2850426
e-mail: depana@entorno.es
www.depana.org

Institutió Catalana d'Història Natural
Carrer del Carme, 47
08001 BARCELONA
Tel: 93 3248582
Fax: 93 2701180
e-mail: ichn@iec.es
www.iec.es/ichn

Institut Català d'Ornitologia
Museu de Zoologia
Passeig Picasso s/n
08080 BARCELONA
Tel: 93 4587893
e-mail: ico@ornitologia.org
www.ornitologia.org

Societat Catalana de Lepidopterologia
Apartat de Correus 35049
08080 BARCELONA
email: e.olivella@altavista.net
http://butterflywebsite.com/Society/scl.htm or www.iec.es/ichn

ORCA (online atlas of the flora of Catalunya, Illes Balears and País Valencià)
www.bio.ub.es/bioveg/orca/WelcomeOrca.html

Balears

Conselleria de Medi Ambient
Departament d'Espais Protegits
Av. Gabriel Alomar i Villalonga, 33
07006 PALMA DE MALLORCA
Tel: 971 176800
Fax: 971 176801
http://mediambient.caib.es/

Grup Balear d'Ornitologia I Defensa de la Naturalesa (GOB)
Verí, 1, 3r
07001 PALMA DE MALLORCA
Tel: 971 721105
Fax: 971 711375
e-mail: info@gobmallorca.com
www.gobmallorca.com

Mallorca

Consell Insular de Mallorca Medi Ambient i Natura
Carrer del General Riera, 111
07010 PALMA DE MALLORCA
Tel: 971 173700
Fax: 971 173732
e-mail: mediambient@
www.conselldemallorca.net

Menorca

Consellar Insular de Menorca Àrea de Medi Ambient
Camí des Castell, 28
07702 MAÓ
Tel: 971 356251
Fax: 971 366199
e-mail: mamb.cime@silme.es

Castilla y León and Madrid

Castilla y León

Dirección General de Medio Natural
c/ Rigoberto Cortejoso, 14
47071 VALLADOLID
Tel: 983 419936
Fax: 983 419933
e-mail: medamb_responde@cma.jcyl.es
www.jcyl.es/jcyl/cmaot/dgmn/svenep/espacios/index.htm

Madrid

Servicio de Información Ambiental
c/ Princesa, 3, planta 2ª
28080 MADRID
Tel: 901 525525 or 91 5801682
Fax: 91 4206695
e-mail: inf.general@maydr.comadrid.es
http://medioambiente.comadrid.es/
biodiversidad/biodibo2.html

Extremadura and Castilla–La Mancha

Extremadura

Servicio de Conservación de la Naturaleza y Espacios Protegidos
Avenida de Portugal, s/n
06800 MÉRIDA
Tel: 924 002408
Fax: 924 002362
e-mail: dgm@aym.juntaex.es
http://www.juntaex.es/consejerias/mut/
dgm/am0401.htm

Asociación para la Defensa de la Naturaleza y los Recursos de Extremadura (ADENEX)
Plaza de Santo Ángel, 1
06800 MÉRIDA
Tel: 924 387189
Fax: 924 387357
e-mail: adenex@bme.es
www.adenex.org

Castilla–La Mancha

See individual site descriptions for contact details, or refer to the website www.jccm.es/turismo/natural/espacios. htm

Esparvel
Portiña de San Miguel, 7, entreplanta B
Apartado de Correos 280
45600 TALAVERA DE LA REINA
Tel. and fax: 925 823860
e-mail: esparvel@teleline.es
www.terra.es/personal/esparvel/

País Valencià and Murcia

País Valencià

Direcció General de Planificació i Gestió del Medi
c/ Francisco Cubells, 7
46011 VALÈNCIA
Tel: 96 3865066
Fax: 96 3863768
e-mail: antonio.ballester@cma.m400.gva.es
www.cma.gva.es/_Planificacion_Gestion_
del_Medio/esp_prin.htm

Instituto Cartográfico Valenciano
Av. de los Naranjos s/n
Edificio Institutos 4
Universidad Politécnica de València
46022 VALÈNCIA
Tel: 96 3877710
Fax: 96 3879789
www.gva.es/icv/

GECEN (Grupo para el Estudio y Conservación de los Espacios Naturales)
Apartado de Correos 22
12600 LA VALL D'UIXÓ
Tel. and fax: 964 691293
e-mail: gecen@gecen.org
www.gecen.org

Murcia

Dirección General del Medio Natural
c/ Catedrático Eugenio Úbeda, 3, 3ª
30008 MURCIA
Tel: 968 228901
Fax: 968 228904
e-mail: mnatural@carm.es
www.carm.es/cma/dgmn/esquema/
indice.htm

Andalucía

Dirección General de la RENPA y Servicios Ambientals
Avenida de Manuel Siurot, 50
41013 SEVILLA
Tel: 955 003473
Fax: 955 003773
e-mail: DGRENPA@cma.junta-
andalucia.es
www.cma.junta-andalucia.es

ANDALUS
El Pedroso 2-Bajo D
41008 SEVILLA
Tel. and fax: 954 356144
e-mail: andalus@bme.es

Colectivo Ornitológico Cigüeña Negra/CPN
Estación Ornitológica de Tarifa
Crt. N-340 km 78,5
11380 TARIFA
e-mail: cocn@tarifainfo.com
www.tarifainfo.com/cocn

Gibraltar Ornithological and Natural History Society
Gibraltar Natural History Field Centre
Jews' Gate
Upper Rock Nature Reserve
PO Box 843
GIBRALTAR
Tel: 72639
Fax: 74022
e-mail: gonhs@gibnet.gi
www.gib.gi/gohns

Cross-border sites

Instituto da Conservação da Natureza (ICN)
Rua da Lapa, 73
1200–701 LISBOA
Tel: 21 3938900/3974044
Fax: 21 3938901/3901048
e-mail: icn@icn.pt
www.icn.it

Sociedade Portuguesa para o Estudo das Aves (SPEA)
(Portuguese BirdLife partner designate)
Rua da Vitória n°53, 3° Esq.
1100–618 LISBOA
Tel: 21 3431847
Fax: 21 3225889
e-mail: spea@spea.pt
www.spea.pt

Quercus – Associação Nacional de Conservação da Natureza
Apartado 4333
1503–003 LISBOA
Tel: 21 7788474
Fax: 21 7787749
e-mail: quercus@quercus.pt
www.quercus.pt

Further reading

Field guides in English

d'Aguilar, J., Dommanget, J-L. and Préchac, R. (1986). *A field guide to the dragonflies of Britain, Europe and North Africa.* Collins.

Arnold, E. N. and Burton, J. A. (1999). *A field guide to the reptiles and amphibians of Britain and Europe.* HarperCollins.

Askew, R. R. (1988). *The dragonflies of Europe.* Harley Books.

Barnes, R. (1979). *The natural history of Britain and Northern Europe: coasts and estuaries.* Book Club Associates.

Blamey, M. and Grey-Wilson, C. (1993). *Mediterranean wild flowers.* HarperCollins.

Buttler, K. P. (1991). *Field guide to orchids of Britain and Europe.* Crowood Press.

Chinery, M. (1989). *Butterflies and day-flying moths of Britain and Europe.* Collins.

Chinery, M. (1993). *Insects of Britain and Western Europe.* HarperCollins.

Chinery, M. (1998). *Butterflies of Britain and Europe.* HarperCollins.

Cortecuisse, R. and Duhem, B. (1995). *Mushrooms and toadstools of Britain and Europe.* HarperCollins.

Davies, P. and Gibbons, B. (1993). *Field guide to the wild flowers of southern Europe.* Crowood Press.

Delforge, P. (1995). *Collins photoguide: orchids of Britain and Europe.* HarperCollins.

Fitter, R., Fitter, A. and Farrer, A. (1995). *Grasses, sedges, rushes and ferns.* HarperCollins.

Grey-Wilson, C. and Blamey, M. (1995). *Alpine flowers of Britain and Europe.* HarperCollins.

Macdonald, D. and Barrett, P. (1993). *Collins field guide to the mammals of Britain and Europe.* HarperCollins.

Miller, P. J. and Loates, M. J. (1997). *Fish of Britain and Europe.* HarperCollins.

Mullarney, K., Svensson, L., Zetterström, D. and Grant, P. J. (1999). *Collins bird guide.* HarperCollins.

Pegler, D. (1990). *Field guide to the mushrooms and toadstools of Britain and Europe.* Kingfisher Books.

Polunin, O. (1969). *Flowers of Europe: a field guide.* Oxford University Press.

Polunin, O. and Smythies, B. E. (1988). *Flowers of south-west Europe: a field guide.* Oxford University Press.

Porter, R. F., Willis, I., Christiensen, S. and Nielson, B. P. (1981*). Flight identification of European raptors.* T. and A. D. Poyser.

Skinner, B. (1998). *Colour identification guide to moths of the British Isles (Macrolepidoptera).* Viking.

Stace, C. (1999). *Field flora of the British Isles.* Cambridge University Press.

Tolman, T. (2001). *Photographic guide to the butterflies of Britain and Europe.* Oxford University Press.

Tolman, T. and Lewington, R. (1997). *Butterflies of Britain and Europe.* HarperCollins.

Spain in general

Finlayson, C. and Tomlinson, D. (1993). *Birds of Iberia.* Santana, Spain.

Grunfeld, F. (1999). *Wild Spain.* Sheldrake Press.

Jödicke, R. (1996). *Studies on Iberian dragonflies.* Advances in Odonatology, Supplement 1, Ursus Scientific Publishers.

Measures, J. (1992). *Wildlife travelling companion: Spain.* Crowood Press.

Paterson, A. (1997). *Las Aves Marinas de España y Portugal.* Lynx Edicions, Barcelona (summaries in English).

Rose, L. (1995). *Where to watch birds in Spain and Portugal.* Hamlyn.

SEO (co-ordinated by de Juana, E.). (1993). *Where to watch birds in Spain.* Lynx Edicions, Barcelona.

Tomkies, M. (1989). *In Spain's secret wilderness.* Jonathan Cape.

Galicia, Asturias, Cantabria, Euskadi and La Rioja

Rebane, M. (1999). *Where to watch birds in north and east Spain.* Christopher Helm.

Navarra and Aragón

Crozier, J. (1998). *A birdwatching guide to the Pyrenees.* Arlequin Press.

Rebane, M. (1999). *Where to watch birds in north and east Spain.* Christopher Helm.

Woutersen, K. and Platteeuw, M. (1998). *Atlas of the birds of Huesca: birdwatching in the central Spanish Pyrenees and the Ebro valley).* Kees Woutersen Publicaciones.

Catalunya

Crozier, J. (1998). *A birdwatching guide to the Pyrenees.* Arlequin Press.

Crozier, J. (1999). *Butterflies of Andorra.* ADN, Andorra.

Crozier, J. and Matschke, A. (reprinting). *Flowers of Andorra.* ADN, Andorra.

Crozier, J., Dubourg-Savage, M. and Clamens, A. (ed.) (1995). *Andorra birds.* ADN, Andorra.

del Hoyo, J. and Sargatal, J. (reprinting). *Where to watch birds in Catalonia.* Lynx Edicions, Barcelona.

Rebane, M. (1999). *Where to watch birds in north and east Spain.* Christopher Helm.

Balears

Beckett, E. (1993). *Illustrated flora of Mallorca.* Editorial Moll, Palma de Mallorca.

Beckett, E. (1998). *Wild flowers of Majorca, Minorca and Ibiza.* Balkema, Netherlands.

Beniston, N. and Beniston, W. (1999). *Wild orchids of Mallorca.* Editorial Moll, Palma de Mallorca.

Bonner, A. (1985). *Plants of the Balearic Islands.* Editorial Moll, Palma de Mallorca.

Busby, J. (1988). *Birds in Mallorca.* Christopher Helm.

Hearl, G. (1996). *A birdwatching guide to Menorca, Ibiza and Formentera.* Arlequin Press.

Hearl, G. (1999). *A birdwatching guide to Mallorca.* Arlequin Press.

Mayol, J. (2002). *Birds of the Balearic Islands.* Editorial Moll, Palma de Mallorca. [Forthcoming.]

Parrack, J. D. (1973). *The naturalist in Mallorca.* David and Charles.

Ramos, E. (1996). *The birds of Menorca.* Editorial Moll, Palma de Mallorca.

Stoba, K. (1990). *Birdwatching in Mallorca.* Cicerone.

Watkinson, E. (1986). *A guide to birdwatching in Mallorca.* J. G. Sanders.

Castilla y León and Madrid

Rebane, M. (1999). *Where to watch birds in north and east Spain.* Christopher Helm.

Extremadura and Castilla–La Mancha

Muddeman, J. (2000). *A birdwatching guide to Extremadura.* Arlequin Press, Chelmsford.

Paterson, A. and García, E. (2001). *Where to watch birds in southern and western Spain.* Christopher Helm.

País Valencià and Murcia

Palmer, M. (1994). *A birdwatching guide to the Costa Blanca.* Arlequin Press.

Palmer, M. and Fidel, L. (2001). *A birdwatching guide to eastern Spain.* Arlequin Press.

Peinado, M., Alcaraz, F. and Martínez-Parras, J. M. (1992). *Vegetation of southeastern Spain.* Gebrüder Borntraeger, Germany.

Andalucía

Finlayson, C. (1993). *A birdwatchers' guide to southern Spain and Gibraltar.* Prion.

Linares, L., Harper, A. and Cortes, J. (1996). *The flowers of Gibraltar: Flora Calpensis.* Gibraltar.

Finlayson, C. (1992). *Birds of the Strait of Gibraltar.* T. and A. D. Poyser.

Molesworth Allen, B. (1993). *A selection of wildflowers of southern Spain.* Santana, Spain.

Paterson, A. and García, E. (2001). *Where to watch birds in southern and western Spain.* Christopher Helm.

Cross-border sites

Moore, C. C., Elias, G. and Costa, H. (1997). *A birdwatchers' guide to Portugal and Madeira.* Prion.

Sunflower 'Landscapes' guides
www.sunflowerbooks.co.uk

Spanish titles include:

- Northern Spain: Picos de Europa
- Pyrenees
- Costa Brava and Barcelona
- Mallorca
- Menorca
- Costa Blanca
- Andalucía and the Costa del Sol

No attempt has been made to include any of the myriad tomes published about Spanish wildlife and protected areas which are not in English. Details of these can be obtained by consulting the following mail-order book suppliers:

NHBS
2–3 Wills Road
TOTNES
Devon TQ9 5XN
Tel: (0)1803 865913
Fax: (0)1803 865280
e-mail: nhbs@nhbs.co.uk
www.nhbs.com

Oryx
Balmes, 71
08007 BARCELONA
Tel: 93 4185511
Fax: 93 4188117
e-mail: oryx@weboryx.com
www.weboryx.com

Species mentioned in the text

In the absence of any more up-to-date or complete work, scientific names of **vascular plants** follow Smythies, B. E. (1984–86), *Flora of Spain and the Balearic Islands: checklist of vascular plants* (Vols I–III). In *Englera* (Veröffentlichungen aus dem Botanischen Garten und Botanischen Museum Berlin-Dahlem, Berlin). Some much-revised genera – for example *Alchemilla, Armeria, Echinospartum, Genista, Helianthemum, Limonium, Petrocoptis, Quercus, Saxifraga* and *Ulex* – follow *Flora Iberica: Plantas Vasculares de la Península Ibérica e Islas Baleares*, published by the Real Jardín Botánico, CSIC, in Madrid (Vols 1–8 and 14 of 21 have appeared since 1986), as do Portuguese endemics up to Leguminosae. Common names, if they exist, are in accordance with Stace (1999) as far as possible, with additions from Buttler (1991), Blamey and Grey-Wilson (1993), Grey-Wilson and Blamey (1995) and Polunin and Smythies (1988). **Fungi** are named from Pegler (1990).

Scientific and common names of **mammals** largely follow Macdonald and Barrett (1993), while **birds** (except Iberian chiffchaff) are in accordance with Snow, D.

W. and Perrins, C. M. (1998), *The birds of the Western Palearctic* (concise edition). Oxford University Press. The scientific names for **reptiles and amphibians** follow Barbadillo, L. J. *et al.* (1999), *Anfíbios y Reptiles de la Península Ibérica, Baleares y Canarias*. Editorial GeoPlaneta, S.A., with common names – as far as possible – taken from Arnold and Burton (1999). **Fish** scientific and common names are taken from the Fishbase website (www.fishbase.org), supplemented by common names from Miller and Loates (1997).

Butterflies are named for the most part in accordance with Tolman and Lewington (1997), while the scientific names of **moths** mentioned are taken from Vives Moreno, A. (1994), *Catálogo Sistemático y Sinonímico de los Lepidópteros de la Península Ibérica y Baleares*. Ministerio de Agricultura, Pesca y Alimentación, Madrid, with common names following Skinner (1998) and Chinery (1993). **Dragonflies** follow d'Aguilar *et al.* (1986). Other invertebrate names have various sources, with the **undersea element** using scientific and common names taken mainly from Riedll, R. (1986), *Fauna y Flora del Mar Mediterráneo*. Ediciones Omega, Barcelona, and Barnes (1979).

Index to place names

Note: *Principal sites* are shown in **bold** text; *general features* are indexed under **Spain**. An index to scientific and English species names used in all the books in this series can be found at www.oup.com/uk/travellersnatureguides

KEY TO SITE MAP SYMBOLS

┣━ ‐ ‐ ━┫	National border		Park or reserve boundary
	River, stream or canal		Reserve or area of interest
	Torrent		Marine reserve
	Road	**i**	Information point
	Dual carriageway	**P**	Parking
	Path or track		Hide or observation point
━○━	Railway		High ground
	Ferry		Indicative landform
✈	Airport, airfield		Sand or mudflats
Î	Lighthouse		Dunes
I	Castle or tower		Marsh
	Ecclesiastical building, disused		Reedbed
	Cliff or crag		Woodland
1155 m ▲	Peak, height in metres		Rock